MW01124665

Scripture and Law in the Dead Sea Scrolls

This book is the first work of its kind to examine legal exegesis in the Dead Sea Scrolls from the perspective of both the history of Jewish law and early Jewish scriptural interpretation. It shows how the Dead Sea Scrolls transform the meaning and application of biblical law to meet the needs of new historical and cultural settings. The Dead Sea Scrolls legal texts are examined through the comparative lens of law and legal interpretation in Second Temple Judaism and rabbinic Judaism. The creative interpretation of scriptural texts in the Dead Sea Scrolls responds to the tension between seemingly rigid authoritative scripture and the need for law and scripture to be perpetually evolving entities. The ongoing legal interpretation of scriptural texts frames the development of Jewish law at the same time as it shapes the nature of the biblical canon.

Alex P. Jassen is Associate Professor of Hebrew and Judaic Studies in the Skirball Department of Hebrew and Judaic Studies at New York University. He previously taught at the University of Minnesota, where he was the recipient of the university's prestigious McKnight Land-Grant Fellowship. Dr. Jassen holds a B.A. in Jewish Studies and Near Eastern Languages and Civilizations from the University of Washington (2001) and a Ph.D. in Hebrew and Judaic Studies from New York University (2006). He has published widely on the Dead Sea Scrolls and ancient Judaism and is a member of the international editorial team responsible for publication of the Dead Sea Scrolls. He is the author of *Mediating the Divine: Prophecy and Revelation in the Dead Sea Scrolls and Second Temple Judaism*, winner of the 2009 John Templeton Award for Theological Promise, as well as many articles in leading journals such as the *Association for Jewish Studies Review*, *Biblical Interpretation*, *Dead Sea Discoveries*, *Journal of Biblical Literature*, *Journal of Jewish Studies*, and *Revue de Qumran*. He is the co-editor of *Scripture, Violence, and Textual Practice in Early Judaism and Christianity*, and co-editor-in-chief of the *Journal of Ancient Judaism*. He served as academic adviser for *The Dead Sea Scrolls: Words That Changed the World* exhibit at the Science Museum of Minnesota. His work on religious violence has been recognized with a fellowship from the National Endowment for the Humanities.

Scripture and Law in the Dead Sea Scrolls

ALEX P. JASSEN
New York University

CAMBRIDGE
UNIVERSITY PRESS

32 Avenue of the Americas, New York NY 10013-2473, USA

Cambridge University Press is part of the University of Cambridge.

It furthers the University's mission by disseminating knowledge in the pursuit of education, learning and research at the highest international levels of excellence.

www.cambridge.org
Information on this title: www.cambridge.org/9780521196048

First published 2014

A catalogue record for this publication is available from the British Library

Library of Congress Cataloguing in Publication data
Jassen, Alex P.
Scripture and law in the Dead Sea scrolls / Alex P. Jassen.
pages cm
Includes bibliographical references and index.
ISBN 978-0-521-19604-8 (hardback)
1. Dead Sea scrolls. I. Title.
BM487.J37 2013
296.1'55–dc23 2013021425

ISBN 978-0-521-19604-8 Hardback

In Loving Memory of

David R. Azose

September 12, 1939–October 26, 2009

ת'נ'צ'ב'ה'

Contents

List of Tables — *page* ix
Acknowledgments — xi
A Note on Style and Translation — xv
Abbreviations and Sigla — xvii

1. Introduction — 1
2. The Dead Sea Scrolls and the History of Jewish Law and Legal Exegesis — 18
3. Jewish Legal Exegesis and the Origins and Development of the Canon — 41
4. Isaiah 58:13 and the Sabbath Prohibition on Speech in the Dead Sea Scrolls, Part 1: The *Damascus Document* — 68
5. Isaiah 58:13 and the Sabbath Prohibition on Speech in the Dead Sea Scrolls, Part 2: *4QHalakha B* — 86
6. Isaiah 58:13 and the Sabbath Prohibition on Speech in the Book of *Jubilees* and Rabbinic Literature — 104
7. Isaiah 58:13 and the Restriction on Thoughts of Labor on the Sabbath in the Dead Sea Scrolls — 131
8. Isaiah 58:13 and the Restriction on Thoughts of Labor on the Sabbath in Philo and Rabbinic Literature — 150
9. Jeremiah 17:21–22 and the Sabbath Carrying Prohibition in the Dead Sea Scrolls — 172
10. Jeremiah 17:21–22 and the Sabbath Carrying Prohibition in *Nehemiah*, *Jubilees*, and Rabbinic Literature — 190

11. Non-Pentateuchal Passages as Prooftexts 216
12. Conclusions 247

Bibliography 253
Index of Ancient Sources 285
Index of Modern Authors 292
Subject Index 296

List of Tables

1. Isa 58:13 and CD 10:17–19 *page* 74
2. Isa 58:13 and CD 10:19 81
3. Isa 58:13 and CD 10:19 and 4Q264a 1 i 6–7 94
4. The Literary Inversion of CD 10:17–21 in 4Q264a 1 i 5–8 102
5. Isa 58:13 and CD 10:17–19 and Jub 50:8 106
6. The Reformulation of Isa 58:13 in CD 10:20–21 136
7. עשה and חפץ in Isa 58:13 and CD 10:20–21 139
8. Exod 16:29 and Jer 17:21–22, 24 and CD, 4Q251, and 4Q265 178
9. The Literary Inversion of Jer 17:21–22 in CD 11:7–9 183
10. The Interpretation of משא (Jer 17:21, 24) in Neh 13:15bc, 19 192
11. Jer 17:21–22 and Jub 50:8 198
12. The Reformulation of Jer 17:21–22 in Jub 2:29 201
13. The Reformulation of Jer 17:22 in Jub 2:30 203
14. 1 Sam 25:26 and CD 9:8–10 223
15. Prov 15:8 and CD 11:20–21 228

Acknowledgments

The book of *Ecclesiastes* concludes with a warning concerning the perils of writing a book: "The making of many books is without limit and much study is a wearying of the flesh" (Eccl 12:12). Any modern scholar can certainly attest to the unending production of books and the significant amount of study that must go into adding yet another contribution. I have been very fortunate not to have embarked upon the present composition in isolation, but with a wonderful supporting cast of family, friends, and colleagues. It is undoubtedly on account of their encouragement and collective wisdom that I hope to have been able to follow in the path of *Ecclesiastes*: "To discover useful sayings and record genuinely truthful sayings" (Eccl 12:10).

The conception and writing of this book coincided with the growth of my family and the development of my professional career. This book was written while I was a member of the Department of Classical and Near Eastern Studies at the University of Minnesota. Its path from conception to completion owes much to the supportive environment of the department and university as well as the enriching intellectual climate provided by my colleagues. This book was completed during my time as a McKnight Land-Grant Professor. I am thankful to the University of Minnesota for this honor and the wonderful resources that came with the professorship. Thanks especially to my departmental colleagues Eva von Dassow, Bernie Levinson, Cal Roetzel, Phillip Sellew, George Sheets, and Jeff Stackert (now of the University of Chicago), who responded to specific queries, lent their wisdom in conversations, or read entire drafts of chapters. A special debt of gratitude goes to my department chair Chris Nappa, whose advocacy for my professional development and unstinting support of my research represent everything a junior faculty member could ask for in a chair. This work owes a great deal to the mentorship, intellectual dialogue, and friendship of Bernie Levinson. Since my arrival at Minnesota, Bernie has been a source of constant support in all my professional and intellectual pursuits. We have shared interests in legal history and biblical exegesis, and his imprint on my approach to these issues is apparent throughout this book. As this book was in its final stages of production, I joined the faculty of the Skirball Department of Hebrew and Judaic Studies at New York University.

Much of the writing of this book coincided with my work as an academic adviser for the exhibition *Dead Sea Scrolls: Words That Changed the World* at the Science Museum of Minnesota. I had the pleasure of working with many talented individuals in creating the exhibit. I learned much from Chris Burda, Ed Fleming, and Joe Imholte on how best to present academic research in a clear and succinct manner. Our constant dialogue on the most effective way to present any particular issue in Dead Sea Scrolls research helped refine my own thinking about many issues. I hope that some of their creative energy and constant attention to the intended audience are reflected in this book. My work on the exhibit provided a wonderful opportunity to learn much from my co-adviser Michael Wise. As we discussed countless issues related to the Dead Sea Scrolls and Qumran, I constantly found his questions and observations challenging and illuminating. My understanding of the Dead Sea Scrolls is much richer because of our friendship and dialogue.

Beyond my local colleagues, I am grateful to many people for their contributions. The two main areas of interest in this study – Jewish law and scriptural interpretation – represent the long-standing areas of research by my two mentors at New York University: Lawrence Schiffman and Moshe Bernstein. I have continued to learn much from both of them, and this book has benefited greatly from our ongoing conversations. Shani Tzoref commented on one of the first drafts of the book and later lent her considerable editorial acumen to an earlier version of Chapters 9 and 10. The broader legal theoretical framework of Chapters 7 and 8 owes much to an inquiry posed to me by Steven Fraade after I presented a paper based on this work in 2009. James VanderKam was very helpful in responding to several queries regarding the text of *Jubilees*.

I am very thankful to Dr. Courtney Friesen of the University of Oxford for his diligent assistance with many aspects of the manuscript preparation. His insightful queries and careful proofreading prevented many infelicities from remaining. Dr. Sarah Shectman completed a very thorough final proofread and compiled the indexes. I am very thankful for her keen attention to detail and meticulous review of the manuscript. I am especially grateful to the wonderful team at Cambridge University Press for their work in diligently shepherding this book from beginning to end. Thank you to Lewis Bateman, Andy Beck, Becca Cain, Brian MacDonald, and Shaun Vigil.

I had the great benefit of presenting many aspects of this book as it was in progress at academic conferences and institutions. Material drawn from the book constituted several papers presented at the annual meetings of the Society of Biblical Literature and the Association for Jewish Studies as well as the Congress of the International Organization for Qumran Studies. I was also very fortunate to be able to share various aspects of my research as a guest lecturer at several universities: the John Cardinal Cody Colloquium at Loyola University Chicago (March 2010); the Open History Seminar at Hebrew Union College–Jewish Institute of Religion (March 2010); Yeshiva University (October 2010); and New York University (October 2010). Thanks to all those in attendance who offered helpful and instructive feedback.

In the course of writing this book, I have published material from my research in progress in several venues. Early versions of Chapters 9 and 10 were published as "Tracing the Threads of Jewish Law: The Sabbath Carrying Prohibition from Jeremiah to the Rabbis," *Annali di storia dell'esegesi* 28:1 (2011): 253–78 (part of the special section "Second Temple Halakhot and the Historical Jesus: Three Contributions toward a Discussion") and "Law and Exegesis in the Dead Sea Scrolls: The Sabbath Carrying Prohibition in Comparative Perspective," in *The Dead Sea Scrolls at Sixty: Scholarly Contributions of the New York University Faculty and Alumni* (ed. L. H. Schiffman and S. L. Tsoref; STDJ 89; Leiden: Brill, 2010), 115–56. I am grateful to the publishers for permission to reprint material from these articles.

Above all, this book could not have been completed without the love and support of my family. My wife Leslie has lived with the Dead Sea Scrolls now for more than a decade. During this time, she has been a constant champion of my research, and together we continue to be enthused by all that the world of the Dead Sea Scrolls offers. She has been a source of great wisdom for our growing family and my work. Indeed, as with Lady Wisdom in the book of *Proverbs*, she "speaks noble things; uprightness comes from [her] lips" (Prov 8:6). She "endows those who love [her] with substance" and "fill[s] their treasuries" (Prov 8:21). Most importantly, Leslie is "a source of delight every day" (Prov 8:30), and together we "rejoice in the world" (Prov 8:31). In deep gratitude of her love and support, let me invoke the praise of the Woman of Valor found later in *Proverbs*: "Many women have done well, but you surpass them all" (Prov 31:29).

While I was writing this book, my now-six-year-old daughter Lila's interest in the stories of the Hebrew Bible developed. As our nighttime story time developed into biblical storytelling, I experienced firsthand the timeless enterprise of scripture and interpretation – both in the way that my own stories were often enhanced by inclusion of midrashic elaboration and by Lila's own observations on the text. The clarity of a young child's perspective attests to the enduring need to make the scriptural text comport with the moral sensibilities of the reader: on Noah cursing Canaan for something his father Ham did in Gen 9:25: "That's not fair!" As with the ancient exegetes, Lila is compelled to "update" the ancient text: on Gen 37:25: "A 'caravan' is a *car* that goes down to Egypt." Her often repeated question "Is that *really* in the Torah?" places her much closer to rabbinic Judaism than Second Temple–period Judaism with regard to the blurring of scripture and its interpretation.

This book is dedicated to the memory of my father-in-law David Azose. He had a strong desire for knowledge and deeper understanding of all things, particularly relating to the history of Judaism. He was a very gracious and perennially curious conversation partner. He possessed a kind and gentle demeanor that made him beloved to all who were around him. The words of 1 Sam 18:14 ring very true for him: ויהי דוד לכל דרכו משכיל, "David was successful in all of his undertakings" (NJPS). Drawing on a technique familiar from rabbinic *midrash* (Y אלה X אל תקרי, "do not read X, rather Y"), we should read משכיל not with its intended intransitive meaning ("be successful"), but with the transitive meaning "to illuminate, give insight" and also render דרך not merely as "undertakings" but with the alternate sense of "manner, behavior." With this midrashic rereading, the scriptural passage becomes an even more fitting epitaph: "David gave insight (to all) in all his ways." David's friends and family can well attest to the many ways in which his demeanor and behavior provided an exemplary model for all to emulate. Indeed, the echo of 1 Sam 18:14 in the Cave 11 *Psalms Scroll* is equally fitting for David: ויהי דויד בן ישי חכם ואור כאור השמש וסופר ונבון ותמים בכול דרכיו לפני אל ואנשים ויתן לו יהוה רוח נבונה ואורה, "Now David (the son of Jesse) was wise and shone like the light of the sun, a scribe and man of discernment, blameless in all his ways before God and men; the Lord gave him a brilliant and discerning spirit" (11QPs[a] 27:2–4). While it certainly stretches credulity to apply this entire encomium to its intended target King David, there is no sense of exaggeration as applied to David Azose.

Unfortunately, David's namesake, my son David, never got to meet his grandfather and learn these attributes from his example. For him, let me take the liberty of revocalizing the verbs in the *Psalms Scroll*. This passage assumes a dramatically different meaning when the verbs are vocalized not as the clearly intended converted imperfect forms, but rather with the consonantally identical jussive forms (וַיְהִי → וִיהִי; וַיִּתֵּן → וְיִתֵּן): "*May David be* wise and shine like the light of the sun, a scribe and man of discernment, blameless in all his ways before God and men; *May the Lord give* him a brilliant and discerning spirit." In so doing, this passage represents my wish that he grow to emulate the kind and gentle spirit of his grandfather.

A Note on Style and Translation

This book on the whole adheres to the style outlined in Patrick H. Alexander, ed., *The SBL Handbook of Style: For Ancient Near Eastern, Biblical, and Early Christian Studies* (Peabody: Hendrickson, 1999). Any modification has been undertaken in the quest for greater clarity in presentation. I have adopted a slightly modified system for abbreviating ancient texts as outlined in the following section. Many of the scholarly articles that I discuss have been reprinted in collected volumes by the authors. In my treatment of these articles in the chapter notes, I cite the article from the most recent printing in the collected volume and indicate the original year of publication in parentheses. Full bibliographic information regarding the original place of publication can be found in the Bibliography.

The translations provided throughout the book represent a combination of my own as well as those of others. In all cases where I rely on other translations, I indicate the source and note if the translation has been modified. Passages from the Hebrew Bible generally follow the New Jewish Publication Society translation (Philadelphia, 1985). As a modern scholarly book about ancient society, this work presents many challenges in striving for inclusive language. As I note several times in the book, biblical and ancient Jewish legal texts nearly always formulate law employing masculine grammatical forms (e.g., "Let no man . . . "). Modern translators sometimes seek to render this decidedly noninclusive language into a gender-neutral translation (e.g., "Let no one . . . "). In an attempt to represent as accurately as possible these ancient texts and the social worlds to which they apply, I have retained the literal translation of the legal formulae with the masculine grammatical forms.

Abbreviations and Sigla

DEAD SEA SCROLLS SIGLA AND TEXTUAL NOTATIONS

2:4–5	Denotes column two, lines four through five. Used for better-preserved larger Dead Sea Scrolls.
2 iii 4–5	Denotes fragment two, column three, lines four through five. Used for fragmentary Dead Sea Scrolls when columns can be reconstructed.
2 4–5	Denotes fragment two, lines four through five. Used for fragmentary Dead Sea Scrolls when columns cannot be reconstructed.
[ ]	Lacuna in ancient manuscript
[א], [a]	Suggested restoration by modern editor
א, a	Overlapping text represented in parallel manuscript
vac, *vacat*	Portion of preserved manuscript with no inscribed text
<א>, <a>	Suggested emendation by modern editor
(a)	Additional words added by modern editor to improve English translation
a // b	Parallel text
par.	Parallel manuscript
frg(s).	Fragment(s)

ABBREVIATIONS OF ANCIENT TEXTS

Hebrew Bible and Second Temple–Period Texts

1–2 Chr	*1–2 Chronicles*	1–2 Kgs	*1–2 Kings*
1–2 Macc	*1–2 Maccabees*	1–2 Sam	*1–2 Samuel*
Amos	*Amos*	Dan	*Daniel*
Deut	*Deuteronomy*	Eccl	*Ecclesiastes*
Exod	*Exodus*	Ezek	*Ezekiel*
Ezra	*Ezra*	Gen	*Genesis*
Hos	*Hosea*	Isa	*Isaiah*
Jer	*Jeremiah*	Job	*Job*
Joel	*Joel*	Jub	*Jubilees*
Lev	*Leviticus*	Mic	*Micah*
Nah	*Nahum*	Neh	*Nehemiah*
Num	*Numbers*	Prov	*Proverbs*
Ps	*Psalms*	Sir	*Wisdom of Ben Sira*
Wis	*Wisdom of Solomon*	Zech	*Zechariah*

Ancient Versions

𝔐	Masoretic Text	⅏	Samaritan Pentateuch
𝔊	Septuagint	𝔗^{J}	Targum Jonathan
𝔗^{N}	Targum Neofiti	𝔗^{O}	Targum Onqelos
𝔗$^{Ps\text{-}J}$	Targum Pseudo-Jonathan		

Dead Sea Scrolls (frequently cited manuscripts)

CD	*Damascus Document* manuscripts from the Cairo Geniza.
1QIsa^{a-b}	*Isaiah* manuscripts from Qumran Cave 1 (superscript numbers indicate individual copies).
1QS	*Rule of the Community* manuscript from Qumran Cave 1.
4QD^{a-h}	*Damascus Document* manuscripts from Qumran Cave 4. Corresponds to 4Q266–273.
4QIsa^{a-r}	*Isaiah* manuscripts from Qumran Cave 4. Corresponds to 4Q55–69b.
4QJer^{a-e}	*Jeremiah* manuscripts from Qumran Cave 4. Corresponds to 4Q70–72b.
4QS^{a-j}	*Rule of the Community* manuscripts from Qumran Cave 4. Corresponds to 4Q255–264.
4QMMT	Composite text of *Miqṣat Ma'ase Ha-Torah* manuscripts from Qumran Cave 4 (4Q394–399).
11QT^{a-b}	*Temple Scroll* from Qumran Cave 11. Corresponds to 11Q19–20.

Rabbinic Texts

Rabbinic Collections

b.	*Babylonian Talmud*	*m.*	*Mishnah*
t.	*Tosefta*	*y.*	*Palestinian Talmud*

Names of Specific Tractates

ʿAbod. Zar.	*ʿAbodah Zarah*	*'Abot*	*'Abot*
B. Bat.	*Baba Batra*	*B. Meṣiʿa*	*Baba Meṣiʿa*
B. Qam.	*Baba Qamma*	*Beṣ.*	*Beṣah*
ʿErub.	*ʿErubin*	*Giṭ.*	*Giṭṭin*
Hor.	*Horayot*	*Ḥag.*	*Ḥagigah*
Ḥul.	*Ḥullin*	*Meg.*	*Megillah*
Men.	*Menaḥot*	*Miqv.*	*Miqva'ot*
Naz.	*Nazir*	*Nid.*	*Niddah*
'Ohal.	*'Ohalot*	*Pe'ah*	*Pe'ah*
Sanh.	*Sanhedrin*	*Shabb.*	*Shabbat*
Sheb.	*Shebuʿot*	*Suk.*	*Sukkah*
Yad.	*Yadayim*	*Yom.*	*Yoma*
Zav.	*Zavim*		

MODERN PUBLICATIONS

AB	Anchor Bible
ABRL	Anchor Bible Reference Library
AGJU	Arbeiten zur Geschichte des antiken Judentums und des Urchristentums
AJSR	*Association for Jewish Studies Review*
ANRW	*Aufstieg und Niedergang der römischen Welt: Geschichte und Kultur Roms im Spiegel der neueren Forschung.* Edited by Hildegard Temporini and Wolfgang Haase. Berlin: de Gruyter, 1972–.
BASOR	*Bulletin of the American Schools of Oriental Research*
Bib	*Biblica*
BIOSCS	*Bulletin of the International Organization for Septuagint and Cognate Studies*
BJRL	*Bulletin of the John Rylands University Library of Manchester*
BJS	Brown Judaic Studies
BZAW	Beihefte zur Zeitschrift für die alttestamentliche Wissenschaft
CBQ	*Catholic Biblical Quarterly*
CBQMS	Catholic Biblical Quarterly Monograph Series

CCWJCW	Cambridge Commentaries on Writings of the Jewish and Christian World, 200 B.C. to A.D. 200
Chi.-Kent L. Rev.	*Chicago-Kent Law Review*
CJA	Christianity and Judaism in Antiquity
CQS	Companion to the Qumran Scrolls
CRINT	Compendia rerum iudaicarum ad Novum Testamentum
CSCO	Corpus scriptorum Christianorum Orientalium
DJD	Discoveries in the Judaean Desert (of Jordan)
DSD	*Dead Sea Discoveries*
EDSS	*Encyclopedia of the Dead Sea Scrolls*. Edited by Lawrence H. Schiffman and James C. VanderKam. 2 vols. Oxford: Oxford University Press, 2000.
EncJud	*Encyclopedia Judaica*. Edited by Michael Berenbaum and Fred Skolnik. 22 vols. 2d ed. Detroit: Macmillan Reference USA, 2007.
ErIsr	*Eretz-Israel*
FAT	Forschungen zum Alten Testament
FIOTL	The Formation and Interpretation of Old Testament Literature
FRLANT	Forschungen zur Religion und Literatur des Alten und Neuen Testaments
HAT	Handbuch zum Alten Testament
HSM	Harvard Semitic Monographs
HSS	Harvard Semitic Studies
HTR	*Harvard Theological Review*
HUCA	*Hebrew Union College Annual*
JAJ	*Journal of Ancient Judaism*
JBL	*Journal of Biblical Literature*
JCS	*Journal of Cuneiform Studies*
JJS	*Journal of Jewish Studies*
JNES	*Journal of Near Eastern Studies*
JQR	*Jewish Quarterly Review*
JSJ	*Journal for the Study of Judaism in the Persian, Hellenistic, and Roman Periods*
JSJSup	Journal for the Study of Judaism in the Persian, Hellenistic, and Roman Periods: Supplement Series
JSOTSup	Journal for the Study of the Old Testament: Supplement Series
JSPSup	Journal for the Study of the Pseudepigrapha: Supplement Series
JSQ	*Jewish Studies Quarterly*
JSRC	Jerusalem Studies in Religion and Culture
JTS	*Journal of Theological Studies*
LCL	Loeb Classical Library

Leš	*Lešonenu*
LSTS	Library of Second Temple Studies
MGWJ	*Monatschrift für Geschichte und Wissenschaft des Judentums*
MHUC	Monographs of the Hebrew Union College
NETS	*New English Translation of the Septuagint*. Edited by Albert Pietersma and Benjamin G. Wright. 2d ed. Oxford: Oxford University Press, 2009.
NJPS	*Tanakh: A New Translation of the Holy Scriptures According to the Traditional Hebrew Text*. Philadelphia: Jewish Publication Society, 1985.
NRSV	New Revised Standard Version
NTL	New Testament Library
OLA	Orientalia lovaniensia analecta
OTL	Old Testament Library
PTSDSSP	Princeton Theological Seminary Dead Sea Scrolls Project
RB	*Revue biblique*
REJ	*Revue des études juives*
RevQ	*Revue de Qumran*
SA	Scriptores Aethiopici
SAOC	Studies in Ancient Oriental Civilizations
SBLDS	Society of Biblical Literature Dissertation Series
SBLSymS	Society of Biblical Literature Symposium Series
SBLWAW	Society of Biblical Literature Writings from the Ancient World
SHR	Studies in the History of Religions
SJ	Scripta Judaica
SJLA	Studies in Judaism in Late Antiquity
STDJ	Studies on the Texts of the Desert of Judah
StPB	Studia post-biblica
StPhA	*Studia Philonica Annual*
SVTP	Studia in Veteris Testamenti pseudepigraphica
TDNT	*Theological Dictionary of the New Testament*. Edited by Gerhard Kittel and Gerhard Friedrich. 10 vols. Grand Rapids: Eerdmans, 1964–76.
TDOT	*Theological Dictionary of the Old Testament*. Edited by G. Johannes Botterweck and Helmer Ringgren. 15 vols. Grand Rapids: Eerdmans, 1974–2006.
ThBN	Themes in Biblical Narrative
TSAJ	Texte und Studien zum antiken Judentum
UCPNES	University of California Publications in Near Eastern Studies
VT	*Vetus Testamentum*

VTSup	Supplements to Vetus Testamentum
WBC	Word Biblical Commentary
WUNT	Wissenschaftliche Untersuchungen zum Neuen Testament
YJS	Yale Judaica Series
ZAW	*Zeitschrift für die alttestamentliche Wissenschaft*
ZfHB	*Zeitschrift für Hebraische Bibliographie*

1

Introduction

> This (alludes to) the study of the Torah which he commanded through Moses to do, according to everything which has been revealed (from) time to time, and according to which the prophets have revealed by his holy spirit.
>
> *Rule of the Community* (1QS) 8:15–16

> Ben Bag-Bag said: "Turn it and turn it again, for everything is in it."
>
> *Mishnah 'Abot* 5:22

1. SCRIPTURE AND LAW IN THE DEAD SEA SCROLLS

In the early phases of Dead Sea Scrolls scholarship, the study of Jewish law was episodic and rarely central to scholarly approaches to the Dead Sea Scrolls.[1] Scholarship on law in the Dead Sea Scrolls long continued to suffer from neglect.[2] The editorial team entrusted with the publication of the Cave 4

[1] My use of the term "Dead Sea Scrolls" here and throughout the book refers to the manuscripts found in the eleven caves near Qumran. Any reference to other scrolls found in the Judean desert will state their place of origin explicitly. The range of civil, criminal, and religious legal material subsumed under the classification "Jewish law" in many respects matches what later rabbinic Judaism refers to as *halakhah* (on which, see Louis Jacobs, "Halakhah," *EncJud* 8:251). As scholars have noted, however, this term does not appear in the Dead Sea Scrolls, and thus its use in reference to the scrolls and the associated sectarian community is anachronistic (see John P. Meier, "Is There *Halaka* (Noun) at Qumran?" *JBL* 122 [2003]: 150–55). At the same time, many scholars have employed the terminology – sometimes with appropriate reservations and sometimes without – as a useful technical term to convey the broad sense of law unique to ancient Judaism. In the context of my discussion of these scholars' work, I employ the term *halakhah*. Otherwise, I use the more general term "Jewish law."

[2] The most significant early analysis of law in the Dead Sea Scrolls was produced before the discovery of the Dead Sea Scrolls in Louis Ginzberg's commentary on the Cairo Genizah manuscripts of what would later be known as the *Damascus Document*. Ginzberg's work was first published in a series of articles entitled "Eine unbekannte jüdische Sekte" in *MGWJ* 55–58 (1911–14),

fragments neither was equipped to analyze the legal material in these texts nor displayed any serious interest in doing so. The lack of availability of the legal texts from Cave 4 prevented scholars with the requisite expertise in Jewish law from introducing this new material into their scholarly work.[3]

Beginning in the 1960s and 1970s, the pioneering work of Joseph Baumgarten, Lawrence Schiffman, and Yigael Yadin turned the sporadic treatment of law that had characterized Dead Sea Scrolls scholarship into a concentrated exploration of the contribution of the Dead Sea Scrolls to the history of Jewish law.[4] In particular, Yadin's publication of the *Temple Scroll* in 1977 dramatically expanded the corpus of relevant material for scholars interested in Jewish law.[5] The appearance of the *Temple Scroll* thus precipitated a renewed interest in Jewish law in the Dead Sea Scrolls.[6] Since then, the combined growth in

and then self-published by Ginzberg as *Eine unbekannte jüdische Sekte* (New York, 1922; repr. Hildesheim: Olms, 1972). An expanded English translation later appeared as *An Unknown Jewish Sect* (Moreshet 1; New York: Jewish Theological Seminary, 1976). After the discovery of the Qumran caves, see especially Saul Lieberman, "Light on the Cave Scrolls from Rabbinic Sources," in *Texts and Studies* (New York: Ktav, 1974), 190–99 (1951); idem, "The Discipline of the So-Called Dead Sea Manual of Discipline," in *Texts and Studies*, 200–7 (1952); Chaim Rabin, *The Zadokite Documents* (Oxford: Clarendon Press, 1954); idem, *Qumran Studies* (SJ 2; Oxford: Oxford University Press, 1957); Jacob Licht, *The Rule Scroll: A Scroll from the Wilderness of Judaea* (Jerusalem: Bialik Institute, 1965) [Hebrew]. On broader trends in early scholarship, see Yaakov Sussman, "The History of Halakha and the Dead Sea Scrolls: Preliminary Talmudic Observations on *Miqṣat Ma'aśe ha-Torah* (4QMMT)," *Tarbiz* 49 (1992): 11–76 (11–22) [Hebrew]; Lawrence H. Schiffman, "Halakhah and History: The Contribution of the Dead Sea Scrolls to Recent Scholarship," in *Qumran and Jerusalem: Studies in the Dead Sea Scrolls and the History of Judaism* (Grand Rapids: Eerdmans, 2010), 63–78 (1999); Steven D. Fraade "Qumran *Yaḥad* and Rabbinic *Ḥăbûrâ*: A Comparison Reconsidered," in *Legal Fictions: Studies of Law and Narrative in the Discursive Worlds of Ancient Jewish Sectarians and Sages* (JSJSup 147; Leiden: Brill, 2011), 125–44 (2009); Alex P. Jassen, "American Scholarship on Jewish Law in the Dead Sea Scrolls," in *The Dead Sea Scrolls in Scholarly Perspective: A History of Research* (ed. D. Dimant; STDJ 99; Leiden: Brill, 2012), 101–54.

3 For discussion of the possible reasons for the lack of interest in legal texts, see Lawrence H. Schiffman, "Confessionalism and the Study of the Dead Sea Scrolls," *Jewish Studies: Forum of the World Union of Jewish Studies* 31 (1991): 3–14; and Fraade, "Qumran *Yaḥad*," 125–28.

4 See especially Joseph M. Baumgarten, *Studies in Qumran Law* (SJLA 24; Leiden: Brill, 1977); Lawrence H. Schiffman, *The Halakhah at Qumran* (SJLA 16; Leiden: Brill, 1975); idem, *Sectarian Law in the Dead Sea Scrolls: Courts, Testimony and the Penal Code* (BJS 33; Chico: Scholars Press, 1983); idem, *Law, Custom, and Messianism in the Dead Sea Scrolls* (Jerusalem: Zalman Shazar Center, 1993) [Hebrew]; idem, *Reclaiming the Dead Sea Scrolls: The History of Judaism, the Background of Christianity, the Lost Library of Qumran* (ABRL; New York: Doubleday, 1995), especially 243–312; idem, *The Courtyards of the House of the Lord: Studies on the Temple Scroll* (ed. F. García Martínez; STDJ 75; Leiden: Brill, 2008); idem, *Qumran and Jerusalem*. On Yadin, see following note. On the contributions of Baumgarten and Schiffman, see further Jassen, "American Scholarship," 132–37, 141–51.

5 The *Temple Scroll* was first published by Yadin in a Hebrew edition: *The Temple Scroll* (3 vols.; Jerusalem: Israel Exploration Society, the Hebrew University, and the Shrine of the Book, 1977). An English edition appeared in 1983.

6 On the importance of the publication of the *Temple Scroll* as a turning point, see Jassen, "American Scholarship," 138–45.

interest and now complete availability of the entire corpus of legal texts has translated into the emergence of Jewish law as a vibrant field of Dead Sea Scrolls scholarship.[7]

Research on Jewish law has focused on two approaches: (1) clarifying the foundations and intricacies of the sectarian system of Jewish law and its relationship to both ancient Israelite law and wider segments of Second Temple–period Judaism,[8] and (2) comparative analysis of Jewish law in the scrolls with rabbinic literature, whereby the scrolls shed important light on our understanding of the origins and development of rabbinic *halakhah* at the same time as rabbinic literature is employed to decipher the meaning and importance of law in the Dead Sea Scrolls.[9]

The study of law in the Dead Sea Scrolls within the broader context of ancient Judaism is clearly an ever-growing field. One area that has received considerably less treatment is discussion of the hermeneutical methods employed in the legal texts among the Dead Sea Scrolls and their relationship to related legal literature in the Second Temple period and rabbinic Judaism. What role does scriptural interpretation play in the formulation of law in the Dead Sea Scrolls, and, if that law was formulated in dialogue with scripture, what exegetical principles and techniques stand behind the legal interpretation of scripture? Moreover, how should the exegetical techniques detected in the Dead Sea Scrolls be

[7] For representative recent work, see especially Lutz Doering, *Schabbat: Sabbathhalacha und praxis im antiken Judentum und Urchristentum* (TSAJ 78; Tübingen: Mohr Siebeck, 1999); Fraade, *Legal Fictions*; Vered Noam, *From Qumran to the Rabbinic Revolution: Conceptions of Impurity* (Jerusalem: Yad Ben Zvi, 2010) [Hebrew]; Schiffman, *Qumran and Jerusalem*; Aharon Shemesh, *Halakhah in the Making: The Development of Jewish Law from Qumran to the Rabbis* (Berkeley: University of California Press, 2009). For a broad overview, see Steven D. Fraade, "The Dead Sea Scrolls and Rabbinic Judaism after Sixty (Plus) Years: Retrospect and Prospect," in *Legal Fictions*, 109–24.

[8] See, for example, Lawrence H. Schiffman, "The Temple Scroll and the Systems of Jewish Law in the Second Temple Period," in *Temple Scroll Studies: Papers Presented at the International Symposium on the Temple Scroll: Manchester, December 1987* (ed. G. J. Brooke; JSPSup 7; Sheffield: JSOT Press, 1989), 239–55; idem, "Pre-Maccabean Halakhah in the Dead Sea Scrolls and the Biblical Tradition," in *Qumran and Jerusalem*, 184–96 (2006); Hannah K. Harrington, "Biblical Law at Qumran," in *The Dead Sea Scrolls after Fifty Years: A Comprehensive Assessment* (ed. J. C. VanderKam and P. W. Flint; 2 vols.; Leiden: Brill, 1998–99), 1:160–85; Aharon Shemesh and Cana Werman, "Halakhah at Qumran: Genre and Authority," *DSD* 10 (2003): 104–29.

[9] Several significant recent trends are surveyed in Fraade "Qumran *Yaḥad*," 128–29; Jassen, "American Scholarship," 146–54. See below, section IV, for fuller discussion of comparative analysis with rabbinic literature. For general overviews of the results of this comparative analysis, see Joseph M. Baumgarten, "Tannaitic Halakhah and Qumran: A Re-evaluation," in *Rabbinic Perspectives: Rabbinic Literature and the Dead Sea Scrolls: Proceedings of the Eighth International Symposium of the Orion Center for the Study of the Dead Sea Scrolls and Associated Literature, 7–9 January, 2003* (ed. S. D. Fraade, A. Shemesh, and R. A. Clements; STDJ 62; Leiden: Brill, 2006), 1–11; Lawrence H. Schiffman, "The Qumran Scrolls and Rabbinic Judaism," in *Qumran and Jerusalem*, 1–11 (1999); Lutz Doering, "Parallels Without 'Parallelomania': Methodological Reflections on Comparative Analysis of Halakhah in the Dead Sea Scrolls," in *Rabbinic Perspectives*, 13–42; Shemesh, *Halakhah in the Making*, especially 1–7.

situated within the broader historical context of ancient Jewish legal-exegetical activity?

The lack of sustained inquiry into legal exegesis in the Dead Sea Scrolls stands in contrast not just to the robust study of Jewish law more generally but also to the study of nonlegal scriptural interpretation in the scrolls. Scholarly analysis of scriptural interpretation appeared in the earliest phases of Dead Sea Scrolls scholarship and has continued unabated.[10] In this area, scholars have located exegetical methods in the Dead Sea Scrolls in the broader context of scriptural interpretation in Second Temple Judaism and explored continuity and discontinuity with later rabbinic exegesis (*midrash*).[11] Yet, the bulk of analysis of scriptural interpretation in the Dead Sea Scrolls has focused on nonlegal material. The study of legal exegesis in the Dead Sea Scrolls both on its own and in a comparative context lags behind both the study of the history of Jewish law and comparative homiletical exegesis. To be sure, important work has been done. The majority of this research, however, has focused on employing the Dead Sea Scrolls in order to trace the historical origins of rabbinic *midrash halakhah* – explicit legal exegesis.[12] This research only secondarily touches upon comparative hermeneutics in ways that have proven so fruitful in the comparative study of nonlegal exegesis.[13]

10 See the review of the development of this field in Moshe J. Bernstein, "The Contribution of the Qumran Discoveries to the History of Early Biblical Interpretation," in *The Idea of Biblical Interpretation: Essays in Honor of James L. Kugel* (ed. H. Najman and J. H. Newman; JSJSup 83; Leiden: Brill, 2004), 215–38.

11 See Paul Mandel, "Midrashic Exegesis and Its Precedents in the Dead Sea Scrolls," *DSD* 8 (2001): 149–68; Lawrence H. Schiffman, "Dead Sea Scrolls, Biblical Interpretation," in *Encyclopedia of Midrash* (ed. J. Neusner and A. J. Avery Peck; 2 vols.; Leiden: Brill, 2005), 1:40–54; Steven D. Fraade, "'Comparative Midrash' Revisited: The Case of the Dead Sea Scrolls and Rabbinic Midrash," in *Higayon L'Yonah: New Aspects in the Study of Midrash, Aggadah, and Piyut in Honor of Professor Yona Fraenkel* (ed. J. Levinson, J. Elbaum, and G. Hasan-Rokem; Jerusalem: Magnes, 2006), 261–84 [Hebrew].

12 For recent attempts, see Steven D. Fraade, "Looking for Legal Midrash at Qumran," in *Legal Fictions*, 145–68 (1998); Menachem Kister, "A Common Heritage: Biblical Interpretation at Qumran and Its Implications," in *Biblical Perspectives: Early Use and Interpretation of the Bible in Light of the Dead Sea Scrolls: Proceedings of the First International Symposium of the Orion Center for the Study of the Dead Sea Scrolls and Associated Literature, 12–14 May, 1996* (ed. M. E. Stone and E. G. Chazon; STDJ 28; Leiden: Brill, 1998), 101–12; Aharon Shemesh, "Scriptural Interpretations in the Damascus Document and Their Parallels in Rabbinic Midrash," in *The Damascus Document: A Centennial of Discovery: Proceedings of the Third International Symposium of the Orion Center for the Study of the Dead Sea Scrolls and Associated Literature, 4–8 February, 1998* (ed. J. M. Baumgarten, E. G. Chazon, and A. Pinnick; STDJ 39; Leiden: Brill, 2000), 161–75; Azzan Yadin, "4QMMT, Rabbi Ishmael, and the Origins of Legal Midrash," *DSD* 10 (2003): 130–49. On earlier approaches, see discussion in Fraade, ibid., 145–47.

13 See especially Elieser Slomovic, "Toward an Understanding of the Exegesis in the Dead Sea Scrolls," *RevQ* 7 (1969): 3–15 (9–12); Michael Fishbane, "Use, Authority, and Interpretation of Mikra at Qumran," in *Mikra: Text, Translation, Reading and Interpretation of the Hebrew Bible in Ancient Judaism and Early Christianity* (ed. M. J. Mulder; CRINT 2/1; Assen:

II. GOALS AND FOCUS OF THIS STUDY

The goal of this study is to engage the larger question of comparative history of law in ancient Judaism through analysis of the hermeneutic strategies and techniques in the Dead Sea Scrolls. My primary focus is the legal literature representing the interrelated set of sectarian communities of the Dead Sea Scrolls.[14] This monograph seeks to address two interconnected questions related to the legal hermeneutics of the Dead Sea Scrolls. The overarching question I explore is the function of non-Pentateuchal scripture in the legal hermeneutics of the Dead Sea Scrolls. While a canon had not yet emerged in the Dead Sea Scrolls and Second Temple Judaism, I argue in Chapter 3 that the sectarian community (and much of Second Temple Judaism) recognized a significant difference between the Pentateuch and all other sacred writings. What distinctions, if any, exist in the way in which non-Pentateuchal material is employed in sectarian legal hermeneutics versus Pentateuchal texts? At the same time, this book represents the first monograph-length study of any aspect of legal-exegetical techniques in the Dead Sea Scrolls. In both inquiries, I situate the evidence of the Dead Sea Scrolls within the broader history of Jewish law and legal exegesis in antiquity.

Scripture, Prophecy, and Law in the Dead Sea Scrolls

My overarching question attempts to explore a fundamental issue of any system of legal hermeneutics – what constitutes an authoritative text? My use of the term "authoritative" here follows the definition provided by Eugene C. Ulrich in his discussion of the emergence of the canon of the Hebrew Bible:

Van Gorcum; Minneapolis: Fortress, 1988), 339–77 (368–71) (both very limited); and more systematic approaches in Schiffman, *Halakhah*; Jacob Milgrom, "The Qumran Cult: Its Exegetical Principles," in *Temple Scroll Studies*, 165–80; idem, "Qumran's Biblical Hermeneutics: The Case of the Wood Offering," *RevQ* 16 (1993–94): 449–56; Moshe J. Bernstein and Shlomo A. Koyfman, "The Interpretation of Biblical Law in the Dead Sea Scrolls: Forms and Methods," in *Biblical Interpretation at Qumran* (ed. M. Henze; Grand Rapids: Eerdmans, 2005), 61–87. This issue has received considerable attention in the recent work of Vered Noam: "Early Signs of Halakhic Midrash at Qumran," *Diné Israel: Studies in Halakhah and Jewish Law* 26–27 (2009–10): 3–26 [Hebrew]; "Embryonic Legal Midrash in the Qumran Scrolls," in *The Hebrew Bible in Light of the Dead Sea Scrolls* (ed. N. Dávid et al.; FRLANT 239; Göttingen: Vandenhoeck and Ruprecht, 2011), 237–62; "Creative Interpretation and Integrative Interpretation in Qumran," in *The Dead Sea Scrolls and Contemporary Culture: Proceedings of the International Conference Held at the Israel Museum (July 6–8, 2008)* (ed. A. D. Roitman, L. H. Schiffman, and S. Tzoref; STDJ 93; Leiden: Brill, 2011), 363–76. See also below, section IV, for further discussion of previous scholarship.

14 Recent research has succeeded in generating a more nuanced portrait of the interrelated sectarian communities represented in the scrolls and their historical development. See especially John J. Collins, *Beyond the Qumran Community: The Sectarian Movement of the Dead Sea Scrolls* (Grand Rapids: Eerdmans, 2010). My focus on the legal literature attempts to take advantage of this renewed understanding at the same time that it seeks to contribute to the conversation.

> A writing, which a group, secular or religious, recognizes and accepts as determinative for its conduct and as of a higher order than can be overridden by the power or will of the group or any member.[15]

Ulrich further qualifies this meaning as unique when the ultimate source of the authority is regarded as God. In such a case, a text is not merely "authoritative" but "a book of scripture." With this type of authoritative text, "The community, as a group and individually, recognizes [it] and accepts [it] as determative for its belief and practice for all time and in all geographical areas."[16]

In the context of the Dead Sea Scrolls, what relative authority did the community attach to Pentateuchal and non-Pentateuchal scripture, and what legal force did these passages possess? My interest in this specific hermeneutic element arose during research conducted for my first book, in which I examined prophecy and revelation in the Dead Sea Scrolls and related segments of Second Temple Judaism.[17] A significant portion of that study focused on the way in which the texts from the Dead Sea Scrolls reconfigure received scriptural models of prophets and prophecy. I argued that the way in which ancient prophecy is reconceptualized in the Dead Sea Scrolls is ultimately reflective of prevailing attitudes toward prophets and prophecy. In my analysis, I found that the most significant way in which the ancient prophets are reconfigured in the Dead Sea Scrolls is their consistent presentation, in both sectarian and nonsectarian texts, as lawgivers. Such a model, while not absent from the Hebrew Bible, is clearly a tendentious portrait crafted by the authors of the Second Temple–period texts.

In assessing the contemporary significance of this feature, I suggested that it must be understood within the context of the community's belief in the progressive revelation of law. Internal textual evidence indicates that the community of the Dead Sea Scrolls conceived of three primary chronological stages in this progressive revelation: (1) Moses, (2) the classical prophets, and (3) the contemporary sectarian community. In particular, I argued that the community fashioned itself as the direct heir to the ancient prophetic lawgivers and therefore constructed a portrait of the ancient law-giving prophets to reflect its own present-day claims to possess the true meaning and application of the Torah based on the receipt of divine revelation.[18]

[15] Eugene C. Ulrich, "The Notion and Definition of Canon," in *The Canon Debate* (ed. L. M. McDonald and J. A. Sanders; Peabody: Hendrickson, 2002), 22–35 (29).

[16] Ulrich, "The Notion and Definition of Canon," 29. See further Chapter 3, section I, for a fuller examination of the meaning of "authority" and "authoritative" texts in ancient Judaism.

[17] Alex P. Jassen, *Mediating the Divine: Prophecy and Revelation in the Dead Sea Scrolls and Second Temple Judaism* (STDJ 68; Leiden: Brill, 2007). This work represents a revised version of my 2006 New York University dissertation.

[18] See further Alex P. Jassen, "The Presentation of the Ancient Prophets as Lawgivers at Qumran," *JBL* 127 (2008): 307–37. Further explorations of the significance of the sectarian belief in progressive revelation can be found in Schiffman, *Halakhah*, 22–32; Shemesh, *Halakhah in the Making*, 39–71.

The conclusions reached at this stage in my research suggested to me that the community of the Dead Sea Scrolls would likely have assigned a significantly elevated legal status to the writings presumed to be the literary record of the classical prophets. If the classical prophets followed Moses as the next authentic recipients of the revealed law, then surely the collection of prophetic scriptures would have been viewed by the community as a textual repository of such legal activity and therefore fertile ground for contemporary legal-exegetical activity.

The present study grows out of my desire to test this working hypothesis in greater detail. Did the community regard non-Pentateuchal scripture as an authoritative legal source, and were these texts considered valid textual bases for contemporary legal exegesis? As I discuss further below, much of the way in which this initial inquiry is framed is based on similar questions proposed in the study of rabbinic legal hermeneutics. In this study, I begin my inquiry into this broad set of questions with the legal texts in the Dead Sea Scrolls. At the same time, I situate my analysis in the larger framework of the history of Jewish law and the relationship among scripture, exegesis, prophecy, and law in ancient Judaism.

The Dead Sea Scrolls and Ancient Jewish Law

This study unfolds as a detailed analysis of fifteen examples in the sectarian Dead Sea Scrolls of legal exegesis on non-Pentateuchal passages. As such, this work represents a more general treatment of several aspects of legal exegesis in the Dead Sea Scrolls. As noted above, the study of sectarian legal exegesis has long lagged behind analysis of the community's nonlegal exegesis. Recent years have witnessed a rightful attempt to remedy this imbalance. This work presents itself as another contribution to this growing scholarly enterprise. Moreover, my analysis seeks to contextualize legal exegesis in the Dead Sea Scrolls within the larger comparative setting of legal exegesis in Second Temple and rabbinic Judaism.

In many ways this work is also representative of the new opportunities available in Dead Sea Scrolls scholarship since the full release of the scrolls in the 1990s and the immense amount of scholarly literature that followed in its wake. Cave 4 yielded a large number of previously unknown sectarian legal documents as well as several copies of the *Damascus Document* and the *Rule of the Community*. The absence of this major group of texts from the publication efforts of the early scholars working on the Cave 4 material had a drastic trickle-down effect. These texts were unavailable and in many cases even unknown to scholars examining Jewish law in the Dead Sea Scrolls and ancient Judaism. Thus, any presentation of Jewish law in the sectarian community or even broader segments of Second Temple Judaism ultimately resulted in an incomplete picture. In taking advantage of a much broader corpus of newly available legal texts, my goal in this study is to provide a fuller portrait of

Jewish law in the community of the Dead Sea Scrolls and its relationship to law in Second Temple and rabbinic Judaism.

Previous treatment of the recently published legal texts from Cave 4 has placed great emphasis on deciphering the meaning of these often fragmentary texts and their legal content. As the work of deciphering their meaning and content has become better established, scholars have begun to situate these legal texts within the broader context of the legal literature of the Dead Sea Scrolls, in particular their relationship to long-known legal texts such as the *Damascus Document* and the *Rule of the Community*, as well as nonsectarian works such as the book of *Jubilees*. This book explores the contribution of the Cave 4 legal texts to the study of the development of modes of legal exegesis within the community of the Dead Sea Scrolls. At the same time, I seek to extend the ongoing scholarly conversation with regard to the literary and redactional relationship of the Cave 4 legal texts to other Dead Sea Scrolls legal literature.

Aside from the newly published Cave 4 texts, my analysis concentrates on many texts that have been widely available since the early days of Dead Sea Scrolls scholarship. In spite of this accessibility, little attention has been paid to their important contribution to the study of legal exegesis. My analysis has the advantage of being able to draw upon the long history of scholarship on texts such as the *Damascus Document* and the *Rule of the Community*. The examination of these documents in conjunction with the recently published texts demonstrates the centrality of the interpretation of scripture to the legal system of the Dead Sea Scrolls and yields a fuller portrait of the community's legal hermeneutics.

III. EARLIER SCHOLARSHIP

Earlier scholarship on the use of non-Pentateuchal scriptural passages in Dead Sea Scrolls legal exegesis has yielded dramatically divergent results. The first attempts to treat this issue stem from research conducted exclusively on the two medieval manuscripts of the *Damascus Document* published by Solomon Schechter in 1910.[19] In the course of his outline of the nature of the sectarian community, Schechter devotes a section to discussing the "biblical Canon" of the sect. As proof that the community accepted the traditional canon, he observes the presence of passages drawn from across the Hebrew Bible throughout the *Damascus Document*. In this context, he notes that the sect "occasionally derives norms for the practice from the prophetic writings" and specifically contrasts this with the rejection of this approach in rabbinic

[19] Solomon Schechter, *Documents of Jewish Sectaries*, volume 1: *Fragments of a Zadokite Work* (Cambridge: Cambridge University Press, 1910; repr. with prolegomenon by Joseph Fitzmyer; Library of Biblical Studies; New York: Ktav, 1970). For a broad overview of pre-Qumran scholarship on law in the *Damascus Document*, see Jassen, "American Scholarship," 101–21.

tradition.[20] Schechter, however, does not elaborate any further on this observation.

R. H. Charles offers the same basic assessment of the *Damascus Document*, though he frames his observation in the context of the suggested identity of the sectarian community. In order to take into account the purported points of correspondence with both the Sadducees and the Pharisees, Charles proposes the existence of a "reformed" group of former Sadducean priests who shared many beliefs and practices with the Pharisees. Charles refers to this group as a "Zadokite Party."[21] In order to make this identification work, Charles offers examples of some shared elements with the Pharisees, though he goes to great lengths to demonstrate that the sect is not identical to the Pharisees. As one example of the latter phenomenon, Charles contrasts the recurring legal use of non-Pentateuchal passages in the *Damascus Document* with the near universal reluctance to do so among the rabbis.[22]

Charles draws on this observation to add further insight into the nature of the purported Pharisaic elements in the sect. He traces the common use of non-Pentateuchal passages for legal purposes to the "higher estimation in which they [i.e., the sect] held the Prophets."[23] This particular comment must be situated in the context of Charles's earlier assertion regarding the reverence for the Prophets among what he terms the "Apocalyptic School of Pharisaism."[24] Charles suggests that the sectarian community should be associated with this presumed branch of Pharisaism. Thus, Charles's observation regarding the relationship between scripture and law in the *Damascus Document* is intimately bound up with his quest to locate the elusive identity of the sect and carve out a distinct form of Pharisaism with which it can be identified. Neither goal, however, serves to locate Charles's correct observation in the broader history of Jewish law and legal exegesis.[25]

The third attempt to address this larger issue also dates to the pre-Qumran period of research on the *Damascus Document*. Louis Ginzberg devotes several

[20] Schechter, *Documents*, 47. As a specific example, he calls attention to the use of 1 Sam 25:26 in CD 9:8–10. On which, see below Chapter 11, section II.

[21] See R. H. Charles, "Fragments of a Zadokite Work," in idem, ed., *Apocrypha and Pseudepigrapha of the Old Testament* (2 vols.; Oxford: Clarendon, 1913), 2:790–92.

[22] Charles, "Fragments," 2:791.

[23] Charles, "Fragments," 2:791.

[24] Charles, "Fragments," 2:789.

[25] A related approach is found in Adolph Büchler's argument that the use of non-Pentateuchal scripture for derivation of law in the *Damascus Document* is influenced by the similar method employed among medieval Karaites (Adolph Büchler, "Schechter's 'Jewish Sectaries,'" *JQR* 3 [1913]: 429–85 [456–67]). This suggestion is one among many that Büchler marshals to argue in favor of a medieval dating of the text. As Schechter correctly notes, the use of non-Pentateuchal scripture for law is not unique to the Karaites, but is clearly found already in rabbinic literature, and thus there is no need to draw the conclusions that Büchler does regarding the dating of the text (Solomon Schechter, "Dr. Büchler's Review of Schechter's 'Jewish Sectaries,'" *JQR* 4 [1914]: 449–74 [467]).

pages to discussion of the authority of non-Pentateuchal material in the legal portion of the text.[26] Ginzberg's approach is far more involved than are the general observations made by Schechter and Charles. Yet, as with Charles, Ginzberg's assessment of the evidence he collects is too heavily colored by his identification of the sect as closely related to the Pharisees.[27] Ginzberg's overarching methodology in his work is to call attention to evidence from rabbinic literature that seems to provide direct correspondence with elements in the *Damascus Document*, thereby reinforcing his suggestion regarding the Pharisaic origin of the *Damascus Document*.

Ginzberg's observations regarding non-Pentateuchal scripture fit this same general approach. He begins by assessing the rabbinic approach to the role of non-Pentateuchal scripture in legal exegesis. Contrary to the common assertion that the rabbis reject the use of all non-Pentateuchal scripture, he provides several examples from rabbinic literature where scriptural passages from the Prophets and Writings are regarded with the same level of legal authority as passages from the Pentateuch.[28] When he turns his attention to the *Damascus Document*, Ginzberg observes the presence of several non-Pentateuchal passages utilized in legal exegesis. In his assessment of these passages, Ginzberg suggests that the *Damascus Document* does not seem to place any greater emphasis on non-Pentateuchal scripture than is found in rabbinic tradition.

Moreover, the reliance upon non-Pentateuchal scripture is never more than "the character of props," equivalent to the rabbinic category of *asmakhta*.[29] In employing this technical term drawn from rabbinic hermeneutics, Ginzberg suggests that all reliance on non-Pentateuchal scripture should only loosely be associated with its purported scriptural prooftext.[30] He clarifies what he means by calling attention to the reference to David's ignorance of the law in CD 5:2–3. This passage, argues Ginzberg, suggests that neither David nor his prophet Nathan – and by extension all prophets – can be treated as legal authorities. Ginzberg thus proposes that prophetic passages that appear in legal contexts in the *Damascus Document* "merely illustrate the ethical content of the law."[31]

In framing the issue in this way, Ginzberg has it both ways. The *Damascus Document* relies on some non-Pentateuchal scripture as in rabbinic literature.

[26] This material first appeared in "Eine unbekannte jüdische Sekte," *MGWJ* 58 (1914): 16–48 (26–38). For the English edition, see Ginzberg, *Jewish Sect*, 182–93.

[27] On Ginzberg's proposal regarding the Pharisaic origins of the *Damascus Document*, see Jassen, "American Scholarship," 116–21.

[28] Ginzberg, *Jewish Sect*, 185–86.

[29] Ginzberg, *Jewish Sect*, 186.

[30] The *asmakhta* in rabbinic legal hermeneutics is understood as "a Biblical interpretation by the Sages to support a given law, though it is not the true purpose of the text." See "אסמכתא ('Asmakhta)," in *Encyclopedia Talmudica* (ed. M. Bar-Ilan and S. Y. Yeiven; trans. H. Freedman; 6 vols. to date; Jerusalem: Yad HaRav Herzog, Talmudic Encyclopedia Institute, 1974–), 2:515–22 (515).

[31] Ginzberg, *Jewish Sect*, 187.

At the same time, the weight accorded to non-Pentateuchal scripture never reaches a critical level so as to erase the distinction between Pentateuchal and non-Pentateuchal scripture. In the *Damascus Document*, as in rabbinic literature, the Pentateuch reigns supreme for legal exegesis. Non-Pentateuchal passages always play a minor and secondary role.

Following the discovery and publication of the Qumran scrolls, few scholars returned to the broad set of questions outlined by Schechter and Ginzberg. In several places, however, Lawrence H. Schiffman has opined that the sectarian community displays no reluctance in using non-Pentateuchal passages for purposes of deriving law.[32] With the benefit of the much fuller Qumran corpus, Schiffman arrives at the same basic conclusions as Schechter. Moreover, Schiffman suggests that the rabbinic reluctance to draw upon non-Pentateuchal scripture is related to contemporaneous Christian use of the Prophets and Writings for messianic prooftexts. Because all the Dead Sea Scrolls texts predate this phenomenon, they show no similar reluctance.[33] In a more recent survey of sectarian legal hermeneutics, Moshe J. Bernstein and Shlomo Koyfman likewise affirm that the community seems to display little hesitation to employ non-Pentateuchal passages for legal purposes. Yet, they assert that the paucity of examples should be taken into consideration when attempting to extrapolate hermeneutic principles.[34]

The two sides in this debate of course cannot both be correct. The widely divergent conclusions can be attributed to a number of factors. In Ginzberg's case, his preconceived notions of the identity of the sectarian community heavily colored his analysis of the material. Moreover, the analyses undertaken by Schechter, Charles, and Ginzberg were limited to passages from the *Damascus Document*, more specifically to only the Cairo Genizah manuscripts. Their knowledge of sectarian legal hermeneutics was therefore extremely limited. The *Damascus Document*, the only available text, in fact differs from most other sectarian legal texts on account of its relative abundance of scriptural citations as legal prooftexts. In Schiffman's case, his argument is found as a secondary assertion in several different places dedicated to treatment of other issues. As with Ginzberg, his initial comments are directed to a very limited set of passages in the *Damascus Document* (Sabbath law). His assertion therefore does not follow a comprehensive analysis of the relevant source materials or a statement of methodological rubrics. Indeed, we should not expect anything of this nature from Charles, Ginzberg, or Schiffman; this is not the stated goal of any of these treatments. Similarly, Bernstein's and Koyfman's caution regarding

32 For the most recent statement, see Schiffman, *Reclaiming*, 222. This same conclusion is asserted in several earlier works: "The Halakhah at Qumran" (2 vols.; Ph.D. diss., Brandeis University, 1974), 1:182; *Halakhah*, 114; "The Temple Scroll in Literary and Philological Perspective," in *Approaches to Ancient Judaism* (ed. W. S. Green; Chico: Scholars Press, 1980), 2:143–58 (151); *Sectarian Law*, 102–3 n. 33.

33 Schiffman, *Reclaiming*, 222.

34 Bernstein and Koyfman, "Interpretation of Biblical Law," 73–74.

the limited nature of the corpus is well intended. Yet, they follow this assertion by only discussing three possible examples.

IV. STATEMENT OF METHOD

The proper treatment of these questions must involve a comprehensive study of all the relevant texts, sensitivity to the larger character of sectarian legal exegesis, and careful consideration of pertinent comparative Second Temple and rabbinic legal texts. In what follows, I gather together fifteen examples of reliance upon non-Pentateuchal sources in Dead Sea Scrolls legal texts. In examining these passages, my attention is first directed to unpacking the legal issues at stake in each passage and then to determining the specific exegetical and legal role of the non-Pentateuchal passage. This is achieved both by close reading of the particular passages and, when applicable, the use of parallel Second Temple and rabbinic legal material.

On Legal Exegesis in the Dead Sea Scrolls

Analysis of the role of scriptural interpretation in Dead Sea Scrolls legal texts has proven to be a formidable task. Nearly all scholars recognize the central role of scriptural language in sectarian legal formulations.[35] With this consideration in mind, many scholars have argued that exegesis of the scriptural text is a defining factor in the expansion of scriptural laws and institutions.[36] At the same time, other scholars argue for a limited role for exegesis in the development of sectarian law.[37] The links to scripture are viewed not as exegesis

35 See especially Steven D. Fraade, "Interpretive Authority in the Studying Community at Qumran," in *Legal Fictions*, 37–68 (1993); Adiel Schremer, "'[T]he[y] Did Not Read in the Sealed Book': Qumran Halakhic Revolution and the Emergence of Torah Study in Second Temple Judaism," in *Historical Perspectives: From the Hasmoneans to Bar Kokhba in Light of the Dead Sea Scrolls: Proceedings of the Fourth International Symposium of the Orion Center for the Study of the Dead Sea Scrolls and Associated Literature, 27–31 January, 1999* (ed. D. Goodblatt, A. Pinnick, and D. R. Schwartz; STDJ 37; Leiden: Brill, 2001), 105–26.

36 See, e.g., Schiffman, *Halakhah*, 54–60; idem, *Reclaiming*, 219–22; Milgrom, "The Qumran Cult: Its Exegetical Principles"; idem, "Qumran's Biblical Hermeneutics"; Hannah K. Harrington, *The Impurity Systems of Qumran and the Rabbis: Biblical Foundations* (Atlanta: Scholars Press, 1993). This discussion focuses on sectarian expansion of ancient Israelite law. Most scholars agree that the rules and regulations related to the admission process and everyday life of the sectarian community are on the whole not based on scriptural exegesis. See Schiffman, *Sectarian Law*, 212. See further discussion in Philip R. Davies, "Halakhah at Qumran," in *A Tribute to Geza Vermes: Essays on Jewish and Christian History and Literature* (ed. P. R. Davies and R. T. White; JSOTSup 100; Sheffield; JSOT Press, 1990), 37–50 (40–42).

37 This particular approach was initially articulated in Joseph M. Baumgarten, "The Unwritten Law in the Pre-Rabbinic Period," in *Studies in Qumran Law*, 13–35 (33) (1972). Baumgarten's later work, however, identifies a much more prominent role for exegesis. See, e.g., idem, "The Laws of the Damascus Document – Between Bible and Mishnah," in *The Damascus Document*, 17–26; and "Common Legal Exegesis in the Scrolls and Tannaitic Sources," in *The Qumran*

but rather as the mere reuse of scriptural language for new law. If sectarian law, however, is formulated as part of a broader engagement with scripture, then what hermeneutic strategies and techniques are operating in this process? Much of this discussion has focused on the quest to find antecedents to rabbinic *midrash halakhah* – explicit legal exegesis – which cites a scriptural text explicitly and often is forthcoming regarding its exegetical techniques and hermeneutic assumptions.[38]

Scholars generally agree that the broader phenomenon of explicit legal exegesis as found in rabbinic legal-exegetical literature is essentially absent from the Dead Sea Scrolls. Indeed, sectarian legal texts regularly contain the formulation of law without explicit citation of any presumed scriptural base or, when a scriptural text is present, without any identification of the exegetical methods applied to the scriptural text.[39] Even when the exegetical foundations are manifest, they do not necessarily follow a logical sequence that can be reproduced.[40]

Notwithstanding the absence of *midrash halakhah* or a coherent system of legal hermeneutics, we can be quite confident that careful exegesis of scripture was not ignored in the sectarian formulation of law but rather played a central role in this process.[41] The community was formed around the ideal of scriptural study and the claim to possess the true meaning of scripture.[42] The *Rule of the Community* refers to the existence of nightly study sessions in which scripture would be expounded under the direction of inspired sectarian leaders (1QS 6:6–8).[43] It was likely during these study sessions that much of the sectarian interpretation of Torah law and the sectarian rules and regulations were formulated. Unfortunately, sectarian literature preserves no accounts of the proceedings of these study sessions. No information is provided concerning the hermeneutical methods applied to scripture during communal study. All

Scrolls and Their World (ed. M. Kister; 2 vols.; Jerusalem: Ben-Zvi, 2009), 2:649–65 [Hebrew]. More recently, an argument for the limited role of exegesis can be found in Shemesh, *Halakhah in the Making*, 24–26.

38 See herein, nn. 12–13.

39 For discussion of some cases where the text spells out its logical principles (CD 4:20–5:11; 4QMMT B 27–33, 75–82), see Shemesh and Werman, "Halakhah at Qumran," 119–23. They observe that all three of these passages are highly polemical. The inclusion of an explanation of the logical basis of the laws is therefore an attempt to justify the correctness of the sectarian position. A similar argument is found in Devorah Dimant, "The Hebrew Bible in the Dead Sea Scrolls: Torah Quotations in the *Damascus Covenant*," in *"Sha'arei Talmon": Studies in the Bible, Qumran, and the Ancient Near East Presented to Shemaryahu Talmon* (ed. M. Fishbane and E. Tov; Winona Lake: Eisenbrauns, 1992), 113*–22* (120*–21*) [Hebrew].

40 See Shemesh and Werman, "Halakhah at Qumran," 113.

41 The view expressed here is indebted to Fraade's analysis of these issues ("Legal Midrash," 150–55).

42 See, for example, 1QS 5:7–12 and 8:12–16 as well as 4QMMT C 7–11 (Fraade, "Legal Midrash," 150–52, 154–55; see also above, n. 13).

43 For this understanding of the description of the nightly study sessions, see Schiffman, *Halakhah*, 32–33; idem, *Reclaiming*, 247–48. See further Fraade, "Legal Midrash," 152–54.

that is available to us is the final product of these sessions as found in the legal material in the community rule books and legal texts.[44]

While the legal hermeneutics are not spelled out in the available material, these texts preserve some sense of the role of scripture in the initial formulation of the laws. Scriptural citations are not completely absent from several of these texts. Indeed, they are often introduced at critical points in the legal texts as prooftexts for already formulated law.[45] In these cases, the scriptural lemma is clearly distinguished from the extrascriptural legal content. Examples of this use of scripture are most prominent in the *Damascus Document*.[46] Moreover, sectarian legal material is replete with the paraphrasing, rewriting, and reformulation of scriptural language and style for legal purposes.[47]

If these particular passages faithfully reflect some sense of what took place in the original law-making study sessions, then the reading and interpretation of scripture make up part of a larger system of legal hermeneutics that stands behind much of the content of sectarian law. Most scholars agree that the sectarian community did not derive law from the scriptural text in a direct way.[48] Rather, sectarian legal formulation and inspired scriptural exegesis represent

44 Furthermore, it is very likely that some of the legal material preserved in sectarian documents was formulated outside of the community, which merely adopted existing law. In this case, the final product reveals little about the distinct hermeneutical methods of the Dead Sea Scrolls community (see Bernstein and Koyfman, "Interpretation of Biblical Law," 63–64).

45 See Fishbane, "Interpretation of Mikra at Qumran," 348–56; Dimant, "The Hebrew Bible in the Dead Sea Scrolls"; Shemesh and Werman, "Halakhah at Qumran," 112–19; Bernstein and Koyfman, "Interpretation of Biblical Law," 71–73. In this category, I am including only passages that explicitly cite a scriptural passage, with or without an introductory citation formula. This form of interpretation is identified by Bernstein and Koyfman as "external interpretation." Fishbane (pp. 351–54) further includes in this larger category instances where exegetical elements are introduced into the scriptural text through reordering of related scriptural passages (the "anthological" form). In these cases, the initial base text and its legal content are interpreted and expanded through the introduction of one or several different scriptural passages (as in the *Temple Scroll*). The deliberate attempt by the authors of these texts to obfuscate the distinction between the base scriptural text and its exegetical amplification from secondary passages recommends against inclusion of these types of passages in the category of explicit citation of scripture. These texts attempt to form a new and more inclusive authoritative scriptural text. See further Chapter 2.

46 The *Damascus Document* contains far more explicit scriptural citations than related sectarian texts in both its homiletical and legal sections. Scholarship on this issue has focused almost exclusively on the nonlegal exegesis: Charles, "Fragments," 2:789; Joseph A. Fitzmyer, "The Use of Explicit Old Testament Quotations in Qumran Literature and in the New Testament," in *Essays on the Semitic Background of the New Testament* (London: G. Chapman, 1971), 3–58 (1960–61); Geza Vermes, "Biblical Proof-Texts in Qumran Literature," in *Scrolls, Scriptures, and Christianity* (LSTS 56; London: T. and T. Clark, 2005), 56–67 (1989); Jonathan G. Campbell, *The Use of Scripture in the Damascus Document 1–8, 19–20* (BZAW 228; Berlin: de Gruyter, 1995). A notable exception to this trend is Devorah Dimant, "The Hebrew Bible in the Dead Sea Scrolls."

47 Bernstein and Koyfman, "Interpretation of Biblical Law," 66–71 (identified as "internal interpretation"). I would include Fishbane's "anthological" form (see n. 45) in this category.

48 See Fraade, "Legal Midrash," 153, 163–64; Noam, "Creative Interpretation."

complementary enterprises in the quest to update and expand scriptural law. Scholars must engage in a process of "reverse engineering" in order to identify the exegetical relationship between the legal material and its scriptural foundations and locate this process within a larger framework of legal-exegetical principles.[49]

The Dead Sea Scrolls and Comparative History of Jewish Law

This work assumes that much profit can be gained by viewing legal exegesis in the Dead Sea Scrolls not merely within the broader framework of the chronologically connected legal texts of Second Temple Judaism, but also against the comparative lens of later rabbinic literature. The benefits of this type of comparative approach are manifold. Indeed, the very emergence of the study of Jewish law in the Dead Sea Scrolls was predicated on the assumption that comparative analysis of Second Temple texts *and* rabbinic literature is a *sine qua non* of any successful attempt to better understand Jewish law in the Dead Sea Scrolls. The scrolls are part of a larger history of Jewish law and thus the often unclear nature of the legal material cannot be approached in isolation. As affirmed by Lawrence H. Schiffman in 1975, "The comparative method is really the only way in which the complex legal texts from Qumran can be unraveled."[50] Schiffman's assertion at the time similarly underpinned much of the work of Baumgarten and Yadin. Indeed, our understanding of law in the Dead Sea Scrolls would hardly have advanced much since the 1970s without the broader prism of rabbinic literature.

This approach continues to resonate as a much fuller corpus of legal literature has emerged from Cave 4. These texts have been met by a guild of scholars seeking to understand them better through the aid of rabbinic legal texts.[51] After a generation of comparative study of law in the scrolls and rabbinic texts, Schiffman's methodological assertion stands at the very foundation of his ongoing work and the recent fruitful labors of Lutz Doering, Steven Fraade,

49 The term "reverse engineering" is adapted from James Kugel's approach to deciphering the exegetical exigencies underlying rabbinic *midrash* (*In Potiphar's House: The Interpretative Afterlife of Biblical Texts* [San Francisco: HarperSanFrancisco, 1990], 251–53). For discussion of the application of this method to the Dead Sea Scrolls legal texts, see Fraade, "Legal Midrash," 148–49; Bernstein and Koyfman, "Interpretation of Biblical Law," 63–64; Noam, "Creative Interpretation," 365.

50 Schiffman, *Halakhah*, 13–14. By "comparative," he means examining not only the scrolls in light of rabbinic texts, but also biblical and Second Temple–period literature. While few would doubt the importance of the latter two corpora, the use of comparative rabbinic evidence is less universally encountered. For further explication of this method, see also idem, *Sectarian Law*, 17–19; idem, *Law, Custom, and Messianism*, 34–44. A similar approach is articulated in Joseph Baumgarten, *Qumran Cave 4.XIII: The Damascus Document (4Q266–273)* (DJD 18; Oxford: Clarendon, 1996), 18–22.

51 On the importance of access to the Cave 4 manuscripts, see Fraade, "The Dead Sea Scrolls and Rabbinic Judaism after Sixty (Plus) Years," 116.

Vered Noam, and Aharon Shemesh.[52] Though some continue to question the viability of this comparative method, the work of these scholars reinforces the more recent claim that "comparison of Qumran law and rabbinic halakah not only benefits our understanding of both, it is essential for reconstructing the history of halakah."[53]

The most common argument found in scholarship on the Dead Sea Scrolls for discounting the importance of rabbinic texts is their "late" nature in relation to the Second Temple–period material. Indeed, the earliest rabbinic texts are at least two centuries later than the latest texts from among the Dead Sea Scrolls. With this chronological gap in mind, Aharon Shemesh has outlined two primary approaches scholars have taken to assessing the contributions of the Dead Sea Scrolls to analysis of the points of contact between rabbinic *halakhah* and its Second Temple–period antecedents. The "reflective" approach assumes that debates that arise in rabbinic literature represent long-standing issues in Jewish legal discourse.[54] In contrast, the "developmental" model locates singular strands in rabbinic *halakhah* as attempts to promote older Second Temple–period legal positions.[55] The material treated in this study supports the general schema crafted by Shemesh and offers further insight into the fruitful and illuminating use of rabbinic literature alongside the Dead Sea Scrolls. Indeed, at times, later rabbinic texts provide an important key to unlocking interpretive cruxes in the Dead Sea Scrolls texts at the same time as the Dead Sea Scrolls shed important light on our understanding of the background of rabbinic Judaism. Thus, the Dead Sea Scrolls and rabbinic literature are exegetically and historically mutually illuminating.

V. OUTLINE OF THE PRESENT STUDY

Chapters 2 and 3 are intended to contextualize the detailed textual analysis that is found in the remainder of the book. In particular, I explore the broader implications of this study for both biblical studies and Jewish studies. Chapter 2 locates my work in the wider setting of previous research on the

[52] For representative bibliography, see above, n. 7.

[53] Vered Noam and Elisha Qimron, "A Qumran Composition of Sabbath Laws and Its Contribution to the Study of Early Halakah," *DSD* 16 (2009): 55–96 (57). It is ironic that the most cautious recent claims regarding the comparative method voiced by Lutz Doering are articulated in the midst of a larger collection of articles that illustrate so well its successful execution, thereby muting many of the very reservations made by Doering ("Parallels Without 'Parallelomania'"). See further methodological discussion in Fraade, "The Dead Sea Scrolls and Rabbinic Judaism after Sixty (Plus) Years," 117–23.

[54] Shemesh, *Halakhah in the Making*, 5. Shemesh identifies the work of Yadin and Schiffman as representative. Though not mentioned by Shemesh, Joseph Baumgarten likewise belongs in this category. A similar approach is highlighted in Fraade, "The Dead Sea Scrolls and Rabbinic Judaism after Sixty (Plus) Years," 118–19.

[55] Shemesh, *Halakhah in the Making*, 3–4. He identifies the work of Yitzḥak Gilat and Noam as examples of this approach.

history of Jewish law and legal exegesis. Chapter 3 examines the generally underutilized role of Jewish legal exegesis for understanding the origins and significance of the canon of the Hebrew Bible. I further explore the blurred boundaries between scripture and interpretation in an attempt to ascertain the role of exegesis in the formation of the canon. In both Chapters 2 and 3, I suggest that my work not only is informed by previous research but also contributes a new and important data set to ongoing conversations.

Beginning in Chapter 4, I turn my attention to the set of fifteen passages under consideration. Chapters 4 through 10 contain three self-contained studies that follow a similar pattern. In each, complementary chapters are devoted to the exposition of the legal-exegetical use of a specific non-Pentateuchal passage first in the Dead Sea Scrolls and then in related Second Temple and rabbinic texts.

Chapters 4 through 6 explore the role of Isa 58:13 as the scriptural basis for restrictions on speech concerning financial or business matters on the Sabbath in the *Damascus Document* (Chapter 4), *4QHalaka B* (Chapter 5), and the book of *Jubilees* and rabbinic legal texts (Chapter 6). Chapters 7 and 8 focus on a related, though distinct, use of Isa 58:13 to restrict not only speech, but also thoughts about prohibited labor on the Sabbath in the *Damascus Document* and *4QHalakha B* (Chapter 7) and the writings of Philo and rabbinic texts (Chapter 8). Chapters 9 and 10 examine the role of Jer 17:21–22 in the development of Sabbath carrying prohibitions in the *Damascus Document*, *4QHalakha A*, and *4QMiscelleanous Rules* (Chapter 9) and *Nehemiah*, *Jubilees*, and rabbinic texts (Chapter 10).

In Chapters 4 through 10 on the Dead Sea Scrolls and related Second Temple texts, the relevant scriptural passages are never cited explicitly but rather are paraphrased. As discussed in Chapter 2, this is the most common method of exegetical engagement with scriptural material in the Second Temple period. At the same time, the legal texts among the Dead Sea Scrolls bear witness to the emerging practice of citing scriptural texts explicitly as legal prooftexts – as commonly found in later rabbinic literature. Chapter 11 analyzes eight examples of non-Pentateuchal passages appearing as explicit citations. I divide these into two categories: (1) independent prooftexts, in which the passage is cited alone; and (2) secondary prooftexts, in which the non-Pentateuchal scriptural passage is cited alongside a Pentateuchal passage. In Chapter 12, I offer some general conclusions based on all the evidence examined and revisit my initial set of questions (and assumptions) regarding the relationship among law, scripture, and canon in the Dead Sea Scrolls and ancient Judaism.

2

The Dead Sea Scrolls and the History of Jewish Law and Legal Exegesis

I. INTRODUCTION

Scholarship on the Dead Sea Scrolls has grown rapidly since the full availability of the Qumran corpus in the early 1990s. An unfortunate consequence of this newfound vibrancy is the sometime insulation of Dead Sea Scrolls scholarship from related fields in biblical and Jewish studies. This book seeks to locate the Dead Sea Scrolls at two meeting points: (1) the ancient crossroads where the Hebrew Bible and Israelite society meet ancient Judaism and its literature and (2) the modern intersection of biblical studies and Jewish studies. The synchronic analysis of the Dead Sea Scrolls will allow the reader to engage with sectarian hermeneutics in a meaningful way. The diachronic analysis of the texts together with biblical, Second Temple, and rabbinic literature will illumine the long and shared history of interpretation and application of ancient Israelite law in ancient Judaism. The present chapter situates the study of the Dead Sea Scrolls in the broader context of the history of Jewish law and legal exegesis.

II. ANCIENT ISRAELITE LAW IN TRANSITION, PART I: THE SECOND TEMPLE PERIOD

The Dead Sea Scrolls are the most significant body of texts available to scholars to illuminate the transition from the sacred writings of ancient Israel to the emergence of new forms of Judaism deeply indebted to these ancient and authoritative writings. Jews in the Second Temple period sought to carve out new cultural and religious identities in a world much different from that of the inherited sacred writings. Yet, the vast majority of Jews and Jewish communities in the Second Temple period were deeply committed to the belief that they were the living embodiment of ancient Israel and that, indeed, a singular arc of history united them with the world of ancient Israel. Thus, as they labored to continue to enliven the sacred writings for their own time, they envisioned themselves as still living within the world of ancient Israel.[1]

The disconnect between the writings of ancient Israel and their new authoritative home within Judaism of the Second Temple period is especially acute in the shifting application of law. To take merely a few among many potential examples, how should the largely agrarian-based system of law envisioned in the Pentateuch apply in the new cosmopolitan Hellenistic world in which Jews now found themselves? How should the often contradictory laws found in the Pentateuch's composite sources be understood in light of the now universal belief in a unified composition of the Pentateuch? How would later Jewish society apply ancient legal institutions that were, for example, oblique in their details, whose practical application was no longer known, or perhaps whose very ideological basis was anathema to the cultural sensibilities of later Judaism? These very issues are compounded by the observation that much of the legal material from ancient Israel should be regarded as literary in nature, rather than having a statutory or prescriptive force.[2] As such, the legal collections were never intended as stand-alone comprehensive law codes in the sense of modern exemplars. Thus, later reformulations of Israelite law are simultaneously engaging and updating law as a literary phenomenon as well as attempting to transform the ancient literary collections into a coherent legal system for Judaism.

This broader set of problematics already faced ancient Israelites as they sought to update their own emerging collection of sacred writings and older legal literature. The evidence from the Second Temple period explored here thus should be viewed as continuous with the process already undertaken in ancient Israel as reflected within biblical literature. Most scholars identify the Covenant Code – the collection of laws found in Exod 20:19–23:33 – as one of the oldest collections of Israelite law.[3] Later Israelite society as evinced in particular by

[1] The most articulate presentation of this dynamic in the Dead Sea Scrolls and related segments of Second Temple Judaism can be found in Shemaryahu Talmon, "Between the Bible and the Mishna," in *The World of Qumran from Within* (Jerusalem: Magnes; Leiden: Brill, 1989), 21–48; see also idem, "The Community of the Renewed Covenant: Between Judaism and Christianity," in *The Community of the Renewed Covenant: The Notre Dame Symposium on the Dead Sea Scrolls* (ed. E. Ulrich and J. VanderKam; CJA 10; Notre Dame: University of Notre Dame Press, 1994), 12–21.

[2] See the recent discussion of this question (with earlier bibliography) in Bruce Wells, "What Is Biblical Law? A Look at Pentateuchal Rules and Near Eastern Practice," *CBQ* 70 (2008): 223–43; and Bernard M. Levinson, *Legal Revision and Religious Renewal in Ancient Israel* (Cambridge: Cambridge University Press, 2008), 23–27.

[3] The precise verse range and dating of the Covenant Code are debated by scholars. On the demarcation of the Covenant Code, see Raymond Westbrook, "What Is the Covenant Code?" in *Law from the Tigris to the Tiber: The Writings of Raymond Westbrook*, volume 1: *The Shared Tradition* (ed. B. Wells and R. Magdalene; Winona Lake: Eisenbrauns, 2009), 97–118 (1994); in dialogue with Bernard M. Levinson, "The Case for Revision and Interpolation within

the book of *Deuteronomy* reenvisions and thus rewrites the earlier authoritative legal material from the Covenant Code.[4] The often dramatic way in which *Deuteronomy* transforms the Covenant Code can be seen in further examples of "inner-biblical exegesis," whereby scriptural works exegetically engage and reformulate older authoritative Israelite literature.[5] Many of the hermeneutic techniques employed in the Second Temple texts can already be detected in earlier "inner-biblical" exegetical settings. Such connections, however, are rarely pursued in the scholarly literature on account of the still-potent canonical divide that separates the analysis of "biblical" works such as *Deuteronomy* and "postbiblical" literature such as the Dead Sea Scrolls or the book of *Jubilees*.[6]

the Biblical Legal Corpora," in *"The Right Chorale": Studies in Biblical Law and Interpretation* (FAT 54; Tübingen: Mohr Siebeck, 2008), 201–23 (1994). Scholars have long identified the Covenant Code as a preexilic composition, in particular pointing to *Deuteronomy*'s apparent dependence on it. Some recent scholars, however, have posited a postexilic date for the Covenant Code. For discussion of these debates in the context of the defense of the preexilic dating, see Levinson, "Is the Covenant Code an Exilic Composition? A Response to John Van Seters," in *Right Chorale*, 276–330 (2004). For a useful overview of the issue of law codes in ancient Israel, see Westbrook, "The Laws of Biblical Israel," in *Law from the Tigris to the Tiber: The Writings of Raymond Westbrook*, volume 2: *Cuneiform and Biblical Sources* (ed. B. Wells and R. Magdalene; Winona Lake: Eisenbrauns, 2009), 317–40 (2008).

4 On *Deuteronomy*, see especially Bernard M. Levinson, *Deuteronomy and the Hermeneutics of Legal Innovation* (New York: Oxford University Press, 1997); and Jeffrey Stackert, *Rewriting the Torah: Literary Revision in Deuteronomy and the Holiness Legislation* (FAT 52; Tübingen: Mohr Siebeck, 2007).

5 The most comprehensive treatment of the phenomenon of inner-biblical exegesis and its hermeneutic models – in both legal and nonlegal settings – is Michael Fishbane, *Biblical Interpretation in Ancient Israel* (Oxford: Clarendon, 1985). For a more recent treatment, see Fishbane, "Inner-Biblical Exegesis," in *Hebrew Bible/Old Testament: The History of Its Interpretation*, volume 1, part 1: *Antiquity* (ed. M. Sæbø; Göttingen: Vandenhoeck and Ruprecht, 1996), 33–48 (especially the topic of law on pp. 38–43). See further Levinson, *Legal Revision*, 95–181, for an updated annotated bibliography on the subject. Scholars have detected a similar process of drawing upon the authority of earlier texts through the process of their rewriting in the vast corpus of cuneiform legal writings from Mesopotamia. See the bibliography gathered in Levinson, *Deuteronomy*, 7 n. 11. On the phenomenon of rewriting more broadly in the Mesopotamian material, see Francesca Rochberg-Halton, "Canonicity in Cuneiform Texts," *JCS* 36 (1984): 127–44. On the debates whether rewriting actually happens in biblical law, see Levinson, "The Case for Revision and Interpolation." Compare also John Van Seters, "Creative Imitation in the Hebrew Bible," *Studies in Religion/Sciences Religieuses* 29 (2000): 395–409, who explores a broad range of biblical literature that reuses earlier texts. He describes this process of "imitation" (i.e., not "rewriting") as the main "creative impulse" throughout biblical texts.

6 The significance of *Deuteronomy* as a model for later trends in Second Temple literature is elucidated by Morton Smith, "Pseudepigraphy in the Israelite Literary Tradition," in *Pseudepigrapha*, volume 1: *Pseudopythagorica, lettres de Platon, littérature pseudépigraphique juive: Huit exposés suivis de discussion* (ed. K. von Fritz; Vandœuvres-Genève: Fondation Hardt pour l'Étude de l'antiquité classique, 1971), 191–215. A few more recent works stand out as further exemplifying this resistance to canonical limitations. See Timo Veijola, "The Deuteronomistic Roots of Judaism," in *Sefer Moshe: The Moshe Weinfeld Jubilee Volume; Studies in the Bible and the Ancient Near East, Qumran, and Post-Biblical Judaism* (ed. Ch. Cohen, A. Hurvitz,

Across the broad cross section of ancient Jewish legal texts examined in this study, the desire to apply ancient Israelite law in new social and historical situations and the associated legal hermeneutics are central. No matter how one addresses the wider set of practical difficulties in "updating" ancient Israelite law, any position articulated must be packaged together with an authoritative voice. In earlier settings, for example, one of the ways in which the Laws of Hammurabi (ca. 1750 BCE) authorizes its legal content is with a literary frame that introduces Hammurabi's rule as stemming from the gods (i.27–49; xlvii.9–58).[7] To be sure, Hammurabi's laws are themselves not identified as divinely revealed.[8] Yet, Hammurabi's stature and authority as a lawgiver are undoubtedly enhanced by this divine approbation, and indeed the two roles are connected at the end of the prologue:

> When the God Marduk commanded me to provide just ways for the people of the land (in order to attain) appropriate behavior, I established truth and justice as the declaration of the land, I enhanced the well-being of the people. (v.14–24)[9]

and S. M. Paul; Winona Lake: Eisenbrauns, 2004), 459–78. See also Hindy Najman, *Seconding Sinai: The Development of Mosaic Discourse in Second Temple Judaism* (JSJSup 77; Leiden: Brill, 2003), who correctly plots *Deuteronomy* along the same literary trajectory as later non-canonical, but generically related, works such as *Jubilees* and the *Temple Scroll*. In Najman's later writings, however, the significance of *Deuteronomy* recedes considerably (see, however, below). More recently, Christophe L. Nihan, "The Emergence of the Pentateuch as 'Torah,'" *Religion Compass* 4 (2010): 353–64 (355), has noted that many of the redactional processes that source criticism has long identified in the formation of the Pentateuch (e.g., harmonization) similarly appear in the many rewritings of the Pentateuch in the Second Temple period. A similar argument for the value of analysis of the rewriting of law across biblical and Second Temple texts is voiced in Bernard M. Levinson, "The Manumission of Hermeneutics: The Slave Laws of the Pentateuch as a Challenge to Contemporary Pentateuchal Theory," in *Congress Volume: Leiden, 2004* (ed. A. Lemaire; VTSup 109; Leiden: Brill, 2006), 281–324 (322–24). These perceptive observations could serve as productive meeting points for biblical scholars and specialists in Second Temple Judaism. Similarly, Matthias Henze observes quizzingly how modern biblical studies displays limited interest in Second Temple–period pseudepigraphic texts while heaping unlimited attention on many canonical yet equally pseudepigraphic writings (e.g., *Deuteronomy*, *Proverbs*, *Psalms*) (*Jewish Apocalypticism in Late First Century Israel* [TSAJ 142; Tübingen: Mohr Siebeck, 2011], 3–4). For a recent forceful argument in favor of breaking down canonical boundaries, see Hindy Najman, "The Vitality of Scripture Within and Beyond the Canon," *JSJ* 43 (2012): 497–515.

7 See Martha T. Roth, *Law Collections from Mesopotamia and Asia Minor* (2d ed.; SBLWAW 6; Atlanta: Scholars Press, 1997), 76–77, 133. On this aspect of the text, see further Roth, "Mesopotamian Legal Traditions and the Laws of Hammurabi," *Chi.-Kent L. Rev.* 71 (1995–96): 13–39 (15–19); David P. Wright, *Inventing God's Law: How the Covenant Code of the Bible Used and Revised the Laws of Hammurabi* (New York: Oxford University Press, 2009), 288–90. A similar prologue can be found in the less famous, though older (ca. 2100 BCE), Sumerian Laws of Ur-Namma (Roth, *Law Collections*, 15–17).

8 On the competing role of divine and royal lawgiver in the Laws of Hammurabi and the Hebrew Bible, see the brief discussion in Marc Z. Brettler, *How to Read the Bible* (Philadelphia: Jewish Publication Society, 2005), 61–63.

9 Roth, *Law Collections*, 80–81.

Similarly, at some redactional stage, the Covenant Code is identified as the culmination of the theophany at Sinai (Exod 19–20), thus drawing further divine approbation from the presumed divine origins.[10] Indeed, as observed by Bernard M. Levinson, "There is not a single law in the Bible that Israelite authors do not attribute to God or to his prophetic intermediary, Moses."[11]

Later legal literature seeks to draw upon the authority that resides in the identification of the divine origins of law by appropriating the very language of such law.[12] The intersecting production of new law through the process of legal exegesis of the sacred scriptures therefore provides the desired authoritative voice. Thus, for example, the authority of *Deuteronomy* and its reshaping of Israelite society are not only predicated on the narrative fiction that identifies *Deuteronomy* as the long-lost – and thus authoritative – "book of the law" (2 Kgs 22–23).[13] Rather, the authority of *Deuteronomy* also rests on the exegetical techniques contained therein that appropriate the older Mosaic word (as the divine proxy) in the service of providing its newest application.[14] Indeed, *Deuteronomy*'s own literary fiction places these new laws in the mouth of the very prophetic lawgiver – Moses – whose original words it seeks to update.[15]

To amplify Ulrich's definition of "authoritative" and "scriptural" introduced in the previous chapter, it is indeed true that authoritative law cannot easily be "overridden by the power or will of the group or any member."[16] Yet, the authoritative nature of the older literature does not by definition render it immutable. The appropriation and transformation of the very words of the older authoritative text serve as the vehicle to produce a new and equally authoritative text. In this way, the seemingly immutable nature of scripture can indeed transcend its limited historical and social origins and become

[10] See, for example, Dale Patrick, "The Covenant Code Source," *VT* 27 (1977): 145–57, especially 156. David P. Wright has argued that the presentation of Yahweh as a lawgiver in the Covenant Code draws from the similar appeal to divine authority in the Laws of Hammurabi (Wright, *Inventing God's Law*, 287–93). Moreover, the very introduction to the Covenant Code (Exod 21:1) mimics the style and thus also the authorizing technique of the prologue to the Laws of Hammurabi (ibid., 77–80).

[11] Levinson, *Legal Revision*, 28.

[12] For a similar phenomenon with regard to the reformulation of earlier prophetic literature, see Alex P. Jassen, *Mediating the Divine: Prophecy and Revelation in the Dead Sea Scrolls and Second Temple Judaism* (STDJ 68; Leiden: Brill, 2007), 213–40.

[13] On the presumed authority tied to the discovery of "long-lost" books, see Moshe Weinfeld, *Deuteronomy 1–11* (AB 5; New York: Doubleday, 1991), 18–19.

[14] On the debate regarding whether *Deuteronomy* should be viewed as a "supplement" or "replacement" relative to its source material, see Levinson, *Deuteronomy*, passim, in dialogue with Najman, *Seconding Sinai*, 5–6, 19–40; and Stackert, *Rewriting the Torah*, 209–25.

[15] See Smith, "Pseudepigraphy," 200–6; Fishbane, *Biblical Interpretation*, 213–16; Levinson, *Deuteronomy*, 6; Najman, *Seconding Sinai*, 36–39.

[16] Eugene C. Ulrich, "The Notion and Definition of Canon," in *The Canon Debate* (ed. L. M. McDonald and J. A. Sanders; Peabody: Hendrickson, 2002), 22–35 (29).

"determinative for [a community's] belief and practice for all time and in all geographical areas."[17]

Closer to the world of Second Temple Judaism, this hermeneutic turn is especially prominent in the books of *Ezra-Nehemiah*. Just as *Deuteronomy* does a few centuries prior, *Ezra-Nehemiah* records a monumental shift in the application of Israelite law. This set of reforms is empowered through the constant appeal to the "Torah of Moses" alongside its legal-exegetical updating. Perhaps the best example is the public interpretation of the Torah in Neh 8 by Ezra, who is identified as both priest (v. 2) and scribe (v. 4).[18] Ezra and his colleagues are described as both reading *and* interpreting the "Torah of Moses":

ויקראו בספר בתורת האלהים מפרש ושום שכל ויבינו במקרא

> They read from the scroll of the Teaching of God, translating it and giving the sense; so they understood the reading. (Neh 8:8; cf. vv. 12, 13)

As observed by Michael Fishbane, this description indicates the technical process of reading the text aloud (ויקראו) with its proper pronunciation, intonation, and phrasing (מפרש) and the "addition of clarifications and interpretations" (ושום שכל ויבינו במקרא).[19] In this setting, the very process of reading is depicted as indistinguishable from its interpretive amplification, which renders the text intelligible.[20] Ezra's act of reading and interpreting the word of Moses

[17] Ulrich, "The Notion and Definition of Canon," 29.

[18] On Ezra's scribal identity, see Joseph Blenkinsopp, *Judaism, the First Phase: The Place of Ezra and Nehemiah in the Origins of Judaism* (Grand Rapids: Eerdmans, 2009), 71–78 and earlier literature cited therein. In verse 9, Ezra is both scribe and priest. Compare also Ezra 7:6, where Ezra's scribal identity is further characterized with language employed elsewhere for prophets ("the hand of the Lord his God upon him"). On the merging of the prophetic character with the priestly and scribal identity of Ezra, see Fishbane, *Biblical Interpretation*, 139–40; Jassen, *Mediating the Divine*, 213–15. For later traditions that identify Ezra as a prophet, see Robert Kraft, "'Ezra' Materials in Judaism and Christianity," *ANRW* II.19.1 (ed. W. Hasse; Berlin: de Gruyter, 1979), 119–36 (127–33).

[19] Fishbane, *Biblical Interpretation*, 108–9. On the technical meaning of מפרש, see also James L. Kugel and Rowan A. Greer, *Early Biblical Interpretation* (Philadelphia: Westminster, 1986), 28.

[20] For a similar understanding of the significance of Neh 8, see also Najman, *Seconding Sinai*, 33–36; idem, "Torah of Moses: Pseudonymous Attribution in Second Temple Writings," in *Past Renewals: Interpretative Authority, Renewed Revelation and the Quest for Perfection in Jewish Antiquity* (JSJSup 53; Leiden: Brill, 2010), 73–86 (76–78) (2004). Many scholars have argued that the hermeneutic techniques in *Ezra-Nehemiah* represent the earliest historical phases of what later becomes rabbinic *midrash halakhah*. See, for example, Yehezkel Kaufman, *The History of Israelite Religion* (4 vols.; Jerusalem: Bialik Institute, 1955), 4:327–51 [Hebrew]; Jacob N. Epstein, *Introduction to the Literature of the Tanaaim* (Tel Aviv: Dvir; Jerusalem: Magnes, 1957), 502–3 [Hebrew]; Lawrence H. Schiffman, "The Halakhah at Qumran," (2 vols.; Ph.D. diss., Brandeis University, 1974), 159–80. Others argue rather that the exegetical process is merely similar. See Wilhelm Bacher, *Die Bibelexegetische Terminologie der Tannaiten* (Leipzig: Hinrichs, 1899), 25–26; M. Gertner, "Terms of Scriptural Interpretation: A Study in Hebrew

elevates him to a status alongside Moses and the people as reenactors of the Sinai experience.[21]

In the context of "seeking to understand the Torah" (v. 13), Ezra and his colleagues find written in the Torah the requirement to celebrate the festival of Booths (v. 14), presumably an allusion to something resembling Lev 23:39–43. The presentation of the ritual aspects of the festival of Booths gives the impression that they merely act out the directives laid out in the Torah. A closer reading of Neh 8:13–18 alongside Lev 23:39–43 – even allowing for likely textual diversity in *Leviticus* – indicates that a subtle amplification of the Torah text is at play.[22] Thus, for example, Neh 8:15 retains the relatively clear directive to take "branches of palm trees, and the boughs of thick trees" found in Lev 23:40. In contrast, the enigmatic "boughs of goodly trees" (Lev 23:40) is provided with practical meaning by the identification of specific types of trees in Neh 8:15 ("olive branches, and pine branches, and myrtle branches"). The base text (*Leviticus*) and its interpretive application (*Nehemiah*) are so closely intertwined that the very intelligibility of the former is now predicated on the subtleties of the latter's exegetical maneuvering. Even more, the preservation of this reading/interpreting process in the books of *Ezra-Nehemiah* retains the same blurred lines of exegetical contact. Without having recourse to the text that Ezra is interpreting, one would never be able to peel away the layers of the twofold process of reading and interpretation.

In an ironic twist, it is likely that the "Torah of Moses" was not even regarded with the same supreme authority by the very people at whom the reforms were targeted.[23] Thus, in one stroke, *Ezra-Nehemiah* establishes the authoritative status of the base text as it simultaneously seeks to authorize its updated understanding and application. Moreover, the central issue here is not

Semantics," *BASOR* 25 (1962): 1–27 (5–6); David Weiss Halivni, *Midrash, Mishnah, and Gemara: The Jewish Predilection for Justified Law* (Cambridge: Harvard University Press, 1986), 15. While the broader historical model I am outlining here certainly supports the phenomenological (if not some historical) points of contact, these are not the same. As observed by Najman, a key distinction divides the two: rabbinic *midrash halakhah* reflects a conscious separation between the text and its interpretation, something absent in *Ezra-Nehemiah* (Najman, "Torah of Moses," 82, 86). Indeed, I am arguing that this very feature is the critical difference between rabbinic hermeneutics and all its predecessors. See further below.

[21] See Najman, *Seconding Sinai*, 35. For further instances in *Ezra-Nehemiah* of reenacting the Mosaic giving of the law on Sinai, see Blenkinsopp, *Judaism, the First Phase*, 125–27. Later Jewish tradition would assign Ezra a status on par with Moses as complementary participants in the promulgation of Torah. See, e.g., 4 Ezra 14; *t. Sanh.* 4:7; *y. Meg.* 1:11 71b; *b. Suk.* 20a; *b. Sanh.* 21b. These traditions regarding Ezra are also preserved in early Christian literature. See Tertullian, *De cultu feminarum* 1.3; Jerome, *Adversus Helvidium de Mariae virginitate perpetua* 7. See Louis Ginzberg, *The Legends of the Jews* (7 vols.; Philadelphia: Jewish Publication Society of America, 1908–38), 4:354–59, 6:443.

[22] For a full explication of the exegetical processes involved, see Kaufmann, *History*, 4:327–29; in dialogue with Fishbane, *Biblical Interpretation*, 109–12.

[23] See, however, some scholarship that regards the Torah as already "canonical" prior to, and thus motivating, Ezra's activity (e.g., Nahum Sarna and S. David Sperling, "Bible: The Canon, Text, and Edition," *EncJud* 3:577–78). See further Chapter 3.

whether the "Torah of Moses" is identical to what we now identify as the Pentateuch.[24] Indeed, there are clear examples of pseudonymous attributions of Mosaic scriptural authority in *Ezra-Nehemiah*, which are then subjected to legal-exegetical modifications.[25] These very phenomena prove the larger point: *Ezra-Nehemiah* sees the key to the stability of the reforms in their exegetical grounding in the authoritative text – whether the real or contrived Mosaic Torah.

A similar set of features has been detected in the scribal transmission and translation of the scriptural texts. In the Septuagint, the pre-Samaritan Pentateuch, and the Targum, the authoritative base text and its updated version are merged together.[26] Renewed interest in scribal practices has reinforced the arguments of nineteenth-century biblical scholarship that scribes and translators actively engaged with their target texts and expended great energy in employing this medium to update the law contained therein.[27] Indeed, in

[24] On this issue, see Sara Japhet, "'Law' and 'The Law' in Ezra-Nehemiah," in *From the Rivers of Babylon to the Highlands of Judah: Collected Studies on the Restoration Period* (Winona Lake: Eisenbrauns, 2006), 137–51 (1988).

[25] See the exploration of this feature in Najman, "Torah of Moses." See also Judson R. Shaver, *Torah and the Chronicler's History Work: An Inquiry into the Chronicler's References to Laws, Festivals, and Cultic Institutions in Relationship to Pentateuchal Legislation* (BJS 196; Atlanta: Scholars Press, 1989), 89–117. See Fishbane, *Biblical Interpretation*, 533–34, for discussion of the larger phenomenon of pseudo-attributive exegesis.

[26] On the Septuagint, see, e.g., Zecharias Frankel, *Über den Einfluss der palästinischen Exegese auf die alexandrinische Hermeneutik* (Leipzig: Verlag von Joh. Ambr. Barth, 1851); Elias Bickerman, "Two Legal Interpretations in the Septuagint," in *Studies in Jewish and Christian History* (AGJU 9; Leiden: Brill, 1976), 201–24 (1956); Lawrence H. Schiffman, "The Septuagint and the Temple Scroll: Shared 'Halakhic' Variants," in *The Courtyards of the House of the Lord: Studies on the Temple Scroll* (ed. F. García Martínez; STDJ 75; Leiden: Brill, 2008), 85–98 (1992); On the Targum, see, for example, Efraim Itzchaky, "The Halacha in Targum Jerushalmi I (Pseudo-Jonathan Ben-Uziel) and Its Exegetical Methods" (Ph.D. diss., Bar Ilan University, 1982) [Hebrew]; David Henshke, "On the Relationship between Targum Pseudo-Jonathan and the Halakhic Midrashim," *Tarbiz* 68 (1999): 187–210 [Hebrew]. On the Samaritan Pentateuch, see Schiffman, "Halakhah," 183–85; Emanuel Tov, "Rewritten Bible Compositions and Biblical Manuscripts, with Special Attention to the Samaritan Pentateuch," *DSD* 5 (1998): 334–54; Sidnie White Crawford, *Rewriting Scripture in Second Temple Times* (Grand Rapids: Eerdmans, 2008), 22–37. In the case of the Samaritan Pentateuch, however, it has been observed that many of the distinctive exegetical features found in narrative portions (e.g., harmonization) are less prominent in legal material. See recent discussion in Tov, ibid., especially 342–43, though see the more nuanced portrait in Michael Segal, "The Text of the Hebrew Bible in Light of the Dead Sea Scrolls," *Materia Giudaica Anno* 12/1–2 (2007): 5–20 (10–17). Especially important are Segal's observations on p. 14: "The (pre-) Samaritan Pentateuch does not contain any large-scale additions in the legal section of the Torah.... Since the laws were binding, their specific formulation was necessarily precise, and less appropriate to change. While this is true of the large-scale changes, there is no indication that in any other characteristics the transmission of the legal material in the (pre-) Samaritan Pentateuch differed in any way from that of the narrative."

[27] See especially the classic treatment of this issue in Abraham Geiger, *Urschrift und Übersetzungen der Bibel in ihrer Abhängigkeit von der inneren Entwicklung des Judentums* (Breslau: Julius Hainauer, 1857); and the work of Frankel cited in the previous note. This question more

Chapter 3 I explore the many ways in which legal exegesis and updating occur within the production and transmission of scriptural texts.

In each of these settings, the sacred writings are the very vehicle to update their limited legal application. Thus, we shall see that the constant appeal to scripture in each of the texts treated stands at the very heart of the broader legislative enterprise. Jewish legal literature in the Second Temple period commonly "rewrites" earlier authoritative scriptural material. I am deliberately casting a wide net in my use of the term "rewrite" in order to characterize it as a legal-exegetical technique rather than only as a literary genre.[28] Some of the literature treated in this study falls under the generic classification "rewritten Bible," as first articulated by Geza Vermes: "In order to anticipate questions, and to solve problems in advance, the midrashist inserts haggadic development into the biblical narrative."[29]

Scholarship on this genre – now commonly called "rewritten scripture" – is mixed with regard to treating legal literature. Vermes began by focusing on narrative texts and accordingly set the tone for further scholarly discussion of the issue. Thus, treatments of "rewritten scripture" rarely have legal texts in view.[30] The absence of legal texts in this discussion was likely compounded by the general lack of interest in law among many scholars of early Jewish biblical interpretation and the ongoing lack of availability of many of the Dead Sea Scrolls legal texts that could contribute to such a discussion. Yet, one could easily substitute "halakhic" for "aggadic" and "law" for "narrative" in Vermes's definition and be able to gather together a wide array of texts from Second Temple Judaism that fit this description, such as the *Temple Scroll*, the legal portions of the Samaritan Pentateuch, and *4QReworked Pentateuch* (4Q158,

broadly is now the subject of a full-length study that has the great advantage of drawing upon a much wider set of data (especially the Judaean Desert scriptural material). See David Andrew Teeter, "Exegesis in the Transmission of Biblical Law in the Second Temple Period: Preliminary Studies" (Ph.D. diss., University of Notre Dame, 2008).

28 On the distinction between "rewritten scripture" as a genre and rewriting as an exegetical technique, see fuller discussion in Molly M. Zahn, "Genre and Rewritten Scripture: A Reassessment," *JBL* 131 (2012): 271–88.

29 Geza Vermes, *Scripture and Tradition: Haggadic Studies* (StPb 4; 2d ed.; Leiden: Brill, 1973), 95. The literature on this genre and its boundaries has grown significantly in recent years. See especially Philip S. Alexander, "Retelling the Old Testament," in *It Is Written: Scripture Citing Scripture; Essays in Honour of Barnabas Lindars, SSF* (ed. D. A. Carson and H. G. M. Williamson; Cambridge: Cambridge University Press, 1988), 99–121, who attempts to outline criteria for inclusion in the genre. See also the survey of scholarship on the genre in Moshe J. Bernstein, "'Rewritten Bible': A Generic Category Which Has Outlived Its Usefulness?" *Textus* 22 (2005): 169–96. Bernstein argues for a very limited generic boundary much like Vermes's initial restricted criteria. More recently, see the broad treatment of the methodological issues and representative texts in Crawford, *Rewriting Scripture*.

30 On this question, see discussion in the context of the *Temple Scroll* in Bernstein, "Rewritten Bible," especially 193–95. Vermes cites the book of *Jubilees* as one of his classic examples, though he likely had in mind the narrative portions of the book (*Scripture and Tradition*, 95).

4Q364–397).[31] Yet, whether the *Temple Scroll* or the other texts should be called "rewritten scripture," for example, is essentially a secondary issue.[32] All would agree that the *Temple Scroll*'s broader literary agenda and authoritative character are achieved through the exegetical technique of "rewriting" significant portions of *Deuteronomy*. As observed by Crawford, the *Temple Scroll* employs the same techniques as narrative "rewritten scripture" to authorize its modification and expansion of *Deuteronomy* (and *Exodus*).[33]

Much as *Deuteronomy* appropriates the very language and literary characteristics of the Covenant Code as it transforms older Israelite legal material, the book of *Jubilees*, the *Temple Scroll*, the *Damascus Document*, and many of the sectarian legal texts among the Dead Sea Scrolls blur the boundaries between scripture and its interpretation.[34] In so doing, all these texts harness the authority of their base texts in order to present a new and improved – sometimes dramatically different – vision of the legal institutions contained therein.[35] Moreover, many of these texts simultaneously tap into the authority

[31] Bernstein, "Rewritten Bible," 184, uses the terminology "legal equivalent" of Vermes's "narrative rewritten Bible." George J. Brooke, "Rewritten Bible," *EDSS* 2:779, classifies the *Temple Scroll* and *4QReworked Pentateuch* (along with other texts) as "reworked Pentateuchal laws." On the Samaritan Pentateuch, see above, n. 26. On *4QReworked Pentateuch*, see Tov, "Rewritten Bible Compositions," 334–54; Crawford, *Rewriting Scripture*, 39–59; Moshe J. Bernstein, "What Has Happened to the Laws? The Treatment of Legal Material in 4QReworked Pentateuch," *DSD* 15 (2008): 24–49. The recent dissertation by Teeter, "Exegesis in the Transmission of Biblical Law in the Second Temple Period," serves to broaden considerably our sense of the nature of the textual transmission of scriptural legal material as a process of rewriting.

[32] The *Temple Scroll* is thus classified in Daniel J. Harrington, "The Bible Rewritten (Narratives)," in *Early Judaism and Its Modern Interpreters* (ed. R. A. Kraft and G. W. E. Nickelsburg; Atlanta: Scholars Press, 1986), 239–47 (244); Tov, "Rewritten Bible Compositions"; Bernstein, "Rewritten Bible," 193–95; Michael Segal, "Between Bible and Rewritten Bible," in *Biblical Interpretation at Qumran* (ed. M. Henze; Grand Rapids: Eerdmans, 2005), 10–28; Crawford, *Rewriting Scripture*, 84–104 (see also idem, "The 'Rewritten Bible' at Qumran: A Look at Three Texts," *ErIsr* 26 [1999; Cross Volume]: 1*–8* [*5]).

[33] Crawford, *Rewriting Scripture*, 86–87. For these techniques, see also Yigael Yadin, *The Temple Scroll* (3 vols.; Jerusalem: Israel Exploration Society, the Hebrew University, and the Shrine of the Book, 1983), 1, passim; Lawrence H. Schiffman, "The Deuteronomic Paraphrase of the Temple Scroll," in *Courtyards of the House of the Lord*, 443–70 (1992); Dwight D. Swanson, *The Temple Scroll and the Bible, The Methodology of 11QT* (STDJ 14; Leiden: Brill, 1995).

[34] The connection between the rewriting of *Deuteronomy* in the *Temple Scroll* and *Deuteronomy*'s own transformation of the Covenant Code is noted in Levinson, *Deuteronomy*, 135.

[35] The debate regarding whether rewritten law should be regarded as supplementary or a replacement is equally apposite here (see n. 14). On the one hand, the *Temple Scroll* retains much of the literary character of earlier Israelite law. As a utopian presentation of law, the *Temple Scroll* was never a binding legal code. On the other hand, even with this utopian character, the *Temple Scroll*, as with related legal texts in the Second Temple period, was drafted in a setting in which law was indeed statutory and binding. Thus, even if the law in the *Temple Scroll* or the book of *Jubilees*, for example, was never fully enacted, its contents were regarded as having the force of law. Thus, there is great significance in the fact that the *Temple Scroll* does not rewrite all of the laws of *Deuteronomy*. As such, both texts are necessary for the ongoing performance of Jewish law. Yet, when they seem to disagree, the assumption is that the rewritten version represents the

vested in the divine origins of the earlier texts. The preamble to the book of *Jubilees* frames the entirety of its rewriting of *Genesis–Exodus* as the record of the divine speech to Moses on Sinai, as dictated by the Angel of Presence – a claim never even made by the Torah itself.[36] The identification of the interpretive content in *Jubilees* as preexistent on the "heavenly tablets" lends it even greater authority.[37] What is even more important about *Jubilees*, observes James VanderKam, is that people seem to have accepted the authoritative claims of the work, thereby lending to it an even more potent layer of authority.[38]

In an even more ambitious claim, the *Temple Scroll* not only rewrites the Mosaic word of *Deuteronomy* but also actually removes the mediating voice of Moses in the Deuteronomic law giving and replaces it with the direct voice of the divine lawgiver.[39] The location of the *Temple Scroll*'s divine revelation,

"correct" meaning. For debates surrounding this question with regard to the *Temple Scroll*, see Yadin, *Temple Scroll*, 1:392; idem, "Is the Temple Scroll a Sectarian Document?" in *Humanizing America's Iconic Books: Society of Biblical Literature Centennial Addresses, 1980* (ed. G. M. Tucker and D. A. Knight; Chico: Scholars Press, 1982), 153–69 (156–57); Baruch A. Levine, "The Temple Scroll: Aspects of Its Historical Provenance and Literary Character," *BASOR* 232 (1978): 5–23 (17–21); Ben Zion Wacholder, *The Dawn of Qumran: The Sectarian Torah and the Teacher of Righteousness* (MHUC; Cincinnati: Hebrew Union College Press, 1983), 1–9; Michael Fishbane, "Use, Authority, and Interpretation of Mikra at Qumran," in *Mikra: Text, Translation, Reading and Interpretation of the Hebrew Bible in Ancient Judaism and Early Christianity* (ed. M. J. Mulder; CRINT 2/1; Assen: Van Gorcum; Minneapolis: Fortress, 1988), 339–77 (351); Lawrence H. Schiffman, "The Temple Scroll and the Halakhic Pseudepigrapha of the Second Temple Period," in *Courtyards of the House of the Lord*, 163–74 (1999). For this discussion in the context of both the *Temple Scroll* and *Jubilees*, see especially Najman, *Seconding Sinai*, 43–50.

36 On the Sinai framework of *Jubilees*, see Najman, *Seconding Sinai*, 53–56. On authorizing techniques in the book of *Jubilees*, see Najman, "Interpretation as Primordial Writing: Jubilees and Its Authority Conferring Strategies," in *Past Renewals*, 39–71 (1999). See also James C. VanderKam, "Studies on the Prologue and *Jubilees* 1," in *For a Later Generation: The Transformation of Tradition in Israel, Early Judaism, and Early Christianity* (ed. R. A. Argall, B. A. Bow, and R. A. Werline; Harrisburg: Trinity Press International, 2000), 266–79.

37 On this function of the heavenly tablets, see Florentino García Martínez, "The Heavenly Tablets in the Book of Jubilees," in *Studies in the Book of Jubilees* (ed. M. Albani, J. Frey, and A. Lange; Tübingen: Mohr Siebeck, 1997), 243–60; and Najman, "Interpretation as Primordial Writing." The internal claims to revelation and heavenly knowledge in *Jubilees* are likewise present in *1 Enoch*. See James C. VanderKam, "Authoritative Literature in the Dead Sea Scrolls," *DSD* 5 (1998): 382–402 (396–97).

38 VanderKam, "Authoritative Literature," 398. He bases this on the large number of manuscripts found among the Qumran scrolls (again, a situation also present for *1 Enoch*).

39 This phenomenon has been much discussed in scholarship on the *Temple Scroll*. See Yadin, *Temple Scroll*, 1:71–73; Fishbane, "Interpretation of Mikra," 351; Moshe Weinfeld, "God versus Moses in the Temple Scroll – 'I Do Not on My Own Authority but on God's Authority' (*Sifrei Deut.* sec. 5; *John* 12:48f)," *RevQ* 15 (1991; Starcky volume): 175–80; Bernard M. Levinson and Molly M. Zahn, "Revelation Regained: The Hermeneutics of כי and אם in the Temple Scroll," *DSD* 9 (2002): 295–346, especially 306–9; Aharon Shemesh and Cana Werman, "Halakhah at Qumran: Genre and Authority," *DSD* 10 (2003): 104–29 (111–12). For discussion of the possible presence and role of Moses in the *Temple Scroll*, see Moshe J. Bernstein, "Pseudepigraphy in the Qumran Scrolls: Categories and Functions," in *Pseudepigraphic Perspectives: The Apocrypha and Pseudepigrapha in Light of the Dead Sea Scrolls: Proceedings*

moreover, is no longer the plains of Moab, as in *Deuteronomy*, but rather Sinai.[40] In both the *Temple Scroll* and the book of *Jubilees*, the rewritten work adopts an authoritative divine voice that is not even explicit in the base text. The re-creation of the Sinai experience – generally alongside appeal to Mosaic authority – thus emerges as a dominant discourse in Second Temple–period texts.[41] The merging of the rewriting of the earlier text and the appeal to its divine origins is a potent combination that imbues the newer texts with unprecedented prestige and authority.

To be sure, not all of the Second Temple–period texts are identical in generic form, exegetical technique, or literary goals. But, amid all the crucial differences, my analysis demonstrates that many groups in ancient Judaism (including the community of the Dead Sea Scrolls) were part of a shared world of scriptural exegesis that sought to make ancient Israelite law portable to new sociological, theological, and geographic contexts.

III. ANCIENT ISRAELITE LAW IN TRANSITION, PART 2: RABBINIC JUDAISM

A substantially different situation presents itself with regard to the engagement with authoritative scripture and Israelite law in rabbinic Judaism. Several critical differences separate rabbinic Judaism and literature from its Second Temple–period antecedents. As observed by Talmon, in contrast to Second Temple Jews who lived in "biblical time," the rabbis were more conscious of the chasm that separated the world of ancient Israel from their own.[42] Closely

of the International Symposium of the Orion Center for the Study of the Dead Sea Scrolls and Associated Literature, 12–14 January, 1997 (ed. E. G. Chazon and M. Stone; STDJ 31; Leiden: Brill, 1999), 1–26 (13–15).

40 The location at Sinai is presumed by the reuse of Exod 34 in column 2 and by the first-person divine speech in 11QT[a] 51:7: "I tell you on this mountain." See further Najman, *Seconding Sinai*, 50, 56; Levinson and Zahn, "Revelation Regained," 320 n. 77. Moreover, it has been suggested that the lost first column of the *Temple Scroll* contained a narrative framework on Sinai similar to the prologue to *Jubilees*. See Florentino García Martínez, "The Temple Scroll," *EDSS* 2:929; Segal, "Between Bible and Rewritten Bible," 22.

41 Literature on the appeal to Sinai in Second Temple Judaism is voluminous. See especially the recent collection of essays in George J. Brooke, Hindy Najman, and Loren T. Stuckenbruck, eds., *The Significance of Sinai: Traditions about Sinai and Divine Revelation in Judaism and Christianity* (ThBN 12; Leiden: Brill, 2008); and also James C. VanderKam, "Sinai Revisited," in *Biblical Interpretation at Qumran*, 44–60. The Sermon on the Mount (Matt 5–7 with parallels) similarly presents Jesus as a new Moses offering an "updated" version of Mosaic law. See especially Bernard S. Jackson, "The Prophets and the Law in Early Judaism and the New Testament," *Cardozo Studies in Law and Literature* 4 (1992): 123–66; and Dale C. Allison Jr., *The New Moses: A Matthean Typology* (Minneapolis: Fortress, 1993), 172–94. For the suggestion that the portrait of Jesus in *Matthew* employs *Deuteronomy*-like exegetical and authorizing techniques, see Bernard M. Levinson, "The Hermeneutics of Tradition in Deuteronomy: A Reply to J. G. McConville," in *Right Chorale*, 256–75 (271–73).

42 Talmon, "Between the Bible and the Mishna," 25. For further nuances to the rabbinic interaction with "biblical time," see James L. Kugel, "Two Introductions to Midrash," in *Midrash*

related to this reality, scripture – now essentially a closed canon – was different for the rabbis, and the rabbis interacted with scripture differently.[43] As has long been noted by scholars of Jewish biblical interpretation, rabbinic Judaism engages with scripture primarily through the commentary form (*midrash*).[44] Rabbinic commentary, whether of an exegetical or a homiletical type, is characterized by a clear distinction drawn between the scriptural text that is the object of commentary and the rabbinic discourse that expounds upon it.[45] Indeed, the genre of "rewritten scripture" so ubiquitous in Second Temple Judaism would not return in rabbinic culture until the second millennium, and thus it is absent from nearly all classical rabbinic *midrash*, both legal and nonlegal.[46] To be sure, rabbinic literature does contain genres – most notably "exegetical narrative" (הסיפור הדרשני) – that approximate the close links to scripture found in "rewritten scripture," but even here the differences are substantial and significant.[47]

In place of the authority that comes with blurring the lines between scripture and its interpretation, the rabbis placed their authority in the claim to possess an authentic ancient tradition stemming from the revelation at Sinai (Oral Torah) and the confidence that their exegetical engagement with scripture could succeed in illuminating the ongoing meaning and application of biblical law. The rabbinic appeal to the "dignity of exegesis," asserts Joshua Levinson,

and Literature (ed. G. H. Hartman and S. Budick: New Haven: Yale University Press, 1986), 77–103 (1983).

43 On the significance of the nature of the canon for understanding rabbinic approaches to scripture, see further below, Chapter 3, section V.

44 The term *midrash* has a long prehistory prior to rabbinic Judaism. Yet, it is commonly employed to refer to the vast corpus of rabbinic interpretive texts. For useful surveys of these works, see H. L. Strack and Günter Stemberger, *Introduction to the Talmud and Midrash* (trans. M. Bockmuehl; Minneapolis: Fortress, 1996); and Jacob Neusner and Alan J. Avery Peck, *Encyclopedia of Midrash* (2 vols.; Leiden: Brill, 2005).

45 To be sure, the lemma-plus-comment form can already be detected in Second Temple–period exegetical literature such as the *Pesharim* and the writings of Philo (though not in any legal literature). While the commentary genre is the exception in Second Temple scriptural interpretation, it dwarfs all other approaches in rabbinic *midrash*. For further exposition on the transition to commentary, see Alex P. Jassen, "The Pesharim and the Rise of Commentary in Early Jewish Scriptural Interpretation," *DSD* 19 (2012): 363–98.

46 The subtleties of the absence of the rewritten form in rabbinic *midrash* are generally explored with regard to nonlegal evidence. For more recent treatment of the possible awareness and employment of "rewritten scripture" in earlier rabbinic literature, see Steven D. Fraade, "Rewritten Bible and Midrash as Commentary," in *Legal Fictions: Studies of Law and Narrative in the Discursive Worlds of Ancient Jewish Sectarians and Sages* (JSJSup 147; Leiden: Brill, 2011), 381–98 (2006); Rachel Adelman, *The Return of the Repressed: Pirqe de Rabbi Eliezer and the Pseudepigrapha* (JSJSup 140; Leiden: Brill, 2009), 7–12.

47 On the genre of "exegetical narrative," see especially Ofra Meir, *The Darshanic Story in Genesis Rabba* (Tel Aviv: Hakibbutz Hameuchad, 1987) [Hebrew]; Yonah Frankel, *The Way of Legend and Midrash* (2 vols.; Tel Aviv: Open University, 1991), 1:287–322 [Hebrew]. On the characteristics that mark this form as significantly different from "rewritten scripture," see Joshua Levinson, "Dialogical Reading in the Rabbinic Exegetical Narrative," *Poetics Today* 25 (2004): 497–528 (500–1).

allows the "quotation of what has already been said . . . [to] express something new," through which rabbinic *midrash* assumes "the cultural authority to be both the same as and different from the verses it represents."[48] Yet, at the same time, the authority of the rabbinic Oral Torah rests on the same principles as the legal texts of the Second Temple period: divine origins. Whereas most of the texts in the Second Temple period claim more immediate access to divine revelation, the Oral Torah traces its divine origins through an unbroken chain of transmission stemming all the way back to Moses at Sinai.

The phenomenon described here is well illustrated by an encounter between Rav Naḥman and Rabbi Isaac recounted in the *Babylonian Talmud*:

> Rav Naḥman and Rabbi Isaac were sitting at a meal and Rav Naḥman said to Rabbi Isaac: "May the Master say something [of Torah]." He replied: "Thus says Rabbi Yoḥanan: 'One should not converse at meals lest the windpipe act before the gullet and one's life will thereby be endangered.'"
>
> After they ended the meal he said, "Thus said Rabbi Yoḥanan: 'Jacob our father did not die.'" He [Rav Naḥman] replied: "Was it then for naught that the wailers wailed, the embalmers embalmed, and the gravediggers dug?!" He [Rabbi Isaac] said: "[It is] a scriptural verse that I expound, as it is said: 'Therefore fear thou not, O Jacob, my servant, says the Lord; neither be dismayed, O Israel. For I will save you from afar, and your seed from the land of captivity' (Jer 30:10). [The verse] likens him [=Jacob] to his progeny [=Israel]; as his progeny is alive, so he too is alive." (*b. Ta'an.* 5b)[49]

This story is as rich in drama as it is in nuance. The drama is what points the reader toward its insights into the meaning and application of *midrash* in rabbinic tradition. After initially responding to Rav Naḥman's request for a word of Torah with a dismissive brief word of Torah, Rabbi Isaac launches into his discourse on the non-death of Jacob. He begins with the audacious statement attributed to his teacher that the patriarch Jacob did not die. On the one hand, as observed by Paul Mandel, Rabbi Isaac is responding to a real exegetical issue posed by the text of *Genesis*: while *Genesis* reports that Abraham and Isaac both breathed their last breath, *died*, and were gathered up to their kin (Gen 25:8; 35:29), Jacob only breathes his last breath and is gathered up to his kin (Gen 49:33) – indeed, scripture never explicitly uses the language "to die" for Jacob.[50]

Yet, Rabbi Isaac never actually frames his approach in this context. Thus, even if he is responding to the clear exegetical issue, his formulation intentionally leaves this part out, likely for the added shock value of his claim

[48] Levinson, "Dialogical Reading," 501. His remarks are specifically directed at "exegetical narrative," but as he notes, they are equally applicable to rabbinic *midrash* more generally.

[49] Translation follows Paul Mandel, "The Origins of 'Midrash' in the Second Temple Period," in *Current Trends in the Study of Midrash* (ed. C. Bakhos; JSJSup 106; Leiden: Brill, 2006), 9–34 (9).

[50] Mandel, "Origins," 10.

that Jacob never died. Indeed, Rav Naḥman does not disappoint. He provides the expected response that all indications are that Jacob did really die. It is interesting, however, that Rav Naḥman does not merely appeal to the apparent narrative of Jacob's death in Gen 49:33. Even if they are responding to the issue of the lack of explicit use of "to die" for Jacob, surely Rav Naḥman could make a strong case for Gen 49:33 pointing toward Jacob's death. Rav Naḥman seems to be playing along and thus both he and Rabbi Isaac suspend the simple meaning of scripture in the service of its larger rereading.

Within the exchange, Rav Naḥman acts the credulous foil for Rabbi Isaac's "transformation, violation, and appropriation" – to borrow Joshua Levinson's terminology – of scripture.[51] Rabbi Isaac's response to Rav Naḥman's assertion that scripture contravenes his claim regarding Jacob strikes at the heart of the midrashic process. Rabbi Isaac unabashedly asserts that his role of exegete allows him to read the scriptural verse as he pleases. Rabbi Isaac's further homiletical reading of Jer 30:10 provides the payoff for his subversive reading of Gen 49:33. Just as Jacob's progeny is brought back from the seeming death of exile in Jer 30:10, so the primogenitor Jacob never truly dies. This rereading of Jer 30:10 offers a powerful message on rabbinic notions of death and renewal and thus serves an important role in broader rabbinic society.

By framing his engagement with the text as "[It is] a scriptural verse that I expound," Rabbi Isaac identifies himself and the entire exegetical process as outside of the text. Indeed, Rav Naḥman knows his scripture just as well as Rabbi Isaac and calls Rabbi Isaac out for his apparent "misreading" of scripture. Rabbi Isaac himself, moreover, cites the verse from *Jeremiah* in full. He allows Gen 49:33 and Jer 30:10 their textual integrity even as he radically transforms their conceptual application. In this sense, he opens himself up to being further challenged by Rav Naḥman. Yet, Rav Naḥman is silent, no doubt because he is convinced by Rabbi Isaac's claim for the validity of his exegetical process.

A second trope can be detected in this pericope that speaks to the issue of rabbinic authority to transform the meaning of scripture. On the one hand, Rabbi Isaac is supremely confident in the correctness of his exegetical method and its results. Rav Naḥman's eventual silence reflects his tacit acceptance of this method, though Rabbi Isaac's acerbic tone no doubt serves to reinforce Rav Naḥman's reluctance to offer any further challenge. At the same time, Rabbi Isaac's entire interpretation, and by extension his confidence, stems from the authority of tracing the source of the exegesis to his teacher Rabbi Yoḥanan. For the rabbis, the appeal to the authority of one's teacher is no small matter. Such a statement locates Rabbi Isaac in the unbroken chain of transmission that the rabbis most famously in *Mishnah 'Abot* trace all the way back to Moses on Sinai:

[51] See Levinson, "Dialogical Reading," 499 and further discussion below.

> Moses received Torah at Sinai and transmitted it to Joshua, Joshua to elders, and elders to prophets, and prophets transmitted it to the men of the great assembly. (*m. 'Abot* 1:1)

The *Mishnah* constructs a literary history that posits a direct connection between the Mosaic receipt of the divine word on Sinai and rabbinic discourse. There are two tendentious processes at work here in support of the rabbinic claims of authority. First, as noted by Moshe Herr, the *Mishnah* deliberately ignores the priests and Levites, the precise class of people most commonly associated with law in the Hebrew Bible and postbiblical tradition.[52] Second, the *Mishnah* reimagines the identity of Moses, Joshua, and the prophets and their role in the history of Israel. In so doing, the *Mishnah* transforms a select group of its predecessors into proto-rabbis and thus faithful tradents of a rabbinic tradition first articulated to Moses on Sinai by God. Thus, in rabbinic imagination, Moses' identity as prophet, lawgiver, and cultic leader recedes in favor of his new identity as משה רבינו, "Moses our Master/Rabbi."[53] So too, Joshua and the prophets become rabbis.[54]

The rabbinic sense of the relationship between their legal and exegetical activity and Moses on Sinai is well articulated by an exposition on the description of the giving of the Torah in Deut 9:10 found in the *Palestinian Talmud*. Deut 9:10 describes how Moses received "two tablets of stone inscribed by the finger of God, and upon them was written according to all these words that the Lord spoke with you on the mountain." Rabbi Joshua ben Levi focuses on the presence in the verse of presumably extraneous particles, which he suggests are intended to indicate the transmission of further content on Sinai:

> Rabbi Joshua ben Levi said "[For] 'upon them [was written,]' [scripture reads] '*and* upon them [was written]' (עליהם ועליהם); [for] 'all [the words],' [scripture reads] '*according* to all [the words]' (כל ככל); [for] 'words,' [scripture reads] '*these* words' (דברים הדברים). [These extra particles indicate that on Sinai was also transmitted] scripture, *Mishnah*, *Talmud*, and *Aggadah*. Even that which a learned student (תלמיד וותיק) someday in the future will recite before his master has been transmitted to Moses on Sinai. What is the reason for this? [Scripture says] "Sometimes there is a phenomenon of which they say, 'Look this one is new' (Eccl 1:10a). His fellow responds to him saying 'It occurred long ago [in ages that went by before us]'" (Eccl 1:10b). (*y. Pe'ah* 2:6 17a)[55]

[52] Moshe D. Herr, "Continuum in the Chain of Tradition of the Torah," *Zion* 44 (1979): 43–56 [Hebrew]. For a more recent discussion of this approach, see Steven D. Fraade, *From Tradition to Commentary: Torah and Its Interpretation in the Midrash Sifre to Deuteronomy* (Albany: SUNY Press, 1991), 70–71.

[53] This designation for Moses first appears in tannaitic literature and is widespread. On this title, see Ginzberg, *The Legends of the Jews*, 5:168–69 n. 68.

[54] On the "rabbinization" of prophets, see the textual evidence collected in Jacob Neusner, *The Rabbis, the Law, and the Prophets* (Lanham: University Press of America, 2008).

[55] Text follows Ms Leiden Or. 4720 (cited from Yaakov Sussman, ed., *Talmud Yerushalmi: Yoṣe le-'Or 'al Pi Ketav Yad Skaliger 3 (Or. 4720) Shebe-Sifriyat ha-Universitah shel Laiden*

A related tradition appears in the later *Exodus Rabbah* based on Exod 20:1:

> "Write for yourself these words" (Exod 34:27). It is written "If I write for him so many things of my law [they are accounted as a stranger]" (Hos 8:12). When God revealed himself at Sinai to give the Torah to Israel, he said to Moses, [it will be] according to the order of scripture, *Mishnah*, *Talmud*, and *Aggada*, as it is said, "And God spoke *all* (כל) of these things" (Exod 20:1). Even that which a student asks his rabbi, God told Moses on Sinai at that time. (*Exodus Rabbah* 47)[56]

This *midrash* asserts that the quantifier "all" (כל) in Exod 20:1 indicates that God articulated much more to Moses on Sinai than what is written down in the Torah.

Both rabbinic traditions reveal how the rabbis envision the "omnisignificance" of the biblical text. This terminology is employed by James Kugel to identify the rabbinic insistence that "nothing in Scripture is said in vain or for rhetorical flourish: every detail is important, everything is intended to impart some teaching."[57] Indeed, in both rabbinic passages, seemingly simple syntactic markers are regarded as conveying a wealth of meaning otherwise unintended by the straightforward meaning of these verses. The subversive readings of Deut 9:10 and Exod 20:1 ultimately pale in comparison to what these "extraneous" words signify for the broader rabbinic hermeneutic model. In what can only be understood as a supreme hyperbole, the rabbis envision every single component of their intellectual and literary creativity as already revealed on Sinai. Thus, Rabbi Isaac's willingness to deny the very simple meaning of scripture draws not only from his own exegetical self-confidence but also from the belief that his exegetical method and associated results represent the very word of God. In this sense, the rabbinic approaches share much with their Second Temple–period forebearers.

'im Tashlamot ve-Tiqunim [Jerusalem: The Academy of the Hebrew Language, 2001], 89–90). Translation (modified) follows Roger Brooks, *The Talmud of the Land of Israel: A Preliminary Translation and Explanation*, volume 2: *Peah* (Chicago: University of Chicago Press, 1990), 128. See parallels in *y. Meg.* 4:1 74a; *Ḥag.* 1:8 76d; *Leviticus Rabbah* 22:1; *Ecclesiastes Rabbah* 1.9.2 (on Eccl 1:10). The passage in *Leviticus Rabbah* and *Ecclesiasties Rabbah* adds to this list of scriptural verses Deut 8:1, where "*the entire* commandment" appears instead of merely "commandment."

56 Translation (modified) follows S. M. Lehrman, *Midrash Rabbah: Exodus* (London: Soncino, 1939), 536. The exact origins of *Exodus Rabbah* are unclear, though most scholars date it to approximately the tenth century (see Strack and Stemberger, *Introduction*, 308–9). A nearly parallel text appears in *Midrash Tanḥuma Shemot, Ki Tissa* 17 (see Solomon Buber, *Midrash Tanḥuma: Exodus* [Vilna, 1885; repr., Jerusalem, 1963], 116). *Exodus Rabbah* 47 comes from the section of the text generally thought to be closely related to the *Tanḥuma* traditions (§§15–52 on Exod 12–40).

57 This definition draws from James Kugel, *Traditions of the Bible: A Guide to the Bible as It Was at the Start of the Common Era* (Cambridge: Harvard University Press, 1998), 17. The terminology was first coined by Kugel in idem, *The Idea of Biblical Poetry: Parallelism and Its History* (New Haven: Yale University Press, 1981), 103–4.

Notwithstanding the divergent literary forms rabbinic legal literature took, it was essentially still grappling with the same questions encountered by its forebearers – how to make ancient Israelite law a living and still timely institution. In an apt, though perhaps more heuristic, observation, Florentino García Martínez notes that the heavenly tablets in the book of *Jubilees* "function in the same way as the Oral Torah in rabbinic Judaism. The HT [heavenly tablets] constitute a hermeneutical recourse which permits the 'correct' interpretation of the Law, adapting it to the changing situations of life."[58] The rabbis shared the view of the Second Temple–period legists that the key to the effective and authoritative updating of ancient Israelite law lay with an intense engagement with scripture, even as the ideological basis and hermeneutic technique differed.

IV. THE DYNAMICS OF ANCIENT JEWISH LAW AND LEGAL EXEGESIS IN DIALOGUE

The foregoing observations have argued in favor of the recognition of the overlapping significance of legal exegesis in Second Temple Judaism *and* rabbinic Judaism. Two particular broader conversations at the interface of the legal hermeneutics of the Dead Sea Scrolls and rabbinic literature are illumined by this study. Much has been made in the study of scriptural interpretation of the Dead Sea Scrolls as a witness to the transition from the purely rewritten form of interpretation to a more explicit commentary genre. Yet, again the imbalance in attention between legal and nonlegal texts persists in this discussion. Thus, scholarship that traces the prehistory of rabbinic methods of exegesis often focuses on nonlegal exemplars in the scrolls. For example, scholars point to the clear example of lemma-plus-commentary interpretation found in the *Pesharim* in attempts to draw lines of continuity to rabbinic exegesis.[59] Similarly, scholars have observed how the *Commentary on Genesis A* (4Q252) blends literary features common to the rewriting style of Second Temple–period exegesis with incipient forms of commentary.[60]

58 García Martínez, "The Heavenly Tablets," 259. Although in principle this observation is correct, see Najman, "Interpretation as Primordial Writing," 71, for several important distinctions.

59 See, e.g., Menachem Kister, "A Common Heritage: Biblical Interpretation at Qumran and Its Implications," in *Biblical Perspectives: Early Use and Interpretation of the Bible in Light of the Dead Sea Scrolls: Proceedings of the First International Symposium of the Orion Center for the Study of the Dead Sea Scrolls and Associated Literature, 12–14 May, 1996* (ed. M. E. Stone and E. G. Chazon; STDJ 28; Leiden: Brill, 1998), 101–12 (103); Bilhah Nitzan, "The Continuity of Biblical Interpretation in the Qumran Scrolls and Rabbinic Literature," in *The Oxford Handbook of the Dead Sea Scrolls* (ed. T. H. Lim and J. J. Collins; Oxford: Oxford University Press, 2010), 337–50. See my treatment of this issue in Jassen, "The Pesharim and the Rise of Commentary."

60 On this aspect of the text, see Moshe J. Bernstein, "4Q252: From Re-Written Bible to Biblical Commentary," *JJS* 41 (1994): 1–27; in dialogue with George J. Brooke, "4Q252 as Early Jewish Commentary," *RevQ* 17 (1996): 385–401.

The transitional method of exegesis opened up by the *Pesharim* and the *Commentary on Genesis A* in a narrative context has a counterpart in the study in legal literature. Beginning with the nineteenth-century *Wissenschaft des Judentums* scholars and continuing long into the twentieth century, scholars expended great energy in seeking to determine in what form early *halakhah* was first transmitted. Over a century of scholarship endlessly debated which method of presenting *halakhah* came first: the apodictic style as reflected in the *Mishnah* or the *midrash*-type form that explicitly linked the law to its presumed scriptural source text, as found in the early halakhic *Midrashim*.[61] Prior to the discovery of the Dead Sea Scrolls, the nature of argumentation on each side drew primarily from competing analyses of the same rabbinic material, with occasional uses of the then-fragmentary data regarding law in the Second Temple period.

The publication of the legal texts among the Dead Sea Scrolls finally seems to provide empirical evidence to put this debate to rest. As observed by Schiffman, on the one hand, the *Damascus Document* is full of legal material presented in the apodictic form familiar from the *Mishnah*. The *Damascus Document* moreover provides headings to its groupings of related apodictic law, thus displaying evidence of a type of topical arrangement familiar from the *Mishnah*. Indeed, the publication of other texts such as *4QMiqṣat Ma'ase Ha-Torah* (4Q394–399), *4QHalakha A* (4Q251), and *4QHalakha B* (4Q264a) provide further examples of a similar form of law.[62] Yet, at the same time, texts such

[61] To be sure, the first attempt to address this issue seems to be Rabbi Sherira Gaon in his *Epistle*, where he argues for the priority of the *midrash*-type presentation. See B. M. Lewin, ed., *Iggeret Rav Sherira Gaon* (Jerusalem: Makor, 1921), 39. For modern scholarship, see, for example, Nachman Krochmal, *More Nebukhe Ha-Zeman* (Lemberg: Josephi Schnayder, 1851), *Sha'ar* 13, in *Kitve Rabbi Naḥman Krokhmal* (ed. S. Rawidowicz; 2d ed.; London: Ararat, 1961), 194–204; David Z. Hoffmann, *Die erste Mischna und die Controversen der Tannaim* (Berlin, 1881–82), 5–26; Jacob Z. Lauterbach, "Midrash and Mishnah: A Study in the Early History of Halakhah," in *Rabbinic Essays* (ed. S. B. Freehof; Cincinnati: Hebrew Union College, 1951), 163–256 (1914–16); Chanokh Albeck, "The Halakhot and the *Derashoth*," in *Alexander Marx: Jubilee Volume on the Occasion of His Seventieth Birthday, Hebrew Volume* (New York: Jewish Theological Seminary, 1950), 1–8 [Hebrew]; idem, *Introduction to the Mishnah* (Jerusalem: Bialik Institute; Tel Aviv: Dvir, 1959), 40–62 [Hebrew]; Solomon Zeitlin, "Midrash: A Historical Study," in *Studies in the Early History of Judaism*, volume 4: *History of Early Talmudic Law* (New York: Ktav, 1978), 41–56 (1953); Ephraim E. Urbach, "The *Derasha* as the Basis of the Halakhah and the Problem of the *Soferim*," *Tarbiz* 27 (1957–58): 166–82 [Hebrew]; Kaufman, *History*, 4:481–85; Yitzḥak D. Gilat, "Halakhic Interpretation (Midrash Halakha) of Scripture in the Post-Talmudic Period," in *Studies in the Development of the Halakha* (Ramat Gan: Bar Ilan University Press, 1992), 374–94 (1978) [Hebrew]; Halivni, *Mishnah, Midrash, and Gemara*; Vered Noam, "Creative Interpretation and Integrative Interpretation in Qumran," in *The Dead Sea Scrolls and Contemporary Culture: Proceedings of the International Conference Held at the Israel Museum (July 6–8, 2008)* (ed. A. D. Roitman, L. H. Schiffman, and S. Tzoref; STDJ 93; Leiden: Brill, 2011), 363–76. Useful summaries of earlier scholarship on this question can be found in Lauterbach, ibid., 163–82; Halivni, ibid., 18–19; and Strack and Stemberger, *Introduction*, 126–29.

[62] On the nature of subject headings and organization, see Lawrence H. Schiffman, *The Halakhah at Qumran* (SJLA 16; Leiden: Brill, 1975), 82–83; idem, "Codification of Jewish Law in the

as the *Temple Scroll* and *4QReworked Pentateuch* reflect a close connection with the scriptural text through its rewriting. The appeal to the authority of scripture thus seems to provide evidence of a prehistory to the later rabbinic *midrash*-type law. Schiffman therefore concludes that the binary nature of the earlier debates had it all wrong. Rather, "It is clear, therefore, that at least for some Jews, already in the second century B.C.E., both forms coexisted among students of the Torah just as they coexisted in tannaitic circles by the second century C.E."[63]

This conclusion is certainly correct and goes a long way in settling the debate. At the same time, by framing our analysis of the forms in the scrolls in light of both later rabbinic norms and the modern debate over origins, we run the risk of misconstruing what the evidence of the scrolls actually does divulge. It is true that the scrolls contain both apodictic *Mishnah*-type law and *midrash*-type scripture-based law. And indeed, they stand side by side in the *Damascus Document*. Furthermore, the *Damascus Document* has long been singled out for its presentation of law with explicit prooftexts. Likewise, *4QMiqṣat Ma'ase Ha-Torah* supports its legal formulations with apparent prooftexts, even though these "citations" are actually paraphrases of scriptural passages.[64]

Dead Sea Scrolls," in *Qumran and Jerusalem: Studies on the Dead Sea Scrolls and the History of Judaism* (Grand Rapids: Eerdmans, 2010), 170–83, especially 176–77, 181 (2007).

[63] Lawrence H. Schiffman, "The Judean Scrolls and the History of Judaism," in *The Dead Sea Scrolls: Fifty Years after Their Discovery: Proceedings of the Jerusalem Congress, July 20–25, 1997* (ed. L. H. Schiffman, E. Tov, and J. C. VanderKam; Jerusalem: Israel Exploration Society in cooperation with the Shrine of the Book, Israel Museum, 2000), 542–57 (552). See the similar point mentioned in the context of the Sadducean/Zadokite approach to law in idem, "Pre-Maccabean Halakhah in the Dead Sea Scrolls and the Biblical Tradition," in *Qumran and Jerusalem*, 194 (2006). On the nature of the coexistence of these forms in early tannaitic literature, see Azzan Yadin, "Resistance to Midrash? Midrash and Halakhah in the Halakhic Midrashim," in *Current Trends in the Study of Midrash*, 35–58. Compare the use of the same evidence from the *Damascus Document* in Halivni, *Mishnah, Midrash, and Gemara*, 38. He discounts the significance of the blended forms by arguing that one cannot compare the sectarian and Pharisaic approaches. This obscures the point. The transmission of law was not merely the prerogative of the Pharisees (or later rabbis). Rather, the *Damascus Document* provides an important snapshot of the presentation of law in a broader Second Temple–period setting. As further observed by Schiffman, it is therefore likely – though ultimately unverifiable absent further source material – that a similar blending of forms was found among Pharisaic literature ("Pre-Maccabean Halakhah," 194). See the strong circumstantial case brought in favor of the use of both forms even among the Pharisees in Joseph M. Baumgarten, "Halivni's *Mishnah, Midrash, and Gemara*," *JQR* 77 (1986): 59–64.

[64] See Elisha Qimron and John Strugnell, *Qumran Cave 4.V: Miqṣat Ma'aśe Ha-Torah* (DJD 10; Oxford: Clarendon, 1996), 140–41; Moshe J. Bernstein, "The Employment and Interpretation of Scripture in 4QMMT: Preliminary Observations," in *Reading 4QMMT: New Perspectives on Qumran Law and History* (ed. J. Kampen and M. J. Bernstein; SBLSymS 2; Atlanta: Scholars Press, 1996), 29–51; George J. Brooke, "The Explicit Presentation of Scripture in 4QMMT," in *Legal Texts and Legal Issues: Proceedings of the Second Meeting of the International Organization for Qumran Studies, Cambridge, 1995; Published in Honour of Joseph M. Baumgarten* (ed. M. J. Bernstein, F. García Martínez, and J. Kampen; STDJ 23; Leiden: Brill, 1997), 67–88. The nature of prooftexts in this text is discussed in more detail in Chapter 11.

At the same time, an important distinction must be made in understanding the prehistory of the *midrash*-type form. The rewriting of the scriptural text in the *Temple Scroll* shares an ideological assumption with later rabbinic *midrash halakhah* that law must be grounded in scriptural authority. Yet, *midrash halakhah* unequivocally creates a distinction between the scriptural base text and its associated *halakhah*. Such a distinction is just as unequivocally absent in the *Temple Scroll*. Whereas the presence of the lemma empowers the *halakhah* with scriptural authority in the halakhic *Midrashim*, its very absence is central to the *Temple Scroll*'s similar appeal to the prestige of scripture. In this hybrid form, laws are presented in the seemingly apodictic style familiar from the *Mishnah*. Yet, even a simple reading of many of these passages reveals the clear influence of scriptural language, thus matching the supporting role of scripture in *midrash halakhah*. Thus, it seems more appropriate to construe legal "rewritten" scripture as yet an additional form in which to present law. Furthermore, the cumulative effect of the evidence of the *Temple Scroll*, the *Damascus Document*, the book of *Jubilees*, and related works indicates that this was the dominant form in which law was presented in the Second Temple period. This should not come as a surprise; the nonlegal literature demonstrates that rewriting was similarly the most common form of scriptural interpretation more generally.

As in contemporaneous texts, the *Damascus Document* shares an appreciation for rewriting scriptural law. But, its many apodictic laws and prooftexts diverge from this dominant model and mark it as a transitional text in the history of Jewish law, thus prefiguring the two norms that would emerge in the *Mishnah* and halakhic *Midrashim*. My synchronic analysis of several legal passages in the *Damascus Document* and related texts offers further light on the competing forms in which law appears, at the same time as it demonstrates the complexity that went into these developing norms.

My diachronic analysis of the material in the Dead Sea Scrolls alongside Second Temple literature and rabbinic texts seeks to nuance the discussion of scripture-based law in each setting. In particular, my analysis offers insight into what happens as the rewritten legal norms of the Second Temple period are abandoned in later rabbinic legal hermeneutics. Many of the examples treated in this study from the *Damascus Document* and related texts fall under the broad rubric I have classified as "rewritten" laws. At the same time, a clear distinction should be drawn between this approach in the *Temple Scroll* and many other texts. While a reader of the *Temple Scroll* would likely recognize the underlying Deuteronomic text, many of the examples treated below from the *Damascus Document*, *4QHalakha A*, *4QHalakha B*, and the book of *Jubilees* display a further distance from the scriptural base text even as they reflect a deep legal-exegetical engagement with that very text. In other words, the creators of the material were well aware of its scriptural basis even as later readers may not have apprehended its full scriptural basis.

An interesting phenomenon is detected when many of these very same laws are traced from the Second Temple period to the rabbinic corpus. As is to be expected, the "rewritten" form is almost entirely abandoned. Thus, rabbinic formulations present the similar laws either in an apodictic style (e.g., in the *Mishnah* or *Tosefta*) or alongside an independent scriptural lemma or prooftext (e.g., in the halakhic *Midrashim*). Yet, in each of these settings, there often exist traces of the exegetical techniques and literary forms that mark the presentation of the laws in their earlier Second Temple–period "rewritten" iterations. At times, rabbinic texts seem to be aware of earlier Second Temple–period exegetical approaches and indeed appropriate them, albeit modified to rabbinic legal norms. In other instances, rabbinic exegesis seems to go to great pains to avoid re-creating the very same exegetical maneuvers. In perhaps the most surprising twist, my analysis below detects several instances where the "rewritten" norms that exist in the Second Temple–period texts persist – to be sure, in a muted manner – in the rabbinic iterations of the related laws. As is always the case, it is not clear where a historical connection exists and where the related evidence is better explained as part of the phenomenological interplay of scripture and interpretation in Jewish legal history. These observations have important implications for understanding the prehistory of rabbinic law and legal exegesis and further demonstrate the lines of development – some direct, others circuitous – between rabbinic legal literature and its Second Temple forebearers.

My analysis also has wider implications for the study of another aspect of the history of Jewish legal hermeneutics. The specific way in which I have formulated the broad research question of the role of non-Pentateuchal scripture draws from similar inquiries in rabbinic literature. Rabbinic legal hermeneutics for the most part rejects the use of non-Pentateuchal scripture in *midrash halakhah*.[65] As is often the case in rabbinic literature, however, there is notable dissent.[66] The general rabbinic rejection of *midrash halakhah* based on non-Pentateuchal texts and the nature of the rabbinic debate over this issue have long occupied rabbinic scholars, both ancient and modern.[67] Do the dominant rabbinic approaches and the associated debates find earlier attestations in Second Temple Judaism? In what ways can analysis of similar issues in a

[65] See, e.g., the rabbinic statement אין דנין דברי תורה מדברי קבלה, "We do not adjudicate the words of Torah from words of tradition (i.e., non-Pentateuchal scripture)" (*b. Nid.* 23a; see *b. Ḥag.* 10b; *b. B. Qam.* 2b for similar formulations).

[66] See, for example, *b. Giṭ.* 36a, where the need for witnesses to sign a deed is supported by a passage from Jer 32:44. A longer list of passages is discussed in Louis Ginzberg, *An Unknown Jewish Sect* (Moreshet 1; New York: Jewish Theological Seminary, 1976), 185–86.

[67] See Zvi H. Chajes, *Torat Nevi'im ha-mekhuneh Eleh ha-Mitsvot* (1836), printed in *Kol Sifre Maharaṣ Chayot* (2 vols.; Jerusalem: Divre Hakhamim, 1958), 1:3–136; Ephraim E. Urbach, "Law and Prophecy," in *The World of the Sages: Collected Studies* (Jerusalem: Magnes, 1988), 21–49 (32–40) (1946–47) [Hebrew]. For a broad overview, see "דברי קבלה," *Enṣiqlopedyah Talmudit* (ed. M. Bar-Ilan and S. Y. Yeiven; 23 vols.; Jerusalem: Mossad ha-Rav Kook, 1947–), 7:112–14 [Hebrew].

Second Temple–period context, particularly in the Dead Sea Scrolls and related texts, provide a fuller picture of this chapter in the history of Jewish legal hermeneutics?

V. CONCLUSIONS

Notwithstanding the several-century chronological gap that divides many of the Second Temple–period and rabbinic texts, my analysis locates them as conversation partners, sometimes historical, at other times phenomenological. As such, this study further contributes to the growing awareness of the shared world of Jewish law and legal exegesis in ancient Judaism. More broadly, the Dead Sea Scrolls, Second Temple legal texts, and rabbinic literature can now be plotted on a larger trajectory of Jewish legal-exegetical activity in antiquity. This study highlights the shared and divergent techniques employed by the varieties of Judaism in the ancient world to continue to enliven the legal writings of ancient Israel for their own time and place.

3

Jewish Legal Exegesis and the Origins and Development of the Canon

I. INTRODUCTION

This book is about the varieties of the reception of the Hebrew Bible in ancient Judaism and the diverse attempts to renew the sacred writings of ancient Israel and the legal material contained therein. As I emphasized in the preceding chapter, this process is undertaken in the Second Temple period through the reformulation of the language and literary features of older texts, and in rabbinic Judaism through the sustained engagement with the text via commentary. Both processes succeed only because the earlier text has attained a degree of authority, which is then transferred to the new texts. Thus, this study is closely focused on questions related to the emerging authority and scriptural status of ancient Israelite literature in Second Temple Jewish settings.[1] The particular emphasis on Pentateuchal versus non-Pentateuchal scripture highlights the complex ways in which diverse types of texts gain authority. More broadly, therefore, this study engages with larger questions related to the emergence and significance of the canon of the Hebrew Bible, in the sense of "the definitive, closed list of the books that constitute the authentic contents of scripture."[2]

This study examines literature on both sides of the historical turn to canon. My analysis of the Second Temple–period material takes into consideration

[1] On the meaning of "authoritative" and "scriptural," see my discussion of Ulrich's definition of these terms above, Chapter 1, section II. See further Eugene C. Ulrich, "The Notion and Definition of Canon," in *The Canon Debate* (ed. L. M. McDonald and J. A. Sanders; Peabody: Hendrickson, 2002), 22–35.

[2] This definition likewise follows Ulrich, "The Notion and Definition of Canon," 34. On the difficulties in applying this terminology to ancient Jewish society, for which no such word existed, see James C. VanderKam, "Revealed Literature in the Second Temple Period," in *From Revelation to Canon: Studies in the Hebrew Bible and Second Temple Literature* (JSJSup 62; Leiden: Brill, 2000), 1–30 (1–3).

the dramatic impact of the Dead Sea Scrolls on modern reconstructions of the historical development of the canon and offers a new data set that can be introduced into these broader discussions.[3] Jews in the Second Temple period were living within a world in which the canon was taking shape. For Second Temple Judaism, individual books were often regarded as authoritative, even as the broader collection of canonical writings still lay in the future. In contrast, any treatment of scriptural authority and legal hermeneutics in rabbinic settings must take into consideration the essentially closed canon that served as the sacred scriptures of rabbinic Judaism. In both Second Temple and rabbinic settings, individuals and communities labored to apply their authoritative texts to new historical and cultural contexts dramatically different from those in which these texts were composed.

In the previous chapter, I explored this same set of problematics within the context of the literary and exegetical development of Second Temple and rabbinic literature. In this chapter, I focus on their implications for understanding

[3] A great deal of scholarly research has developed in recent years. For a sampling since merely the mid-1990s, see Eugene Ulrich, "The Bible in the Making: The Scriptures at Qumran," in *The Dead Sea Scrolls and the Origins of the Bible* (Grand Rapids: Eerdmans, 1999), 17–33 (1994); idem, "The Qumran Biblical Scrolls – The Scriptures of Late Second Temple Judaism," in *The Dead Sea Scrolls in Their Historical Context* (ed. T. Lim; Edinburgh: T. and T. Clark, 2000), 67–87; idem, "Methodological Reflections on Determining Scriptural Status in First Century Judaism," in *Rediscovering the Dead Sea Scrolls: An Assessment of Old and New Approaches and Methods* (ed. M. L. Grossman; Grand Rapids: Eerdmans, 2010), 145–61; idem, "Clearer Insight into the Development of the Bible – A Gift of the Scrolls," in *The Dead Sea Scrolls and Contemporary Culture: Proceedings of the International Conference Held at the Israel Museum (July 6–8, 2008)* (ed. A. D. Roitman, L. H. Schiffman, and S. Tzoref; STDJ 93; Leiden: Brill, 2011), 119–37; Frank Moore Cross, "The Stabilization of the Canon of the Hebrew Bible," in *From Epic to Canon: History and Literature in Ancient Israel* (Baltimore: Johns Hopkins University Press, 1998), 219–29; Julio C. Trebolle Barrera, "Origins of a Tripartite Old Testament Canon," in *The Canon Debate*, 128–45; James C. VanderKam, "Authoritative Literature in the Dead Sea Scrolls," *DSD* 5 (1998): 382–402; idem, "Revealed Literature," 1–30; idem, "Questions of Canon as Viewed through the Dead Sea Scrolls," in *The Canon Debate*, 91–109 (2001); Shemaryahu Talmon, "The Crystallization of the 'Canon of Hebrew Scriptures' in the Light of Biblical Scrolls from Qumran," in *Text and Canon of the Hebrew Bible* (Winona Lake: Eisenbrauns, 2010), 419–42 (2002); Armin Lange, "The Status of the Biblical Texts in the Qumran Corpus and the Canonical Process," in *The Bible as Book: The Hebrew Bible and the Judaean Desert Discoveries* (ed. E. D. Herbert and E. Tov; London: British Library; New Castle: Oak Knoll Press, 2002), 21–30; George J. Brooke, "Between Authority and Canon: The Significance of Reworking the Bible for Understanding the Canonical Process," in *Reworking the Bible: Apocryphal and Related Texts at Qumran: Proceedings of a Joint Symposium by the Orion Center for the Study of the Dead Sea Scrolls and Associated Literature and the Hebrew University Institute for Advanced Studies Research Group on Qumran, 15–17 January, 2002* (ed. E. G. Chazon, D. Dimant, and R. A. Clements; STDJ 53; Leiden: Brill, 2005), 85–104; idem, "New Perspectives on the Bible and Its Interpretation in the Dead Sea Scrolls," in *The Dynamics of Language and Exegesis at Qumran* (ed. D. Dimant and R. Kratz; FAT 2/35; Tübingen: Mohr Siebeck, 2009), 19–37; Florentino García Martínez, "Rethinking the Bible: Sixty Years of Dead Sea Scrolls Research and Beyond," in *Authoritative Scriptures in Ancient Judaism* (ed. M. Popović; JSJSup 141; Leiden: Brill, 2010), 19–36.

both the canonical process and the intersection of scriptural formation and scriptural interpretation in ancient Judaism. The robust scholarly conversation about canon since the 1990s on the whole has not taken into consideration the significance of Jewish legal-exegetical activity or legal literature more broadly. The evidence explored in this and the following chapters suggests that the literary and exegetical updating of law in Second Temple literature should be regarded as part of the very production of scripture.

II. THE "OLD" MODEL OF CANON FORMATION

Prior to the full impact of the Dead Sea Scrolls, studies on the emergence of the canon of the Hebrew Bible followed a relatively standard formula. Scholars sought to identify the precise historical time frame in which each unit of the tripartite canon was stabilized and thus reached a canonical status.[4] The origins of the Pentateuch (Torah) were placed in the early Persian period, with its canonization often identified with Ezra. Likewise, the Prophets (Nebi'im) were regarded as stabilized by the Hellenistic period. The third part of the tripartite canon, the Writings (Ketubim), were often seen as the product of first-century CE canonical conversations.[5] Within this framework, scholars sought to recover the "standardized" text of the "Bible" as constituted in each of these literary units.[6] Even as some pieces of the puzzle – such as the idea of a

[4] The history of modern research on the canon is summarized in Steven B. Chapman, *The Law and the Prophets* (FAT 27; Tübingen: Mohr Siebeck, 2000), 1–70. Much of the older approach can still be detected in Roger Beckwith, *The Old Testament Canon of the New Testament Church and Its Background in Early Judaism* (Grand Rapids: Eerdmans, 1985) (see also idem, "Formation of the Hebrew Bible," in *Mikra: Text, Translation, Reading and Interpretation of the Hebrew Bible in Ancient Judaism and Early Christianity* [ed. M. J. Mulder; CRINT 2/1; Assen: Van Gorcum; Minneapolis: Fortress, 1988], 39–86); and Sid Z. Leiman, *The Canonization of Hebrew Scripture: The Talmudic and Midrashic Evidence* (Transactions of the Connecticut Academy of Arts and Sciences 47; 2d ed.; New Haven: Connecticut Academy of Arts and Sciences, 1991). Unlike his predecessors, Leiman places great emphasis on the rabbinic evidence. On Leiman and Beckwith, see further VanderKam, "Revealed Literature," especially 12–19. As asserted by VanderKam, the second-century BCE dating for a final closed canon as argued by both Beckwith and Leiman has little merit. Indeed, further evidence from the Dead Sea Scrolls not available to Leiman and Beckwith (or VanderKam in 1988, when his paper was first delivered) only makes their arguments even less plausible.

[5] See VanderKam, "Revealed Literature," 10–11, for further elements and common evidence adduced in the "early standard theory" (his terminology).

[6] See Ulrich, "Qumran Biblical Scrolls," 69–70; Emanuel Tov, "The History and Significance of a Standard Text of the Hebrew Bible," in *Hebrew Bible/Old Testament: The History of Its Interpretation*, volume 1, part 1: *Antiquity* (ed. M. Sæbø; Göttingen: Vandenhoeck and Ruprecht, 1996), 49–66; Armin Lange, "'They Confirmed the Reading' (y. Ta'an 4.68a): The Textual Standardization of Jewish Scriptures in the Second Temple Period," in *From Qumran to Aleppo: A Discussion with Emanuel Tov about the Textual History of Jewish Scriptures in Honor of His Sixty-Fifth Birthday* (ed. A. Lange, M. Weigold, and J. Zsengellér; FRLANT 230; Göttingen: Vandenhoeck and Ruprecht, 2009), 29–80.

deliberative council of Yabneh (Jamnia) – were discarded after closer scrutiny, the basic overall model persisted.[7]

This scholarly model rests on a number of assumptions regarding the development of sacred literature and its transformation into authoritative scripture and canon. First, the canon of scripture develops in a linear fashion. Thus, the canonization of the Pentateuch was complete prior to the Prophets, and the Prophets prior to the Writings. Second, each of these scriptural units is a singular entity; the Pentateuch, for example, thus refers to a singular form of the Pentateuch. Though scholars were aware of variation in its textual character, this very feature was viewed as obfuscating the "original" text, which was regarded as the "biblical" text. Third, canon can have a clear and ascertainable endpoint.

III. TOWARD A NEW MODEL OF CANON FORMATION: LITERARY AND TEXTUAL DIVERSITY

The Dead Sea Scrolls have undermined everything we thought we once knew about the origins of the canon and simultaneously reveal a wealth of new ways to consider its historical development and cultural significance. The Dead Sea Scrolls are the product of a time when the text of the Hebrew Bible was still being crafted and the authoritative collection of books later identified as the canon of the Hebrew Bible had not yet been fully decided. Different collections of authoritative writings existed in distinct Second Temple–period communities, including the community of the Dead Sea Scrolls. What is most interesting is the textual diversity that characterizes collections of scriptural writings in the late Second Temple period. This phenomenon has long been known from such examples as the Greek versions of *Jeremiah* or *Daniel* and other Greek (Septuagint) and Hebrew (Samaritan Pentateuch) textual traditions that differ considerably from the Hebrew Masoretic version.[8] Yet, these divergent literary traditions were generally regarded as reflective of distinct social settings. More problematic, one would often be considered the "canonical" text (almost universally the Masoretic Text) and the others merely repositories of potential textual variants (i.e., the Septuagint or Samaritan Pentateuch).[9]

7 On Yabneh, see Jack P. Lewis, "What Do We Mean by Jabneh?" in *The Canon and Masorah of the Hebrew Bible: An Introductory Reader* (ed. S. Z. Leiman; New York: Ktav, 1974), 254–61 (1964); idem, "Jamniah Revisited," in *The Canon Debate*, 146–62; David E. Aune, "On the Origins of the 'Council of Javneh' Myth," *JBL* 110 (1991): 491–93. The rejection of the notion of a council at Yabneh is central to the broader arguments in Leiman, *Canonization*, 120–24; and Beckwith, *Old Testament Canon*, 274–77.

8 On *Jeremiah*, see Emanuel Tov, "The Literary History of the Book of Jeremiah in Light of Its Textual History," in *The Greek and Hebrew Bible: Collected Essays on the Septuagint* (VTSup 72; Leiden: Brill, 1999), 363–84 (1985). For other examples in the Septuagint and ancient versions, see discussion in idem, *Textual Criticism of the Hebrew Bible* (3d ed.; Minneapolis: Fortress, 2012), 283–326.

9 On the dominance of the Masoretic Text in scholarly conceptions of the meaning of "*the* Bible," see Ulrich, "Clearer Insight," 121–24 (cf. idem, "Qumran Biblical Scrolls," 71–72; "The Notion

Scholars were therefore quite surprised when they found within the Dead Sea Scrolls Hebrew copies of *Jeremiah* that corresponded with both the longer Masoretic Text (4QJer^{a,c}) and the shorter Septuagint text (4QJer^{b,d}).[10] Although each version of *Jeremiah* overlaps enough to be considered the book of *Jeremiah*, their literary divergence clearly marks them as distinct "versions" of *Jeremiah* from antiquity. In the scrolls, both versions stand alongside each other as authoritative versions of the prophetic word of *Jeremiah*. As more and more scrolls became available and were subjected to closer scrutiny, it became clear that the situation with the *Jeremiah* scrolls was true of nearly every book that would later be considered part of the Hebrew Bible.[11] This phenomenon is no small matter in the broader social landscape. If *Jeremiah*, for example, was regarded as the prophetic word of God, then the very word of God was still fluid and dynamic.

In the early years following the discovery of the Dead Sea Scrolls, the most comprehensive attempt to explain the coexistence of all these text types can be found in Frank Moore Cross's theory of "local texts." Cross suggests that the Masoretic Text, Septuagint, and Samaritan Pentateuch represent the scriptural texts of the Jewish communities in Babylonia, Egypt, and Palestine, respectively.[12] Cross's model was initially formulated based on a limited number of manuscripts. As more scrolls have come to light, Cross's theory no longer adequately explains why all of these textual traditions, and others, coexist in one setting – the Dead Sea Scrolls.[13]

More recently, Eugene Ulrich has repeatedly demonstrated how the "biblical" scrolls reflect evidence of "variant literary editions," whereby individual

and Definition of Canon," 31; "Determining Scriptural Status," especially 152–53); Arie van der Kooij, "The Textual Criticism of the Hebrew Bible before and after the Qumran Discoveries," in *The Bible as Book*, 167–77.

[10] These manuscripts are published in Emanuel Tov, "4QJer^{a-e}," in *Qumran Cave 4.X: The Prophets* (ed. E. Ulrich et al.; DJD 15; Oxford: Clarendon, 1997), 145–208. See also idem, "Jeremiah Scrolls from Cave 4," *RevQ* 14 (1989): 189–206; idem, "Three Fragments of Jeremiah from Qumran Cave 4," *RevQ* 15 (1992): 531–42. Tov's research is also summarized in *Textual Criticism*, 286–94.

[11] See Ulrich, "Qumran Biblical Scrolls," especially 76–78; idem, "Determining Scriptural Status," 158–60.

[12] See Frank Moore Cross, "The History of the Biblical Text in the Light of Discoveries in the Judaean Desert," in *Qumran and the History of the Biblical Text* (ed. F. M. Cross and Sh. Talmon; Cambridge: Harvard University Press, 1975), 177–95 (1964); idem, "The Contribution of the Qumrân Discoveries to the Study of the Biblical Text," in *Qumran and the History of the Biblical Text*, 278–92 (1966); idem, "The Evolution of a Theory of Local Texts," in *Qumran and the History of the Biblical Text*, 306–20.

[13] In the wake of Cross's proposal, Emanuel Tov formulated a theory of five text types that circulated in the Second Temple period – all of which are represented in the "biblical" Dead Sea Scrolls. See Emanuel Tov, "A Modern Textual Outlook Based on the Qumran Scrolls," *HUCA* 53 (1982): 11–27; idem, "Hebrew Biblical Manuscripts from the Judaean Desert: Their Contribution to Textual Criticism," *JJS* 39 (1988): 5–37; idem, "The Biblical Texts from the Judaean Desert: An Overview and Analysis of the Published Texts," in *The Bible as Book*, 139–66.

books are transmitted in multiple textual attestations – all of which are deemed scripture. Ulrich defines a variant literary edition as the following:

> A literary unit – a story, pericope, narrative, poem, book – appearing in two or more parallel forms (whether by chance extant or no longer extant in our textual witnesses), which one author, major redactor, or major editor completed and which a subsequent redactor or editor intentionally changed to a sufficient extent that the resultant form should be called a revised edition of that text.[14]

For Ulrich, therefore, the Septuagint, Masoretic Text, Samaritian Pentateuch, and additional textual traditions found in the Dead Sea Scrolls are merely snapshots of the broader landscape of the authoritative scriptures in the late Second Temple period. In this model, textual diversity becomes the hallmark of authoritative scripture.

IV. THE CANONICAL PROCESS AND AUTHORITY IN SECOND TEMPLE JUDAISM

Individual Scriptural Books and the Canonical Process

In spite of all the diversity that marks the authoritative scriptures of Second Temple Judaism, significant evidence serves as a harbinger of the more fully developed future canon, which can best be characterized as a "canonical process."[15] Jews in the Second Temple period clearly assigned greater authority and prestige to certain books over against others. Thus, for example, *Genesis* was likely a universally agreed-upon scriptural book among Jews in the Second

[14] Ulrich, "The Canonical Process, Textual Criticism, and Latter Stages in the Composition of the Bible," in *Origins of the Bible*, 51–78 (63) (1992). Ulrich has articulated this approach in several publications: "Double Literary Editions of Biblical Narratives and Reflections on Determining the Form to Be Translated," in *Origins of the Bible*, 34–50 (1988); idem, "Pluriformity in the Biblical Text, Text Groups, and Questions of Canon," in *Origins of the Bible*, 79–98 (1992); idem, "Multiple Literary Editions: Reflections toward a Theory of the History of the Biblical Text," in *Origins of the Bible*, 99–120 (1996); idem, "The Dead Sea Scrolls and the Biblical Text," in *The Dead Sea Scrolls after Fifty Years: A Comprehensive Assessment* (ed. J. C. VanderKam and P. W. Flint; 2 vols.; Leiden: Brill, 1998–99), 1:79–100; idem, "The Qumran Scrolls and the Biblical Text," in *The Dead Sea Scrolls Fifty Years after Their Discovery: Proceedings of the Jerusalem Congress, July 20–25, 1997* (ed. L. H. Schiffman, E. Tov, and J. C. VanderKam; Jerusalem: Israel Exploration Society in cooperation with the Shrine of the Book, Israel Museum, 2000), 51–59. Other scholars have also taken up Ulrich's observations. See Julio Trebolle Barrera, "Qumran Evidence for a Biblical Standard Text and for Non-Standard and Parabiblical Texts," in *The Dead Sea Scrolls in Their Historical Context*, 89–106; James C. VanderKam, "The Wording of Biblical Citations in Some Rewritten Scriptural Works," in *The Bible as Book*, 41–56; Hans Debel, "Greek 'Variant Literary Editions' to the Hebrew Bible," *JSJ* 41 (2010): 161–90.

[15] My use of this term draws from Ulrich, "The Notion and Definition of Canon," 30. See also idem, "Clearer Insight," 132–33, for an attempt to sketch out the stages by which a text moves from individual literary creation to scripture.

Temple period. A similar status was enjoyed for many of the books that would later be regarded as "canonical" within the rabbinic biblical canon as well as others. In this precanonical state, individual books more broadly enjoyed a heightened degree of authority, even if that authority extended to the multiple literary iterations of the work.[16]

Even with the pluriformity described above, all books were not treated equally.[17] Many works composed in the late Second Temple period were likely written with the intention of joining the elite class of authoritative scripture – a situation that likely did transpire to some degree for many such writings. Yet, distinctions in authority still existed. For example, there is significant evidence to suggest that the book of *Jubilees* was very popular and no doubt regarded as scripture by many, including the sectarian community of the Dead Sea Scrolls.[18] But, there is no evidence to suggest that it was ever regarded as on par with *Genesis*. Thus, for example, while *Genesis* is cited myriad times in the Dead Sea Scrolls, the similarly authoritative *Jubilees* is cited explicitly fewer than a handful of times (CD 16:3–4; 4Q228 1 i 9; 4Q384 9 2).[19] To

[16] See further Ulrich, "The Notion and Definition of Canon," 32.

[17] This point is similarly emphasized in VanderKam, "Revealed Literature," 3–4.

[18] See VanderKam, "Authoritative Literature," 396–402; idem, "Revealed Literature," 23–29; idem, "Questions of Canon," 105–7; Charlotte Hempel, "The Place of the Book of Jubilees at Qumran and Beyond," in *The Dead Sea Scrolls in Their Historical Context*, 187–96; Sidnie White Crawford, *Rewriting Scripture in Second Temple Times* (Grand Rapids: Eerdmans, 2008), 60–61; Aharon Shemesh, "4Q265 and the Authoritative Status of Jubilees at Qumran," in *Enoch and the Mosaic Torah: The Evidence of Jubilees* (ed. G. Boccaccini and G. Ibba; Grand Rapids: Eerdmans, 2009), 247–60; Todd R. Hanneken, "The Status and Interpretation of *Jubilees* in 4Q390," in *A Teacher for All Generations: Essays in Honor of James C. VanderKam* (ed. E. Mason et al.; 2 vols.; JSJSup 153; Leiden: Brill, 2011), 1:407–28. See, however, the overly cautious reservations on the authoritative status of the book of *Jubilees* outside the community of the Dead Sea Scrolls in Hindy Najman, "Reconsidering Jubilees: Prophecy and Exemplarity," in *Past Renewals: Interpretative Authority, Renewed Revelation and the Quest for Perfection in Jewish Antiquity* (JSJSup 53; Leiden: Brill, 2010), 189–206 (191–92) (2009). Najman notes that the evidence marshaled in favor of the universally authoritative status of *Jubilees* all stems from the Dead Sea Scrolls, and thus the authority of *Jubilees* should be limited to "some of the authors and copyists at Qumran." While this is true with regard to the commonly cited evidence of an abundance of *Jubilees* manuscripts, it misapprehends the fact that the authority of *Jubilees* is also evinced from its common use in more general nonsectarian Jewish literature *preserved* in the Dead Sea Scrolls. Thus, for example, Hanneken, ibid., demonstrates the authoritative nature of *Jubilees* for the author of 4Q390 (*Apocryphon of Jeremiah C*), which is representative of a now lost stream of Judaism that once existed outside of the sectarian community of the Dead Sea Scrolls. Moreover, VanderKam, "Authoritative Literature," 399–400, advances another, less empirical argument. He suggests that Christians likely would not have regarded as canonical a work not otherwise sacred in at least some Jewish circles. Thus, the very preservation of the book in a Christian canon attests to its significance in some Jewish communities.

[19] See VanderKam, "Authoritative Literature," 399; Hanneken, "Status and Interpretation," 418–21. On the *Damascus Document*, see, however, Devorah Dimant, "Two 'Scientific' Fictions: The So-Called Book of Noah and the Alleged Quotation of Jubilees in CD 16:3–4," in *Studies in the Hebrew Bible, Qumran, and the Septuagint: Essays Presented to Eugene Ulrich on the*

be sure, *Jubilees* is introduced in 4Q228 (*4QText with a Citation of Jub*) with the same citation formula (כי כן כתוב) as elsewhere employed for the Pentateuch (1QS 5:15 – Lev 22:16; CD 11:18 – Lev 23:38).[20] Yet, the singular nature of this attestation again is itself suggestive. Even as the book of *Jubilees* enjoys a heightened authoritative status, this hardly reaches the stature of *Genesis*.

A similar situation exists for other Second Temple works. The *Apocryphon of Joshua* is cited in *4QTestimonia* (4Q174 21–23).[21] Moreover, the *Aramaic Levi Document* may be cited in the *Damascus Document* one time as well (CD 4:15–19), but these two examples pale in comparison to citations of other books.[22] Moreover, VanderKam has demonstrated that if we focus even more closely on books introduced with citation formulae, the numbers shrink even further.[23] Even if we were to expand this criterion to include paraphrase – as noted, the far more common method of drawing upon earlier works – the discrepancies persist.[24]

Occasion of His Sixty-Fifth Birthday (ed. P. W. Flint, J. C. VanderKam, and E. Tov; VTSup 101; Leiden: Brill, 2003), 242–48.

20 The fragmentary nature of 4Q228 precludes learning much more about the nature of the citation. 2Q25 1 3 also employs this citation formula to introduce something written in the "book of Moses," though the text breaks off. Thus, it may have in mind either the Pentateuch or perhaps *Jubilees*. On this citation formula, see further VanderKam, "Authoritative Literature," 392.

21 On the citation of the *Apocryphon of Joshua* (= 4Q379 22 7–15), see Carol A. Newsom, "4Q378 and 4Q379: An Apocryphon of Joshua," in *Qumranstudien: Vorträge und Beiträge der Tailnehmer des Qumranseminars auf dem internationalen Treffen der Society of Biblical Literature, Münster 25.–26. Juli 1993* (ed. H.-J. Fabry, A. Lange, and H. Lichtenberger; Göttingen; Vandenhoeck and Ruprecht, 1996), 35–85 (74–77). An argument in favor of the *Apocryphon of Jeremiah* citing from *4QTestimonia* is advanced by Hanan Eshel, "The Historical Background of the Pesher Interpreting Joshua's Curse on the Rebuilder of Jericho," *RevQ* 15 (1992): 409–20 (411–12).

22 On use of the *Aramaic Levi Document*, see Jonas Greenfield, "The Words of Levi Son of Jacob in Damascus Document IV 15–19," *RevQ* 13 (1988): 319–22. Michael Stone has further suggested that the *Aramaic Levi Document* serves as a source for the book of *Jubilees*. He therefore suggests that the *Aramaic Levi Document* "was ascribed a certain authority and standing" in the third and second centuries BCE. See Stone, "Aramaic Levi in Its Contexts," in *Apocrypha, Pseudepigrapha and Armenian Studies: Collected Papers*, volume 1 (OLA 144; Leuven: Peeters, 2006), 275–94 (287) (2002). See further the (short) list of "noncanonical" works cited or alluded to in sectarian writings in Johann Lust, "Quotation Formulae and Canon in Qumran," in *Canon and Decanonization* (ed. A. van der Kooij and K. van der Toorn; SHR 82; Leiden: Brill, 1998), 67–77 (68–70); Lange, "Status of Biblical Texts," 23; García Martínez, "Rethinking the Bible," 22–24.

23 VanderKam, "Authoritative Literature," 394–95.

24 See George J. Brooke, "'The Canon within the Canon' at Qumran and in the New Testament," in *The Dead Sea Scrolls and the New Testament* (Minneapolis: Fortress, 2005), 27–51 (1997); Julio Trebolle (Barrera), "A 'Canon Within a Canon': Two Series of Old Testament Books Differently Transmitted, Interpreted and Authorized," *RevQ* 19 (2000): 383–99. On the specific issue of citations, see Joseph A. Fitzmyer, "The Use of Explicit Old Testament Quotations in Qumran Literature and in the New Testament," in *Essays on the Semitic Background of the*

While *Jubilees* does spawn a small collection of rewriting (e.g., *Pseudo-Jubilees* – 4Q225–227), it in no way compares with the cottage industry of *Genesis* rewritings and parascriptural works (e.g., *Jubilees*, the *Genesis Apocryphon*, *Commentary on Genesis A*).[25] The long time span between *Genesis* and its rewritten admirers cannot be employed to explain the discrepancy. The book of *Daniel*, which reaches its final form only in the second century BCE, around the time of the composition of *Jubilees*, serves as the inspiration for a large collection of reformulations.[26]

The cumulative evidence does not suggest that what later becomes the canonical rabbinic Bible predominates in the textual orbit of Second Temple Judaism. On the contrary, a similar dearth of manuscripts, citations, and reuses exists for many of the historical books (e.g., *Samuel*, *Kings*, *Chronicles*, *Ezra-Nehemiah*).[27] In this sense, the authority of the book of *Jubilees* dwarfs that of many of the historical writings that are preserved in the later canon.

Even as the authoritative collection of writings in the Second Temple period was expansive and pluriform, the evidence suggests that – across later canonical

New Testament (London: G. Chapman, 1971), 3–58 (1960–61); Geza Vermes, "Biblical Proof-Texts in Qumran Literature," in *Scrolls, Scriptures, and Christianity* (LSTS 56; London: T. and T. Clark, 2005), 56–67 (1989); VanderKam, "Authoritative Literature." Early assessments of the scrolls incorrectly argued for little distinction between so-called biblical and apocryphal books (the regnant terminology of the time): Bleddyn J. Roberts, "The Dead Sea Scrolls and the Old Testament Scriptures," *BJRL* 36 (1953–54): 75–96; J. Carmignac, "Les citations de l'Ancien Testament dans 'La guerre des fils de lumière contre les fils de ténèbres," *RB* 63 (1956): 234–60.

25 See Moshe J. Bernstein, "Contours of Genesis Interpretation at Qumran: Contents, Context, and Nomenclature," in *Studies in Ancient Midrash* (ed. J. Kugel; Cambridge: Harvard University Press, 2001), 57–85. For the possibility that *4QMiscellaneous Rules* (4Q265) rewrites material from *Jubilees*, see Shemesh, "4Q265 and the Authoritative Status of Jubilees at Qumran," 247–60. For a different explanation of the relationship of *4QMiscellaneous Rules* to the book of *Jubilees*, see below, Chapter 10, section III.

26 Material related to *Daniel* includes the Greek additions to *Daniel* preserved in the Septuagint (*Susanna*, *Bel and the Dragon*) and previously unknown Aramaic works found in the Dead Sea Scrolls: *4QPrayer of Nabonidus* (4Q242), *4QPseudo-Daniel*$^{a-b}$ (4Q243–244), *4QPseudo-Daniel*^{c} (4Q245), *4QApocryphon of Daniel* (4Q246), *4QFour Kingdoms*$^{a-b}$ (4Q552–553), *4QDaniel-Susanna?* (4Q551). On the latter collection of texts, see Klaus Beyer, *Die aramäischen Texte vom Toten Meer* (Göttingen: Vandenhoeck and Ruprecht, 1984), 223–25; Peter W. Flint, "The Daniel Tradition at Qumran," in *The Book of Daniel: Composition and Reception* (ed. J. J. Collins and P. W. Flint; FIOTL 2; VTSup 83; 2 vols.; Leiden: Brill, 2001), 2:329–67. To be sure, in this case, some of the para-Daniel material may actually predate the canonical *Daniel*. Even still, it is inspired by some form of the proto-Daniel writings from the late Second Temple period.

27 This point is likewise emphasized in VanderKam, "Questions of Canon," 91–92; Lange, "Status of Biblical Texts," especially 23–24; Sidnie White Crawford, "The Use of the Pentateuch in the Temple Scroll and the Damascus Document in the Second Century B.C.E.," in *The Pentateuch as Torah: New Models for Understanding Its Promulgation and Acceptance* (ed. G. N. Knoppers and B. M. Levinson; Winona Lake: Eisenbrauns, 2007), 301–18 (305). Lange argues for the non-authoritative status of *Song of Songs*, *Ecclesiastes*, *Ruth*, *Esther*, *Ezra-Nehemiah*, and *Chronicles*.

lines – certain books enjoyed much greater prestige and authority. In order to comprehend this situation fully, we must abandon the powerful assumptions that the later canon ingrains in our notions of how to characterize and classify authoritative writings in the Second Temple period. As scholars have significantly advanced our understanding of the diversity in the precanonical stage, old habits die hard. Even as new terminology such as "scripture" emerges to replace the anachronistic "Bible," the conceptual categories are still very much guided by old canonical boundaries.[28]

The Pentateuch and the Canonical Process

A similar situation exists for larger collections of books. It is not only *Genesis* that possesses a heightened authority in Second Temple Judaism but also its accompanying books in the Pentateuch, and the Pentateuch as a whole. Second Temple texts from the second and first centuries BCE evince several different expressions employed to classify emerging collections of scriptural books:

> **Prologue to the *Wisdom of Ben Sira*:** (1) the Law, (2) the Prophets, and (3) the later authors/other books of our ancestors/rest of the books.[29]
>
> ***4QMiqṣat Ma'ase Ha-Torah* (4QMMT):** (1) the book of Moses, (2) the books of the Prophets, and (3) (the writings of) David [and (4) the events of] ages past (C 9–11 = 4Q397 14–21 9–11; 4Q398 14–17 i 2–3).[30]

28 A good example of the still powerful models of canon can be found in Trebolle (Barrera), "Canon Within a Canon," 383–99, who marshals a great deal of evidence indicating the greater prestige accorded to the Pentateuch, *Isaiah*, the Minor Prophets, *Psalms*, *Job*, and *Proverbs* in contrast to *Joshua*, *Judges*, *Samuel*, *Kings*, *Jeremiah*, *Ezekiel*, and *Daniel*. This study, however, is effectively incomplete in not taking into consideration so-called noncanonical works. Surely, the criteria employed in this study would locate at least the book of *Jubilees* in the first category (and likely other books). While not responding directly to Trebolle Barrera, this basic point is cogently affirmed by VanderKam, "Authoritative Literature"; idem, "Questions of Canon"; Lange, "Status of Biblical Texts"; Ulrich, "Determining Scriptural Status."

29 The division of books is mentioned three times in the prologue. Each time, the first two categories are constant while the third appears in three different variations (see VanderKam, "Revealed Literature," 5–6). See the argument in favor of reading a bipartite canon in the prologue in Eugene Ulrich, "The Non-attestation of a Tripartite Canon in *4QMMT*," *CBQ* 65 (2002): 202–14 (212–13).

30 This translation follows Elisha Qimron and John Strugnell, *Qumran Cave 4.V: Miqṣat Ma'aśe Ha-Torah* (DJD 10; Oxford: Clarendon, 1996), 58–59. On this much-discussed passage, see VanderKam, "Authoritative Literature," 387–88; Jonathan G. Campbell, "*4QMMT*[d] and the Tripartite Canon," *JJS* 51 (2000): 181–90; Timothy H. Lim, "The Alleged Reference to the Tripartite Division of the Hebrew Bible," *RevQ* 20 (2001): 23–37; Ulrich, "Non-attestation," 202–14. Lim disputes not the reconstruction but rather its implications for the origins of the canon. Ulrich, in contrast, notes the difficulties in the physical reconstruction and cautions against too quickly accepting the reconstruction of the text as presented by Qimron and Strugnell in the interest of seeing a reference to the tripartite canon.

Rule of the Community: (1) Moses and (2) the Prophets (1QS 1:3; 8:15–16).[31]

2 Maccabees 2:13–14: (1) books about the kings and prophets, (2) and the writings of David, (3) and letters of kings about votive offerings.[32]

The significance of these passages for the origins of the tripartite canon is debated and ultimately outside the scope of the present inquiry.[33] This debate, however, generally focuses on the nebulous meaning of the third or further categories in the passages. When we read across the several passages, it becomes clear that the distinct categories of "Law/Torah/Moses" and "Prophets" are well attested.[34] The predilection to discuss sacred writing in these broad categorizations at the very least suggests that Jews in the second century BCE were beginning to think not just about individual books but how those books cohered with others in order to generate larger bodies of authoritative writings. The coherence of the first two categories suggests that they were the only (near) universally agreed-upon categories.[35]

The references to the "Torah/Law/Moses" in the passages cited here point to the growing significance of the Pentateuch as a self-contained authoritative scripture of Second Temple Judaism. The abundance of manuscripts of Pentateuchal books in the Qumran scrolls and other Judean Desert sites and their widespread citation and allusion in other Second Temple writings is evidence of their emerging authoritative status.[36] Beyond this, the evidence suggests that not only were the individual books authoritative, but also the five books were increasingly regarded as a unified collection. Already in *Ezra-Nehemiah*, as discussed in the previous chapter, the "Torah of Moses" – resembling in some form what later is identified as the Pentateuch – enjoys great prestige and appears with a distinct citation formula.[37] This evidence suggests that at

[31] See VanderKam, "Authoritative Literature," 390.

[32] See also the first-century CE references in Luke 24:44; Philo, *On the Contemplative Life* 25; Josephus, *Against Apion* 1.37–43; 4 Ezra 14:23–48; and the much later *b. Bab. Bat.* 14b–15a (see VanderKam, "Revealed Literature," 7–10). These and related passages may conveniently be consulted in Lee M. McDonald, "Appendix A: Primary Sources for the Study of the Old Testament/Hebrew Bible Canon," in *Canon Debate*, 580–82.

[33] See Beckwith, *Old Testament Canon*, especially 110–80; John Barton, "The Significance of a Fixed Canon of the Hebrew Bible," in *Hebrew Bible/Old Testament*, 67–83; Trebolle (Barrera), "Canon within a Canon"; idem, "Origins of a Tripartite Old Testament Canon"; Lim, "Alleged Reference"; Ulrich, "Non-attestation"; VanderKam, "Revealed Literature."

[34] Only the passage in 2 Macc 2:13–14 lacks any reference to the law.

[35] Thus, many scholars consider the existence of a bipartite canon – "law" and "prophets" – prior to the emergence of a tripartite canon. See, e.g., Beckwith, *Old Testament Canon*; Cross, "Stabilization of the Canon," 228; Ulrich, "Non-attestation," 212–13; idem, "Determining Scriptural Status," 140.

[36] See, e.g., VanderKam, "Questions of Canon," 92–93; Crawford, "Use of the Pentateuch," 302–3.

[37] On the citation formulae, see further Sebastian Grätz, "The Second Temple and the Legal Status of the Torah: The Hermeneutics of the Torah in the Books of Ruth and Ezra," in *Pentateuch as Torah*, 273–87.

least by the early Persian period some form of the Pentateuch existed as a self-contained collection of writings associated with Moses.[38]

The Persian period data finds further support in later Second Temple–period evidence, which reinforces the earlier authoritative status of the Pentateuch and attests to its growing scriptural – indeed canonical – status. The coherence and scriptural status of the Pentateuch are corroborated by its unified translation in the Septuagint in the third century BCE.[39] Already by the late third century BCE, the Greek chronographer Demetrius employed the Septuagint Pentateuch in his *On the Kings of Judea*.[40] The earliest Septuagint manuscripts (second–first centuries BCE) from among the Qumran Dead Sea Scrolls are nearly all of Pentateuchal books.[41] The unity of the Pentateuch is further presumed in the adoption of the pre-Samaritan text of the Pentateuch as the exclusive sacred scripture of the Samaritans. Recent scholarship generally locates the transition

38 A large body of literature on this issue exists. Most recently, see Christophe L. Nihan, "The Emergence of the Pentateuch as 'Torah,'" *Religion Compass* 4 (2010): 353–64, and the various essays collected in Knoppers and Levinson, *The Pentateuch as Torah*. On the theory of the Persian authorization of the Pentateuch, see the essays collected in James W. Watts, ed., *Persia and Torah: The Theory of Imperial Authorization of the Pentateuch* (SBLSymS 17; Atlanta: Society of Biblical Literature, 2001); and Konrad Schmid, "The Persian Imperial Authorization as a Historical Problem and as a Biblical Construct: A Plea for Distinctions in the Current Debate," in *Pentateuch as Torah*, 23–38.

39 The *Letter of Aristeas* refers to the object of translation as "the laws" (*Letter of Aristeas* 10; cf. Philo, *Life of Moses* 2.31). See further Joseph Blenkinsopp, *The Pentateuch: An Introduction to the First Five Books of the Bible* (ABRL; New York: Doubleday, 1992), 42–43; Tov, *Textual Criticism*, 128–32.

40 Demetrius utilizes a Greek translation of *Genesis* and likely also *Exodus*. See the text in Carl R. Holladay, *Fragments from Hellenistic Jewish Authors*, volume 1: *Historians* (Chico: Scholars Press, 1983), 51–91. On the significance of Demetrius for the Septuagint Pentateuch, see Natalio Fernández Marcos, *The Septuagint in Context: Introduction to the Greek Versions of the Bible* (trans. W. G. E. Watson; Leiden: Brill, 2000), 260–61.

41 7Q1 – *Exodus* (cf. the *Greek Paraphrase of Exodus* – 4Q127); 4Q119–120 – *Leviticus*; 4Q121 – *Numbers*; 4Q122 – *Deuteronomy*. The absence of *Genesis* is likely an accident of preservation. 4Q126 is too fragmentary to identify with certainty but may represent a Septuagint manuscript as well. The one clear non-Pentateuchal Septuagint manuscript among the Qumran scrolls is the copy of the *Epistle of Jeremiah* (7Q2). 7Q4 likely represents a Greek translation of portions of *1 Enoch* 103 and 105 (see Émile Puech, "Notes sur les fragments grecs du manuscript 7Q4 = 1 Hénoch 103 et 105," *RB* 103 [1996]: 592–600). If this identification is correct, this text would likely have been included among the scriptural Greek texts. The Cave 4 manuscripts are found in Patrick W. Skehan, Eugene Ulrich, and Judith E. Sanderson, *Qumran Cave 4.IV: Palaeo-Hebrew and Greek Biblical Manuscripts* (DJD 9; Oxford: Clarendon, 1992), 17–157, 219–42. The Cave 7 manuscripts appear in M. Baillet, J. T. Milik, and R. de Vaux, *Les "Petites Grottes" de Qumrân* (DJD 3; Oxford: Clarendon, 1962), 142–43. The manuscript finds at Naḥal Ḥever yielded a first-century CE copy of the Greek Minor Prophets (8Ḥev 1). See Emanuel Tov, with the collaboration of Robert A. Kraft and a contribution by Peter Parsons, *The Greek Minor Prophets Scroll from Naḥal Ḥever (8ḤevXIIgr)* (DJD 8; Oxford, Clarendon, 1990). On the Judean Desert Greek manuscripts more broadly, see Leonard J. Greenspoon, "The Dead Sea Scrolls and the Greek Bible," in *Dead Sea Scrolls after Fifty Years*, 1:101–27.

from pre-Samaritan Pentateuch to Samaritan Pentateuch sometime within the second–first centuries BCE.[42]

The scribal practices of the Hebrew scrolls preserved in the Dead Sea Scrolls offer further evidence regarding the Pentateuch. Several manuscripts contain two, and possibly three, books of the Pentateuch copied together.[43] At the same time the inverse is true; no manuscripts preserve Pentateuchal books copied together with non-Pentateuchal books. Moreover, the overwhelming majority of the paleo-Hebrew manuscripts among the Dead Sea Scrolls are of books within the Pentateuch.[44] The use of paleo-Hebrew reflects an attempt to infuse the particular manuscript with a heightened degree of esteem, a feature that also seems to be present in the use of paleo-Hebrew to render divine names (אל and the Tetragrammaton).[45] If the full copying of a manuscript in

42 Esther Eshel and Hanan Eshel, "Dating the Samaritan Pentateuch's Compilation in Light of the Qumran Biblical Scrolls," in *Emanuel: Studies in the Hebrew Bible, Septuagint, and Dead Sea Scrolls in Honor of Emanuel Tov* (ed. S. M. Paul et al.; VTSup 94; Leiden, Brill, 2003), 215–40, especially 239–40, argue for a second-century date. A second/first-century date is asserted by Reinhard Pummer, "The Samaritans and Their Pentateuch," in *Pentateuch as Torah*, 237–69. A first-century BCE date is affirmed by James D. Purvis, *The Samaritan Pentateuch and the Origins of the Samaritan Sect* (HSM 2; Cambridge: Harvard University Press, 1968), especially 85.

43 4QGen–Exod[a] (4Q1); 4QPaleoGen–Exod[l] (4Q11); 4QExod–Lev[f] (4Q17); 4QLev–Num[a] (4Q23). Each of the manuscripts contains blank space between the book divisions. 4QExod[b] (4Q13) preserves two midcolumn blank lines prior to the opening verses of *Exodus*. Tov therefore suggests that this manuscript likewise contained *Genesis* (he identifies it as 4Q[Gen–] Exod[b]). Mur 1 clearly has both *Genesis* and *Exodus* and may also contain material from *Numbers*. Tov further suggests that the size of five additional scrolls containing only one book indicates that they also preserved at least two or more books. See full evidence in Emanuel Tov, *Scribal Practices and Approaches Reflected in the Texts Found in the Judean Desert* (STDJ 54; Leiden: Brill, 2004), 75–76. Another relevant witness to this phenomenon is the placement of multiple Pentateuchal verses in the *tefillin* and *mezuzot* found in the Qumran caves. On the various verse arrangements, see Emanuel Tov, "Excerpted and Abbreviated Biblical Texts," in *Hebrew Bible, Greek Bible, and Qumran: Collected Essays* (TSAJ 121; Tübingen: Mohr Siebeck, 2008), 27–41 (30–31) (1995).

44 Twelve are of Pentateuchal books. Four are clearly not Pentateuchal: one copy of *Job* (4Q101), one text possibly associated with *Joshua* (4Q123), and two fragmentary manuscripts (4Q124–125). These texts are published in Skehan, Ulrich, and Sanderson, *Qumran Cave 4.IV*, 161–215. See also Eugene C. Ulrich, "The Paleo-Hebrew Biblical Manuscripts from Qumran Cave 4," in *Origins of the Bible*, 121–47 (1995) (with earlier publication information and bibliography cited therein); Emanuel Tov, "Scribal Practices Reflected in the Paleo-Hebrew Texts from the Judean Desert," *Scripta Classica Israelica* 15 (1996): 268–73; idem, "The Socio-Religious Background of the Paleo-Hebrew Biblical Texts Found at Qumran," in *Geschichte – Tradition – Reflexion: Festschrift für Martin Hengel zum 70. Geburtstag* (ed. H. Cancik et al.; 2 vols.; Tübingen: Mohr Siebeck, 1996), 1:353–74.

45 See Tov, "The Socio-Religious Background," 369–70. Tov likewise remarks that all of the paleo-Hebrew texts are written on leather, with none on papyrus (*Scribal Practices*, 48), and that the manuscripts were copied with great care (*Scribal Practices*, 239, 241). Ulrich, "Paleo-Hebrew Biblical Manuscripts," 123, suggests that the presence of *Job* may be linked to a tradition later found in the *Babylonian Talmud* that *Job* was composed by Moses (*b. Bab. Bat.* 14b).

paleo-Hebrew is a marker of esteem for the text, then clearly the Pentateuch reigns supreme.

The rewritings of the Pentateuch in the book of *Jubilees* and the *Temple Scroll* have long been adduced as support for the authority of the Pentateuch.[46] *4QReworked Pentateuch* (4Q158, 4Q364–367) likewise attests to the authority and unity of the Pentateuch in the late Second Temple period. Scholars debate whether this text is a copy of the Pentateuch or an exegetically motivated reworking of the Pentateuch.[47] Either way, the various manuscripts preserve content from across the five books of the Pentateuch. Moreover, unlike the so-called biblical manuscripts introduced above that contain two or sometimes three books of the Pentateuch copied together, *4QReworked Pentateuch* combines content from all five books in a single manuscript. Even as significant portions of these five books are omitted in *4QReworked Pentateuch*, the location of content from across the five books in a single collection is significant. Of the best-preserved manuscripts, 4Q158 preserves material from *Genesis*, *Exodus*, and *Deuteronomy*, and 4Q364 contains material from *Genesis*, *Exodus*, *Numbers*, and *Deuteronomy*, while 4Q365 has content from all five books.[48]

By the Second Temple period, the Pentateuch was authoritative scripture (status) and stable in the general outline of its five books (form). Indeed, a frustratingly fragmentary text among the Dead Sea Scrolls may refer to the Pentateuch as "f]ive books ([ס]פרים חמשים)" (1Q30 1 4).[49] The cumulative effect of this evidence affirms that we should agree with Ulrich that there was

Less significance is attached to the paleo-Hebrew script in VanderKam, "Questions of Canon," 272–73. He does suggest that the use of the script is an attempt to place the origins of the text in the distant (Mosaic) past.

46 See Crawford, "The Use of the Pentateuch," 301–17.

47 For the *editiones principes*, see John M. Allegro, with Arnold A. Anderson, "4Q158: Biblical Paraphrase: Genesis, Exodus," in *Qumran Cave 4.I (4Q158–4Q186)* (ed. J. M. Allegro; DJD 5; Oxford: Clarendon, 1968), 1–6; and Emanuel Tov and Sidnie White (Crawford), "4Q364–367: 4QReworked Pentateuch[b-e]," in *Qumran Cave 4.VIII: Parabiblical Texts*, part 1 (ed. H. Attridge et al.; DJD 13; Oxford: Clarendon, 1994), 187–351. For the debate surrounding the scriptural status of the text, see especially Molly M. Zahn, "The Problem of Characterizing the 4QReworked Pentateuch Manuscripts: Bible, Rewritten Bible, or None of the Above?" *DSD* 15 (2008): 315–39.

48 The precise material contained in each manuscript is presented in Emanuel Tov, "4QReworked Pentateuch: A Synopsis of Its Contents," in *Hebrew Bible, Greek Bible*, 21–26 (1995). See also Crawford, *Rewriting Scripture*, 40.

49 This text was published in J. T. Milik, "1Q30–31: Textes liturgiques (?)," in *Qumrân Cave 1* (ed. D. Barthélemy and J. T. Milik; DJD 1; Oxford: Clarendon, 1955), 132–34. Milik presents both the Pentateuch and the Psalter as the possible collection in view, though he prefers the latter without explanation (so followed in Mitchell Dahood, *Psalms 1–50* [AB 16; Garden City: Doubleday, 1965], xxxi). Others (Blenkinsopp, *Pentateuch*, 44; Lim, "Alleged Reference," 28–29) have argued in favor of seeing a reference to the Pentateuch on account of the presumed later time frame for the fivefold arrangement of the Psalter (on which, see following note). On this terminology in rabbinic texts to refer to the Pentateuch, see Leiman, *Canonization*, 57.

"certainly full agreement that the Torah was canonical in the sense of *norma normans*, and on the five books that constituted the Torah."[50]

At the same time, this set of observations must be qualified by everything else we now know about the emergence of scripture in Second Temple Judaism and the textual variation that characterizes its transmission. The Pentateuch must be regarded as a fluid literary category. The existence of pseudo-Mosaic attributions in *Ezra-Nehemiah* already points to the fluid nature of the broader classificatory heading of the Pentateuch. A similarly dynamic understanding of the meaning of the Pentateuch persists into later Second Temple Judaism. For example, Ulrich notes that *Exodus*, in particular, was transmitted in multiple literary editions: manuscripts that match the text as preserved in the Masoretic Text alongside a distinct version of *Exodus* as represented by 4QpaleoExod^{m}.[51] Thus, while the Septuagint, Samaritan Pentateuch, and *4QReworked Pentateuch* attest to the "canonical" status of the Pentateuch, they simultaneously affirm the diversity that characterizes the central text of Second Temple Judaism.[52]

The "Prophets" and the Canonical Process

The situation is dramatically different for the broader heading of "Prophets" and the various further classifications found in the previously cited references to scriptural collections. Here, not only does the fluid nature of the literary and textual traditions match the wider set of evidence from Second Temple

[50] Ulrich, "Qumran Biblical Scrolls," 85. Later first-century CE evidence demonstrates the unequivocal unity of the Pentateuch. Thus, Josephus's listing of the sacred scriptures of Judaism begins with "five are the books of Moses" (*Against Apion* 1.39). Philo similarly refers to the five books of Moses (*On the Eternity of the World* 19). Moreover, the fivefold division of the Pentateuch may have inspired similar fivefold literary units in the late Second Temple period. For example, the Ethiopic *1 Enoch* is divided into five books, possibly on the model of the Pentateuch (G. H. Dix, "The Enochic Pentateuch," *JTS* 27 [1925–26]: 29–42; J. T. Milik, *The Books of Enoch: Aramaic Fragments of Qumrân Cave 4* [Oxford: Clarendon, 1976], 77–78, 183–84). Yet, how early this arrangement was understood is unclear and ultimately speculative prior to the Ethiopic manuscript tradition. The same situation is present for the Pentateuchal inspiration for the fivefold division of the Psalter. To be sure, some scholars have argued for a fivefold division of *Psalms* based on internal indicators (see Gerard H. Wilson, *The Editing of the Hebrew Psalter* [SBLDS 76; Chico: Scholars Press, 1985], 199–228). Explicit testimony to this perceived arrangement, however, cannot be detected prior to rabbinic and patristic evidence. A fivefold division is assumed in Jerome, *Prologus Galeatus*; and *b. Qid.* 33a, while the explicit connection with the fivefold division of the Pentateuch is found in *Midrash on Psalms* 1. See further Beckwith, *Old Testament Canon*, 112–15, 438–47; and Nahum Sarna, *On the Book of Psalms: Exploring the Prayers of Ancient Israel* (New York: Schocken, 1993), 16–18.

[51] See Ulrich, "Double Literary Editions," 105–6; "Canonical Process," 278–80. For more analysis within the context of a detailed study of 4QpaleoExod^{m}, see Judith A. Sanderson, *An Exodus Scroll from Qumran: 4QpaleoExod^{m} and the Samaritan Tradition* (HSS 30; Atlanta: Scholars Press, 1986).

[52] See further Crawford, *Rewriting Scripture*, 21; idem, "Use of the Pentateuch," 304–5.

Judaism, but also even what books were subsumed within this broader category is never clarified. Notwithstanding the great efforts of many scholars, it is extremely difficult to ascertain the precise meaning of Ben Sira's grandson's reference to "other books of our ancestors" or even what precisely is intended by the reference to "David" in 4QMMT. To be sure, the stability of the term "Prophets" likely points at least to a core of generally agreed-upon books contained therein. Beyond that, however, the empirical evidence is lacking.[53] The lack of clarity regarding what is contained in these categories likely points to the still fluid nature of their identification. Thus, the second half of Ulrich's comment cited above is apposite. In contrast to the Pentateuch, in the case of the "Prophets," there was "virtually complete agreement by all except the Samaritans and possibly the Sadducees that the Prophets was a collection of Sacred Scriptures, though the specific contents of the collection was not fixed."[54]

The bulk of the literature that I examine in this study stems from the period of the "canonical process" described above. In this sense, any engagement with the literature of Second Temple Judaism (in later terms, texts that form the Hebrew Bible, so-called apocryphal works, and the broader set of texts preserved in the Dead Sea Scrolls) must constantly be sensitive to the terms of working "behind" the canon. Indeed, this book attempts to draw upon the wealth of new data regarding the canonical process to offer an informed assessment of the relative authority of the different corpora of scriptural writings and consider the intersecting foci of scripture, canon, and authority in ancient Judaism.

At the same time, my analysis seeks to offer a new data set – drawn from previously underutilized legal texts – to be considered in unraveling the still mysterious layers of the canonical process. I have alluded several times to various methods employed by modern scholars to determine the authoritative or scriptural status of particular works. Scholars commonly point to citation, paraphrase, or general influence of a particular text as helpful indices of its status.[55] For example, as noted above, *Genesis* is commonly cited in the literature of Second Temple Judaism, and its influence is pervasive in rewritten

53 See VanderKam, "Revealed Literature," 20.

54 Ulrich, "Qumran Biblical Scrolls," 85.

55 See Leiman, *Canonization*, 14; Sidnie White Crawford, "The 'Rewritten Bible' at Qumran: A Look at Three Texts," *ErIsr* 26 (1999; Cross Volume): 1*–8*, especially 4*; Trebolle (Barrera), "Canon within a Canon," especially 389–96; idem "Origins of the Tripartite Canon," 138; VanderKam, "Authoritative Literature"; idem, "Questions of Canon," 98–99; Emanuel Tov, "From 4QReworked Pentateuch to 4QPentateuch (?)," in *Authoritative Scriptures in Ancient Judaism*, 73–91 (85–90). At the same time, this approach must be wary of the hyper-reliance on citations as found, for example, in Beckwith, *Old Testament Canon*, especially 71–76 (idem, "Formation of the Hebrew Bible," 46, 48–49). He operates with the basic principle that any text cited by a later author was regarded as part of the canon of the later author. Aside from the problematic schema of canon employed here, the methodology is flawed. While in many cases the cited text was scriptural for the later writer, a single citation cannot be employed as an adequate criterion. See further Lee M. McDonald and James A. Sanders, "Introduction," in *The Canon Debate*, 5.

works. Thus, in addition to all the other evidence pointing in the same direction, we can rely upon this evidence to argue for the scriptural – indeed, canonical – status of *Genesis*. As suggested by James VanderKam, "Some books were regarded by certain writers as sufficiently authoritative that they could be cited to settle a dispute, explain a situation, provide an example, or predict what would happen."[56]

Discussions that explore the implications of the use of texts tend to focus on narrative or other nonlegal examples. We might assume that VanderKam's category of "settle a dispute" would encompass the use of earlier textual material for the purposes of determining the norms of Jewish law and ritual. Law was a primary part of Jewish society, and its proper determination was a central concern of Jewish creative activity. The significance attached to the divine origins of law makes the appeal to scriptural authority all the more urgent. Indeed, in the Second Temple period, drawing upon a given text for purposes of law was often tantamount to assigning it a divine origin – hence an authoritative scriptural status. In the analysis that follows, I consider this very question as I explore the role of texts and their redeployment as exegetical touchstones for the formation of Jewish law. My broader inquiry into the relative authority of Pentateuchal and non-Pentateuchal scriptural texts is poised to offer a new contribution to the consideration of the ongoing esteem and authority of the Pentateuch. At the same time, my analysis of the non-Pentateuchal texts provides a new data set with which to consider the emerging authority of the individual prophetic books and the broader collection of the Prophets as a whole.

V. THE CANONICAL PROCESS AND AUTHORITY IN RABBINIC JUDAISM

The situation described above changes dramatically for rabbinic Judaism in the first century CE and onward. The rabbis inherit an essentially closed canon. Late first-century evidence outside rabbinic literature attests to the growing acceptance of a closed list of sacred books, thereby signaling the turn from a canonical process to a canon. Most notably, Josephus and 4 *Ezra* describe a twenty-two- or twenty-four-book collection.[57] To be sure, early rabbinic literature preserves evidence of ongoing engagement in issues that seem to relate to the canon, most famously in the debate regarding what books "defile the hands."[58] Though the exact reason for the use of this locution seems to

[56] VanderKam, "Questions of Canon," 91.

[57] See Josephus, *Against Apion* 1.37–43; and 4 Ezra 14:22–48. See further Leiman, *Canonization*, 30–34; Beckwith, *Old Testament Canon*, 235–73; VanderKam, "Revealed Literature," 8–9; Steve Mason, "Josephus and His Twenty-Two Book Canon," in *The Canon Debate*, 110–27.

[58] Rabbinic texts bearing on issues of canon are collected and analyzed in Leiman, *Canonization*, 51–125. See further Beckwith, *Old Testament Canon*, 274–337; Jack N. Lightstone, "The Rabbis' Bible: The Canon of the Hebrew Bible and the Early Rabbinic Guild," in *The Canon*

be unclear even to the rabbis, this terminology is employed in early rabbinic literature as a code word for writings deemed sacred.[59] Thus, for example, one finds this terminology employed to frame disputes regarding the status of the *Song of Songs* and *Ecclesiastes*:

> All sacred scriptures impart uncleanness to hands. The *Song of Songs* and *Ecclesiastes* impart uncleanness to hands. Rabbi Judah says, "The *Song of Songs* imparts uncleanness to hands, but as to *Ecclesiastes* there is dispute." Rabbi Yose says, "*Ecclesiastes* does not impart uncleanness to hands, but as to *Song of Songs* there is dispute." (*m. Yad.* 3:5)

Further rabbinic sources preserve discussions regarding the status of other books, most notably, *Ezekiel*, *Ruth*, *Esther*, and *Proverbs*.[60]

Early scholarship explained these passages as part of a larger systematic rabbinic discourse on canon undertaken by a council at Yabneh (Jamnia). As noted above, the idea of a council at Yabneh deliberating over the scope of the canon is now universally recognized as a modern scholarly fiction and is completely absent from the rabbinic evidence.[61] Scholars have further called into question the broader significance of this evidence for reconstructing even a streamlined rabbinic dialogue on canon. As observed by Sid Leiman in his treatment of the rabbinic discussions regarding *Song of Songs* and *Ecclesiastes* cited above, no party to these rabbinic debates questions the canonical status of the two books. Rather, Leiman suggests, their place in the canon is secure, and the debate merely focuses on their inspired status.[62] Leiman presents a similar argument for rabbinic discussions regarding the potential withdrawal (גנז) of *Ezekiel* and *Proverbs*.[63] The very nature of the discussion points to their canonical and sacred status. Leiman suggests that the critical issue is the rabbinic sense that these books contain problematic content, and thus the rabbis

Debate, 163–84; David Stern, "On Canonization in Rabbinic Judaism," in *Homer, the Bible, and Beyond: Literary and Religious Canons in the Ancient World* (ed. M. Finkelberg and G. G. Stroumsa; JSRC 2; Leiden: Brill, 2003), 227–52.

59 On this terminology and attempts to explain its meaning, see Leiman, *Canonization*, 102–20; John Barton, *Oracles of God: Perceptions of Ancient Prophecy in Israel after the Exile* (London: Darton, Longman, and Todd, 1986), 68–72; Martin D. Goodman, "Sacred Scripture and 'Defiling the Hands,'" *JTS* 41 (1990): 99–107; Shamma Friedman, "The Holy Scriptures Defile the Hands – The Transformation of a Biblical Concept in Rabbinic Theology," in *Minḥa le-Naḥum: Biblical and Other Studies Presented to Nahum M. Sarna in Honour of His Seventieth Birthday* (ed. M. Brettler and M. Fishbane; JSOTSup 154; Sheffield: Sheffield Academic Press, 1993), 117–32; Stern, "On Canonization in Rabbinic Judaism," 231–35; Timothy H. Lim, "The Defilement of the Hands as a Principle Determining the Holiness of Scriptures," *JTS* 61 (2010): 501–15.

60 See Leiman, *Canonization*, 102–24; Lightstone, "The Rabbis' Bible," 175–78.

61 See bibliography above, n. 7.

62 Leiman, *Canonization*, 120–24; so also Beckwith, *Old Testament Canon*, 276–77; Barton, *Oracles of God*, 69; VanderKam, "Revealed Literature," 11–12; Talmon, "Crystallization," 438–39.

63 Leiman, *Canonization*, 72–86.

wish to limit their circulation and influence.[64] A similar approach is taken by John Barton, who argues that the debates focus on the use of certain books for liturgical purposes.[65]

Indeed, closer scrutiny of the broader rabbinic evidence indicates that rabbinic discussions about specific books are all "postcanonical" and represent discussions regarding the rabbinic attitudes toward the role of these books in rabbinic society.[66] The very fact that these are the questions that frame rabbinic discourse on canon demonstrates that they did not possess the ability to influence the scope of the canon. At best, some of these discussions may have been targeted at marginalizing specific books within the canon.

At the same time as the rabbis seek to minimize the cultural impact of some books, they promote the enhanced sanctity of the Pentateuch. This primacy of the Torah is indicated in rabbinic statements regarding its compositional history versus that of the Prophets and Writings. Thus, rabbinic Judaism views the Torah, unlike all the other books of the Bible (except *Job*), as stemming from Mosaic authorship.[67] Rabbinic terminology for the division of the canon always distinguishes the Torah from the Prophets and Writings, whereas the latter two categories are often lumped together with regard to both their compositional history and canonical status.[68] Moreover, rabbinic *halakhah* serves to emphasize further the sanctity of the scroll (or codex) of the Torah over those of the Prophets and Writings.[69] Some rabbinic traditions assert that the Prophets and the Writings will be annulled in the future (end of days?), while the Torah will remain eternally valid and sacred.[70]

There is a secondary – though equally significant – issue that is often overlooked in discussions of rabbinic approaches to the canon. Alongside the

[64] Leiman, *Canonization*, 79–80.

[65] Barton, *Oracles of God*, 68–72.

[66] This interpretation therefore explains the curious presence of *Ben Sira* in many of these discussions. The long history of rabbinic discourse on the status of this book reflects an ongoing rabbinic debate regarding the role of *Ben Sira*. The scribal transmission of the book in Hebrew attests to its continued popularity in some Jewish circles, including among the rabbis. For full evidence, see Jenny R. Labendz, "The Book of Ben Sira in Rabbinic Literature," *AJSR* 30 (2006): 347–92 (with earlier literature cited therein).

[67] See *b. B. Bat.* 14b–15a; *Midrash on Psalms* 90:4. Medieval rabbinic Judaism closely identified the tripartite divisions with varying levels of authorial inspiration, in which the Torah was regarded as possessing the most authorial inspiration. This view, however, does not seem to be found in any classical rabbinic sources. See bibliography of the medieval sources and discussion in Leiman, *Canonization*, 169–70 n. 294.

[68] See Leiman, *Canonization*, 56–72 (especially 56–58).

[69] For example, a copy of the Torah may be placed on top of a copy of the Prophets, but the reverse is forbidden (*t. Meg.* 4:20). See further examples collected in Leiman, *Canonization*, 60–63.

[70] *Y. Meg.* 1:1 70d. This view is ascribed to Rabbi Joḥanan. Rabbi Simeon b. Lakish, however, includes the book of *Esther* among those books that will likewise not be annulled. As scholars have noted, this may reflect a rabbinic attempt to bolster the status of *Esther* (see Leiman, *Canonization*, 171 n. 301).

inheritance of a canon of books, the rabbis also inherited an established text of these books – the proto-Masoretic Text. The move toward a stabilized text of scripture is reflected in the growing emergence of the proto-Masoretic Text as the text of the sacred scriptures within Judaism. A bird's-eye view of the text of scriptural books among the Judean Desert manuscripts provides a useful way of accessing this phenomenon. As discussed above, the scriptural texts found in the Qumran caves attest to the diversity and plurifomity of the scriptural text in the late Second Temple period. In contrast, all the manuscripts of scriptural books found at sites from the first century CE (Masada) and the second century CE (Wadi Sdeir, Naḥal Ṣe'elim, Naḥal Ḥever, and Wadi Murabba'at) are, based on the recent assessment by Tov, "almost identical to the medieval consonantal text of Masoretic Text."[71] Scholars continue to debate whether this was part of a concerted effort at stabilizing the text by the rabbis or merely a situation where the rabbis were left with the proto-Masoretic Text as their sacred scripture.[72] The end result, however, is the same: rabbinic interaction with the sacred scriptures existed within the framework of a limited number of sacred books and a much more uniform text of those books.

VI. BETWEEN SCRIPTURAL FORMATION AND SCRIPTURAL INTERPRETATION

Alongside my focus on the canonical process, I am interested in its creative force for ancient Jews operating within the world in which the canon was developing and formalizing. Notwithstanding the diverse states of their scriptural canon, Jews in both the Second Temple and rabbinic periods encountered a set of authoritative writings, with which they grappled to update and enliven the contents therein. In this sense, this book explores how the categories of scriptural formation and scriptural interpretation converge and begin to take on a mutually creative force. How does the emerging notion of authoritative texts and textual collections contribute to the very growth of the canon and its ongoing transformation?

In an insightful analysis of the role of canon in religious traditions, Jonathan Z. Smith calls attention to the interplay of canon – in Smith's definition, fixed authoritative entities – and exegesis.[73] Smith is primarily interested in fixed canons, and thus his insights are especially helpful for understanding the

71 Emanuel Tov, "The Biblical Texts from the Judaean Desert – An Overview and Analysis of the Published Texts," in *Hebrew Bible, Greek Bible*, 128–54 (135) (2002). Tov identifies twenty-three texts from the non-Qumran Judean Desert sites. See also idem, "The Many Forms of Hebrew Scripture: Reflections in Light of the LXX and 4QReworked Pentateuch," in *From Qumran to Aleppo*, 11–28 (11–15).

72 See bibliography above, n. 6. See especially the review of scholarship in Lange, "Textual Standardization," 31–45; and discussion in Ulrich, "Clearer Insight," 125–26.

73 Jonathan Z. Smith, "Sacred Persistence: Toward a Redescription of Canon," in *Imagining Religion: From Babylon to Jonestown* (Chicago: University of Chicago Press, 1982), 36–52

rabbinic response to canon. His approach is equally useful for thinking about precanonical authoritative texts and indeed helps us better understand how a text can be both authoritative and textually fluid. He notes the tension between the "radical and arbitrary reduction" generated by canon and the need for individuals and societies to adapt the canon in constant and meaningful ways. This is not merely a matter of choice. Because of its seemingly rigid status in a dynamic society, every canon will produce the "*necessary* occurrence of a hermeneute, of an interpreter whose task it is continually to extend the domain of the closed canon over everything that is known or everything that exists without altering the canon in the process."[74] Thus, he argues for a renewed interest among historians of religion in "the exegetical enterprise of applying the canon to every dimension of human life," which he characterizes as the "most characteristic, persistent, and obsessive religious activity."[75]

Smith's insights can be detected in Joshua Levinson's recent treatment of rabbinic *midrash*. He argues that the entire body of rabbinic and contemporary *midrash* (loosely defined) is not only a response to exegetical exigencies in the scriptural text but also reflective of the larger demand for canon to be in a constant state of resignification: "It is precisely the canonical status of the text – that which acts as the foundation for its cultural legitimacy – that invites its constant transformation, violation, and appropriation."[76]

In a recent study, Bernard M. Levinson has offered two important addenda to Smith's argument, which may also be employed to consider further the significance of the observations made by J. Levinson. First, Smith assumes that societies only engage in the creative exegetical response to canon after it is complete. Indeed, at first glance this supposition seems logical. If canon reflects rigidity, then anything precanon can be modified before it assumes a rigid state. Thus, for Smith, canon is only resignified after it has achieved its final character. Yet, as noted in my discussion of the origins of the biblical canon, all canons have a long prehistory that is best characterized as a "canonical process." Within these stages, various segments of what becomes the more fully developed canon emerge with their own individualized canonical status. In other words, a text need not be absolutely complete for it to be authoritative, and authoritative texts are themselves not always complete.

What Levinson observes is that "the ingenuity of the interpreter operates even in the formative period of the canon, while those texts that will

(1978). Smith is deliberately broad in his use of "canon" to designate any fixed authoritative entity, whether textual or nontextual.

74 Smith, "Sacred Persistence," 48 (emphasis original).

75 Smith, "Sacred Persistence," 43.

76 Joshua Levinson, "Dialogical Reading in the Rabbinic Exegetical Narrative," *Poetics Today* 25 (2004): 497–528 (499). Levinson's approach is indebted to the theoretical model of "literary transduction" as articulated in Lubomír Doležel, *Heterocosmica: Fiction and Possible Worlds* (Baltimore: Johns Hopkins University Press, 1998), 202–5.

subsequently win authoritative status are still being composed and collected."[77] Moreover, for Levinson, the ongoing dialectic of the emerging canon and its simultaneous interpretation ultimately constitute the building blocks of the final canon and shape its very character. Thus, the final form of the canon is itself the byproduct of this long process of development and rethinking that happens within the boundaries of the canon.

Levinson makes an important second observation. As interpreters seek to alter radically the contours of their inherited canon, they do so in ways that seek to minimize their very presence and conceal the transformative nature of their endeavors.[78] In other words, they strive to create the impression that their modifications are inherent in the original text – and therefore also representative of the original divine intent – and thus their activities are merely illuminating what has always been there. To return to Smith's formulation, creative interpretation succeeds in "extend[ing] the domain of the closed canon . . . without altering the canon in the process."

The Hebrew Bible serves as the primary historical and conceptual world in which Levinson frames his observations, and thus it functions as the textual basis for ensuing analysis that draws out the implications of these observations. Levinson's two basic observations on canon and creativity can profitably be expanded into the world of Second Temple Judaism and its literature. As I have repeatedly underscored, our modern – by which I mean two-thousand-year-old – canonical categories merely get in the way of seeing the phenomena that Levinson describes in *Deuteronomy* and elsewhere as commensurate with similar literary and exegetical features in Second Temple Judaism. As suggested in Chapter 2, *Deuteronomy* is to the Covenant Code what the *Temple Scroll* is to *Deuteronomy*. Both strive to update the earlier authoritative text in a culturally meaningful way through exegetical and literary refinement under the cloak of concealment.

The terms of working within the canonical process in the late Second Temple period render the mechanism of canon renewal more intrusive than anything observed by Levinson in the literature of ancient Israel. Second Temple Jewish literary activity not only resignifies the meaning of the scriptural text through interpretation but also changes the very textual integrity of the authoritative texts through its constant rewriting and reformulation. The diversity and pluriformity that mark the sacred scriptures of Second Temple Judaism are not merely on account of scribal errors and other vagaries of textual transmission. Rather, these features are indicative of Jews working within the canon of authoritative scripture to renew and resignify its cultural import and impact. Thus, Jews in the Second Temple period were still living in "biblical times" – using Talmon's terminology – because in many ways they were still crafting the biblical story.

[77] Bernard M. Levinson, *Legal Revision and Religious Renewal in Ancient Israel* (Cambridge: Cambridge University Press, 2008), 18.

[78] Levinson, *Legal Revision*, 16–17.

Exegetical engagement is present in works that we commonly classify as Pentateuchal: the Masoretic Text Pentateuch, the Septuagint Pentateuch, the pre-Samaritan Pentateuch, many of the Pentateuchal manuscripts discovered at Qumran, and *4QReworked Pentateuch*.[79] In these cases, the renewed scripture should be regarded as an "updated" version of the same text, thus corresponding to Ulrich's conceptual model of "variant literary editions."[80] Exegesis is likewise identified as the distinctive feature of closely related texts that scholars traditionally have identified as "rewritten" works, such as the *Temple Scroll* and the book of *Jubilees*. Yet, the *Temple Scroll* and *Jubilees* are commonly regarded as qualitatively and quantitatively distinct from the more explicitly Pentateuchal texts in their exegetical and literary content.[81] Thus Sidnie Crawford has recently suggested that the rewriting of scripture in Second Temple Judaism should be located on a continuum, with some activity identified within scriptural texts and some outside.[82]

Crawford's model is quite helpful in highlighting the pervasiveness of rewriting across the wide plane of Second Temple–period literature. Yet, its focus on charting literary activity from an exegetical vantage point should be expanded to understand its implications for understanding the interplay of canon and creativity in Second Temple Judaism. As I have repeatedly suggested, the ubiquitous rewriting observed by Crawford is distinctive of attempts by Jews in the Second Temple period to work within the canon to transform it. While some of the final products retain enough of the character of the target text to be regarded as another copy of it, others are best characterized as distinct exegetical works. Yet, all of these texts are united by the desire to transform their target texts through exegetical engagement within the text. The end result is to renew the target text in ways that obscure the voice of the exegete.

The evidence of the Dead Sea Scrolls attests to the success of canon renewal in at least one segment of Second Temple Judaism. As I have repeatedly emphasized, the community of the Dead Sea Scrolls possessed a set of

79 On the ancient versions, see the bibliography cited above, Chapter 2, section II. For interplay of scriptural formation and scriptural interpretation in *4QReworked Pentateuch*, see especially Ulrich, "The Dead Sea Scrolls and the Biblical Text," 88–89 (more recently, see idem, "Clearer Insight," 130); Michael Segal, "4QReworked Pentateuch or 4QPentateuch," in *The Dead Sea Scrolls Fifty Years after Their Discovery*, 391–99; Emanuel Tov, "Three Strange Books of the LXX: 1 Kings, Esther, and Daniel Compared with Similar Rewritten Compositions from Qumran and Elsewhere," in *Hebrew Bible, Greek Bible*, 283–308 (2008); idem, "The Many Forms of Hebrew Scripture."

80 On this concept, see above, section III.

81 My emphasis on "quantity" and "quality" of difference draws from Molly M. Zahn, *Rethinking Rewritten Scripture: Composition and Exegesis in the 4QReworked Pentateuch Manuscripts* (STDJ 95; Leiden: Brill, 2011), 11 (see following note).

82 Crawford, *Rewriting Scripture*, 13–15. Zahn, *Rethinking Rewritten Scripture*, 7–11, correctly voices the need for appropriate criteria to determine where individual texts should be plotted on this continuum and indeed embarks on this very directive in her study. Compare, however, Brooke, "New Perspectives," 24–25, who argues for an even closer connection between scriptural works and their rewritten versions.

authoritative scriptural writings that no doubt included many of the books that would later constitute the rabbinic Bible and many other works such as *Jubilees*, the *Temple Scroll*, and *4QReworked Pentateuch*. Through a long process of canon renewal, the authors of these texts succeeded in transforming the very meaning of the Pentateuch and its application in Second Temple Judaism. The unified preservation of these texts in the library of the sectarian community of the Dead Sea Scrolls demonstrates the degree to which these renewed scriptures succeed in becoming authoritative scripture. The end result is an expanded "canon" suitable for the new cultural and social settings of the sectarian community. While our evidence is lacking for other groups in Second Temple Judaism, undoubtedly other renewed scriptures accumulated in distinct social groups and provided a powerful agent for cultural and religious transformation.

I began Chapter 2 by remarking on Talmon's insightful observation regarding the different ways in which Jews in the Second Temple period versus the rabbis engage with the world of ancient Israel.[83] As further observed in this chapter, Second Temple Judaism's view of itself in continuity with the past is reinforced by the still fluid nature of the canon and text of scripture, which makes possible widespread exegetical and literary intrusion into the text. In contrast, the rabbinic engagement with the world of ancient Israel reflects a keen awareness of the deep divide between their world and that of their predecessors. The rabbis found themselves in a seemingly impossible situation. The closed nature of scripture did not allow for the type of internal processes observed in the Second Temple period. Yet, the rabbis were no less aware of the need to renew the scriptures for their own time. Talmon calls attention to a rabbinic dictum that captures the rabbinic tension between the world of ancient Israel and the rabbis: "The language of the Torah is one matter, the language of the Sages is another" (*b. 'Abod. Zar.* 58b; *b. Men.* 65a). As suggested by Talmon, this is not merely an issue of linguistic barriers. Rather, it hints at the rabbinic awareness of "the incompatibility of the world of the Sages and the world of the Bible."[84]

As with Jews in the Second Temple period, the rabbis engage in an equally ambitious and audacious program of canon renewal. Unlike the Jews of the Second Temple period, who operate within the world of the emerging canon, the rabbis are constantly working with an essentially complete canon. Thus, all rabbinic actions in the pursuit of canon renewal respect the textual and canonical integrity of scripture. In this sense, their actions are more akin to the postcanon process of canon renewal outlined by Smith. The rabbis develop a system of exegetical processes that transform the canon from the outside. When Joshua Levinson speaks of the "transformation, violation, and appropriation" of scripture in the context of *midrash*, he refers to the many ways in which

[83] See Chapter 2, section II.
[84] Talmon, "Crystallization" 437.

rabbinic *midrash* makes the scriptural text signify something that otherwise seems quite foreign to the text. Herein lies the major difference between Second Temple–period and rabbinic exegesis: Second Temple Jews give new meaning by changing the text (rewriting), while the rabbis change the meaning of the text (rereading). Both are equally subversive and equally effective.

This phenomenon I am here describing for the development of law in both Second Temple and rabbinic contexts is well illustrated by the interpretation of Amos 5:26–27 in the *Damascus Document* (CD 7:14–18). This passage explains the meaning of two expressions from the scriptural text – "the booth of the king" (סכות מלכים) and "the *kywn* of your images" (כיון צלמיכם) – as the "books of the Torah" and the "books of the Prophets," respectively. The identification of two general categories of scriptural books comports with similar presentations of the emerging divisions of the tripartite canon presented earlier in this chapter. The previously treated passages, however, follow with one or more terms generally identified as additional textual categories (e.g., "David," "other books"). The *Damascus Document*, in contrast, introduces a third scriptural component – the "star" – which is interpreted as referring to a person identified as the "Interpreter of the Law" (דורש התורה).[85]

I have suggested in a previous treatment of this passage that the alignment of the "books of the Torah," the "books of the Prophets," and the "Interpreter of the Law" locates the sectarian community as the most recent recipients of the progressive revelation of law previously vouchsafed to Moses and the prophets.[86] As further observed by Florentino García Martínez, there is an equally powerful claim offered here regarding the method employed for the formation of law in the sectarian community. The third category does not refer to a set of scriptural writings but rather to "a person and his function," namely the sectarian exegetical engagement with the Torah.[87]

The placement of the "Interpreter of the Law" alongside the two scriptural categories reflects a keen awareness by the sectarian authors of the *Damascus Document* of the central role played by exegesis in the formation of scripture. In this sense, the "Interpreter of the Law" actually does serve as a further "scriptural" category alongside the Torah and the Prophets. The exegetical activity of the "Interpreter of the Law" infuses the Torah and the Prophets with new meaning and dramatically transforms the very application of these sacred texts

85 The "star" likely refers back to the expression "star of your God" in Amos 5:26 (in both 𝔐 and 𝔊), though this particular portion of the lemma is not explicitly cited in the *Damascus Document*. García Martínez, "Rethinking the Bible," 34, therefore suggests that this portion of the lemma may have been lost in the medieval copy of the *Damascus Document* (so also Chaim Rabin, *The Zadokite Documents* [Oxford: Clarendon, 1954], 28). At the same time, the use of the term "star" looks ahead to its appearance in the newly introduced lemma of Num 24:17 in CD 7:19–20.

86 See Alex P. Jassen, "The Presentation of the Ancient Prophets as Lawgivers at Qumran," *JBL* 127 (2008): 307–37 (334–35).

87 García Martínez, "Rethinking the Bible," 34.

in Jewish society. In the Second Temple–period setting, this exegetical activity is indeed part of the ongoing production of scripture, and thus the "Interpreter of the Law" rightfully takes its place alongside the other canonical categories.

VII. CONCLUSIONS

I began this book by asserting that one of its primary payoffs is its placement of the Dead Sea Scrolls within the broader history of Jewish law and legal exegesis. In so doing, this work contributes to two vibrant fields of Dead Sea Scrolls scholarship – law and scriptural interpretation – in new and productive ways. The material treated in this chapter suggests that the broader legal and exegetical currents examined in this study must likewise be located in a third vibrant field of Dead Sea Scrolls scholarship – the origins and development of the canon. More specifically, the study asserts that these three fields must become more integrated in order to provide a full and accurate portrait of the evidence from the Dead Sea Scrolls and Second Temple Judaism. Jewish legal exegesis as reflected in the Dead Sea Scrolls and related Second Temple–period texts is a central part of the process of canon formation. In contrast to older scholarly models of a linear development for the canon, the new evidence provided by the Dead Sea Scrolls points toward a far more circular and mutually enriching relationship between scriptural formation and scriptural interpretation in ancient Judaism.

I have repeatedly suggested that the production of scripture and its interpretation can no longer be approached as distinct enterprises. The Dead Sea Scrolls have demonstrated that these processes occur alongside each other in a mutually enriching manner. It is the modern observer, heavily informed by long-standing canonical boundaries, who too quickly seals off one set of texts as "scripture" and another as "rewritten." Exegetical engagement with a target scriptural text should not deny a text its own scriptural status. As remarked by Emanuel Tov, had we first encountered *Chronicles* among the Dead Sea Scrolls, we surely would have labeled and classified it as "rewritten scripture" on account of its literary and exegetical relationship with *Samuel–Kings*.[88] The new evidence provided by the Dead Sea Scrolls and the renewed analysis of long-known texts (e.g., the book of *Jubilees*) yield a new vantage point for charting the intersecting histories of scripture, interpretation, and canon in ancient Judaism. As asserted by George Brooke, any assessment of scripture in the Second Temple period must make room for the totality of so-called biblical, parabiblical, and rewritten material. It is not for us to impose our canonical sensibilities on these ancient texts. When working "within" the canonical process, Brooke argues, "text and interpretation belong together in a symbiotic relationship."[89] To see Second Temple Jewish literary activity in its

[88] Tov, "Many Forms of Hebrew Scripture," 27 n. 54.

[89] Brooke, "New Perspectives," 27 (cf. idem, "Between Authority and Canon").

fullest expression, we must free ourselves from the limitations so appropriately labeled by Robert Kraft as the "tyranny of canonical assumptions."[90]

To be sure, the dynamic interplay of text and interpretation in the formation of the canon does eventually subside, as the rabbinic evidence demonstrates. Yet, even here, the rabbis succeed in continuing the transformative exegetical approaches of their Second Temple forebearers. As I asserted earlier, Jews in the Second Temple period change the meaning of the text by changing the text itself. In contrast, the rabbis change the meaning of the text through the seemingly less invasive commentary form. Yet, the end results of the rabbinic commentary yield a new meaning for the scriptural text that is no less intrusive than that produced in the Second Temple period. Thus, Second Temple–period exegetical activity shapes the text of scripture and in turn leaves a deep imprint on the canon itself. Rabbinic exegetical activity frames the ultimate meaning and significance of the canon through its exegetical resignification.

The chapters that follow seek to introduce the legal literature of ancient Judaism into the broader set of conversations outlined here. The diversity and pluriformity that mark the sacred scriptures of Second Temple Judaism find further reverberations in their ongoing use in Jewish legal-exegetical activity. The Dead Sea Scrolls have amply demonstrated the extent to which Jews in the Second Temple period debated the particulars of Jewish law. Scripture and its interpretation are central to this set of conversations. At the same time, the evidence treated in this book outlines the many ways in which scriptural texts are read and reread in order to fit legal and exegetical exigencies. In so doing, these later writers contribute to the diversity of the very text for which they are claiming to possess the singular interpretation. As in its narrative counterpart, this legal-exegetical activity becomes the textual foundation for the emerging canon – and more broadly, the meaning – of scripture.

90 See Robert A. Kraft, "Para-mania: Beside, Before and Beyond Bible Studies," *JBL* 126 (2007): 5–27, especially 10–18. This approach is strongly echoed in Hindy Najman, "The Vitality of Scripture Within and Beyond the Canon," *JSJ* 43 (2012): 497–515. For further examples of scholarship that embodies this approach, see above, Chapter 2, n. 6.

4

Isaiah 58:13 and the Sabbath Prohibition on Speech in the Dead Sea Scrolls, Part 1

The *Damascus Document*

1. INTRODUCTION

The following three chapters seek to address the broader goals of this book through comparative analysis of the sectarian prohibition against certain forms of speech on the Sabbath. The most extensive sectarian formulation of these laws is found in the *Damascus Document* (10:17–19). Scholarly treatments have focused on deciphering the precise details of the sectarian laws as well as identifying parallel formulations in Second Temple and rabbinic legal texts.[1] Nearly all of these analyses observe that the laws in the *Damascus Document*

[1] See Louis Ginzberg, *An Unknown Jewish Sect* (Moreshet 1; New York: Jewish Theological Seminary, 1976), 57–59, 108–9; Chanokh Albeck, *Das Buch der Jubiläen und die Halacha* (Berichte der Hochschule für die Wissenschaft des Judentums 47; Berlin: Hochschule für die Wissenschaft des Judentums, 1930), 9; Boaz Cohen, "Sabbath Prohibitions Known as *Shebut*," in *Law and Tradition in Judaism* (New York: Ktav, 1969), 127–66 (145–46) (1949); Yitzḥak D. Gilat, "Regarding the Antiquity of Several Sabbath Prohibitions," in *Studies in the Development of the Halakha* (Ramat Gan: Bar Ilan University Press, 1992), 249–61 (255–58) [Hebrew] (1963); S. T. Kimbrough Jr., "The Concept of Sabbath at Qumran," *RevQ* 5 (1966): 483–502 (487–88); Lawrence H. Schiffman, *The Halakhah at Qumran* (SJLA 16; Leiden: Brill, 1975), 87–90; Baruch Sharvit, "The Sabbath of the Judean Desert Sect," *Immanuel* 9 (1979): 42–48 (44–45); Lutz Doering, "New Aspects of Qumran Sabbath Law from Cave 4 Fragments," in *Legal Texts and Legal Issues: Proceedings of the Second Meeting of the International Organization for Qumran Studies, Cambridge, 1995; Published in Honour of Joseph M. Baumgarten* (ed. M. J. Bernstein, F. García Martínez, and J. Kampen; STDJ 23; Leiden: Brill, 1997), 251–74 (252–56); idem, *Schabbat: Sabbathhalacha und -praxis im antiken Judentum und Urchristentum* (TSAJ 78; Tübingen: Mohr Siebeck, 1999), 138–43; Ben Zion Wacholder, *The New Damascus Document: The Midrash on the Eschatological Torah of the Dead Sea Scrolls; Reconstruction, Translation, and Commentary* (STDJ 56; Leiden: Brill, 2007), 331–32; Vered Noam and Elisha Qimron, "A Qumran Composition of Sabbath Laws and Its Contribution to the Study of Early Halakah," *DSD* 16 (2009): 55–96 (60–61).

represent a reformulation of Isa 58:13.[2] Yet, no significant study has focused on the legal and exegetical relationship between Isa 58:13 and CD 10:17–19 or the relevant comparative Second Temple and rabbinic legal sources.[3] In this chapter, I explore this relationship in the *Damascus Document* and compare it to related uses of Isa 58:13 in the ancient versions.

As in so many other aspects of Dead Sea Scrolls studies, the Cave 4 materials have significantly broadened the scope of inquiry on this subject. *4QHalakha B* (4Q264a 1 i 5–8; par. 4Q421 13+2+8 1–5) contains several laws that overlap in varying degrees with the Sabbath prohibitions. In the following chapter, I therefore explore the relationship between the laws in *4QHalakha B* and those in the *Damascus Document*, with particular attention to the shared and divergent exegetical relationship to Isa 58:13. In Chapter 6, I expand the historical and literary setting of this inquiry by examining related legal-exegetical applications of Isa 58:13 in the book of *Jubilees* and rabbinic literature. Throughout, my discussion focuses on three interrelated issues: (1) the specific aspects of speech that are regulated on the Sabbath, (2) the exegetical relationship of each text to Isa 58:13 and related scriptural passages, and (3) the relationship between the sometimes similar, while at other times dissimilar, exegetical techniques employed within each of these texts to expand the legal application of Sabbath law in Isa 58:13.

II. SABBATH "LAW" IN ISAIAH 58:13

Isa 58:13 contains a general condemnation of individuals who violate the Sabbath, though what specific activities are condemned is not entirely clear:[4]

אם תשיב משבת[5] רגלך עשות[6] חפציך ביום קדשי וקראת לשבת ענג ולקדוש[7] יהוה מכבד וכבדתו מעשות דרכיך
ממצוא[8] חפצך ודבר דבר

[2] See below, n. 24.

[3] One notable exception with regard to exegetical technique is the brief treatment in Elieser Slomovic, "Toward an Understanding of the Exegesis in the Dead Sea Scrolls," *RevQ* 7 (1969): 3–15 (9–10) (see below). Slomovic's observations can also be found in Schiffman, *Halakhah*, 88–89; Doering, *Schabbat*, 140 (with minimal amplification).

[4] Portions of Isa 58:13 are preserved in 1QIsa^{a}, 1QIsa^{b} (1Q8), and 4QIsa^{n} (4Q67). My analysis calls attention to relevant non-orthographic variants from these manuscripts. On the general meaning of the passage, in addition to the various commentaries, see H. A. Brongers, "Einige Bemerkungen zu Jes 58 13–14," *ZAW* 87 (1975): 212–26.

[5] 4QIsa^{n} preserves מהשבת. The definite article is represented in $\mathfrak{G}$.

[6] מעשות is found in 1QIsa^{a}, 4QIsa^{n}, and some $\mathfrak{T}^{J}$ manuscripts but does not appear in $\mathfrak{M}$ or 1QIsa^{b}. The appearance of the *mem* may be the result of analogy with מעשות at the end of the verse. Its basic sense is presumed in nearly all translations of the first appearance of עשות.

[7] The *waw* appears in 1QIsa^{a}, 1QIsa^{b}, and 4QIsa^{n}, but not $\mathfrak{M}$.

[8] וממצוא is found in 1QIsa^{a} and $\mathfrak{T}^{J}$, but the conjunctive *waw* does not appear in $\mathfrak{M}$, 1QIsa^{b}, or 4QIsa^{n}. 4QIsa^{n} displays an odd feature for this word, whereby the following letters are preserved: מל[מ]צ◦]. Aside from the *lamed*, this seemingly should be reconstructed as $\mathfrak{M}$ ממצוא. Yet, there is no erasure mark for the *lamed*.

> If you refrain from trampling the Sabbath, from pursuing your affairs on my holy day; If you call the Sabbath "delight," the Lord's holy day "honored"; And if you honor it and go not your ways nor look to your affairs, nor speak a word. (modified NJPS)

The general language of the condemned activities – pursuing (עשה) and looking to (מצא) one's affairs (חפצ[י]ך), doing (עשה) one's ways (דרכיך), and speaking (דבר) a word (דבר) – is quite vague. Indeed, both ancient and modern commentators have struggled with how to classify and understand the presumed condemned Sabbath activities in this passage. Modern commentators in particular have focused on the twofold use of חפץ, "business, affair," in the context of related uses of this term in the Hebrew Bible and comparative Semitic evidence.[9] In particular, Moshe Weinfeld observes that the two expressions employing חפץ possess Akkadian cognates that are employed to refer to mercantile pursuits: עשות חפצך – *epēš ṣibûti*, "doing business"; ממצוא חפצך – *kašād ṣibûti*, "completing the enterprise."[10] חפץ in Isa 58:13 is therefore understood as alluding to business dealings, and thus at least part of the condemned activity focuses on business-related activity.[11]

While this understanding of the verse illuminates the general condemnation, many of its specific details are still unclear. One of the many difficulties involves the meaning of the expression ודבר דבר, literally "(Nor) speak a word/matter." Philological analysis of this clause is not uniquely challenging; a *pi'el* infinitive construct "to speak/speaking" is followed by the noun "word/matter." The negation is provided by virtue of ellipsis from the earlier prefixed *mems* on מעשות דרכיך and ממצוא חפצך. This yields the likely translation "Nor speak a

9 On the late biblical Hebrew meaning of חפץ as "business, affair," see Eccl 3:1, 17; 5:7; 8:6; 1QS 3:17 (cf. Prov 31:13; Sir 11:21); and W. E. Staples, "The Meaning of *ḤḖP̱EṢ* in Ecclesiastes," *JNES* 24 (1965): 110–12; G. J. Botterweck, "חפץ," *TDOT* 5:92–107 (99–100); Moshe Weinfeld, "The Counsel of the 'Elders' to Rehoboam and Its Implications," in *Reconsidering Israel and Judah: Recent Studies on the Deuteronomistic History* (ed. G. N. Knoppers and J. G. McConville; Sources for Biblical and Theological Study 8; Winona Lake: Eisenbrauns, 2000), 516–39 (531–32) (1982). This meaning is likely also intended in Isa 58:3 (see Brongers, "Bemerkungen," 213).

10 Weinfeld, "The Counsel of the 'Elders,'" 531–32. Weinfeld makes a similar comparative argument for the expression עשות דרכיך – *ḫarrānu epēšu*, "to undertake a business journey." Cf. Michael Fishbane, *Biblical Interpretation in Ancient Israel* (Oxford: Clarendon, 1985), 304–5 n. 31.

11 See, e.g., J. Skinner, *Isaiah: Chapters XL–LXVI* (Cambridge: Cambridge University Press, 1898), 186; John L. McKenzie, *Second Isaiah* (AB 20; New York: Doubleday, 1968), 164; Claus Westermann, *Isaiah 40–66: A Commentary* (OTL; Philadelphia: Westminster, 1969), 340–41; Brongers, "Bemerkungen," 213; R. N. Whybray, *Isaiah 40–66* (NCBC; Grand Rapids: Eerdmans; London: Marshall, Morgan, and Scott, 1981), 218. Others have found allusions to other specific Sabbath restrictions. J. D. Watts, *Isaiah 34–66* (WBC 25; Waco: Word Books, 1987), 276; Joseph Blenkinsopp, *Isaiah 56–66* (AB 19B; New York: Doubleday, 2003), 181, interpret אם תשיב משבת רגלך as an allusion to the restriction on Sabbath travel (based on Exod 16:29), a suggestion already made by the medieval Jewish exegete Rabbi David Kimḥi (ad loc., s.v. אם תשיב משבת רגלך).

word." The larger question is, what type of speech is condemned here? As many scholars have noted, this passage is certainly not condemning all speech on the Sabbath. Modern interpretations of this clause, observes H. A. Brongers, tend to fall into two general categories.[12] One group of commentators suggests it refers to profane or idle talk.[13] This interpretation, however, as further observed by Brongers, lacks coherence with the larger sense of the verse, which seems to prohibit business dealings. Thus, he argues in favor of the second group of interpretations that assert that the speech is somehow related to the condemned business dealings.[14] Indeed, Weinfeld has argued based on comparative biblical and Akkadian evidence that the verb דבר + direct object דבר in the Hebrew Bible is a technical expression meaning "to arrive at a decision through bargaining (usually at a gathering)." In the context of Isa 58:13, Weinfeld therefore suggests, the expression refers to business transactions or bargaining.[15]

The full meaning and legal application of this expression already eluded ancient readers of scripture, as evinced by the divergent translations found in the ancient versions. Ancient readers were faced with a secondary problem beyond merely understanding the simple meaning of the condemned actions. Isa 58:13–14 forms part of a broader general prophetic invective against the neglect of the Sabbath. In this sense, its language is not intended to be prescriptive for the particulars of Sabbath observance. Yet, this is almost certainly how readers in the Second Temple period would have regarded this passage. Thus, ancient readers were forced to "translate" the highly allusive and rhetorical prophetic invective into prescriptive Sabbath law.

Two illustrative examples of this approach can be found in the Septuagint and Targum. The Septuagint surmises that Isa 58:13 condemns individuals who speak in anger: οὐδὲ λαλήσεις λόγον <u>ἐν ὀργῇ</u> ἐκ τοῦ στόματός σου, "Nor speak a word <u>in anger</u> out of your mouth" (NETS). In addition to the clear exegetical expansion, the Septuagint renders the entire expression as an explicit

[12] Brongers, "Bemerkungen," 214.

[13] In addition to the examples furnished by Brongers, see, e.g., August Dillman, *Der Prophet Jesaja* (HAT; Leipzig: S. Hirzel, 1890), 497; Skinner, *Isaiah*, 186; McKenzie, *Second Isaiah*, 165; Blenkinsopp, *Isaiah 56–66*, 175 (see also RSV, NIV). Medieval Jewish exegetes generally understand the expression, following rabbinic tradition (see below, Chapter 6, section III), as a proscription against excessive or idle conversation on the Sabbath (see Rabbi David Kimḥi and Rabbi Abraham ibn Ezra, ad loc.). See also the suggestion of David N. Freedman that this refers to legal proceedings (cited in McKenzie, *Second Isaiah*, 165).

[14] See, e.g., Skinner, *Isaiah*, 186: "arranging a matter (of business)" (as a second interpretation; see above, n. 13); Arnold B. Ehrlich, *Mikra Kifshuṭoh* (3 vols.; New York: Ktav, 1969), 1:145; Westermann, *Isaiah 40–66*, 340: "trading" ("verhandelst"); Botterweck, "חפץ," 99: "conducting transactions"; Raphael Weiss, "Two Notes," *Leš* 37 (1972–74): 306; Brongers, "Bemerkungen," 214: "Abkommen triffst" ("conclude an agreement"); NJPS (H. L. Ginsberg): "striking bargains"; Brevard S. Childs, *Isaiah* (OTL; Louisville: Westminster John Knox, 2001), 474: "business."

[15] Weinfeld, "The Counsel of the 'Elders'" 530–32.

prohibition. Thus, the negation, which is implied in the Hebrew, is made explicit in the Greek with the inclusion of οὐδέ. Moreover, in place of the Hebrew infinitive construct, the Septuagint provides a second-person singular future indicative. In so doing, the Septuagint makes explicit that this is a prohibition against angry speech on the Sabbath.[16]

In contrast, the Targum renders the clause as ומלמללא מלין דאונים, "And from speaking words of wickedness." The Targum is likely influenced by the similar language in Isa 58:9, which condemns speaking wickedness (לדבר און), for which it provides the same translation.[17] Both versions recognize that the text of *Isaiah* lacks meaning without greater context and thus try to remedy this problem by adding some nuance to the proscribed speech. While the Septuagint focuses on the state of mind of the speaker, the Targum is concerned with the content of the words. Yet, neither of these translations provides any further elaboration on the relationship of the condemned speech to the more general restriction on Sabbath activity. The limited attempts of the Targum and the Septuagint stand in contrast to other ancient readers of Isa 58:13, for whom this broader context was a central preoccupation. It is to this question that we now turn.

III. TEXT AND TRANSLATION: DAMASCUS DOCUMENT (CD) 10:17–19 (PAR. 4Q270 6 V 3–4)[18]

17 וביום השבת אל ידבר איש דבר
18 נבל ורק אל ישה ברעהו כל אל ישפוט על הון ובצע
19 אל ידבר בדברי המלאכה והעבודה לעשות למשכים

[16] An additional modification is the further identification of the speech as coming "out of your mouth." This does not seem to reflect any specific exegetical agenda here but rather is reflective of the translation technique of the Septuagint (see, e.g., 𝔊 2 Sam 14:13; 1 Kgs 20:33; cf. 1 Kgs 17:1). The Septuagint's understanding of Isa 58:13 is similarly found in the Christian *Apostolic Constitutions*: "So no one might be willing to send one word out of his mouth in anger on the day of the Sabbath" (VII.36). See Alexander Roberts and James Donaldson, *The Ante-Nicene Fathers*, Volume 7 (Buffalo: Christian Literature Company, 1886), 474.

[17] See also the identical translation for דברו דברים in Hos 10:4. In Targumic Aramaic, אונס generally has the meaning of "wrong" or "accident" (see Michael Sokoloff, *A Dictionary of Jewish Palestinian Aramaic* [2d ed.; Ramat Gan: Bar Ilan University Press; Baltimore: Johns Hopkins University Press, 2002], 40, s.v. אונס). That it implies "wickedness" in Isa 58:13 is certain based on the evidence of the Targum's translation of און in Isa 58:9 as אונים. This connection was observed by medieval Jewish exegetes (see Rabbi David Kimḥi ad loc.) and has been further noted by modern scholars (see Gilat, "Sabbath Prohibitions," 255 n. 27; Weinfeld, "The Counsel of the 'Elders,'" 531 n. 81; Schiffman, *Halakhah*, 90).

[18] Hebrew text follows Elisha Qimron, "The Text of CDC," in *The Damascus Document Reconsidered* (ed. M. Broshi; Jerusalem: Israel Exploration Society, the Shrine of the Book, Israel Museum, 1992), 29. For 4Q270, see Joseph M. Baumgarten, *Qumran Cave 4.XIII: The Damascus Document (4Q266–273)* (DJD 18; Oxford: Clarendon, 1996), 160 (no variants are present). Additional philological analysis can be found in Schiffman, *Halakhah*, 87–88; Doering, *Schabbat*, 138–43.

17. And on the Sabbath, let no man speak
18. A vile and empty word: He shall not demand any payment from his fellow;[19] He shall not enter into a dispute concerning money or profit;[20]
19. He shall not speak about matters relating to work and labor that need to be done on the following morning.[21]

IV. ISAIAH 58:13 IN THE DAMASCUS DOCUMENT

This passage contains a series of laws relating to financial and business matters on the Sabbath. The unit begins with a general classificatory statement: "Let no man speak a vile and empty word."[22] This general prohibition is followed by three specific laws that all include activity performed primarily through

[19] This clause is subject to different interpretations. I am following Schechter and several later commentators who understand this law as prohibiting an individual from demanding the repayment of a loan from the debtor. See Solomon Schechter, *Documents of Jewish Sectaries*, volume 1: *Fragments of a Zadokite Work* (Cambridge: Cambridge University Press, 1910; repr. with prolegomenon by Joseph Fitzmyer; Library of Biblical Studies; New York: Ktav, 1970), 80; I. Lévi, "Un Écrit Sadducéen Anterieur à la Destruction du Temple," *REJ* 61 (1911): 161–205 (197); Ginzberg, *Jewish Sect*, 108–9 especially n. 13, 292; Chaim Rabin, *The Zadokite Documents* (Oxford: Clarendon, 1954), 52 (as a second translation option); Slomovic, "Exegesis," 10; Joseph M. Baumgarten and Daniel R. Schwartz, "Damascus Document (CD)," in *The Dead Sea Scrolls: Hebrew, Aramaic, and Greek Texts with English Translations; Damascus Document, War Scroll and Related Documents* (ed. J. H. Charlesworth; PTSDSSP 2; Tübingen: Mohr Siebeck; Louisville: Westminster John Knox, 1995), 47; Wacholder, *New Damascus Document*, 89 n. 13 (as a second translation option). This translation understands ב + נשה\א (either *qal* or *hiph'il*) with the general meaning "to be a creditor" and the specific sense of "to press on a loan" as in Neh 5:7, 10 (cf. 1 Kgs 8:31//2 Chr 6:22; without the ב, see Exod 22:24; Ps 89:23). Other scholars render ב + נשה\א as a *hiph'il* imperfect with the meaning "to lend" (see Deut 15:2; 24:10). In this sense, the law prohibits an individual from lending anything on the Sabbath (R. H. Charles, "Fragments of a Zadokite Work," in idem, ed., *Apocrypha and Pseudepigrapha of the Old Testament* [2 vols.; Oxford: Clarendon, 1913], 2:826; Rabin, *Zadokite Documents*, 52; Schiffman, *Halakhah*, 87; Doering, *Schabbat*, 139). While the philological evidence can be read in support of either interpretation, as argued by Ginzberg, the former interpretation is required by the context, "which here certainly requires forbidden 'words' and not 'actions'" (ibid., 109 n. 13). See the similar Sabbath restriction in Philo, *On the Migration of Abraham*, 91. See also Lévi, "Un Écrit Sadducéen," 197 n. 2; and Leonhard Rost, *Die Damascusschrift: Neu Bearbeitet* (Klein Texte für Vorlesungen und Übungen 167; Berlin: de Gruyter, 1933), 20, who note the possible emendation of ישה to ישיח ("to converse"). This reading would render the entire clause as related to verbal communication (presumably business related). There is little textual evidence, however, to support this emendation.

[20] This law was initially understood by Schechter as a proscription against formal court proceedings on the Sabbath as in *m. Beṣ.* 5:2 (*Documents*, 80). Ginzberg, followed by Schiffman, however, correctly understands it as prohibiting a private dispute concerning business matters (Ginzberg, *Jewish Sect*, 58, 109 n. 12; Schiffman, *Halakhah*, 88). On the range of possible meanings for הון and בצע, see Doering, *Schabbat*, 141. It seems certain that these terms refer to financial matters here.

[21] On this understanding of למשכים (as known from rabbinic Hebrew), see Charles, "Fragments," 2:826; Ginzberg, *Jewish Sect*, 58; Schiffman, *Halakhah*, 88 n. 25.

[22] On this understanding of the initial clause, see full discussion below.

TABLE 1. *Isa 58:13 and CD 10:17–19*

Isa 58:13	CD 10:17–19
אם תשיב משבת רגלך עשות חפציך ביום קדשי וקראת לשבת ענג ולקדוש יהוה מכבד וכבדתו מעשות דרכיך ממצוא חפצך ודבר דבר	וביום השבת אל ידבר איש דבר נבל ורק And on the Sabbath, let no man speak a vile and empty word.
If you refrain from trampling the sabbath, from pursuing your affairs on my holy day; If you call the Sabbath "delight," the Lord's holy day "honored"; And if you honor it and go not your ways nor look to your affairs, nor speak a word.	אל ידבר בדברי המלאכה והעבודה לעשות למשכים He shall not speak about matters relating to work and labor that need to be done on the following morning.

speech: (1) demanding repayment of a loan, (2) entering into a dispute about money, (3) and speaking about work matters related to the following week.[23] None of these laws is identified with any scriptural source.

Though never cited, it is certain that the general statement and the third specific law reformulate language from Isa 58:13, as illustrated by the correspondence in Table 1.[24]

The "Vile and Empty Word"

Let me begin with what I have identified as the general classificatory statement – אל ידבר איש דבר נבל ורק. As is illustrated by Table 1, the language of this clause

[23] To be sure, these actions will likely at some point involve nonverbal activity. For example, if one demands from a debtor the repayment of a loan, this may lead to a physical exchange of money or goods. The initial act in each of these three cases, however, always involves a verbal undertaking.

[24] See also Schechter, *Documents*, 80; Charles, "Fragments," 2:826; Ginzberg, *Jewish Sect*, 59; Rost, *Damascusschrift*, 20; Rabin, *Zadokite Documents*, 53; Kimbrough, "Sabbath," 487–88; Slomovic, "Exegesis," 9–10; Weiss, "Two Notes," 306; Schiffman, *Halakhah*, 89–91; Michael Fishbane, "Use, Authority, and Interpretation of Mikra at Qumran," in *Mikra: Text, Translation, Reading and Interpretation of the Hebrew Bible in Ancient Judaism and Early Christianity* (ed. M. J. Mulder; CRINT 2/1; Assen: Van Gorcum; Minneapolis: Fortress, 1988), 339–77 (370); Steven D. Fraade, "Looking for Legal Midrash at Qumran," in *Legal Fictions: Studies of Law and Narrative in the Discursive Worlds of Ancient Jewish Sectarians and Sages* (JSJSup 147; Leiden: Brill, 2011), 145–68 (160) (1998); Baumgarten and Schwartz, "Damascus Document," 47 n. 158; Moshe J. Bernstein and Shlomo A. Koyfman, "The Interpretation of Biblical Law in the Dead Sea Scrolls: Forms and Methods," in *Biblical Interpretation at Qumran* (ed. M. Henze; Grand Rapids: Eerdmans, 2005), 61–87 (72); Doering, *Schabbat*, 139; Wacholder, *New Damascus Document*, 331; Aharon Shemesh, *Halakhah in the Making: The Development of Jewish Law from Qumran to the Rabbis* (Berkeley: University of California Press, 2009), 165 n. 7; George J. Brooke, "Prophetic Interpretation in the *Pesharim*," in *A Companion to Biblical Interpretation in Early Judaism* (ed. M. Henze; Grand Rapids: Eerdmans, 2012), 235–54 (142–43).

draws from the key phrase ודבר דבר in Isa 58:13. Two larger questions are critical here: (1) What are the literary and exegetical foundations of the reformulation? (2) What does the clause mean within the immediate context of the *Damascus Document*'s Sabbath law?

Several modifications are present in the *Damascus Document*'s reformulation. First, the *Damascus Document* alters the scriptural infinitive construct to bring it in line with the apodictic legal formulae employed throughout the *Damascus Document* – אל + jussive (masc. sg.), with the further inclusion of איש as the expressed subject (*Isaiah*: ודבר → CD: אל ידבר איש).[25] In so doing, the *Damascus Document* makes the enigmatic passage from *Isaiah* look like a standard scriptural apodictic law at the same time as it makes it conform to the *Damascus Document*'s own literary form for Sabbath law.[26] Second, as with the Septuagint and the Targum, the *Damascus Document* seeks to create a more specific meaning for the proscribed speech through an expansive reformulation. As with the Targum more specifically, the *Damascus Document* focuses on the nature of the spoken words, thus interpreting ודבר דבר as a reference to conversation with contemptible content. This is achieved through the inclusion of the two adjectives נבל (vile) and רק (empty): *Isaiah*: ודבר דבר → CD: אל ידבר איש דבר [נבל ורק].

Two exegetical steps are operating in the reformulation. First, the *Damascus Document* takes for granted that Isa 58:13 does not mean that all speech is proscribed on the Sabbath, but rather only a limited type of speech is condemned. In making this assumption, the *Damascus Document* likely draws upon Isa 58:9b: אם תסיר מתוכך מוטה שלח אצבע ודבר און, "If you banish the yoke from your midst, the menacing hand, and evil speech." As in 58:13, Isa 58:9b serves as the protasis of a conditional clause that outlines the reward of abandoning iniquitous ways (אם + verb of turning away + מ), including some form of contemptible speech. The one critical difference is that the speech in verse 9 is specifically identified as wicked:

> **Isa 58:9:** אם תסיר מתוכך מוטה שלח אצבע ודבר [און], "If you banish the yoke from your midst, the menacing hand, and [evil] speech."
>
> **Isa 58:13:** אם תשיב משבת ... ודבר דבר, "If you refrain from ... nor speak a word."

Later readers of Isa 58, as evinced by the Targum's identical translation of ודבר און (58:9) and ודבר דבר (58:13), saw the correspondence between these two verses as a clue to understanding the nature of the condemned speech in verse 13. Similarly, the *Damascus Document* uses Isa 58:9 as part of a much broader

[25] See Schiffman, *Halakhah*, 80–83. For further discussion of exegetical techniques involved in the modification of scriptural content into the apodictic legal formulae of Dead Sea Scrolls legal texts, see Chapter 9.

[26] A similar formal modification is found in the Septuagint. See above, n. 16.

exegetical reformulation. Yet, unlike the Targum, the *Damascus Document* turns elsewhere for the specific language employed in its own amplification of the meaning of דבר.

The use of the particular adjectives רק and נבל in the *Damascus Document* is based on several scriptural verses in which each of these words appears together with the root דבר.[27] Each of the intertextual links contains the keyword דבר together with the desired descriptive adjective (either נבל or רק). In one case, moreover, there is an attempt to underscore the correspondence between ודבר דבר in Isa 58:13 and the related expression ודבר און in Isa 58:9. For both נבל and רק, two specific verses function as intertextual links. In each case, Isa 32:6 functions as the primary intertextual link.[28] Both formulations in the *Damascus Document* also reflect one further influence from related verses with the combination of דבר and the specific adjective, either נבל or רק.

Isa 32:6 contains the root דבר with the meaning "to speak" together with reference to a *villain* and *villainy* (נבל):[29]

> **CD 10:17–18:** אל ידבר איש דבר נבל ורק, "Let no man speak a vile and empty word."
>
> **Isa 32:6a:** כי נבל נבלה ידבר ולבו יעשה און לעשות חנף, "For the villain speaks villainy and his mind plots wickedness to act impiously."

Moreover, the villainous speech of the villain in the first half of this clause parallels the *wicked* plotting (און) of the villain in the second half of the clause (as marked by double underlining). The perceived correspondence between Isa 58:9 (ודבר און) and 58:13 (ודבר דבר) therefore reinforces the suitability of נבל from Isa 32:6 as the descriptive adjective for the reformulation of דבר in the *Damascus Document*.

A similar combination of דבר and נבל is likewise found in Isa 9:16:

> **CD 10:17–18:** אל ידבר איש דבר נבל ורק, "Let no man speak a vile and empty word."
>
> **Isa 9:16:** וכל פה דבר נבלה "And every mouth speaks villainy."

In this case, the exegetical link is not through Isa 58:9 but rather through Isa 58:14, which concludes with כי פי יהוה דבר, "For the mouth of the Lord

[27] This general phenomenon is observed on a limited scale by Slomovic, "Exegesis," 10, who identifies the exegetical technique as identical to the later rabbinic *gezera shawah* (argument from analogous expression). Slomovic is followed by Fishbane, "Use, Authority, and Interpretation," 370; Brooke, "Prophetic Interpretation," 242. On other possible attestations of *gezera shawah* in Dead Sea Scrolls legal texts, see Bernstein and Koyfman, "Interpretation of Biblical Law," 84–86.

[28] Isa 32:6 appears in *Pesher on Isaiah E* (4Q165 6 3–4) as part of a larger lemma from Isa 32:5–7. Unfortunately, virtually nothing from the pesher interpretation survives. Line 7 preserves the introductory pesher formula, and line 8 has a fragmentary reference to "the Torah" (cf. 𝔗J Isa 32:6, which introduces the "words of the Torah").

[29] See also Schiffman, *Halakhah*, 87 n. 20.

speaks." Ancient readers of Isa 58:13–14 likely recognized the inverse relationship between the contemptible speech in verse 13 and the divine speech in verse 14. The appeal to Isa 9:16 underscores this exegetical relationship by employing the specific language describing the divine speech in verse 14 to illuminate the broader context for the condemned speech in verse 13. Abandonment of one's villainous speech (Isa 58:13 + 9:16) will bring about the rewards of the divine speech (Isa 58:14).[30]

The use of רק likewise draws its exegetical inspiration from Isa 32:6.

> **CD 10:17–18:** אל ידבר איש דבר נבל ורק, "Let no man speak a vile and empty word."
>
> **Isa 32:6b:** ולדבר אל יהוה תועה להריק נפש רעב ומשקה צמא יחסיר, "And to preach disloyalty against the Lord; to leave unsatisfied the hungry and deprive the thirsty of drink."

Isa 32:6b presents the two infinitive constructs דבר and ריק (*hiph'il*) in poetic parallelism.[31] In this case, the *Damascus Document* transforms the parallel verbal use of ריק into an adjective, which then supplies the second explanation for the condemned speech in the *Damascus Document* (דבר נבל ורק).

רק, as its pair נבל, likely has a second exegetical basis for its appearance in the *Damascus Document*:

> **CD 10:17–18:** אל ידבר איש דבר נבל ורק, "Let no man speak a vile and empty word."
>
> **Deut 32:47:** כי לא דבר רק הוא מכם כי הוא חייכם ובדבר הזה תאריכו ימים על האדמה אשר אתם עברים את הירדן שמה לרשתה, "For this is not a trifling (lit. empty) matter for you, it is your very life; through it (lit. this thing) you shall long endure on the land that you are to possess upon crossing the Jordan."

In this verse, the root דבר, here used in the sense of "matter" – and contextually referring back to the Torah of the previous verse – is described as something that is not empty (רק). This verse continues by identifying "this thing" (דבר הזה) as the critical item that must be observed in order to ensure survival on the land. In drawing on Deut 32:47, the *Damascus Document* inverts the sense

[30] As noted by Schiffman, 𝔗[J] Isa 9:16 and 32:6 render נבל with words that denote wickedness (32:6: רשעה; 9:16: שקר [cf. 𝔊 ἄδικα]) (*Halakhah*, 87 n. 20).

[31] In the citation of this passage in *Pesher on Isaiah E* (4Q165), the fragmentary word corresponding to 𝔐 ולהריק clearly does not have a *reš* as its fourth letter. The visible traces allow for a *kap*, *pe*, or *mem*, thus yielding a range of possible suggestions: e.g., ולהכ]רית, ולהמ]ית, ולהכ]ות, ולהפ]ריד, ולהפ]יץ (see Maurya P. Horgan, *Pesharim: Qumran Interpretations of Biblical Books* [CBQMS 8; Washington, D.C.: The Catholic Biblical Association of America, 1979], 136–37). ולהריק is found in 1QIsa[a]. The Septuagint has διαπεῖραι ("to scatter"), and the Targum translates as לשלאהא ("to weaken"), though both of these seem to be exegetical attempts to render the sense of the Hebrew ריק.

of רק. Failure to adhere to the Sabbath law in the *Damascus Document* is an "empty word," the exact opposite of the Torah in Deut 32:47, which is not empty.[32]

The combination of all the intertextual links – all grounded in the combined use of דבר, נבל, and רק in Isa 32:6 and related verses – provides the desired literary form for the *Damascus Document*'s reformulation of the scriptural ודבר דבר.[33] On the basis of this reformulation of Isa 58:13, the second question to address is, what does the *Damascus Document* mean when it condemns vile and empty speech? As already noted, the inclusion of these two adjectives indicates that the *Damascus Document* does not understand Isa 58:13 as condemning all speech on the Sabbath but merely a specific form of contemptible speech. Several early commentators argued that the identification of this condemned speech as "vile and empty" indicates that the *Damascus Document* intends to prohibit idle or secular talk on the Sabbath, and thus this clause is regarded as the first of four prohibitions related to speech on the Sabbath.[34]

This approach, however, seems to be too heavily influenced by later rabbinic interpretations of ודבר דבר in Isa 58:13 as a prohibition against engaging in idle talk on the Sabbath or in profane discussion that would normally transpire during the week.[35] Chaim Rabin notes that this understanding is problematic in light of the similar restriction on "foolish speech" (דבר נבל) in the sectarian penal code found in the *Rule of the Community*. 1QS 7:9 condemns general foolish speech: ואשר ידבר בפיהו דבר נבל שלושה חודשים, "Whoever speaks a foolish word: three months (of reduced food rations)." For Rabin, the *Damascus Document* and the *Rule of the Community* are directed at the same community.

32 The link to Deut 32:47 is noted by Slomovic, "Exegesis," 10; and Schiffman, *Halakhah*, 87 n. 20. The combination of ריק and negative speech may also appear in Matt 5:22: ὃς δ᾽ἂν εἴπῃ τῷ ἀδελφῷ αὐτοῦ ῥακά (Ms Sinaiticus: ραχα) – "anyone who says to his brother, '*raqa*' ..." ῥακά is generally rendered as "fool, empty-head," and its derivation is traced back to the Aramaic ריקא, "empty one." See linguistic evidence with bibliography in William F. Arndt and F. Wilbur Gingrich, *A Greek-English Lexicon of the New Testament and Other Early Christian Literature* (Chicago: University of Chicago Press; Cambridge: Cambridge University Press, 1957), 741.

33 Another possible intertextual source is suggested by early commentators based on the emendation of the *Damascus Document* from נבל ורק to הבל ורק (see Charles, "Fragments," 2:826; W. Bacher, "Zu Schechters neuestem Geniza-Funde," *ZfHB* 15 [1911]: 13–26 [25]; Ginzberg, *Jewish Sect*, 57; Rost, *Damascusschrift*, 20; Rabin, *Zadokite Documents*, 52). This emendation is proposed based on the identical phrase in Isa 30:7: ומצרים הבל וריק יעזרו ("For the help of Egypt shall be vain and empty"). The verse, however, does not contain any use of דבר, which seems to be critical to the *Damascus Document*'s exegetical technique. Moreover, there is no textual basis for the emendation (no variant is found in 4Q270).

34 Schechter, *Documents*, 80; Ginzberg, *Jewish Sect*, 108–9, cf. 57; Cohen, "Sabbath Prohibitions," 146 n. 51; Gilat, "Sabbath Prohibitions," 255; Kimbrough, "Concept of Sabbath," 487–88; Sharvit, "Sabbath," 44; Weinfeld, "The Counsel of the 'Elders,'" 531 n. 81; Wacholder, *New Damascus Document*, 331. Cohen follows Schechter's incorrect division and translation of the line (with ורק – rendered as "and surely" – belonging to the next clause) and understands נבל as an adverb: "no man shall utter a word foolishly."

35 On the rabbinic texts, see Chapter 6.

CD 11:17 therefore would seem to be prohibiting on the Sabbath an action that is otherwise forbidden throughout the week in 1QS 7:9.[36] More recent scholarship on the Dead Sea Scrolls has demonstrated that the Sabbath law of the *Damascus Document* and the penal code of the *Rule of the Community* are likely directed at different communities.[37] Lutz Doering, however, has further noted that a parallel restriction on דבר נבל appears in the expanded penal code found in one of the Cave 4 copies of the *Damascus Document* (4Q266 [4QD[a]] 10 ii 3–4): ואשר ידבר בפיה[ו] דבר נבל ונענש ע[שר]ים [יום והובדל] שלושה חודשי[ם, "Whoever speaks a foolish word shall be punished t[went]y [days (of reduced food rations) and excluded] three month[s]."[38]

The twofold appearance of the general restriction on foolish speech in the penal codes reinforces the understanding of this expression in sectarian literature as referring more generally to condemned speech, and therefore the *Damascus Document* does not use it to outlaw contemptible speech alone on the Sabbath.[39] Moreover, the interpretation of CD 10:17–18 as an independent law disrupts the structural and exegetical integrity of the broader literary unit. This supposed first law becomes contextually removed from the following three laws that all focus on speech related to business or financial matters. Why would the *Damascus Document* introduce its paraphrase of Isa 58:13 with a law related to idle talk and then move directly to what is clearly the core of its legal-exegetical application of Isa 58:13 as a restriction on financial- and business-related speech?

Accordingly, it seems best to follow more recent analysis of this literary unit that identifies the expression אל ידבר איש דבר נבל ורק as a general classificatory statement regarding the meaning of ודבר דבר in Isa 58:13 – only a specific type of speech is prohibited – followed by three specific examples of this legal application.[40] Thus, the *Damascus Document* partially agrees with later rabbinic traditions that identify Isa 58:13 as limiting profane speech on the Sabbath. For the *Damascus Document*, however, the nature of this profane speech is restricted to financial and business matters.[41] This also clarifies the reason for the corresponding language in 1QS 7:9 and 4Q266 10 ii 3. The

[36] Rabin, *Zadokite Documents*, 52.

[37] The fullest explication of the social location of the penal codes can be found in Alison Schofield, *From Qumran to the Yaḥad: A New Paradigm of Textual Development for the Community Rule* (STDJ 77; Leiden: Brill, 2008), 162–90.

[38] Doering, *Schabbat*, 139–40. Hebrew text follows Baumgarten, *Qumran Cave 4.XIII*, 74–75.

[39] Doering, *Schabbat*, 139–40. Note that Wacholder, *New Damascus Document*, 331, argues the opposite logic – CD 10:18 draws upon the same language as 1QS 7:9 and 4Q266 in order to restrict general foolish speech. Rabin's original counterargument, however, still stands. According to Wacholder's logic, there would be no compelling reason why the *Damascus Document* singles out this specific law as uniquely applying on the Sabbath.

[40] See Schiffman, *Halakhah*, 88–89; Doering, *Schabbat*, 139–40.

[41] See, however, my discussion in the next chapter of *4QHalakha B*, which extends the application of this understanding of Isa 58:13.

Damascus Document draws upon stock sectarian language condemning inappropriate speech as a fitting introduction to its own statement on the specific types of speech that are uniquely forbidden on the Sabbath (but not during the week) and are thus likewise "vile and empty."

Schiffman suggests an even stronger connection: transgression of these laws is perhaps subject to the same punishment for the similar "foolish speech" as prescribed in the sectarian penal code.[42] The specific desire to link this Sabbath prohibition and the general sectarian restriction on "foolish speech" likely provides the impetus for the protracted series of exegetical processes that yield the final formulation in CD 10:17–18 with the identical keyword נבל. The simplest exegetical amplification for Isa 58:13 is seemingly to add און as found in Isa 58:9. Yet, the *Damascus Document* merely uses this locution as an exegetical step to get to Isa 32:6 and its use of און *and* נבל. In so doing, the final reformulation of Isa 58:13 corresponds with the passage in 1QS 7:9 and 4Q266 10 ii 3–4.

Isaiah 58:13 and Laws 1 and 2 in the *Damascus Document*

Following the formulation of the general heading for this Sabbath law, the *Damascus Document* continues by providing three specific examples of prohibited conversation. Each of these examples, following the general tenor of the passage in *Isaiah* and its interpretation in the *Damascus Document*, condemns financial- or business-related activity on the Sabbath that is performed merely through verbal communication. The specific content of the first two laws, as in the initial classificatory statement, is formulated through intertextual links between the root דבר (supplied by Isa 58:13) and other scriptural passages that contain laws regarding lending and adjudication of difficult cases.[43]

Deut 15:2 contains the keyword from *Isaiah*, דבר, together with the exhortation for all *creditors* (בעל משה) to forgive any outstanding loans to their *fellows* (אשר ישה ברעהו).

> **CD 10:18:** אל ישה ברעהו כל, "He shall not demand any payment from his fellow."
>
> **Deut 15:2:** וזה דבר השמטה שמוט כל בעל משה ידו אשר ישה ברעהו, "This shall be the nature of the remission: every creditor shall remit the due that he claims from his fellow."

Similarly, Deut 17:8 speaks about a matter (דבר) concerning a judicial case (למשפט).

42 Schiffman, *Halakhah*, 88 (commenting only on 1QS 7:9; 4Q266 was not available at the time). 1QS levies a three-month punishment on anyone engaging in "foolish speech." 4Q266 contains a double punishment – one is punished (נענש) for twenty days and separated (הובדל) for three months.

43 These connections and their larger exegetical implications were first noted in Slomovic, "Exegesis," 10. The linguistic correspondence with Deut 15:2 was earlier noticed by Schechter, *Fragments*, 80; Charles, "Fragments," 2:826.

TABLE 2. *Isa 58:13 and CD 10:19*

Isa 58:13	CD 10:19
אם תשיב משבת רגלך עשות חפציך ביום קדשי וקראת לשבת ענג ולקדוש יהוה מכבד וכבדתו מעשות דרכיך ממצוא חפצך ודבר דבר If you refrain from trampling the sabbath, from pursuing your affairs on my holy day; If you call the Sabbath "delight," the Lord's holy day "honored"; And if you honor it and go not your ways nor look to your affairs, nor speak a word.	אל ידבר בדברי המלאכה והעבודה לעשות למשכים He shall not speak about matters relating to work and labor that need to be done on the following morning. ➢ המלאכה והעבודה – see Exod 20:9//Deut 5:13: ששת ימים תעבד ועשית כל מלאכתך, "Six days you shall labor and do all your work."

CD 10:18: אל ישפוט על הון ובצע, "He shall not enter into a dispute concerning money or profit."

Deut 17:8: כי יפלא ממך דבר למשפט, "If a case is too baffling for you to decide."

These two passages illustrate the extremely malleable nature of legal exegesis in the Dead Sea Scrolls. In both intertextual passages, the root דבר is employed not with the meaning "to speak" or "a word" as in *Isaiah* but rather with another of its meanings – "thing, matter."

Isaiah 58:13 and Law 3 in the *Damascus Document*

The third law, as with the initial classificatory statement, is based on a reformulation of Isa 58:13. Table 2 re-presents this correspondence as previously highlighted in Table 1.

The reformulation of Isa 58:13 in this third law shares many similarities with the initial classificatory statement in the *Damascus Document*. Foremost, the third law begins by transforming the scriptural language into the desired legal apodictic formula:

Isaiah: ודבר דבר, "Nor speak a word" → CD: אל ידבר, "He shall not speak."[44]

As with the initial statement, the third law follows the exegetical technique of the Septuagint and Targum in attempting to add nuance to the scriptural noun דבר, which in Isa 58:13 is best translated as "word." The *Damascus Document* adopts the meaning of "matter," though now as a plural noun introducing a construct clause. The elements that complete the construct clause provide two specific examples of "matters" concerning which one should not speak – matters related to work and labor:

44 Note that unlike CD 10:17, this formula does not include the subject איש.

Isaiah: ודבר דבר, "Nor speak a word" → CD: אל ידבר בדברי המלאכה והעבודה, "He shall not speak about matters relating to work and labor."

The *Damascus Document* goes one step further than its exegetical counterparts by adding a further nuance. It is work that is intended to be carried out following the Sabbath once the work week resumes (לעשות למשכים). Thus, the specific focus on this law is speaking about post-Sabbath work plans.

As with the content that precedes it, the form of the third law in CD 10:19 is grounded in an exegetical reformulation of ודבר דבר in Isa 58:13. The initial classificatory statement and the first two laws draw upon other scriptural language that contains the keyword דבר. The third law engages in a similar technique, except that it draws its additional language from intertextual links with another keyword from Isa 58:13 – עשה. In particular, the *Damascus Document* attempts to explain the twofold use of עשות in Isa 58:13. In both cases, this word is used to describe some type of condemned activity on the Sabbath. As noted above, the specific actions – עשות חפצך and עשות דרכיך – clearly refer to personal affairs but at the same time are quite vague in their specific application. The *Damascus Document* suggests that the key to understanding the vagueness of the twofold use of עשה and ודבר דבר is to read them together. For the *Damascus Document*, the prohibited speech refers back to the general actions similarly condemned earlier in the passage. More specifically, the twofold use of עשות – and likely also the duplication of the root דבר in ודבר דבר – indicates that there are *two* specific types of actions about which one is forbidden to speak.

The two specific words employed to describe the prohibited work – עבודה and מלאכה – are chosen based on the same exegetical principles that generated the first two laws. These words appear in other scriptural verses alongside the keyword עשה from Isa 58:13. This keyword appears in Exod 20:9//Deut 5:13 in the Decalogue's Sabbath law: ששת ימים תעבד ועשית כל מלאכתך, "Six days you shall labor and do all your work."[45] These verses thus contribute specific language for the two proscribed actions – מלאכה and עבודה – that comports with the scriptural language of Sabbath restrictions. Following the *Damascus*

[45] This verse as the source of the Sabbath law in the Decalogue makes it the most likely intertextual link. See also Lev 23:3, in which the same language is used to describe the Sabbath. The combination of עשה and עבד/מלאכה is found in several other places as well. See, in particular, the common expression כל מלאכת עבדה לא תעשו, but this combination is only employed to restrict labor on the festivals (Lev 23:7, 8, 21, 25, 35, 36; Num 28:18, 25, 26; 29:1, 12, 35). The terminological distinction between labor restricted on the Sabbath (כל מלאכה) and on the festivals (כל מלאכת עבודה) is continued in the Second Temple period. Thus, the former language is employed with regard to the Sabbath in CD 10:15 (par. 4Q270 6 v 1); Jub 2:27 = 4Q218 1 3, while the latter is applied to the festivals in the *Temple Scroll* (11QT[a] 14:10; 17:11, 16; 19:8//11QT[b] III 3ii, 5–7 25; 25:9) (following scriptural precedent, the language of the Day of Atonement is as that of the Sabbath – 11QT[a] 27:6, 7, 10). Rabbinic literature likewise follows scriptural precedent in preferring מלאכה as the general designation for Sabbath labor (see, e.g., *m. Shabb.* 7:1).

Document's broader understanding of Isa 58:13, it is these specific actions about which one is also forbidden to speak on the Sabbath. In this third law, the *Damascus Document* simultaneously solves two exegetical problems in Isa 58:13 – what is forbidden to do and what is forbidden to say.

One final question remains in the interpretation of CD 10:19: What is the precise meaning of מלאכה and עבודה, and how does it relate to the broader Sabbath restrictions in this passage? מלאכה is easily identifiable as the general term employed in scriptural and Second Temple literature to designate work that is prohibited on the Sabbath. Indeed, the opening law in the *Damascus Document*'s Sabbath Code uses this very term in its extension of the time frame for the beginning of the Sabbath (CD 10:14–17). Yet, in the law restricting speech that immediately follows, a second term – עבודה – is introduced. The use of both of these terms in the *Damascus Document* likely follows scriptural terminology, in which מלאכה denotes general work on the Sabbath, while עבודה refers to a more restricted type of labor, perhaps specifically physical labor.[46] Indeed, the next law in the *Damascus Document* prohibits an individual from traveling in his field in order to determine any necessary work to be done (עבודת חפצו), surely a reference to physical labor in the field (CD 10:20).[47] Thus, it is likely that a similar understanding of עבודה as restricted physical labor is intended in CD 10:19.

The other uses of עבודה in reference to physical labor in the Dead Sea Scrolls, both on the Sabbath and in a more general sense, provide further insight into its meaning in CD 10:19.[48] CD 20:7 and 1QS 5:14 both condemn the mingling of sectarians with outsiders. In both cases, the specific items singled out are the sectarian interaction with outsiders with regard to הון (wealth) and עבודה (labor). These two terms also appear together elsewhere in sectarian Sabbath laws. The fragmentary *4QHalakha B*, which will be discussed in greater detail in the next chapter, condemns speaking about matters relating to wealth and labor: אל ידבר]בכול דבר או עבודה או בהון או במק[ח], "He shall not speak] about any matter of labor, or money, or buyin[g]" (4Q264a 1 i 6). This passage contains several points of contact with CD 10:18–19 that will be treated below. What is particularly interesting is that it has moved the restriction on speaking about labor to the earlier list as found in the second law in the *Damascus Document*, which as suggested above refers specifically to financial- or business-related

[46] On עבודה as a subdesignation, see the festival passages cited in the previous note. On these distinctions, see further Jacob Milgrom and David P. Wright, "מלאכה," *TDOT* 8:325–31 (328). This meaning for עבודה is consistent with more general uses of the root עבד and the noun עבודה elsewhere in the Hebrew Bible to denote physical labor. See Jacob Milgrom, "The Levitical 'Aboḏā," *JQR* 61 (1970): 132–54; idem, *Studies in Levitical Terminology*, volume 1: *The Encroacher and the Levite, the Term 'Aboda* (UCPNES 14; Berkeley: University of California Press, 1970), 60–87.

[47] On this passage, see Chapter 7.

[48] See Shemaryahu Talmon, "A Further Link between the Judean Covenanters and the Essenes," *HTR* 56 (1963): 313–19 (316–17).

matters. Moreover, CD 10:20 weaves together the language of physical labor (עבודה) with the scriptural language of business activity (חפץ) as drawn from Isa 58:13. The close connection between עבודה and uniquely financial terminology (הון and חפץ), both in the immediate context of related Sabbath laws and in more general sectarian legislation, suggests that the עבודה intended in CD 10:19 is uniquely associated with some aspect of financial gain or more general business dealings.

Based on this interpretation of the meaning of מלאכה and עבודה, two specific types of speech are prohibited in CD 10:19. One may not speak about general work prohibited on the Sabbath that one intends to perform on the following day (מלאכה).[49] Alongside this general law, the *Damascus Document* introduces a narrower application. One also may not speak about physical activities related to financial gain that one will undertake on the following day (עבודה). The twofold law follows the similar double use of עשות in Isa 58:13, where one refers to general affairs (דרכיך) and the other more narrowly to business pursuits (חפציך).[50]

V. CONCLUSIONS

I began this chapter by observing the ambiguity that pervades the condemnation of activity on the Sabbath in Isa 58:13. Comparative biblical and Semitic evidence suggests that Isa 58:13 condemns business dealings that are regarded as inappropriate on the Sabbath. Even with this degree of clarity, Isa 58:13 is couched in highly allusive prophetic language. Later readers of this passage, however, turned to passages such as Isa 58:13 for direction on prescriptive Sabbath law. As such, Jews in the Second Temple period attempted to transform the ambiguous language of Isa 58:13 into explicit Sabbath law. The examples from the Septuagint, Targum, and *Damascus Document* illustrate the diverse ways in which Isa 58:13 is rewritten in order to achieve these goals. The reuse of language from Isa 58:13 is central to the method of rewriting scripture

[49] Note that מלאכה is also associated with הון in sectarian legislation. See 1QS 6:2, 19. In 1QS 6:2, the interchangeable ממון is used, but the Cave 4 manuscripts contain הון (4Q258 1a ii 7; 4Q263 3). No such association, however, is made specifically with regard to Sabbath law (as is the case with עבודה), and thus it is unlikely that any such further nuance is intended in CD 10:19.

[50] If I am correct that the twofold use of מלאכה and עבודה reuses the two scriptural expressions עשות חפצך and עשות דרכיך, this would constitute an example of "Zeidel's law," whereby scriptural paraphrases are inverted in their exegetical reformulation. Thus, the first scriptural expression עשות חפצך (= business) corresponds to the second term in the *Damascus Document* (עבודה), while the second scriptural clause עשות דרכיך (= general restriction) corresponds to the first term in the *Damascus Document* (מלאכה). On literary inversion, see Moshe Zeidel, "Parallels between Isaiah and Psalms," *Sinai* 38 (1955–56): 149–72, 229–40, 272–80, 335–55 [Hebrew]; Shemaryahu Talmon, "The Textual Study of the Bible: A New Outlook," in *Qumran and the History of the Biblical Text* (ed. F. M. Cross Jr. and Sh. Talmon; Cambridge: Harvard University Press, 1975), 321–400 (360–62); Pancratius Beentjes, "Inverted Quotations in the Bible: A Neglected Stylistic Pattern," *Bib* 63 (1982): 506–23.

as found throughout Second Temple literature. The *Damascus Document*, in particular, employs a host of exegetical techniques to amplify the meaning of the "word" that may not be spoken on the Sabbath. More specifically, the *Damascus Document* uses the keyword דבר ("word") in order to create intertextual connections with other scriptural passages that provide the desired textual nuance for the meaning of Isa 58:13, "Nor speak a word." In so doing, the *Damascus Document* creates an entire set of Sabbath restrictions regarding business-related speech that are grounded in a legal-exegetical reformulation of Isa 58:13.

5

Isaiah 58:13 and the Sabbath Prohibition on Speech in the Dead Sea Scrolls, Part 2

4QHalakha B

I. INTRODUCTION

The publication of the Cave 4 legal texts has expanded considerably our knowledge of sectarian Sabbath law.[1] Among these texts, *4QHalakha B* is particularly distinctive on account of its apparent exclusive focus on Sabbath law. This chapter explores the speech-related Sabbath restrictions in *4QHalakha B*, both in their own regard and in dialogue with the related material from the *Damascus Document* introduced in Chapter 4.

4QHalakha B is represented in two highly fragmentary manuscripts – 4Q264a and 4Q421. 4Q421 was initially published under the title *4QWays of Righteousness* and classified as a sapiential text.[2] This particular manuscript, however, contains significant textual overlap with the 4Q264a as first detected by Lutz Doering and further outlined by Eibert J. C. Tigchelaar.[3] Doering and

[1] On the Cave 4 texts specifically, see Lutz Doering, "New Aspects of Qumran Sabbath Law from Cave 4 Fragments," in *Legal Texts and Legal Issues: Proceedings of the Second Meeting of the International Organization for Qumran Studies, Cambridge, 1995; Published in Honour of Joseph M. Baumgarten* (ed. M. Bernstein, F. García Martínez, and J. Kampen; STDJ 23; Leiden: Brill, 1997), 251–74; idem, *Schabbat: Sabbathhalacha und –praxis im antiken Judentum und Urchristentum* (TSAJ 78; Tübingen: Mohr Siebeck, 1999), 215–55.

[2] Torleif Elgvin, "4Q421: *4QWays of Righteousness^b*," in *Qumran Cave 4.XV: Sapiential Texts*, part 1 (ed. J. A. Fitzymer et al.; DJD 20; Oxford: Clarendon, 1997), 183–202.

[3] Doering, *Schabbat*, 217–19. Doering's observations first appear in his 1997 Göttingen dissertation that serves as the basis for his later book. His earlier treatment of the text does not consider the textual overlap ("New Aspects," 252–56). See further Eibert J. C. Tigchelaar, "Sabbath Halakha and Worship in 4QWays of Righteousness: 4Q421 11 and 13+2+8 par 4Q264(a) 1–2," *RevQ* 18 (1998): 359–72. These observations were integrated into the *editio princeps*: Joseph Baumgarten, "4Q264a: 4QHalakha B," in *Qumran Cave 4.XXV: Halakhic Texts* (ed. J. M. Baumgarten et al.; DJD 35; Oxford: Clarendon, 1999), 53–56. The edition by James

Tigchelaar identify textual overlap among fragments 2, 8, and 13 of 4Q421 and 4Q264a 1, thereby providing a much fuller picture of the text and its Sabbath law. Subsequent to the publication of Joseph Baumgarten's *editio princeps*, Tigchelaar published a previously neglected photograph of portions of 4Q264a (PAM 40.626), which corresponds to the missing left-hand portion of 4Q264a 1 and further corroborates the textual overlap in 4Q421.[4] Vered Noam and Elisha Qimron have recently presented an even more substantial composite text, at the same time seeking to situate several of the Sabbath laws in *4QHalakha B* within the broader setting of the history of *halakhah*. They propose that the combined text of 4Q264a and 4Q421 (reclassified by them as 4Q421a) should be understood as an independent work, which they title "Sabbath Laws."[5] My presentation of the text here takes into consideration all this previous research on the two manuscripts that make up *4QHalakha B*.

II. TEXT AND TRANSLATION: 4Q264A 1 I 5–8 (PAR. 4Q421 13+2+8 1–5)[6]

5 אל יחשב איש [ב]פ[יהו] [7]

H. Charlesworth and Carsten Claussen, "Halakah B: 4Q264a," in *The Dead Sea Scrolls: Hebrew, Aramaic, and Greek Texts with English Translations; Damascus Document II, Some Works of the Torah, and Related Documents* (ed. J. H. Charlesworth; PTSDSSP 3; Tübingen: Mohr Siebeck; Louisville: Westminster John Knox, 2006), 286–89, incorporates research on the text up to Baumgarten's DJD volume.

4 Eibert J. C. Tigchelaar, "More on *4Q264a* (*4QHalakha A* or *4QWays of Righteousness*[c]?)," *RevQ* 19 (2000): 453–56. He also provides several corrections to Baumgarten's *editio princeps*.

5 Vered Noam and Elisha Qimron, "A Qumran Composition of Sabbath Laws and Its Contribution to the Study of Early Halakah," *DSD* 16 (2009): 55–96. They further suggest the existence of additional joins between the two manuscripts, even where textual overlap is not visible. For the text under consideration here – frg. 1 – Tigchelaar's observations are the most crucial because they provide the basis for the composite text. Noam and Qimron offer several suggestions for improved readings and restoring lacunae that will be noted in my discussion of the text. See also Baumgarten's posthumously published response to some of Noam's and Qimron's suggestions in Joseph M. Baumgarten, "A Proposed Re-interpretation of Qumran Shabbat Regulations," in *Zaphenath-Paneah: Linguistic Studies Presented to Elisha Qimron on the Occasion of His Sixty-Fifth Birthday* (ed. D. Sivan, D. Talshir, and C. Cohen; Beer-Sheva: Beer-Sheva University Press, 2009), 9*–13*.

6 The composite text presented here follows the preserved content in 4Q264a. Extant material from 4Q421 is presented in the brackets with overlining. Content in the brackets without underlining represents a suggested restoration based on the surrounding preserved content of 4Q264a or 4Q421.

7 As will be clear below, the inclusion of this word in the composite text is critical for a full understanding of the law. Its inclusion was first suggested based on its appearance in the textual overlap from 4Q421. The correctness of its placement here is now corroborated by the photograph (PAM 40.626) treated in Tigchelaar, "More on *4Q264a*," which preserves traces of the *pe*.

6 [. . . [8]אל ידבר[9]בכול דבר או[10] עבודה או בהון או במק[ח][11]
7 [. . . [12]]ביום המ[וחר]ת[13] ואל יד[בר ד]בר כי אם לדבר[י][14]
8 [קודש כחוק ויד]בר לברך אל אך ידבר [דבר][15] לאכול ולש[תות]

5. Let no man consider [with his]m[outh]
6. [. . . He shall not speak] about any matter of labor, or money, or buyin[g]
7. [. . .] on the next d[a]y. He shall not sp[eak wo]rds, except to tal[k of holy]
8. [things as is lawful, and to ut]ter blessings of God. Yet, he may speak a [word] (in order) to eat and to dr[ink]

[8] Noam and Qimron, "Qumran Composition," 57, restore here [לעשות חפצו בשבת], "[to pursue his affairs on the Sabbath]." See further below, n. 26.

[9] The text is reconstructed here following common sectarian Sabbath apodictic law (אל + jussive). The specific verb is suggested based on the parallel clause in CD 10:19 (as based on Isa 58:13). See Doering, "New Aspects," 254; Tigchelaar, "Sabbath Halakha," 367; Baumgarten, "4Q264a: 4QHalakha B," 55; Noam and Qimron, "Qumran Composition," 57.

[10] Reconstruction follows Noam and Qimron, "Qumran Composition," 57–58. Previous editions reconstruct בכול דברי עבודה.

[11] The restoration at the end of the line was first proposed by Tigchelaar based on the extant remains of]במק on PAM 40.626 ("More on *4Q264a*," 455). He also suggests the possibility of במק[נה, "about property." Noam and Qimron, "Qumran Composition," 57, reconstruct here במק]ח וממכר (following on to line 7). The most common other suggestion – בצע (based on CD 10:18) – is now regarded as unlikely based on the paleographical evidence (see Doering, *Schabbat*, 226; Tigchelaar, "Sabbath Halakha," 367; Florentino García Martínez and Eibert J. C. Tigchelaar, *The Dead Sea Scrolls Study Edition* [2 vols.; Leiden: Brill, 1997–98], 1:546).

[12] Noam and Qimron, "Qumran Composition," 57, restore in the lacuna: [לצאת לדרך], "traveling." Based on their reading of the extant material after the lacuna (see following note), this refers to traveling after the Sabbath. This specific prohibition does not have an exact parallel in the speech-related restrictions in CD 10:17–19, but Jub 50:8 does prohibit speaking about a post-Sabbath business trip (see Chapter 6, section II).

[13] This reconstruction follows Noam and Qimron, "Qumran Composition," 58–59. Previous editions restore here: ביום הש[ב]ת, "on the Sa[bba]th day" – presumably a reference to when the prohibited speech transpires. As observed by Noam and Qimron, the ink traces prior to the lacuna are better deciphered as a *mem*. This expression is thus parallel to למשכים ("the next morning") in CD 10:19 – i.e., it refers to the time in which the specific action that is being spoken about will take place, and therefore *4QHalakha B* similarly represents a general prohibition on verbal planning for post-Sabbath business or financial matters.

[14] דבר is clearly present on the photograph published by Tigchelaar ("More on *4Q264a*," 455), seemingly confirming the initial suggestion to restore here with the text from 4Q421: ל]דבר דברי קודש (Doering, *Schabbat*, 225; Tigchelaar, "Sabbath Halaka," 367; Baumgarten, "4Q264a: 4QHalakha B," 54). Yet, as noted by Tigchelaar, traces of the downstroke of a letter can be seen to the immediate left of the *reš* of לדבר. Thus, he suggests that the scribe either omitted the word space between לדבר and דברי or accidentally wrote לדברי. The latter suggestion works best with the presumed left-hand margin of the lines (so also Noam and Qimron, "Qumran Composition," 57).

[15] Restoration follows Tigchelaar, "Sabbath Halakhah," 368; García Martínez and Tigchelaar, *Dead Sea Scrolls Study Edition*, 1:546; Noam and Qimron, "Qumran Composition," 59. Noam and Qimron note that the manuscript has been distorted, thus reducing the space in the lacuna. Once the manuscript has been properly stretched out, the lacuna allows for this reconstruction based on Isa 58:13. Baumgarten, "4Q264a: 4QHalakha B," 54; and Doering, *Schabbat*, 225, do not reconstruct דבר.

III. ISAIAH 58:13 IN 4QHALAKHA B

The extant text in fragment 1, lines 5–8, contains several laws that restrict various forms of speech on the Sabbath.[16] Two general observations are important to note: (1) The legal content of this fragment contains significant textual and thematic overlap with the Sabbath law in CD 10:17–19, which similarly proscribes speech on the Sabbath. As in the *Damascus Document*, *4QHalakha B* forbids speech related to financial and business matters (ll. 6–7). *4QHalakha B*, however, extends this restriction to include even more types of prohibited speech that are not found in the *Damascus Document* (ll. 7–8).[17] (2) Another important similarity between the two texts is the pervasiveness of language from Isa 58:13. As in CD 10:17–19, *4QHalakha B* reuses the important keyword דבר in order to provide a legal-exegetical application of the enigmatic expression ודבר דבר, "Nor speak a word," in Isa 58:13. In so doing, *4QHalakha B* seeks to explain what types of words may actually not be spoken on the Sabbath. In lines 5–8, the keyword דבר from Isa 58:13 is employed in six preserved places and plausibly reconstructed in two or three additional places.

My treatment of this fragment seeks to examine the exegetical role of Isa 58:13 in these lines. This analysis simultaneously explores the literary relationship between the respective textual units of the *Damascus Document* and *4QHalakha B*. The fragmentary nature of *4QHalakha B* precludes any full-scale assessment of the literary and redactional relationship between *4QHalakha B* and the *Damascus Document* or their individual units. Yet, my analysis here, with its focus on the role of Isa 58:13 in each text, presents evidence to suggest that 4Q264a 1 i 5–8 represents a deliberate legal and exegetical reformulation of its corresponding material in the *Damascus Document*.[18]

4Q264a 1 i 5, CD 10:17–21, and the Absence of Isaiah 58:13

The section on speech in *4QHalakha B* clearly begins in the middle of line 5: אל יחשב איש [ב]פ[יהו], which I have translated here as "Let no man consider [with

[16] For treatment of the entire manuscript and its Sabbath laws in the broader context of ancient Sabbath legislation, see Noam and Qimron, "Qumran Composition," 55–96. The specific laws in fragment 1, lines 5–8, however, are only episodically examined by Noam and Qimron.

[17] See also Doering, *Schabbat*, 217–19, 225–27; Tigchelaar, "Sabbath Halakha," 366–67; Noam and Qimron, "Qumran Composition," 60–61.

[18] See the initial proposal in this direction voiced by Doering, "New Aspects," 256. 4Q264a is written in a Herodian hand, suggesting the possibility of a first-century BCE date of composition. See Charlesworth and Claussen, "Halakah B: 4Q264a," 286. The oldest copies of the *Damascus Document* are from the early first century BCE, thus suggesting that the text as a whole is somewhat earlier (see Joseph M. Baumgarten, "Damascus Document," *EDSS* 1:166–70). This suggested dating makes it possible that *4QHalakha B* represents a reformulation of content from the *Damascus Document*.

his]m[outh]."[19] The specific details of this law are highly elusive due to both the long lacuna that follows and the multiple possible meanings of the verb יחשב. My translation follows earlier scholars' reading of this verb as a *qal* form, thus meaning "to plan, consider, think of."[20]

The morpheme יחשב is a third-person masculine singular jussive verb from the root חשב. This form, however, can be interpreted in multiple ways: (1) *qal*, (2) *pi'el*, or (3) *niph'al*. The *niph'al* meaning ("to be regarded as, to be counted as") was originally proposed by Elgvin for the translation of the independent 4Q421 on account of cultic elements outlined elsewhere in the manuscript. The new context provided by the combined text of 4Q264a and 4Q421, however, makes this interpretation unlikely.[21] The *pi'el* meaning ("to calculate") represents one viable possibility.[22] Indeed, a parallel rabbinic law treated in the next chapter (*t. Shabb.* 17:9) likewise restricts the calculation of accounts on the Sabbath. Moreover, the broader setting for the rabbinic law is likewise the restriction of speech on the Sabbath.[23] The *qal* meaning ("to plan, consider, think of"), however, seems to provide the best fit for the wider context.[24] As a general introductory statement, this passage would likely draw upon the widest possible semantic range (*qal*), rather than one specific type of application (*pi'el*).

The formulation "Let no man consider [with his]m[outh]" is intended to articulate a general restriction on speech. In this sense, the opening passage in 4Q264a 1 i 5 mirrors the initially classificatory statement in CD 10:17–18 ("let no man speak a vile and empty word") – both introduce a series of laws that restrict certain types of speech on the Sabbath. Unlike CD 10:17–18, however, *4QHalakha B* employs an initial formulation that is both semantically unexpected and syntactically awkward. The odd word choice is rendered even odder by the failure to employ the common verbal root for speech – דבר – as found in Isa 58:13 and throughout the remainder of the following three lines.

[19] Lines 3–4, though fragmentary, clearly refer to restrictions on reading a scroll on the Sabbath (cf. 4Q251 1–2 5; see further Noam and Qimron, "Qumran Composition," 80–88). Note as well the suggestion of Tigchelaar, "Sabbath Halakha," 369, that all of 4Q264a 1 i 1–8 is concerned with speech on the Sabbath. While lines 1–5 deal with appropriate speech on the Sabbath (e.g., prayer), lines 5–8 are specifically focused on prohibited speech. This proposal, not taken up by later scholarship on the text, deserves more careful consideration as a possible way to understand the organizing principle of the fragment.

[20] Discussion of the various possible interpretations of this word is found in Doering, "New Aspects," 252–54; idem, *Schabbat*, 225–27 (see also Tigchelaar, "Sabbath Halakha," 366–67; Baumgarten, "4Q264a: 4QHalakha B," 54; Noam and Qimron, "Qumran Composition," 59).

[21] See Doering, "New Aspects," 252 n. 9. It is not discussed in idem, *Schabbat*, 225–27.

[22] So Charlesworth and Claussen, "Halakah B: 4Q264a," 289: "Let no man count."

[23] See further Doering, "New Aspects," 252–53; idem, *Schabbat*, 226.

[24] Doering, "New Aspects," 253; idem, *Schabbat*, 225–26; Tigchelaar, "Sabbath Halakha," 366–67; García Martínez and Tigchelaar, *Dead Sea Scrolls Study Edition*, 1:547; Baumgarten, "4Q264a: 4QHalakha B," 54; Noam and Qimron, "Qumran Composition," 59.

In the combination of בפה + חשב, the preposition *bet* likely functions as a location marker for the verbal action. Common biblical Hebrew idiom, however, would normally locate the heart as the physical location of thought. Indeed, the root חשב appears several times with a prepositional clause beginning with *bet*, where the prepositional clause identifies the heart as the locus of internal consideration.[25] The construction that appears in *4QHalakha B* therefore indicates that one's initial mentally formulated thoughts are verbally articulated through speech. The formal language employed in *4QHalakha B* presents two related questions. First, why does the text employ such a cumbersome and syntactically unexpected construction to indicate speech? Second, if indeed this law parallels the related Sabbath law in CD 10:17–19, why does it not also draw upon the language of Isa 58:13, with its far more logical verbal root דבר, which is employed later in *4QHalakha B* with clear dependency on Isa 58:13? As observed above, the keyword דבר from Isa 58:13 appears in lines 6–8 anywhere between six and nine times – but not in the precise location where it makes the most semantic, structural, and exegetical sense!

The answer to both of these questions is related. *4QHalakha B* is indeed parallel to the laws regarding speech in CD 10:17–19. But, we must also consider this passage in light of the law that follows in CD 10:20–21. In Chapter 7, I examine the reformulation of Isa 58:13 in CD 10:20–21 at length and argue that this passage restricts travel through a field on the Sabbath in order to assess its needs (which will be performed after the Sabbath). Not all thoughts, however, are prohibited in the *Damascus Document*. Rather, the specific case of planning for future work in the field – perhaps indicating more generally planning for future business-related labor – is outlined. In the *Damascus Document*, this law is presented as the natural next step after the restriction on speech related to future business or financial affairs in CD 10:17–19. CD 10:20–21 provides a setting in which not only speech but even thoughts about prohibited labor are forbidden. *4QHalakha B*, however, expounds upon the underlying legal principle in the *Damascus Document* by asserting its own position on the law regarding thoughts about labor on the Sabbath. The specific case of the individual in the field is not found in the preserved text of *4QHalakha B*, though the highly fragmentary nature of the manuscript suggests that much of its content is missing.[26] In all likelihood, *4QHalakha B* would agree with the legal position of the *Damascus Document* because the rest of its preserved content in this fragment is more stringent than the related laws in the *Damascus Document*. More generally, however, *4QHalakha B* does seem to weigh in

[25] See Zech 7:10; 8:17; Ps 140:3; Prov 19:21; Sir 12:16 (cf. Prov 17:9).

[26] See, however, the reconstruction of lines 5–6 found in Noam and Qimron, "Qumran Composition," 57–59: אל יחשב איש [ב]פ[יהו לעשות חפצו בשבת, "No one shall reckon [with his] m[outh to pursue his affairs on the Sabbath" (see above, n. 8). This reconstruction is clearly motivated by the desire to see further correspondence with CD 10:20–21.

on the larger question of whether thoughts about labor are prohibited on the Sabbath.

The semantic representation of speech as "verbally articulated thought" suggests that the author of *4QHalakha B* has employed very deliberate language in order to reject implicitly the opposite legal position. Thus, mental consideration (חשב) is in fact forbidden – however, only when it progresses into formal speech (בפיהו). *4QHalakha B* has modified the physical locus of the mental consideration such that it is now not only an internal thought process but also formally articulated speech. Moreover, 4Q264a 1 i 5 avoids any use of language from Isa 58:13 in order to affirm the legal and exegetical limitations of the scriptural verse. While CD 10:20–21 reformulates Isa 58:13 to restrict thoughts about labor in one's field, 4Q264a 1 i 5 avoids all language from Isa 58:13 in order to assert that this scriptural passage cannot be extended to include a general restriction on thoughts on the Sabbath.

In broader structural perspective, 4Q264a 1 i 5 must be understood as related both to the initial classificatory statement restricting speech in CD 10:17–18 and to the specific case in which thoughts about labor are prohibited in CD 10:20–21. 4Q264a 1 i 5 mirrors CD 10:17–18 by providing an opening statement outlining the section that follows as a set of restrictions related to speech on the Sabbath. CD 10:17–18 draws on language from Isa 58:13 to assert that not all speech is prohibited, but rather only speech with "vile and empty" content – understood in CD 10:18–19 as speech related to business or financial matters. Similarly, 4Q264a 1 i 5 asserts that the unit that follows likewise presents a range of circumstances in which speech is prohibited. In contrast to CD 10:17–18, the initial statement in *4QHalakha B* is not as descriptive as its counterpart in the *Damascus Document*.

At the same time, the specific language employed in 4Q264a 1 i 5 and the non-use of Isa 58:13 are intended to be read in concert with the final law in the combined unit of CD 10:17–19 and CD 10:20–21. More specifically, it seeks to limit the potential implication of the related law in CD 10:20–21. Structurally, 4Q264a 1 i 5 mirrors the initial clause in the *Damascus Document*'s legal-exegetical amplification of Isa 58:13 in CD 10:17–21 at the same time as it inverts the literary structure of the broader set of laws in CD 10:17–21.

4Q264a 1 i 6–7, CD 10:18–19, and Isaiah 58:13

Lines 6–7 of *4QHalakha B*, as with line 5, closely parallel the *Damascus Document*'s Sabbath laws discussed above. In examining this passage, several questions present themselves. First, how should the various lacunae in the fragmentary 4Q264a 1 i 6–7 be reconstructed? Second, how do we understand the relationship between this passage and the seemingly parallel material in CD 10:18–19? In particular, 4Q264a 1 i 6–7 displays close textual and thematic parallels with the third law related to proscribed speech in CD 10:19 (עבודה, "labor"). Yet, additional content is parallel to the second law in CD 10:18

(הון, "money"). What significance should be assigned to this double parallelism? Third, what is the exegetical relationship between Isa 58:13 and 4Q264a 1 i 6–7? Moreover, how should this exegetical relationship be understood in the broader context of the closely related – but subtly different – use of Isa 58:13 in the overlapping material in CD 10:18–19?

Based on the extant text in *4QHalakha B*, this passage proscribes the general articulation of speech related to one's future financial affairs and describes specific circumstances in which such proscribed speech might occur. The fragmentary lines 6–7 contain examples of cases of the general proscription articulated in line 5 (אל יחשב איש [ב]פ[יהו], "Let no man consider [with his]m[outh]") and reiterated at the beginning of line 6 (אל ידבר] בכול דבר, "He shall not speak] about any matter . . . "). *4QHalakha B* clearly prohibits communication regarding labor (עבודה) and money (הון). The list of proscribed topics in *4QHalakha B* is followed by an additional "or" (או) and traces of what is most plausibly reconstructed as במק[ח], "buyin[g]."[27]

Following the lacuna in line 7, Noam and Qimron restore ביום המ[וחר]ת, "On the next d[a]y."[28] Unfortunately, the preceding lacuna makes it difficult to contextualize the precise legal application of this expression. In light of the textual and thematic parallels with CD 10:18–19 – the third law in CD 10:19 in particular – it is likely that this expression merely is parallel to למשכים ("the next morning") in CD 10:19. As in CD 10:19, it functions as part of a broader prohibition on verbal planning for post-Sabbath business or financial matters. In this sense, it is not clear if the temporal qualifier should be applied to all of the items listed in lines 6–7 (i.e., one may not speak about labor – עבודה, wealth – הון, buying – מקח), or merely the final item(s) now lost in the lacuna of line 7. The answer to this question is both found in closer examination of the relationship between *4QHalakha B* and CD 10:18–19 and complicated by this very analysis.

As in CD 10:18–19, 4Q264a 1 i 6–7 proscribes the general articulation of speech related to one's future financial affairs and describes specific circumstances in which such proscribed speech might occur. Moreover, both passages draw heavily upon the language of Isa 58:13. Though these similarities indicate that CD 10:18–19 and 4Q264a i 6–7 contain overlapping Sabbath legislation, several significant differences exist. Table 3 outlines the literary relationship between the two texts and the shared dependence on Isa 58:13 (identified by the single underlining; correspondence between the two texts is marked by other types of underlining).

The bulk of the literary correspondence is with CD 10:19. As discussed above, CD 10:19 specifically restricts any articulation of speech that concerns

27 See above, n. 11. The length of the lacuna would allow for the possibility of even a fourth item, for which Noam and Qimron suggest [או לצאת לדרך], "or traveling."

28 Contra the previous reconstruction ביום הש[ב]ת. See above, n. 13.

TABLE 3. *Isa 58:13 and CD 10:19 and 4Q264a 1 i 6–7*

CD 10:18–19	4Q264a 1 i 6–7
18 אל ישפוט על הון ובצע He shall not enter into a dispute concerning money or profit 19 אל ידבר בדברי המלאכה והעבודה לעשות למשכים He shall not speak about matters relating to work and labor that need to be done on the following day.	אל ידבר]בכול דבר או עבודה או בהון או במק[ח . . .] ביום המ[וחר]ת He shall not speak] about any matter of labor, or money, or buyin[g . . .] on the next d[a]y.

work that will be undertaken in the coming week. Though 4Q264a 1 i 6–7 employs slightly different language to represent the post-Sabbath temporal context (CD: משכים // *4QHalakha B*: ביום המ[וחר]ת), both are concerned with speech on the Sabbath regarding post-Sabbath business or financial undertakings. As discussed above, in formulating this aspect of the law, the *Damascus Document* engages in two legal-exegetical applications of Isa 58:13. First, CD 10:19 transforms the twofold use of the keyword דבר from *Isaiah* (infinitive + object) into a negative prohibition:

> *Isaiah*: ודבר דבר, "Nor speak a word" → CD: אל ידבר בדברי, "He shall not speak about matters . . . "

In the *Damascus Document*, however, the precise meaning and legal application of the second דבר are provided through its transformation into the first part of a larger construct clause (. . . דברי, "matters relating to . . . "). As in the larger clause in CD 10:17–19, the remaining elements of the construct clause in CD 10:19 provide practical meaning for the elusive דבר of Isa 58:13. Second, CD 10:19 draws upon the keyword עשה ("to perform") from Isa 58:13 in order to generate explicit language for types of actions about which one may not speak on the Sabbath. The keyword עשה provides an intertextual link with the Sabbath law in the Decalogue, thereby identifying מלאכה and עבודה as the specific actions about which speech is forbidden.

4QHalakha B engages in a closely related set of legal-exegetical re-applications of Isa 58:13 in order to generate a similar set of Sabbath restrictions. As in CD 10:19, *4QHalakha B* attempts to provide a fuller context for the proscribed speech (דבר) in Isa 58:13. As in the *Damascus Document*, *4QHalakha B* retains the twofold use of דבר in Isa 58:13 as both verb and object, though similarly transformed into a negative prohibition:

> *Isaiah*: ודבר דבר, "Nor speak a word" → *4QHalakha B*: אל ידבר]בכול דבר, "He shall not speak] about any matters . . . "

Rather than create a larger construct phrase, however, *4QHalakha B* follows the enigmatic דבר with a serial או... או... או (either X or Y or Z) clause. As in the *Damascus Document*'s construct clause, the specific elements in the list represent the issues about which one may not speak on the Sabbath.

The most significant difference between CD 10:19 and *4QHalakha B* is the specific items on the list, with regard to both their exegetical relationship to Isa 58:13 and the range of practical legal application.[29] Of the two fully preserved elements in the list, one finds correspondence in the second law in CD 10:18 (הון, "money"), while the other is found exclusively in the third law in CD 10:19 (עבודה, "labor"). A third element ([מק[ח) does not parallel the language of the *Damascus Document* at all. Moreover, the temporal designator (ביום המ[וחר]ת, "On the next day") is likewise parallel to the similar expression in CD 10:19. In this sense, 4Q264a 1 i 6–7 looks most like a close reformulation of CD 10:19, with content from CD 10:18 interpolated alongside new material. If indeed this is correct, then we must also explain the modified exegetical reuse of Isa 58:13. While both CD 10:19 and *4QHalakha B* seek to provide fuller meaning for the enigmatic דבר in Isa 58:13, the latter adds two specific elements not found in the related content in the *Damascus Document*: (1) the inclusion of כול ("any") prior to דבר, and (2) the use of the serial או... או... או (either X or Y or Z) construction, rather than the much more common amplifying construct clause.

The best explanation for both the exegetical context and legal formulation in *4QHalakha B* is to view the passage in *4QHalakha B* as not exegetically linked directly to Isa 58:13. Rather, it functions as a legal reformulation of the related passage in the *Damascus Document*. As observed by Doering, מלאכה in CD 10:19 is a general designation for proscribed work on the Sabbath (as found in CD 10:15), while עבודה and הון represent specific aspects of prohibited Sabbath labor.[30] As discussed above, עבודה likely alludes to physical labor, while הון indicates general financial dealings. As I suggested above, the inclusion of מלאכה in CD 10:19 is intended to proscribe speech regarding general post-Sabbath work, while עבודה has in view specifically physical labor involved in one's financial livelihood. In this sense, the conflation of עבודה and הון in *4QHalakha B* removes any potential ambiguity regarding the practical application of עבודה in CD 10:19. Moreover, *4QHalakha B* is likely responding to several lingering questions in the combined law of CD 10:18–19. The second law in CD 10:18 prohibits engaging in disputes regarding money or profit. The third law in CD 10:19 forbids engaging in discussion of future labor. What about discussion of הון or בצע that will transpire in the coming week? What about more general discussion of מלאבה or עבודה not necessarily tied to events that will unfold in the coming week? In other words, the individual laws found in CD 10:18 and CD 10:19 allow for sufficient legal ambiguity, to which *4QHalakha B* responds.

[29] See also Doering, "New Aspects," 254–55; idem, *Schabbat*, 225–27.

[30] Doering, "New Aspects," 255; idem, *Schabbat*, 225.

The specific nature of the response is embedded in the manner in which 4Q264a 1 i 6–7 modifies the exegetical reformulation of Isa 58:13 in CD 10:18–19 and the associated list of items. As in the *Damascus Document*, *4QHalakha B* transforms ודבר דבר from Isa 58:13 into a negative prohibition. *4QHalakha B*, however, adds the significant quantifier כול ("any") in order to qualify the nature of the prohibited word:

> CD: אל ידבר בדברי, "He shall not speak about matters" → *4QHalakha B*: [אל ידבר] בכול דבר, "He shall not speak] about any matters."

4Q264a 1 i 6–7 does not intend that all words are prohibited, but rather all words that are included under the general headings of proscribed business and financial speech fall under the aegis of this law. The broad range of this law is then reinforced by the serial או . . . או . . . או construction that follows, which carries an epexegetical function for דבר.[31] Rather than closely follow the construct clause of CD 10:19, *4QHalakha B* opens up the situational possibilities by including an expansive set of circumstances.[32] Indeed, the further inclusion of מק[ח], "buying" – not found in the *Damascus Document* – reinforces the sense that *4QHalakha B* is attempting to expand the parameters of the restrictions on business-related speech as articulated in CD 10:18–19 to closely related cases.

The first two examples, as previously noted, draw from both the second and third laws in the *Damascus Document*. These two specific elements employed are inverted from their original context. The first item in the list of *4QHalakha B* is עבודה as drawn from CD 10:19, while the second aspect is הון as found in CD 10:18. Literary inversion is a common technique in scriptural and Second Temple Jewish literature that draws upon and reorients the meaning and application of the target text.[33] In *4QHalakha B*, the literary inversion both calls attention to the reuse of CD 10:18–19 in *4QHalakha B* and affirms the legal

[31] A similar construction can be found in the *Temple Scroll*'s subtle linguistic-exegetical reformulation of Deut 17:13: Deut: וילך ויעבד אלהים אחרים וישתחו להם ולשמש או לירח או לכל־צבא השמים, "By going to serve other gods and worshiping them – whether the sun or the moon or any of the host of heaven" (NRSV) → 11QT^{a} 55:17–18: הלך ועבד אלוהים אחרים וההשתחוה להמה או לשמש או לירח או לכול צבא השמים, "(A man or woman who does what I consider evil, transgressing my covenant in) going to serve other gods, worshiping them – whether sun, moon, or any of the host of heaven." In *Deuteronomy*, the celestial entities represent possible objects of worship and thus serve as practical possibilities for the object להם. This is undoubtedly the correct interpretation of the clause. Yet, the prefixed *waw* and preposition *lamed* on the first item in the list (ולשמש) make the entire construction syntactically cumbersome and potentially difficult to discern. The *Temple Scroll* removes any ambiguity by employing the serial או construction as explicitly epexegetical for להמה.

[32] For more general expansive lists employing the serial או, see 1QS 5:25–26; 1QSa 2:5–6; 1QM 7:4; 4Q266 8 i 8; 11QT^{a} 50:6; 52:10; 54:19–20.

[33] On the exegetical technique of literary inversion (commonly known as "Zeidel's law"), see bibliography, Chapter 4, n. 50.

reformulation of the former in the latter. With this technique, *4QHalakha B* implicitly asserts that all the situations contained in the two sets of laws in CD 10:18–19 are in view in the more precise and systematic outline of types of prohibited Sabbath work about which one is similarly forbidden to speak.

4Q264a 1 i 7–8, CD 10:17–18, and Isaiah 58:13

The final two lines of this passage restrict conversation of a nonsacred and nonessential manner. As in the preceding content, these two lines partially parallel CD 10:17–19.[34] The mere presence of a law prohibiting all nonsacred and nonessential speech at the end of this literary unit is perplexing. If lines 7–8 prohibit all nonessential speech, would not the proscribed business and financial speech in lines 6–7 also be included? Accordingly, the more restrictive law found in lines 7–8 is almost certainly a secondary legal formulation. More specifically, it represents a secondary legal application of the closely related Sabbath laws in CD 10:17–19.

4Q264a 1 i 5–7 reformulates the extant Sabbath law in CD 10:17–19. As such, it preserves and subtly rewrites the limited range of restricted types of speech on the Sabbath (i.e., business- or finance-related matters). It then extends the entire legal and exegetical foundation of CD 10:17–19 to its logical conclusion: not only is business- or finance-related speech prohibited on the Sabbath, but all nonsacred speech is likewise restricted. In so doing, *4QHalakha B* draws on some of the very same exegetical principles operating in CD 10:17–19 with regard to its legal-exegetical application of Isa 58:13. Moreover, *4QHalakha B* applies some of these identical techniques to its own reformulation of CD 10:17–19. Accordingly, *4QHalakha B* harnesses the authority of Isa 58:13 and the *Damascus Document* in its legal-exegetical amplification of both texts.

The first clause articulates a general legal principle that one may not speak (i.e., on the Sabbath) except for "holy matters" (ואל יד]בר ד[בר כי אם ל[דברי קודש כחוק; ll. 7–8). Line 8 proceeds to provide an example of such "holy" speech; one may bless God (i.e., prayer) (ויד]בר לברך אל, "ut]ter blessings of God").[35] The text continues with an additional exception to the general legal principle. One may also engage in conversation that is specifically for the purpose of eating and drinking (אך ידבר [דבר] לאכול ולש[תות, "Yet, he may speak a [word] (in order) to eat and to dr[ink]"). This may relate either to the process of preparing the food or to the time of the meal. That this particular exception is introduced with the particle אך ("yet") indicates that speech related to food and

[34] See general treatment in Doering, "New Aspects," 255–56; idem, *Schabbat*, 226–27; Baumgarten, "4Q264a: 4QHalakha B," 55; Noam and Qimron, "Qumran Composition," 60.

[35] As noted by Doering, prayer in the Dead Sea Scrolls is heavily doxological in form, and therefore the reference to blessing God most likely indicates formal prayer ("New Aspects," 255; idem, *Schabbat*, 227).

drink is not considered an additional "holy" exception.[36] Rather, such speech is permitted presumably for practical purposes and therefore forms its own exception.[37]

This entire legal clause contains a general legal principle followed by two exceptions. The first of the exceptions follows very closely the general principle. Because prayer is "holy" speech, it is permitted. The second exception does not fall under the "holy" exemption. Speech related to food and drink is exempted from this law for purely practical purposes. Following the general legal principle, *4QHalakha B* would have likely also permitted other examples of "holy" speech on the Sabbath (e.g., Torah study). It is not clear, however, whether the exemption for practical purposes would have been extended to additional comparable cases.

The saturation of this clause with the root דבר suggests that this law is deliberately drawing upon the language of Isa 58:13 and therefore offering an additional explication of the legal meaning of the scriptural expression ודבר דבר and its implications for Sabbath observance.[38] As noted earlier, commentators have long observed that the expression ודבר דבר cannot refer to a complete rejection of speech on the Sabbath. Thus, ancient readers of scripture offered their own interpretations through the application of various exegetical and rewriting techniques.

In 4Q264a 1 i 7, the ambiguous scriptural clause ודבר דבר is reformulated as a negative prohibition (*Isaiah*: ודבר דבר → *4QHalakha B*: ואל יד]בר ד[בר). This same technique was observed for the exegetical reformulation of Isa 58:13 in the *Damascus Document* and elsewhere in *4QHalakha B*. Yet, in those cases, the reformulated text was amplified through the creation of broader construct clauses or serial או clauses that include examples of specific types of condemned words (as also in the Targum). 4Q264a 1 i 7, in contrast, lets the reformulated negative prohibition stand alone. By not following the other exegetical models for reformulating Isa 58:13, *4QHalakha B* employs explicit legal language to make Isa 58:13 say exactly what commentators argue that it must not be saying – speech on the Sabbath is indeed forbidden.

4QHalakha B inverts the widespread exegetical technique not to provide specific examples of proscribed speech but rather to furnish exceptions to the

[36] See Exod 12:16 for a similar formulation on a festival (Baumgarten, "4Q264a: 4QHalakha B," 55).

[37] As further noted by Doering, eating and drinking constitute central aspects of the observance of the Sabbath and therefore engendered such legal liberties ("New Aspects," 266; idem, *Schabbat*, 227). Note as well that 4Q264a, frgs. 2–3 open with the expression]תענוג בי[ום שבת. Though it is not clear how close this expression would have been located to lines 7–8 of frg. 1 (Baumgarten identifies them as different columns), the former may serve as an explanation for the exception in the latter.

[38] Based on the reconstruction provided above, six (possibly seven – see n. 14) out of the sixteen words in this clause are derivatives of the root דבר (37.5 percent).

universal restriction on speech. In these exceptions, the root from *Isaiah* (דבר) is further employed in order to indicate that these very exceptions are likewise implicit in *Isaiah*'s original Sabbath restriction:

> *general restriction*: ואל יד]בר ד[בר, "He shall not sp[eak wo]rds"; *general exception*: כי אם לדבר]י קודש כחוק[, "Except to tal[k of holy things as is lawful]"; *specific exception 1*:]ויד[בר לברך, "[And to ut]ter blessings of God"; *specific exception 2*: אך ידבר]דבר[לאכול ולש]תות[, "Yet, he may speak a [word] (in order) to eat and to dr[ink]."

Both the general restriction and the exceptions are written in order to appear as the precise application of Isa 58:13 ודבר דבר. In reformulating Isa 58:13 in this way, *4QHalakha B* has added a new voice to the cacophony of ancient and modern interpretations of the elusive meaning of ודבר דבר. Nonsacred and nonessential speech is forbidden on the Sabbath.

One final point must be discussed – the relationship of the law in 4Q264a 1 i 7–8 to CD 10:17–18. In the earlier discussion of CD 10:17–19, I argued that the expression אל ידבר איש דבר נבל ורק in CD 10:17–18 is not a general prohibition on idle or profane speech on the Sabbath, as suggested by several scholars. Rather, this clause functions only as a general classificatory designation for the laws that follow. Speech about business-related matters on the Sabbath is the specific type of profane speech that is proscribed in the *Damascus Document*. In contrast, *4QHalakha B* offers a far more expansive understanding of the Sabbath speech restrictions by taking the implications of CD 10:17–19 to their logical conclusions. While the *Damascus Document* only condemns business-related speech, *4QHalakha B* extends this restriction to all nonsacred and nonessential conversation.

The reformulation of the initial classificatory statement in CD 10:17–18 is reinforced by the inversion of the very exegetical techniques operating in the *Damascus Document*. As noted above, the *Damascus Document* expands the meaning of the דבר from *Isaiah* with additional words (נבל ורק) and three specific legal cases. In contrast, the close reformulation of Isa 58:13 in *4QHalakha B* (ואל יד]בר ד[בר) effectively erases the force of the modifying words in the *Damascus Document* as the correct meaning of Isa 58:13 (*4QHalakha B*: ואל יד]בר ד[בר = CD: אל ידבר איש דבר ~~נבל ורק~~). As such, the specific cases further outlined in CD 10:17–19 do not serve as the correct amplification of the broader legal application of Isa 58:13. Rather, the initial classificatory statement in *4QHalakha B* is now followed by its own set of specific exceptional cases cast in the context of the new legal and exegetical understanding of Isa 58:13.

This observation reinforces my suggestion made above that 4Q264a 1 i 7–8 is a secondary legal formulation. The exceptional cases in lines 7–8 serve to undo the legal and exegetical force of the three specific cases in CD 10:18–19 as the practical application of the initial classificatory statement in CD 10:17–18. Yet, these very cases are explicitly and implicitly in view in the earlier lines of *4QHalakha B*! Thus, it seems likely that 4Q264a 1 i 5–7 has preserved faithfully a set of laws that are intended to parallel very closely the similar Sabbath laws in CD 10:17–19. The law in lines 7–8, therefore, is an additional law that is unique to *4QHalakha B* and formulated as a coda to the set of speech-related restrictions drawn from the *Damascus Document*.

IV. CONCLUSIONS

Chapters 4 and 5 have focused on two texts from among the Dead Sea Scrolls – the *Damascus Document* (CD 10:17–19) and *4QHalakha B* (4Q264a 1 i 5–8) – and their exegetical reformulation of Isa 58:13. Both texts draw on exegesis of Isa 58:13 in order to articulate a formalized set of Sabbath restrictions related to speech. Both texts recognize the inherent – no doubt intended – ambiguity in the prophetic condemnation of Sabbath violation in Isa 58:13. The evasive language of Isa 58:13 provided a rich body of exegetical material to work with as later Jewish readers of scripture sought to establish the parameters of Sabbath observance and ground their innovations in authoritative scripture. The language of Isa 58:13 both invited and demanded the legal-exegetical intrusion and transformation of the meaning of this text at the hands of ancient exegetes. My analysis of the legal and exegetical appropriation of Isa 58:13 in the *Damascus Document* and *4QHalakha B* provides a window into this transformative process. For these ancient readers, Isa 58:13 no longer represented a vague prophetic invective against Israelite violation of the Sabbath. Rather, it came to constitute the scriptural statement for the Jewish law restricting a range of speech on the Sabbath.

In these chapters, I have explored the ancient reading and reformulation of the enigmatic expression ודבר דבר, "Nor speak a word," at the end of Isa 58:13. The *Damascus Document* and *4QHalakha B* share a general legal and exegetical assumption: ודבר דבר does not proscribe all forms of speech but rather has a limited application. The evidence from the Septuagint and the Targum indicates that the conceptual framework and the exegetical enterprise of the *Damascus Document* and *4QHalakha B* are part of a much broader attempt to infuse meaning and practical legal application into the unclear scriptural language. Even as the legal and exegetical agendas of the texts explored in this chapter diverge, they overlap with regard to several exegetical techniques and legal formulations.

In the *Damascus Document*, the general assumption that ודבר דבר does not condemn all speech is underscored by the initial classificatory statement in CD 10:17–18, which asserts that only "vile and empty" content is prohibited. This is then followed by three specific examples of such forbidden speech. In all three laws, the specific condemned action is speech that is related to financial or business matters. My analysis of the exegetical and structural basis of CD 10:17–19 underscores the central role of Isa 58:13 in the formulation of these Sabbath laws in the *Damascus Document*. The passage in the *Damascus*

Document begins with an interpretation of the legal application of Isa 58:13. The three laws in the *Damascus Document* provide specific applications of the unclear Sabbath proscription in Isa 58:13. The language of Isa 58:13 is pervasive, in both explicit reformulation and intertextual allusion. In all cases, the *Damascus Document* recognizes the semantic ambiguity of ודבר דבר and related content in Isa 58:13 and exploits it to develop its own understanding of what exactly cannot be spoken. In so doing, the *Damascus Document* identifies Isa 58:13 as foundational for the exegetical, structural, and legal content of CD 10:17–19.

My analysis of *4QHalakha B* demonstrates its significant exegetical dependence on Isa 58:13 and close textual and thematic links to CD 10:17–21. These texts are more than mere parallel formulations of sectarian Sabbath law. Rather, *4QHalakha B* represents a deliberate reformulation of the legal and exegetical foundations of the corresponding Sabbath law in the *Damascus Document*. CD 10:17–21 contains two primary sets of Sabbath law: restrictions on business-related speech (ll. 17–19) and mental consideration of work on the Sabbath (ll. 20–21). Both of these two larger legal categories and their specific legal elements are reformulated in *4QHalakha B*. This reformulation is guided by a desire to clarify ambiguities in CD 10:17–21, and both limit and expand the contours of the *Damascus Document*'s Sabbath law.

4QHalakha B "engages" CD 10:17–21 in two overarching ways. First, just as Isa 58:13 is pervasive in the *Damascus Document* as the scriptural foundation of the Sabbath law, this same scriptural verse constitutes the legal and exegetical thread throughout 4Q264a 1 i 5–8 (indeed, even when it is absent, as in line 5). Second, the entire structure of 4Q264a 1 i 5–8 represents a literary and structural inversion of the legal content in CD 10:17–21, as outlined in Table 4.

The first clause in *4QHalakha B*, [E'] אל יחשב איש בפיהו, represents a double structural modification of the corresponding content in CD 10:17–21. As noted above, the first clause in *4QHalakha B* should be regarded as closely related to the final law in the *Damascus Document* (CD 10:20–21 [E]). While CD 10:20–21 restricts thoughts on the Sabbath in a limited context, *4QHalakha B* offers its own statement on the broader legal theory underlying the law in the *Damascus Document*. The identification of speech as "verbally articulated thought" dispels any notion that thought is restricted on the Sabbath in a general sense. The avoidance of any trace of exegetical dependence on Isa 58:13 – as is found in the parallel passage in CD 10:20–21 – reinforces the position that Isa 58:13 cannot be extended beyond speech to include the restriction on thoughts. At the same time, the formulation in *4QHalakha B* fulfills much the same function as the initial classificatory statement in CD 10:17–18 – notwithstanding the lack of exegetical dependence on Isa 58:13. As with CD 10:17–18, 4Q264a 1 i 5 functions as an initial legal statement articulating the general principle that certain types of speech are forbidden on the Sabbath. As

TABLE 4. *The Literary Inversion of CD 10:17–21 in 4Q264a 1 i 5–8*

CD 10:17–21	4Q264a 1 i 5–8
[A] (17) וביום השבת אל ידבר איש דבר (18) נבל ורק [A] (17) And on the Sabbath, let no man speak (18) a vile and empty word	[E'] (5) אל יחשב איש ב]פ[יהו [E'] (5) Let no man consider [with his]m[outh]
[B] אל ישה ברעהו כל [B] He shall not demand any payment from his fellow	[D'] (6) [. . . אל ידבר]בכול דבר או עבודה [D'] (6) [. . . He shall not speak] about any matter of labor
[C] אל ישפוט על הון ובצע [C] He shall not enter into a dispute concerning money or profit	[C'] או בהון או במק[ח] (7) [. . .]ביום המ[וחר]ת [C'] or money, or buyin[g] (7) [. . .] on the next d[a]y
[D] (19) אל ידבר בדברי המלאכה והעבודה לעשות למשכים [D] (19) He shall not speak about matters relating to work and labor that need to be done on the following morning.	[E'] ואל יד[בר ד]בר כי אם ל[דברי (8) קודש כחוק ויד]בר לברך אל אך ידבר [דבר] לאכול ולש[תות] [E'] He shall not sp[eak wo]rds, except to [talk of holy things as is lawful, and to ut]ter (8) blessings of God. Yet, he may speak a [word] (in order) to eat and to dr[ink]
[E] (20) אל יתהלך איש בשדה לעשות את עבודת חפצו (21) <ביום> השבת [E] (20) He shall not walk in the field in order to do his desired labor (20) <on> the Sabbath <day>.	

in the *Damascus Document*, the initial statement is then followed by specific examples.

The double structural modification in *4QHalakha B* serves several important functions. First, as in the corresponding unit in the *Damascus Document*, the initial clause in 4Q264a 1 i 5 frames the content that follows as the amplification and clarification of the parameters of the Sabbath law restricting speech. Second, by diverging from the language of Isa 58:13 to reject the general prohibition on thoughts, *4QHalakha B* not so subtly asserts that there are clear limits to the restrictions on speech and thoughts. The legal, exegetical, and structural modification of the *Damascus Document* that opens this unit in *4QHalakha B* clues the reader into the further reformulation of the *Damascus Document* that follows in the following lines of *4QHalakha B*.

The next unit in *4QHalakha B* [ll. 6–7 = D' + C'] provides the first set of examples of restricted speech on the Sabbath, following the structural model of CD 10:18–19 [B–D]. More specifically, as noted above, this unit of *4QHalakha B* is actually made up of at least two subunits that conflate the second and third laws in CD 10:18–19 [C–D]. Moreover, the keywords from these two laws in the *Damascus Document* are inverted in the new literary formulation in *4QHalakha B* (C → C': הון; D → D': עבודה).[39]

The final unit in *4QHalakha B* [A'] likewise represents a structural reformulation of corresponding content in the *Damascus Document* [A]. As noted above, *4QHalakha B* takes the opening statement in CD 10:17–18 to its fullest implications. The restriction on "vile and empty" words is not limited to business-related speech but rather is expanded to all nonsacred and nonessential speech. Moreover, as observed above, the exegetical modification of Isa 58:13 in the final clause of *4QHalakha B* mimics the exegetical technique of the reformulation of Isa 58:13 in CD 10:17–18, even as it makes the legal force of the scriptural verse dramatically different.

The structural, legal, and exegetical modification of CD 10:17–21 in *4QHalakha B* has a potent cumulative effect. Through its subtle reformulation of CD 10:17–21, *4QHalakha B* modifies and updates the corresponding Sabbath law in the *Damascus Document*. There are actually two different levels of reformulation operating in *4QHalakha B*. At one level, it reformulates CD 10:17–21 in much the same way that the *Damascus Document* and related texts rewrite their own scriptural base texts (e.g., literary inversion = Zeidel's law). At the same time, *4QHalakha B* engages in its own legal-exegetical reformulation of Isa 58:13. Yet, even here, the methods and techniques mirror the exegetical relationship of CD 10:17–21 to Isa 58:13. Again, the point is clear. Not only does *4QHalakha B* represent an "updated" version of the content in CD 10:17–21, but it simultaneously authorizes this new formulation through reframing the meaning of the very scriptural text that underpins CD 10:17–21.

39 Note that the first law in CD 10:18 [B] is not reformulated in *4QHalakha B*, though possibly could be represented in some way in the lacuna.

6

Isaiah 58:13 and the Sabbath Prohibition on Speech in the Book of *Jubilees* and Rabbinic Literature

I. INTRODUCTION

The preceding two chapters examined a range of restrictions on speech on the Sabbath in the sectarian Dead Sea Scrolls. While both the *Damascus Document* and *4QHalakha B* focus their attention on speech directly related to one's business or financial affairs, the latter extends this law to include all nonsacred and nonessential speech on the Sabbath. Moreover, I explored the exegetical interplay with Isa 58:13 in both these texts. The restriction on different types of speech on the Sabbath in the *Damascus Document* and *4QHalakha B* is grounded in a legal-exegetical reformulation of Isa 58:13.

The Sabbath law and exegetical techniques in the Dead Sea Scrolls do not stand in isolation. Rather, one of the major assumptions of this book is that Jewish law and legal exegesis in the Dead Sea Scrolls are part of a broader historical and phenomenological framework that extends from the Second Temple period through rabbinic Judaism. This principle is in practice with regard to the restriction on speech on the Sabbath in ancient Judaism. This chapter explores several iterations of this law as found in one contemporaneous Second Temple–period text – the book of *Jubilees* – and several different passages from the broad scope of rabbinic literature.

Two wider conclusions emerge from my analysis that follows. First, the legal formulation and exegetical techniques found in the Dead Sea Scrolls find close points of correspondence with the presentation of speech-related laws in the book of *Jubilees*. Second, while both the legal content and exegetical presentation of the speech restrictions in rabbinic literature share less in common with their Second Temple antecedents, it is clear that the issue of what type of speech is prohibited on the Sabbath and the scriptural basis for these laws continued to constitute a lively debate well beyond the Second Temple period. Indeed, we shall see that the broad sweep of rabbinic texts examined in this chapter affirms my assumptions that Jewish law and legal exegesis in the Dead Sea Scrolls must be plotted along a much wider trajectory in ancient Judaism.

II. ISAIAH 58:13 AND THE RESTRICTION ON SPEECH IN THE BOOK OF JUBILEES

Sabbath law appears in two places in the book of *Jubilees* (2:29–30; 50:6–13).[1] As part of the second list of Sabbath laws, Jub 50:8 presents Sabbath laws related to business dealings:

> *wa-za-hi yetnāgar nagara megbār*[2] *bāti kama yegbar bāti*[3] *gayiso wa-ba-'enta-ni kʷellu šayiṭ wa-tašāyeṭo*
>
> Who speaks a word[4] about work on it: That he is to set out on a trip on it or[5] about any selling or buying. (Jub 50:8)[6]

The formulation of these laws is closely related to the *Damascus Document* in both its exegetical use of Isa 58:13 and the formal structure in which the laws are presented. This correspondence is outlined in Table 5, with content drawn from Isa 58:13 underlined.[7]

1 On the Sabbath in general in *Jubilees*, see Lutz Doering, "The Concept of the Sabbath in the Book of *Jubilees*," in *Studies in the Book of Jubilees* (ed. M. Albani, J. Frey, and A. Lange; TSAJ 65; Tübingen: Mohr Siebeck, 1997), 179–205. On Sabbath law in particular, see Chanokh Albeck, *Das Buch der Jubiläen und die Halacha* (Berichte der Hochschule für die Wissenschaft des Judentums 47; Berlin: Hochschule für die Wissenschaft des Judentums, 1930), 7–12; Louis H. Finkelstein, "The Book of Jubilees and the Rabbinic Halakha," *HTR* 16 (1923): 39–61 (45–51); Liora Ravid, "The Laws of Sabbath in the Book of Jubilees," *Tarbiz* 69 (2000): 161–66 [Hebrew]; Lutz Doering, *Schabbat: Sabbathhalacha und –praxis im antiken Judentum und Urchristentum* (TSAJ 78; Tübingen: Mohr Siebeck, 1999), 70–108. For consideration of the literary and redactional relationship between the two lists of Sabbath law, see my discussion of the two appearances of the Sabbath carrying prohibition in Chapter 10.

2 For the manuscript evidence in favor of this reading, see James C. VanderKam, *The Book of Jubilees: A Critical Text* (CSCO 510–11; SA 87–88; 2 vols.; Leuven: Peeters, 1989), 2:326. For discussion of earlier alternative readings, see Doering, *Schabbat*, 84.

3 The expression "on it" (*bāti*) is omitted in one manuscript (Ms EMML 4750), while another manuscript omits the entire clause regarding the trip (Ms Ethiop. 51 = Charles's "A"). See VanderKam, *Jubilees*, 1:253. In addition, the clause regarding the trip until *bāti* is missing in some additional late manuscripts (Mss EMML 1163, 101, 2532), though this seems to be a clear case of haplography (*bāti . . . bāti*).

4 VanderKam's main translation renders this clause as "who says anything," though he notes that the literal translation is "who speaks a word" (*Jubilees*, 2:326). I have adopted the literal translation because it more clearly expresses the exegetical dependence on Isa 58:13. The literal translation is likewise preferred in James L. Kugel, *A Walk through* Jubilees: *Studies in the* Book of Jubilees *and the World of Its Creation* (JSJSup 156; Leiden: Brill, 2012), 204.

5 Charles omits the conjunction (*The Book of Jubilees* [London: Adam and Charles Black, 1902], 259). Hence, his translation: "That he will set out on a journey thereon in regard to any buying or selling."

6 Text and translation of *Jubilees* follow VanderKam, *Jubilees*, 1:253, 2:326.

7 My interest here is primarily in the shared exegetical, literary, and legal elements of the text discussed here as they relate to discussion of business on the Sabbath and the interpretation of

TABLE 5. *Isa 58:13 and CD 10:17–19 and Jub 50:8*

CD 10:17–19	Jubilees 50:8
And on the Sabbath, let no man speak a vile and empty word (אל ידבר איש דבר נבל ורק):	Who speaks a word (*yetnāgar nagara*) about work on it
(I) He shall not demand any payment from his fellow	(i) that he is to set out on a trip on it
(II) He shall not enter into a dispute concerning money or profit	(ii) or about any buying or selling
(III) He shall not speak about matters (אל ידבר בדברי) relating to work and labor that need to be done on the following day.	

As in the *Damascus Document*, Jub 50:8 opens with a general classificatory statement that is based on an exegetical reading and reformulation of ודבר דבר in Isa 58:13: "Who speaks a word about work on it." Although the original Hebrew for this portion of *Jubilees* is not extant, the Ge'ez *yetnāgar nagara* is equivalent to Isa 58:13 "speak a word," even preserving the cognate accusative.[8]

In its reformulation of ודבר דבר, *Jubilees* includes two interpretive elements: (1) a more explicit notion of the time in which the speech takes place ("on it") and (2) the general subject of the speech ("about work"). In this clause, "on it," following the scriptural verse, clearly indicates the time in which one speaks about the work – on the Sabbath.[9] The second interpretive element (*megbār* – "about work") functions similarly to the expanded construct clauses attached to דבר in the *Damascus Document* and *4QHalakha B*. In all three texts, the additional content serves to clarify the nature of the Sabbath restriction in the scriptural passage. The presence of two specific cases that follow in Jub 50:8 suggests that the opening clause is not intended to proscribe

Isa 58:13. For fuller discussion of the text-critical and literary issues, see Doering, *Schabbat*, 83–84.

[8] On the relationship to Isa 58:13, see also Albeck, *Jubiläen*, 9; Doering, *Schabbat*, 86; Kugel, *A Walk through* Jubilees, 204.

[9] Charles renders this first clause as "whoever says he will do something on it" (*Jubilees*, 259; see the similar translation in Ephraim Isaac, "Jubilees," in *Old Testament Pseudepigrapha* [ed. J. H. Charlesworth; 2 vols.; ABRL; New York: Doubleday, 1983–85], 2:142). In Charles's translation, the temporal designation "on it" indicates the future Sabbath in which the work will transpire. It would seem that the speech therefore takes place during the week. Finkelstein was troubled by this passage's assumption that an individual would be condemned to death for merely stating his or her intention to violate the Sabbath ("Jubilees," 48). He therefore suggests that "on it" in this clause refers to the time when the statement is articulated and not to the time when the proscribed labor may occur. This indeed seems to be the correct understanding and is now supported by the manuscript evidence employed by VanderKam in his edition and translation.

all speech regarding prohibited Sabbath work. Rather, it merely frames the nature of *Jubilees*' interpretation of Isa 58:13 as a prohibition of specific types of speech.[10]

Similar to the structural presentation of the legal material in the *Damascus Document* (and in a modified way in *4QHalakha B*), the initial general statement is followed by two specific laws, which provide concrete examples of the prohibited speech. The first of these passages prohibits the discussion of a trip (i). This passage never explicitly states the nature of the trip. R. H. Charles understands this clause as related to the prohibition against traveling beyond the Sabbath limit based on Exod 16:29.[11] More recently, Lutz Doering has argued that this prohibition restricts merely talking about a journey. Taking such a trip would be forbidden on the Sabbath. Thus, any conversation about it would also be forbidden because this would detract from the sanctity of the Sabbath.[12]

Neither of these proposals adequately explains this law in the context of the wider Sabbath prohibition. The placement of a law regarding Sabbath boundaries here is unlikely, as this law appears explicitly in Jub 50:12. Moreover, Charles's explanation does not comport with his broader understanding of the trip as directly related to the commercial activities at the end of the passage.[13] Doering's interpretation does not explain why the law singles out the specific case of a trip. Something about the trip marks it as a unique case, for which discussion of its details is specifically highlighted as forbidden. The juxtaposition of this clause with the following clause regarding commerce-related speech suggests that the trip is likewise somehow related to financial dealings. The inclusion of this specific activity is likely an exegetical application of Isa 58:13 מעשות דרכיך, "Go not your ways." Jub 50:8 understands the passage in a very literal way as condemning an individual for going on one's way – that is, a trip – on the Sabbath.[14] In this sense, *Jubilees* understands the travel as directly related to the condemned business dealing found elsewhere in Isa 58:13.[15] The prohibited action on the Sabbath is combined with the expectation of restricted

[10] See also Doering, *Schabbat*, 85.

[11] Charles, *Jubilees*, 259.

[12] Doering, *Schabbat*, 86.

[13] See Charles's translation provided above, n. 9.

[14] As previously noted, the original Hebrew is not preserved for Jub 50:8. However, the Ge'ez *kama yegbar bāti gayiso* may reflect an underlying Hebrew reformulation of מעשות דרכיך from Isa 58:13. Similar to the Hebrew root עשה, the Ge'ez *gabra* has a wide semantic range. See Wolf Leslau, *Comparative Dictionary of Ge'ez (Classical Ethiopic)* (Wiesbaden: Otto Harrassowitz, 1987), 178–79. Thus, *yegbar* could render some form of *Jubilees*' reuse of עשה. In that case, the Hebrew underlying *gayiso* would represent an exegetical reformulation clarifying the precise nature of "your ways" (דרכיך) in Isa 58:13.

[15] On this understanding of Isa 58:13, see above, Chapter 4, section II. Note as well Moshe Weinfeld's argument that מעשות דרכיך in Isa 58:13 refers specifically to a business-related trip. See above, Chapter 4, n. 10.

speech on the Sabbath from Isa 58:13 to proscribe speech about this particular activity.

The expression "on it" (*bāti*) in this clause can be interpreted in two different ways. Its placement at the end of the clause suggests that it identifies the time in which the proposed trip will take place – that is, on the Sabbath. The inclusion of this law following the preceding general statement indicates that the verbal articulation likewise transpired on a Sabbath. The specific prohibition therefore concentrates on an individual's declaration of intent to take a business trip on the Sabbath, though it is not clear if the trip will occur on the same Sabbath or a future one.

A second possible understanding is that "on it" does not refer to the time in which the trip will transpire. Rather, as in the preceding general clause, it refers only to the specific time in which the verbal articulation takes place – namely, on the Sabbath. Thus, the business trip will take place not on the Sabbath but more likely sometime during the following week. James Kugel's annotation of VanderKam's translation points toward this understanding: "That is, discussing on the sabbath a voyage he is to set out on."[16]

To be sure, this understanding produces a slightly awkward syntax because "on it" would refer back to the implied act of speaking, rather than the explicit statement regarding taking a trip. Indeed, some manuscript evidence omits the expression "on it" entirely.[17] Thus, the speech that is articulated on the Sabbath is merely a declaration to set out on a trip in the future. The proposed trip, however, would most likely not transpire on a future Sabbath but rather is intended to take place sometime in the following week.[18] Thus, *Jubilees* forbids planning ahead for business related to the coming week. According to this second interpretation, *Jubilees* would closely parallel the restriction on speech related to future business dealings as articulated in the *Damascus Document*, *4QHalakha B*, and, as discussed below, *Mishnah Shabbat* 23:3.[19]

The second specific law in Jub 50:8 (ii) is much clearer. As with the first specific law, this law provides an explicit example of the work-related speech that is condemned. Any speech that is related to business transactions – whether buying or selling – is proscribed.[20] The law does not provide any information about when this buying or selling would take place. Presumably, the law seeks to prohibit verbal business transactions on the Sabbath that may not necessarily involve monetary exchanges or other explicit violations of Sabbath law.[21] In this respect, this law parallels laws I and II in the *Damascus Document*

[16] Kugel, *A Walk through* Jubilees, 204.

[17] See above, n. 3.

[18] As argued by Finkelstein, "Jubilees," 49. See also Albeck, *Jubiläen*, 9.

[19] See the *Mishnah* text cited below, section III.

[20] See Kugel, *A Walk through* Jubilees, 204. See, however, Charles, *Jubilees*, 259, where the translation suggests that the buying and selling represent the circumstances of the business trip (based on his omission of the conjunction "or"; see above, n. 5).

[21] Though not clear, it is possible that the law similarly condemns discussion of business transactions that will transpire in the coming week.

and related content in *4QHalakha B*, which proscribe fiscal activities that are engaged in merely through verbal communication.[22]

The presentation of Sabbath law in Jub 50:8 closely resembles the related Sabbath laws articulated in the *Damascus Document* and to a lesser extent *4QHalakha B* in content, structure, and exegetical dependency on Isa 58:13. The initial clause in Jub 50:8 is a general prohibition of work-related discussion on the Sabbath. As with the general classificatory statement found in CD 10:17–18, this passage is an exegetical reformulation of Isa 58:13 that establishes a general legal rubric related to the prohibition of discussing business matters on the Sabbath. The second half of the passage in *Jubilees*, similar to the three laws that follow in the *Damascus Document* and the examples provided in *4QHalakha B*, provides two concrete examples of instances in which one would speak about work-related matters on the Sabbath.

The relationship between the passages in the *Damascus Document* and *Jubilees* bears evidence of an even closer literary connection. The two specific laws in Jub 50:8 reflect an inverse relationship with the three specific laws in the *Damascus Document*. Broadly speaking, the first specific law in Jub 50:8 condemns speech related to future commercial activity. The second specific law proscribes business-related speech that transpires on the Sabbath. In the three specific laws found in CD 10:17–19, the first two prohibit speech on the Sabbath related to financial matters, while the third forbids speech related to business activity during the coming week. Thus, the restrictions on speech in Jub 50:8 and CD 10:17–19 both begin with a general classificatory statement condemning specifically business-related speech. Of the specific laws outlined, the first two in the *Damascus Document* match the second law in *Jubilees*, while the third law in the *Damascus Document* is related to the first law in *Jubilees*. The composition of *Jubilees* predates the *Damascus Document*, and the *Damascus Document* reflects a high degree of familiarity with both the legal and nonlegal content of *Jubilees*.[23] In this case, therefore, CD 10:17–19 seems to have drawn upon the well-established exegetical technique of literary

[22] See also the suggestion to restore 4Q264a 1 i 6–7 as במק]ח, "buyin[g" (Tigchelaar) or במק]ח וממכר, "buyin[g and selling" (Noam and Qimron). See Chapter 5, n. 11.

[23] The chronological priority of *Jubilees* is assured based on the citation of it found in CD 16:3–4 (see above, Chapter 3, section IV). Most scholars date *Jubilees* to the first half of the second century BCE (though some date it later in the second century BCE), while the *Damascus Document* is generally located toward the end of the second century BCE or early first century BCE. For discussion of the date of *Jubilees*, see James C. VanderKam, "Recent Scholarship on the Book of Jubilees," *Currents in Biblical Research* 6 (2008): 405–31 (407–9). On the date of the *Damascus Document*, see above, Chapter 5, n. 18. The issue of the *Damascus Document*'s use of *Jubilees* was first treated in Solomon Schechter, *Documents of Jewish Sectaries*, volume 1: *Fragments of a Zadokite Work* (Cambridge: Cambridge University Press, 1910; repr. with prolegomenon by Joseph Fitzmyer; Library of Biblical Studies; New York: Ktav, 1970), 47–48, and the many parallels noted in his comments to the text (which can be accessed easily through the source index). Todd R. Hanneken has recently revisited this issue as part of a broader study on the use and influence of the book of *Jubilees*. Hanneken addressed the influence of *Jubilees* in the *Damascus Document* in a paper delivered at the 2011 Annual Meeting of the

inversion in order to re-present in a subtly modified way its own version of the speech-related restrictions found in Jub 50:8.[24]

III. THE RESTRICTION ON SPEECH IN RABBINIC LITERATURE

Rabbinic exegesis of Isa 58:13 contains many points of correspondence with the *Damascus Document*, *4QHalakha B*, and the book of *Jubilees*, and it indeed likely reflects an awareness of some of the earlier exegetical traditions found in these texts. At the same time, rabbinic approaches to Isa 58:13 often display significant exegetical and legal developments. Two broad legal-exegetical applications of Isa 58:13 are reflected in the tannaitic corpus and later amoraic interpretive traditions. While these traditions agree that one must not engage in activity related to one's weekday affairs, they differ in the specific details of the nature of the prohibited activity and its exegetical foundations in Isa 58:13. One thread in rabbinic literature follows the dominant approach of the Second Temple–period texts that regards Isa 58:13 as restricting speech on the Sabbath related specifically to business or financial matters. A second trend extends the restriction to all idle or nonessential speech that is deemed inconsistent with the sacred nature of the Sabbath. In this sense, the passages that condemn general inappropriate conversation often distinguish between speech-oriented actions that would normally transpire during the week and more general idle conversation. Both are equally regarded as inconsistent with the sanctity of the Sabbath, and thus both are forbidden. To be sure, business-related speech is conceptualized in rabbinic literature as falling under the broader rubric of inappropriate speech. Yet, the rabbinic texts themselves often treat business-related speech as a distinct category. Thus, my narrow focus on business-related speech is guided both by the independent treatment it receives in rabbinic texts and by the importance that the related set of Second Temple–period texts provide in framing the contours of the rabbinic evidence.

These two broad legal approaches represent the same two positions detected in the Second Temple–period texts. Both legal positions, moreover, attest to counter-exegetical traditions in other rabbinic texts, whereby Isa 58:13 is ignored as the scriptural source. My discussion of the rabbinic material highlights the legal and exegetical points of contact while outlining the various ways in which the rabbinic texts differ from their Second Temple–period antecedents.

Isaiah 58:13 and the Restriction on Business-Related Speech

Rabbinic discussion of prohibited speech on the Sabbath is found in *Mishnah Shabbat* 23:3, which forbids an individual from hiring laborers for the following week:

Association for Jewish Studies: "The Use of Jubilees in the Damascus Document." Thank you to Dr. Hanneken for sharing with me his conference paper and ongoing research in this area.

24 On the exegetical technique of literary inversion (commonly known as "Zeidel's law"), see bibliography, Chapter 4, n. 50.

לא ישכור אדם[25] פועלים בשבת ולא יאמר אדם לחבירו לשכור לו פועלים

A man may not hire laborers on the Sabbath or say to his fellow that he should hire laborers for him (for work related to the week).[26]

The *Mishnah* proscribes two types of verbal exchanges. In the first half, an individual is prohibited from directly hiring another individual as a worker. In the second half, the *Mishnah* forbids the hiring of workers even through an agent. In both cases, the prohibited act is not employing a laborer on the Sabbath; rather, the *Mishnah* proscribes the *verbal* act of hiring a worker. While the hiring occurs on the Sabbath, the individual is hired for work that will commence during the coming week.[27] Thus, this law restricts speech that involves planning for future business dealing, as similarly found in the Second Temple–period texts treated in the previous two chapters. Whereas the *Damascus Document* and *4QHalakha B* contain general prohibitions against speech related to future planning, the *Mishnah* provides a specific case in which one would engage in speech on the Sabbath.

While Isa 58:13 is regarded by later commentators as the scriptural source of the *Mishnah*'s law, consistent with its apodictic style, the *Mishnah* does not refer in any way to the scriptural passage.[28] The legal and exegetical relationship of the *Mishnah* to Isa 58:13, however, is taken for granted in the *Babylonian Talmud*'s discussion of the *Mishnah*. The exegetical relationship to Isa 58:13, though still somewhat opaque, is more clearly discernible:

הא קמ"ל לא יאמר אדם לחבירו שכור לי פועלים אבל אומר לו[29] הנראה שתעמוד עמי לערב ומתני' מני כרבי יהושע היא דתניא לא יאמר אדם לחבירו הנראה שתעמוד עמי לערב רבי יהושע בן קרחה אומר אומר אדם לחבירו הנראה שתעמוד עמי לערב אמר רבה בר בר חנה אמר רבי יוחנן הלכה כרבי יהושע בן קרחה ואמר רבה בר בר חנה אמר רבי יוחנן מאי טעמיו דרבי יהושע בן קרחה דכתיב ממצוא חפצך ודבר דבר דיבור אסור הרהור מותר

It was taught, "One may not say to his fellow, 'Hire me workers,' but one may say to his fellow, 'We shall see if you stand with me (i.e., join me) this evening.'" With whom does the *Mishnah* agree? With Rabbi Joshua (ben Korḥah), as it was taught, One may not say to his fellow, "We shall see if you stand with me (i.e., join me) this evening." Rabbi Joshua ben Korḥah said, "One may not say to

25 Following Cambridge T-S E1.50. Ms Kaufmann A 50 has לא ישכור לו; Cambridge T-S E1.51 has only לא יסכור. See Abraham Goldberg, *Commentary to the Mishna Shabbat* (Jerusalem: Jewish Theological Seminary of America, 1976), 386 [Hebrew].

26 Aside from the one variant indicated in the previous note, the Hebrew text follows Ms Kaufmann A 50. See Georg Beer, *Faksimile-Ausgabe des Mischnacodex Kaufmann A 50* (Haag: M. Nijhoff, 1929; repr. Jerusalem: 1969), 99; and the critical edition found in Goldberg, *Commentary to the Mishna Shabbat*, 386.

27 On this understanding, see Chanokh Albeck, *Shishah Sidre Mishnah*, volume 2: *Seder Mo'ed* (Jerusalem: Bialik Institute; Tel Aviv: Dvir, 1958), 70, and the discussion of the *Babylonian Talmud* below.

28 On the identification of Isa 58:13 as the source, see Rashi ad loc. s.v. לא ישכור אדם פועלין; Rabbi Obadiah of Bartenoro ad loc. s.v. לא ישכור אדם פועלין. The view of the medieval commentators is clearly influenced by the *Babylonian Talmud*'s association of Isa 58:13 with this law.

29 The Vilna printed edition and Ms Vatican ebr. 108 have אומר אדם לחבירו.

> his fellow, 'We shall see if you stand with me (i.e., join me) this evening.'" Said Rabba ben Bar Ḥanna in the name of Rabbi Yoḥanan, "The law follows Rabbi Joshua ben Korḥah." Furthermore, Rabba ben Bar Ḥanna in the name of Rabbi Yoḥanan, "What is Rabbi Joshua ben Korḥah's reasoning? As it says, 'Nor look to your affairs, nor speak a word': Speech is prohibited; thought is permitted." (*b. Shabb.* 150a)[30]

In addressing the issue of whether it is permitted for an individual to hire workers through indirect communication, the *Babylonian Talmud* asserts that while direct verbal communication is prohibited, one may do so through indirect hinting ("We shall see if you stand with me [i.e., join me] this evening"). A *baraita* (tannaitic tradition) found in *t. Shabb.* 17:11 attributing this opinion to Rabbi Joshua ben Korḥah is then cited as tannaitic support for this ruling. The scriptural basis for Rabbi Joshua ben Korḥah's position (not found in the *Tosefta*) is traced to exegesis of ודבר דבר in Isa 58:13. The *Babylonian Talmud* explains that because the root דבר is employed, *Isaiah* should be understood as only explicitly prohibiting business transactions that involve speech; transactions involving only thought are not proscribed ("Speech is prohibited; thought is permitted"). Because the first individual only hints at the need to hire workers, the second individual is forced to decipher on his own that the full intent of the first individual is to hire him.[31]

Several interconnecting observations should be made regarding the legal-exegetical application of Isa 58:13 in the *Babylonian Talmud*. The primary focus of the exegetical engagement with Isa 58:13 is not to identify it as the source of the *Mishnah*'s ruling or even more generally as the scriptural source for the prohibition on business-related speech. This legal application of Isa 58:13 is taken for granted in the *Babylonian Talmud* and perhaps in the *Mishnah* if indeed Isa 58:13 is lurking behind the apodictic formulation. It is only because Isa 58:13 is assumed to restrict business-related speech that it can then be employed for its primary legal and exegetical role in the *Babylonian Talmud*. The keyword דבר in Isa 58:13 limits the legal application of this scriptural passage to explicit speech; thus, thoughts alone are not under the purview of this law. The internal debate over thoughts versus speech is part of the same long-standing debate that surfaced in the polemical language of *4QHalakha B*, as discussed in the previous chapter. As with *4QHalakha B*, the *Babylonian Talmud* limits the legal and exegetical application of Isa 58:13 to explicit speech.[32]

In light of the appeal to Isa 58:13 to draw the boundaries of this law, it is surprising that no trace is found of an exegetical application of Isa 58:13 to

30 Hebrew/Aramaic text follows Ms Munich 95.

31 See Rashi ad loc. s.v. הנראה.

32 Below in Chapter 8, I treat the rabbinic material – including this passage – in greater detail in the broader context of the history of the restriction on thoughts on the Sabbath and its exegetical dependence on Isa 58:13.

the primary Sabbath law under discussion – the restriction on business-related speech. The evidence of the *Babylonian Talmud* and its tannaitic conversation partner suggests that the pervasiveness of Isa 58:13 as the scriptural source for restricting business-related speech in Second Temple Judaism was retained in rabbinic law. Moreover, this legal and exegetical application of Isa 58:13 was so firmly entrenched in Jewish legal exegesis in antiquity that no further exegetical argument needed to be advanced. On the contrary, rabbinic legal exegesis is concerned with establishing the limits of this legal-exegetical application of Isa 58:13.

A closely related law regarding permitted and prohibited calculations (חשבונות) is found in *Tosefta Shabbat* 17:9:

> כל חשבונות שהו צריך להן בין שעברו ובין לעתיד לבא אין מחשבין אותן בשבת חשבונות שאינן אלא מה בכך מחשביו אותן בשבת
>
> Any account which one requires, whether concerning matters in the past or concerning matters in the future, they do not reckon on the Sabbath. Accounts which are of no purpose can be reckoned on the Sabbath.[33]

This passage contains a general law prohibiting individuals from calculating (מחשבין) their necessary accounts (חשבונות שהו צריך להן) on the Sabbath.[34] These accounts may refer to expenditures in the past or the future. Nonessential accounts (שאינן אלה מה בכך), however, may be calculated on the Sabbath.[35] The *Tosefta* is decidedly silent on how one would conduct the proscribed calculations and the precise nature of these calculations. In this respect, it is not clear if the *Tosefta* is at all concerned about engaging in speech related to one's past or future financial expenditures. In addition, consistent with the apodictic form of the *Tosefta*, we are provided with no scriptural source.

As was the case with the *Mishnah* discussed above, the *Babylonian Talmud*'s expansion of the tannaitic law clarifies several of these questions. In *b. Shabb.* 150a–b, consideration of permitted and prohibited calculations follows the treatment of prohibited and permitted commercial speech discussed above. The *Babylonian Talmud* prefaces this second discussion with the

33 The Hebrew text follows Saul Lieberman, *The Tosefta: The Order of Mo'ed* (New York: Jewish Theological Seminary of America, 1962), 82. Translation (slightly modified) follows Jacob Neusner, *The Tosefta*, volume 1 (Peabody: Hendrickson, 2002), 424.

34 Further rabbinic consideration of calculations on the Sabbath is found in *Mekhilta de-Rabbi Shim'on b. Yoḥai* on Exod 35:2 and the parallel tradition in *Mishnat Rabbi Eli'ezer* 20, though neither reflects any exegetical dependence on Isa 58:13. These passages are treated below.

35 My understanding of this expression follows Lieberman, *Tosefta*, 82, who explains the term as financial considerations that are entirely unrelated to the speaker, such as the expenses of rich people or a king. This explanation can also be found (with slightly different examples) in Rabbi David Pardo, *Ḥasde David*, volume 1 (Livorno, 1776), ad loc. (on 18:7). Note, however, the different meaning of the nearly identical term in the *Babylonian Talmud* as discussed below, where it means past expenses (see n. 39). This particular explanation, however, does not work in the *Tosefta* as a contrast to the prohibited "necessary" calculations.

question וכי דיבור אסור ("Now, is speech forbidden?"). This rhetorical question seeks to explore the full parameters of the restriction on speech. The *Babylonian Talmud* identifies the issue of calculations as an expansion of the question of what type of speech one may engage in on the Sabbath. The response to the initial question is to single out a range of calculations that may indeed be the object of speech on the Sabbath, notwithstanding the inevitable discussion of financial matters involved in their performance. According to the *Babylonian Talmud*, all calculations that are for the sake of a religious obligation (חשבונות של מצוה) are permitted, while those that are for personal benefit are not. Several examples of verbal calculations for the sake of religious obligation are cited in the name of different rabbis: determining charity disbursements, attending to individual and communal life and death matters, general communal matters (in different venues), making arrangements for betrothal of young women, and matters related to education of young children.

Each of the examples is cited on account of the central role of speech in their performance and the associated discussion of financial affairs. Isa 58:13 is identified as the scriptural source for this allowance. The *Babylonian Talmud* focuses on the final section of the verse: "Nor look to your affairs (חפציך), nor speak a word." The proscribed word is limited to one's own words – those in which the speaker has a personal financial stake. One's own affairs are prohibited, but the "affairs of heaven" (חפצי השמים) are permitted, even if they involve speech.[36] As observed in several examples from the *Damascus Document* and *4QHalakha B* discussed in the previous two chapters, the *Babylonian Talmud*

[36] This legal-exegetical understanding is also found in *b. Shabb.* 113a, though without the full elaboration found here (on this passage, see below). Several of the same "heavenly affairs" (charity disbursements, betrothal of young women, and education of young children, along with praying for the sick) are presented in *t. Shabb.* 16:21–22 and *b. Shabb.* 12a as prohibited by the House of Shammai, though permitted by the House of Hillel. Rashi, *b. Shabb.* 12a (s.v. וב"ה מתירין) explains the position of the House of Hillel as the application of the legal-exegetical principle of Isa 58:13 in *b. Shabb.* 150a – these actions are the affairs of heaven (חפצי שמים), not personal affairs. See Yitzḥak D. Gilat, "Regarding the Antiquity of Several Sabbath Prohibitions," in *Studies in the Development of the Halakha* (Ramat Gan: Bar Ilan University Press, 1992), 249–61 (256), who understands this debate in light of earlier Second Temple restrictions on speech. My analysis supports Gilat's assumption that the general contours of the debate between the House of Hillel and the House of Shammai can indeed be traced to pre-rabbinic Jewish law. *B. Shabb.* 12a includes several speech-oriented actions that have no financial component, e.g., praying for the sick, comforting mourners, and visiting the sick. As noted by Gilat (ibid., especially n. 34), the debate regarding the permissibility of the latter two seems to center on their speech element (contra Rashi, ad loc., s.v. ואין מנחין, who suggests that such actions would be disquieting to all parties on the Sabbath). These actions were likely a concern because they were regarded as forms of speech normally undertaken during the week and therefore, according to the House of Shammai, inconsistent with the sanctity of the Sabbath (on this category of prohibited speech, see below). Indeed, the formulation employed to allow for general greetings on the Sabbath (התירו לשאול שלום בשבת מדוחק; *y. Shabb.* 15:3 15c, see below) appears in *b. Shabb.* 12b to explain the rabbinic concession to allow for both comforting mourners and visiting the sick (בקושי התירו לנחם אבלים ולבקר חולים).

infuses an enigmatic word from Isa 58:13 (חפץ) with practical legal meaning by reorienting the word as part of a larger construct clause.

The *Babylonian Talmud* has reformulated the *Tosefta*'s laws of calculations on the Sabbath as something that is specifically related to articulating one's calculations through speech, simultaneously identifying Isa 58:13 as the scriptural source for this law. Moreover, as in the earlier unit in the *Babylonian Talmud*, there is no attempt to provide an exegetical link to Isa 58:13 for the general prohibition of business-related speech. Once again, the legal-exegetical connection is assumed, and Isa 58:13 is marshaled as exegetical proof for the exception to the rule. As I suggested above, it is likely that the presumed legal-exegetical force of Isa 58:13 in the later rabbinic texts is a result of its pervasive influence in earlier Jewish exegetical traditions.[37]

In what follows, the *Babylonian Talmud* narrows the application of the law even further, in such a way that the law is even closer to the Second Temple–period formulations. The *Babylonian Talmud* cites Rabbi Judah in the name of Samuel as permitting calculation of all accounts of no practical value (מה לך)[38] and past accounts (מה בכך).[39] A *baraita* is then cited that is intended to support Rabbi Judah's statement:

> תניא נמי הכי חשבונות שעברו ושעתידין להיות אסור לחשבן של מלך ושל מה בכך מותר לחושבן
>
> It was likewise taught, past and future calculations are forbidden to calculate on the Sabbath; unimportant or past (calculations) are permitted to calculate on the Sabbath. (*b. Shabb.* 150a–b)

An immediate discrepancy is now noted. The second half of the *baraita*, as with Rabbi Judah, seems to permit calculations of past accounts, while the first half of the *baraita* clearly prohibits calculations of both future and past expenditures.[40] The contradiction is resolved by suggesting that the prohibition

[37] See, in particular, my discussion of the possible morphological form of יחשב in *4QHalakha B* (4Q264a 1 i 5). Doering has noted the possibility that this should be understood as a *pi'el* form and thus represents a direct parallel to the restriction found in the *Tosefta*. See above, Chapter 5, section III.

[38] מה לך (following Ms Munich 95) appears in several editions as מלך or מילך. For treatment of the variants, see Saul Lieberman, *Tosefta Kifshuṭah*, part 3: *Seder Mo'ed* (Jerusalem: Jewish Theological Seminary of America, 1962), 285–86. Lieberman concludes that there is no practical semantic difference among the various formulations.

[39] On the meaning of מה לך, see Rashi on *b. Shabb.* 150a (s.v. מלך). He explains it as financial information that is of no significance to the speaker (lit. "what is to you"). For example, how much would it cost for somebody else to build a house. The latter term – מה בכך – following Rashi (ad loc.) refers to the calculation of expenses for the speaker that took place in the past (lit. "what is in this?" – i.e., how much did I spend on this?). See also the different meaning of the nearly identical term in the *Tosefta* as discussed above (n. 35). Rashi's interpretation, however, seems to be correct here – otherwise there would be no contradiction in the *baraita*.

[40] Indeed, this contradiction is seemingly already present in the *Tosefta*. *T. Shabb.* 17:5 permits a person to calculate different types of past expenditures, including money for one's home, hiring of workers, and expenses related to guests. Presumably, the first two categories would

regarding calculation of past accounts only applies in instances where a laborer is still owed money for past work. In such a case, while the work was already completed, the specific individual's financial obligation is still a pending future business transaction. Thus, in its narrowest application in the *Babylonian Talmud*, the law of calculations on the Sabbath prohibits discussion of any business-related expenditures that one will incur in the future or that will only be fully resolved in the future.

This particular formulation of the prohibition of calculations thus serves to connect the entire law with the earlier treatment in *b. Shabb.* 150a regarding speech related to hiring a worker. In both cases, the immediate concern is speech on the Sabbath for financial or business affairs that will transpire during the following week. In the earlier case, the intention is to hire the workers for post-Sabbath activity. In this case, the speaker will calculate the remaining payments needed to be released to his worker in the following week. Thus, a central concern throughout *b. Shabb.* 150a–b is with speech on the Sabbath related to post-Sabbath business or financial dealing. As noted in my discussion of the earlier talmudic unit, this very same issue stands out in the Second Temple–period texts treated above. Yet, unlike the Second Temple texts that go to great lengths to ground their legal rulings in the exegetical application of Isa 58:13, neither rabbinic iteration of the related law is compelled to do so. On the contrary, I observed how in both cases the legal application of Isa 58:13 is taken for granted, such that the scriptural verse is instead employed in the service of articulating some other finer points of the law.

Isaiah 58:13 and the General Restriction on Idle and Nonsacred Speech

Rabbinic exegetical traditions expand the legal and exegetical application of Isa 58:13 to multiple Sabbath law restrictions just as in the Dead Sea Scrolls legal texts treated in the previous two chapters. In particular, as in *4QHalakha B*, rabbinic tradition extends the prohibition from certain types of speech (i.e., business) to all types of speech that would normally transpire during the regular week.[41] As noted above, rabbinic law seems to distinguish between two different types of proscribed speech: (1) speech that would normally transpire during the week and is thus forbidden on account of the sacred nature of

be classified as "necessary accounts." Yet, the similar calculation of necessary past accounts is clearly forbidden in *t. Shabb.* 17:9. See Boaz Cohen, *Mishnah and Tosefta: A Comparative Study*, part 1: *Shabbat* (New York: Jewish Theological Seminary, 1935), 143.

41 See the brief overview of some of the rabbinic evidence in Boaz Cohen, "Sabbath Prohibitions Known as *Shebut*," in *Law and Tradition in Judaism* (New York: Ktav, 1969), 127–66 (145–46) (1949); Gilat, "'Sabbath Prohibitions," 255–58. Gilat conflates the more general laws regarding idle speech with the law restricting specific types of speech (e.g., business) in both the rabbinic and Second Temple sources. My analysis of both sets of evidence suggests that both the rabbinic and Second Temple texts see a distinction between these two sets of speech-related laws.

the Sabbath, and (2) entirely idle conversation that carries no practical value. Three different primary iterations of this law based on Isa 58:13 are present in rabbinic literature (*Babylonian Talmud*, *Leviticus Rabbah*, *Mishnat Rabbi Eli'ezer*), each with different legal, exegetical, and literary emphases.

The *Babylonian Talmud* contains a general restriction on all types of speech that would normally transpire during the week and are thus inappropriate for the Sabbath. This formulation is found within a broader talmudic discussion in *b. Shabb.* 113a–b focused on laws that enhance the sanctity of the Sabbath. This entire treatment appears as an exegetical discourse on the lemmata from Isa 58:13, whereby the *Babylonian Talmud* cites an excerpted lemma followed by its legal application with regard to the Sabbath. The talmudic unit is initially concerned with various laws related to garments on the Sabbath. In particular, special Sabbath garments are identified as a way to distinguish between the sanctity of the Sabbath and the mundane nature of the rest of the week. This tradition is traced back to exegesis of Isa 58:13 וכבדתו מעשות דרכיך, "And if you honor it and go not your ways."[42] By marking a distinction in one's dress between the Sabbath and the normal week, one fulfills the scriptural directive to sanctify (וכבדתו) the Sabbath.

The interest in marking the sanctity of the Sabbath in contrast to the profanity of the week is further asserted through exegesis of the remaining textual units in Isa 58:13. Thus, the second part of the previously cited scriptural lemma מעשות דרכך, "Go not your ways," is interpreted as a directive to walk in a different manner on the Sabbath than how one would walk normally during the week (שלא יהא הילוכך של שבת כהילוכך של חול, "Your walking on the Sabbath shall not be like your weekday walking").[43] This is followed by a reiteration of the law discussed above in *b. Shabb.* 150a–b that restricts personal calculations, again exegetically linked to Isa 58:13 (ממצוא חפצך חפציך אסורין חפצי שמים מותרין, "'Nor look to your affairs': your affairs are prohibited, but the affairs of heaven are permitted").

The exegetical discourse concludes by offering an interpretation of the enigmatic final lemma ודבר דבר:

> ודבר דבר שלא יהא דבורך של שבת כדבורך של חול דבור אסור הרהור מותר
>
> "Nor speak a word" (Isa 58:13): [this means that] your speech on the Sabbath shall not be like your speech during the week – speech is prohibited, thought is permitted.

This particular interpretation of Isa 58:13 shares much in common with the related exegetical tradition in *b. Shabb.* 150a that restricts business-related

[42] Note the disjunctive division of the scriptural verse. Literarily, וכבדתו belongs with the preceding clause, while מעשות דרכיך is part of a parallel clause that follows. Yet, in the service of the rabbinic exegetical agenda, these literary aspects are rendered secondary.

[43] The precise application of this directive is explained below in *b. Shabb.* 113b.

speech. Both share a concern for clearly affirming that the law under consideration applies exclusively to speech and not thought. Yet, this legal formulation expands the parameters of the speech law far beyond the limited restriction on business-related speech in *b. Shabb.* 150a.

The relationship between these two legal formulations should be understood in much the same way that I explained the similar dual presence in the Dead Sea Scrolls of laws restricting a specific type of profane speech (i.e., business related) and *all* profane speech. As in the scrolls, the more general restriction likely develops as an outgrowth of the limited restriction. Thus, *b. Shabb.* 113a–b proscribes not just speech related to financial affairs but all speech deemed to be inconsistent with the sacred character of the Sabbath.[44] Moreover, the dual manifestations of the law appear alongside one another in *b. Shabb.* 113a–b, just as in *4QHalakha B*. Thus, in both Second Temple and rabbinic Judaism, speech related to business or financial affairs is a unique type of nonsacred speech that receives its own prohibition on the Sabbath, even as eventually all such nonsacred speech is proscribed.

As in the related law in *b. Shabb.* 150a, this law is identified as a legal-exegetical explanation for the scriptural clause ודבר דבר. Yet, *b. Shabb.* 113a–b is somewhat more forthcoming with regard to its exegetical technique. Similar

44 Note that the *Babylonian Talmud* never provides concrete examples. *4QHalakha B* similarly does not give specific applications of its even more restrictive law, though it does provide examples of exceptions to the rule. Even later halakhic tradition does not offer specific examples of speech deemed inappropriate for the Sabbath (see, e.g., Maimonides, *Mishneh Torah*, *Hilkhot Shabbat*, 24:4, who merely restates the general law). In contrast, Maimonides's restatement of the restriction on business-related speech contains several newly fashioned examples, likely specific to his contemporary mercantile setting (ibid., 24:1). This phenomenon is likely related to the practical concerns with determining what is considered sacred versus profane speech. While some topics could clearly be identified as such, in practice this law likely was applied in a very subjective way. The neutral language of the *Babylonian Talmud* may be an attempt to underscore the intention that this law would be applied differently in diverse settings. Some commentators understand the restriction on idle talk in *b. Shabb.* 113a–b as applying specifically to business-related speech (see Rashi on *b. Shabb.* 113b s.v. שלא יהא דבורך של שבת כדבורך של חול). It is more likely, however, that this passage refers to the general discussion of mundane matters that are more commonly spoken about during the week, which would include financial affairs (see Maimonides, ibid., 24:4). As noted by Tosafot (on *b. Shabb.* 113a s.v. שלא יהא דבורך של שבת כדבורך של חול; repeated in Cohen, "Sabbath Prohibitions," 145 n. 47), the prohibition against business-related speech is articulated in the immediately preceding clause in connection with the scriptural lemma ממצוא חפצך, and thus it does not make sense to see it repeated here. Moreover, the other iterations of this law (see below, next section) clearly indicate that other types of profane speech are intended as well (Tosafot call attention specifically to both the story in *Leviticus Rabbah* and the allowance for personal greeting in the *Palestinian Talmud*; see below). Rabbinic sources identify several restrictions on the Sabbath that are performed through speech. See *t. Shabb.* 16:21–22 and *b. Shabb.* 12a (see above, n. 36); *t. Beṣ.* 4:2; *Sifra Aḥare Mot* 7:9. In some cases, these restrictions are grouped together (e.g., *m. Beṣ.* 5:2: legal proceedings, betrothal, divorce, Levirite marriage), thus suggesting that speech may be understood as their common denominator (so Gilat, "Sabbath Prohibitions," 256–57). Yet, none of these texts explicitly identifies speech as the critical factor in the Sabbath prohibitions as found in the set of texts treated here.

to the Targum and the Second Temple–period exegetical traditions, *b. Shabb.* 113a–b assumes that not every type of דבר is presumed in the scriptural passage. Thus, similar to these earlier exegetical traditions, it offers an example of the intended type of proscribed word – all words not deemed to be of a nature consistent with the sacred character of the Sabbath. In so doing, *b. Shabb.* 113a–b – as with the *Damascus Document* and the Targum – restricts the practical application of דבר. At the same time, as with *4QHalakha B*, it makes Isa 58:13 into the universal restriction on speech that follows from a straightforward reading of ודבר דבר.

Leviticus Rabbah 34 contains an extended exegetical discourse on Isa 58:7–14. While much of the content is focused on homiletical exegesis, the unit on verses 13–14 (§16) contains several legal interpretations.[45] A twofold exegesis of the final portion of Isa 58:13 is present. First, the lemma ממצוא חפצך ודבר דבר is cited in support of the prohibition against beseeching one's material needs (חפציו בשבת) in prayer on the Sabbath. The exegetical assumption is that the proscribed דבר refers to any word that pertains to "your needs" (חפצך). However, an exception is made for certain types of prayers that contain fixed beseeching formulae (טופס ברכות כך הוא).

The next clause contains a re-citation of the final portion of the lemma ודבר דבר, which is followed by the often repeated story of Rabbi Shim'on ben Yoḥai and his mother.[46] He would chastise her whenever she engaged in too much idle conversation on the Sabbath:

> אימיה דר' שמעון בן יוחי כד הוות משתעייא מותר מילה בשובתא הווה אמ' לה אימא שובתא היא והיא שתקא
>
> When the mother of Rabbi Shim'on ben Yoḥai would talk excessively on the Sabbath, he would say to her "Mother, it is the Sabbath." And she would shut up. (*Leviticus Rabbah* 34:16)[47]

The assumption is that her actions – excessive speech – are a violation of the Sabbath law in the scriptural passage. The introduction of this story, however, distinguishes this law from the restriction on speech found in *b. Shabb.* 113a–b.

45 See Mordechai Margaliot, *Midrash Vayyikra Rabbah* (5 vols.; New York: Jewish Theological Seminary, 1993), 814–17.

46 The printed edition of *Midrash Tanḥuma, Bereshit* 2 incorporates the story of Rabbi Shim'on b. Yoḥai and his mother into the exegetical discourse on lemmata from Isa 58:13 found in *b. Shabb.* 113a–b. Thus, the lemma ודבר דבר is followed by the story of Rabbi Shim'on b. Yoḥai and his mother rather than the general statement restricting profane speech that appears in the *Babylonian Talmud*. This unit is not present in the recension published by Solomon Buber. On the other appearances of this story (without appeal to Isa 58:13), see below.

47 Margaliot, *Midrash Vayyikra*, 816. Translation (slightly modified) follows Jacob Neusner, *Judaism and Scripture: The Evidence of Leviticus Rabbah* (Chicago: University of Chicago Press, 1986), 577. The specific word employed to describe Rabbi Shim'on b. Yoḥai's mother being quiet has a wide range of closely related variant forms in the manuscripts and medieval attestations of this story. See the collation of the variant forms in Margaliot, *Vayyikra Rabbah*, 816. With the exception of clear errors (e.g., שובה), all the variants agree on the same basic idea: She stopped speaking.

Whereas the *Babylonian Talmud* is concerned with general speech that would normally transpire during the week, *Leviticus Rabbah* focuses on the idle nature of Rabbi Shim'on ben Yoḥai's mother's conversation.

Leviticus Rabbah never clarifies the exegetical process by which it reads ודבר דבר as a restriction on idle conversation. It is possible that the ancient rabbis read the passage in much the same manner as some modern commentators, who regard its straightforward meaning as applying to idle talk.[48] As such, no exegetical reformulation was necessary. Yet, the story of Rabbi Shim'on ben Yoḥai's mother provides some hint of the exegetical process of the rabbis. Her speech is characterized as מותר מילה, which I have translated as "talk excessively."[49] But, this phrase literally means "excess words," with מילה as the Aramaic equivalent of Hebrew דבר.[50] The rabbis saw the doubling of the word דבר in Isa 58:13 (ודבר דבר) as the exegetical key to understanding its practical legal application. The two appearances of דבר – that is, excess *words* – indicate that all such unnecessary words on the Sabbath are likewise prohibited. Indeed, as we shall see below, this particular characterization of her speech is not found in the version of the story linked to Exod 20:10 in the *Palestinian Talmud* and likely is uniquely grounded in the exegetical relationship between the story and Isa 58:13.

Rabbinic tradition preserves an additional iteration of this law with a closely related exegetical application of Isa 58:13. *Mishnat Rabbi Eli'ezer* 20, as in *Leviticus Rabbah* and *b. Shabb.* 113a–b, contains a series of Sabbath laws that are arranged in the sequence of exegetical applications of individual textual units in Isa 58:13–14.[51] The interpretation of ודבר דבר similarly understands the passage to restrict idle conversation:

> מניין שאין מדברין דברים יתרים ולא דברים של בטלה בשבת ת"ל ודבר דבר
>
> From where do we know that one should not speak extraneous words or idle words on the Sabbath? Scripture says, "Nor speak a word."[52]

48 See above, Chapter 4, n. 13.

49 Compare Neusner, *Judaism and Scripture*, 577: "blather on too long."

50 On the Aramaic מילה, see Michael Sokoloff, *A Dictionary of Jewish Palestinian Aramaic* (2d ed.; Ramat Gan: Bar Ilan University Press; Baltimore: Johns Hopkins University Press, 2002), 305. Compare 𝔗ᴶ Isa 58:13 cited in Chapter 4, section II. All manuscripts of *Leviticus Rabbah* and printed versions agree on some version of this formulation: מותר with מילה\מילא\מילין. The *Midrash Tanḥuma* version has מילי סגי, likely influenced by the use of סגי in the other appearances of the story (though without any form of "word"; see below).

51 This exegetical discourse on Isa 58:13–14 immediately follows a similar list of Sabbath laws that are all introduced by inquiring about their scriptural sources. The initial list draws from the *Mekhilta de-Rabbi Shim'on b. Yoḥai* on Exod 35:2. See below for discussion of content from this list in the *Mekhilta*.

52 H. G. Enelow, *Mishnat Rabbi Eli'ezer: Midrash Sheloshim u-Shetayim Middot* (New York: Block, 1933), 369. Enelow dates this text to the tannaitic period (see p. 60 of his introduction). Further analysis suggests that it stems from the late first millennium (see H. L. Strack and Günter Stemberger, *Introduction to the Talmud and Midrash* [trans. M. Bockmuehl; Minneapolis: Fortress, 1996], 22–23). In particular, J. N. Epstein demonstrates how much of the content in

As in the talmudic tradition, *Mishnat Rabbi Eli'ezer* interprets Isa 58:13 as prohibiting all idle conversation on the Sabbath. This passage seems to share with *Leviticus Rabbah* the assumption that the multiple appearances of דבר in Isa 58:13 indicate that all excessive speech is proscribed on the Sabbath. Indeed, *Mishnat Rabbi Eli'ezer* identifies the prohibited speech as דברים יתרים, "extraneous words" – the Hebrew equivalent of the identical Aramaic formulation מותר מילה in *Leviticus Rabbah*.

Mishnat Rabbi Eli'ezer is also more forthcoming with regard to the manner in which it reformulates the relevant clause in Isa 58:13. This exegetical tradition shares with both the Second Temple and talmudic texts an approach that seeks to offer further insight into the meaning of the enigmatic דבר. The particular approach in *Mishnat Rabbi Eli'ezer* actually bears striking similarities to the exegetical technique of the Targum, *Damascus Document*, and *4QHalakha B*. In these texts, as observed in the previous two chapters, the scriptural formulation ודבר דבר is retained in a slightly modified manner followed by explanatory glosses linguistically tagged to דבר. So too, *Mishnat Rabbi Eli'ezer* reformulates the scriptural language into a negative prohibition. The keyword דברים is then infused with further meaning through the inclusion of two explanatory clauses (יתרים and של בטלה) that replicate the twofold appearance of דבר in the scriptural passage. Consistent with the general non-use of the construct state in rabbinic Hebrew, *Mishnat Rabbi Eli'ezer* modifies דברים through the use of an attribute adjective and a של genitive clause:[53]

> *Isaiah*: ודבר דבר, "Nor speak a word" → *Mishnat Rabbi Eli'ezer*: אין מדברין דברים יתרים ולא דברים של בטלה בשבת, "One should not speak extraneous words or idle words on the Sabbath."

In so doing, *Mishnat Rabbi Eli'ezer* – as in the related Second Temple–period and rabbinic exegetical traditions – provides practical meaning for the nature of the restricted דבר in Isa 58:13.

Rabbinic Counter-Exegetical Traditions: The Absence of Isaiah 58:13

In the preceding two sections, I have argued that rabbinic literature preserves a range of exegetical traditions related to Isa 58:13 and Sabbath law that are best understood in dialogue with related legal-exegetical applications of Isa 58:13 in Second Temple Judaism. As such, all of these texts belong to a broader history of Jewish law and legal exegesis. Rabbinic tradition preserves an equally important set of related texts that similarly display a concern for restriction of business-related speech or idle conversation on the Sabbath. Yet,

Mishnat Rabbi Eli'ezer is dependent on the *Babylonian Talmud* and other late rabbinic works (J. N. Epstein, "Mishnat Rabbi Eliezer," *HUCA* 23, part 2 [1950–51]: *1–*15 [Hebrew]).

53 On the general non-use of the construct state in rabbinic Hebrew, see Miguel Pérez Fernández, *An Introductory Grammar of Rabbinic Hebrew* (trans. J. Elwolde; Leiden: Brill, 1999), 32.

in these texts, no exegetical trace of Isa 58:13 is present. Rather, alternative scriptural verses are harnessed in support of the legal formulations. As we shall see, these counter-exegetical traditions similarly must be situated in the larger history of Jewish law and legal exegesis that I have outlined here.

The tenuous link to Isa 58:13 in the law of calculations in the *Tosefta* and *Babylonian Talmud* is exploited in other rabbinic iterations of this law in order to detach the rabbinic law from its presumed exegetical roots in Isa 58:13. The *Mekhilta de-Rabbi Shim'on ben Yoḥai* on Exod 35:2 contains a list of Sabbath prohibitions and their purported scriptural sources.[54] The *Mekhilta* inquires as to the scriptural source of the prohibited calculations: מנין לחשבונות שנקראו מלאכה, "Based on what scriptural source are calculations considered work?" The answer provided is not Isa 58:13 but rather Gen 39:11: ויבא הביתה לעשות מלאכתו, "He [Joseph] went into the house in order to perform his work." As in Targums Onqelos, Neofiti, and Pseudo-Jonathan on this verse, the *Mekhilta* identifies Joseph's "work" as "calculations."[55] Thus, the latter fall under the general heading of prohibited Sabbath work (מלאכה). To be sure, this exegetical connection does not focus on the speech component. At the same time, the complete absence of any appeal to Isa 58:13 at the very least suggests that a parallel legal-exegetical tradition existed that saw no connection between Isa 58:13 and the restriction on calculations as articulated in the *Tosefta* and *Babylonian Talmud*.

In a similar way, the exact formulation from *t. Shabb.* 17:9 forbidding necessary calculations is reiterated in *Midrash ha-Gadol* on Exod 20:10.[56] *Midrash ha-Gadol* dates to much later than many of the rabbinic texts treated here and anthologizes much of this earlier content.[57] As such, it can be a useful text to gauge the reception of earlier rabbinic exegetical traditions. In *Midrash ha-Gadol*, Isa 58:13 is nowhere identified as a scriptural source for the restriction on calculations. At the same, there is no exegetical connection made between the restriction and Exod 20:10. Indeed, this entire passage represents a pastiche of related rabbinic rulings on the Sabbath. Yet, the indexing of this formulation with Exod 20:10 suggests that the editor of *Midrash ha-Gadol* perceives the exegetical connection to be with Exod 20:10, rather than

54 See J. N. Epstein and E. Z. Melamed, *Mekhilta de Rabbi Shimon ben Yoḥai* (Jerusalem: Mekitse Nirdamim, 1955), 224. The same passage is also found in *Mishnat Rabbi Eli'ezer* 20 (Enelow, *Mishnat Rabbi Eli'ezer*, 368). As noted above (n. 51), the formulation in *Mishnat Rabbi Eli'ezer* comes immediately prior to a series of legal-exegetical applications of the textual units in Isa 58:13. Thus, it is unlikely that the appeal to Exod 20:10 in *Mishnat Rabbi Eli'ezer* is a deliberate avoidance of Isa 58:13. Rather, *Mishnat Rabbi Eli'ezer* is likely following an earlier source text – most likely the *Mekhilta*.

55 $\mathfrak{T}^{O}$: על לביתא למדבק בכתבי חושבניה, "He went in the house to check his accounting books"; $\mathfrak{T}^{N}$: על לגו ביתא למחשבה חשבונוי, "He went into the midst of the house to calculate his accounts"; $\mathfrak{T}^{Ps\text{-}J}$ ועל לביתא למבחוש בפינקסי חושבניה, "He went into the house to check his accounting books."

56 Mordechai Margaliot, *Midrash ha-Gadol: Shemot* (Jerusalem: Mossad ha-Rav Kook, 1956), 416.

57 See Strack and Stemberger, *Introduction*, 354–55.

Isa 58:13. Indeed, the examples discussed below from the *Palestinian Talmud* further attest to the popularity of Exod 20:10 as an alternative scriptural source to Isa 58:13.[58]

Perhaps the most interesting counter-exegetical tradition is found in the other iterations of the story of Rabbi Shim'on ben Yoḥai and his mother and the restriction on idle speech on the Sabbath. This story as found in *Leviticus Rabbah* was treated above in connection with its exegetical links to Isa 58:13. The other two iterations of this story and its associated legal formulation in the *Palestinian Talmud* (*y. Shabb.* 15:3 15b–c) and *Pesiqta Rabbati* 23:8 are nearly identical with the version presented in *Leviticus Rabbah*. Yet, neither version reflects any traces of exegetical dependence on Isa 58:13. Rather, both versions are exegetically linked to Exod 20:10.

The broader context of the version in the *Palestinian Talmud* is important for situating it in the larger development of the law limiting idle conversation on the Sabbath:[59]

> לא ניתנו שבתות וימים טובים אלא לאכילה ולשתייה על ידי שהפה זה טריח התירו לו לעסוק בהן בדברי תורה ר' ברכיה בשם ר' חייא בר בא לא ניתנו שבתות וימים טובים אלא לעסוק בהן בדברי תורה. . . אמ' ר' אבהו שבת לי'י שבות כי'י מה הקב"ה שבת ממאמר אף את שבות ממאמר[60] אמ' ר' חנינא מדוחק התירו לשאול שלום בשבת אמ' רבי חייא בר בא ר' שמעון בן יוחי כד הוה חמי לאימיה משתעיא סגין הוה אמ' לה אימא שובתא היא
>
> Sabbaths and festivals have been given only for the purpose of eating and drinking. Because the mouth is weary, they also permitted one to be engaged on them in study of Torah. Rabbi Berachia said in the name of Rabbi Ḥiyya son of Ba: "Sabbaths and festivals have been given only in order to engage in study of Torah on them." . . . Rabbi Abbahu said, "'A Sabbath for the Lord' (Exod 20:10). (This means) rest as the Lord. Just as the Holy One Blessed be He ceased from speech (on the Sabbath), so too you should cease from speech." Rabbi Ḥannina said, "Only under pressure did they permit greetings on the Sabbath." Rabbi

[58] See also the passage from *Pesiqta Rabbati* discussed below, Chapter 8, section III.

[59] The discussion below focuses primarily on the version in the *Palestinian Talmud*. The story is nearly identical in *Pesiqta Rabbati*. The *Palestinian Talmud* version contains much more of the broader legal context that is instructive for comparing it to both the other rabbinic versions of this story/law treated above and the Second Temple–period evidence. Moreover, it is undoubtedly more original and thus is closer to the original context of the literary techniques that I observe below. For the version in *Pesiqta Rabbati*, see Rivka Ulmer, *Pesiqta Rabbati: A Synoptic Edition of Pesiqta Rabbati Based on All Extant Manuscripts and the Editio Princeps* (3 vols.; SJ; Lanham: University Press of America, 2009), 1:558–59; and William G. Braude, *Pesiqta Rabbati; Discourses for Feasts, Fasts, and Special Sabbaths* (YJS 18; 2 vols.; New Haven: Yale University Press, 1968), 1:477–78. I treat the passage in which this story/law appears in *Pesiqta Rabbati* in Chapter 8. The *Palestinian Talmud* version is also repeated in *Midrash ha-Gadol* on Exod 20:10 (see Margaliot, *Midrash ha-Gadol*, 417).

[60] The printed editions (and also *Pesiqta Rabbati* and *Midrash ha-Gadol*) include the story of the pious man in his field immediately after Rabbi Abbahu's statement (on this story, see full treatment below, Chapter 8). On the textual evidence and the argument that the story of the pious man is a secondary introduction in the *Palestinian Talmud*, see Chapter 8, n. 41.

> Ḥiyya son of Ba said: "When Rabbi Shim'on ben Yoḥai saw his mother engaged in excessive talk on the Sabbath, he said to her 'Mother, it is the Sabbath!'" (*y. Shabb.* 15:3 15a)[61]

The restriction on speech comes directly after the *Palestinian Talmud*'s assertion that on the Sabbath one should only engage in essential human needs such as eating or drinking in concert with persistent study of Torah. This view of the Sabbath is traced to exegesis of Exod 20:10: "A Sabbath for the Lord" – that is, one should engage in heavenly pursuits on the Sabbath.[62]

Within this context, the *Palestinian Talmud* offers a second application of the scriptural verse and the God-oriented nature of Sabbath activities. Humans should mimic the divine cessation (i.e., at creation) from speech on the Sabbath. The placement of this legal formulation immediately following the promotion of engaging in Torah and the permission to undertake the necessary steps for consumption on the Sabbath indicates that the cessation from speech is clearly not universal. Rather, speech that is not directed at essential human needs or heavenly pursuits is condemned. Indeed, the *Palestinian Talmud* asserts that only begrudgingly did the rabbis permit general greetings on the Sabbath.[63]

[61] Text follows Ms Leiden Or. 4720 (cited from Yaakov Sussman, ed. *Talmud Yerushalmi: Yoṣe le-'Or 'al Pi Ketav Yad Skaliger 3 (Or. 4720) Shebe-Sifriyat ha-Universitah shel Laiden 'im Tashlamot ve-Tiqunim* [Jerusalem: The Academy of the Hebrew Language, 2001], 436). Note that Ms Leiden Or. 4720 does not have the final clause of the story of Rabbi Shim'on b. Yoḥai's mother indicating that she was quiet (as found in *Leviticus Rabbah* and *Pesiqta Rabbati*). Several medieval attestations of the *Palestinian Talmud*, however, do contain the final clause in various different forms, thus reflecting the same variance attested in *Leviticus Rabbah* (see above n. 50). On the evidence, see Baer Ratner, *Ahavath Ṣiyyon Vi-Yerushalayim: Shabbat* (Vilna: F. Garber, 1902), 143; Saul Lieberman, *Yerushalmi Kifshuṭoh*, volume 1 (Jerusalem: Darom, 1935), 191. It was most likely added to the *Palestinian Talmud* editions on analogy with its presence in the other versions of the story (thus also explaining the presence of the variant forms when it does appear in the *Palestinian Talmud*).

[62] Compare, however, the fuller explanation of the directive to engage in Torah study in the Genizah fragment published in J. N. Epstein, "Additional Fragments of the Yerushalmi," *Tarbiz* 3 (1932): 15–26, 121–36, 237–48 (241) [Hebrew]: לא ניתנו ימים טובים ושבתות אלא לעסוק בהן בדיברי תורה ובחול על ידי שהוא טורח ואין לו פנאיי לעסוק בדברי תורה ניתנו לו ימים טובים ושבתות לעסוק בהן בדברי תורה, "Festivals and Sabbaths have been given only in order to engage in Torah study on them. On account of the fact that during the week it is considered a burden and one does not have free time to engage in Torah study, festivals and Sabbaths have been given in order to engage in Torah study on them." This formulation is also found in several medieval citations of the *Palestinian Talmud* (see Epstein, ibid., and Ratner, *Ahavath Ṣiyyon*, 142–43). Lieberman also calls attention to a passage in *Pesiqta Rabbati* 23:29 (Ulmer, *Pesiqta Rabbati*, 586–87), which refers to laborers who are so busy during the week that they only have time on the Sabbath to engage in Torah study (see Lieberman, *Yerushalmi Kifshuṭoh*, 191). The explanation is less focused on the desire to maintain the heavenly character of the Sabbath than it is on the purely practical reality that one is freer to engage in such pursuits. This does not preclude the assumption that these activities still succeed in preserving the sanctity of the Sabbath.

[63] Compare *b. Shabb.* 12b, as discussed above (n. 36), where the language of the allowance is employed for consolation of mourners and visiting the sick.

This extended legal-exegetical discussion is then supported by the illustrative story of Rabbi Shim'on ben Yoḥai and his loquacious mother discussed above.

As noted above, the formulation of the story of Rabbi Shim'on ben Yoḥai's mother is nearly identical to the version found in *Leviticus Rabbah*. Yet, while *Leviticus Rabbah* attaches the story to the legal-exegetical application of Isa 58:13 to restrict idle conversation, this scriptural source is nowhere in view in the *Palestinian Talmud*. As noted in my discussion of *Leviticus Rabbah*, the exegetical basis of this story is the duplicate דבר ("word") in Isa 58:13, thus indicating that excessive "words" on the Sabbath are likewise condemned. The *Palestinian Talmud* likewise condemns Rabbi Shim'on ben Yoḥai's mother for talking excessively (משתעיא סגין). Closer examination of the version of the story in the *Palestinian Talmud* indicates that the key exegetical link to Isa 58:13 is absent. While the mother's words are still described as "excessive" (סגין), this terminology is not explicitly connected to "words" as in *Leviticus Rabbah*.[64]

IV. CONCLUSIONS: ISAIAH 58:13 AND THE RESTRICTION ON SPEECH IN COMPARATIVE PERSPECTIVE

The sources discussed in the last three chapters all treat the same question: What does the locution ודבר דבר in Isa 58:13 mean, and what are its practical implications with respect to Sabbath law? My discussion began with the *Damascus Document* and the related sectarian legal text *4QHalakha B* and expanded to include related laws in the book of *Jubilees* and rabbinic literature. In each case, my analysis focused on the exegetical techniques employed to interpret the meaning of this scriptural expression and its larger literary context. I examined the various ways in which these different texts reemploy language from Isa 58:13 in their own Sabbath law formulations. The above analysis has demonstrated many important points of contact in the legal-exegetical explication of Isa 58:13 across these various textual and social worlds. These similarities apply to content, structure, and exegetical use of Isa 58:13. At the same time, numerous differences exist among the various texts discussed. These distinctions most often relate to the precise legal parameters each text draws in its use of Isa 58:13. Even as each of these texts sometimes arrives at different legal conclusions, the exegetical technique is often strikingly similar.

The *Damascus Document* employs the most common form of scriptural interpretation in the Second Temple period – paraphrase – to make Isa 58:13 into a foundational text for a series of laws prohibiting speech related to business on the Sabbath. In so doing, the text builds from the semantic and

64 Some medieval attestations of this passage describe her words as משתעיא טובא. See Lieberman, *Yerushalmi Kifshuṭoh*, 191. Note that *Pesiqta Rabbati* does match the language of *Leviticus Rabbah*, but this is to be expected on account of the more common literary conflation in this later stage of rabbinic midrashic literature. *Midrash ha-Gadol*, which follows the *Palestinian Talmud* much more closely, retains סגין.

syntactical ambiguity of the scriptural passage. Through intertextual links to several Pentateuchal passages that employ the key root דבר from Isa 58:13, the *Damascus Document* formulates a set of three specific laws related to the proscribed speech following a general classificatory statement that realigns the precise legal application of Isa 58:13. These very same techniques were likewise observed in *4QHalakha B*, though in the service of a slightly different legal agenda. Where there is overlap with CD 10:17–19, the laws in *4QHalakha B* are more detailed and precise at the same time as they are more expansive. As in the *Damascus Document*, *4QHalakha B* draws freely upon the language of Isa 58:13 in its legal-exegetical formulation. In one instance, we would expect to see Isaianic language but do not (l. 5). This exegetical non-use of Isa 58:13 seems to reflect a deliberate polemic against Second Temple (and rabbinic) traditions that expanded the speech prohibition to include also thoughts about business matters. Finally, the last two lines of *4QHalakha B* reflect the most significant development from the *Damascus Document*. All nonsacred and nonessential speech is proscribed. This law represents another attempt to make sense of Isa 58:13 and provide a real-life application. As in other laws discussed above, this understanding of Isa 58:13 also finds several points of exegetical and legal contact in Second Temple and rabbinic texts.

My analysis of *Jubilees* highlighted several significant similarities in exegetical technique with the *Damascus Document* and *4QHalakha B*. Moreover, *Jubilees*' exegetical reformulation of Isa 58:13 follows the same structural pattern as the *Damascus Document*. The closely related rabbinic traditions discussed provide additional evidence for the pervasiveness of Isa 58:13 as the scriptural source for prohibitions regarding business-related speech on the Sabbath. In this respect, as in *Jubilees*, they indicate that the legal-exegetical explication of Isa 58:13 in CD 10:17–19 is not unique to the community of the Dead Sea Scrolls.

As with Jub 50:8, the rabbinic texts reflect various points of legal and exegetical correspondence with CD 10:17–19, though in varying degrees and sometimes with critical developments. As is to be expected in any study of rabbinic literature, the rabbinic texts explored above give voice to myriad different legal and exegetical approaches to the question of the restriction on speech on the Sabbath and its scriptural foundations. Three primary legal positions are articulated in the rabbinic texts: (1) speech related to business is prohibited on the Sabbath, (2) all forms of speech deemed inconsistent with the sacred nature of the Sabbath are prohibited, and (3) idle or excessive speech is prohibited on the Sabbath. In all three cases, rabbinic texts identify Isa 58:13 as the scriptural source. In some cases, an explicit exegetical argument is advanced, while in others, Isa 58:13 is merely taken for granted as the scriptural source. When distinct exegetical techniques are discernible, they also vary across the rabbinic texts.

My analysis has demonstrated that the rabbinic texts share much with their Second Temple–period antecedents with regard to the broad strokes in which these laws are framed in both corpora. The central role of the restriction on business-related speech in Second Temple Judaism seems to have been retained in rabbinic law. Indeed, the rabbinic concern for planning for post-Sabbath business dealings as articulated in the law of hiring workers in the *Mishnah* and *Babylonian Talmud* and the law of calculations in the *Babylonian Talmud* reiterates earlier Second Temple concerns with speech on the Sabbath regarding post-Sabbath business dealings. Rabbinic texts identify speech related to business or financial matters as a unique form of proscribed speech, even as additional types of nonsacred speech began to be outlawed on the Sabbath. As in the Second Temple texts, Isa 58:13 plays a central exegetical role in framing the scriptural foundations of this law. Yet, as observed in my analysis of several of the rabbinic texts, Isa 58:13 rarely functions as the exegetical cornerstone for the restriction on business-related speech as it does in the Second Temple–period texts. I suggested that rabbinic literature essentially takes for granted the close relationship between Isa 58:13 and the restriction on speech, whereby it draws upon the scriptural verse to delineate further aspects of the law. The perceived centrality of Isa 58:13 and its concomitant exegetical versatility is likely the result of its still influential legal and exegetical status in the transition from Second Temple–period Jewish law to rabbinic *halakhah*.

Two additional wider features in the rabbinic texts can help frame better our understanding of the Second Temple–period texts and provide insight into the position of all of this textual material in the broader history of Jewish law and legal exegesis. The first of these features is the curious proliferation of rabbinic laws restricting various forms of speech on the Sabbath. As in *4QHalakha B*, rabbinic law proscribes speech related to business on the Sabbath at the same time as it prohibits *all* forms of speech deemed inconsistent with the sacred nature of the Sabbath. While *4QHalakha B* is fragmentary and opaque, the rabbinic texts are a bit more forthcoming regarding the historical development of these legal categories and their continued coexistence.

In my treatment of *4QHalakha B*, I suggested that the general restriction on nonsacred and nonessential speech must be viewed as secondary to the more specific restriction on business-related speech. This historical development likely reflects a growing strictness applied to Sabbath observance that was then cast back into the scriptural foundational text of Isa 58:13. The fact that the straightforward reading of Isa 58:13 seemed to restrict general speech likely facilitated this legal transformation. Yet, in *4QHalakha B*, these laws restricting business speech and all nonsacred speech stand alongside each other, seemingly without any awareness that the latter law renders the former unnecessary.

The rabbinic texts provide a useful mirror of the phenomenon observed in *4QHalakha B*. The appearance of the various speech restrictions in rabbinic texts reinforces my suggestion regarding the historical reconstruction of the related set of laws in the Dead Sea Scrolls. In the rabbinic texts surveyed above, the tannaitic texts only contain legal formulations concerning the restrictions on speech related to business or financial affairs. Thus, the laws proscribing hiring future workers and calculations are found in the *Mishnah* and *Tosefta*, respectively, with an additional appearance in the *Mekhilta de-Rabbi Shim'on ben Yoḥai*. No traces of the more general law restricting nonsacred or idle speech on the Sabbath are found in any tannaitic texts. To be sure, this nuance of the speech restrictions does make its appearance in early amoraic works such as *Leviticus Rabbah* and the *Palestinian Talmud*. Yet, if the mere location in which these various laws first appear can be regarded as some reflection of their historical origins, it is clear that rabbinic law experiences a legal expansion of Sabbath speech restrictions in much the same way that the evidence of the Dead Sea Scrolls suggests. Thus, the earliest rabbinic law as enshrined in the tannaitic texts only restricts speech on the Sabbath related to business or financial affairs. Later rabbinic law, as attested by the many amoraic and late rabbinic texts treated above, expands the speech restrictions to include all speech of a nonsacred character.

Moreover, the rabbinic evidence provides further insight into the peculiar phenomenon observed above in *4QHalakha B*, whereby a general restriction on all nonessential speech on the Sabbath stands alongside a more limited prohibition of specific types of speech (i.e., business).

Two rabbinic texts treated above display a similar phenomenon. First, the exegetical discourse on the lemmata of Isa 58:13 in *b. Shabb.* 113a–b positions the restriction on calculations (based on עשות חפצך) directly alongside the expectation that one's speech on the Sabbath should be different from speech during the week (based on ודבר דבר).

The twofold presentation of these laws is also found in the passage in *Mishnat Rabbi Eli'ezer* (§20) treated above. The particular passage in *Mishnat Rabbi Eli'ezer* restricting "extra" or "idle" words appears near the end of a long list of Sabbath laws that are introduced with the question "From where (i.e., scriptural source) do we learn X?" followed by the identification of the purported scriptural source. The first part of this list, as noted above, first appears in the *Mekhilta de-Rabbi Shim'on ben Yoḥai* (§35). Gilat observes that the first portion of the list of laws contains a range of actions that would be performed on the Sabbath through words (e.g., business dealings, judicial proceedings, and betrothal or divorce proceedings). He therefore opines that *Mishnat Rabbi Eli'ezer* seeks to ensure that even exclusively speech actions are indeed considered equivalent to prohibited labor on the Sabbath.[65] Following this initial list is a second list of Sabbath prohibitions presented as part of an exegetical discourse on the various lemmata of Isa 58:13–14, including the restriction on idle speech as well as other non–speech-related actions. While the second part of the list in its full form is unique to *Mishnat Rabbi Eli'ezer*, its individual components are all drawn from earlier rabbinic texts.[66] Thus, the

[65] Gilat, "Sabbath Prohibitions," 255.

[66] See Epstein, "Mishnat Rabbi Eliezer," *8–*9.

composite list is a deliberate literary creation of the author/editor of *Mishnat Rabbi Eli'ezer*.

The initial list in *Mishnat Rabbi Eli'ezer* shares formal characteristics with the lists of speech-oriented prohibitions in CD 10:17–19 and *4QHalakha B*. As in these two texts, speech focused on business or financial matters figures largely in the list in *Mishnat Rabbi Eli'ezer* as drawn from the *Mekhilta de-Rabbi Shim'on ben Yoḥai*. As suggested above, this iteration of the speech prohibition is the earliest that appears in rabbinic law and literary sources. *Mishnat Rabbi Eli'ezer* deliberately attaches this manifestation of the law alongside the more general restriction on speech as found in the exegetical discourse on Isa 58:13–14 that follows. Undoubtedly, *Mishnat Rabbi Eli'ezer*, as in rabbinic legal thought more generally, recognized a practical distinction between the two sets of laws. In other words, the restrictions on business-related speech and other actions prohibited on the Sabbath are not deemed commensurate with the more general restriction on idle speech. The initial list of speech-oriented prohibitions consists of all actions that normally do serve a practical function, such as the execution of a business deal or legal proceedings. Yet, they are prohibited on the Sabbath. The restriction on "extra words" is framed in such a way that it is directed at conversation that serves no practical or sacred purpose. Indeed, this is the sense of the anecdote about Rabbi Shim'on ben Yoḥai's mother found elsewhere: her words are mere idle chatter and thus inappropriate for the Sabbath. While each set of speech-related restrictions has a distinct social context, they are both identified as inconsistent with the sacred nature of the Sabbath and thus prohibited. Thus, in the end, all of the specific examples of prohibited speech can be classified as inappropriate speech. Yet, the formal and structural presentations of these laws in rabbinic texts indicate that they enter into the halakhic tradition in distinct stages for unique reasons.

A second unique phenomenon observed in the rabbinic texts is the emergence of counter-exegetical traditions that do not ground any of these laws in Isa 58:13. My discussion of the *Damascus Document* demonstrates the central exegetical role of other scriptural passages, particularly from the Pentateuch. Yet, in none of these settings does the Pentateuchal passage stand alone. On the contrary, its mere presence is only as part of a broader intertextual bridge grounded in Isa 58:13. The absence of Isa 58:13 from several rabbinic texts is likely the result of the incipient unease in rabbinic Judaism with drawing upon non-Pentateuchal material for legal-exegetical purposes. As discussed above in Chapter 2, several rabbinic texts proscribe this very process.[67] A similar slow effacing of appeal to non-Pentateuchal texts will be detected in nearly all the rabbinic material treated in this study. In these cases, rabbinic texts often display an exegetical counternarrative in which legal-exegetical priority is given to a Pentateuchal prooftext. Yet, this very phenomenon serves to highlight the inverse reality. Many rabbinic texts show no compunction

[67] See discussion above, Chapter 2, section IV.

about employing non-Pentateuchal passages as prooftexts. What will become apparent through the course of this study is that this phenomenon is most pronounced when the rabbinic texts stand at the tail end of robust exegetical engagement with the particular scriptural verses in earlier Second Temple–period texts. As already suggested, the pervasiveness of these very same non-Pentateuchal verses in rabbinic literature is due to their long-standing presence as the primary scriptural sources – as evinced by the Second Temple–period material.

Jubilees and the later rabbinic traditions do not provide exact parallels to the laws restricting business-related conversation on the Sabbath in the Dead Sea Scrolls and their exegetical relationship to Isa 58:13. Indeed, such a phenomenon would be entirely unexpected. What these two sets of traditions do provide, however, is a larger legal and exegetical framework in which the sectarian hermeneutics found in the *Damascus Document* and *4QHalakha B* should be situated. The exegetical reading of Isa 58:13 in both texts and its legal application of this scriptural passage are not restricted to the community of the Dead Sea Scrolls. Rather, they represent a much more widespread tradition that is reflected in numerous legal-exegetical contexts in the Second Temple–period and in later rabbinic Judaism.

7

Isaiah 58:13 and the Restriction on Thoughts of Labor on the Sabbath in the Dead Sea Scrolls

I. INTRODUCTION

My particular focus in the next two chapters is the question of whether thoughts regarding forbidden labor are proscribed on the Sabbath. I begin this chapter by examining the legal-exegetical reformulation of Isa 58:13 in CD 10:20–21, which I argue supports the general interpretation of this passage as restricting thoughts about labor on the Sabbath. I then place this text into dialogue with similar presentations of law related to thoughts about work on the Sabbath elsewhere in sectarian literature (*4QHalakha B*). In the following chapter, I expand my scope of inquiry to other Second Temple (Philo) and rabbinic texts, the majority of which are also exegetically related to Isa 58:13. Within this broader literary setting, I am interested in three interconnected issues: (1) the specific contours of this Sabbath law in these different contexts, (2) the scriptural foundations of the legal formulations, and (3) approaches to the broader question of creating legislation regarding one's internal thoughts.

As in the previous three chapters, the Second Temple and rabbinic evidence explored in the following two chapters further attests to the broad history of Jewish law and legal exegesis in ancient Judaism. Prior to the discovery of the Dead Sea Scrolls, scholars could point to both Second Temple and rabbinic texts that address the prohibition against thoughts about labor on the Sabbath and its scriptural foundations. The new evidence provided by the Dead Sea Scrolls frames the disparate texts in ancient Judaism into a coherent dialogue and counterdialogue regarding these questions. My tour through these texts highlights the tension among the various texts regarding the application of this law and its scriptural basis. Throughout, we shall see how later rabbinic texts provide an important key to unlocking interpretive cruxes in the Dead Sea Scrolls texts at the same time as the Dead Sea Scrolls, Second Temple legal texts, and rabbinic literature can now be plotted on a larger trajectory of Jewish legal-exegetical activity in antiquity.

II. THE DEAD SEA SCROLLS AND THE NATURE OF LAW IN ANCIENT JUDAISM

The comparative analysis in the following two chapters moves beyond merely charting the historical development of the restriction on thought from the Second Temple period to rabbinic Judaism. The evidence also provides an opportunity to gain greater insight into approaches to both legal theory and the nature of law in ancient Judaism. In a broader perspective, many of the texts explored in these two chapters engage a larger question in the theory of law – how can a legal system legislate regarding one's mental status? What we shall see is that implicit in the various ways in which the contours of this law are expressed is a statement on legal theory. Is it realistic and sustainable to create legislation that is so restrictive, ultimately difficult for an individual to implement, and surely impossible for any possible legal authorities to enforce?

The role of legislation regarding thoughts is an issue treated in both ancient and modern legal systems.[1] In the legal literature of ancient Israel, for example, one finds legislation that proscribes coveting one's neighbor's wife (Exod 20:17; Deut 5:18) or hating one's brother in one's heart and bearing a grudge (Lev 19:17–18).[2] Other unequivocal examples of punishment or reward for mere

1 My interest in these two chapters is specifically legislation directed at thoughts where no attendant action is assumed to transpire. A closely related issue is the assessment of whether a completed criminal action (*actus reus*) matches the intention (*mens rea*) of the actor. This issue is clearly present in legal material of the Hebrew Bible (e.g., the distinction drawn between murder and manslaughter in Exod 21:12–14; Num 35:6–34; Deut 19:4–5) and later Jewish legal literature. See fuller discussion in David Daube, *The Deed and the Doer in the Bible* (Gifford Lectures, volume 1; edited and compiled by Calum Carmichael; West Conshohocken: Templeton Foundation, 2008), 31–52; Bernard S. Jackson, "Liability for Mere Intention in Early Jewish Law," in *Essays in Jewish and Comparative Legal History* (SJLA 10; Leiden: Brill, 1975), 202–34 (222–28) (1971). Moreover, this very question continues to loom large in modern legal theory and jurisprudence. See, e.g., Gerard Coffey, "Codifying the Meaning of 'Intention' in the Criminal Law," *Journal of Criminal Law* 79 (2009): 394–413, and earlier literature cited therein.

2 Both ancient rabbinic interpretation and many biblical scholars construe "covet" (חמד) in the Decalogue law as implying the associated act of appropriation. In so doing, this law is interpreted in much the same way as most modern law regards intention – one is only culpable when intention is combined with action (see previous note). The various approaches are deftly summarized and critiqued by Jackson, who defends the interpretation of the commandment as applying only to intention ("Liability for Mere Intention," especially 202–13). Note that the statement regarding hating one's brother is intimately connected to failure to offer reproof, perhaps suggesting that the latter is the specific action tied to the condemned thoughts (i.e., hate) indicated in the former. Similarly, bearing a grudge is associated with taking vengeance, again possibly suggesting that the thought (grudge) commonly develops into external action (vengeance). Yet, in both cases (hate, grudge), the presumed chain of causation is never explicitly outlined, thereby marking these two restrictions as independent legislative categories.

intention are not in the realm of human law, but rather involve the dispensing of divine justice: for example, the response of the flood for humanity's evil intentions (Gen 6:5) and the divine blessing of David for mere intention to build the temple (1 Sam 16:7). Thus, Bernard S. Jackson suggests that intention was never actually applied as a basis for liability in ancient Israelite law, but that the Israelite notion of divine justice did assign culpability to wrong thoughts.[3]

Closer to the world of ancient Judaism explored in this book, perhaps the most famous example where guilt can be assigned based on thoughts is found in Matt 5:27–28 (cf. Mark 9:47). In this passage, Jesus is presented as condemning lust as equivalent to adultery.[4] Similarly, Josephus mentions that mere intention to commit wrongdoing against one's parents warrants the death penalty (*Against Apion* 2.217), though Jackson asserts that this example is exceptional on account of the importance assigned to parents. Thus, it should not be regarded as representative of broader legal trends.[5]

Rabbinic evidence regarding legislation against mere thoughts is, as expected, not uniform, though it generally rejects the position that thought alone renders an individual guilty.[6] In particular, scholars have noted a distinction between the legal reasoning of the School of Shammai, which minimizes the legal force for intention, and the School of Hillel, for which intention can act as a determining factor.[7] A good example can be found in the discussion in *Mishnah 'Ohalot* 4:3 of the impurity of openings in a house containing a corpse. The openings are all regarded as impure in the present because it is not known through which one the corpse will be removed in the future. The act of opening one pathway is sufficient to isolate the impurity to that opening and render all others safe from impurity. Even more, the School of Hillel and the School of Shammai debate to what extent mere intention to remove the corpse through one of the openings has the same effect. While they disagree on the

[3] Jackson, "Liability for Mere Intention," 212–13.

[4] Further narrative examples are found in Jackson, "Liability for Mere Intention," 213–15.

[5] Jackson, "Liability for Mere Intention," 216–17. Indeed, elsewhere (*Jewish Antiquities* 12.358), Josephus mentions the opinion of Polybius of Megalopolis, who suggested that Antiochus died because he intended to plunder the temple of Diana in Persia. In response, Josephus asserts that mere intention to commit a crime does not render one liable for punishment.

[6] A significant amount has been written on this issue in rabbinic literature. See Solomon Zeitlin's many articles devoted to the topic collected in *Studies in the Early History of Judaism*, volume 4: *History of Early Talmudic Law* (New York: Ktav, 1978); Michael Higger, "Intention in Talmudic Law," in *Studies in Jewish Jurisprudence* (ed. E. M. Gershfield; New York: Hermon, 1971), 235–93 (1927); Yitzḥak D. Gilat, "Intention and Action in Tannaitic Literature," in *Studies in the Development of Halakha* (Ramat Gan: Bar Ilan University Press, 1992), 72–84 [Hebrew] (1967–68); Robert Goldenberg, "Commandment and Consciousness in Talmudic Thought," *HTR* 68 (1975): 261–72; Jackson, "Liability for Mere Intention," 218; Howard Eilberg-Schwartz, *The Human Will in Judaism: The Mishnah's Philosophy of Intention* (BJS 103; Atlanta: Scholars Press, 1986); Shana Strauch-Schick, "Intention in the Babylonian Talmud: An Intellectual History" (Ph.D. diss., Yeshiva University, 2011).

[7] In addition to Zeitlin's many studies on this issue (see previous note), see especially Gilat, "Intention and Action."

details, both the School of Shammai and the School of Hillel agree on the legal force of intention.[8]

Thus, the broader legal context of the Second Temple and rabbinic material that I treat in these two chapters is aware of the notion that law can be enacted to limit thoughts. At the same time, this approach is clearly in the minority in both literary representation and practical jurisprudence.[9] In a similar way, modern legal theory and practical jurisprudence generally rejects any consideration of legislation regarding thoughts.[10] Indeed, in American jurisprudence, the Supreme Court has consistently interpreted the First Amendment as offering the opposite effect – one is free to *think* whatever one desires.[11]

The texts that I examine in these two chapters never explicitly enter into this broader theoretical debate. Yet, the question they address – whether thoughts regarding forbidden labor on the Sabbath are similarly prohibited – stands at the heart of this wider legal debate. At times, some texts seem to polemicize against other perspectives in the specific debate on Sabbath law, thereby simultaneously engaging the broader question of legal theory. In such cases, the polemical tone is always voiced by the more lenient positions in an attempt to demonstrate the implausibility of the more restrictive positions. In mapping out the various voices in this debate, I demonstrate that the history of Jewish law on this question reflects a gradual shift away from the more restrictive position in favor of the more lenient approach. Such a trend is already visible in the Second Temple–period material and resurfaces in the rabbinic texts.

These two chapters contribute to another broader set of theoretical questions in the comparative study of the nature of law in the Dead Sea Scrolls and rabbinic Judaism – the degree to which sectarian law reflects a "realistic" conception of law versus the presumed "nominalism" of later rabbinic law. As applied initially by Daniel R. Schwartz to qualify the distinction in the two sets of law, the "realism" of law in the Dead Sea Scrolls is guided by viewing the "commandments as guidelines based in independently existing situations, which man, due to the grace of the wisdom-giving God, may introduce among his considerations by accepting the yoke of the commandment." In contrast,

8 For an insightful analysis of this passage and its significance for understanding rabbinic notions of intention, see Vered Noam, "Ritual Purity in Tannaitic Literature: Two Opposing Perspectives," *JAJ* 1 (2010): 65–103 (86–87).

9 A similar situation seems to be present in Roman law. See the evidence collected in Jackson, "Liability for Mere Intention," 214, 218–19. It is of note, however, that Cicero, in his treatment of moral law, regards lust (*in libidine esse*) as one misdeed for which culpability requires no action (see *De finibus bonorum et malorum*, III.ix.32).

10 In the realm of legal theory, see Herbert Morris, "Punishment for Thoughts," in *On Guilt and Innocence: Essays in Legal Philosophy and Moral Psychology* (Berkeley: University of California Press, 1976), 1–29; compared with Meir Dan-Cohen, "Harmful Thoughts," *Law and Philosophy* 18 (1999): 379–405. For practical jurisprudence, see Marbree D. Sullivan, "The Thought Police: Doling out Punishment for Thinking about Criminal Behavior in John Doe v. City of Lafayette," *New England Law Review* 40 (2005): 263–301.

11 See Sullivan, "The Thought Police," 264–65 (especially the cases collected in nn. 12–13), 271–82.

rabbinic "nominalism" regards the "commandments as orders resultant from the will of the commanding God."[12] Schwartz has been criticized for his portrait of rabbinic law as universally nominalist and for seeing sharp distinctions between realism and nominalism in both corpora where the evidence is equivocal at best.[13] My analysis in this chapter strengthens the arguments of Schwartz and others regarding sectarian law in the Dead Sea Scrolls. Indeed, the material in this chapter corresponds well with the "core claim" of American legal realism that laws "respond primarily to the stimulus of the facts of the case, rather than to legal rules of reason."[14] At the same time, my analysis of rabbinic literature in the next chapter reinforces the notion that rabbinic law cannot simply be defined as nominalist but rather displays tensions between realism and nominalism.[15] The interweaving of realism and nominalism in both the Second Temple and rabbinic material examined in this study further complicates attempts to create a sharp historical disconnect between the law and legal exegesis of the Second Temple period and that of rabbinic Judaism.

III. THOUGHTS ABOUT WORK ON THE SABBATH IN THE DAMASCUS DOCUMENT

In a separate study on CD 10:20–21, I treat the textual difficulties in the medieval manuscript (Ms A) and explain the specific aspects of Sabbath law outlined in the passage.[16] I argue that a greater sensitivity to the exegetical techniques operating in the passage represents the key to unlocking the difficulty

[12] Daniel R. Schwartz, "Law and Truth: On Qumran-Sadducean and Rabbinic Views of Law," in *The Dead Sea Scrolls: Forty Years of Research* (ed. D. Dimant and U. Rappaport; STDJ 10; Leiden: Brill; Jerusalem: Magnes Press and Yad Izhak Ben-Zvi, 1992), 229–40 (231 n. 8). The terminology draws on Yochanan Silman, "Halakhic Determinations of a Nominalist and Realistic Nature: Legal and Philosophical Considerations," *Diné Israel: Studies in Halakhah and Jewish Law* 12 (1984–85): 249–66 (251) [Hebrew]. For a fuller explanation of this terminology informed by its philosophical origins, see Jeffrey L. Rubenstein, "Nominalism and Realism in Qumranic and Rabbinic Law: A Reassessment," *DSD* 6 (1999): 157–83 (158–59 n. 5). See further Aharon Shemesh, *Halakhah in the Making: The Development of Jewish Law from Qumran to the Rabbis* (Berkeley: University of California Press, 2009), 107–28; Christine Hayes, "Legal Realism and the Fashioning of Sectarians in Jewish Antiquity," in *Sects and Sectarianism in Jewish History* (ed. S. Stern; Leiden: Brill, 2011), 119–46.

[13] See especially Rubenstein, "Nominalism and Realism." See also Yaakov Elman, "Some Remarks on 4QMMT and the Rabbinic Traditions: Or, When Is a Parallel not a Parallel?" in *Reading 4QMMT: New Perspectives on Qumran Law and History* (SBLSymS 2; ed. J. Kampen and M. J. Bernstein; Atlanta: Scholars Press, 1996), 99–128 (100–2, 124–25); Shemesh, *Halakhah in the Making*, 107–8.

[14] See Brian Leiter, "American Legal Realism," in *The Blackwell Guide to the Philosophy of Law and Legal Theory* (ed. M. P. Golding and W. A. Edmundson; Malden: Blackwell, 2005), 50–66 (52).

[15] This tension is observed by Silman, "Halakhic Determinations," 250, though is not incorporated into Schwartz's assessment of rabbinic law. See Rubenstein, "Nominalism and Realism," 158–61.

[16] Alex P. Jassen, "What Exactly Is Prohibited in the Field? A New Suggestion for Understanding the Text and Context of CD 10:20–21," *RevQ* 25 (2011): 41–62.

TABLE 6. *The Reformulation of Isa 58:13 in CD 10:20–21*

	Isa 58:13		CD 10:20–21	
a	אם תשיב משבת רגלך If you turn away your foot from the Sabbath	→	אל יתהלך איש בשדה Let no man walk in the field	a'
b	עשות חפציך	→	לעשות את עבודת חפצו	b'
+	from pursuing your affairs מעשות דרכיך ממצוא חפצך go not your ways nor look to your affairs		in order to do his desired labor	
c	ביום קדשי on my holy day	→	<ביום> השבת <on> the Sabbath <day>	c'

surrounding the textual and legal issues. As has been noted by many scholars, CD 10:20–21 represents a legal-exegetical reformulation of Isa 58:13.[17]

My analysis of this passage below demonstrates that the *Damascus Document* transforms the vague prophetic invective against violation of the Sabbath in Isa 58:13 into a clear case of Sabbath legislation – in much the same way that ודבר דבר from Isa 58:13 becomes the scriptural foundation for the restriction on speech in CD 10:17–19 and 4Q264a 1 i 5–8 as explored in Chapters 4 and 5. My treatment of CD 10:20–21 agrees with Louis Ginzberg's proposal – based on a parallel rabbinic law – that CD 10:20–21 restricts the act of traveling through one's field on the Sabbath in order to assess what future work needs to be undertaken in the field. The primary issue here is neither the mere act of walking in the field nor the possibility that one will engage in the work on the Sabbath. The former is not regarded as problematic, while the latter is otherwise covered under more general Sabbath restrictions on Sabbath labor. The specific issue in the *Damascus Document* is the restriction on thoughts regarding labor that will transpire as one travels through the field with the explicit intent of surveying its needs. Careful attention to the reformulation

[17] The connection is observed, with varying degrees of elaboration, in Solomon Schechter, *Documents of Jewish Sectaries*, volume 1: *Fragments of a Zadokite Work* (Cambridge: Cambridge University Press, 1910; repr. with prolegomenon by Joseph Fitzmyer; Library of Biblical Studies; New York: Ktav, 1970), 80; Louis Ginzberg, *An Unknown Jewish Sect* (Moreshet 1; New York: Jewish Theological Seminary, 1976), 59; Chaim Rabin, *The Zadokite Documents* (Oxford: Clarendon, 1954), 53; Lawrence H. Schiffman, *The Halakhah at Qumran* (SJLA 16; Leiden: Brill, 1975), 91; Joseph M. Baumgarten and Daniel R. Schwartz, "Damascus Document (CD)," in *The Dead Sea Scrolls: Hebrew, Aramaic, and Greek Texts with English Translations; Damascus Document, War Scroll and Related Documents* (ed. J. H. Charlesworth; PTSDSSP 2; Tübingen: Mohr Siebeck; Louisville: Westminster John Knox, 1995), 47; Lutz Doering, *Schabbat: Sabbathhalacha und –praxis im antiken Judentum und Urchristentum* (TSAJ 78; Tübingen: Mohr Siebeck, 1999), 144; Ben Zion Wacholder, *The New Damascus Document: The Midrash on the Eschatological Torah of the Dead Sea Scrolls: Reconstruction, Translation, and Commentary* (STDJ 56; Leiden: Brill, 2007), 332.

of Isa 58:13 in CD 10:20–21 reveals the exegetical techniques at work in the *Damascus Document*.

Text and Translation: Damascus Document (CD) 10:20–21[18]

20 אל יתהלך איש בשדה לעשות את עבודת חפצו[19]

21 <ביום> השבת

20. Let no man walk in the field in order to do his desired labor

21. <on> the Sabbath <day>

What Exactly Is Prohibited in the Field?

A simple reading of CD 10:20–21 demonstrates why its full understanding has long been elusive.[20] The first half of the clause describes a situation in which an individual is walking through a field on the Sabbath, an act that by itself is clearly not forbidden. The text proceeds to prohibit the performance of some type of labor presumably undertaken in the field. The final portion of the text seems to add an additional explanation of the presumed time frame for the proscribed labor. Yet, this particular formulation – השבת – is grammatically and syntactically incoherent and only further obfuscates the full meaning of the passage.

A full understanding of CD 10:20–21 is only possible when this passage is read in the context of its broader legal-exegetical reformulation of Isa 58:13. In Table 6, I isolate specific textual elements from Isa 58:13 that have been reformulated in CD 10:20–21.

As in other passages in the *Damascus Document* and sectarian legal literature, the scriptural language is reformulated in the *Damascus Document* to align with the specific aspect of Sabbath law articulated. This reformulation operates at both the structural and exegetical levels. Structurally, the first three textual units in Isa 58:13 serve as the textual foundations for the three syntactic units in CD 10:20–21. Thus, (1) Isa 58:13a is reformulated as CD 10:20 (a'), and (2) Isa 58:13b provides the core language for CD 10:20 (b'). In this

[18] The Hebrew text follows Elisha Qimron, "The Text of CDC," in *The Damascus Document Reconsidered* (ed. M. Broshi; Jerusalem: Israel Exploration Society, the Shrine of the Book, Israel Museum, 1992), 29. The material in brackets represents my suggested emendation based on my understanding of the text as presented below and as more fully developed in Jassen, "What Exactly Is Prohibited in the Field?" 4Q270 6 v preserves all the surrounding text but contains a lacuna in the very place where this passage would be found. See Joseph M. Baumgarten, *Qumran Cave 4.XIII: The Damascus Document (4Q266–273)* (DJD 18; Oxford: Clarendon, 1996), 160–61.

[19] On the debate whether to transcribe this word as חפצו or חפצי, see Jassen, "What Exactly Is Prohibited in the Field?" 43–44 n. 10. The *waw* is clearly visible on the manuscript.

[20] This section draws on my much fuller analysis of CD 10:20–21 and engagement with previous approaches to the text presented by Solomon Schechter, Louis Ginzberg, and Chaim Rabin as found in Jassen, "What Exactly Is Prohibited in the Field?"

particular case, CD 10:20 is likewise influenced by the second use of עשה and חפץ later in Isa 58:13, and (3) Isa 58:13c is reformulated in CD 10:20–21 (c'). My discussion of this passage explores how each of these three legal-exegetical reformulations operates and how a full understanding of these techniques yields a better sense of both the text and context of CD 10:20–21.

(1) Isa 58:13a: אם תשיב משבת רגלך ("If you turn away your foot from the Sabbath") → CD 10:20 (a'): אל יתהלך איש בשדה ("Let no man walk in the field"). At first glance, these two formulations seem to have little to do with each other. Closer analysis, however, reveals that two legal-exegetical reformulations are operating. The passage in *Isaiah* employs a highly rhetorical exhortation to restrain one's foot as a way to enjoin its audience to cease violating the Sabbath. While some commentators have suggested that *Isaiah* has in mind the literal restraint of one's foot through the cessation of travel, the meaning of this metaphor is likely the more general condemnation of Sabbath violations.[21] In the Second Temple period, this type of ambiguous exhortation couched in metaphorical language becomes fodder for exegetical reformulation.

The *Damascus Document* understands the rhetorical expression in *Isaiah* in its most literal sense, whereby the movement of one's foot is regarded as walking. The exhortation to cease from this "walking" in *Isaiah* is carried over to the reformulation in CD 10:20–21. The *Damascus Document*, however, has reformulated the rhetorical exhortation into clear apodictic legal language familiar from elsewhere in the legal portions of the *Damascus Document* and related sectarian legal literature. Thus, the negation is combined with the masculine singular jussive form and an explicit general subject (איש + יתהלך + אל). The *Damascus Document* articulates in explicit legal language ("Let no man walk") what *Isaiah* asserts in characteristically evasive prophetic language ("Turn away your foot").

One additional modification is present in the inclusion of שדה in the *Damascus Document*. Isa 58:13 has no specific space in mind for its exhortation, which is likely to be extended to all settings in which Sabbath violations occur. CD 10:20–21, in contrast, frames its reformulation in the context of the specific setting of the field. This expansion is consistent with the more general reformulation of Isa 58:13 in CD 10:20–21 from a general prophetic exhortation to a more clearly defined case of Sabbath restriction.

(2) Isa 58:13b: עשות חפציך + מעשות דרכיך ממצוא חפצך ("From pursuing your affairs" + "Go not your ways nor look to your affairs") → CD 10:20 (b'): לעשות את עבודת חפצו ("In order to do his desired labor"). While Isa 58:13a is reformulated in order to articulate the restriction on movement, the *Damascus Document* clearly does not merely prohibit one from walking through a field. The core aspect of the Sabbath restriction can be found in the legal-exegetical reformulation of the next element in Isa 58:13 – the combination of the keywords עשה and חפץ, which appear twice in the scriptural source text.

[21] For the suggestion that the clause refers to the restriction on travel in some form, see Chapter 5, n. 11. See further Jassen, "What Exactly Is Prohibited in the Field?" 52–53.

TABLE 7. *עשה and חפץ in Isa 58:13 and CD 10:20–21*

Twofold Use of עשה and חפץ in Isa 58:13	עשה and חפץ + עבודה in CD 10:20–21
First Use in Isa 58:13 עשות חפציך ביום קדשי "From pursuing your affairs on my holy day" *Second Use in Isa 58:13* מעשות ~~דרכיך ממצוא~~ חפצך "Go not ~~your ways nor look to~~ your affairs"	לעשות את [עבודת] חפצו "To pursue his desired [labor]" עבודה – *Analogy* See **Exod 20:9//Deut 5:13:** ששת ימים [תעבד] ועשית כל מלאכתך, "Six days [you shall labor] and do all your work." חפץ – *Semantic Reorientation* חפץ – Isa = "business, affair" → CD = "delight, pleasure, desire" (cf. 𝔗^J, 𝔊)

One can immediately detect that these two keywords serve as the textual basis of CD 10:20 (b'), with the further inclusion of עבודה. As in Isa 58:13a, the ambiguity of the prophetic language compels its exegetical refinement at the same time as it allows for significant latitude in how this is applied. Several different legal-exegetical reformulations are operating, which I have outlined in Table 7.

Let me begin with the first use of the keywords עשה and חפץ in *Isaiah*. Isa 58:13b condemns the pursuit of one's affairs (עשות חפציך) on the Sabbath. As in the first clause in the verse, the prophetic language is deliberately vague as it seeks to condemn a wide range of Sabbath violations. As observed in Chapter 4, the specific use of חפץ with its late biblical Hebrew meaning of "business, affair" has prompted several commentators to suggest that the passage condemns mercantile pursuits.[22] Later readers of *Isaiah* sought to provide clarity as to what specific action falls under the purview of the Sabbath restriction.

The inclusion of עבודה in CD 10:20 provides a solution that is exegetically woven into the literary fabric of the scriptural language from Isa 58:13. In Isa 58:13, חפץ is the direct object of the condemned actions (עשות + חפציך). In CD 10:20, it remains the direct object, but now as the second half of a construct clause – appropriately modified to reflect the third-person language of the *Damascus Document* (*Isaiah*: חפציך → CD: חפצו). The introduction of עבודה as the first half of the construct clause with חפץ (עבודת חפצו) serves to modify the broader meaning of חפץ, particularly as the entire construct clause now functions as the direct object of עשות. In so doing, the *Damascus Document* has resolved the lingering legal and exegetical dilemma in the interpretation and application of Isa 58:13. For the *Damascus Document*, a specific type of "business, affair" (חפץ) is condemned here – one that involves "labor" (עבודה).

A similar exegetical reformulation occurs with regard to the second appearance of עשה and חפץ in Isa 58:13. In the second appearance, these two words

[22] See above, Chapter 4, section II.

appear as the first and last elements in a clear example of binary poetic parallelism: מעשות דרכיך // ממצוא חפצך. CD 10:20 collapses the parallelism in a way that negates the intended parallelism in order to merge עשה and חפץ as in their first appearance in Isa 58:13b. At the same time, עבודה is introduced as the lexical substitute for the displaced words, thereby offering the semantic nuance for חפץ as outlined above (*Isaiah*: מעשות ~~דרכיך ממצוא~~ חפצך → CD: לעשות את עבודת חפצו).

The introduction of עבודה in CD 10:20 is motivated by both exegetical and semantic factors. Exegetically, the introduction of this word is based on textual analogy with the Sabbath law in the Decalogue, as outlined in Table 7. Exod 20:9//Deut 5:13 refers to the performance (עשה) of work with the language of engaging in one's labor (עבד) during the week: "Six days you shall labor (תעבד) and do (ועשית) all of your work." CD 10:20 appeals to the appearance of the keyword עשה in both Isa 58:13 and Exod 20:9//Deut 5:13 to draw out the related keyword עבד in Exod 20:9//Deut 5:13 and apply it to its exegetical reformulation of Isa 58:13. A similar intertextual alignment of Isa 58:13 and Exod 20:9//Deut 5:13 was observed in Chapter 4 as the exegetical basis for CD 10:19.[23]

Semantically, it is likely that the use of עבודה is intended to refer to *physical* labor. As discussed in Chapter 4, this meaning is consistent with the use of עבודה in the Hebrew Bible to refer to both general labor and proscribed physical labor on the Sabbath. This semantic range seems to be replicated in the Dead Sea Scrolls.[24] Indeed, the emphasis on physical labor is appropriate to the setting in the field, where it is precisely physical labor that is most commonly undertaken. The reformulated language of Isa 58:13b in CD 10:20 thus provides clear direction on the nature of the condemned חפץ by identifying it with physical labor in the field in which one is walking.

The foregoing discussion has revealed much of the exegetical technique of CD 10:20, but we seem to be no closer to understanding the practical application of the Sabbath restriction. A simple reading of CD 10:20–21 in light of its reformulation of Isa 58:13 – putting aside for the moment the textual corruption at the end – suggests that the passage proscribes walking in one's field in order to do some type of physical labor in the field. Indeed, Solomon Schechter understood the passage in this way in the *editio princeps* of the *Damascus Document*, and he has since been followed by many others.[25] Yet,

[23] See Chapter 4, section IV.

[24] See Chapter 4, section IV.

[25] Schechter, *Documents*, 80, translates: "One may not walk in the field to do the work of his affairs *on the day of* the Sabbath" (italics representing his textual emendation; see below). His basic sense of the passage is reflected in the presentation of the text in R. H. Charles, "Fragments of a Zadokite Work," in idem, ed., *Apocrypha and Pseudepigrapha of the Old Testament* (2 vols.; Oxford: Clarendon, 1913), 2:826; A. Dupont-Sommer, *The Essene Writings From Qumran* (trans. G. Vermes; Cleveland: Meridian, 1962), 152; Baumgarten and Schwartz, "Damascus Document," 47; Geza Vermes, *The Complete Dead Sea Scrolls in English*

on this very point, Louis Ginzberg long ago questioned Schechter's explanation by noting that it is incongruous for the *Damascus Document* to restrict general labor in the field. This type of action is clearly forbidden on account of more general restrictions on labor on the Sabbath. Something unique to the situation in the field must be in view in CD 10:20–21.[26]

Ginzberg's own approach seeks to respond to his criticism of Schechter and resolve the textual difficulty at the end of the passage. In my opinion, he is successful in the first task but fails in the second.[27] Ginzberg calls attention to an important rabbinic legal formulation that seems to offer a strikingly similar case: לא יהלך אדם בתוך שדהו לידע מה היא צריכה, "A man may not go into his field (on the Sabbath) in order to see what work is necessary (after the Sabbath)" (*b. 'Erub* 38b).[28] He argues that the "almost verbal parallel" between the rabbinic passage and the *Damascus Document* indicates that we can draw upon the clear circumstances of the rabbinic law to understand the obscure meaning of the law in the *Damascus Document*. Thus, for Ginzberg, the *Damascus Document* restricts an individual from traveling through a field to assess what specific actions need to be undertaken in the field after the Sabbath concludes.

Ginzberg is well aware that the simple sense of the *Damascus Document* seems to suggest otherwise. Thus, he offers a host of textual emendations to bring the textual evidence in line with his conceptual explanation of the passage. Most significantly, he proposes emending לעשות to לידע to make the *Damascus Document* more explicitly conform to the rabbinic law. At the same time, he attempts to make the text more clearly indicate that the labor itself is undertaken not on the Sabbath but rather during the week that follows. He offers two suggestions in this regard. First, he proposes emending the incoherent השבת to אחר השבת ("after the Sabbath"). He seems to embrace more enthusiastically a second possibility. He emends חפצו to חפצי, whereby it now forms the first half of a construct phrase with השבת. Ginzberg then suggests that שבת here does not convey its usual meaning of "Sabbath" but rather an alternate meaning of "week." Thus, the labor in the *Damascus Document* is that which pertains to the "needs of the week."[29]

(London: Penguin, 2004), 141; Edward Cook, "Damascus Document," in Michael Wise, Martin Abegg Jr., and Edward Cook, *The Dead Sea Scrolls: A New Translation* (2d ed.; San Francisco: HarperSanFrancisco, 2006), 71. It is not always clear if those who offer a translation similar to Schechter's subscribe to the same basic meaning or merely retain the ambiguity of the Hebrew in translation.

26 Ginzberg, *Jewish Sect*, 58. Schechter seems to anticipate this criticism and tentatively suggests in his notes that the issue is "probably" planning for work (contrary to the sense of his translation). See Schechter, *Documents*, 80.

27 On Ginzberg, see further Jassen, "What Exactly Is Prohibited in the Field?" 47–49.

28 Ginzberg, *Jewish Sect*, 58 (following Ms Munich 95; the Vilna printed edition and Ms Vatican ebr. 109 have בסוף שדהו; the translation is Ginzberg's). This passage appears in several different rabbinic texts, which are discussed in greater detail in the following chapter.

29 Ginzberg, *Jewish Sect*, 58.

Ginzberg's textual and semantic dissection of CD 10:20–21 is by all accounts unwarranted. The emendation of לעשות to לידע is guided less by textual plausibility than by a desire to make the *Damascus Document* say exactly what Ginzberg wants it to say, thereby making an "almost verbal parallel" even more parallel. The reorientation of the meaning of שבת from "Sabbath" to "week" is similarly unlikely based on our fuller knowledge of Hebrew lexicography. While the latter meaning appears with increasing frequency in rabbinic Hebrew, it is likely absent in biblical Hebrew, and שבת never means "week" in the Dead Sea Scrolls.[30]

The approaches of Schechter and Ginzberg differ on whether the prohibition pertains to labor actually performed on the Sabbath or the act of planning for future labor. While Schechter's translation of the passage makes little sense, Ginzberg's forced emendations are equally unsatisfying. Neither Schechter nor Ginzberg includes any discussion of the scriptural basis for the law or engages with the exegetical reformulation of Isa 58:13 that forms the core language of the passage. A closer examination of CD 10:20–21 in dialogue with its exegetical basis in Isa 58:13 reinforces Ginzberg's sense of the legal parameters of the Sabbath law.

I noted above that the expression עשות חפציך in Isa 58:13b employs the relatively rare late biblical Hebrew meaning of חפץ as "business, affair." The perceived ambiguity surrounding the precise meaning of this expression can be detected in the various ways in which the ancient translators render this clause. In searching for a nuance to attach to the clause, both the Septuagint and the Targum appeal to the more common biblical Hebrew meaning of חפץ as "delight, pleasure, desire." Thus, the Septuagint renders עשות חפציך as μὴ ποιεῖν τὰ θελήματά σου ("nor pursuing your desire"). θέλημα is the common word used by the Septuagint to render Hebrew חפץ when it denotes "delight, pleasure, desire."[31] In contrast, when חפץ appears with the meaning of "business, affair," the Septuagint translates it as πρᾶγμα.[32] Similarly, the Targum translates the same clause as למעבד צרכך, "Performing your needs (i.e., that which you desire)." The Aramaic צרוך commonly appears in the Targum as the equivalent

30 For possible attestations of the alternate meaning of שבת as "week" in biblical Hebrew, see Lev 23:15; 25:8; Isa 66:23; and F. Brown, S. R. Driver, and C. A. Briggs, *Hebrew and English Lexicon* (Peabody: Hendrickson, 1997), 992b; Ludwig Koehler and Walter Baumgartner, *The Hebrew and Aramaic Lexicon of the Old Testament* (2 vols.; Leiden: Brill, 2001), 1411. For the more explicit evidence in rabbinic Hebrew, see Marcus Jastrow, *A Dictionary of the Targumim, the Talmud Babli and Yerushalmi, and the Midrashic Literature* (Peabody: Hendrickson, 2005), 1520.

31 See e.g., 𝔊 2 Sam 23:5; 1 Kgs 5:22; Isa 48:14; 2 Chr 9:12.

32 See, e.g., Eccl 3:1, 17; 5:7; 8:6 (except in Sir 10:26 as noted below, Chapter 8, n. 15). Moreover, the Greek translation of *Ecclesiastes* is careful to distinguish this meaning of חפץ from its other appearances with the meaning of "delight, pleasure, desire," which is correctly rendered with θέλημα (Eccl 5:3; 8:13; 12:1, 10). Thus, the possibility of a translation mistake in Isa 58:13 is unlikely. On broader uses of θέλημα in the Septuagint, see G. Schrenk, "θέλω, θέλημα, θέλησις," *TDNT* 3:44–62 (53–54).

of the Hebrew חפץ ("desire, delight, pleasure").[33] Both translations are likely influenced by other appearances of עשה and חפץ together in *Isaiah*, where חפץ clearly conveys its more common meaning of "delight, pleasure, desire" (Isa 46:10; 48:14; 55:11).

I am suggesting that the use of חפץ in the *Damascus Document* reflects the same semantic reorientation that is found in the Targum and Septuagint.[34] In this sense, the work alluded to in CD 10:20–21 is not work that will actually be performed on the Sabbath (Schechter), but rather it is the work that one desires to do – that is, future work (Ginzberg). Unlike in the Septuagint and the Targum, the semantic reorientation of חפץ in the *Damascus Document* carries with it implications for the contours of the Sabbath law articulated in CD 10:20–21. The *Damascus Document* retains the scriptural עשות even as it creates the impression that the restriction applies to the performance of physical labor in the field on the Sabbath. The alignment of עשות with the semantically reoriented חפץ, however, contextually reorients עשות from its basic meaning of "to do, perform" into a more nuanced meaning of "to plan" for future work.[35] The close rabbinic parallel adduced by Ginzberg provides the most plausible scenario for the content of the Sabbath restriction in CD 10:20–21. As in the rabbinic case, the *Damascus Document* is concerned that an individual passing through the field will mentally note what work needs to be undertaken in the field after the Sabbath.

Here, we see a significant difference between the formal presentation of law in rabbinic Judaism versus in sectarian literature (and by extension related segments of Second Temple Judaism). Scripture forms the basis for the literary presentation of law in the Dead Sea Scrolls, and thus both keywords from Isa 58:13 are retained in the reformulation of this verse in CD 10:20–21. Through a variety of exegetical techniques, the *Damascus Document* reorients and expands the meaning of חפץ. The *Damascus Document*'s fidelity to the scriptural language compels it to retain עשות in spite of its potential for

33 See $\mathfrak{T}^{J}$ 1 Kgs 5:22, 23, 24; 9:11; Jer 48:38; Hos 8:8. See also the parallel use of Hebrew צורך and חפץ in Sir 10:26. See further Jassen, "What Exactly Is Prohibited in the Field?" 58 n. 56.

34 My understanding of the meaning of חפץ in CD 10:20–21 as some form of "delight, pleasure, desire" follows similar translations in Rabin, *Zadokite Documents*, 52; É. Cothenet, "Le Document de Damas," in *Les Textes de Qumran traduits et annotés*, volume 2 (ed. J. Carmignac, É. Cothenet, and H. Lignée; Paris: Letouzey et Ané, 1963), 192; Eduard Lohse, *Die Texte aus Qumran* (München: Kösel, 1964); Schiffman, *Halakhah*, 90; Baruch Sharvit, "The Sabbath of the Judean Desert Sect," *Immanuel* 9 (1979): 42–48 (45); Florentino García Martínez and Eibert J. C. Tigchelaar, *The Dead Sea Scrolls Study Edition* (2 vols.; Leiden: Brill, 1997–98), 1:569; Cook, "Damascus Document," 71.

35 In my earlier study of CD 10:20–21, I explore the possibility that עשה has also experienced a semantic reorientation (as with חפץ). I examine alternative meanings of עשה that convey the sense of future planning. I also reexamine the possibility first suggested by Cothenet that the use of עשה in CD 10:20–21 may draw on the meaning of the closely related root עשת ("to think, devise"). See further Jassen, "What Exactly Is Prohibited in the Field?" 59–60.

obscuring the broader meaning of the passage. In contrast, the parallel rabbinic formulation introduced by Ginzberg is not bound at all by the scriptural language of Isa 58:13 or any other scriptural passage. Thus, it presents the situation with the much more contextually appropriate verb ידע, thereby making explicit its concern with one's thoughts, not physical actions.

(3) Isa 58:13c: ביום קדשי ("On my holy day") → CD 10:21 (c'): <ביום> השבת ("<On> the Sabbath <day>"). The third and final legal-exegetical reformulation of Isa 58:13 provides the key to resolving the textual difficulty in CD 10:20–21 at the same time as it provides a sharper understanding of the time frame for the proscribed activity. Isa 58:13c condemns the pursuit of one's affairs "on my holy day." Though this expression is rare in the Hebrew Bible, it almost certainly is employed in *Isaiah* to designate the Sabbath day.[36] More specifically, the expression is employed in Isa 58:13 to refer to the time frame in which the condemned activity transpires – that is, on the Sabbath itself. As such, it seems most likely that this same temporal sense should be carried over to the exegetical reformulation of Isa 58:13c in the *Damascus Document*. CD 10:20–21, however, clearly does not employ the identical temporal expression. Rather, the *Damascus Document* modifies the scriptural designation of the Sabbath (יום קדשי) in order to make it comport with more standard terminology for the Sabbath in sectarian literature. In both legal and nonlegal sectarian texts, the Sabbath is referred to as either השבת or יום השבת.[37]

Most important, all of the prohibitions surrounding CD 10:20–21 that have temporal designations proscribe the specific action "on the Sabbath day" (ביום השבת).[38] In particular CD 11:2 contains a closely related reformulation of Isa 58:13 in order to proscribe the use of a foreign agent on the Sabbath. In this passage, ביום השבת clearly refers to the time in which the prohibited action would take place: אל ישלח את בן הנכר לעשות את חפצו ביום השבת, "One may not send a foreigner to do his business on the Sabbath day." CD 11:2 reformulates the scriptural ביום קדשי to comport with sectarian technical terminology for the Sabbath – hence, ביום השבת. As in this passage, CD 10:20–21 represents a reformulation of ביום קדשי from Isa 58:13 to match general sectarian designations for the Sabbath as well as the specific language employed in this section of the *Damascus Document*'s Sabbath Code.[39]

36 A related locution, יום קדש, appears in Neh 10:32 to refer to the festivals. This particular formulation is likely influenced by the combination of יום and קדש in the Pentateuchal presentation of the festivals (e.g., Lev 23; Num 28; cf. 11QT^a 43:17).

37 For the *Damascus Document*, see the following note. Outside of the *Damascus Document*, ביום השבת is almost universally employed in legal texts treating the Sabbath: 4Q251 1–2 6; 4Q265 6 2, 4, 5, 7 (rec.), 8 (rec.); 4Q274 2 i 2; 4Q513 3–4 3. Outside of the *Damascus Document*, בשבת appears only in 4Q251 1–2 5. Another form – כל השבת ("all of the Sabbath") – is employed once in 4Q251 1–2 4 (see Chapter 9).

38 See CD 10:17, 22; 11:2, 13. In contrast, the terminological designation בשבת is employed in CD 11:5, 9, 10, 11, 12, 14, 15, 17.

39 A similar modification of scriptural language can be detected in the exegetical reformulation of Exod 16:29 in 4Q251 1–2 4–5 (*4QHalakha A*) and 4Q265 6 4–5 (*4QMiscellaneous Rules*).

In light of the textual and exegetical features of CD 10:20–21, the best solution to the textual difficulty at the end of the passage is to emend the text to read ביום השבת, "On the Sabbath day," as first suggested by Schechter in the *editio princeps*.[40] This temporal designator merely replaces *Isaiah*'s ביום קדשי, and accordingly the expression retains its use in reference to the time in which the proscribed actions would take place. Thus, similarly to Schechter, I suggest that whatever is undertaken in the field will indeed transpire on the Sabbath. Unlike Schechter, however, I am suggesting that the work is the planning, not the execution.

IV. THOUGHTS ABOUT WORK ON THE SABBATH IN 4QHALAKHA B

The presentation of Sabbath law in 4Q264a 1 i 5–8 was discussed at length in Chapter 5. Two important points emerged from that discussion. First, as in CD 10:17–19, *4QHalakha B* contains a range of laws that restrict specific types of speech on the Sabbath. Moreover, my analysis of *4QHalakha B* demonstrates how this text expands the restrictions on speech in CD 10:17–19 in order both to add greater clarity to the presentation of the laws and in some cases to offer a more stringent application of the restriction on speech on the Sabbath. Second, both CD 10:17–19 and *4QHalakha B* draw upon Isa 58:13 as their scriptural base text. Each seeks to provide a practical meaning for the enigmatic expression ודבר דבר, "Nor speak a word," in Isa 58:13. Through a variety of related and divergent techniques, each text reformulates the scriptural language in the service of its larger legal interests. The pervasiveness of the keyword דבר from Isa 58:13 in *4QHalakha B* is clear – it appears between six and nine times in a mere four lines.

As I outlined in my initial discussion of this passage in Chapter 5, 4Q264a 1 i 5–8 is directly linked to the formal structure of CD 10:17–19. The first clause in CD 10:17–18 reformulates the scriptural verse ודבר דבר to indicate that not all speech is forbidden, but only speech with "vile and wicked" content. The passage follows with several examples, all of which focus on business or financial matters. Similarly, *4QHalakha B* opens with a general condemnation of speech: אל יחשב איש [ב]פ[יהו], "Let no man consider [with his]m[outh]" (l. 5).[41] Based on the parallel text in the *Damascus Document* and the content that follows in *4QHalakha B*, the prohibition focuses on the general consideration of work on the Sabbath. The inclusion of the prepositional phrase בפיהו ("with his mouth"), however, indicates that the proscribed mental

Exod 16:29 identifies the Sabbath as ביום בשביעי, while both 4Q251 (כל השבת) and 4Q265 (ביום השבת) modify the scriptural language to comport with more common sectarian designations for the Sabbath. See below, Chapter 9, section III.

40 Schechter, *Documents*, 80. Schechter does not articulate why he emends the text as such, though it is likely based on the similar expression in CD 11:2.

41 See Chapter 5 for fuller discussion of the manuscript and paleographical evidence and for further treatment of the range of possible meanings of יחשב.

consideration here is actually performed verbally. Following this general restriction, *4QHalakha B* continues with several examples of prohibited speech. As discussed, the formulation in *4QHalakha B* is strange for two reasons. First, classical Hebrew locates thought not in one's mouth but rather as a process undertaken in one's heart. As such, the combination of thought (חשב) and one's mouth (בפיהו) to represent speech is semantically odd. Second, the opening statement in *4QHalakha B* is quite distinctive in its non-use of דבר, which represents the far more logical choice based on semantic consideration, and in light of its appearance in Isa 58:13 and throughout its legal-exegetical reformulation in 4Q264a 1 i 5–8.

As I proposed in my discussion of this passage in Chapter 5, the specific reason for describing the general restriction on speech as "verbally articulated thought" is closely linked to a wider set of literary and exegetical correspondences between *4QHalakha B* and CD 10:17–19 as well as the law that follows in CD 10:20–21. As examined at length in this chapter, CD 10:20–21 outlines a specific case in which even thinking about labor on the Sabbath is prohibited. The limited case of an individual in the field in the *Damascus Document* raises the obvious question – how far does the restriction on thoughts expand?

The emphasis on thought (חשב) in the language of 4Q264a 1 i 5 is part of a broader engagement with the law in CD 10:20–21. 4Q264a 1 i 5 deliberately avoids the expected language of speech (דבר) as drawn from Isa 58:13 in order to offer an assessment of its approach to the theoretical issue of how far the restriction on thoughts extends. While Isa 58:13 generates a wide range of restrictions pertaining to speech in the *Damascus Document* and *4QHalakha B*, 4Q264a 1 i 5 affirms that Isa 58:13 cannot be employed to sustain a widespread restriction on thoughts on the Sabbath. In order to achieve its desired polemical tone, *4QHalakha B* must diverge from the language of Isa 58:13 as found in the *Damascus Document* and indeed in the following lines of *4QHalakha B*. The degree to which *4QHalakha B* diverges from its own exegetical reformulation of Isa 58:13 in favor of semantically obfuscating language is indicative of the significance it attaches to affirming the exegetical limitations of Isa 58:13.

V. CONCLUSIONS

In this chapter, I have focused on two sectarian legal texts – CD 10:20–21 and 4Q264a 1 i 5 – and their legal perspectives on restricting thoughts on the Sabbath and the exegetical use of Isa 58:13. Moreover, my treatment of these two texts has begun to consider their contribution to a broader discussion of the theory of law in ancient Judaism. In this chapter, I have examined each law in its own literary context. At the same time, my treatment of *4QHalakha B* has already hinted at the wider conversation that these two texts are part of in ancient Jewish legal literature.

My analysis of CD 10:20–21 has argued that this particular passage prohibits an individual from walking through a field in order to assess what post-Sabbath actions need to be undertaken in the field. The concern of this law is neither the mere act of walking through the field nor the possibility that the work would be performed on the Sabbath. Rather, this law is directed at a very specific situation that could arise as an individual travels through a field. This particular field presumably contains crops critical to the livelihood of the person walking through it. It is important to underscore two key elements of the law. First, this law very clearly does not restrict all thoughts about forbidden labor on the Sabbath. On the contrary, CD 10:20–21 has in mind a limited application. To be sure, it is not entirely clear if the setting of the field is intended to be exclusive or merely representative of a particular setting in which one might engage in consideration of labor directly related to one's livelihood. Even if the latter is the case, the *Damascus Document* has framed the law within a restricted set of parameters.

The limited nature of the law is directly related to the second critical element. The formulation of a law prohibiting thoughts about labor on the Sabbath emerges from a real-life situation, and its literary presentation is articulated with this framework in mind. This law responds to the very real concern that individuals would have for their financial well-being and the realization that an individual walking through a field that provides this livelihood would not ignore any problems detected in the field. While a person might be fastidious not to tend to the labor-related needs on the Sabbath, it is hard to imagine that someone would not make a mental note to return to it after the Sabbath ends. Herein lie the internal difficulties present in this reality-based law. It responds to a real and common situation – the mental checklist that will arise as one walks through the field. At the same time, the very nature of this real situation makes it difficult to respond to with measured and effective legislation. The carefully restrained nature of the law as presented in CD 10:20–21 ultimately does it best to respond to this situation.

This broader understanding of the legal factors operating in CD 10:20–21 offers further insight into the organizational logic of this section of the *Damascus Document*'s Sabbath Code. CD 10:20–21 is placed immediately after a set of laws regarding restricted speech on the Sabbath in CD 10:17–19. These two passages share two significant features. Foremost, both CD 10:17–19 and CD 10:20–21 present their legal content in the framework of legal-exegetical reformulations of Isa 58:13. At the same time, both sets of laws are directed at activities on the Sabbath that intersect with one's financial well-being. CD 10:17–19 restricts a range of speech on the Sabbath that relates to one's business or financial matters. CD 10:20–21 continues this theme by restricting thoughts that are related to one's financial affairs. The interconnected nature of these two sets of law is reinforced by the manner in which they are juxtaposed. The final law in CD 10:17–19 prohibits speech on the Sabbath regarding business dealings that will transpire during the coming week (l. 19: אל ידבר בדברי המלאכה והעבודה לעשות למשכים, "He shall not speak about matters relating to work and labor that need to be done on the following morning").

CD 10:20–21 continues by asserting that even thoughts about future labor are prohibited in some situations.

At the same time, it is important to underscore what legal aspects CD 10:17–19 and CD 10:20–21 do not treat. In both sets of laws, the more direct act of Sabbath violation is not in view. CD 10:17–19 does not concern itself with direct business transactions, which would have already been regarded as prohibited on the Sabbath based on Amos 8:5 and Neh 13:15–22. Similarly, CD 10:20–21 is not directed at actual work in the field. Both sets of laws take for granted these general restrictions and respond to the more practical and legally ambiguous situations that undoubtedly were presented to people as they sought to balance their observance of the Sabbath and their concern for their financial well-being. Both laws restrain themselves to the real-life matter at hand: CD 10:17–19 only restricts a specific type of speech, and CD 10:20–21 prohibits only a limited range of thoughts. In both cases, business or financial matters direct the legislative agenda.

If we consider the cumulative evidence of sectarian Sabbath law as found in these passages from the *Damascus Document* and *4QHalakha B*, two related viewpoints can be found regarding the restriction of thoughts on the Sabbath. Moreover, we can also detect the presence of alternative approaches that are indirectly engaged by the sectarian legal texts. The *Damascus Document* restricts the future planning of work as represented by a specific case (or perhaps limited set of circumstances). *4QHalakha B* contains no record of its position on this specific case. However, it asserts the position that thoughts more generally are not prohibited. The identification of speech in *4QHalakha B* as "verbally articulated thought" employs polemically charged language to respond to the broader legal issue. On the whole, *4QHalakha B* represents a more stringent approach regarding speech on the Sabbath than the parallel laws in CD 10:17–19. Indeed, *4QHalakha B* goes well beyond the *Damascus Document* with its prohibition of all nonessential and nonsacred speech (l. 8). Yet, *4QHalakha B* affirms that there is a clear limit to its own expanded stringencies. The limited case in which thoughts on the Sabbath are prohibited is not expanded alongside the speech laws.

The expanded speech laws in *4QHalakha B* provide insight into this critical legislative decision. While the restriction on speech is expanded beyond only business-related speech, it too has limitations. 4Q264a 1 i 8 provides two broad exceptions to the restriction on speech: words articulated to bless God (likely prayer) and verbal communication related to food and/or drink (i.e., preparation and/or consumption). Here, *4QHalakha B* adopts a realism-based approach to a set of restrictions – prohibitions on human communication – that are decidedly antirealism in their broader orientation. Just as *4QHalakha B* recognizes that a widespread restriction on speech is impractical, it affirms the difficulties associated with even an expanded general prohibition on thoughts. The assertion that thoughts are only prohibited when they are verbally articulated provides a clear and discernible rubric for an otherwise unenforceable and impractical law.

The semantic representation of speech as "verbally articulated thought" responds to literary and legislative considerations in both the *Damascus Document* and *4QHalakha B*. The nature of the interaction between 4Q264a 1 i 5 and CD 10:20–21 differs from the more general literary and exegetical correspondence between the two texts explored in Chapters 4 and 5, whereby *4QHalakha B* clarifies and expands the material in the *Damascus Document*. As treated in Chapter 5, *4QHalakha B* follows closely the *Damascus Document* and its legal-exegetical use of Isa 58:13 in the service of providing an updated formulation of the laws regarding speech on the Sabbath. With the restriction on thought, however, *4QHalakha B* diverges from the language of both the *Damascus Document* and Isa 58:13. This very change in practice hints at the larger setting in which the polemical tone employed in *4QHalakha B* should be situated. It is not reacting specifically to the related law in the *Damascus Document*. Rather, *4QHalakha B* is directed at legal perspectives outside of the sectarian community of the Dead Sea Scrolls.

Lurking behind the legal formulations in the Dead Sea Scrolls is a much broader set of trends regarding restrictions on thoughts on the Sabbath and the realization that this issue was the subject of a much wider debate in Second Temple Judaism. In order to find traces of this debate, we must widen the scope of our inquiry to related texts in Second Temple and rabbinic Judaism.

8

Isaiah 58:13 and the Restriction on Thoughts of Labor on the Sabbath in Philo and Rabbinic Literature

I. INTRODUCTION

In the previous chapter, I explored two texts from among the Dead Sea Scrolls that present related perspectives on the restriction on thoughts of forbidden labor on the Sabbath. The *Damascus Document* outlines a limited case in which thoughts would be prohibited. *4QHalakha B*, though containing no clear legislation regarding prohibited thoughts on the Sabbath, engages in a broader polemic with legal traditions that advocate an expanded prohibition on thoughts. *4QHalakha B* counters these other legal traditions with its representation of speech as "verbally articulated thought." As I suggested at the end of the last chapter, the polemical language of *4QHalakha B* is indicative of wider traditions in ancient Judaism that both affirm an expanded restriction on thoughts and ground this restriction in an exegetical reformulation of Isa 58:13.

In this chapter, I examine one Second Temple–period text and several different rabbinic texts that are representative of these wider legal traditions. Each of these texts reflects points in the broader dialogue and counterdialogue in ancient Judaism. As in my discussion of the material from the Dead Sea Scrolls, my interest is in both the precise contours of the application of the law and its scriptural basis. Moreover, we shall see that several rabbinic texts in particular couch their legal formulations in a polemical tone. As in *4QHalakha B*, the rabbinic texts reflect internal debates regarding the full range of the restriction on thoughts on the Sabbath, thus engaging in a debate that has its roots in earlier Second Temple legal debates. My analysis of Philo and the rabbinic evidence contributes both to charting the historical development of this law and its exegetical foundations and to the broader discussion of legal theory and the nature of law in ancient Judaism.

II. BROADER TRENDS IN SECOND TEMPLE JUDAISM: PHILO

Philo and the Prohibition on Thoughts on the Sabbath

In the Second Temple period, the outright prohibition on thoughts about labor is alluded to by Philo:

> ταύτης ἕνεκα τῆς αἰτίας ὁ πάντα μέγας Μωυσῆς ἐδικαίωσε τοὺς ἐγγραφέντας αὐτοῦ τῇ ἱερᾷ πολιτείᾳ θεσμοῖς φύσεως ἑπομένους πανηγυρίζειν ἐν ἱλαραῖς διάγοντας εὐθυμίαις ἀνέχοντας μὲν ἔργων καὶ τεχνῶν τῶν εἰς πορισμὸν καὶ πραγματειῶν ὅσαι κατὰ βίου ζήτησιν ἄγοντας δ᾽ ἐκεχειρίαν καὶ διαφειμένος πάσης ἐπιπόνου καὶ καματηρᾶς φροντίδος.
>
> For this cause, Moses, great in everything, determined that all who were written on his holy burgess-roll and who followed the laws of nature should hold high festival through the hours of cheerful gaiety, abstaining from work and profit-making crafts and professions, and business pursued to get a livelihood, and enjoy a respite from all wearisome and toilsome thought and care. (*Life of Moses* 2.211)[1]

Philo's description of the various aspects of Sabbath restrictions contains a range of terms appropriate to the restriction of labor on the Sabbath.[2] The list begins with a general reference to abstention from "work" (ἔργον), which employs the term commonly found in the Septuagint as the equivalent of the Hebrew term for prohibited Sabbath labor – מלאכה.[3] The list continues with several additional examples of more specific types of proscribed professional activities. One is similarly prohibited to engage in "crafts and professions"

[1] Greek text and translation (slightly modified) follow F. H. Colson, *Philo*, volume 6 (LCL 289; Cambridge: Harvard University Press; London: William Heinemann, 1935), 552–53. In particular, I have translated φροντίδος as "thought and care" (Colson: "care") in order to express more clearly the cognitive element involved. The associated verb φροντίζω carries with it the connotation of "planning" or "worrying," which transpires as a direct result of the more general act of thinking about something. See Henry C. Liddell and Robert Scott, revised and augmented by Henry Scott Jones, *A Greek-English Lexicon: With Revised Supplement* (Oxford: Clarendon, 1996), 1957, s.v. φροντίς, ίδος, ἡ. Compare the translation of C. D. Yonge, *The Works of Philo* (Peabody: Hendrickson, 2000), 509: "all laborious and fatiguing thought and care."

[2] General discussion of the legal contents of this passage can be found in Samuel Belkin, *Philo and the Oral Law: The Philonic Interpretation of Biblical Law in Relation to Palestinian Halakhah* (HSS 11; Cambridge: Cambridge University Press, 1940), 200–1; Yitzḥak D. Gilat, "Regarding the Antiquity of Several Sabbath Prohibitions," in *Studies in the Development of the Halakha* (Ramat Gan: Bar Ilan University Press, 1992), 249–61 (256) [Hebrew]; Lutz Doering, *Schabbat: Sabbathhalacha und –praxis im antiken Judentum und Urchristentum* (TSAJ 78; Tübingen: Mohr Siebeck, 1999), 348–53.

[3] See, e.g., 𝔊 Exod 20:10; Deut 5:13; Jer 17:22. See further Edwin Hatch and Henry A. Redpath, *A Concordance to the Septuagint* (2d ed.; Grand Rapids: Baker, 1998), 541–44. Elsewhere, Philo also draws upon this terminology with regard to restricted Sabbath labor (e.g., *Life of Moses* 2.220; *The Special Laws* 2.59, 64, 66).

(τεχνῶν) and "business" (πραγματειῶν). Following this passage, Philo provides an explanation for why these specific acts are prohibited in the course of his analysis of the Pentateuchal incident of the individual charged with gathering sticks on the Sabbath (Num 15:32–37).[4] In his explanation of why gathering sticks is forbidden, he identifies this act as preparatory to the explicitly prohibited creation of fire (Exod 35:3) and hence also forbidden. In the same vein, "other arts and occupations" (ἄλλαι τέχναι καὶ πραγματεῖαι) require fire and are therefore similarly forbidden on the Sabbath.[5]

Philo's twofold use of these two specific terms (τέχνη, πραγματεία) for related Sabbath prohibitions is deliberate. Each of these terms is employed in the Septuagint as equivalent to עבדה and מלאכה, respectively, and thus as with ἔργον represent appropriate terminological categories for proscribed labor.[6] Yet, unlike ἔργον, neither of these terms ever appears specifically in the context of prohibited Sabbath labor. Thus, Philo (or whatever source he is drawing upon) is expanding the contours of prohibited Sabbath activities with terminology fitting for the general restriction of labor.

Closer examination of the specific prohibited acts (τέχνη, πραγματεία) reveals two important points for our broader discussion. First, both prohibited activities are related to business or financial matters. This characteristic is indicated by the linguistic range of each term as well as Philo's explicit clarification of their application in the context of Sabbath law. Thus, τέχνη refers more generally to a "skill, trade" that would be employed for financial gain, a semantic range that is reflected in both the few occurrences in the Septuagint as well as broader linguistic usage.[7] Moreover, Philo makes this aspect explicit by

4 *Life of Moses* 2.213–20. Philo also discusses the incident in *The Special Laws* 2.250–51. See general treatment in Belkin, *Philo and the Oral Law*, 194–200 (attempting to demonstrate Philo's acquaintance with rabbinic interpretation of the same incident); Herold Weiss, "Philo on the Sabbath," *StPhA* 3 (1991; Hilgert Festschrift): 83–105 (90–92); Doering, *Schabbat*, 331–34.

5 *Life of Moses* 2.219. The same explanation is provided in *The Special Laws* 2.251. Philo elsewhere (*The Special Laws* 2.65; cf. *On the Migration of Abraham* 91) comments on the prohibition of fire and its central role in other related acts that are likewise forbidden (including πραγματεία). On the prohibition of fire more generally in Philo (including discussion of connections to the Prometheus myth), see Yitzḥak D. Gilat, "The Sabbath and Its Laws in the World of Philo," in *Torah and Wisdom: Studies in Jewish Philosophy, Kabbalah, and Halacha: Essays in Honor of Arthur Hyman* (ed. R. Link-Salinger; New York: Shengold, 1992), 61–73 (65–66); Weiss, "Philo on the Sabbath," 86, 91–92; Doering, *Schabbat*, 328–31.

6 See Hatch and Redpath, *Concordance*, 1200 (s.v. πραγματεία), 1347 (s.v. τέχνη).

7 This term is employed in the Septuagint to denote the professional capabilities of craftsmen (𝔊 Exod 28:11; 30:25; 1 Kgs 7:2[14]; 1 Chr 28:21; Sir 38:34). In Wis 13:10; 14:19, this craftsmanship is condemned as part of the process of the production of idols. On broader usage, see Liddell, Scott, and Jones, *Greek-English Lexicon*, 1784–85; William F. Arndt and F. Wilbur Gingrich, *A Greek-English Lexicon of the New Testament and Other Early Christian Literature* (4th ed.; Chicago: University of Chicago Press; Cambridge: Cambridge University Press, 1952), 821.

identifying the τέχνη as "profit making" (πορισμόν).[8] Similarly, πραγματεία has a more general meaning of "undertakings," alongside a more specific application as "business, affairs."[9] Philo further reinforces the more narrow meaning by identifying these undertakings as "pursued to get a livelihood" (ὅσαι κατὰ βίου ζήτησιν). By singling out these two specific activities as representative examples of the broader category of proscribed labor (ἔργον), Philo identifies professional pursuits related to business and financial gain as a specific category of prohibited labor on the Sabbath.

The second significant point regarding these two prohibited acts is the range of their practical application. Clearly, Philo has in mind that any professional *actions* undertaken in pursuit of "crafts and professions" (τέχνη) or "business" (πραγματεία) are prohibited. At the same time, Philo restricts further elements associated with the performance of these professional actions – specifically, mental consideration of such prohibited labor. This further aspect is encoded in the semantic range of each word as well as made explicit by Philo's own summation statement at the end of the passage. τέχνη commonly applies to professional crafts undertaken with one's hands, though it also conveys the mental acumen and process that likewise contributes to such professional accomplishments.[10] Similarly, πραγματεία expresses not only the general pursuit of professional endeavors, but also the desire that stands behind that very undertaking.[11] Within this broader linguistic context, Philo's concluding statement that on the Sabbath one must abstain from "all wearisome and toilsome thought and care" (πάσης ἐπιπόνου καὶ καματηρᾶς φροντίδος) encapsulates both the physical and the closely related mental nature of the restrictions on professional activity and related labor.

In contrast to the expected cessation of labor, Philo advocates for the exclusive pursuit of wisdom on the Sabbath. In particular, he instructs individuals to pursue the true philosophy of "three strands – thoughts (βουλευμάτων), words

8 See especially Wis 13:19; 14:2; and Arndt and Gingrich, *Greek-English Lexicon*, 699 (with further references cited therein).

9 See 𝔊 1 Kgs 7:19; 9:1; 10(9):22(19); 1 Chr 28:21; Dan 6:4 (cf. 2 Tim 2:4). See further Arndt and Gingrich, *Greek-English Lexicon*, 704; C. Maurer, "πράσσω, πρᾶγμα, πραγματεία," *TDNT* 6:632–44 (640–41). This word is a derived noun from πρᾶγμα, which carries a similar semantic range. πραγματεία stands behind the Jewish Palestinian Aramaic loanword פרגמטייה, "commerce, merchandise" (see Michael Sokoloff, *A Dictionary of Jewish Palestinian Aramaic* [2d ed.; Ramat Gan: Bar Ilan University Press; Baltimore: Johns Hopkins University Press, 2002], 444).

10 See especially 𝔊 1 Kgs 7:2(14); Dan 1:17 (standing for the Hebrew חכמה). This range of meaning is clear from the varied uses of the noun and associated verb (τεχνάζω) in classical Greek (see Liddell, Scott, and Jones, *Greek-English Lexicon*, 1784–95). Thus, Colson, *Philo*, 553, comments on the passage in Philo that the term includes both "manual and mental arts" (calling attention to such a use in *Life of Moses* 2.219, as noted above).

11 See especially 𝔊 1 Kgs 9:1, 10(9):22(19) (contains noun and associated verb πραγματεύω, rendering the Hebrew חשק). Cf. 𝔊 1 Kgs 7:19(33), where the translator seems to have mistakenly identified חשקיהם ("their spokes") as similarly related to חשק, "desire."

(λόγων), and deeds (πράξεων)" (*Life of Moses* 2.212).[12] The same three elements that encompass the performance of proscribed labor on the Sabbath are now transformed into the three elements of prescribed undertakings on the Sabbath.[13]

Philo's statement on cessation from action and thought on the Sabbath is far-reaching. One should not only abstain from proscribed labor on the Sabbath but also refrain from even mental consideration of it. At the same time, Philo's placement of the general prohibition in the context of the specific examples of the restriction on business and professional activities should be located within the broader setting of the Second Temple–period articulation of this law as found in the Dead Sea Scrolls (and also rabbinic literature to be discussed below). In both the *Damascus Document* and *4QHalakha B*, the restriction on thoughts is intimately connected to laws related to business. In these texts, the sectarian position on restricted thoughts is articulated alongside the restriction on speech regarding business and financial affairs on the Sabbath. Moreover, the *Damascus Document* limits the restriction on thoughts to a specific type of business venture – the assessment of the needs of one's field. This limited application does not seem to be operating in Philo. Indeed, Philo explicitly states that one should remove *all* thoughts of labor from one's mind in order to busy oneself with wisdom alone.

Philo and the texts from the Dead Sea Scrolls share a common approach to business and professional pursuits on the Sabbath in their assessment of how such pursuits are actually conducted and the associated Sabbath restrictions. Both recognize that business and financial pursuits will undoubtedly involve consideration of such undertakings. Moreover, even if business dealings themselves are proscribed on the Sabbath, people will still engage in the associated thoughts. Accordingly, both the community of the Dead Sea Scrolls and Philo share a desire to curb both physical and mental aspects related to the performance of business.

Is Isaiah 58:13 the Exegetical Basis of the Law in Philo?

As discussed in the previous chapter on the *Damascus Document* and *4QHalakha B*, the interest in business and its close relationship to the prohibited speech and thought is grounded in the exegetical reformulation of Isa 58:13.

[12] For βουλεύω rendering Hebrew חפץ, see 𝔊 Isa 42:21; 46:10; Jer 49(42):22. For Hebrew חשב, see 𝔊 Gen 50:20; Isa 55:7, 8 (the nominal form is not represented in 𝔊). Indeed, the semantic range of this word in Greek encompasses both desire and internal consideration (i.e., thoughts). See Liddell, Scott, and Jones, *Greek-English Lexicon*, 324–25; Arndt and Gingrich, *Greek-English Lexicon*, 145–46 (s.v. βούλημα, βούλομαι); G. Schrenk, "βούλημαι, βουλή, βούλημα," *TDNT* 1:629–37 (629–33).

[13] To be sure, Philo never explicitly prohibits speech about the prohibited work. Such actions, no doubt, are encapsulated by his general restriction on both the performance and thinking about prohibited work.

Both the *Damascus Document* and *4QHalakha B* see the implicit condemnation of financial matters in Isa 58:13 and draw upon this sense to provide a specific application for the vague condemnations found throughout the scriptural passage. Can any trace of the use of Isa 58:13 be found in Philo's articulation of this law?

In the particular passage under analysis, Philo traces all Sabbath law back to Moses, a feature consistent with both Philo's high regard for Moses as a lawgiver and his general exegetical predilection for the Pentateuch.[14] Moreover, Philo explains the logic of the restriction on business and professional pursuits as related to the Pentateuchal prohibition against kindling a fire on the Sabbath (based on Exod 35:3). All related acts therefore also fall under the purview of this restriction.

Yet, Philo's outline of the specific examples of actions that may not be performed on the Sabbath and the language employed to express these restrictions echo a similar constellation of exegetical applications of Isa 58:13 found in the Dead Sea Scrolls. As in the discussion of the scrolls, my focus here is on the twofold use of the restriction on pursuing one's "affairs" (חפץ) in Isa 58:13. In my treatment of the *Damascus Document*, I observed that חפץ from Isa 58:13 has been semantically reformulated to articulate the restriction of thoughts regarding labor on the Sabbath. As noted in that discussion, a closely related exegetical reorientation is likewise operating in the Septuagint, which represents the version of Isa 58:13 that Philo would have been reading:

> ἐὰν ἀποστρέψῃς τὸν πόδα σου ἀπὸ τῶν σαββάτων τοῦ μὴ ποιεῖν τὰ θελήματά σου ἐν τῇ ἡμέρᾳ τῇ ἁγίᾳ καὶ καλέσεις τὰ σάββατα τρυφερά, ἅγια τῷ θεῷ σου, οὐκ ἀρεῖς τὸν πόδα σου ἐπ᾽ ἔργῳ οὐδὲ λαλήσεις λόγον ἐν ὀργῇ ἐκ τοῦ στόματός σου.
>
> If you turn your foot away from the sabbaths, so as not to do the things you wish on the holy day, and you shall call the sabbaths delightful, holy to your God, you shall not lift your foot for work nor speak a word in anger out of your mouth. (NETS)

The second twofold restriction on pursuing one's affairs (מעשות דרכיך ממצוא חפצך) is collapsed into one clause in the Septuagint in such a way that חפץ is understood as alluding to general work on the Sabbath (ἔργον): οὐκ ἀρεῖς τὸν πόδα σου ἐπ᾽ <u>ἔργῳ</u>, "You shall not lift your foot for <u>work</u>."[15] ἔργον likewise appears as

[14] The former theme is particularly pronounced in the second book of *Life of Moses*, in which Philo identifies Moses as lawgiver, high priest, and prophet. On the latter trend, see Yehoshua Amir, "Authority and Interpretation of Scripture in the Writings of Philo," in *Mikra: Text, Translation, Reading and Interpretation of the Hebrew Bible in Ancient Judaism and Early Christianity* (ed. M. J. Mulder; CRINT 2/1; Assen: Van Gorcum; Minneapolis: Fortress, 1988), 421–53.

[15] The Septuagint does not otherwise render חפץ with ἔργον. Aside from Isa 58:13, the only other instance of this phenomenon is Sir 10:26 (Ms B): לעשות חפצך → ποιῆσαι τὸ ἔργον (Ms A לעבד), which may reflect influence from the similar clause in Isa 58:13. The use of ἔργον for Hebrew חפץ in Isa 58:13 therefore suggests that this is an intentional legal-exegetical rendering.

the general designation for the prohibited Sabbath work in Philo.[16] To be sure, ἔργον appears throughout the Septuagint and Philo for Sabbath restrictions and by itself cannot demonstrate a link between Isa 58:13 and the passage in Philo.

This desired link may be found in the Septuagint's exegetical reformulation of the first restriction on pursuing one's affairs in Isa 58:13 (עשות חפציך). As discussed above, the Septuagint is similar to the Targum and the *Damascus Document* in its translation of חפץ not with the contextually warranted meaning of "business, affair," but rather with the meaning more generally applied to the more common use of חפץ in the Hebrew Bible as "desire" (θέλημα): μὴ ποιεῖν τὰ θελήματά σου, "So as not to do the things you wish."[17] With this reorientation of the semantic nuance of חפץ, the Targum, the Septuagint, and the *Damascus Document* are able to read into Isa 58:13 a prohibition concerning thoughts. Philo does not employ θέλημα, as found in the Septuagint, because this term would be imprecise in the context of his broader legal formulation. At the same time, he does draw upon several different terms that are linguistically and thematically linked to "thought" and "desire," in both Hebrew and Greek: πραγματειῶν (= חשק), φροντίδος (= חשב), and βουλευμάτων (= חשב and חפץ).[18]

III. BROADER TRENDS IN RABBINIC LITERATURE

The vast corpus of rabbinic literature yields the richest set of conversations regarding the full range of the prohibition on thoughts on the Sabbath. As in the earlier Second Temple–period material, the rabbinic texts present diverse voices debating across texts whether such a restriction is realistic in its orientation and sustainable in its implementation. Moreover, the overlapping contours of the rabbinic debates and the Second Temple antecedents indicate that the later rabbis are taking up a set of questions that had long occupied Jewish juridical thought – for which no consensus was ever reached. The two opinions voiced in the Second Temple texts – an outright prohibition (Philo) and a limited prohibition (*Damascus Document*) – are similarly found in the rabbinic texts,

[16] See above, n. 3.

[17] On the translation of the two meanings of חפץ in the Septuagint, see above, Chapter 7, nn. 31–32.

[18] On the semantic range and Septuagint equivalencies, see the notes above for each word. Note that the 𝔊 1 Kgs 9:1 renders the Hebrew כל חשק שלמה אשר חפץ לעשות as πᾶσαν τὴν πραγματείαν Σαλωμων ὅσα ἠθέλησεν ποιῆσαι. The second half of both 𝔐 and 𝔊 contains the same two keywords as the clause in Isa 58:13 (though inverted). It is possible that the Septuagint's rendering of this closely related clause provided textual support for Philo's (or his source's) introduction of πραγματεία. Furthermore, this intertextual reference would serve as a link between the Septuagint of Isa 58:13 and the precise language of Philo's formulation.

alongside the explicit rejection of any restriction on thoughts. Moreover, the rabbinic texts retain some of the polemical undertone detected in the Second Temple–period texts, further reinforcing my assertion that this topic was deeply contested throughout this long period in the formation of Jewish law.

In addition to debating the specific contours of the Sabbath law, the rabbinic texts enter a new variable into the question of its underlying scriptural authority. Isa 58:13 no longer is the exclusive scriptural source for the restriction on thoughts. The entry of new exegetical sources reflects internal rabbinic conversations about what constitutes authoritative scripture. At the same time, these very debates over the role of Isa 58:13 and other texts further demonstrate the close contacts between the rabbinic texts and the earlier Second Temple–period treatments of the exegetical foundations of the law. In what follows, I explore three different iterations of the law in rabbinic texts: (1) the general prohibition on thoughts, (2) the limited prohibition on thoughts, and (3) the explicit rejection of any such prohibition. Within this broader discussion, I examine the exegetical role of Isa 58:13 and related scriptural passages.

General Prohibition: *Mekhilta de-Rabbi Ishma'el*

The first set of rabbinic texts to be discussed comes from the *Mekhilta de-Rabbi Ishma'el*. In two instances, the *Mekhilta* explicitly prohibits all thoughts of labor on the Sabbath. Such an outright condemnation finds close correspondence with the similarly far-reaching prohibition articulated by Philo and also seemingly is lurking behind the polemical language of *4QHalakha B*. In this sense, it is not inconsequential that the strictest position articulated in the rabbinic texts is found in the earliest of the texts chronologically (third century CE).[19] Indeed, my analysis of the *Mekhilta* calls attention to further evidence that suggests that it is keenly aware of earlier iterations of the law and its scriptural basis in the Second Temple period. The first passage is found in an exegetical comment on the Sabbath law in the Decalogue (Exod 20:9):

> ששת ימים תעבוד ועשית כל מלאכתך וכי איפשר לו לאדם לעשות כל מלאכתו בששה ימים אלא שבות כאלו מלאכתך עשויה דבר אחר שבות במחשבת עבודה ואומר אם תשיב משבת רגליך וגו' ואומר אז תתענג על יי'

> "Six days thou shall labor and do all thy work" (Exod 20:9). But is it possible for a human being to do all his work in six days? It simply means: rest on the Sabbath as if all your work were done.

> Another interpretation: rest even from thought of labor. And it says: "If thou turn away thy foot because of the Sabbath..." (Isa 58:13). And then it says:

19 On issues involved in the dating of the *Mekhilta*, see H. L. Strack and Günter Stemberger, *Introduction to the Talmud and Midrash* (trans. M. Bockmuehl; Minneapolis: Fortress, 1996), 253–55.

"Then shalt you delight thyself in the Lord..." (Isa 58:13–14). (*Mekhilta Ba-Ḥodesh* 7)[20]

As with Philo, the *Mekhilta* seeks to reorient the nature of Sabbath observance. Not only must one abstain from performance of work, but one must also remove from one's consciousness all aspects related to non-Sabbath activity. The first unit of the *Mekhilta* articulates this in a very general sense – on the Sabbath, one must operate under the pretense that all non-Sabbath work is indeed complete. Undoubtedly, this general attempt to reorient the attitude toward work on the Sabbath extends from performance to contemplation of work. Thus, the second unit in the *Mekhilta* clearly articulates the related actualization of the broader principle by prohibiting even thoughts of labor. This formulation, echoing earlier legal positions in the Second Temple period, explicitly cites Isa 58:13 as its scriptural prooftext.

The *Mekhilta* shares two important components with its Second Temple–period forebearers. First, as with Philo and the counterposition in view in *4QHalakha B*, the *Mekhilta* seeks to restrict thoughts regarding all forbidden labor on the Sabbath. Second, the *Mekhilta* seemingly identifies Isa 58:13 as the scriptural basis for this legal position. The first shared component attests to the long history of this aspect of Sabbath law and thus provides a critical meeting point for the history of Jewish law between Second Temple and rabbinic Judaism. The second shared component, in contrast, identifies both the overlapping worlds of legal exegesis in Second Temple and rabbinic Judaism at the same time as it affirms critical distinctions between the two enterprises.

Close analysis of the exegetical technique of the second unit in the *Mekhilta* demonstrates that not only is there no discernible exegetical connection to *Isaiah*, but also the keyword עבודה in the legal formulation is much more closely exegetically linked to Exod 20:9 (as marked by single underlining). This explains why the *Mekhilta* contains an abrupt shift in the terminology used to describe restricted labor from מלאכה (first unit) to עבודה (second unit). The first two uses of the form מלאכה in the first unit are clearly intended as exegetical elaborations of the identical term in the scriptural passage (as marked by double underlining). Accordingly, the second exegetical application of Exod 20:9 draws upon the other keyword in the verse used to describe prohibited labor (עבד), a less frequent term in rabbinic Sabbath law to express proscribed Sabbath labor. In this context, the two scriptural keywords have been inverted in their reuse in the *Mekhilta*.[21]

[20] Hebrew text follows H. S. Horowitz and I. A. Rabin, *Mekhilta' d'Rabbi Ishmael* (Frankfurt: J. Kaufman, 1931; repr., Jerusalem: Shalem, 1997), 230. English translation follows Jacob Z. Lauterbach, *Mekilta de-Rabbi Ishmael* (3 vols.; Philadelphia: Jewish Publication Society, 1976), 2:253.

[21] On the exegetical technique of literary inversion (commonly known as "Zeidel's law"), see bibliography, Chapter 4, n. 50.

Isa 58:13 is seemingly cited as the sole prooftext for the second legal formulation. Yet, the exegetical connection is clearly with Exod 20:9. Indeed, the formal introduction of Isa 58:13 with ואומר ("and it says . . .") suggests that it is introduced as a secondary prooftext, even as no initial prooftext is explicitly stated in connection with the second legal formulation. In this sense, the appeal to Isa 58:13 as the source is likely based on the long-standing awareness of this passage as the primary scriptural source – as reflected in the *Damascus Document* and possibly Philo (and implicit in *4QHalakha B*). The lack of interest in the exegetical connection with Isa 58:13 is likely a reflection of broader rabbinic resistance to drawing upon prophetic passages for legal exegesis.[22] The pervasiveness of Isa 58:13 as the widely acknowledged source, however, ensures its presence here. The connection between Isa 58:13 and the restriction on thoughts, moreover, provides a basis for reorienting the exegetical application of Exod 20:9 to include thought (מחשבה) as well.

Other early rabbinic approaches do not tie this law to *Isaiah* at all. A later passage in the *Mekhilta* – attested only in some manuscripts but reflecting a related exegetical tradition in other rabbinic texts – links the law to Exod 31:17:

כי ששת ימים [עשה יהוה את השמים ואת הארץ] וביום השביעי שבת וינפש שבת ממחשבת עבודה

> "For in six days [the Lord made the heavens and the earth] and on the seventh day he ceased from work and refreshed himself" (Exod 31:17): he ceased from the thought of work. (*Mekhilta Shabbata* 1)[23]

The formulation in this passage is nearly identical to the other *Mekhilta* passage and thus shares with it the expectation that one will cease from thoughts about work on the Sabbath. *Mekhilta Ba-Ḥodesh* frames this expectation as prescriptive Sabbath law. In contrast, *Mekhilta Shabbata* describes cessation from work as part of the divine experience at the first Sabbath, though it implicitly exhorts humans to mimic this aspect of the divine Sabbath observance. The formulation restricting thoughts in each passage is distinguished only by the subtle shift in vocalization and change in mood/tense in the first verbal root שבת: *Mekhilta Ba-Ḥodesh*: שבות ממחשבת עבודה ("rest" – imperative) // *Mekhilta Shabbata*: שבת ממחשבת עבודה ("he rested" – perfect). Moreover, both use the less common rabbinic formulation for prohibited labor as עבודה.

[22] See fuller discussion above, Chapter 2, section IV.

[23] Lauterbach, *Mekilta*, 3:205. This passage is found in Mss Oxford 151, Munich Cod. Hebr. 117, and Vatican ebr. 299 (and thus appears in Lauterbach's eclectic edition) and is cited in *Yalquṭ Shim'oni* on Exod 31:17 (see note in Horowitz and Rabin, *Mekhilta*, 344). Moreover, a closely related formulation appears in *'Abot de-Rabbi Nathan* B 21 (see below, n. 26).

The exegesis in *Mekhilta Shabbata* is likely based on a twofold understanding of the scriptural word וינפש in Exod 31:17. While this *niph'al* verb likely means "to refresh oneself," the exegetical traditions on Exod 31:17 commonly render it with the basic meaning of "to rest."[24] The *Mekhilta* therefore interprets this verb in both its contextual sense of "to rest" as well as the more common meaning of נפש as "soul." Thus, the "rest" found in this passage also indicates rest of the soul – that is, cessation from all internal activities, including thought.[25] The shared formulation among the two passages suggests that one is dependent upon the other (or both on a third source).[26] Yet, *Mekhilta Shabbata* shows no awareness of the role of Isa 58:13 as the long-standing scriptural prooftext, as in *Mekhilta Ba-Ḥodesh*.[27]

24 See, in particular, the Septuagint (κατέπαυσεν) and the Targum (ונח). Indeed, rabbinic Hebrew reflects a shift whereby the verbal root נפש, while retaining the biblical Hebrew meaning of "to breathe," now also means "to rest." Yet, it does not retain the further biblical Hebrew meaning of "to refresh oneself" (see Marcus Jastrow, *A Dictionary of the Targumim, the Talmud Babli and Palestinian Talmud, and the Midrashic Literature* [Peabody: Hendrickson, 2005], 926). For discussion of the meaning of נפש in Exod 31:17 in the broader context of Pentateuchal Sabbath law and in the exegetical traditions, see Jeffrey Stackert, "The Sabbath of the Land in the Holiness Legislation: Combining Priestly and Non-priestly Perspectives," *CBQ* 73 (2011): 239–50.

25 The wide semantic range applied to נפש as "soul" in biblical Hebrew includes one's will or desire. In this sense, there may be some connection (likely unintended) between the exegetical application of Exod 31:17 treated here and the earlier discussion of Isa 58:13. As I noted in the previous chapter, the Septuagint, Targum, and the *Damascus Document* reorient the meaning of חפץ in Isa 58:13 from its contextual meaning of "business, affair" to its more common biblical Hebrew usage as "delight, pleasure, desire." In so doing, the Sabbath restriction in Isa 58:13 can apply to one's internal activity. A similar exegetical technique is applied in the *Mekhilta* to נפש in Exod 31:17.

26 The related passage in *'Abot de-Rabbi Nathan* B 21 provides a slightly different exegetical basis: שנאמר שבת וינפש שבת מן המלאכה וינפש מן המחשבה, "As it says: 'he ceased from work and rested' (Exod 31:17): he ceased from work and rested from thought" (see Solomon Schechter, *Avoth de-Rabbi Nathan* [New York: Jewish Theological Seminary of America, 1997], 23). Even as it divides up the two components of rest and their scriptural keywords, *'Abot de-Rabbi Nathan* shares with the *Mekhilta* the twofold meaning of וינפש, thus also indicating the internal "rest" of the soul. Yet, *'Abot de-Rabbi Nathan* further distances itself from the *Mekhilta* traditions by employing the more common rabbinic designation for work as מלאכה, rather than עבודה as found in the *Mekhilta*.

27 A closely related formulation is found in the *Mekhilta de-Rabbi Shim'on b. Yoḥai* on Exod 12:16 and 20:10. In the context of treatment of the similarities between labor on the Sabbath and labor required for building the Tabernacle, the *Mekhilta* notes that both involve "forethought" (מחשבה). See J. N. Epstein and E. Z. Melamed, *Mekhilta de Rabbi Shimon ben Yoḥai* (Jerusalem: Mekitse Nirdamim, 1955), 19, 150 (the translation "forethought" follows W. David Nelson, *Mekhilta de Rabbi Shimon bar Yoḥai* [Philadelphia: Jewish Publication Society, 2006], 32, 246). In this context, the primary issue does not seem to be the restriction on thoughts alone but rather the recognition that prior mental planning is necessary for the execution of labor. The underlying principle, however, is related to the more general restriction on thoughts. Rabbinic legislation is worried that thoughts would lead to action, and therefore even thoughts alone are prohibited.

Limited Prohibition: *Babylonian Talmud ('Erubin)*, *Leviticus Rabbah*, and *Pesiqta Rabbati*

The next rabbinic voice in this debate is the various iterations of the law noted by Ginzberg as parallel to the *Damascus Document* – one may not walk through the field in order to assess its needs. In all iterations of this law, the issue is never performing labor in the field but rather the mental planning of such labor. The rabbinic legislation seeks to prevent the individual from being in a situation in which such planning may transpire. Moreover, as I have suggested should also be the understanding in the *Damascus Document*, this law forbids thoughts in a restricted set of circumstances related to one's livelihood. Ginzberg calls attention to the simplest explication of the law in the *Babylonian Talmud*:

לא יהלך אדם בתוך שדהו לידע מה היא צריכה

> A man may not go into his field (on the Sabbath) in order to see what work is necessary (after the Sabbath). (*b. 'Erub.* 38b)[28]

The verbal and thematic parallels with the passage in the *Damascus Document* were noted in the previous chapter. While both Ginzberg and I draw upon these similarities to illuminate the enigmatic passage from the *Damascus Document*, the earlier Second Temple–period material can now be employed in order to understand the broader context in which this rabbinic formulation is articulated. This rabbinic legal formulation is striking a middle ground in the debate over thoughts about labor on the Sabbath. As in the *Damascus Document*, the *Babylonian Talmud* restricts this prohibition to a specific set of circumstances, in particular a situation intimately tied to one's financial livelihood. Moreover, by implicitly rejecting the alternative positions found in the *Mekhilta*, as in *4QHalakha B*, it rejects the notion that all thoughts should (or can) be restricted. To be sure, no polemical tone is found in the *Babylonian Talmud*. Yet, if we examine more carefully two rabbinic articulations of related aspects of this law – in *Leviticus Rabbah* and *Pesiqta Rabbati* – the polemical tone is much more explicit.[29]

An extended legal and homiletical interpretation of Isa 58:13 is found in *Leviticus Rabbah* 34. As in the *Mekhilta*, *Leviticus Rabbah* identifies Isa 58:13 as the scriptural source for the prohibition against thinking about labor on the Sabbath. This law is presented in the form of a general prohibition followed by a story. The scriptural passage "from pursuing your affairs" is

[28] Following Ms Munich 95 (see Chapter 7, n. 28).

[29] A further iteration of the law can be found in *Mishnat Rabbi Eli'ezer* 20: מניין שאינן יוצאין בשדות לידע מה הן צריכות לתקנן ת"ל עשות חפציך ביום קדשי, "From where do we know that one may not go into fields in order to determine their needs so as to fix them? scripture says, 'from pursuing your affairs on my holy day.'" See H. G. Enelow, *Mishnat Rabbi Eli'ezer: Midrash Sheloshim u-Shetayim Middot* (New York: Block, 1933), 368. This formulation combines the apodictic language of the *Babylonian Talmud 'Erubin* with the scriptural source text (Isa 58:13).

interpreted as a proscription against entering into one's vineyard to see what work needs to be done:

> עשות חפציך ביום קדשי מיכן אסור לאדם לצאת בכרמו[30] בשבת ולידע מהו צריך[31] מעשה בחסיד אחד שיצא לטייל בתוך כרמו בשבת לידע מה הוא צריך וראה שם פרצה אחת וחשב עליה לגודרה בשבת במוצאי שבת אמ' הואיל וחשבתי עליה לגודרה בשבת חס ושלום איני גודרה עולמית מה פרע לו הקב"ה זימן לו אילן אחד שלנצפה ועלת בתוכה וגדרתה והיה מתפרנס ממנה כל ימי חייו
>
> "From pursuing your affairs on my holy day" (Isa 58:13): On the basis [of this statement, we learn that] a person is forbidden to walk about in his vineyard on the Sabbath so as to find out what it needs.
>
> There is a tale of a pious man who went out to take a walk in his vineyard on the Sabbath to find out what it might require. He saw a breach there [in the wall] and on the Sabbath gave thought to fencing it up. At the end of the Sabbath he said, "Because I gave thought on the Sabbath to fencing it up, God forbid, I shall never fence it up."
>
> How did the Holy One, Blessed be He, pay him back? He set up a caper bush there and it grew and filled up the breach, and the man made his living from the caper bush for the entire rest of his life. (*Leviticus Rabbah* 34:16)[32]

The exegetical basis for this law is the expression "your affairs" (חפציך) in Isa 58:13. *Leviticus Rabbah* identifies *Isaiah*'s "your affairs" as a restriction against pursing all *personal* financial affairs – thus, one is restricted from entering his vineyard/field.[33] In this particular case, the primary problem is the individual's mental processes about the needs of the vineyard. In this respect, this case legislates specifically concerning thoughts about labor on the Sabbath directly related to one's financial livelihood.

The text then cites an often reported story about a pious man who enters his vineyard to assess its needs.[34] When he sees a breach in the wall, he thinks about (וחשב עליה) fixing it. After the Sabbath ends, he resolves that because he had thought about fixing the breach on the Sabbath, he would never carry out

30 Several manuscripts (Mss Vatican ebr. 32, Oxford Bodleian Opp. Add. fol. 3, Jerusalem JNUL Heb 24° 5977, Heb 8° 515) and the early printed editions have "his field" (שדהו) rather than "his vineyard" (see the law in the *Babylonian Talmud* cited above). The appearance of שדה (as in the *Babylonian Talmud*) makes the entire passage an even closer parallel to the formulation in the *Damascus Document*.

31 The expression appears as מה היא צריכה (feminine) in Mss Vatican ebr. 32, Oxford Bodleian Opp. Add. fol. 3, Jerusalem JNUL Heb 24° 5977, Heb 8° 515, Ms Oxford Add. fol. 51, and early editions of *Yalquṭ Shim'oni*. The use of the feminine would seem to refer back to the antecedent noun שדה (see previous note), which sometimes appears in rabbinic Hebrew as feminine.

32 Hebrew text follows Mordechai Margaliot, *Midrash Vayyikra Rabbah* (5 vols.; New York: Jewish Theological Seminary, 1993), 814–15. Translation follows Jacob Neusner, *Judaism and Scripture: The Evidence of Leviticus Rabbah* (Chicago: University of Chicago Press, 1986), 576–77.

33 The same exegetical tradition is found in *Mishnat Rabbi Eli'ezer* 20 (see above, n. 29). A similar exegetical application of חפציך is employed in *b. Shabb.* 150a in order to condemn the calculation of one's personal affairs. See above, Chapter 6, section III.

34 For further uses of the story of the pious man in other rabbinic traditions, see the parallels adduced by Margaliot, *Vayyikra Rabbah*, 815.

these intentions. In reward for this pious activity, God produces a caper bush on the very spot of the breach, and the bush provides permanent sustenance for the pious man.

The story is clearly furnished in order to provide a specific example of activity on the Sabbath that could result in the proscribed act of thinking about labor on the Sabbath. What is most interesting for our purposes is that the example is nearly identical with the specific case furnished in the *Damascus Document*. While *Leviticus Rabbah* moves from general law to illustrative example, the *Damascus Document* provides a specific case from which one is expected to identify its larger legal implications. At the same time, both texts seem to indicate that the proscribed thoughts apply only in the specific circumstances under consideration. The case of the pious man in his vineyard is introduced in order to limit the specific application of the prohibition against thoughts on the Sabbath. Similarly, the *Damascus Document* provides the example of the individual in his field to indicate this same narrow application of the law. Both attestations of this law therefore disagree with the more general prohibition articulated in Philo and the *Mekhilta*.

The polemical tone in *Leviticus Rabbah* can be detected in both its exegetical technique and homiletical style. By linking the law to Isa 58:13, *Leviticus Rabbah* simultaneously rejects the notion that this passage can be employed in the service of the more restrictive position (as in the *Mekhilta*). On the contrary, for *Leviticus Rabbah*, Isa 58:13 states that this law only applies with regard to one's financial livelihood (חפציך). Perhaps most important, the story attached to the law in *Leviticus Rabbah* serves as a further statement regarding rabbinic attitudes toward the sustainability of this law. The association of the law with the pious man is likely intended as a further counternarrative to its widespread application. Not only should this law only apply to one's livelihood, but it is something to which only a truly pious person can aspire. Yet, even the pious person fails to follow the law to its fullest extent. Thus, the formulation of this law in *Leviticus Rabbah* is implicitly aware of its limited applicability.

The appearance of the law restricting thoughts on the Sabbath in *Pesiqta Rabbati* further reinforces the polemical tone detected in *Leviticus Rabbah*. As in *Leviticus Rabbah*, *Pesiqta Rabbati* combines a legal formulation restricting thoughts with the story of the pious man. Both texts introduce the story of the pious man in order to emphasize the difficulties involved in any law restricting thoughts. In *Pesiqta Rabbati*, however, the polemical tone is even more pronounced:

> שבת ליי אלהיך אמ"ר חייא בר אבא ר' מנחמיה ר' ביבי ר' אלעז' בשם ר' לוי שבות כאלהיך[35] מה אלהיך שבת ממאמר אף אתה שבות מן המאמר... אמ"ר אייבו שבות מן המחשבה[36] אמ"ר ברכי(ה)

[35] Mss Casanata 3324 and Dropsie 26 have the clearly incorrect באלהיך. I follow here Mss Parma 3122, JTS 8195, and the *editio princeps*.

[36] The text here follows Mss Casanata 3324, Dropsie 26, JTS 8195, and the *editio princeps*. Ms Parma 3122 has the clearly incorrect שבות והמחשבה.

מעשה בחסיד אחד שיצא לטייל[37] בתוך כרמו בשבת לידע מה צריך וראה שם פרצה אחת וחשב עליה לגודרה במוצאי שבת אמ' הואיל וחשבתי עליה בשבת איני גודרה עולמית מה פרע לו הב"ה[38] זימן לו מתוכה אילן אחד של נצפה וגדרה והיה מתפרנס ממנו כל ימיו

"A rest for the Lord thy God" (Exod 20:10): Said Rabbi Ḥiyya son of Ba, Rabbi Menaḥemiah, Rabbi Bibi, Rabbi Eli'ezer, in the name of Rabbi Levi: "The words mean, rest like your God. Even as God rested from saying, so are you to rest from saying..." [followed by story of Rabbi Shim'on ben Yoḥai chastising his mother for speaking too much and the statement that the rabbis only begrudgingly allowed greetings on the Sabbath].[39]

Rabbi Aibu said: Rest even from the thought [of labor]

A story is told, said Rabbi Berechiah, of a pious man who took a walk in his vineyard to find out what it required. He saw a breach there [in the wall] and on the Sabbath gave thought to fencing it up. At the end of the Sabbath he said, "Because I gave thought on the Sabbath to fencing it up, God forbid, I shall never fence it up."

How did the Holy One, Blessed be He, pay him back? He set up a caper bush there and it grew and filled up the breach, and the man made his living from the caper bush for the entire rest of his life. (*Pesiqta Rabbati* 23:8)[40]

The story of the pious man is essentially identical in *Pesiqta Rabbati* and *Leviticus Rabbah*.[41] Yet, while *Leviticus Rabbah* mirrors the *Babylonian Talmud* (*b. 'Erub.* 38b) in the language of the legal formulation (i.e., focusing on the field), *Pesiqta Rabbati* follows closely the general legal formulation found in *Mekhilta Ba-Ḥodesh* (*Mekhilta*: שבות ממחשבת עבודה → *Pesiqta Rabbati*:

[37] Here as well Ms Parma 3122 diverges from all text witnesses with what is likely a mistake: שרצא לטייל.

[38] I.e., הקדוש ברוך הוא. The expression is spelled out in Ms JTS 8195 and the *editio princeps*.

[39] On these two elements, see discussion in the context of their appearance in the *Palestinian Talmud*, above, Chapter 6, section III.

[40] Hebrew text follows Rivka Ulmer, *Pesiqta Rabbati: A Synoptic Edition of Pesiqta Rabbati Based on All Extant Manuscripts and the Editio Princeps* (3 vols.; SJ; Lanham: University Press of America, 2009), 1:558–59. The text presented above follows on the whole Ms Casanata 3324. Aside from the minor divergences listed in the previous notes, the manuscripts and the *editio princeps* attribute some of the statement to different rabbis. Translation (slightly modified) follows William G. Braude, *Pesiqta Rabbati: Discourses for Feasts, Fasts, and Special Sabbaths* (YJS 18; 2 vols.; New Haven: Yale University Press, 1968), 1:477–78 (the homily division follows Ulmer; Braude's identification of this unit as §3 follows Meir Friedmann, *Midrash Pesikta Rabbati* [Vienna, 1880; repr., Tel Aviv, 1963], 116b). An identical version of this homily appears in *Midrash Ha-Gadol* on Exod 20:10 (see Mordechai Margaliot, *Midrash Ha-Gadol: Shemot* [Jerusalem: Mossad ha-Rav Kook], 416).

[41] The story also appears in the printed editions of the *Palestinian Talmud* (*y. Shabb.* 15:3 15b), though this is almost certainly not original. Foremost, the story of the pious man in the field is not universally attested in the manuscripts. It appears only in the margin of Ms Leiden Or. 4720 and is absent in many other important witnesses (especially a Genizah fragment published by J. N. Epstein, "Additional Fragments of the Yerushalmi," *Tarbiz* 3 [1932]: 15–26, 121–36, 237–48 [241] [Hebrew]). A general summary of evidence of the manuscripts and printed editions is found in Margaliot, *Vayyikra Rabbah*, 815.

שבות מן המחשבה).[42] Two critical distinctions, however, can be detected. First, *Pesiqta Rabbati* has expunged any traces of Isa 58:13 as the scriptural source for the law. This feature is likely based on the same hesitation to turn to a prophetic source for law as detected above in *Mekhilta Shabbata*.

The second major distinction is the inclusion of the story of the pious man, which radically changes the law as first articulated in *Mekhilta Ba-Ḥodesh*. The anonymous statement outlawing all thoughts about labor on the Sabbath in the *Mekhilta* is attributed to Rabbi Aibu in *Pesiqta Rabbati*. Whereas the *Mekhilta* follows this apodictic law with the appeal to Isa 58:13, *Pesiqta Rabbati* instead introduces the story of the pious man in the field. The combination of these two elements produces a conceptual and legal disconnect. The first formulation, based on the *Mekhilta*, restricts thoughts entirely, while the second formulation – the story of the pious man – provides a specific setting in which thoughts would be prohibited and affirms the limited applicability of the law. The apodictic legal formulation restricting movement in a field/vineyard articulated in the *Babylonian Talmud ʿErubin* and *Leviticus Rabbah* would seem to be a much better fit with the illustrative example of the pious man.

The story of the pious man in *Pesiqta Rabbati* fulfills a slightly different function than does its appearance in *Leviticus Rabbah*. *Leviticus Rabbah* affirms the limited applicability of the restriction on thoughts and draws upon the story of the pious man to assert that even these limited circumstances are impractical. By attaching the story of the pious man to a slightly modified version of the general prohibition from the *Mekhilta*, *Pesiqta Rabbati* effectively erases any sense that the law found in the *Mekhilta* can in fact be implemented. If a pious man cannot withhold his improper thoughts on the Sabbath, how can anyone else be expected to do so? As in *Leviticus Rabbah*, *Pesiqta Rabbati* offers another voice affirming the implausible nature of a law that restricts thoughts.

No Prohibition: *Babylonian Talmud (Shabbat)*

Rabbinic tradition preserves yet a third manifestation of this law. Though they disagree about the specific details and the feasibility of their implementation, all the rabbinic texts I have examined assume the extension of the scriptural base texts to include the prohibition of even thinking about labor on the Sabbath. The *Babylonian Talmud Shabbat* is explicit in its rejection of any notion that thoughts regarding labors are prohibited or that this law can be traced to Isa 58:13.

In Chapter 6, I examined *Babylonian Talmud Shabbat* 150a, which expounds upon the restriction on hiring workers for post-Sabbath labor

[42] As noted by Horowitz and Rabin, *Mekhilta*, 230; Braude, *Pesiqta Rabbati*, 478 n. 26. עבודה is likely intended as the subject matter of the thought in *Pesiqta Rabbati*. At the same time, its absence may be intended to underscore the universal nature of the restriction on thoughts.

articulated in *Mishnah Shabbat* 23:3.[43] According to the *Babylonian Talmud*, the key element in the prohibition is the restriction on *speaking* about post-Sabbath work during the Sabbath. By clearly articulating the terms of the hiring, the individual is violating the rabbinic requirement to abstain from speech on the Sabbath related to one's business or financial matters. At the same time, the *Babylonian Talmud* affirms that one can hire a worker through indirect language: אבל אומר לו הנראה שתעמוד עמי לערב, "But one may say to him, 'we shall see if you stand with me (i.e., join me) this evening.'" The identification of the scriptural basis for the law affirms the underlying logic of the permissibility of indirect hiring. After asserting that this law represents the opinion of Rabbi Joshua ben Korḥah, the *Babylonian Talmud* grounds its legal reasoning in exegesis of ודבר דבר in Isa 58:13. Business activity that involves speech – דבר, the keyword from Isa 58:13 – is forbidden on the Sabbath. Thus, the *Mishnah* prohibits an individual from clearly hiring a worker on the Sabbath. The indirect language of the second case attributed to Rabbi Joshua ben Korḥah avoids this difficulty because the first individual never engages in the hiring with explicit words. Rather, the worker is required to decipher through his mental faculties the intentions of the first individual. Thus, the case of indirect hiring illuminates the underlying legal principle of the *Babylonian Talmud*: "Speech is prohibited, thought is permitted" (דיבור אסור הרהור מותר).

The extended discussion regarding the legality of Rabbi Joshua ben Korḥah's position is no doubt the result of still lingering positions to the contrary – that both speech *and* thought are restricted. Rather, the *Babylonian Talmud* categorically rejects this legal position and its exegetical basis in Isa 58:13.[44] The emphasis on speech to the exclusion of thoughts finds points of contact with the polemical language found in *4QHalakha B* to express a legal position similar to that of the *Babylonian Talmud*. Moreover, the specific setting in which this statement is articulated further suggests that the *Babylonian Talmud* is concerned with the sustainability of the law. While it is reasonable to restrict an individual from verbally hiring a worker on the Sabbath for post-Sabbath labor, it is unrealistic to extend this restriction to include limiting the thoughts of these individuals. As such, the indirect speech that yields thoughts is rendered permissible, as are all thoughts about labor on the Sabbath.

This approach to the law is embedded in new language employed to express thought. Whereas all the previously discussed rabbinic texts refer to the proscribed mental activity with some form of the verbal root חשב, the *Babylonian Talmud* here identifies the mental process as הרהור. The verbal root חשב articulates a process of mental deliberation on a topic. In contrast, הרהור in this context likely represents more spontaneous thought. The rabbinic Hebrew הרהור is a loanword from Aramaic. In Dan 4:2, הרהר refers to "dream-fantasies"

[43] See Chapter 6, section III.

[44] See also the discussion that immediately follows between Rav Aḥa and Raba, which reinforces the conceptual and legal distinction between speech and thought.

(in parallelism with חלם). Rabbinic Hebrew employs the root הרהר for all types of thought processes, including improper thoughts of a sexual nature (e.g., *m. Naz.* 9:4; *Zav.* 2:2; *b. Yom.* 29a; *Nid.* 13b). The use of הרהר to describe the uncontrollable nature of dreams is retained in several instances where it likewise is employed to describe the uncontrollable nature of nocturnal sexual thoughts (see especially *m. Miqv.* 8:3; *b. Ḥul.* 37b). As in its use to describe spontaneous dreams or uncontrollable nocturnal sexual fantasies, the *Babylonian Talmud*'s lexical choice of הרהור draws on a similar semantic range.[45] By rejecting any prohibition on thoughts with this language, the *Babylonian Talmud* affirms part of its reasoning. In contrast to speech (דיבור), thought (הרהור) cannot always be controlled. As such, it is unreasonable and impractical to create Sabbath law directed at controlling one's thoughts.[46]

IV. CONCLUSIONS

The broader premise of the last two chapters is that the legal formulations in CD 10:20–21 and 4Q264a 1 i 5 do not stand alone. Rather, both passages must be situated within a wider context of Jewish law and legal exegesis in antiquity. Other texts from Second Temple and rabbinic Judaism likewise address the question of whether certain thoughts are restricted on the Sabbath. These texts engage in similar exegetical techniques in order to frame their legal positions as grounded in the authoritative scripture of Judaism. At the same time, the texts analyzed enter into a larger debate regarding legal theory – can one create legislation that seeks to proscribe mental consideration?

In the previous chapter, I suggested that the polemical tone of *4QHalakha B* is indicative of a wider setting in which the more restrictive position was applied and was likely exegetically linked to Isa 58:13. The writings of Philo examined in this chapter provide a manifestation of the stricter position and

[45] Thus, while the terminology can refer to thoughts more generally (as with חשב), its semantic range allows for an understanding that highlights the uncontrollable and spontaneous nature of some thoughts (perhaps better translated as "fantasies").

[46] Later halakhic tradition would follow the most lenient formulation found in the *Babylonian Talmud Shabbat*. See, e.g., Maimonides, *Mishneh Torah*, *Hilkhot Shabbat*, 24:1; *Shulḥan 'Arukh*, *'Oraḥ Ḥayyim*, 306:1, 8. At the same time, the halakhic tradition would codify the tension detected in the classical rabbinic texts and thus preserve this earlier dialogue. While thoughts about work are permitted in the *Shulḥan 'Arukh* (*'Oraḥ Ḥayyim*, 306:8), one is encouraged to abstain even from such thoughts. In contrast to the rabbinic texts discussed here, the source of this law is identified as the requirement to enjoy a pleasant Sabbath: הרהור בעסקיו מותר ומ"מ משום עונג שבת מצוה שלא יחשוב בהם כלל ויהא בעיניו כאילו כל מלאכתו עשויה, "Thoughts about one's work are permitted. Nonetheless, on account of 'delight of the Sabbath,' one should not think about work at all and consider it as if all of his work is completed." This formulation conflates the restrictive language of *Mekhilta Ba-Ḥodesh* and the permissive language of the *Babylonian Talmud Shabbat*. Note that the expectation of "delight of the Sabbath" (עונג שבת) is generally traced to Isa 58:13: וקראת לשבת ענג, "If you call the Sabbath 'delight'" (e.g., *b. Shabb.* 118b).

offer possible insight into its exegetical roots. Philo, as with his Second Temple–period contemporaries, turns to scripture to authorize this approach. The evidence provided by Philo is important for understanding the broader legal and exegetical setting of the texts in the Dead Sea Scrolls. The *Damascus Document* and *4QHalakha B* represent a snapshot of what was clearly a much livelier debate about how far the restriction on thoughts about proscribed labor extends. *4QHalakha B*, in particular, not only rejects the outright condemnation of such thoughts but also seems to polemicize against adherents of what was likely an impractical legal position. The Sabbath law preserved by Philo represents a snapshot of one of those very adherents. Philo's restriction on thoughts is framed within the same broader legal setting as that of the Dead Sea Scrolls – business and financial pursuits. Moreover, there is some evidence to support the proposition that the Sabbath law in Philo is at least aware of the exegetical basis of this law in Isa 58:13.

The points of correspondence between Philo and the Dead Sea Scrolls should not be regarded as evidence of any presumed direct contact. Rather, they are both representative of an approach to Sabbath law grounded in a response to social reality. Both recognize the need to expand Sabbath law to cover business-related activities. The *Damascus Document* and *4QHalakha B* take for granted the broader prohibition against conducting business and expand this law to include both speech and thoughts about business or financial matters. Philo explicitly extends the restriction against work on the Sabbath to include activity related to business. As in the *Damascus Document* and *4QHalakha B*, Philo expands the restriction even further by similarly emphasizing the cognitive elements that go along with such work. While the restriction on speech is not clearly delineated, it is likely that it would also be covered by the range of prohibitions articulated by Philo. Unlike the *Damascus Document* and *4QHalakha B*, however, Philo extends the restriction even further by proscribing thoughts of *all* activity restricted on the Sabbath.

The extant Second Temple–period texts reflect differing viewpoints on how far this aspect of Sabbath law reaches, the exegetical techniques applied to the scriptural sources, and the very philosophical foundations of a law that restricts thoughts. No doubt there were other voices in Second Temple Judaism entering into this contentious debate; their voices, however, are not preserved in the literary remains. It is only with later rabbinic literature that this ancient debate receives its fullest expression and the battle lines are clearly demarcated.

My analysis of the Second Temple–period material in conjunction with the rabbinic texts demonstrates that the questions encountered by the rabbis and the divergent approaches taken were not new. The rabbinic texts have their own internal debates that mirror those of the Second Temple–period texts. The rabbinic texts discussed in this chapter depict three divergent approaches to the broad question of whether thoughts about labor on the Sabbath are prohibited. The three viewpoints represent a set of internal debates occurring within rabbinic culture. As such, they often engage with one another, at times reflecting a polemical tone no doubt inspired by the contentious nature of this debate. The viewpoints expressed in these three approaches are not merely about legislating the minutiae of Sabbath law. Rather, they reflect significant questions encountered in the practical application of Sabbath law and Jewish law more generally – can legislation be enacted to restrict one's thoughts? The rabbinic texts outline three responses: yes, in some circumstances, and no.

The two formulations in the *Mekhilta* reject all thoughts of labor on the Sabbath. In contrast, the *Babylonian Talmud 'Erubin* introduces a specific case – walking in one's field – in which such thoughts are restricted. Yet, *Leviticus Rabbah* attaches to this case a story of a pious man who, even with his great piety, cannot resist the urge to think about labor on the Sabbath. The message is clear – restricting thoughts on the Sabbath must be limited to a real context, and even then, a thoroughly pious person has difficulty refraining. Indeed, the formulation of this law in *Pesiqta Rabbati* adds the story of the pious man as a gloss on the overly restrictive law in the *Mekhilta*. Finally, the *Babylonian Talmud Shabbat* offers an unequivocal rejection of any restriction on thoughts on the Sabbath. As in the Second Temple–period texts, the rabbinic texts all reflect a deep engagement with the question of the scriptural sources for this law. As with its antecedents, rabbinic literature relies on Isa 58:13 – likely continuing from its Second Temple–period usage – even as it introduces new possible scriptural sources. In dialogue with one another, the rabbinic texts bear witness to a long history of development regarding this law. We can also detect the resurfacing of some of the same polemics already observed in the Second Temple period.

The cumulative effect of these two chapters has been to locate Second Temple–period texts and rabbinic literature as part of a broader history of Jewish law and legal exegesis. When we place the two corpora alongside each other, it becomes clear that these texts are part of a continuous period of debate regarding the specific contours of this law, its exegetical foundations, and its theoretical underpinning. This observation reinforces the growing recognition that rabbinic juridical activity should be viewed as continuous with its Second Temple–period antecedents. The pairing of the rabbinic texts alongside the Second Temple–period evidence reinforces the view of rabbinic law as "reflective" of earlier active debates in Second Temple–period legal culture. Indeed, the passage from the *Babylonian Talmud 'Erubin* has striking textual and thematic correspondences with the case in the *Damascus Document*.

At the same time, the earliest rabbinic voice on this question (*Mekhilta*) is most closely aligned with the strictest approach detected in Second Temple texts. In this case, the *Mekhilta* may be representative of the "developmental" model of Jewish law, whereby singular strands in rabbinic law reach back into pre-rabbinic law to rehearse older Second Temple–period legal positions. Indeed, my analysis of the exegetical foundations of *Mekhilta Ba-Ḥodesh* suggests that it is knowledgeable of at least some aspects of the Second Temple–period legal-exegetical application of Isa 58:13 to proscribe thoughts about labor on the Sabbath.[47]

These two sets of texts offer insight into another theoretical issue involved in the comparative study of Second Temple and rabbinic law. As discussed at the beginning of the previous chapter, scholars debate the degree to which Second Temple and rabbinic texts reflect legal perspectives of realism versus nominalism. My analysis reinforces some common assumptions in this debate at the same time as it complicates others. The two Dead Sea Scrolls texts examined in the previous chapter should be offered as further evidence of the realism of sectarian law. The law in the *Damascus Document* is directly tied to a real-life – and likely, very common – situation. Its legislation is realistic in both its conception and implementation. Moreover, the negative assertion in *4QHalakha B* is grounded in the very same principles. The *Damascus Document* legislates for a very specific case where thoughts are of central concern, while *4QHalakha B* rejects the juridical approach that would expand this localized case into a universal legal principle.

When we examine closely the representation of the universal legal principle in Philo, traces of its initial realism-based origins can be detected. As in the Dead Sea Scrolls texts, the law in Philo is closely connected with business and financial affairs. The various formulations of this Sabbath law are the formal legal response to the real-world setting that recognizes that individuals will pay careful attention to their financial and professional well-being – even on the Sabbath. The *Damascus Document* limits the juridical response to the specific case to which it responds. Philo expands it into a universal law even as he reflects awareness of the original setting. *4QHalakha B* frames its opposition to the universal law in the context of exegesis of Isa 58:13 and its application for business-related speech. In so doing, it rejects the universal law at the same time as it redirects the law to the specific context for which it was first formulated.

In the case of this particular law, the rabbis were grappling with a similar set of practical realities as their predecessors had – how far should the restriction on thoughts move from a limited set of practical cases to a universal legal principle? More generally as a question of legal principle, is it realistic and sustainable to restrict one's thoughts? The rabbinic approaches share much in common with the earlier responses to this question detected in the Second Temple–period sources. As in the Second Temple–period materials themselves, the rabbinic texts display a movement away from the strict approach and similarly contain both implicit and explicit polemics against its applicability and feasibility. This development should also be framed within the debate over Second Temple–period and rabbinic realism versus nominalism. As in Philo, the

[47] On the "reflective" and "developmental" models of *halakhah* as formulated by Aharon Shemesh, see my discussion above, Chapter 1, section IV.

Mekhilta frames the law in the nominalist realm. In the three sets of rabbinic texts I have examined here, the rabbinic approach moves from the nominalist to the purely realistic. Thus, the legislation of the *Babylonian Talmud* permitting all manner of thought and outlawing speech alone is grounded in the simple reality that laws cannot be removed from their practical human context. In an intermediate state, the rabbis share with the *Damascus Document* the suggestion that one's thoughts can be dictated in a specific setting (i.e., the field – relating to one's livelihood). Yet, even this approach comes to be regarded as implausible and unfeasible within the context of practical human activity. For the rabbis, the restriction on thoughts can only be applied by the exceptionally pious, who even struggle with carrying out this difficult directive. The *Babylonian Talmud Shabbat*'s rejection of any restriction on thoughts on the Sabbath and its possible exegetical roots in Isa 58:13 represent a final utterance in a nearly millennium-long cacophony of legal and exegetical voices.

9

Jeremiah 17:21–22 and the Sabbath Carrying Prohibition in the Dead Sea Scrolls

I. INTRODUCTION

In the following two chapters, I turn my attention to another set of Sabbath restrictions articulated in the Dead Sea Scrolls and other ancient Jewish literature – the prohibition against carrying on the Sabbath. As in previous chapters, my analysis focuses on illuminating the specific contours of the law as articulated in legal texts from among the Dead Sea Scrolls (*Damascus Document*, *4QHalakha A*, *4QMiscellaneous Rules*), related Second Temple texts (*Nehemiah*, *Jubilees*), and rabbinic literature (*Mishnah Shabbat*). Alongside my treatment of the historical development of the carrying law and its specific components, I explore the exegetical foundations of the carrying prohibition as articulated in each of the distinct legal corpora from ancient Judaism.

The fullest sectarian formulation of the laws regarding carrying on the Sabbath is found in the *Damascus Document* (11:7–9; par. 4Q270 6 v 13–14; 4Q271 5 i 3–4). Scholarship on the carrying prohibition has focused on deciphering the precise details of the sectarian laws as well as identifying parallel legal formulations in Second Temple and rabbinic legal texts.[1] Nearly all of

[1] See Louis Ginzberg, *An Unknown Jewish Sect* (Moreshet 1; New York: Jewish Theological Seminary, 1976), 65–66, 186–87; Chanokh Albeck, *Das Buch der Jubiläen und die Halacha* (Berichte der Hochschule für die Wissenschaft des Judentums 47; Berlin: Hochschule für die Wissenschaft des Judentums, 1930), 8; Chaim Rabin, *Qumran Studies* (SJ 2; Oxford: Clarendon, 1957), 109–10; S. T. Kimbrough Jr., "The Concept of Sabbath at Qumran," *RevQ* 5 (1966): 483–502 (493); Lawrence H. Schiffman, *The Halakhah at Qumran* (SJLA 16; Leiden: Brill, 1975), 113–15; Lutz Doering, "New Aspects of Qumran Sabbath Law from Cave 4 Fragments," in *Legal Texts and Legal Issues: Proceedings of the Second Meeting of the International Organization for Qumran Studies, Cambridge, 1995; Published in Honour of Joseph M. Baumgarten* (ed. M. J. Bernstein, F. García Martínez, and J. Kampen; STDJ 23; Leiden: Brill, 1997), 241–74 (252–56); idem, *Schabbat: Sabbathhalacha und -praxis im antiken Judentum und Urchristentum* (TSAJ 78; Tübingen: Mohr Siebeck, 1999), 178–82, 229–31; Charlotte Fonrobert, "From Separatism

these analyses observe that the laws in the *Damascus Document* represent a reformulation of Jer 17:21–22.[2] In spite of this long-recognized connection, no significant study has focused on the legal and exegetical relationship between Jer 17:21–22 and CD 11:7–9 or the relevant comparative Second Temple and rabbinic legal sources.[3] The Cave 4 legal texts have also furnished us with an intriguing set of similarly formulated laws that must now be considered in conjunction with the *Damascus Document*. *4QHalakha A* (4Q251) and *4QMiscellaneous Rules* (4Q265) contain several closely related Sabbath regulations that overlap in varying degrees with the carrying prohibition in the *Damascus Document*.

These two chapters seek to contribute further to our understanding of the sectarian prohibition by identifying the scriptural basis of CD 11:7–9 and the Cave 4 legal texts and clarifying their legal and exegetical relationship to Jer 17:21–22 and related scriptural passages, particularly Exod 16:29. This relationship is then located within the larger framework of the legal and exegetical employment of these verses in the broader context of Second Temple and rabbinic legal texts.

II. THE SABBATH CARRYING PROHIBITION IN THE DEAD SEA SCROLLS

Laws regarding the prohibition against carrying on the Sabbath are found in three places in the sectarian legal texts:

Damascus Document (CD) 11:7–9 (par. 4Q270 6 v 13–14; 4Q271 5 i 3–4)[4]

7 *vac* אל יוציא[5] איש מן הבית

8 לחוץ ומן החוץ אל בית ואם בסוכה יהיה אל יוצא ממנה

9 ואל יבא[6] אליה

7. *vac* Let no man carry out (anything) from the house

to Urbanism: The Dead Sea Scrolls and the Origins of the Rabbinic ‘Eruv,” *DSD* 11 (2004): 43–71.

[2] See below, n. 17.

[3] For example, Schiffman, *Halakhah*, 113, simply remarks that “from the wording, it is clear that the law is a rephrasing of Jer. 17:21 and 22.”

[4] Hebrew text follows Elisha Qimron, “The Text of CDC,” in *The Damascus Document Reconsidered* (ed. M. Broshi; Jerusalem: Israel Exploration Society, the Shrine of the Book, Israel Museum, 1992), 31. Parallel Cave 4 texts can be found in Joseph M. Baumgarten, *Qumran Cave 4.XIII: The Damascus Document (4Q266–273)* (DJD 18; Oxford: Clarendon, 1996), 161, 180 (significant variants are noted below). For general discussion, see Schiffman, *Halakhah*, 113–15; Doering, *Schabbat*, 178–82.

[5] 4Q270–271 preserve יוציאה.

[6] 4Q271 has the plene spelling יביא.

8. outside and from the outside into the house. And if he is in a booth (*sukkah*)[7] he shall not carry out (anything) from it
9. and he shall not bring in it (anything).

4QHalakha A (4Q251) 1–2 (olim frg. 1) 4–5[8]

4 אל] יוצא איש ממקומו כל השבת
5 [מן החוץ אל הבית] ומן הבית אל הח[וץ]

4. [Let no] man carry out[9] (anything) from his place for the entire Sabbath
5. [from the outside to the house] and from the house to the ou[tside]

4QMiscellaneous Rules (4Q265) 6 4–5[10]

4 אל יו[צא אי]ש מאהלו כלי ומאכ[ל]
5 ביום *vac* השבת

4. Let no ma[n] ca[rry out] from his tent any vessel or foo[d]
5. on the day *vac* of the Sabbath.

The shared content and overlapping language suggest that these passages represent a single Sabbath law expressed in three separate

[7] The term סוכה can be understood here as a general term for a temporary dwelling or in its more technical sense as the temporary dwelling used on the festival of Tabernacles (see further Schiffman, *Halakhah*, 114 n. 197; Doering, *Schabbat*, 179). In support of the latter understanding, Schiffman elsewhere explains that its introduction here is based on the inevitable problem posed by the construction of a *sukkah*. If it is built in a field (or any distance from the home), then one would need to carry items from one's home to the outside in order to transfer them to the *sukkah* on the Sabbath. Thus, the *Damascus Document* reiterates that the carrying restriction is still in force, notwithstanding the attendant inconvenience. It is not clear if the community allowed for the construction of an *'erub* in order to alleviate the problem, as is done by the rabbis (Lawrence H. Schiffman, *Reclaiming the Dead Sea Scrolls: The History of Judaism, the Background of Christianity and the Lost Library of Qumran* [ABRL; New York: Doubleday, 1995], 277–78).

[8] Text and translation (slightly modified) follow Erik Larson, Manfred R. Lehmann, and Lawrence Schiffman, "4Q251: 4QHalakha A," in *Qumran Cave 4.XXV: Halakhic Texts* (ed. J. M. Baumgarten et al.; DJD 35; Oxford: Clarendon, 1999), 28–30.

[9] See the translation of יוצא as "go out" in James H. Charlesworth and Carsten Claussen, "Halakah A: 4Q251," in *The Dead Sea Scrolls: Hebrew, Aramaic, and Greek Texts with English Translations; Damascus Document II, Some Works of the Torah, and Related Documents* (ed. J. H. Charlesworth; PTSDSSP 3; Tübingen: Mohr Siebeck; Louisville: Westminster John Knox, 2006), 275. Presumably, they understand the form as a *qal* participle. Yet, the standard sectarian legal formula requires a jussive form. Thus, the *mater lectionis waw* identifies this form as *hiph'il* ("carry out").

[10] Text and translation (slightly modified) follow Joseph Baumgarten, "4Q265: Miscellaneous Rules," in *Qumran Cave 4.XXV*, 68–69.

texts.[11] Before turning to the scriptural basis of these passages and their exegetical amplification in the Dead Sea Scrolls, let me first clarify the legal content of these three related passages. Three specific components of the law are introduced in these passages: (1) the precise locations to and from which carrying is forbidden, (2) the definition of what constitutes one's personal space, and (3) what specific objects may not be carried.

In the *Damascus Document*, individuals are prohibited from carrying an item from one's house (i.e., personal space) outside (i.e., public space) and vice versa.[12] A nearly identical formulation is found in *4QHalakha A*. In contrast, *4QMiscellaneous Rules* prohibits only the act of taking an item outside of one's tent. The *Damascus Document* adds an additional element to the law by stating that the entire prohibition is also applicable if one carries from a temporary dwelling (or a technical *sukkah*) outside and vice versa. This second clause in the *Damascus Document* thereby extends the precise parameters of prohibited areas of carrying to include additional personal spaces that are equivalent to one's home. Similarly, in *4QMiscellaneous Rules*, the law of carrying is expressed by referring to an individual's "tent," with no mention of a house. Presumably, this passage is also intended to extend the notion of personal space beyond merely the house.[13] The inclusion of the possessive suffix

[11] The possibility of a fourth iteration of the carrying law in *4QHalakha B* has recently been suggested in Vered Noam and Elisha Qimron, "A Qumran Composition of Sabbath Law and Its Contribution to the Study of Early Halakah," *DSD* 16 (2009): 55–96 (61–63). Noam and Qimron propose combining 4Q264a and 4Q421 (relabeled by them as 4Q421a) beyond where overlapping language is visible (see above, Chapter 5, n. 5). The newly combined 4Q264a 3 + 4Q421 12 6 contains a clause that presumably refers to the prohibition against carrying on the Sabbath (I have indicated here material from 4Q264a with a single underline and content from 4Q421 with a double underline; anything not underlined represents a suggested restoration by Noam and Qimron): א]ל יוצא ואל יבא בשער חצרו ובשער עירו], "N[o one shall take out or bring in the gate of his courtyard and in the gate of his city" (ibid., 61–62). The lack of a physical manuscript join and the general fragmentary nature of both manuscripts make the restored text speculative. In an earlier study, I treat the plausibility of the restoration and its possible implications for the carrying law. See Alex P. Jassen, "Law and Exegesis in the Dead Sea Scrolls: The Sabbath Carrying Prohibition in Comparative Perspective," in *The Dead Sea Scrolls at Sixty: The Scholarly Contributions of the New York University Faculty and Alumni* (ed. L. H. Schiffman and S. Tsoref; STDJ 89; Leiden: Brill; 2010), 115–56 (especially 118 n. 11).

[12] On the debate regarding the categories of personal and private space in sectarian law, see my discussion in Jassen, "Law and Exegesis," 119 n. 12.

[13] In this sense, *4QMiscellaneous Rules* likely does not exclude the house or temporary dwelling from the prohibited areas of carrying. Doering suggests that "tent" here should be understood as equivalent to a house ("New Aspects," 260–61; *Schabbat*, 230). It seems more likely that the inclusion of a tent in *4QMiscellaneous Rules* is intended to extend the already known restriction of the *Damascus Document* (and *4QHalakha A*) to an additional private dwelling. This is similar to the inclusion of *sukkah* in the *Damascus Document*. All of this is responding to restrictive scriptural language of Jer 17:22, where only a "house" is mentioned (see below). See also Jub 50:8, which restricts carrying out of both a house and a tent (see Chapter 10, section III).

in *4QMiscellaneous Rules* ("his tent") may also call attention to the sectarian understanding that personal space cannot be extended.[14]

4QHalakha A is the only passage that does not contain any additional designation regarding what constitutes personal space. This passage, however, is also the only text that paraphrases ממקומו ("from his place") from Exod 16:29.[15] This additional inclusion in *4QHalakha A* (ממקומו, "from his place") therefore fulfills a function similar to *sukkah* and "tent" in the *Damascus Document* and *4QMiscellaneous Rules*; it serves to indicate that one's personal space extends beyond merely the home.

Neither the *Damascus Document* nor *4QHalakha A* provides specific information regarding what types of items are being carried. This silence suggests an inclusive prohibition, proscribing the carrying of all items on the Sabbath. Once again, *4QMiscellaneous Rules* provides the exception in that it singles out a "vessel" and "food" as specific items that may not be carried.[16] It is unlikely that *4QMiscellaneous Rules* restricts the prohibition on carrying to include only vessels and food. Rather, these are being singled out just as *4QMiscellaneous Rules* also includes the tent among the areas of prohibited carrying. Let me now turn to the exegetical basis for the various legal formulations in these three texts.

III. EXODUS 16:29 AND JEREMIAH 17:21–22, 24 IN THE DAMASCUS DOCUMENT, 4QHALAKHA A, AND 4QMISCELLANEOUS RULES

Introductory Observations and Synoptic Comparison

No scriptural source is cited for any of the three Dead Sea Scrolls legal texts. Nearly all of the specific legal content in these three passages as well as their

[14] Doering, "New Aspects," 261.

[15] The *Damascus Document* and *4QMiscellaneous Rules* only paraphrase the initial part of the interdiction: אל יצא (Exod: "Let him not go out)" → אל יוציא (CD, 4Q265: "Let no man carry out"). See below for full discussion of the legal-exegetical reading of Exod 16:29.

[16] See below for fuller treatment of this issue. A different explanation for these anomalies in *4QMiscellaneous Rules* is offered by Baumgarten ("4Q265: Miscellaneous Rules," 69; cf. Doering, *Schabbat*, 231). He suggests that the primary focus of the clause in *4QMiscellaneous Rules* concerns restrictions on moving certain items on the Sabbath within one's home (*muqṣe* cf. CD 11:10–11; Josephus, *Jewish War* 2.147). *4QMiscellaneous Rules*, argues Baumgarten, represents an additional provision for this law, specifically regarding items that may not be carried out of the home. He suggests that כלי ומאכל should be understood as hendiadys and therefore a reference to a "food vessel." Such an item, declares *4QMiscellaneous Rules*, may not be carried outside of the home but may be carried within the home (i.e., it is not subject to the laws of *muqṣe*). Other vessels can be carried neither in the home nor outside of the home. The indirect way in which such a formulation functions recommends against its understanding as part of the *muqṣe* laws. Furthermore, the close literary correspondence with the carrying laws in the *Damascus Document* and *4QHalakha A* (and also Jer 17:21–22 and Exod 16:29) suggests that it should rather be grouped with these other passages as a restriction against carrying.

literary form, however, are grounded in the interpretation and reformulation of scriptural content. All three passages contain significant overlap in legal content and shared language with Exod 16:29 and Jer 17:21–22, 24. These features suggest that the scriptural passages represent the legal and exegetical source for the passages in the *Damascus Document*, *4QHalakha A*, and *4QMiscellaneous Rules*. The shared language is outlined in Table 8.

The shared language between Jer 17:21–22, 24 and CD 11:7–9 suggests that the latter represents a paraphrase of the former.[17] *4QHalakha A* and *4QMiscellaneous Rules* also share language with Jer 17:21–22, though in a more limited sense consistent with their shorter presentation of the carrying prohibition. At the same time, the literary correspondence between all three passages and Exod 16:29 is unmistakable. The initial formulation of all three passages, with a slight grammatical shift to be discussed below, is nearly identical to Exod 16:29.[18]

Because both Exod 16:29 and Jer 17:21–22 seemingly function as the basis for the paraphrase in the sectarian legal texts, a number of questions arise. First, how are the legal texts in the Dead Sea Scrolls reading and reformulating the scriptural passages with their legal interests in mind? Second, what is the relationship between scriptural verses as they interface in the sectarian reformulation? I first introduce the scriptural passages and then turn to deciphering the mechanics of their reformulation in the sectarian legal texts.

Exodus 16:29 and Jeremiah 17:21–22 in Context

Exod 16:29 forms part of the larger pericope that narrates the Israelites' receipt of the manna in the desert (Exod 16). After the Israelites go out to collect manna on the Sabbath, Moses reminds them that they had previously been commanded not to do so. Exod 16:29 contains Moses' instruction to them not to leave

[17] Most scholars have recognized the connection to vv. 21–22. See R. H. Charles, "Fragments of a Zadokite Work," in idem, ed., *Apocrypha and Pseudepigrapha of the Old Testament* (2 vols.; Oxford: Clarendon, 1913), 2:827; Leonhard Rost, *Die Damascusschrift: Neu Bearbeitet* (Klein Texte für Vorlesungen und Übungen 167; Berlin: de Gruyter, 1933), 21; Chaim Rabin, *The Zadokite Documents* (Oxford: Clarendon, 1954), 55; Kimbrough, "Sabbath at Qumran," 493; Schiffman, *Halakhah*, 114; Charlotte Hempel, *The Laws of the Damascus Document: Sources, Traditions, and Redaction* (STDJ 29; Leiden: Brill, 1998), 12; Doering, "New Aspects," 258; idem, *Schabbat*, 178. Contra Ginzberg, *Jewish Sect*, 186–87, who argues that the *Damascus Document* "maintains a complete silence about the source" of the law of carrying. He contrasts the presumed silence of the *Damascus Document* with rabbinic tradition, which freely draws upon Jer 17:21–22. The material in verse 24 clearly overlaps with language from vv. 21–22 and is thus secondary. There does seem to be some direct exegetical use of verse 24 in the sectarian texts (see below).

[18] For Exod 16:29 and *4QHalakha A*, see Doering, "New Aspects," 257; idem, *Schabbat*, 229; Larson, Lehmann, and Schiffman, "4Q251: Halakha A," 29; Charlesworth and Claussen, "Halakah A: 4Q251," 275 (though see above, n. 9). On *4QMiscellaneous Rules*, see Baumgarten, "4Q265: Miscellaneous Rules," 69.

TABLE 8. *Exod 16:29 and Jer 17:21–22, 24 and CD, 4Q251, and 4Q265*

Hebrew Bible	Dead Sea Scrolls
Exod 16:29[a] ראו כי יהוה נתן לכם השבת על כן הוא נתן לכם ביום הששי לחם יומים שבו איש תחתיו אל יצא איש ממקמו ביום השביעי Mark that the Lord has given you the Sabbath; therefore he gives you two days' food on the sixth day. Let everyone remain where he is: let no one leave his place on the seventh day.	**CD 11:7–9** אל יוציא איש מן הבית לחוץ ומן החוץ אל בית ואם בסוכה יהיה אל יוצא ממנה ואל יבא אליה Let no man carry out (anything) from the house outside and from the outside into the house. And if he is in a booth, he shall not carry out (anything) from it and he shall not bring in it (anything).
Jer 17:21–22, 24[b] 21 כה אמר יהוה השמרו בנפשותיכם ואל תשאו משא ביום השבת והבאתם בשערי ירושלם 22 ולא תוציאו משא מבתיכם ביום השבת וכל מלאכה לא תעשו וקדשתם את יום השבת כאשר צויתי את אבותיכם (21) Thus said the Lord: Guard yourselves for your own sake against carrying burdens on the Sabbath day, and bringing them through the gates of Jerusalem. (22) Nor shall you carry out burdens from your houses on the Sabbath day, or do any work, but you shall hallow the Sabbath day, as I commanded your fathers. 24 והיה אם שמע תשמעון אלי נאם יהוה לבלתי הביא משא בשערי העיר הזאת ביום השבת ולקדש את יום השבת לבלתי עשות בה [בו][c] כל מלאכה If you obey me – declares the Lord – and do not bring in burdens through the gates of this city on the Sabbath day, but hallow the Sabbath day and do no work on it	**4Q251 1–2 4–5** אל] יוצא איש ממקומו כל השבת [מן החוץ אל הבית] ומן הבית אל הח[וץ [Let no] man carry out (anything) from his place for the entire Sabbath [from the outside to the house]and from the house to the ou[tside. **4Q265 6 4–5** אל יו[צא אי]ש מאהלו כלי ומאכ[ל] ביום *vac* השבת Let no ma[n] ca[rry out] from his tent any vessel or foo[d] on the day *vac* of the Sabbath.

[a] Exod 16:29 is partially preserved in 4QpaleoGen–Exod[l] (4Q11) 16 6–8. For this text, see Patrick W. Skehan, Eugene Ulrich, and Judith E. Sanderson, "4Q11: 4QpaleoGen–Exod[l]," *Qumran Cave 4.IV: Palaeo-Hebrew and Greek Biblical Manuscripts* (ed. P. W. Skehan, E. Ulrich, and J. E. Sanderson; DJD 9; Oxford: Clarendon, 1992), 37. Neither 4QpaleoGen–Exod[l] nor any of the ancient versions preserve any significant textual variants.

[b] Jer 17:21–24 is partially preserved in 4QJer[a] (4Q70) 26–28 xi 11–15. See Emanuel Tov, "4Q70: 4QJer[a]," in *Qumran Cave 4.X: The Prophets* (ed. E. Ulrich et al.; DJD 15; Oxford: Clarendon, 1997), 163. No significant variants are found in this manuscript or in the ancient versions.

[c] 4QJer[a] preserves the 𝔐 *ketiv* form בה.

(אל יצא) their place on the Sabbath. As is readily apparent, there is nothing in this passage regarding carrying or any hint of its proscription. Indeed, Exod 16:29 does not constitute a legal imperative at all. The command for "everyone to remain in his place" forms part of the literary narrative and in its original context carries no prescriptive force for more general Sabbath observance.

In contrast, Jer 17:21–22 represents an explicit prohibition against carrying on the Sabbath, something absent in the Pentateuchal Sabbath laws. As Michael Fishbane has observed, this passage is an expanded reformulation of the Sabbath law of the Decalogue in *Deuteronomy*. In so doing, Jer 17:21–22 has imparted its own expanded Sabbath law with Sinaitic authority.[19] The specific parameters of *Jeremiah*'s prohibition on carrying are not as certain. While *Jeremiah* opens with a general condemnation of "carrying burdens" on the Sabbath (v. 21b), two more specific aspects are thereafter delineated. *Jeremiah* warns against carrying through the city gates (v. 21c) and outside of one's house (v. 22a). Does the condemnation apply only to these two specific cases, or is it a more general proscription for all carrying on the Sabbath? What precise types of "burdens" are proscribed here? As a prophetic invective, the language of Jer 17:21–22 fulfills its task. As a Sabbath prohibition – the capacity in which it was clearly understood in later Judaism – it fails to provide the desired explicit legal language.

Exodus 16:29 and Jeremiah 17:21–22 Recontextualized

The synoptic comparison of Jer 17:21–22 and the three Dead Sea Scrolls texts in Table 8 indicates that the sectarian legal texts draw much of their language from two specific clauses in *Jeremiah*:

> **Jer 17:21bc:** ואל תשאו משא ביום השבת והבאתם בשערי ירושלם, "(Guard yourselves) against carrying burdens on the Sabbath day, and bringing them through the gates of Jerusalem."

> **Jer 17:22a:** ולא תוציאו משא מבתיכם ביום השבת, "Nor shall you carry out burdens from your houses on the Sabbath day."

All three Dead Sea Scrolls texts make repeated use of several keywords from these clauses, with the clear exception of the expressions משא ("burden") and שערי ירושלם ("gates of Jerusalem"). The Dead Sea Scrolls texts subtly modify keywords from *Jeremiah* (indicated in Table 8 with different forms of underlining), simultaneously transforming the meaning of the unused words (משא and שערי ירושלם).

[19] Michael Fishbane, *Biblical Interpretation in Ancient Israel* (Oxford: Clarendon, 1985), 131–33. For a different understanding of the relationship between Deut 5:12–14 and Jer 17:21–22, see Jerry A. Gladson, "Jeremiah 17:19–27: A Rewriting of the Sinaitic Code?" *CBQ* 62 (2000): 33–40. On source-critical questions regarding the provenance of this pericope, see below, Chapter 10, n. 1.

The original prophetic language is more precisely defined and expanded to include several new features. In so doing, these texts infuse Jer 17:21–22 with a dramatically different application, while still claiming to represent the full meaning of *Jeremiah*. As we shall see in the next chapter, similar principles are operating in the other Second Temple and rabbinic texts. In this sense, all these texts utilize *Jeremiah* in much the same way that *Jeremiah* employs *Deuteronomy* – in order to provide divine sanction for the newly formulated law. The following discussion focuses on three exegetical issues in the Dead Sea Scrolls texts: (1) a precise definition of the space in which carrying is proscribed, (2) a precise definition of items that may not be carried on the Sabbath, and (3) the exegetical relationship of Jer 17:21–22 and Exod 16:29 in all three Dead Sea Scrolls texts.

Defining the Space in Which Carrying Is Prohibited

The first aspect of the exegetical reformulation of *Jeremiah* consists of delineating in greater detail the precise physical space affected by the carrying prohibition. Three legal-exegetical developments are discernible in the sectarian reformulations. The first legal-exegetical development focuses on a more precise application of *Jeremiah*'s statement regarding personal space and public space. The *Damascus Document* and *4QHalakha A* preserve the scriptural language of carrying from a house (*Jeremiah*: מבתיכם, "From your houses" → CD, 4Q251: מן הבית "From the house") with the root יצא in the *hiph'il* form (*Jeremiah*: ולא תוציאו "Nor shall you carry out"→ CD, 4Q251: אל יוצ[י]א איש, "Let no man carry out"). In so doing, the *Damascus Document* and *4QHalakha A* reinforce *Jeremiah*'s emphasis on the house as one's personal space. At the same time, all three texts expand this parameter so as to include additional personal dwellings. This legal expansion is accomplished by including the additional statement that the law applies as well in a temporary dwelling (*sukkah* – CD), in a tent (4Q265), and perhaps in additional personal spaces ("his place" – 4Q251).

In the case of the *Damascus Document*'s extension of the law to a *sukkah*, the *Damascus Document* contains a lengthy addendum that repeats the entire legal formulation found in lines 7–8 regarding a house (itself paraphrasing *Jeremiah*) as it would apply to a *sukkah*:

> **House** (ll. 7–8): אל יוציא איש מן הבית לחוץ ומן החוץ אל בית, "Let no man carry out (anything) from the house outside and from the outside into the house."
>
> ***Sukkah*** (ll. 8–9): ואם בסוכה יהיה אל יוצא ממנה ואל יבא אליה, "And if he is in a booth, he shall not carry out (anything) from it and he shall not bring in it (anything)."

The inclusion of the *sukkah* in the *Damascus Document* therefore is "authorized" by a repetition of the full scriptural language from *Jeremiah* referring to a house. As in *Jeremiah*'s "house clause" (and the *Damascus Document*'s reformulation), the *Damascus Document*'s "*sukkah* clause" includes the root יצא in the *hiph'il* form followed by the preposition *mem* and the pronoun referring back to the *sukkah*:

> Jer 17:22a: ולא תוציאו משא מבתיכם, "Nor shall you carry out burdens from your houses."
>
> CD 11:7: אל יוציא איש מן הבית, "Let no man carry out (anything) from the house."
>
> CD 11:8: אל יוצא ממנה, "He shall not carry out (anything) from it."[20]

A similar reuse of *Jeremiah*'s language is found in *4QMiscellaneous Rules* to expand the law to include one's tent as well. While this passage contains no reference to one's house, its inclusion of a tent employs language from *Jeremiah* in much the same way that the *Damascus Document* expands its law to include a *sukkah*. Thus, *4QMiscellaneous Rules* preserves *Jeremiah*'s יצא–*hiph'il* followed by the preposition *mem*. Rather than a house, however, *4QMiscellaneous Rules* applies the scriptural language to a tent:

> Jer 17:22a: ולא תוציאו משא מבתיכם, "Nor shall you carry out burdens from your houses."
>
> 4Q265 6 4: אל יו[צא אי]ש מאהלו, "Let no ma[n] ca[rry out] from his tent."

Thus, *4QMiscellaneous Rules* further expands the initially limited application of *Jeremiah*'s words.

It is not clear if *4QHalakha A* is following a similar legal-exegetical application of *Jeremiah* with its similar formulation: אל] יוצא איש ממקומו, "[Let no] man carry out (anything) from his place" (l. 4). This clause closely reformulates Exod 16:29 (אל יצא איש ממקמו, "let no one leave his place"), which would suggest that it is not an exegetical formulation of *Jeremiah*. At the same time, it also follows *Jeremiah*'s formula of יצא–*hiph'il* followed by the preposition *mem* and the specific space under consideration. If this is intentional, then *4QHalakha A* would be employing this exegetical technique to expand *Jeremiah*'s words to include further personal spaces:

> Jer 17:22a: ולא תוציאו משא מבתיכם, "Nor shall you carry out burdens from your houses."
>
> 4Q251 1–2 4: אל] יוצא איש ממקומו, "[Let no] man carry out (anything) from his place."

The restricted language of *Jeremiah* is also expanded with regard to the meaning of public space. Jer 17:22a merely condemns the carrying of an item out of one's home, with no indication that any specific outside space is intended. This limited language is expanded in the *Damascus Document* and *4QHalakha A*

[20] The second half of the clause in the *Damascus Document* (ואל יבא אליה) further reinforces the scriptural support by paraphrasing Jer 17:21c (see further below).

by making explicit the presumed implications of Jer 17:22a. Thus, both texts include the word חוץ ("outside") as a general designation for outside space.

The second legal-exegetical development regarding space focuses on the ownership of the specific space. The clause in Jer 17:22a that serves as the foundation for the later determination of space employs the second-person plural verbal form and possessive suffix. While the emphasis on "your homes" (מבתיכם) is likely rhetorical in the original context of *Jeremiah*, later readers may have regarded the possessive pronoun as uniquely condemning individuals for carrying items through their own homes. The Dead Sea Scrolls legal texts evince two distinct modes of reformulating this scriptural language.

The *Damascus Document* and *4QHalakha A* retain the scriptural language of a "house," though they remove any reference to the possessive suffix as found in *Jeremiah*. On the one hand, the entire modification is consistent with both texts' general transformation of the *Jeremiah* clause from the second-person masculine plural to the third-person masculine singular in order to present the law in the formal style of sectarian legal texts.[21] At the same time, however, neither text makes an attempt to transform the possessive suffix accordingly (i.e., *Jeremiah*: מבתיכם, "from your houses" → CD, 4Q251: הבית, "the house" ≠ מביתו, "from his house"). To be sure, we do find in *4QHalakha A* the third-person possessive suffix (ממקומו, "his place"), though its presence is likely explained based on the text's close reuse of the language of Exod 16:29 (אל יצא איש ממקמו, "Let no one leave his place").

The only attempt to represent in any way *Jeremiah*'s possessive suffix is found in *4QMiscellaneous Rules*, which adds the possessive suffix to its designated space (מאהלו, "from his tent").[22] It is not clear how we should explain this phenomenon. It is possible that the *Damascus Document* and *4QHalakha A* represent legal traditions that expand Jer 17:22a to include any home (i.e., personal space), even if it is not associated with the individual carrying the object. Accordingly, *4QMiscellaneous Rules* would represent a countertradition that limits the proscription to one's own personal space (similar to the literal understanding of the formulation in *Jeremiah*).

The third legal-exegetical development regarding the affected space concerns the specification of spaces to and from which the carrying is prohibited. As is apparent from the preceding discussion, Jer 17:22a (ולא תוציאו משא מבתיכם, "Nor shall you carry out burdens from your houses") forms the core scriptural language from which all three Dead Sea Scrolls texts reformulate their own laws. The scriptural language, however, is significantly limiting because it only refers to carrying items *out* of one's home with no further proscription on carrying items *into* one's home. The *Damascus Document* and *4QHalakha A* interpret the words in *Jeremiah* to imply that the reverse action is also

[21] As noted in several places already, sectarian legal texts render the verbal element of the law in the third-person singular jussive form. See further below.

[22] I.e., rather than מן האהל, which would correspond to the formulation in the *Damascus Document* and *4QHalakha A*.

TABLE 9. *The Literary Inversion of Jer 17:21–22 in CD 11:7–9*

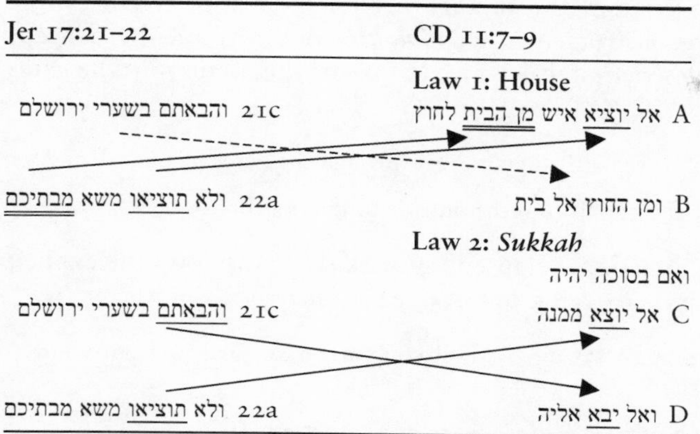

Jer 17:21–22	CD 11:7–9
	Law 1: House
והבאתם בשערי ירושלם 21c	אל יוציא איש מן הבית לחוץ A
ולא תוציאו משא מבתיכם 22a	ומן החוץ אל בית B
	Law 2: *Sukkah*
	ואם בסוכה יהיה
והבאתם בשערי ירושלם 21c	אל יוצא ממנה C
ולא תוציאו משא מבתיכם 22a	ואל יבא אליה D

prohibited. Thus, both very clearly delineate the prohibition of carrying an item from outside into one's house.

In both cases, *Jeremiah* provides the rationale and exegetical basis for this expansion. Jer 17:21c (והבאתם בשערי ירושלם, "And bringing them through the gates of Jerusalem") does indeed condemn the carrying of items *into* the gates of Jerusalem. The *Damascus Document* and *4QHalakha A* merge the general proscription regarding carrying into the city gates in Jer 17:21c (והבאתם בשערי ירושלם) with the specific prohibition regarding carrying out of one's house in Jer 17:22a (ולא תוציאו משא מבתיכם). As such, carrying into *and* out of one's house is prohibited. The exegetical reformulation of the two scriptural passages in the *Damascus Document* is achieved by the literary inversion of their content and textual elements as outlined in Table 9.

In the first law in the *Damascus Document*, the first clause [A] draws its two key textual elements (יצא–*hiph'il* and בית) from Jer 17:22a (as marked by solid arrows). The second clause [B] expands the law to include the restriction on carrying into one's home. This aspect of the law draws its conceptual framework from the condemnation of carrying items into the gates of Jerusalem in Jer 17:21a (as marked by a dashed arrow). A similar inverted literary reformulation of Jer 17:21c and 17:22a is found in the second law in the *Damascus Document*. The first clause [C] draws its key textual element (יצא–*hiph'il*) from the identical verbal root in Jer 17:22a (as marked by a solid arrow). Unlike the first law in the *Damascus Document*, the second clause in the second law [D] employs the precise textual element from Jer 17:21c (בוא–*hiph'il*) (as marked by a solid arrow). In each law, the two passages from *Jeremiah* are inverted. I have noted several instances of this exegetical technique in earlier chapters for similar legal-exegetical reformulations of scriptural content in legal texts.[23]

[23] On the exegetical technique of literary inversion (commonly known as "Zeidel's law") in exegetical traditions, see bibliography, Chapter 4, n. 50.

While the *Damascus Document* inverts its reformulation of *Jeremiah*, *4QHalakha A* evinces a nearly identical legal-exegetical reformulation of *Jeremiah* yet does not contain the literary inversion. The first half of the directional clause as reconstructed in *4QHalakha A* draws on the conceptual framework of the restriction in Jer 17:21c on carrying items *into* the gates of Jerusalem:

> Jer 17:21c: והבאתם בשערי ירושלם, "Bringing them through the gates of Jerusalem."
>
> 4Q251 1–2 5: [מן החוץ אל הבית] "[From the outside to the house]."

The second half of the directional clause in *4QHalakha A* follows the explicit restriction in Jer 17:22a on carrying out of one's home:

> Jer 17:22a: ולא תוציאו משא מבתיכם, "Nor shall you carry out burdens from your houses."
>
> 4Q251 1–2 5: ומן הבית אל הח]וץ, "And from the house to the ou[tside."

4QMiscellaneous Rules reflects a much different exegetical expansion of *Jeremiah*. It closely follows Jer 17:22a in only restricting carrying outside and not the reverse:

> Jer 17:22a: ולא תוציאו משא מבתיכם, "Nor shall you carry out burdens from your houses."
>
> 4Q265 6 4: אל יו]צא אי[ש מאהלו, "Let no ma[n] ca[rry out] from his tent."

Defining What Items May Not Be Carried

The second broad aspect of the exegetical reformulation of *Jeremiah* involves a more precise identification of the items that may not be transported on the Sabbath. The prophetic invective in *Jeremiah* is highly restricted in that only the carrying of one's "burden" (משא) is explicitly condemned. Commentators on *Jeremiah* have suggested that this word does not refer to any item but rather has in view a more limited meaning – most likely commercial goods.[24] It seems that some later readers of this text were aware of this specialized meaning (e.g., Neh 13:15–19). For most readers, however, the reference to a משא would have been entirely ambiguous and thus insufficient for the needs of a carefully formulated Sabbath restriction. In much the same way that the limited conception of space is dramatically expanded in the Dead Sea Scrolls texts, these three passages also reformulate the restricted language of *Jeremiah*'s "burden."

The *Damascus Document* and *4QHalakha A* solve the legal and exegetical dilemma by omitting any direct object in their reformulation of Jer 17:22. Thus,

[24] See discussion of this question in Jack R. Lundbom, *Jeremiah 1–20* (AB 21A; New York: Doubleday, 1999), 806. He suggests that it may refer to the transfer of produce to Jerusalem for sale. This proposal echoes similar understandings of this verse by earlier commentators.

the "burden" of *Jeremiah* is absent in these two texts at the exact syntactic place it would be expected in the reformulation of Jer 17:22:

Jer 17:22a: ולא תוציאו [משא] מבתיכם, "Nor shall you carry out [burdens] from your houses."

CD 11:7: אל יוציא איש [ ] מן הבית, "Let no man carry out [ ] from the house."

CD 11:8: אל יוצא [ ] ממנה, "He shall not carry out [ ] from it."

4Q251 1–2 4: אל יוצא איש [ ] ממקומו, "Let no] man carry out [ ] from his place."[25]

Similarly, the secondary formulation in CD 11:9, which draws upon the use of בוא–*hiph'il* in Jer 17:24, likewise omits any reference to the משא that follows:

Jer 17:24: הביא [משא], "Bring in [burdens]."

CD 11:9: ואל יבא אליה, "And he shall not bring in it."

The exclusion of any explicit item – specifically *Jeremiah*'s משא – as the direct object in the *Damascus Document* and *4QHalakha A* indicates that these texts did not wish to leave any doubt as to the comprehensiveness of the prohibition; all items are forbidden to be carried. The syntax of the clauses in the *Damascus Document* and *4QHalakha A* suggests that the direct object is intended to be understood by virtue of ellipsis. The nature of the exegetical reformulation of Jer 17:22, 24 in these two texts indicates that the direct object should be rendered as "anything." Thus, in the full translation provided above for the *Damascus Document* and *4QHalakha A*, I have followed other translators in expressing this sense through the inclusion of the word "anything" in parentheses following the verb of conveyance: "Let no man carry out (anything)."

In contrast, *4QMiscellaneous Rules* identifies two specific items – food and vessels – that may not be carried on the Sabbath. In its reformulation of Jer 17:22, these two terms stand in place of the scriptural משא:

Jer 17:22: ולא תוציאו [משא] מבתיכם, "Nor shall you carry out [burdens] from your houses."

4Q265 6 4: אל יו[צא אי]ש מאהלו [כלי ומאכ[ל]], "Let no ma[n] ca[rry out] from his tent [any vessel or foo[d]]."[26]

[25] To be sure, such an explicit statement may be lost in the lacuna in *4QHalakha A*. The conjunction that directly follows the lacuna in line 5, however, suggests that the lacuna contains an additional reference to carrying from one space to another (in reverse from the extant text in line 5, as in the *Damascus Document*). If this restoration is correct, there is not enough additional space to include a description of proscribed "burdens."

[26] Because מאהלו is a reformulation of מבתיכם, *4QMiscellaneous Rules* evinces another example of literary inversion in the reuse of Jer 17:22. The equivalent terms in *4QMiscellaneous Rules* of *Jeremiah*'s משא and מבתיכם are inverted in *4QMiscellaneous Rules* (Jer: משא^{A} מבתיכם^{B} → 4Q265: מאהלו$^{B'}$ כלי ומאכ[ל]$^{A'}$). On the exegetical technique of literary inversion (commonly known as "Zeidel's law") in exegetical traditions, see bibliography, Chapter 4, n. 50.

At first glance, this seems to limit the application of the prohibition to these two items, perhaps understanding them as the meaning of *Jeremiah*'s "burden." It seems more likely that this aspect of the law should be understood similar to my earlier interpretation of the appearance of "tent" in *4QMiscellaneous Rules*. Above, I suggested that *4QMiscellaneous Rules* is aware of the more general prohibition on carrying (as articulated in the *Damascus Document* and *4QHalakha A*) and its wider set of details. Thus, the "tent" in *4QMiscellaneous Rules* is intended to be understood as a supplement to the house and *sukkah* of the *Damascus Document* and *4QHalakha A*. Similarly, *4QMiscellaneous Rules* refers to food and vessels not because they are the only focus of the proscription but because they are uniquely singled out as items that may not be carried on the Sabbath.[27]

In this sense, *4QMiscellaneous Rules* is also responding to the legal-exegetical difficulty presented by *Jeremiah*'s "burden." The mercantile nuance of משא in *Jeremiah* could potentially suggest that items that have no commercial use or value – items that are explicitly used in the home – may in fact be transported on the Sabbath. *4QMiscellaneous Rules* therefore highlights two of the more ubiquitous such items and singles them out for inclusion in the prohibition.

On the Exegetical Role of Exodus 16:29

The legal and exegetical influence of Jer 17:21–22, 24 is pervasive through all of the Dead Sea Scrolls texts. What, however, is the role of Exod 16:29, which as observed above is also closely related to the three Dead Sea Scrolls passages? The literary form for the presentation of the carrying prohibition in all three passages follows Exod 16:29 very closely, as indicated by the text boxes in Table 8. These passages reflect only the slight exegetical variant involving the transformation of the scriptural יצא ("to go"; *qal*) to יוצא/יוציא ("to bring out"; *hiph'il*).[28] In so doing, these texts are able to transform a scriptural proscription against individuals leaving their dwelling places into a

[27] The inclusion of "food" as one of the singled-out items may be connected to the influence of Exod 16:29 (on which, see below). As noted by Baumgarten, Exod 16 explicitly proscribes the collection of manna on the Sabbath. The special inclusion of food in *4QMiscellaneous Rules* may be a further reflection of this interdiction ("4Q265: Miscellaneous Rules," 69). The additional inclusion of vessels may be related to the fact that vessels would have been needed in order to gather the manna.

[28] יצא is found in 4QpaleoGen–Exod^{l} (4Q11 16 7) and reflected in the ancient versions, thus making it unlikely that the form in the *Damascus Document*, *4QHalakha A*, and *4QMiscellaneous Rules* is a textual variant (Larson, Lehmann, and Schiffman, "4Q251: Halakha A," 29; cf. Doering, *Schabbat*, 229). Note also that Exod 16:29 has ביום השביעי. As noted by Doering, the Sabbath is not identified in sectarian literature by this designation but rather by השבת or יום השבת ("New Aspects," 257), and thus *4QHalakha A* and *4QMiscellaneous Rules* "update" *Exodus* accordingly. See the similar phenomenon for the reformulation of Isa 58:13 in CD 10:20–21 as treated in Chapter 7.

prohibition against individuals transporting items out of their homes.[29] There is no indication, however, that the *Damascus Document*, *4QHalakha A*, or *4QMiscellaneous Rules* considered Exod 16:29 to be the scriptural source for the prohibition of carrying.[30] On the contrary, the explicit legal-exegetical reconfiguration of Jer 17:21–22, 24 indicates that the community viewed this passage as the scriptural source and the basis for all further developments in the legal institution.

While the intended centrality of Jer 17:21–22, 24 can be seen in the reuse of several key words from this passage, it was insufficient with respect to the formal literary character of the Sabbath law in the *Damascus Document* and the related sectarian legal texts. As I have noted several times in earlier chapters, sectarian law follows a distinct formal literary structure. Law in the *Damascus Document* and sectarian legal literature is formulated as אל + jussive (masc. sg.), sometimes with the inclusion of the general subject איש following the jussive.[31] This literary form is lacking in Jer 17:21–22, 24. The *Jeremiah* passage is formulated in apodictic style characteristic of law in the Hebrew Bible (לא + indicative – ולא תוציאו). This form corresponds to what John Bright identified as the standard scriptural form to express an eternally binding proscription.[32] Moreover, Jer 17:21–22, 24 is formulated in the second-person masculine plural form rather than the desired third-person form employed throughout sectarian legal literature.

In earlier chapters, I discussed several passages in which scriptural language is modified to comport with sectarian legal formulae. In all those examples, the sectarian texts worked with the language of the base scriptural texts. Thus, for example, in Chapters 4 and 5, I noted how Isa 58:13 ודבר דבר, "Nor speak a word," is reformulated in both the *Damascus Document* and *4QHalakha B* in order to present a clear prohibition in sectarian legal language: אל ידבר דבר (CD 10:17); אל ידבר בדברי (CD 10:19); אל ידבר [בכול דבר או (4Q264a 1 i 6); ואל יד[בר ד]בר (4Q264a 1 i 7). The formation of the standard sectarian legal formula for the carrying law in the *Damascus Document*, *4QHalakha A*, and *4QMiscellaneous Rules* follows a different strategy. Rather than working exclusively with the scriptural language of Jer 17:21–22, 24, these texts appeal to the intertextual link supplied by the root יצא in Jer 17:21–22, 24 in order to draw upon the

29 Note, however, that Exod 16:29 was also understood by the sectarian community in its more straightforward manner as the source for the prohibition against Sabbath travel (see below, n. 34).

30 Contra Doering, "New Aspects," 258: "the *Yaḥad* derived the prohibition of carrying out without hesitation also from this [i.e., Exod 16:29] Pentateuchal passage."

31 See further Schiffman, *Halakhah*, 80–83. As in legal passages in the Hebrew Bible, the default formulation is masculine. Specific laws that apply only to women are formulated with the feminine singular jussive (e.g., laws regarding menstruation in 4Q266 [4QD^a] 6 ii 3–4).

32 John Bright, "The Apodictic Prohibition: Some Observations," *JBL* 92 (1973): 185–204 (especially 186–87).

specific language and structure of Exod 16:29: אל יצא איש ממקמו ביום השביעי, "Let no one leave his place on the seventh day."

Exod 16:29 is formulated in the alternative apodictic style common in the Hebrew Bible (אל + jussive – אל יצא). Exod 16:29 therefore provides the exact literary form employed throughout the *Damascus Document*'s Sabbath Code as well as the Cave 4 legal texts.[33] Exod 16:29 even supplies the additional term איש. With a minor exegetical shift of the root from the *qal* to the *hiph'il*, Exod 16:29 provides the *Damascus Document*, *4QHalakha A*, and *4QMiscellaneous Rules* with the precise desired literary form.

The prohibition against carrying on the Sabbath is grounded in Jer 17:21–22, 24 and its interpretation and amplification, while Exod 16:29 supplies the formal language of its presentation. It is almost certain that the sectarian legal texts do not represent that first exegetical use of Exod 16:29 in the context of the Sabbath carrying prohibition. Rather, the very appeal to Exod 16:29 suggests that this passage was already being interpreted in this sense in the Second Temple period. At the same time, by explicitly merging the legal-exegetical reading of Jer 17:21–22, 24 with the formal language of Exod 16:29, the *Damascus Document*, *4QHalakha A*, and *4QMiscellaneous Rules* have simultaneously reinforced the growing legal-exegetical understanding of Exod 16:29 as a prohibition against carrying on the Sabbath. Indeed, when Exod 16:29 is read with the *hiph'il*, it too forbids an individual from transporting items outside of one's home on the Sabbath.[34]

IV. CONCLUSIONS

My goal is this chapter has been to demonstrate the complex exegetical processes involved in the development of the Sabbath carrying prohibition. My analysis has examined the diverse approaches found in the Dead Sea Scrolls

33 In contrast to the לא + indicative form, Bright argues that the אל + jussive structure "expresses a specific command for a specific occasion" ("The Apodictic Prohibition," 187). Indeed, this understanding fits the simple meaning of Exod 16:29. For discussion of why the sectarian community adopted this latter form, see Schiffman, *Halakhah*, 82.

34 This new understanding of Exod 16:29 may have been made easier by the larger context of the manna pericope, where the Israelites are censured for attempting "to collect" (v. 27) manna on the Sabbath. This act would of course require them to transport the manna (see Rabbi Abraham ibn Ezra, ad loc.; on the use of this logic to explain the similar rabbinic transformation of this verse, see Tosafot on *b. 'Erub* 17b, s.v. לאו שניתן לאזהרת מיתת ב"ד). Besides the expansion to a carrying prohibition, Second Temple and rabbinic texts also reorient the meaning of Exod 16:29 to include additional Sabbath proscriptions. Thus, the restriction on movement in Exod 16:29 is understood in rabbinic literature as a reference to the restriction on Sabbath travel (תחום שבת). See 𝔗[Ps-J] Exod 16:29; *Mekhilta de-Rabbi Ishma'el Wa-Yassa* 6; *b. 'Erub* 51a. A similar application of Exod 16:29 can also be found in Jub 50:12 (see Albeck, *Jubiläen*, 9; Doering, *Schabbat*, 87–94); CD 10:21; 11:5 (par. 4Q271 5 i 2) (see Schiffman, *Halakhah*, 91–98; Doering, ibid., 145–51); 4Q264a 1 i 1; cf. 4Q264a 3 + 4Q421 12 7 (see Noam and Qimron, "Qumran Composition," 61–62).

legal texts regarding the nature of the Sabbath carrying prohibition and its scriptural basis. All attempts to clarify the type of item under the purview of the carrying prohibition involve exegetical engagement with Jer 17:21–22 (and vv. 23–27). Jer 17:21–22 condemns carrying on the Sabbath as part of a broader prophetic invective. As this passage came to be understood as the scriptural source for the carrying prohibition, the prophetic invective lacked the necessary elements to function as an explicit articulation of Sabbath law. Thus, readers in the Second Temple period turned to this text in order to understand its basic meaning at the same time as they transformed its meaning through exegetical reformulation.

My analysis of the sectarian legal texts in this chapter has focused on several key issues: (1) the precise locations to and from which carrying is forbidden, (2) the definition of what constitutes one's personal space, (3) what specific objects may not be carried, and (4) the exegetical relationship between Jer 17:21–22 and Exod 16:29. The *Damascus Document*, *4QHalakha A*, and *4QMiscellaneous Rules* reflect several intersecting exegetical techniques and legal conclusions. At the same time, one can detect a significant amount of divergence across the three texts. The legal and exegetical features found in these three texts are part of broader attempts in the Second Temple and rabbinic periods to transform Jer 17:21–22 into a clearly articulated scriptural basis for the Sabbath carrying restriction. In this sense, the sectarian scrolls do not stand alone. Rather, as in the exegetical material regarding Isa 58:13 treated in earlier chapters, the evidence of the Dead Sea Scrolls must be positioned within the broader history of Jewish law and legal exegesis in ancient Judaism.

10

Jeremiah 17:21–22 and the Sabbath Carrying Prohibition in *Nehemiah*, *Jubilees*, and Rabbinic Literature

I. INTRODUCTION

In the previous chapter, I explored the exegetical reformulation of Jer 17:21–22 (and 24) and Exod 16:29 in three legal texts from among the Dead Sea Scrolls. The Sabbath carrying law as articulated in the *Damascus Document*, *4QHalakha A*, and *4QMiscellanous Rules* finds additional expression in several Second Temple and rabbinic sources. Comparative legal sources provide close parallels to the legal-exegetical use of Jer 17:21–22 and Exod 16:29 in the Dead Sea Scrolls. These comparative sources attest to wider currents in Second Temple and rabbinic legal traditions. In the comparative material, as in the Dead Sea Scrolls texts, Jer 17:21–22 is clearly the legal and exegetical scriptural source for the Sabbath law of carrying. At the same time, the comparative evidence diverges on the role of Exod 16:29. The Second Temple–period texts (*Nehemiah* and *Jubilees*) show no influence of Exod 16:29. In the *Mishnah* and related rabbinic texts, however, Exod 16:29 seems to supply some of the scriptural language for the formulation of the law.

II. THE RESTRICTION ON CARRYING IN NEHEMIAH

Neh 13:15–19 recounts the attempt to combat commercial activity transpiring in Jerusalem on the Sabbath. This passage embeds a condemnation of carrying on the Sabbath within its broader critique of mercantile pursuits on the Sabbath. In the condemnation of carrying, *Nehemiah* draws upon language and imagery from Jer 17:21–22, 24 (as marked by underlining):[1]

[1] Several scholars have argued that the passage in *Jeremiah* is in fact formulated as prophetic support for the Sabbath law in *Nehemiah*. See discussion and bibliography in Jack R. Lundbom, *Jeremiah 1–20* (AB 21A; New York: Doubleday, 1999), 802–4. The strongest argument in favor of the primacy of *Jeremiah*, as asserted by Michael Fishbane, is that *Nehemiah*, unlike

(15) בימים ההמה ראיתי ביהודה דרכים גתות בשבת ומביאים הערמות ועמסים על החמרים ואף
יין ענבים ותאנים וכל משא ומביאים ירושלם ויבם השבת ואעיד ביום מכרם ציד (16) והצרים ישבו בה
מביאים דאג וכל מכר ומכרים בשבת לבני יהודה ובירושלם (17) ואריבה את חרי יהודה ואמרה להם מה
הדבר הרע הזה אשר אתם עשים ומחללים את יום השבת (18) הלוא כה עשו אבתיכם ויבא אלהינו עלינו
את כל הרעה הזאת ועל העיר הזאת ואתם מוסיפים חרון על ישראל לחלל את השבת (19) ויהי כאשר צללו
שערי ירושלם לפני השבת ואמרה ויסגרו הדלתות ואמרה אשר לא יפתחום עד אחר השבת ומנערי העמדתי
על השערים לא יבוא משא ביום השבת

(15) At that time I saw men in Judah treading winepresses on the Sabbath, and others bringing heaps of grain and loading them onto asses, also wine, grapes, figs, and all sorts of goods, and bringing them into Jerusalem on the Sabbath. I admonished them there and then for selling provisions. (16) Tyrians who lived there brought fish and all sorts of wares and sold them on the Sabbath to the Judahites in Jerusalem. (17) I censured the nobles of Judah, saying to them, "What evil thing is this that you are doing, profaning the Sabbath day! (18) This is just what your ancestors did, and for it God brought all this misfortune on this city; and now you give cause for further wrath against Israel by profaning the Sabbath!" [See Jer 17:27.] (19) When shadows filled the gateways of Jerusalem at the approach of the Sabbath, I gave orders that the doors be closed, and ordered them not to be opened until after the Sabbath. I stationed some of my servants at the gates, so that no goods should enter on the Sabbath. (𝔐 Neh 13:15–19)

The explicit use of language and imagery drawn from Jer 17:21–22, 24 indicates that *Nehemiah* intends to condemn these individuals for violating the prohibition of carrying on the Sabbath in addition to the more direct invective against general business activity on the Sabbath.[2] *Nehemiah* retains the basic contours of the condemnation of carrying in *Jeremiah*. Thus, as in Jer 17:21c (והבאתם בשערי ירושלם, "And bringing them through the gates of Jerusalem"), *Nehemiah* focuses on both the act of "bringing" items into Jerusalem and the "gates of Jerusalem." Neh 13:15–19 engages in a subtle modification of Jer 17:21c. The act of "bringing" (בוא–*hiph'il*) goods into Jerusalem is mentioned twice in verse 15, though no reference is made to the "gates" of Jerusalem. Rather, the "gates" appear twice later in the pericope, in verse 19, as the location through which no goods should be conveyed. Thus, the key language and imagery of Jer 17:21–22 are spread throughout the pericope in Neh 13:15–19 in an attempt to accentuate the adoption of *Jeremiah*'s carrying prohibition.

The one significant legal and exegetical amplification in *Nehemiah* concerns the identification of what items may not be carried on the Sabbath. In two instances, *Nehemiah* refers to the "burden" (משא) from *Jeremiah* (vv. 15, 19). As noted in my discussion of *Jeremiah* in the previous chapter, the term משא

Jeremiah, includes the issue of selling (see below). It is thus more likely that *Nehemiah* expanded upon *Jeremiah* than that *Jeremiah* shortened *Nehemiah* (*Biblical Interpretation in Ancient Israel* [Oxford: Clarendon, 1985], 131 n. 70). See the additional arguments collected by Lundbom.

2 On the specific offenses singled out in this pericope and their relationship to the covenantal declaration against buying goods on the Sabbath in Neh 10:32, see discussion in Joseph Blenkinsopp, *Ezra-Nehemiah: A Commentary* (OTL; Philadelphia: Westminster, 1988), 359.

TABLE 10. *The Interpretation of* משא *(Jer 17:21, 24) in Neh 13:15bc, 19*

Jer 17:21bc, 24	Neh 13:15bc, 19
21 ואל תשאו משא ביום השבת והבאתם בשערי ירושלם	15 ומביאים הערמות ועמסים על החמרים ואף יין ענבים ותאנים וכל משא ומביאים ירושלם ביום השבת . . .
(Guard yourselves) against carrying burdens on the Sabbath day, and bringing them through the gates of Jerusalem.	Bringing heaps of grain and loading them onto asses, also wine, grapes, figs, and all sorts of goods, and bringing them into Jerusalem on the Sabbath day . . .
24 לבלתי הביא משא בשערי העיר הזאת ביום השבת	19 לא יבוא משא ביום השבת
And do not bring in burdens through the gates of this city on the Sabbath day.	So that no goods should enter on the Sabbath day.

likely has some mercantile pursuits in mind. At the same time, the vagueness of the term makes it difficult to apply to actual circumstances of Sabbath activity. *Nehemiah*'s Sabbath restriction is thus an exegetical expansion of *Jeremiah*'s proclamation, such that *Jeremiah*'s original prophetic invective now includes the explicit added element of carrying for commercial purposes.[3] Jer 17:21, 24 forbids the act of carrying a burden through the gates of Jerusalem. No specific details, however, are provided concerning the specific nature of this burden. *Nehemiah* rewrites the passage from *Jeremiah*, adding specific details regarding what constitutes a "burden," as outlined in Table 10.

Neh 13:15 draws its language from Jer 17:21 and 24, as indicated by the various forms of underlining. Regarding the general condemnation of carrying, Neh 13:15c follows Jer 17:21c in focusing on the act of "bringing" items into Jerusalem, though with slightly modified language:

> Jer 17:21c: והבאתם בשערי ירושלם, "Bringing them through the gates of Jerusalem."
>
> Neh 13:15c: ומביאים ירושלם, "Bringing them into Jerusalem."

The reformulation of the meaning of "burden" in *Jeremiah* (as marked by single underlining) is found in the rewriting of Jer 17:21b in Neh 13:15b:

> Jer 17:21b: ואל תשאו משא ביום השבת, "(Guard yourselves) against carrying burdens on the Sabbath day."
>
> Neh 13:15b: ומביאים הערמות ועמסים על החמרים ואף יין ענבים ותאנים וכל משא, "Bringing heaps of grain and loading them onto asses, also wine, grapes, figs, and all sorts of goods."

3 See Fishbane, *Biblical Interpretation*, 131–33, especially n. 68.

Neh 13:15b reuses language from Jer 17:21b, though three fundamental modifications are discernible:

(1) The use of "carrying" (תשאו) with the "load" in Jer 17:21b is modified in Neh 13:15b to "bringing" (ומביאים), the same verbal root found in Jer 17:21c (והבאתם) (as marked by double underlining).

(2) Neh 13:15b interjects a long list of items (as marked by the text box) between the first verb of conveyance (ומביאים, "bringing") and the general term for items that may not be carried (משא, "goods"). This passage adds the further qualification that this list is not exhaustive (וכל משא, "and all sorts of goods").

(3) The time frame indicated in Jer 17:21b (ביום השבת, "on the Sabbath day") is transposed to the end of Neh 13:15c (as marked by wavy underlining).

These three modifications should be understood as *Nehemiah*'s attempt to provide a functional definition for משא in Jer 17:21–22 and the associated Sabbath prohibition. The modification of the main verb in the reformulation (Jer 17:21b: תשא, "carrying" → Neh 13:15b: ומביאים, "bringing") should be understood as a deliberate exegetical technique.[4] והבאתם ("bringing") is employed in Jer 17:21c to refer to the transfer of items through the gates of Jerusalem. This is indeed the primary concern of the prophetic invective throughout this pericope, as is apparent from the repeated reference to both Jerusalem and the gates of Jerusalem in the ensuing verses. Thus, the verb in Jer 17:21c that refers to the transfer of items through the gates of Jerusalem is employed in *Nehemiah* for the general prohibition of carrying that reformulates Jer 17:21b. In making this exegetical modification, Neh 13:15b draws upon the similar use of the verb "bring in" (הביא) in Jer 17:24, where it governs the direct object משא ("burdens").

In the second modification, the expansive list of items in Neh 13:15b is placed at the exact location in the rewriting of Jer 17:21b where משא ("burdens") appears. Thus, these specific items (heaps of grain, wine, grapes, and figs) provide practical examples of the משא from *Jeremiah*. Moreover, *Nehemiah* modifies the term in order to indicate that even the previously enumerated list is not exhaustive:

Jeremiah: משא, "Burdens." → *Nehemiah*: וכל משא, "And all sorts of goods."

The inclusion of כל "all" here may be an analogy with Jer 17:24, which, following the secondary condemnation of carrying a load, warns against performing "any (כל) work on it."

Neh 13:16 seems to add further examples of proscribed items: דאג וכל מכר, "Fish and all sorts of wares." This second list employs the same open-ended language to allow for more "wares" to be included under the purview of the

[4] It is possible that this shift also reflects linguistic updating. See, e.g., 1 Kgs 10:11 (וגם אני חירם אשר נשא זהב מאופיר) compared with 2 Chr 9:10 (וגם עבדי חירם ועבדי שלמה אשר הביאו זהב מאופיר).

carrying prohibition: וכל מכר, "And all sorts of wares." The common thread that binds all of the individual "burdens/goods" enumerated is their role in the broader mercantile pursuits condemned in *Nehemiah*. *Jeremiah* describes the "burdens/goods" in general terms, while *Nehemiah* employs language that is simultaneously more specific and general enough to allow for the inclusion of even further specific items.

The merging of Jer 17:21b–c in Neh 13:15 is further evident in the third modification. The time frame in Jer 17:21b (ביום השבת, "on the Sabbath day") is transferred to the end of Neh 13:15, such that it now forms part of *Nehemiah*'s reformulation of Jer 17:21c. In so doing, the entirety of Neh 13:15 is more explicitly identified as an attempt to explain the intervening content of Jer 17:21b – the meaning of "burdens." Once again, Jer 17:24 provides the literary basis for this modification. Jer 17:24 likewise begins with the verb of "bringing" and ends with the time frame, with "load" appearing in the middle:

> Jer 17:21b: ואל תשאו משא ביום השבת, "(Guard yourselves) against carrying burdens on the Sabbath day."

> Jer 17:24: לבלתי הביא משא בשערי העיר הזאת ביום השבת, "Do not bring in a load through the gates of this city on the Sabbath day."

> Neh 13:15: ומביאים הערמות ועמסים על החמרים ואף יין ענבים ותאנים וכל משא ומביאים ירושלם ביום השבת, "Bringing heaps of grain and loading them onto asses, also wine, grapes, figs, and all sorts of goods, and bringing them into Jerusalem on the Sabbath day."

Through these three legal-exegetical reformulations of Jer 17:21–22, Neh 13:15 has adapted and transformed the meaning of the prophetic invective against carrying on the Sabbath. In so doing, *Nehemiah* harnesses the authority of *Jeremiah* in order to condemn both general business on the Sabbath and the specific act of carrying. At the same time, *Nehemiah* expands the meaning of the "burdens" that may not be carried on the Sabbath. This is achieved through the appropriation and modification of the language of Jer 17:21–22. Even as it transforms this aspect of Jer 17:21–22, *Nehemiah* draws upon the authority that inheres in the ancient prophetic word.

III. THE RESTRICTION ON CARRYING IN THE BOOK OF JUBILEES

Sabbath law regarding carrying is found in two places in *Jubilees* – 2:29–30 and 50:8.[5] These two passages are part of two larger lists of Sabbath law in *Jubilees* (2:29–30 and 50:6–13). The presence of two separate units for Sabbath law is often introduced into larger questions of the literary history of

[5] On the Sabbath and Sabbath law in the book of *Jubilees*, see bibliography, Chapter 6, n. 1.

Jubilees. Most research on the authorship of *Jubilees* has advocated a singular authorship.[6] In recent years, some scholars have argued for multiple redactional layers to the book (continuing a line of reasoning episodically encountered in earlier scholarship).[7] In particular, several scholars have suggested that the Sabbath material in Jub 50:6–13 comes from the hands of a later author/editor.[8]

The debate over the redactional history of *Jubilees* has important implications for understanding the nature of the relationship between Sabbath law in Jub 2 and 50.

Scholars positing a singular authorship must explain why the Sabbath law appears twice and why the presentations differ in their overall details (while still having overlapping content). It has therefore been suggested that the author drew upon multiple earlier sources for Sabbath law and that the distinct lists are reflections of the diverse source material employed. In particular, Lutz Doering has proposed that the overlapping material – the restriction on drawing water and the carrying prohibition – are intentional markers by the author to call attention to the use of multiple sources.[9]

[6] See the review of scholarship in James C. VanderKam, "The End of the Matter? Jubilees 50:6–13 and the Unity of the Book," in *Heavenly Tablets: Interpretation, Identity and Tradition in Ancient Judaism* (ed. L. LiDonnici and A. Lieber; JSJSup 119; Leiden: Brill, 2007), 267–84; idem, "Recent Scholarship on the Book of Jubilees," *Currents in Biblical Research* 6 (2008): 405–31 (410–16).

[7] The trajectory of arguments for redactional history can be found in Michael Segal, *The Book of Jubilees: Rewritten Bible, Redaction, Ideology, and Theology* (JSJSup 117; Leiden: Brill, 2007), 14–21. See now also James L. Kugel, *A Walk through* Jubilees: *Studies in the* Book of Jubilees *and the World of Its Creation* (JSJSup 156; Leiden: Brill, 2012), 11–16, who argues for an "interpolator" who inserted twenty-nine passages into the otherwise complete book. He also suggests the presence of a later editor/copyist (see following note).

[8] The most prominent exponent of this view is Liora Ravid, "Sabbath Laws in the Book of *Jubilees* 50:6–13," *Tarbiz* 69 (2000): 161–66 [Hebrew]. See also the supporting view of Menachem Kister as reported in Segal, *The Book of Jubilees*, 20–21, and Kugel, *A Walk through* Jubilees, 204, who assign these passages to a later editor or copyist (note that Kugel identifies the Sabbath law in Jub 2:25–33 as coming from the hands of the secondary interpolator [35–36]). Jub 50:6–13 is also assigned to a second editor by Gene Davenport, though with little argument in support of this assertion (*The Eschatology of the Book of Jubilees* [StPB 20; Leiden: Brill, 1971], 68, 75). In response to Ravid, see the defense of the singular authorship in Lutz Doering, "Jub 50:6–13 als Schlussabschnitt des 'Jubiläenbuchs' – Nachtrag aus Qumran oder ursprünglicher Bestandteil des Werks?" *RevQ* 20 (2002): 359–87; and VanderKam, "The End of the Matter?"

[9] Lutz Doering, "New Aspects of Qumran Sabbath Law from Cave 4 Fragments," in *Legal Texts and Legal Issues: Proceedings of the Second Meeting of the International Organization for Qumran Studies, Cambridge, 1995; Published in Honour of Joseph M. Baumgarten* (ed. M. J. Bernstein, F. García Martínez, and J. Kampen; STDJ 23; Leiden: Brill, 1997), 241–74 (182); idem, *Schabbat: Sabbathhalacha und –praxis im antiken Judentum und Urchristentum* (TSAJ 78; Tübingen: Mohr Siebeck, 1999), 59–60. Doering likewise calls attention to a similar earlier argument by Louis Finkelstein with respect to the material in Jub 50:8, 12–13 ("Some Examples of Maccabean Halaka," *JBL* 49 [1930]: 20–42 [28–29]).

For those scholars who argue for a separate authorship for Jub 50:6–13, it is taken for granted that the Sabbath laws in Jub 50 come from a different source than those in Jub 2. Indeed, Ravid opines that the composition of Jub 50:6–13 stems from the hand of a scribe at Qumran.[10] To be sure, Doering has rightly criticized this argument based on the presence of several contradictory Sabbath laws in *Jubilees* and the sectarian Dead Sea Scrolls.[11] What is important for this study is that Ravid has called attention to the differences between the two sets of laws and their implications for tracing the literary history of the material.[12] Yet, Ravid and others do not engage in the question of the author's sources for the Sabbath law in Jub 50:6–13. If indeed Jub 50:6–13 is secondary, its laws either would draw upon another preexisting list of Sabbath legal material or would have been newly composed by the later author. It is not clear if the secondary author of Jub 50:6–13 would have likewise taken into account the preexisting set of Sabbath laws in Jub 2:29–30 in addition to other known Sabbath legal traditions.[13] However one understands the literary relationship of the Sabbath law in Jub 50 to the material in Jub 2, it seems likely that these two passages represent distinctive sets of Sabbath law that draw upon multiple earlier lists of Sabbath law.

The original Hebrew of Jub 2:29–30 and 50:8 is not preserved.[14] It is clear, however, that both passages employ Ge'ez equivalents of several keywords from Jer 17:21–22 (e.g., יצא, בוא, בית, שער) found in other Second Temple and

[10] Ravid, "Sabbath Laws," 165. Ravid does not marshal much support for this proposal. She merely notes that *Jubilees* was continuously copied there. Davenport, *Eschatology*, 16, had earlier likewise identified his second redactor as a Qumran scribe based on his suggested time frame for the second editor and the overlapping ideology of *Jubilees* and the sectarian community at Qumran (though for Davenport, this redactor is not the author of Jub 50:6–13). Note that Davenport discounts the importance of the presence of copies of *Jubilees* in the Dead Sea Scrolls as a viable criterion for ascribing a Qumran provenance for the second redactor.

[11] Doering, "Jub 50:6–13 als Schlussabschnitt des 'Jubiläenbuchs,'" 385–87. Below, I highlight similarities among the laws of carrying in Jub 50:8 and 4Q*Miscellaneous Rules* (in contrast to the *Damascus Document* and 4Q*Halakha A*). This limited correspondence, however, cannot support Ravid's assertion (see further discussion below).

[12] See especially her synoptic comparison of the material in each list (Ravid, "Sabbath Laws," 165).

[13] As suggested by Kugel, *A Walk through* Jubilees, 204.

[14] J. T. Milik argues that the highly fragmentary 4Q217 3 preserves portions of Jub 2:28–30. James VanderKam, Milik's coeditor of the *editio princeps* of this manuscript, disagrees with the very identification of 4Q217 as a copy of *Jubilees* based on the significant divergence between the Hebrew and Ge'ez texts. See their contrasting views in J. T. Milik and James C. VanderKam, "4Q217: 4QpapJubilees[b]?" in *Qumran Cave 4.VIII: Parabiblical Texts*, part 1 (ed. H. Attridge et al.; DJD 13; Oxford: Clarendon, 1994), 24–33; and further James C. VanderKam, "The Manuscript Tradition of Jubilees," in *Enoch and the Mosaic Torah: The Evidence of Jubilees* (ed. G. Boccaccini and G. Ibba; Grand Rapids: Eerdmans, 2009), 3–21 (6). Whether or not 4Q217 is a copy of *Jubilees*, the purported content in fragment 3, corresponding to Jub 2:29–30, yields only a handful of letters and one full word. Thus, it is of no value for the present analysis.

rabbinic texts.[15] This linguistic correspondence suggests that the underlying Hebrew text likewise contained these very keywords drawn from *Jeremiah*. As in other Second Temple–period and rabbinic texts discussed in this study, *Jubilees* transforms *Jeremiah*'s prophetic pronouncement into an explicit legal formulation regarding the restriction on carrying on the Sabbath. As such, it likewise must further clarify particular aspects of *Jeremiah*'s words and articulate in greater detail the precise parameters of the carrying prohibition. As we shall see, *Jubilees* employs some of the same exegetical techniques in the service of this goal. Because the two *Jubilees* passages differ in their overall details as well as exegetical technique, I treat each separately before discussing their relationship to each other.

The Carrying Prohibition in Jubilees 50:8

Of the two iterations of the carrying prohibition in *Jubilees*, Jub 50:8 provides the most straightforward formulation with regard to both its content and its exegetical use of Jer 17:21–22:

> *wa-za-hi 'anše'a za-yeṣawwer k^{w}ello kama yāwḍe' 'em-dabtarāhu 'em-bētu*
>
> Or who lifts any load to bring (it) outside his tent or his house.[16]

[15] Doering, *Schabbat*, 76. My understanding of the Hebrew equivalents of the Ge'ez draws upon Wolf Leslau, *Comparative Dictionary of Ge'ez (Classical Ethiopic)* (Wiesbaden: Otto Harrassowitz, 1987). I call attention to the comparative Semitic evidence when the specific words are first encountered.

[16] Text and translation of *Jubilees* follow James C. VanderKam, *The Book of Jubilees: A Critical Text* (CSCO 510–11; SA 87–88; 2 vols.; Leuven: Peeters, 1989), 1:253, 2:326. Further textual analysis can be found in Doering, *Schabbat*, 75–79. Immediately following this clause, the verse ends with the declaration "is to die" – affirming the expectation of death for transgressors of this Sabbath commandment as well as the others enumerated in Jub 50:8. This declaration frames the punishment for general Sabbath violation articulated at the beginning of Jub 50:8: "The man who does any work on it is to die." As observed by VanderKam, the literary frame of Jub 50:8 follows Exod 31:14–15, into which *Jubilees*' list of transgressions is interpolated. The twofold reference to death as the penalty for transgression in *Exodus* is replicated in *Jubilees* (VanderKam, "The End of the Matter?" 282). As such, the clause "is to die" following the carrying prohibition is not part of the direct legal-exegetical reformulation of Jer 17:21–22. On the death penalty for Sabbath transgression in the book of *Jubilees*, see Lutz Doering, "The Concept of the Sabbath in the Book of Jubilees," in *Studies in the Book of Jubilees* (ed. M. Albani, J. Frey, and A. Lange; TSAJ 65; Tübingen: Mohr Siebeck, 1997), 179–205 (199–200); idem, *Schabbat*, 68–69. The approach of *Jubilees* should be contrasted with the *Damascus Document* (CD 12:3–6), which removes the death penalty as punishment even for violation of Sabbath law that would be considered capital crimes according to scriptural law. See further Joseph M. Baumgarten, "The Avoidance of the Death Penalty in Qumran Law," in *Reworking the Bible: Apocryphal and Related Texts at Qumran: Proceedings of a Joint Symposium by the Orion Center for the Study of the Dead Sea Scrolls and Associated Literature and the Hebrew University Institute for Advanced Studies Research Group on Qumran, 15–17 January, 2002* (ed. E. G. Chazon, D. Dimant, and R. A. Clements; STDJ 53; Leiden: Brill, 2005), 31–38.

TABLE 11. *Jer 17:21–22 and Jub 50:8*

Jeremiah 17:21–22		Jubilees 50:8
ואל תשאו משא ביום השבת	21b	*wa-za-hi 'anše'a za-ye-ṣawwer kʷello*
Against carrying burdens on the Sabbath day.		Or who lifts any load.
והבאתם בשערי ירושלם	21c	– – – – – – – – – –
And bringing them through the gates of Jerusalem.		
ולא תוציאו משא מבתיכם ביום השבת	22a	*kama yāwḍe' 'em-dabtarāhu 'em-bētu*
Nor shall you carry out burdens from your houses on the Sabbath day.		To bring (it) outside his tent or his house.

Jub 50:8 forbids the carrying of an item from one's house or tent to outside.[17] In its exegetical reformulation of Jer 17:21–22, Jub 50:8 focuses specifically on the general condemnation of carrying burdens on the Sabbath (Jer 17:21b) and the specific reference to carrying items out of the house (Jer 17:22a). *Jubilees* conflates these two scriptural clauses in order to produce a general prohibition regarding carrying from one's personal space (מבתיכם, "from your houses"), simultaneously ignoring the broader context implied in Jer 17:21c (בשערי ירושלם, "through the gates of Jerusalem"). The exegetical reformulation of Jer 17:21b and 22a is outlined in Table 11.

As in the Dead Sea Scrolls texts, the legal-exegetical reformulation of *Jeremiah* in *Jubilees* focuses on two general elements of the law: (1) a precise definition of the space in which carrying is proscribed and (2) a precise definition of items that may not be carried on the Sabbath.

Regarding the affected personal space, Jub 50:8 preserves the emphasis on one's home in Jer 17:22a through the reuse of יצא–*hiph'il* followed by the

[17] Jub 50:8, as with 4Q*Miscellaneous Rules* (see above, Chapter 9, n. 16), contains several anomalies that have led scholars to question understanding it simply as a prohibition against carrying. Albeck initially observed that *Jubilees* seems to condemn the individual for merely picking up an item in the home with the intention to take it outside, even if this act was never fully carried out (*Das Buch der Jubiläen und die Halacha* [Berichte der Hochschule für die Wissenschaft des Judentums 47; Berlin: Hochschule für die Wissenschaft des Judentums, 1930], 41 n. 35). Accordingly, several scholars have suggested that Jub 50:8 refers to items that may not even be carried within the home, equivalent to the rabbinic category of *muqṣe* (Yitzḥak D. Gilat, *The Teachings of R. Eliezer ben Hyrcanus and Their Place in the History of Halakha* [Tel Aviv: Dvir, 1968], 127–28 [Hebrew]; Joseph M. Baumgarten, "4Q265: Miscellaneous Rules," in *Qumran Cave 4.XXV* [ed. J. M. Baumgarten; DJD 35; Oxford: Clarendon, 1999], 77). The issue here, however, is not one of intention. It seems that *Jubilees* assumes that the act will in fact be carried out and thus represents a violation of the Sabbath carrying restriction. See further discussion in Doering, *Schabbat*, 78–79.

preposition *mem*.[18] At the same time, *Jeremiah*'s definition of personal space is expanded to include one's tent as well. *Jubilees* articulates this expansion by similarly employing the יצא–*hiph'il* + מ construction for the reference to a tent. The reformulation is further reinforced by the interjection of "tent" between the reused scriptural terms יצא–*hiph'il* and בית ("house"):

Jer 17:22a: ולא תוציאו משא מבתיכם, "Nor shall you carry out burdens from your houses."

Jub 50:8: *kama yāwḍe' 'em-dabtarāhu 'em-bētu*, "To bring (it) outside his tent or his house."

Jubilees also provides more details regarding the ownership of these specific spaces. In each case, the third-person possessive suffix is added to the personal space designation (*dabtarāhu*, "his tent"; *bētu*, "his house"), presumably indicating the personal space of the individual engaging in the carrying. In the previous chapter, I noted how this very technique seems to have been avoided in the *Damascus Document* and *4QHalakha A*.

One further important detail regarding space can be detected in Jub 50:8. As noted, Jub 50:8 merges Jer 17:21b and 22a in order to focus on the specific laws associated with one's personal space and carrying. In so doing, *Jubilees* preserves faithfully the straightforward reading of Jer 17:22a as only proscribing carrying items *out* of one's personal space (for *Jubilees*, either a home or a tent). By ignoring the intervening material in Jer 17:21c, there is no implication that carrying *into* one's personal space is similarly prohibited.[19]

The second major exegetical expansion found in *Jubilees* is a more precise identification of the meaning of the משא ("burden") in *Jeremiah*. As already encountered, this is a central concern of both the Dead Sea Scrolls texts and *Nehemiah*, though each has a different technique for solving the exegetical problem. Jub 50:8 resolves this issue through its reformulation of Jer 17:21b. In rewriting this clause as a general condemnation of carrying on the Sabbath, *Jubilees* adds the quantifier *kʷello* ("all, each, every"), thereby transforming *Jeremiah*'s reference to *a* load into *any* load:

'anše'a (= משא) *za-yeṣawwer* (= תשאו) *kʷello*, "Or who lifts any load."[20]

[18] Ge'ez *waḍ'a* = BH יצא (Leslau, *Comparative Dictionary*, 605). The form in Jub 50:8 is the causative (*'awḍe'a*), thus equivalent to BH יצא–*hiph'il*.

[19] Contra Chaim Rabin, *Qumran Studies* (SJ 2; Oxford: Clarendon, 1957), 109, who suggests that the reverse is intended to be assumed by the reader.

[20] According to this understanding, the Ge'ez *yeṣawwer* represents תשאו from the scriptural verse. The Ge'ez root, meaning "to carry," is related to biblical Hebrew נשא (Leslau, *Comparative Dictionary*, 567). Yet, the Ge'ez *naš'a* would seem to be a much closer cognate (ibid., 404). As such, the text of *Jubilees* as preserved in Ge'ez lacks the cognate accusative found in the Hebrew of Jer 17:21. It is not clear if this modification was already present in the Hebrew text of Jub 50:8 or was perhaps introduced in either the Greek or Ge'ez translation.

The presence of *k*[w]*ello* in the Ge'ez text presumably reflects a Hebrew *Vorlage* כל משא. *Jubilees*' technique therefore bears a striking resemblance to the inclusion of כל in Neh 13:15 to expand the list of items that may not be carried on the Sabbath.

The Carrying Prohibition in Jubilees 2:29–30

The restriction on carrying is articulated a second time in the book of *Jubilees*, in the earlier list of Sabbath law in chapter 2:

> **Jub 2:29:** *wa-la-'ābe'o wa-la-'awḍe'o bāti k*[w]*ello za-yeṣawwer ba-'anāqeṣihomu*
>
> (Not) to bring in or remove on it anything which one carries in their gates.[21]
>
> **Jub 2:30:** *wa-'iyāwedḍe'u wa-'iyabe'u 'em-bēt bēta ba-zāti 'elat*
>
> They are not to bring (anything) out or in from house to house on this day.[22]

These two passages contain two specific formulations of the Sabbath carrying laws: (1) "(Not) to bring in or remove on it anything which one carries in their gates" (Jub 2:29) and (2) "They are not to bring (anything) out or in from house to house on this day" (Jub 2:30). Jub 2:29 clearly restricts carrying items in and out, though it does not articulate which specific spaces are affected by the two-way prohibition. In contrast, Jub 2:30 locates the house as the locus of activity. Presumably, the issue here is that in order to carry from one's house to another, one would have to transfer an object from one's house to the outside and likewise from outside into the house. This would therefore be in violation of the law restricting carrying in either direction.

The perceived redundancy in the text is the result of a faithful reformulation of the twofold structure of Jer 17:21–22. As outlined in Table 12, keywords (as marked by the various forms of underlining) from Jer 17:21 are reused in Jub 2:29.[23]

[21] The end of Jub 2:29 continues with the clause "(any) work that they had not prepared for themselves in their dwellings on the sixth day." As several commentators have noted, the clause is clearly out of place here and most likely is related to the earlier laws in Jub 2:29 regarding food preparation. For a range of approaches to solving this issue, see Charles, *Jubilees*, 20; O. S. Wintermute, "Jubilees," in *Old Testament Pseudepigrapha* (ed. J. H. Charlesworth; 2 vols.; ABRL; New York: Doubleday, 1983–85), 1:58. Doering, "Concept," 183 n. 17, following an earlier suggestion by Albeck (*Jubiläen*, 8), opines that the final clause of Jub 2:29 may represent an editorial insertion intended to underscore that all work (i.e., not just food preparation) must be done on the sixth day.

[22] Text and translation follow VanderKam, *Jubilees*, 1:14, 2:15.

[23] In addition to the exegetical reformulation outlined here, it is possible that the continuation of Jub 2:30, which identifies the Sabbath as "more holy and more blessed" than any of the Jubilees, is influenced by the continuation of Jer 17:22, which enjoins the sanctification (וקדשתם) of the Sabbath. In general, the identification of the Sabbath as "holy" in *Jubilees* draws upon scriptural references to the divine sanctification of the Sabbath in Gen 2:3 and Exod 20:11 (see Doering, *Schabbat*, 66–67). The use of this motif in this specific context, however, may be motivated by Jer 17:22.

TABLE 12. *The Reformulation of Jer 17:21–22 in Jub 2:29*

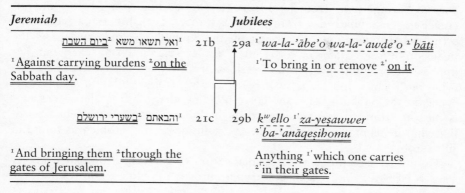

Jeremiah			*Jubilees*
¹ואל תשאו משא ²ביום השבת	21b	29a	¹' *wa-la-'ābe'o wa-la-'awḍe'o* ²' *bāti*
¹Against carrying burdens ²on the Sabbath day.			¹'To bring in or remove ²'on it.
¹והבאתם ²בשערי ירושלם	21c	29b	*kʷello* ¹'*za-yeṣawwer* ²'*ba-'anāqeṣihomu*
¹And bringing them ²through the gates of Jerusalem.			Anything ¹'which one carries ²'in their gates.

In its exegetical reformulation of Jer 17:21, Jub 2:29 evinces three structural modifications: (1) The first expression of each verset in Jer 17:21 is inverted in the reformulated content in Jub 2:29 (as marked by single underlining and with arrows):

> Jer 17:21b¹: ואל תשאו משא, "Against carrying burdens." → Jub 2:29b¹': *za-yeṣawwer*, "Which one carries."
>
> Jer 17:21c¹: והבאתם, "And bringing them." → Jub 2:29a¹': *wa-la-'ābe'o*, "To bring in."[24]

(2) The final elements in each scriptural verset are retained as the final elements in each reformulated clause in *Jubilees* (as marked by double underlining):

> Jer 17:21b²: ביום השבת, "On the Sabbath day." → Jub 2:29a²': *bāti*, "On it."
>
> Jer 17:21c²: בשערי ירושלם, "Through the gates of Jerusalem." → Jub 2:29b²': *ba-'anāqeṣihomu*, "In their gates."

(3) One completely new word is introduced into each of the units in Jub 2:29 (as marked by the dashed underlining). In one case (Jub 2:29a: *wa-la-'awḍe'o*, "or remove"), the word has migrated from Jer 17:22a, which has its primary exegetical reformulation in Jub 2:30:

> Jer 17:22a: תוציאו, "Carry out." → Jub 2:29a: *wa-la-'awḍe'o*, "Or remove."

In the other case (Jub 2:29b: *kʷello*, "anything"), the word is not drawn from any language in *Jeremiah*.

These structural modifications are part of a larger exegetical transformation of Jer 17:21 into a legal statement regarding carrying on the Sabbath. Jeremiah 17:21b and 21c are merged in *Jubilees* and become one clause, and

[24] On the latter equivalency, see Leslau, *Comparative Dictionary*, 114–15. On the exegetical technique of literary inversion (commonly known as "Zeidel's law"), see bibliography, Chapter 4, n. 50.

simultaneously one element is drawn from Jer 17:22. By moving the reference to "bringing in" from Jer 17:21c (והבאתם) and placing it before the reference to the Sabbath day from Jer 17:21b (ביום השבת), Jub 2:29a retains the scriptural denunciation of carrying on the Sabbath. At the same time, the inclusion of *wa-la-'awḍe'o*, "or remove" (= Jer 17:22a: תוציאו, "carry out"),[25] applies the prohibition to both directions of movement (carrying *in* and carrying *out*). Thus, Jub 2:29a now reads as a general prohibition against carrying on the Sabbath. The one corresponding element from Jer 17:21 that is missing from this general regulation in Jub 2:29a is a statement regarding what items may not be carried. The solution to this problem is found in Jub 2:29b.

The transfer of the general condemnation of carrying a burden from Jer 17:21b (ואל תשאו משא, "against carrying burdens") to Jub 2:29b resolves the issues of the precise meaning of *Jeremiah*'s "burden" (משא). *Jubilees* removes the ambiguous word "burden" and adds in its place *kʷello* ("anything"). The associated verbal form is then transformed from a negated imperfect into a relative pronoun and imperfect:

> Jer 17:21b^{1}: ואל תשאו, "Do not carry." → Jub 2:29b$^{1'}$: *za-yeṣawwer*, "Which one carries."

Based on the structural reorganization of Jer 17:21, this entire clause in now merged with בשערי ירושלם ("through the gates of Jerusalem") from Jer 17:21c. In *Jubilees*, however, this expression is generalized such that it no longer refers to the gates of Jerusalem but rather to "their gates" (*ba-'anāqeṣihomu*), presumably an allusion to the entrance to one's home. As such, the new possessive suffix refers to any individual involved in carrying items on the Sabbath.

In the reformulated Jer 17:21, *kʷello* ("anything") functions as the direct object of the two infinitives referring to carrying (*wa-la-'ābe'o*, "to bring in"; *wa-la-'awḍe'o*, "to remove") and is the antecedent of the relative pronoun (*za-*, "which"). Thus, the entire relative clause in Jub 2:29b attempts to explain the meaning of *kʷello* and therefore provides the precise meaning for *Jeremiah*'s "burden." According to *Jubilees*, anything that one would carry through one's gates – presumably intended to refer to any item – may not be carried on the Sabbath.[26]

The transformation of שערי ירושלם ("the gates of Jerusalem") from a reference to *where* one may not carry in items (as in *Jeremiah*) to part of a larger understanding of *what* items may not be carried creates a new problem – what areas fall under the rubric of the carrying proscription? Jub 2:30 resolves this

[25] On this linguistic correspondence, see above, n. 18.

[26] Note the alternative translation found in Charles, *Jubilees*, 20, who ignores the relative pronoun: "or bring in or take out thereon *through* their gates any burden" (my emphasis). He therefore understands the reference to gates in much the same way as it appears in *Jeremiah* – the location where carrying may not take place.

TABLE 13. *The Reformulation of Jer 17:22 in Jub 2:30*

	Literary Frame				
Jer 17:22	ולא תוציאו "Nor shall you carry out"	*draws from Jer 17:21c:* והבאתם "bringing"	משא "burdens"	מבתיכם "from your houses"	ביום השבת "on the Sabbath day"
Jub 2:30	*wa-'iyāwed̤e'u* "They are not to bring (anything) out"	*wa-'iyabe'u* "or (bring anything) in"	---	*'embēt bēta* "from house to house"	*ba-zāti 'elat* "on this day"

question. As outlined in Table 13, Jub 2:30 employs several keywords from Jer 17:22a.

The literary frame of the reformulated passage follows the language of *Jeremiah* very closely, with little exegetical modification. Within the literary frame provided by Jer 17:22, three exegetical modifications are visible. (1) There is no corresponding reference in Jub 2:30 to "burdens" (משא) from Jer 17:22. (2) "Or [bring anything] in" (*wa-'iyabe'u*), drawn from Jer 17:21c, is interjected into the reformulation of Jer 17:22. (3) *Jeremiah*'s reference to "from your houses" (מבתיכם) is rendered in *Jubilees* as "from house to house" (*'embēt bēta*).

The explanation for the first two exegetical transformations is readily discernible. Because Jub 2:29 has solved the problem of the meaning of *Jeremiah*'s "burden," there is no need to retain this scriptural language in Jub 2:30. Indeed, its non-inclusion in Jub 2:30 reinforces the conclusion of Jub 2:29 that all items may not be carried. The inclusion of "or (bring anything) in" (*wa-'iyabe'u* = Jer 17:21c והבאתם) in Jub 2:30 mirrors the inclusion of "or remove" (*wa-la-'awd̤e'o*) in Jub 2:29. As in Jub 2:29, verse 30 formulates its legal ruling as applicable to carrying both inside and outside. The twofold language of Jer 17:21–22 (21c: בוא–*hiph'il* + 22a: יצא–*hiph'il*) provides the lexical basis for both passages in *Jubilees*.

In adding a second verbal element, the reformulation in Jub 2:30 disrupts the syntax of Jer 17:22. As previously noted, the carrying element in Jer 17:22 is marked by the root יצא–*hiph'il* + מ in order to articulate the idea of carrying an item out of one's home. The inclusion of *wa-'iyabe'u* ("or [bring anything] in" = בוא–*hiph'il*) renders this understanding of the preposition *mem* impossible. Instead, the second-person plural possessive suffix on מבתיכם ("from your houses") is no longer understood as a general reference to one's house from which carrying is proscribed. Rather, it is understood as referring to carrying "from house to house." The *mem* preposition therefore indicates carrying *from* one of *your* houses to another of *your* houses. In so doing, Jub 2:30 renders Jeremiah's מבתיכם compatible with the reorientation of the carrying prohibition as applying to carrying both into and out of locations.

Jubilees 2:29–30 and 50:8 in Context

Through a variety of exegetical techniques, both Jub 2:29–30 and 50:8 transform Jer 17:21–22 into a fully developed statement on Sabbath carrying law. They resolve several central questions regarding the specific spaces affected by the carrying prohibition and the precise meaning of the "burden" that one may not carry on the Sabbath. In the preceding discussion, I treated the two carrying laws in *Jubilees* independently. While they agree in some details (e.g., the wide range of items that may not be carried), other elements (e.g., the direction of proscribed carrying) are distinct. These two passages seemingly represent two different applications of the Sabbath carrying law and evince distinct exegetical techniques in their reformulation of Jer 17:21–22.

The differences between these two passages should now be understood within the wider context of the distinct presentations of the Sabbath carrying prohibition in Dead Sea Scrolls legal texts and their exegetical relationship to Jer 17:21–22. Throughout the earlier discussion of the Dead Sea Scrolls texts, I repeatedly noted that the *Damascus Document* and *4QHalakha A* are often in agreement in their general details as well as their exegetical techniques. In contrast, the carrying prohibition in *4QMiscellaneous Rules* diverges from the *Damascus Document* and *4QHalakha A* both in some of its basic details and its exegetical application of Jer 17:21–22. When the sectarian legal texts and *Jubilees* are read together, the dissimilarities that exist within each collection of documents find intriguing points of contact across the literary collections. Many aspects of *4QMiscellaneous Rules* seem to find additional expression in Jub 50:8, while elements from the *Damascus Document* and *4QHalakha A* appear in Jub 2:29–30.

With regard to the space affected by the carrying prohibition, I addressed three elements. *4QMiscellaneous Rules* introduces the "tent" as a specific personal space in which the carrying restriction applies. So too, this exact space is the one new element introduced in Jub 50:8.[27] In both cases, this expansion is achieved by the introduction of the new element following the use of the scriptural יצא–*hiph'il* + מ construction (likewise employed in the *Damascus Document* and *4QHalakha A*). Similarly, I observed that *4QMiscellaneous Rules* is the only one of the three Dead Sea Scrolls texts to personalize the affected space ("*his* tent"). This detail is supplied in *4QMiscellaneous Rules*

[27] Jub 50:8 similarly retains the scriptural reference to a "house." If there is some relationship between Jub 50:8 and *4QMiscellaneous Rules*, as suggested here, this would support my assertion in Chapter 9 that *4QMiscellaneous Rules* assumes that the carrying law applies with regard to a tent *in addition* to a house (which goes unmentioned).

by the modification of the possessive suffix on Jer 17:22 "your houses." The *Damascus Document* and *4QHalakha A*, in contrast, omit a possessive suffix, thereby suggesting that personalized space is not an issue. In my earlier discussion, I proposed that this discrepancy could perhaps be traced to different stages in the understanding and application of the carrying prohibition. The multiple presentations of the carrying law in *Jubilees* add additional support to this assertion. Jub 50:8 once again agrees with *4QMiscellaneous Rules* in adding a possessive suffix to its affected spaces ("his tent," "his house"), while Jub 2:30 lacks any such reference ("from house to house").[28]

Perhaps the most striking difference among all these texts is the question of the direction of proscribed carrying. The *Damascus Document* and *4QHalakha A* prohibit carrying items both *into* and *out of* the affected spaces. In contrast, *4QMiscellaneous Rules* condemns only carrying items *out* of one's tent. As discussed, the *Damascus Document* and *4QHalakha A* formulate their presentations of the law as an application of the twofold language of carrying in Jer 17:21c (בוא–*hiph'il*) and 22a (יצא–*hiph'il*). This requires the alteration of בוא–*hiph'il* from a reference to carrying through "gates" to carrying into "homes." In contrast, *4QMiscellaneous Rules* appears as a straightforward application of Jer 17:21–22 with regard to one's home and carrying. Thus, consistent with the reference to homes in Jer 17:22 (יצא–*hiph'il* + מ), *4QMiscellaneous Rules* only proscribes carrying items out of one's home and not the reverse.

The direction of the prohibited carrying is likewise the most prominent difference between Jub 50:8 and 2:29–30. Jub 50:8 completely ignores Jer 17:21c and its use of בוא–*hiph'il* + ב (i.e., carrying items in). Rather, it preserves a very straightforward application of Jer 17:22a and thus only prohibits carrying items out of one's home or tent. Jub 2:29–30, similar to the *Damascus Document* and *4QHalakha A*, explicitly forbids carrying items in both directions. In formulating the law this way, Jub 2:29–30 similarly draws upon the twofold language of Jer 17:21c and 22a. As in the corresponding passages in the *Damascus Document* and *4QHalakha A*, Jub 2:29–30 achieves this exegetical modification by inverting the keywords from *Jeremiah* and reorienting their meaning for a new legal context.

To be sure, there is dissimilarity among the respective passages in *Jubilees* and the Dead Sea Scrolls texts. For example, both passages in *Jubilees* clarify and expand the meaning of *Jeremiah*'s "burden" through creative uses of *k*^{w}*ello* ("anything" = כל). In principle, the *Damascus Document* and *4QHalakha A* agree with this expansion but evince a different exegetical technique. Moreover, *4QMiscellaneous Rules* likely agrees with the expanded understanding of the "burden," but singles out two specific items for special mention. Such a feature is not present in Jub 50:8.

[28] Note that Jub 2:29 does evince a related type of exegetical modification in its transformation of Jer 17:21c, "gates of Jerusalem" to "your gates."

Despite these dissimilarities, there seems to be enough correspondence to suggest that *4QMiscellaneous Rules* and Jub 50:8, on the one hand, and the *Damascus Document* and *4QHalakha A* and Jub 2:29–30, on the other hand, emerge from shared legal-exegetical contexts. There is precious little evidence to ascertain whether the Dead Sea Scrolls texts are directly relying upon *Jubilees* or if each is dependent upon the same independent source.[29] This suggestion, however, works well with the assertion that the multiple Sabbath lists in Jub 2 and 50 represent independent Sabbath legal traditions – whether as separate lists utilized by one author or multiple authors/editors or as independent compositions of multiple authors/editors.

IV. THE RESTRICTION ON CARRYING IN RABBINIC LITERATURE

Mishnah Shabbat 1:1 and Jeremiah 17:21–22

> יציאות השבת שתים שהן ארבע בפנים ושתים שהן ארבע בחוץ כיצד העני עומד בחוץ ובעל הבית בפנים פשט העני את ידו לפנים ונתן לתוך ידו של בעל הבית או שנטל מתוכה והוציא העני חייב ובעל הבית פטור פשט בעל הבית את ידו לחוץ ונתן לתוך ידו של עני או שנטל מתוכה והכניס בעל הבית חייב והעני פטור פשט העני את ידו לפנים ונטל בעל הבית מתוכה או שנתן לתוכה והוציא שניהם פטורין פשט בעל הבית את ידו לחוץ ונטל העני מתוכה או שנתן לתוכה והכניס שניהם פטורין
>
> (Acts of) transporting objects from one domain to another (which violate) the Sabbath are two which (indeed) are four (for one who is) inside, and two, which are four (for one who is) outside. How so? (If on the Sabbath) the beggar stands outside and the householder inside, (and) the beggar stuck his hand inside and put (a beggar's bowl) into the hand of the householder, or if he took (something) from inside it and brought it out, the beggar is liable, the householder is exempt. (If) the householder stuck his hand outside and put (something) into the hand of the beggar, or if he took (something) from it and brought it inside, the householder is liable, and the beggar is exempt. (If) the beggar stuck his hand inside, and the householder took (something) from it, or if (the householder) put something in it and he (the beggar) removed it, both of them are exempt. (If) the householder put his hand outside and the beggar took (something) from it, or if (the beggar) put something into it and (the householder) brought it back inside, both of them are exempt.[30]

The opening *Mishnah* of tractate *Shabbat* treats several aspects of the prohibition against carrying. In comparison to the Second Temple texts, the *Mishnah*'s presentation is quite well developed. The *Mishnah* has a clear sense

[29] See my earlier discussion of the relationship between Jub 50:8 and CD 10:17–19 (Chapter 6, section II).

[30] The Hebrew text follows Ms Kaufmann A 50. See Georg Beer, *Faksimile-Ausgabe des Mischnacodex Kaufmann A 50* (Haag: M. Nijhoff, 1929; repr., Jerusalem, 1969), 84; and the critical edition found in Abraham Goldberg, *Commentary to the Mishna Shabbat* (Jerusalem: Jewish Theological Seminary of America, 1976), 1 [Hebrew]. Translation follows Jacob Neusner, *The Mishnah: A New Translation* (New Haven: Yale University Press, 1988), 179.

of the space affected by this prohibition. Two general domains are envisioned, for which the two characters "householder" (private domain) and "beggar" (public domain) are representative.[31] Furthermore, the *Mishnah* very clearly formulates the law as applying to carrying items both *into* and *out of* the affected spaces. Regarding the extent of the items that may not be conveyed on the Sabbath, the *Mishnah* is decidedly silent. Indeed, in all cases where the verb of conveyance could reasonably follow with a direct object, it does not. This silence therefore suggests that all items are intended to fall under the rubric of this law.

Similar to the legal texts treated thus far, the *Mishnah* seems to reuse language from Jer 17:21–22 (as marked by single underlining). At the same time, the *Mishnah* amplifies and clarifies the precise parameters of *Jeremiah*'s prohibition against carrying on the Sabbath. While the shared language is less prominent than in related texts, the use of the root יצא in the *hiph'il* (והוציא) to describe the act of transporting an item out of one's home suggests that the *Mishnah* recognizes Jer 17:21–22 as the scriptural starting point for the carrying prohibition.[32] Indeed, in the list of the thirty-nine proscribed labors on the Sabbath found later in *Mishnah Shabbat*, the *Mishnah* follows Jer 17:22 in identifying carrying with יצא–*hiph'il* + מ: המוציא מרשות לרשות, "He who transports an object from one domain to another" (*m. Shabb.* 7:2).[33]

At the same time, the *Mishnah* opens by identifying the laws of carrying with the general terminological rubric יציאות השבת ("goings out"). As ancient and modern commentators have noted, the expression "goings out" (*qal*) is strange here. The *Mishnah* proceeds to explain that violation of the law of carrying requires transporting an item out of one domain and into another domain. The use of the term "goings out" therefore seems inappropriate because it excludes the critical act of "bringing in" an object to the other domain.[34] At the very least, one would have expected this process of conveyance to be described with the *hiph'il* הוצאות, meaning "carryings (out)."[35]

[31] The *Mishnah* intends these two characters as individuals who would most often be found in these two specific spaces. As suggested by Maimonides, the use of these two characters is the result of the *Mishnah*'s pursuit of brevity. The one word "householder" conveys the sense of the longer expression "a man standing in private domain," as does "beggar" for "a man standing in public domain" (*Commentary on the Mishnah*, *Shabbat* 1:1).

[32] See also Lawrence H. Schiffman, *The Halakhah at Qumran* (SJLA 16; Leiden: Brill, 1975), 114; Doering, "New Aspects," 258 (cf. Rabin, *Zadokite Documents*, 55).

[33] See further *y. Shabb.* 1:1 2b, which contains a discussion of the scriptural source of the *Mishnah*. Rabbi Ḥezekiah in the name of Rabbi Aḥa identifies *Jeremiah* as the source of the *Mishnah*'s ruling. See below for the opposing view tracing the law to Exod 36:6. See also *b. Hor.* 4a as found in the Vilna printed edition, which likewise identifies Jer 17:22 as the scriptural source. See, however, below for treatment of the variant reading found in Ms Munich 95, which identifies Exod 16:29 as the source.

[34] See *b. Shabb.* 2b and discussion below.

[35] See Tosafot on *b. Shabb.* 2a, s.v. יציאות. For this general use of the *hiph'il*, see, e.g., *m. Shabb.* 7:2; *b. Hor.* 4a.

The strange word choice of the *Mishnah* is somewhat clarified by the *Babylonian Talmud*'s suggestion that the expression "goings out" (*qal*) encompasses the act of both taking an item out of one domain (הוצאה) and bringing an item into another domain (הכנסה), the two elements of the rabbinic prohibition of carrying (as illustrated in *Mishnah Shabbat* 1:1). יציאות (*qal*) is therefore a technical term for both of these acts. While this answer is clearly not in accord with the precise grammatical meaning of the word, the talmudic understanding of יציאות has some support from similar uses of this expression elsewhere in rabbinic literature.[36]

We are still left with the question of why יציאות was specifically chosen as the terminological rubric in the *Mishnah*. In this respect, it is likely that the expression יציאות (יצא–*qal*) was employed in order to correspond with the scriptural language of Exod 16:29 (also יצא–*qal*): אל יצא איש ממקמו ביום השביעי, "Let no man leave his place on the seventh day."[37] A laconic reference to exegesis of Exod 16:29 in the *Babylonian Talmud* (*b. 'Erub.* 17b) indicates that this scriptural passage is associated with the carrying prohibition based on the same exegesis as is found in the Dead Sea Scrolls.[38]

Exod 16:29 is regarded in rabbinic law as a general restriction on travel on the Sabbath.[39] The talmudic discussion in *'Erubin* 17b centers around whether violation of the Sabbath travel restriction is liable for flogging. According to rabbinic jurisprudence, flogging cannot be administered for a noncapital biblical prohibition that simultaneously serves as a "warning" (אזהרה) against a capital offense.[40] The *Babylonian Talmud* advances the opinion of Rabbi Yonatan that the travel prohibition is a secondary understanding of Exod 16:29; the primary understanding is that this passage prohibits carrying, which is a capital offense. According to Rabbi Yonatan, therefore, one cannot receive flogging as punishment for violating the Sabbath travel restriction. This entire view, however, is rejected by Rav Ashi by asserting that the scriptural text very clearly says "go out" (*qal*; e.g., travel) not "take out" (*hiph'il*; e.g., carrying):

36 See Chanokh Albeck, *Shishah Sidre Mishnah*, volume 2: *Seder Mo'ed* (Jerusalem: Bialik Institute; Tel Aviv: Dvir, 1958), 405 (cf. Rabin, *Qumran Studies*, 109–10).

37 This opinion is first advanced by Tosafot, on *b. Shabb.* 2a, s.v. יציאות. The same argument (drawing from the language of Tosafot) is adduced in the commentary on the *Mishnah* of Rabbi Obadiah of Bertinoro (s.v. יציאות השבת). See also Herbert Danby, *The Mishnah* (Oxford: Oxford University Press, 1933), 100 n. 2; Doering, "New Aspects," 258.

38 See also the brief discussion of this passage in Doering, "New Aspects," 258.

39 See the sources cited above, Chapter 9, n. 34.

40 Rabbinic law presumes that every capital offense articulated in the Hebrew Bible appears as both an explicit "warning" (אזהרה) and a formulated "punishment" (עונש). On these categories, see "אזהרה ('Azharah)," in *Encyclopedia Talmudica* (ed. M. Bar-Ilan and S. Y. Yeiven; trans. H. Freedman; 6 vols. to date; Jerusalem: Yad HaRav Herzog, Talmudic Encyclopedia Institute, 1974–), 1:517–23; Devora Steinmetz, *Punishment and Freedom: The Rabbinic Construction of Criminal Law* (Divinations; Philadelphia: University of Pennsylvania Press, 2008), 15–18, 40–52.

אמר רב אשי מי כתיב אל יוציא אל יצא כתיב

> Rav Ashi said, is it written, "Let no man carry out?" It is written "Let no man go out." (*b. 'Erub.* 17b)

According to Rav Ashi, the straightforward reading of Exod 16:29 identifies it as a restriction against Sabbath travel, not carrying. While the talmudic discussion rejects the understanding of Exod 16:29 as an explicit prohibition against carrying, this passage very clearly indicates that the rabbis saw in Exod 16:29 an allusion to the prohibition and recognized the closely related lexical constructions. The very rejection of this exegetical reading of Exod 16:29 attests to its viability at least in some rabbinic settings.

Mishnah Shabbat 1:1 likely represents a strand of rabbinic tradition that was well acquainted with the rejected exegetical tradition in the later *Babylonian Talmud*. Exod 16:29 provides part of the scriptural language employed by the *Mishnah*. יציאות ("goings out") is neutral enough so as not to indicate exclusively carrying either out or in, while specific enough to convey both aspects of the prohibited carrying. At the same time, Exod 16:29 is not presented as the scriptural source for the carrying prohibition or even the exegetical starting point for its rabbinic development. Moreover, there is no indication that the *Mishnah* draws upon the scriptural language of Exod 16:29 in order to prioritize Pentateuchal language over non-Pentateuchal language (i.e., Jer 17:21–22). As in the texts from the Dead Sea Scrolls, Jer 17:21–22 is the guiding legal and exegetical scriptural source, while Exod 16:29 provides part of the formal language in which this law is expressed.

The Rabbinic Carrying Prohibition and the Non-use of Jeremiah 17:21–22

In earlier treatments of the restriction on speech and thought on the Sabbath in rabbinic literature, I observed tension in rabbinic tradition regarding the scriptural source of these laws. Several significant strands in rabbinic literature follow the Second Temple–period sources in identifying Isa 58:13 as the source for the Sabbath restrictions on speech and thought. Other rabbinic texts, however, appeal to different scriptural passages. In some cases, I observed that the counter-exegetical traditions deliberately avoid Isa 58:13 in favor of the alternative scriptural sources. I have repeatedly suggested that this broader phenomenon should be traced to a growing hesitation among the rabbis to employ non-Pentateuchal passages in support of legal formulations.

A similar trend in favor of passages other than Jer 17:21–22 can be detected in rabbinic presentations of the carrying law. The rabbinic hesitation to identify Jer 17:21–22 as the basis of the carrying prohibition, however, is different from the other examples examined in previous chapters. For both speech and thought on the Sabbath, Isa 58:13 is far from equivocal as the scriptural basis for these

Sabbath laws. Jer 17:21–22, in contrast, is explicit in its condemnation of carrying on the Sabbath. Moreover, no other scriptural passage prohibits carrying on the Sabbath in such clear terms. Thus, any rabbinic appeal to scriptural passages other than Jer 17:21–22 by the rabbis represents a divergence from the most readily available scriptural source. The alternative sources offered by the rabbis all require significant exegetical modification just so that they can say what Jer 17:21–22 articulates clearly!

Already in *Mishnah Shabbat* 1:1 we can see movement among the rabbis away from turning to Jer 17:21–22 as the scriptural source. As suggested, the use of יצא–*hiph'il* in order to describe the prohibited act of carrying an item outside seems to paraphrase the identical use of this root in Jer 17:22. At the same time, however, the verbal root in Jer 17:21 employed to represent the act of bringing an item inside, בוא–*hiph'il*, is not used in the *Mishnah*. Rather, the *Mishnah* describes this act with כנס–*hiph'il*. It is not entirely clear if this modification represents linguistic updating, or perhaps כנס–*hiph'il* is regarded as more appropriate to the precise circumstances outlined in the *Mishnah*. Even if either of these situations is the case, the clear avoidance of the verb of conveyance from Jer 17:21 would not have gone unnoticed by either the formulator of the *Mishnah* or its audience.

Other rabbinic traditions not only avoid Jer 17:21–22 but also offer alternative scriptural sources. As is to be expected, Exod 16:29 is regularly cited as the scriptural basis for the carrying prohibition. The evidence provided by *Babylonian Talmud 'Erubin* 17b cited above indicates that the appeal to Exod 16:29 in rabbinic sources follows the same exegetical pattern as the Second Temple sources. Thus, אל יצא, "Let no man go out," is reread as אל יוציא, "Let no man take out." In the context of its discussion, the *Babylonian Talmud 'Erubin*, however, rejects Exod 16:29 as a source for the carrying prohibition. The identification of Exod 16:29 as the scriptural source for the carrying prohibition is also found in *Babylonian Talmud Horayot* 4a, as preserved in MS Munich 95. In the course of a discussion regarding whether the restriction on carrying is scripturally based, the talmudic text preserved in Ms Munich 95 cites Exod 16:29.[41]

Elsewhere, however, the *Babylonian Talmud* unequivocally embraces Exod 16:29 as the scriptural source. A different legal tradition in *Babylonian Talmud 'Erubin* discusses the scriptural source for the restriction on traveling more than 2,000 cubits on the Sabbath. As we would expect, Exod 16:29 is presented as the source. The specific formulation found in the *Babylonian Talmud* presents a tannaitic ruling that identifies Exod 16:29 as the source of both the travel restriction *and* carrying:

41 See Raphael Rabbinovicz, *Sefer Dikduke Sofrim = Variae Lectiones in Mischnam et in Talmud Babylonicum* (2 vols.; New York: M. P. Press, 1976]), vol. 2, ad loc. The Vilna edition cites Jer 17:22. On a third manuscript tradition that cites Exod 36:6, see below, n. 46.

הני אלפים אמה היכן כתיבן דתניא שבו איש תחתיו אלו ארבע אמות אל יצא איש ממקומו אלו אלפים אמה

What is the scriptural source for the 2,000 cubits? It has been taught on tannaitic authority: "Let everyone remain where he is" (Exod 16:29) – this refers to four cubits; "Let no one leave his place on the seventh day" (Exod 16:29) – this refers to 2,000 cubits. (*b. 'Erub.* 51a)

The primary interest of this passage is the scriptural source for the travel restriction ("2,000 cubits"), for which Exod 16:29 is cited as the obvious source. The *Babylonian Talmud* interjects with a related law that shares both a scriptural source (Exod 16:29) and a unit of measurement (cubit).

The reference to "four cubits" in this passage alludes to the earlier view likewise based on Exod 16:29 that an individual possesses a personal space of four cubits (*b. 'Erub.* 48a). This principle functions in two ways. With regard to the Sabbath travel restriction, one who involuntarily leaves the Sabbath boundary must remain within a space of four cubits until the conclusion of the Sabbath.[42] With regard to the carrying restriction, rabbinic law allows one to carry an item a distance of four cubits within the public domain.[43] This particular aspect of the carrying law is regarded as distinct from the elements of conveyance from one domain to another as articulated in *Mishnah Shabbat* 1:1.

Unlike all the sources treated thus far, the tannaitic source cited here does not appeal to the modified exegesis of יצא, "go out," in Exod 16:29. This part of the verse is rendered with its much simpler meaning as a restriction on movement, hence travel. Rather, the tannaitic authority appeals to the earlier element in the verse, שבו איש תחתיו, "Let everyone remain where he is." The rabbinic interpretation of this lemma understands תחתיו in a very literal sense, whereby this individual must remain in the place that is "under him." The rabbis calculate this space as four cubits (*b. 'Erub.* 48a). Thus, this individual outside of the Sabbath boundary or holding an item is exhorted to stay put – that is, do not move even within public domain more than four cubits.

Targum Pseudo-Jonathan on Exod 16:29 presents a conflation of both legal traditions regarding the meaning of this verse for the carrying law alongside the rabbinic restriction on traveling beyond 2,000 cubits:

שרון גבר באתריה ולא תטלטלון מידעם מרשותא לרשותא בר מארבעה גרמידי ולא יפוק אינש מאתריה לטיילא לבר מתרין אלפין גרמידי ביומא שביעאה

Let everyone remain in his place. One may not convey anything from one domain to another, (nothing) beyond four cubits. And let no man go out from his place to travel beyond 2,000 cubits on the seventh day.[44]

42 See also *m. 'Erub.* 4:1, 5.

43 See also *m. Shabb.* 11:1–4; *b. Shabb.* 153b.

44 Aramaic text follows E. G. Clarke, *Targum Pseudo-Jonathan of the Pentateuch: Text and Concordance* (Hoboken: Ktav, 1984), 87.

This first unit in the Targum alludes to both elements of the rabbinic carrying law: (1) a restriction on conveying an item from one domain to another and (2) movement of an item within one domain more than four cubits. Yet, both elements of the law are presented as a translation of the scriptural lemma, שבו איש תחתיו, "Let everyone remain where he is." As in the tannaitic source cited in *Babylonian Talmud 'Erubin* 51a, the final portion of Exod 16:29 – אל יצא איש ממקומו, "Let no one leave his place" – is rendered in Targum Pseudo-Jonathan as an allusion to the travel restriction.

Rabbinic tradition attests to the emergence of a third scriptural source for the carrying law. In this particular case, Exod 36:6 appears as an alternative scripture source alongside Jer 17:21–22. A tradition reported in the *Palestinian Talmud* attempts to identify the source of *Mishnah Shabbat* 1:1 (*y. Shabb.* 1:1 2b; *y. Sheb.* 1:1 32c). This first scriptural origin is suggested by Rabbi Samuel ben Naḥman in the name of Rabbi Yonatan, who traces the law to Exod 36:6:

> ויצו משה ויעבירו קול במחנה לאמר איש ואשה אל יעשו עוד מלאכה לתרומת הקדש ויכלא העם מהביא
>
> Moses thereupon had this proclamation made throughout the camp: "Let no man or woman make further effort toward gifts for the sanctuary." So the people stopped bringing.

The association with Exod 36:6 is based on a broader rabbinic exegetical tradition that identifies the specific Sabbath prohibitions with the labor necessary to construct the Tabernacle.[45] A second approach in the *Palestinian Talmud* is advocated by Rabbi Ḥezekiah in the name of Rabbi Aḥa, who identifies Jer 17:21–22 as the source of the *Mishnah*'s ruling.

An additional passage in the *Babylonian Talmud* likewise identifies Exod 36:6 as the scriptural source, though no mention is made of Jer 17:21–22 (*b. Shabb.* 96b).[46] This particular tradition attempts to explain the connection between carrying and Exod 36:6 by projecting rabbinic categories of public and private domains onto the Israelite desert camp. The talmudic passage asserts that Exod 36:6 refers to a situation in which Moses was standing in the Levite camp, which is regarded as public domain. The donations that the Israelites had been bringing for the construction of the Tabernacle came from their dwellings, which are regarded as private domain. Thus, when Moses instructs the Israelites to cease bringing gifts, he is likewise telling them to refrain from carrying items from private domain to public domain. As noted at the beginning of this section, the rabbinic traditions that link the carrying restriction to Exod 36:6 exert a considerable amount of exegetical energy to make this verse say what Jer 17:21–22 says explicitly. As such, the passages

45 On the use of the Tabernacle material to generate the prohibited labors, see, e.g., *b. Shabb.* 39b.

46 In the passage from *b. Hor.* 4a discussed above, Exod 36:6 is cited as the scriptural source of the carrying prohibition in Ms Paris Suppl. Heb. 1337.

explored in this section offer further evidence to the growing rabbinic reluctance to appeal to non-Pentateuchal passages for legal support.

V. CONCLUSIONS

My analysis in the last two chapters has been guided by two overarching themes: (1) Jer 17:21–22 is the scriptural source for later Jewish formulations of a restriction against carrying on the Sabbath. In this role as a scriptural Sabbath law, however, Jer 17:21–22 is lacking in many of the necessary details, and thus the Second Temple and rabbinic texts reflect a careful exegetical modification of much of the content of Jer 17:21–22. (2) The legal-exegetical application of Jer 17:21–22 in the Dead Sea Scrolls legal texts is not an isolated phenomenon. Rather, these texts must be situated within the broader context of the interpretation of Israelite scriptures and law in ancient Judaism. Indeed, the interpretation of Jer 17:21–22 in *Nehemiah*, *Jubilees*, and the *Mishnah* reflects several parallels with the use of *Jeremiah* in the *Damascus Document*, *4QHalakha A*, and *4QMiscellaneous Rules*.[47]

All these texts identify Jer 17:21–22 as the scriptural source for the prohibition of carrying on the Sabbath. For all of these sources, however, *Jeremiah* provided an incomplete formulation of this law. Thus, all of these texts attempt to delineate in more precise detail the wider application of *Jeremiah*'s condemnation of carrying on the Sabbath. This amplification is achieved through the exegetical formulation and expansion of Jer 17:21–22. Keywords from *Jeremiah* are interwoven into the new, more precise and expanded legal formulation. My discussion focused on three general aspects: (1) the range of the space affected by the carrying prohibition, (2) the meaning of *Jeremiah*'s "burden," and (3) the relationship of the use of Jer 17:21–22 in these texts to the influence of Exod 16:29 in some of them.

The last two chapters have reinforced my earlier assertion regarding the interconnected nature of legal exegesis in ancient Judaism. With regard to the space affected by the carrying restriction, each of the texts attempts to provide more details regarding what specific spaces are under the rubric of the carrying

[47] Moreover, the *Gospel of John* preserves an anecdote that indicates familiarity with both the Sabbath carrying prohibition and its expansion in contemporaneous Second Temple Judaism. In John 5:10, a man who had just been cured by Jesus is queried by "the Jews": σάββατόν ἐστιν καὶ οὐκ ἔξεστι σοι ἆραι τὸν κράββατον, "It is the Sabbath; it is not lawful for you to carry your mat" (NRSV). The verb employed to describe the condemned carrying (αἴρω) corresponds to the Hebrew verb employed for carrying in Jer 17:21: "Against carrying (Heb: תשאו; 𝔊: αἴρετε) loads on the Sabbath day." This would suggest that the legal source that stands behind the formulation in John 5:10 recognizes Jer 17:21 as the scriptural source for the prohibition against carrying. In this adaptation of Jer 17:21, the "mat" takes the place of the "load" in Jer 17:21. In this sense, the legal source behind John 5:10 likely is in agreement with the broader approach detected in the Second Temple texts that regard all items under the rubric of the meaning of "load" in Jer 17:21–22. Thus, the passage applies this general principle to the specific case of the "mat."

law. Thus, the Dead Sea Scrolls texts specifically include a *sukkah* and a tent, while *Jubilees* likewise adds a tent. In all of these cases, the more significant issue is that both sets of texts employ nearly identical exegetical techniques to expand the law. Similarly, all these texts grapple with the seemingly limited application of *Jeremiah*'s words to proscribe only carrying items out of one's home. Once again, the legal-exegetical amplification of this aspect of the law in the Dead Sea Scrolls texts finds additional expression in *Jubilees*. Here, however, we find an even more interesting phenomenon. Two of the Dead Sea Scrolls texts (*Damascus Document* and 4*QHalakha A*) agree with one passage in *Jubilees* (2:29–30), while another (4*QMiscellaneous Rules*) agrees with a different passage in *Jubilees* (50:8). I suggested above that this is not merely a coincidence, but rather the corresponding source material is drawing from a shared collection of Sabbath law based on similar legal-exegetical readings of *Jeremiah*. Indeed, this particular issue seems to have been a subject of much dispute in Second Temple Judaism.

In this respect, the implications of Lutz Doering's correct observation that Sabbath law in *Jubilees* often disagrees with corresponding material in the sectarian Dead Sea Scrolls texts should be nuanced.[48] The material treated here suggests that the situation is far more complex. The Cave 4 texts have opened up a wider context for law in the Dead Sea Scrolls and the sectarian community. Discussions of sectarian Sabbath law must take a more nuanced perspective on the development of legal traditions in the community of the Dead Sea Scrolls and their relationship to other Second Temple texts. In the issue under discussion, it is indeed true that some elements in *Jubilees* and the scrolls are in disagreement. At the same time, however, other material in *Jubilees* and the scrolls does agree. As suggested here, we must peel apart the layers of tradition in these texts in search of smaller units of correspondence, which must then be analyzed for evidence of a historical relationship.

All of these texts likewise share a concern for identifying with more precision the nature of *Jeremiah*'s "burden" that may not be carried on the Sabbath. Here as well, the various texts reflect overlapping legal formulations and shared exegetical amplifications of *Jeremiah*. In principle, all the texts treated here agree that the Sabbath carrying restriction applies to all items. At the same time, the various texts reflect two distinct exegetical techniques to represent this legal position. The *Damascus Document*, 4*QHalakha A*, and the *Mishnah* follow one route by omitting any reference to the term משא from *Jeremiah*, thereby indicating that all items are to be included.[49] In contrast, Neh 13:15 and both passages in *Jubilees* modify the meaning of משא by the

48 Doering, "Jub 50:6–13 als Schlussabschnitt des 'Jubiläenbuchs,'" 385–87.

49 4*QMiscellaneous Rules* should likely be grouped with this collection. Because the text singles out two specific items, the assumption is that the carrying prohibition applies likewise to all items. In addition, as in the *Damascus Document*, 4*QHalakha A*, and the *Mishnah*, it does not retain the scriptural term משא.

introduction of a quantifier כל//*k^w ello* in order to expand it to a wider range of items.[50]

The last two chapters have also examined the exegetical interplay between Jer 17:21–22 and Exod 16:29 in several of the texts. The Dead Sea Scrolls texts rely upon Exod 16:29 for the formal language in which the laws are presented. As suggested, the use of *Exodus* is motivated by the formal literary aspects of the sectarian legal texts. Neither *Nehemiah* nor *Jubilees* reflects any influence from Exod 16:29. The *Mishnah*, however, draws upon Exod 16:29 for part of its literary formulation as it simultaneously reformulates Jer 17:21–22. As in the sectarian legal texts, Exod 16:29 provides the formal literary aspects desired by the *Mishnah*.

50 Neh 13:15 and Jub 50:8 in particular retain the scriptural term משא while simultaneously modifying it.

11

Non-Pentateuchal Passages as Prooftexts

I. INTRODUCTION

In the previous chapters, I have explored the reformulation of Isa 58:13 and Jer 17:21–22 in legal texts from among the Dead Sea Scrolls. In all the texts I have examined, neither of these scriptural passages is cited explicitly. Rather, general language and specific keywords from both passages are employed in their reformulated contexts. In some cases, language from these passages is retained with minimal or no modification. In other contexts, the Dead Sea Scrolls legal texts modify the scriptural language as part of a broader deliberate legal and exegetical reuse of these texts. The emphasis on reformulation of scriptural language rather than explicit citation is consistent with the centrality of paraphrase as the primary method of scriptural interpretation in the Second Temple period in both legal and nonlegal contexts. As noted in Chapter 2, the explicit citation of prooftexts is considerably less prominent in Second Temple–period texts.[1]

This chapter explores the use of non-Pentateuchal passages as prooftexts in sectarian legal texts.[2] In this context, I have detected two different types of prooftexts: (1) citations of non-Pentateuchal passages as independent prooftexts and (2) non-Pentateuchal passages that are cited as secondary prooftexts alongside Pentateuchal passages. In the first category, the non-Pentateuchal passages appear following, or in one case preceding, the apodictic formulation of sectarian law. What larger function do they serve as prooftexts? In these passages, the non-Pentateuchal passages appear as prooftexts in much the same way as Pentateuchal passages. One often encounters in sectarian legal

[1] See above, Chapter 2, section IV, and bibliography in nn. 59–60.

[2] Prooftexts in the Dead Sea Scrolls have been the object of considerable attention, though rarely with a particular focus on legal texts. See bibliography above, Chapter 1, nn. 45–46.

texts the explicit formulation of a law followed by a citation from the Pentateuch. These citations, generally introduced by citation formulae, are connected to the preceding law in varying degrees. Sometimes, the exegetical foundations are manifest though not necessarily logical. Other times, the exegetical relationship is not immediately apparent. The evidence examined in this chapter demonstrates that non-Pentateuchal prooftexts function in the same way.[3]

The second category of texts that I have identified contains non-Pentateuchal passages that are cited alongside Pentateuchal passages. In these texts, both the Pentateuchal and non-Pentateuchal passages function as scriptural prooftexts for the sectarian legal formulation. In each case, however, the non-Pentateuchal passage is cited only after the Pentateuchal passage, which is already suggestive of the relative authority of each passage. Indeed, the examples I discuss each indicate that the non-Pentateuchal passage fulfills a secondary function.

II. NON-PENTATEUCHAL PASSAGES AS INDEPENDENT PROOFTEXTS

Concerning Bans: CD 16:14–15 (par. 4Q271 4 ii 14–15)[4]

14 [אל] יקדש איש את מאכל
15 פיהו[5] [לא]ל כי אשר אמר איש את רעהו יצ[ו]דו חרם

[3] My treatment of prooftexts in this chapter does not address the question of the degree to which the prooftext is formulated as scriptural support for the legal ruling versus its function as the scriptural "source" for the legal ruling. On this issue, see discussion in Vered Noam, "Creative Interpretation and Integrative Interpretation in Qumran," in *The Dead Sea Scrolls and Contemporary Culture: Proceedings of the International Conference Held at the Israel Museum (July 6–8, 2008)* (ed. A. D. Roitman, L. H. Schiffman, and S. Tzoref; STDJ 93; Leiden: Brill, 2011), 363–76.

[4] Hebrew text follows Elisha Qimron, "The Text of CDC," in *The Damascus Document Reconsidered* (ed. M. Broshi; Jerusalem: Israel Exploration Society, the Shrine of the Book, Israel Museum, 1992), 41. The end of column 16 is extremely fragmentary. The Cave 4 manuscripts indicate that column 16 was followed by column 9. For 4Q271, see Joseph M. Baumgarten, *Qumran Cave 4.XIII: The Damascus Document (4Q266–273)* (DJD 18; Oxford: Clarendon, 1996), 178 (no variants exist). On this passage in particular, see Moshe Benovitz, "The Origin and Meaning of the Prohibitive Vow in Second Temple and Tannaitic Literature," *Tarbiz* 64 (1995): 203–28 (219–21) [Hebrew].

[5] Only slight traces of this word appear on the manuscript. The *pe* and the *yod* seem certain, though the *he* and *waw* are very unclear. The parallel text in 4Q271 unfortunately contains a lacuna in this very place. Several early commentators restore here מאכל פעלו, "the food of his worker." See Louis Ginzberg, *An Unknown Jewish Sect* (Moreshet 1; New York: Jewish Theological Seminary, 1976), 100; Leonhard Rost, *Die Damascusschrift: Neu Bearbeitet* (Klein Texte für Vorlesungen und Übungen 167; Berlin: de Gruyter, 1933), 28; K. H. Rengstorf, "κορβᾶν, κορβανᾶς," *TDNT* 3:860–66 (864). This restoration is partially motivated by Ginzberg's interpretation of the text as discussed below. The reconstruction, however, seems to be impossible based on the clear presence of the *yod* in the Genizah manuscript of the *Damascus Document*. See discussion in Benovitz, "Prohibitive Vow," 220–21 n. 65.

14. Let no man sanctify the food of
15. [his] mouth [to Go]d, for this is what he said "Each one traps his neighbor (with) a net" (Mic 7:2).

This passage is difficult to decipher on account of both its laconic formulation and its fragmentary character.[6] Based on the text as reconstructed here, the *Damascus Document* forbids an individual from sanctifying his food. This law is then supported by a scriptural prooftext from the end of Mic 7:2:

אבד חסיד מן הארץ וישר באדם אין כלם לדמים יארבו איש את אחיהו יצודו חרם

> The pious are vanished from the land, none upright are left among men; all lie in wait to commit crimes, one traps the other in his net. (𝔐)[7]

A number of difficulties arise, however, in the interpretation of the passage in the *Damascus Document*. First, what are the specific parameters and precise application of this law? Second, as I have been asking throughout this study, what is the legal-exegetical relationship between the scriptural citation and the law for which it serves as prooftext? Third, whenever a scriptural text is cited as a prooftext in the *Damascus Document*, we must consider why this specific law warranted the inclusion of a scriptural citation.

In his analysis of this law, Louis Ginzberg notes the rabbinic law that laborers are permitted to partake of any produce in the fields where they are working (*m. B. Meṣiʿa* 7:2–8). He surmises that the law in the *Damascus Document* refers to a situation in which the employer wishes to prevent this from happening. In order to do so, the landowner would declare the food sanctified (חרם), whereby it would be forbidden even to the workers.[8] Indeed, a similar act is mentioned in the Gospels, where it is likewise condemned. In Matt 15:5 and Mark 7:11, the Pharisees are condemned for consecrating their property

[6] See, for example, Solomon Schechter, *Documents of Jewish Sectaries*, volume 1: *Fragments of a Zadokite Work* (Cambridge: Cambridge University Press, 1910; repr. with prolegomenon by Joseph Fitzmyer; Library of Biblical Studies; New York: Ktav, 1970), 88, who states that he is entirely uncertain as to the meaning of the law in this passage.

[7] The lemma of Mic 7:2 cited in the *Damascus Document* has רעהו, while the Masoretic Text preserves אחיהו. Fragmentary portions of Mic 7:2 are preserved in 4QXII^{g} (4Q82) 96 9–10 and Mur 88 15 17–18, both of which agree with 𝔐. The section containing רעהו/אחיהו is completely lost in the lacuna in Mur 88. 4QXII^{g} preserves the final section of this verse, but the extant possessive suffix could reflect either 𝔐 or the version cited in the *Damascus Document*:]הו יצודו חרם[. Russell E. Fuller restores according to 𝔐 ("4Q82: 4QXIIg," in *Qumran Cave 4.X: The Prophets* [ed. E. Ulrich et al.; DJD 15; Oxford: Clarendon, 1997], 284).

[8] Ginzberg, *Jewish Sect*, 100–1. See also Chaim Rabin, *The Zadokite Documents* (Oxford: Clarendon, 1954), 77; Fitzmyer, "The Use of Explicit Old Testament Quotations in Qumran Literature and in the New Testament," in *Essays on the Semitic Background of the New Testament* (London: G. Chapman, 1971), 3–58 (42) (1960–61). The often suggested reconstruction מאכל פעלו, therefore, works perfectly with this understanding, although it is textually implausible (see above, n. 5).

to God, whereby they are not required to use this property to support their parents.

Aharon Shemesh has suggested an alternative understanding of this passage. Shemesh notes that Ginzberg's interpretation requires that the word פיהו ("his mouth") in line 15 must be understood not in its simple sense as a reference to the mouth of the one who owns the food. Instead, it refers to the mouth of the second party, who is denied access to the food.[9] Shemesh prefers the simple interpretation of the passage and therefore contends that it proscribes any individual from consecrating too much of his or her own food such that there is nothing left.[10] He further asserts that this understanding fits well with the focus of the larger literary unit, which attempts to curtail the excessive issuance of vows and oaths.[11]

The legal-exegetical function of the citation from *Micah* is relatively straightforward if one follows Ginzberg's explanation. In Mic 7:2 one traps an enemy by use of a net (חרם). The *Damascus Document* applies an alternative meaning for חרם as a "ban." The scriptural verse is now reformulated to describe the very case in the *Damascus Document*. The employer "traps" his workers from partaking of any of his food through imposing a "ban" on the food.[12] The law itself as formulated in the *Damascus Document* is not readily intelligible. The passage from *Micah*, read with the double meaning of חרם, clarifies the meaning of the law by suggesting that the law assumes the existence of a second party (רעהו, "his neighbor") who is unable to benefit from the food as a result of the ban.[13]

If one follows Shemesh's interpretation of the law, the legal-exegetical function of Mic 7:2 is less clear. While the wordplay with חרם (net → ban) is still present, the two conflicting parties found in *Micah* bear little exegetical meaning for the *Damascus Document*. In fact, Shemesh argues that Mic 7:2 has very little to do with this specific law in the *Damascus Document*. Rather, he opines that the scriptural citation functions as the general scriptural source for

[9] See, however, Benovitz, "Prohibitive Vow," 220–21 n. 65. Benovitz notes that the antecedent of פיהו could also be the Israelite mentioned in the previous law (16:14). This would remove some of the awkwardness identified by Shemesh. Benovitz further proposes that the lacuna in line 13 could be restored: מאכל פי]ן ישראל. This as well would favor Ginzberg's initial understanding of the passage.

[10] Aharon Shemesh, "Scriptural Interpretations in the Damascus Document and Their Parallels in Rabbinic Midrash," in *The Damascus Document: A Centennial of Discovery: Proceedings of the Third International Symposium of the Orion Center for the Study of the Dead Sea Scrolls and Associated Literature, 4–8 February, 1998* (ed. J. M. Baumgarten, E. G. Chazon, and A. Pinnick; STDJ 39; Leiden: Brill, 2000), 161–75 (172–73). Shemesh cites the parallel evidence of *Sifra, Be-Ḥuqotai* 12 in support of this understanding. He is following the earlier understanding of this passage in Benovitz, "Prohibitive Vow," 220.

[11] Shemesh, "Scriptural Interpretations," 169.

[12] This wordplay has long been noted by commentators. See Ginzberg, *Jewish Sect*, 101; Rabin, *Zadokite Documents*, 77; Fitzmyer, "Old Testament Quotations," 43.

[13] See Baumgarten, *Qumran Cave 4.XIII*, 180.

the entire literary unit. Following the wordplay on חרם, the *Damascus Document* employs Mic 7:2 to illustrate that a similar disastrous outcome follows from excessive vows and oaths.[14] Shemesh further observes that the wordplay with חרם also links the final literary unit of column 16 with the closely related literary unit that follows at the beginning of column 9.[15] The first law of column 9 condemns any individual who "destroys" (יחרים) a fellow Jew by the "statutes of the gentiles." This presumably refers to an individual who causes the death of a fellow Jew by reporting him or her to the non-Jewish authorities.[16] The use of the root חרם here no doubt is part of the same wordplay with the root from Mic 7:2. In the scriptural verse, one traps one's brother with a "net" (חרם); in the *Damascus Document*, the trapping of one's brother is performed through a destructive act (יחרים).[17]

The larger exegetical function of the citation from Mic 7:2 in CD 9:1, as proposed by Shemesh, is certainly correct. The additional use of the wordplay based on Mic 7:2 in CD 9:1 serves to link these two literary units that treat different legal elements. His assessment of the role of Mic 7:2 in column 16, however, should be rethought. While he may be correct that Mic 7:2 serves as a scriptural warning for the larger message of the literary unit, it is specifically tied to the law that appears in lines 14–15. In this exegetical capacity, the scriptural verse corresponds better with the interpretation of the law as proposed by Ginzberg and others. This is the only law that treats the specific issue of a חרם, the keyword from Mic 7:2. Moreover, if Mic 7:2 fulfills the larger role suggested by Shemesh, we would expect it at either the very beginning or the very end of the literary unit. Mic 7:2 serves foremost as the scriptural prooftext for the law against bans in lines 14–15 while also providing a critical literary link to the set of laws that follow in column 9.

14 Shemesh, "Scriptural Interpretations," 170.

15 On the different approaches to the division of these literary units, see Shemesh, "Scriptural Interpretations," 168. This observation can likewise be found in Charlotte Hempel, *The Laws of the Damascus Document: Sources, Traditions, and Redaction* (STDJ 29; Leiden: Brill, 1998), 31–32.

16 On this meaning, see Joseph M. Baumgarten and Daniel R. Schwartz, "Damascus Document (CD)," in *The Dead Sea Scrolls: Hebrew, Aramaic, and Greek Texts with English Translations; Damascus Document, War Scroll and Related Documents* (ed. J. H. Charlesworth; PTSDSSP 2; Tübingen: Mohr Siebeck; Louisville: Westminster John Knox, 1995), 43 n. 139. For a more general treatment of this clause, see Ze'ez W. Falk, "*Beḥuqey hagoyim*: Damascus Document IX,1," *RevQ* 6 (1969): 569; J. D. M. Derrett, "*Beḥuqey hagoyim*: Damascus Document IX,1 Again," *RevQ* 11 (1983): 409–15. A similar penalty for such activity is found in the *Temple Scroll* (11QT[a] 64:7–8).

17 A similar legal-exegetical application of Mic 7:2 is found in the Targum on this verse. See Joseph M. Baumgarten, "Qumran and the Halakah in the Aramaic Targumim," in *Proceedings of the Ninth World Congress of Jewish Studies: Panel Sessions, Bible Studies and Ancient Near East* (ed. M. Goshen-Gottstein; Jerusalem: World Congress of Jewish Studies, Magnes, the Hebrew University, 1985), 45–60 (47).

Concerning Oaths: CD 9:8–10 (par. 4Q267 9 i 4–5; 5Q12 1 3–4)[18]

8 על השבועה אשר
9 אמר לא תושיעך ידך לך איש אשר ישביע על פני השדה
10 אשר לא לפנים[19] השפטים או מאמרם[20] הושיע[21] ידו לו

8. Concerning oaths: as to that which
9. he said, "Let not your hand help you" (≈ 1 Sam 25:26): A man who causes (another) to swear in the open field
10. that is not in the presence of the judges or by their bidding has let his hand help him.

Under the subject heading "concerning oaths," the *Damascus Document* provides a specific case regarding proscribed oaths that simultaneously articulates its more general attitude toward oaths.[22] The specific case described here involves one individual causing another individual to administer an oath "in the open field," meaning that the oath is without judicial oversight.[23] The emphasis on the lack of judicial oversight indicates that the *Damascus Document* wishes to curtail the excessive administration of oaths not in the presence of judges, especially because these oaths have greater potential to be false or in vain.[24] This specific law, with its larger implications regarding the community's views on oaths, provides an appropriate literary bridge between the preceding literary unit that paraphrases Num 30:15 for the law of reproof (CD 9:6) and the subsequent laws regarding various types of oaths and vows.[25]

[18] Hebrew text follows Qimron, "CDC," 27. For 4Q267, see Baumgarten, *Qumran Cave 4.XIII*, 105. Most of 4Q267 is reconstructed (with plene orthography), though no variants exist in the extant portion. 5Q12 is extremely fragmentary, though likewise preserves no variants in the extant text. See J. T. Milik, "5Q12: Document de Damas," in M. Baillet, J. T. Milik, and R. de Vaux, *Les "Petites Grottes" de Qumran* (DJD 3; Oxford: Clarendon, 1962), 181.

[19] This word is usually emended to לפני or לפי. See, however, Lawrence H. Schiffman, *Sectarian Law in the Dead Sea Scrolls: Courts, Testimony and the Penal Code* (BJS 33; Chico: Scholars Press, 1983), 50 n. 150.

[20] On this form, see discussion in Schiffman, *Sectarian Law*, 50 n. 151.

[21] This should be הושיעה (Qimron, "CDC," 27; Baumgarten, *Qumran Cave 4.XIII*, 105).

[22] On oaths and vows more broadly in the Dead Sea Scrolls, see Lawrence H. Schiffman, "The Law of Vows and Oaths (Num. 30,3–16) in the Zadokite Fragments and the Temple Scroll," in *The Courtyards of the House of the Lord: Studies on the Temple Scroll* (ed. F. García Martínez; STDJ 75; Leiden: Brill, 2008), 557–72 (1991).

[23] On this understanding of ישביע, see Rabin, *Zadokite Documents*, 46 (cf. Baumgarten, *Qumran Cave 4.XIII*, 106). For discussion of parallel rabbinic traditions, see Rabin, ibid., together with Schiffman, *Sectarian Law*, 38.

[24] See Schiffman, *Sectarian Law*, 38.

[25] For the text of CD 9:6, see below. On the location of this law following CD 9:2–8, see also above, n. 4. Note that 5Q12 preserves additional text preceding this passage that is not represented in the Genizah manuscript (see Milik, "5Q12: Document de Damas," 181).

The law of oaths in CD 9:8–10 is presented in the *Damascus Document* as the real-world application of what appears to be a scriptural citation. Following the subject heading, we find a citation formula (אשר אמר), which would normally precede a scriptural passage.[26] The text that follows (לא תושיעך ידך לך), however, is not equivalent to any known scriptural verse. Both Schechter and Ginzberg note the similarities between this passage and 1 Sam 25:26.[27] Ginzberg, however, argues against the identification of this passage as a citation. He advocates instead for an approach that views this citation as stemming from a now-lost sectarian work, with the book of Hagu as the most plausible candidate.[28] He attempts to explain the textual proximity of this passage to 1 Sam 25:26 by suggesting that the sectarian document that serves as the *Damascus Document*'s source (likely the book of Hagu) had already reformulated 1 Sam 25:26 to serve its legal purposes.[29]

To be sure, 1 Sam 25:26 is not cited according to any known ancient witness.[30] The textual modifications present in the *Damascus Document*, however, point to a carefully constructed exegetical reformulation of 1 Sam 25:26 for its present legal purposes. In this sense, this passage further underscores the creative and often manipulative exegetical techniques of the *Damascus Document* even as it "cites" scripture:

1 Sam 25:26 represents part of Abigail's speech to David.[31] This particular passage reports her formal oath to David that she did not see the messengers sent by David (v. 25) and her desire that all of David's enemies falter (v. 26). Verse 26 reproduces the formal language of her oath. The specific expression employed by Abigail – והושע ידך לך, "Gaining your victory with your own hands" – is an idiom denoting the vanquishing of one's enemies, generally

[26] See Fitzmyer, "Old Testament Quotations," 10–11.

[27] Schechter, *Documents*, 78; Ginzberg, *Jewish Sect*, 189–90. See also Rost, *Damaskusschrift*, 18.

[28] Ginzberg, *Jewish Sect*, 189–90. This basic approach can also be found in Rabin, *Zadokite Documents*, 45; Schiffman, *Sectarian Law*, 39. Ginzberg's discussion of this question is found in his larger treatment of the legal authority of non-Pentateuchal passages in the *Damascus Document* (see above, Chapter 1, section III). Consistent with his already formulated conclusions that the *Damascus Document* never relies on non-Pentateuchal passages for legal exegesis, he asserts that it is therefore impossible that this is a direct citation of 1 Sam 25:26.

[29] Thus, according to Ginzberg, the very same sectarian community did in fact turn to a non-Pentateuchal passage for legal purposes! See also the proposal of Jacob Licht discussed below, n. 36.

[30] 4QSam[a] (4Q51) 36 is extremely fragmentary at this point and preserves none of the pertinent part of the verse. See Frank Moore Cross, Donald W. Parry, and Richard J. Saley, "4Q51: 4QSam[a]," in *Qumran Cave 4.XII: 1–2 Samuel* (ed. F. M. Cross et al.; DJD 17; Oxford: Clarendon, 2005), 89 (they restore according to 𝔐).

[31] Some commentators note the textual incongruity of 1 Sam 25:26 in the larger story (P. Kyle McCarter Jr., *I Samuel* [AB 8; Garden City: Doubleday, 1980], 394). This textual issue, however, has little bearing on the way in which the particular passage is reformulated in the *Damascus Document*.

TABLE 14. *1 Sam 25:26 and CD 9:8–10*

1 Sam 25:26 (𝔐)	CD 9:8–10
ועתה אדני חי יהוה וחי נפשך אשר מנעך יהוה מבוא בדמים והושע ידך לך ועתה יהיו כנבל איביך והמבקשים אל אדני רעה	9 אשר אמר לא תושיעך ידך לך
	As to that which he said, "Let not your hand help you
	10 הושיע ידו לו
I swear, my lord, as the Lord lives and as you live – the Lord who has kept you from bloodguilt and from gaining your victory with your own hands – let your enemies and all who would harm my lord fare like Nabal!	has let his hand help him

Note: The translation of the underlined portion of 1 Sam 25:26 follows McCarter Jr., *I Samuel*, 391.

through violent means.[32] This formal language identifies God as the one who prevented David from seeking redress from his enemies through violent means.[33]

As outlined in Table 14, the *Damascus Document* has reformulated the context of Abigail's oath such that it now describes a more general situation of an oath administered without judicial oversight. The fact that 1 Sam 25:26 is itself a formal oath was likely the primary motivation for the *Damascus Document* to turn to this passage.[34] In 1 Sam 25:26, God is identified as one who has prevented the execution of violent vigilante justice. This act is construed in the *Damascus Document* as equivalent to the administration of an oath not before judges. Just as Abigail condemns delivering one's hand for personal redress, so too the *Damascus Document* denounces raising one's hand in order to articulate a judicially unsupervised oath. In both these situations, the shared physical act of raising one's hand is highlighted. The exegetical link may have also been strengthened by the visually and aurally similar roots ישע ("to raise") and שבע ("to swear"). The *Damascus Document* identifies raising one's hand for a judicially unsupervised oath as equivalent to raising one's hand for violent ends.[35] The passage in the *Damascus Document* therefore concludes by

32 The expression is found as well in 1 Sam 25:31 (following 𝔊; see McCarter, *I Samuel*, 395) and 33 and Jud 7:2. See also Job 40:14, where the expression appears with ימין rather than יד, and Ps 44:4, where זרוע is employed.

33 The emphasis on preventing violent and unwarranted redress in Abigail's oath is likely an additional motivation for placing this law immediately following the sectarian interpretation of the laws of revenge and bearing of grudge in Lev 19:18 found earlier in CD 9:2–8.

34 Thus, I view 1 Sam 25:26 as the source of the *Damascus Document* and not 1 Sam 25:31, 33, which contain nearly identical formulations of this expression.

35 See also Joseph M. Baumgarten, "A 'Scriptural' Citation in 4Q Fragments of the Damascus Document," *JJS* 43 (1992): 95–98 (97); idem, *Qumran Cave 4.XIII*, 106; Moshe J. Bernstein

asserting that if an individual engages in this proscribed act, he "has let his hand help him" (הושיע ידו לו), the very act condemned in 1 Sam 25:26. Thus, the more precise scriptural citation from 1 Sam 25:26 actually appears at the end of the passage, rather than immediately following the citation formula in lines 8–9.[36]

How then should we understand the legal and exegetical role of the initial "citation" of 1 Sam 25:26 and interpret its significantly modified character? The *Damascus Document* views 1 Sam 25:26 as the scriptural basis for this larger law and draws upon this scriptural language in order to articulate its specific real-world application. In so doing, the *Damascus Document* has retained some of the contextual meaning of 1 Sam 25:26 but ultimately provides it with an entirely new meaning and application. Drawing upon this newly construed legal application of 1 Sam 25:26, the *Damascus Document* reformulates the scriptural language such that it now expresses in clear and precise language the prohibition against administering oaths without judicial oversight. לא תושיעך ידך לך is a citation neither of a textually corrupt version of 1 Sam 25:26 nor of a secondary sectarian work; it is a citation of 1 Sam 25:26 reformulated to express its new meaning as understood by the sectarian community. Because this is the "real" meaning of 1 Sam 25:26, the reformulated passage is introduced with the standard citation formula that one would expect for all direct scriptural citations.

Concerning Sacrifice through Agents: CD 11:18–21 (par. 4Q271 5 i 12–15)[37]

18 אל ישלח
19 איש למזבח עולה ומנחה ולבונה ועץ ביד איש טמא באחת

and Shlomo A. Koyfman, "The Interpretation of Biblical Law in the Dead Sea Scrolls: Forms and Methods," in *Biblical Interpretation at Qumran* (ed. M. Henze; Grand Rapids: Eerdmans, 2005), 61–87 (74).

[36] The minimal transformation of *1 Samuel*'s second-person possessive suffixes to the third person in the *Damascus Document* is clearly driven by the formal language (i.e., third person) in which the law is presented in the *Damascus Document*. The closely related expression והו[שיעה ידו לוא [=לו] is found in 1QS 6:27 to describe an individual who has taken the law into his own hands. Based on the shared language of the *Rule of the Community* and the *Damascus Document* and the inexact correspondence with the scriptural text in the *Damascus Document*, Jacob Licht argues that both texts are drawing upon a third sectarian work, which they each employ for different legal purposes (*The Rule Scroll: A Scroll from the Wilderness of Judaea* [Jerusalem: Bialik Institute, 1965], 159–60 [Hebrew]). This argument is likewise advanced in Schiffman, *Sectarian Law*, 39–40, who follows Ginzberg's original understanding of the "apocryphal" source of the "citation" (see above, n. 28). It is more likely, however, that 1QS 6:27 is merely drawing upon the common scriptural idiom (see P. Wernberg-Møller, *The Manual of Discipline* [STDJ 1; Leiden: Brill, 1957], 112). The appearance of the citation formula in CD 9:8–9 indicates that, while it is also employing the scriptural idiom, this passage is specifically intended as a scriptural citation.

[37] Hebrew text follows Qimron, "CDC," 31. For 4Q271, see Baumgarten, *Qumran Cave 4.XIII*, 180–81 (no variants exist).

20 מן הטמאות להרשותו לטמא את המזבח כי כתוב זבח
21 רשעים תועבה ותפלת צדקם כמנחת רצון

18. Let no man send
19. to the altar a burnt offering, a meal offering, frankincense, or wood through a man defiled with one
20. of the impurities, so as to permit him to defile that altar, for it is written: "The sacrifice of
21. wicked ones is an abomination, but the prayer of righteous ones is like a pleasing meal offering" (Prov 15:8).

This passage represents the first law in the *Damascus Document* following the close of the Sabbath Code.[38] It describes a situation in which an individual appoints an agent to present an offering in the Temple. In these circumstances, the agent must not be defiled with any impurity. In such a case, the impure agent would thereby defile the altar. Following this legal formulation, the text introduces a modified citation from Prov 15:8 preceded by a citation formula that identifies the function of the scriptural passage as a prooftext (כי כתוב, "for it is written"). Prov 15:8 as preserved in the Masoretic Text and ancient versions reflects a slightly different ending than the text cited in the *Damascus Document*: זבח רשעים תועבת יהוה ותפלת ישרים רצונו, "The sacrifice of the wicked is an abomination to the Lord, but the *prayer of the upright* pleases him."[39]

Three interrelated questions present themselves in the interpretation of this passage. First, what is the real-world application of this case, if any? If the sectarian community withdrew from participation in the Temple cult, then what is the nature of this legislation? Second, what role does the prooftext from *Proverbs* play in the larger legal formulation? Third, what legal-exegetical significance, if any, should be attached to the seemingly modified character of the scriptural citation?

[38] Commentators have noted that this alignment is clearly not an accident. The final passage in the Sabbath Code legislates concerning sacrifices on the Sabbath (CD 11:17–18). The shared focus on sacrificial altar laws likely contributed to the placement of the law of agents for sacrifice here. See Ginzberg, *Jewish Sect*, 70; Baumgarten and Schwartz, "Damascus Document," 51 n. 177; Hempel, *Laws*, 34.

[39] Prov 15:8 is partially preserved in 4QProv^{b} (4Q103) 5–6, 7 i + 8–10 13, though the second half of the verse is lost in the lacuna. Patrick W. Skehan and Eugene Ulrich restore according to 𝔐 (Patrick W. Skehan and Eugene Ulrich, "4Q103: 4QProv^{b}," in *Cave 4.XI: Psalms to Chronicles* [ed. E. Ulrich et al.; DJD 14; Oxford: Clarendon, 2000], 185). The Septuagint and Targum both essentially match 𝔐. Note, however, that the Vulgate preserves a text that reflects the *Damascus Document*'s absolute use of רצון rather than 𝔐's form with a possessive suffix (*vota justorum placabilia*). Two minor variants exist in the citation of Prov 15:8 in the *Damascus Document*: (1) תועבת יהוה in 𝔐 *Proverbs* appears in the *Damascus Document* merely as תועבה. This likely reflects a deliberate attempt to avoid reproducing the Tetragrammaton (see further below). (2) ישרים in 𝔐 *Proverbs* appears as צדקם in the *Damascus Document*. This may reflect a citation error. Rabin notes the possible influence of Prov 15:29: ותפלת צדיקים ישמע (*Zadokite Documents*, 58).

In his treatment of this passage, Schechter suggests that it indicates that the sect offered sacrifices at its own sanctuary.[40] The implausibility of this proposal has been repeatedly demonstrated.[41] In contrast, Ginzberg argues that when the sect initially withdrew from Jerusalem and the Temple, some community members remained faithful to the Temple and continued to send sacrifices through emissaries. It is this specific practice that the *Damascus Document* condemns.[42] If Ginzberg is correct, it is not clear why this act would be condemned only if the agent possessed some impurity. Would not all forms of contact with the Temple and its cult be denounced?

Ginzberg's analysis of this passage seems to be too heavily influenced by the belief that the community shunned all aspects of sacrifice and related sacrificial laws. The mass of material in some of the sectarian Dead Sea Scrolls (e.g., *4QMiqṣat Ma'ase Ha-Torah* and the *Damascus Document*) indicates a heightened interest in sacrifice and its attendant rules and regulations. Three approaches have been taken in response to this feature, each of which reflects assumptions regarding the nature of the sectarian community and its historical development. Philip Davies argues that the *Damascus Document* describes a particular community that continued to participate in the Temple to some extent and therefore legislated accordingly.[43] Similarly, Joseph Baumgarten suggests that these laws stem from a period before the sect withdrew completely from Jerusalem and Temple worship. For Baumgarten, however, the *Damascus Document* reflects the later sectarian preservation of these laws in anticipation of a future time in which they would return to a purified temple.[44] In contrast, Lawrence Schiffman views both the *Damascus Document* and these particular laws as stemming from the sectarian community after it had already shunned all participation in the Jerusalem Temple. As such, the laws do not come from a time in which the sect was active in the cult. Rather, drawing a parallel to rabbinic literature, he suggests that, following its withdrawal from the Temple, the sectarian community legislated for a time in the future when

40 Schechter, *Documents*, 47.

41 See especially Joseph M. Baumgarten, "Sacrifice and Worship among the Jewish Sectarians of the Dead Sea (Qumran) Scrolls," in *Studies in Qumran Law* (SJLA 24; Leiden: Brill, 1977), 39–56 (43) (1953); Jodi Magness, "Communal Meals and Sacred Space at Qumran," in *Debating Qumran: Collected Essays on Its Archaeology* (Leuven: Peeters 2004), 81–112 (92–99) (2001); Magness, "Dogs and Chickens at Qumran," in *The Dead Sea Scrolls and Contemporary Culture*, 349–62. For an attempt to defend the presence of animal sacrifice among the sectarians, see Frank Moore Cross, *The Ancient Library of Qumran* (3d ed.; Minneapolis: Fortress, 1995), 85–86.

42 Ginzberg, *Jewish Sect*, 70. Ginzberg refers to Josephus, *Jewish Antiquities* 18.18–19, where Josephus notes that some Essenes offered sacrifices in the Temple through emissaries (cf. Rabin, *Zadokite Documents*, 58).

43 See Philip R. Davies, "The Ideology of the Temple in the Damascus Document," *JJS* 33 (1982): 287–301; idem, "The Judaism(s) of the Damascus Document," in *The Damascus Document: A Centennial of Discovery*, 27–43 (34).

44 Baumgarten, "Sacrifice," 43–44.

the sanctity of the sacrificial cult would be restored.[45] According to Davies and Baumgarten, CD 11:18–21 represents prescriptive legislation, while Schiffman regards the laws as framed in idealistic terms. Yet, for all three approaches, CD 11:18–21 represents a serious attempt to provide legislation related to sacrificial worship.

What is the *Damascus Document* actually legislating here? The emphasis on the defiled status of the emissary is the central element in this passage. The use of the defiled emissary creates a situation in which the altar will also be defiled. Thus, the *Damascus Document* does not condemn the sacrificial system outright but merely legislates against the bringing of sacrifices by unclean parties.[46]

How are we to understand the role of the citation from *Proverbs*? Prov 15:8 creates an oppositional relationship between the offerings of the righteous and those of the wicked. Those of the former are readily accepted, while those of the latter are rejected. The "wicked" individual in *Proverbs* is construed as the "defiled" emissary in the *Damascus Document*.[47] The scriptural passage is introduced in the *Damascus Document* in order to reinforce the notion that the sacrificial offerings of those who are unfit (*Proverbs* "wicked" = CD "defiled") are illegitimate and proscribed.[48] As abominations administered by impure individuals, they will ultimately result in the defilement of the altar.

In drawing upon the passage from *Proverbs*, however, the *Damascus Document* achieves more. While lending scriptural support to its sacrificial legislation, it draws upon the same scriptural passage in order to present its broader approach to the optimal way of divine worship. This is achieved by the exegetical expansion that appears in the citation of Prov 15:8b:

Proverbs creates an oppositional relationship between the wicked and the upright – the prayers of the former are acceptable, while the sacrifices of the latter are an abomination. The theological position articulated in *Proverbs* is part of a larger critique of a sacrificial cult that is inattentive to the inner disposition of the worshipper. It simultaneously acknowledges the historical reality of the emergence of prayer as a modified mode of ritual piety. The opposition generated in the passage, however, indicates that prayer had not yet

45 Lawrence H. Schiffman, "The Dead Sea Scrolls and Rabbinic *Halakhah*," in *The Dead Sea Scrolls as Background to Postbiblical Judaism and Early Christianity: Papers from an International Conference at St. Andrews in 2001* (ed. J. R. Davila; STDJ 46; Leiden: Brill, 2003), 3–24 (16–17). On the rabbinic evidence, see Jacob Neusner, "Map Without Territory: Mishnah's System of Sacrifice and Sanctuary," in *Method and Meaning in Ancient Judaism* (Atlanta: Scholars Press, 1979), 133–54.

46 See also Baumgarten, "Sacrifice," 43; Fitzmyer, "Old Testament Quotations," 42; Hempel, *Laws*, 37; Bernstein and Koyfman, "Interpretation of Biblical Law," 74.

47 This equation is consistent with the common sectarian association of ritual impurity with moral sin. See Jonathan Klawans, *Impurity and Sin in Ancient Judaism* (Oxford: Oxford University Press, 2000), 67–91.

48 See Hempel, *Laws*, 37.

TABLE 15. *Prov 15:8 and CD 11:20–21*

Prov 15:8 (𝔐)	Prov 15:8 in CD 11:20–21
זבח רשעים תועבת יהוה ותפלת ישרים רצונו	זבח רשעים תועבה ותפלת צדקם כמנחת רצון
The sacrifice of the wicked is an abomination to the Lord, but the prayer of the upright pleases him.	The sacrifice of wicked ones is an abomination, but the prayer of righteous ones is like a pleasing meal offering.

emerged as a serious challenge to the ritual piety of sacrifice. The key element in *Proverbs* is that it is always better to be upright than wicked. The upright receive divine favor even if they engage in a less-than-optimal mode of worship – prayer. Sacrifice alone cannot guarantee the well-being of the wicked.

As outlined in Table 15, the *Damascus Document* takes the implications of *Proverbs* one step further and applies it to the cultic ideology of the community. For the *Damascus Document*, *Proverbs* asserts that the prayer of the righteous one is not only pleasing (ותפלת ישרים רצונו). Prayer is now entirely equivalent to sacrifice as a mode of cultic piety (ותפלת צדקם כמנחת רצון, "But the prayer of righteous ones is like a pleasing meal offering"). The interpretive variant found in the citation of *Proverbs* emphasizes the sect's belief that prayer has replaced sacrifice while the Temple remains defiled.[49] The modified text of Prov 15:8 does not state that prayer is better than a meal offering. Rather, it clearly maintains that prayer is "like" an agreeable meal offering. Prayer functions as a viable substitute for sacrifice until the sacrificial cult is purified and reconstituted under sectarian aegis. Indeed, in the law that follows, the *Damascus Document* (l. 22) refers to the "house of prostration" (בית השתחות), likely a reference to a physical space where prayer was offered in lieu of Temple worship.[50]

Based on this understanding of the role of the citation of Prov 15:8, can we better ascertain the legal force of the scriptural source? First, it is intended to lend scriptural support to the exclusion of defiled persons from acting as emissaries for sacrifices. In this sense, it functions as a scriptural prooftext. The second half of the scriptural passage is introduced in order to articulate more clearly the sectarian attitude toward the state of the sacrificial cult and the community's promotion of alternative modes of cultic piety.

49 It is therefore significant that this passage reflects parallel language with 1QS 9:4–5, the classical statement on the sectarian emphasis on prayer as a substitute for sacrifice (noted by Rabin, *Zadokite Documents*, 58; É. Cothenet, "Le Document de Damas," in *Les Textes de Qumran traduits et annotés*, volume 2 [ed. J. Carmignac, É. Cothenet, and H. Lignée; Paris: Letouzey et Ané, 1963], 2:195).

50 On this expression, see Annette Steudel, "The Houses of Prostration – CD XI,21–XII,1: Duplicates of the Temple," *RevQ* 16 (1993): 49–68; Daniel K. Falk, *Daily, Sabbath, and Festival Prayers in the Dead Sea Scrolls* (STDJ 27; Leiden: Brill), 242–46.

Why, however, is the *Damascus Document* compelled to provide a scriptural prooftext for this particular law? Surely, this law could be presented like so many others in the *Damascus Document* in a purely apodictic form. The treatment of Temple and sacrificial law in this passage, however, demanded more. The previous law, the last in the Sabbath Code, introduces laws regarding sacrifices on the Sabbath. As suggested above, the discussion of sacrificial laws likely served as the bridge to the present law regarding defiled emissaries. Both of these laws legislate for a situation when the sacrificial cult would be fully functional and presumably administered under sectarian aegis. Yet, in its current sectarian form, the *Damascus Document* was well aware of the fact that the Temple was not currently operating according to sectarian standards and that the two laws introduced here were ideal at best. The citation from Prov 15:8, with its promotion of prayer as an alternative and equivalent mode of cultic piety, therefore serves as a coda to these two ideal sacrificial laws. While the citation acts as the scriptural prooftext for the prohibition against unclean emissaries, it fulfills a much larger theological and ideological function.

Concerning Interaction with Outsiders: 1QS 5:16–18 (par. 4Q256 4 ix 10–11; 4Q258 1a i, 1b i 9–10)[51]

16 ואשר לוא יוכל[52] מהונם כול ולוא ישתה[53] ולוא יקח מידם כול מאומה[54]
17 אשר לוא במחיר כאשר כתוב <u>חדלו לכם מן האדם אשר נשמה באפו כי במה נחשב הואה</u> כיא
18 כול אשר לוא נחשבו בבריתו להבדיל אותם ואת כול אשר להם

16. No one must eat or drink anything of their property, or accept anything whatever from their hand
17. without payment, as it is written: "<u>Have nothing to do with the man whose breath is in his nostrils, for wherein can he be accounted?</u>" (Isa 2:22) For
18. all those who are not accounted within his covenant, they and everything they have must be excluded.

[51] Hebrew text and translation follow Elisha Qimron and James H. Charlesworth, "Rule of the Community (1QS; cf. 4QMSS A–J, 5Q11)," in *The Dead Sea Scrolls: Hebrew, Aramaic, and Greek Texts with English Translations; Rule of the Community and Related Documents* (ed. J. H. Charlesworth; PTSDSSP 1; Tübingen: Mohr Siebeck; Louisville: Westminster John Knox, 1994), 22–23. For 4Q256 and 4Q258, see Philip S. Alexander and Geza Vermes, *Qumran Cave 4.XIX: Serekh Ha-Yaḥad and Two Related Texts* (DJD 26; Oxford: Clarendon, 1998), 53, 94.

[52] 4Q258: ואל יואכל איש מאנשי הקדש. 4Q256 preserves]נשי הקודש[and likely contained the same text as 4Q258. יואכל is the more common form in Qumran Hebrew.

[53] Space does not permit the reconstruction of כול or ולוא ישתה in the lacunae in 4Q256 and 4Q258.

[54] 4Q258 preserves the initial *lamed* of ולוא and traces of the final *he* of מאומה, though with only approximately sixteen letter spaces in between. There is therefore not enough space to reconstruct this entire clause. Alexander and Vermes therefore do not reconstruct כול in the lacuna. Following this clause, 4Q256 and 4Q258 do not contain any text parallel to 1QS 5:16b–18b. The text continues with the law that follows in 1QS 5:18b: ...ולא ישען.

I have reproduced the text here as it appears in the Cave 1 version of the *Rule of the Community* (1QS). The parallel text in 4Q256 (4QS^{b}) and 4Q258 (4QS^{d}) contains significant variants and does not reflect text equivalent to lines 16b–18b, which is indicative of the different recensional character of these two manuscripts.[55] Therefore, I analyze this text first according to the Cave 1 recension before commenting on the Cave 4 recension.

This passage forbids certain interactions with nonsectarians that will jeopardize the ritual integrity of the community – accepting food or drink from nonsectarians or any gifts without full payment.[56] Exception is allowed only in the case of purchase because the item now becomes the full property of the sectarian.[57] The law is then supported by a passage from Isa 2:22, which enjoins against the glorification of mortal "man" at the expense of God: חדלו לכם[58] מן האדם אשר נשמה באפו כי במה נחשב הוא, "Oh, cease to glorify man, who has only a breath in his nostrils! For by what does he merit esteem?" (𝔐; 1QIsa^{a}).[59]

The legal-exegetical reading of *Isaiah* is twofold and builds upon two key-words from the two stichs in the scriptural passage. The "man" in verse 22a is the larger segment of humanity that persists in misdirected worship – the "other" more broadly in *Isaiah*. The *Rule of the Community* has reformulated the scriptural passage such that this condemned "man" is now an equally illegitimate nonsectarian. This exegesis is reinforced by the reconfiguration of נחשב in verse 22b, which identifies that "man" as unworthy of esteem ("for by what does he merit esteem"). The *Rule of the Community* retains this verb with the "man" still as the subject. Now, however, the nonsectarian "man" is one who is not "accounted" (נחשבו) as one among the covenanters (l. 18). In so doing, the *Rule of the Community* draws upon identical language employed earlier in the column to describe nonsectarians: כיא לוא החשבו בבריתו, "For they are not accounted within his covenant" (1QS 5:11).[60] Just as *Isaiah*'s audience

[55] See further Sarianna Metso, *The Textual Development of the Qumran Community Rule* (STDJ 21; Leiden: Brill, 1997), 82–83; Alexander and Vermes, *Qumran Cave 4.XIX*, 97. These two manuscripts are generally shorter than other versions of the *Rule of the Community*. The large degree of agreement between 4Q256 and 4Q258 (especially versus other manuscripts) suggests that they belong to a single recension. There are, however, some significant differences between these two manuscripts. Alexander and Vermes therefore posit two further subrecensions for this single recension (see *Qumran Cave 4.XIX*, 10). On this specific passage, see the brief treatment in Sarianna Metso, *The Serekh Texts* (CQS 9; LSTS 62; London: T. and T. Clark, 2007), 42–43.

[56] See Licht, *Megillat ha-Serakhim*, 132–33. On the concern of mingling with the property of outsiders, see also 1QS 6:17; 7:25; 8:23.

[57] See A. R. C. Leaney, *The Rule of Qumran and Its Meaning* (NTL; Philadelphia: Westminster, 1966), 174–75; Michael A. Knibb, *The Qumran Community* (CCWJCW 2; Cambridge: Cambridge University Press, 1987), 112.

[58] 1QIsa^{a}: להמה.

[59] This passage is not present in the Septuagint, and commentators often regard it as a gloss in *Isaiah*. The passage, however, is present in 1QIsa^{a} and 𝔐. The citation in the *Rule of the Community* follows 𝔐 and 1QIsa^{a} closely (with minimal variants, as noted above).

[60] This wordplay has long been noted by commentators. See Licht, *Megillat ha-Serakhim*, 134; Fitzmyer, "Old Testament Citations," 34; Knibb, *Qumran Community*, 112; Metso, *Textual*

is instructed to pay no attention to the ephemeral "man" who spurns God, so too the sectarian community is exhorted to maintain a safe distance from those outside of the community. As such, Isa 2:22, as understood according to its sectarian interpretation, functions as the scriptural prooftext for the sectarian rules regarding contact with nonsectarians.

One issue that remains to be considered is the significance of the recension of the *Rule of the Community* represented by the Cave 4 manuscripts (4Q256, 4Q258). As noted, these manuscripts preserve a truncated version of the passage in the Cave 1 version (1QS). In this recension, the sectarians are only instructed not to eat with nonsectarians or accept anything from them:

[וא]שר לוא יוחד [עמו בהון ובעבודה ואל יואכל איש מא]נשי הקודש [מהונם ולוא יקח מידם מאומה]

> [Further]more, he shall not be united [with him in possessions or in work. Neither shall eat any man of the m]en of holiness [from their possessions, nor take from their hand anything]. (4Q256 4 ix 10–11; par. 4Q258 1a i, 1b i 9–10)[61]

In the Cave 4 recension, there is no mention of drinking or of the allowance that exists if the transferred item is purchased by the sectarian. Moreover, the passage from *Isaiah* is not cited. It is tempting to interpret this omission as a deliberate attempt to refrain from employing a non-Pentateuchal passage as a legal prooftext. If the 4Q256 and 4Q258 recension is earlier than 1QS, as argued by Sarianna Metso, then 1QS would indicate that the community gradually accepted the use of non-Pentateuchal passages in this way.[62] If the recension of 1QS is earlier, as argued by Philip Alexander, then the community would have grown to reject the use of non-Pentateuchal passages in its legal hermeneutics.[63] Either of these models, however, seems unlikely. The shorter recension merely reflects a more underdeveloped version of this sectarian rule. Moreover, the *Rule of the Community* generally does not cite scriptural prooftexts. Thus, it seems more likely that the significant issue is the mere introduction of an explicit prooftext in the Cave 1 recension. Indeed, the use of Isa 2:22 in 1QS 5:16–18 is part of a broader introduction of scriptural prooftexts in the expanded version of the *Rule of the Community* preserved in 1QS 5.[64] Thus, while Isa 2:22 is clearly tied to its legal context in 1QS 5:16–18 through the

Development, 82–83; Qimron and Charlesworth, "Rule of the Community," 23 n. 114. For an attempt to find an exegetical basis in the broader setting of Isa 2, see Alec J. Lucas, "Scripture Citations as an Internal Redactional Control: 1QS 5:1–20a and Its 4Q Parallels," *DSD* 17 (2010): 30–52 (49–50).

[61] Hebrew text and translation follow Alexander and Vermes, *Qumran Cave 4.XIX*, 58. The text is cited from 4Q256, with parallel material from 4Q258 (as marked by overlining) aiding in a fuller restoration of the passage.

[62] See Metso, *Textual Development*, 144.

[63] See Philip S. Alexander, "The Redaction-History of the *Serekh Ha-Yaḥad*: A Proposal," *RevQ* 17 (1996; Milik volume): 437–56 (especially 447).

[64] See further Sarianna Metso, "Biblical Quotations in the Community Rule," in *The Bible as Book: The Hebrew Bible and the Judaean Desert* (ed. E. D. Herbert and E. Tov; London:

wordplay associated with the root חשב, there is nothing in the law itself that suggests the need for a scriptural prooftext.

Concerning Measurements: 4Q159 1 ii 13; 4Q513 1–2 i 4; 4Q271 2 2

4Q159[65]]האיפה והבת תכון א[חד
4Q513[66]]האיפה והב[ת תכון אחד
4Q271[67]]האיפה והבת תכון אחד

4Q159, 4Q513, 4Q271: the *ephah* and the *bath* are one measure.

The three texts identify the *ephah* and *bath* as equivalent measurements based on language from Ezek 45:11:

<u>האיפה והבת תכן אחד</u> יהיה לשאת מעשר החמר הבת ועשירת החמר האיפה אל החמר יהיה מתכנתו

<u>The *ephah* and the *bath* shall comprise the same volume</u>, the *bath* a tenth of a *ḥomer* and the *ephah* a tenth of a *ḥomer* their capacity shall be gauged by the *ḥomer*. (𝔐)

In each case, the scriptural passage is understood to be a source of normative law regarding measurements. In *4QOrdinances*[a] (4Q159), the passage appears in an extremely fragmentary context. Schiffman suggests that the larger pericope treats "fair and honest measures."[68] Accordingly, it includes the precise measurements of the *ephah* and *bath*. A similar concern for identifying the precise meaning of measurements is found in the related text known as *4QOrdinances*[b] (4Q513). This text seems to be a longer recension of the text reflected in *4QOrdinances*[a].[69] 4Q513 1–2 i, similar to the text just discussed, is devoted entirely to clarifying the precise character of several measurements. Here as well (l. 4), the passage from *Ezekiel* is cited verbatim.

One final citation of Ezek 45:11 is found in a portion of the Qumran fragments of the *Damascus Document* (4Q271). The passage deals with various

British Library; New Castle: Oak Knoll Press, 2002), 81–92; Lucas, "Scripture Citations as an Internal Redactional Control," 30–52.

65 See Lawrence H. Schiffman, "Ordinances and Rules," in *Rule of the Community*, 152. See also the *editio princeps* in John M. Allegro with Arnold A. Anderson, "4Q159: Ordinances," in *Qumran Cave 4.I (4Q158–4Q186)* (ed. John M. Allegro with A. A. Anderson; DJD 5; Oxford: Clarendon, 1968), 7.

66 See Schiffman, "Ordinances and Rules," 158. See the *editio princeps* in Maurice Baillet, "4Q513: Ordonnances (ii)," in *Qumrân grotte 4.III (4Q282–4Q520)* (ed. M. Baillet; DJD 7; Oxford: Clarendon, 1982), 287.

67 See Baumgarten, *Qumran Cave 4.XIII*, 173. See also Hempel, *Laws*, 56–59.

68 Schiffman, "Ordinances and Rules," 153 n. 26.

69 Baillet, *Qumrân grotte 4.III*, 287; Schiffman, "Ordinances and Rules," 147.

laws regarding tithing. Line 1 states that the farmer should take a tenth of a *ḥomer* from the threshing floor. This measurement, according to Baumgarten's reconstruction, is equated with both the *ephah* and *bath*. The extant text resumes with the citation of the passage from *Ezekiel*. Immediately preceding the passage, Baumgarten restores a citation formula (כאשר הקים אל, "as God established"). Whether or not we accept Baumgarten's reconstruction here, the force of the citation of *Ezekiel* is clear. As in the employment of this passage in *4QOrdinances$^{a\text{-}b}$*, the verse serves to identify the precise parameters of these measurements and their relationship to the larger legal context.

None of these passages reflects any exegetical interpretation and reformulation of Ezek 45:11. On the contrary, they seem to view Ezek 45:11 merely as an authoritative source for precise data concerning measurements and their equivalencies. The pervasiveness of this precise formulation suggests that it may have already been known to the community as a standard statement regarding measurements. In this respect, while Ezek 45:11 is the original scriptural source, its legal and exegetical influence is minimal.[70]

III. NON-PENTATEUCHAL PASSAGES AS SECONDARY PROOFTEXTS

Concerning Illegal Marriages: 4QMiqṣat Ma'ase Ha-Torah (4QMMT) B 75–82 (= 4Q396 1–2 iv 4–11; 4Q397 6–13 12–15)[71]

75 ועל הזונות הנעסה בתוך העם והמה ב[ני זרע]
76 קדש משכתוב[72] קודש ישראל ועל בה[מתו הטהור]ה
77 כתוב שלוא לרעבה[73] כלאים ועל לבוש[ו כתוב לוא]
78 יהיה שעטנז ושלוא לזרוע שדו וכ[רמו כלאים]

[70] For further treatment of divinely ordained measurements in the Dead Sea Scrolls, including discussion of the role of the language of Ezek 45:11 in nonlegal contexts, see Menahem Kister, "Physical and Metaphysical Measurements Ordained by God in the Literature of the Second Temple Period," in *Reworking the Bible: Apocryphal and Related Texts at Qumran: Proceedings of a Joint Symposium by the Orion Center for the Study of the Dead Sea Scrolls and Associated Literature and the Hebrew University Institute for Advanced Studies Research Group on Qumran, 15–17 January, 2002* (ed. E. G. Chazon, D. Dimant, and R. A. Clements; STDJ 58; Leiden: Brill, 2005), 153–76, especially 168.

[71] Text follows the composite text of Elisha Qimron and John Strugnell, *Qumran Cave 4.V: Miqṣat Ma'aśe Ha-Torah* (DJD 10; Oxford: Clarendon, 1996), 54–57. The composite text here follows closely 4Q396. In addition to the translation from Qimron and Strugnell, I include Christine Hayes's translation for lines 80–82. On these distinctions, see discussion below.

[72] 4Q397 has כשכתוב.

[73] 4Q397 has להרביע]ה. On the linguistic significance of the *hiph'il* infinitive rather than the *pi'el*, see George J. Brooke, "The Explicit Presentation of Scripture in 4QMMT," in *Legal Texts and Legal Issues: Proceedings of the Second Meeting of the International Organization for Qumran Studies, Cambridge, 1995; Published in Honour of Joseph M. Baumgarten* (ed. M. J. Bernstein, F. García Martínez, and J. Kampen; STDJ 23; Leiden: Brill), 67–88 (75).

79 [ב]גלל שהמה קדושים ובני אהרון ק[דושי קדושים]
80 [ו]אתם יודעים שמקצת הכהנים ו[העם מתערבים]
81 [והם]מתוככים ומטמאי[ם] את זרע [הקודש ואף]
82 את [זרע]ם עם הזונות כ[י לבני אהרון]

75. And concerning the practice of illegal marriage (lit. unlawful intercourse) that exists among the people: (this practice exists) despite their being so[ns] of holy [seed]
76. as it is written, "<u>Israel is holy</u>" (Jer 2:3). And concerning his (i.e., Israel's) [clean ani]mal,
77. it is written that one must not let it mate with another species; and concerning his clothes [it is written that they should not]
78. be of mixed stuff; and he must not sow his field and vine[yard with mixed specie]s.
79. Because they (Israel) are holy, and the sons of Aaron are [most holy.]

Strugnell/Qimron	**Hayes**[74]
80. But you know that some of the priests and [the laity mingle with each other	80. And you know that some of the priests and [the people intermarry
81. and they] unite with each other and pollute the [holy] seed [as well as]	81. and] mix and defile the [holy] seed and also even]
82. their own [seed] with women whom they are forbidden to marry. Since [the sons of Aaron should . . .]	82. their own (i.e., the priests' most holy) [seed], with female outsiders. Since [the sons of Aaron should . . .]

This passage, the last of *4QMiqṣat Ma'ase Ha-Torah*'s list of laws, condemns the practice of illegal marriages (זונות), which is regarded as equivalent to the forbidden mixture of species. The nature of the illicit relations is not immediately clear and has been the subject of a long-standing scholarly debate. Elisha Qimron and John Strugnell understand the restriction as a reference to marriage between priests and nonpriests.[75] They note that the extant text on line 80 refers to "some of the priests," and they restore the following lacuna with the condemnation of the commingling of the priests and nonpriests. Moreover, they call attention to a range of plausible evidence suggesting that this practice was condemned in the Second Temple period.[76] Since the publication

[74] See Christine Hayes, *Gentile Impurities and Jewish Identities: Intermarriage and Conversion from the Bible to the Talmud* (Oxford: Oxford University Press, 2002), 84. I have added brackets in the translation to correspond with the lacunae.

[75] Qimron and Strugnell, *Qumran Cave 4.V*, 171–75.

[76] To be sure, the historical origins of such a law are unclear. Lev 21:14 requires the high priest to marry only priestly women. No such law, however, exists for the normal priest. Qimron and Strugnell adduce several possible scriptural sources for this expanded law. See further discussion in Lawrence H. Schiffman, "Prohibited Marriages in the Dead Sea Scrolls," in

of the *editio princeps* of 4QMMT, several scholars have voiced agreement with Qimron's and Strugnell's interpretation and often augment their admittedly speculative proposal.[77] Martha Himmelfarb, for example, observes that marriage between Jews and non-Jews was rare in the Second Temple period, and thus it is unlikely that 4QMMT would polemicize against a practice with limited application.[78]

Joseph M. Baumgarten, however, suggests that the prohibition here condemns marriage between Jews and non-Jews.[79] He correctly observes that much of the comparative evidence cited by Qimron and Strugnell is either lacking as substantial support or equivocal at best. He also notes the incongruity created in line 75 where the heading "exists among the people" (בתוך העם) introduces a law specifically targeting priests. Thus, Baumgarten proposes that the condemned illicit relations in 4QMMT fit better with the more general meaning of זנות as relations between Jews and non-Jews.

Baumgarten's criticisms are well founded and severely challenge Qimron's and Strugnell's general interpretation of this passage. Yet, Baumgarten's rereading of the passage never fully considers the meaning of the clearly preserved references to the "sons of Aaron" in line 79 and "some of the priests" in line 80. He merely notes that the condemned intermarriage defiles the holy status of Israel and thus also the priesthood.[80] At least two lines of this passage refer specifically to priests (ll. 79–80), with the strong likelihood that priests are also

Rabbinic Perspectives: Rabbinic Literature and the Dead Sea Scrolls: Proceedings of the Eighth International Symposium of the Orion Center for the Study of the Dead Sea Scrolls and Associated Literature, 7–9 January, 2003 (ed. S. D. Fraade, A. Shemesh, and R. A. Clements; STDJ 62; Leiden: Brill, 2006), 113–25 (121–22).

77 See Moshe J. Bernstein, "The Employment and Interpretation of Scripture in 4QMMT: Preliminary Observations," in *Reading 4QMMT: New Perspectives on Qumran Law and History* (ed. J. Kampen and M. J. Bernstein; SBLSymS 2; Atlanta: Scholars Press, 1996), 29–51 (46); John Kampen, "4QMMT and New Testament Studies," in *Reading 4QMMT*, 129–44 (135–36); Cana Werman, "Jubilees 30: Building a Paradigm for the Ban on Intermarriage," *HTR* 90 (1997): 1–22 (14 n. 60); Hannah K. Harrington, "Biblical Law at Qumran," in *The Dead Sea Scrolls after Fifty Years: A Comprehensive Assessment* (ed. J. C. VanderKam and P. W. Flint; 2 vols.; Leiden: Brill, 1998–99), 1:160–85 (175). More tentative discussions are found in Eileen Schuller, "Women in the Dead Sea Scrolls," in *The Dead Sea Scrolls after Fifty Years*, 2:117–44 (134–35); Schiffman, "Prohibited Marriages," 121–22.

78 Martha Himmelfarb, "Levi, Phinehas, and the Problem of Intermarriage at the Time of the Maccabean Revolt," *JSQ* 6 (1999): 1–24.

79 Baumgarten's understanding is reported in Qimron and Strugnell, *Qumran Cave 4.V*, 55 n. 75, 171 n. 178a, and is discussed in greater detail in his review of DJD 10: "The 'Halakah' in Miqṣat Ma'aśe Ha-Torah," *JAOS* 116 (1996): 512–16 (515–16). Baumgarten's approach is further developed in Carolyn Sharp, "Phinehan Zeal and Rhetorical Strategy in 4QMMT," *RevQ* 18 (1997): 207–22; Hayes, *Gentile Impurities*, 82–89; William Loader, *The Dead Sea Scrolls on Sexuality: Attitudes towards Sexuality in Sectarian and Related Literature at Qumran* (Grand Rapids: Eerdmans, 2009), 65–75.

80 Baumgarten, "The 'Halakah' in Miqṣat Ma'aśe Ha-Torah," 515. My point is also observed in Hayes, *Gentile Impurities*, 83.

the subject of lines 81–82. Thus, it seems much more likely that a significant element of the condemned relations refers to priests.

The most plausible way to understand this fragmentary passage is to follow Christine Hayes in viewing it as consisting of two condemnations of illicit relations.[81] The first part is directed at lay Jews (ll. 75–78), while the second part of the passage focuses specifically on priests (ll. 79–82). Line 79 refers to the holiness of both lay Jews and priests, and it thus acts as a bridge between the two sections. Hayes thus suggests an alternative way to understand the reconstructed passage in line 80: [ו]אתם יודעים שמקצת הכהנים ו[העם מתערבים]. Qimron and Strugnell argue that in order for this passage to refer to intermarriage with non-Jews, the verb מתערבים ("to mingle") requires a prepositional phrase such as בגוים, "with non-Jews," to indicate a third group involved in the mingling. Yet, they assert that the length of the lacuna does not allow for its inclusion.[82] In contrast, Hayes proposes that both the priests and lay Jews are the subject of מתערבים, and the prepositional phrase is found in line 82: עם הזונות, "with (female) outsiders [i.e., gentile women]."[83] Lines 80–82 expand on the reference to intermarriage among lay Jews in lines 75–79 by asserting that the same practice exists among priests.

Thus, 4QMMT condemns the marriage of both lay and priestly Jews with non-Jews. Hayes suggests that the polemical nature of the legislation in 4QMMT is that it condemns these marriages even when the non-Jewish party has undertaken a conversion process.[84] The scriptural support for the institution of illegal marriages is arrived at by means of an analogy with the forbidden mixtures of unlike agricultural and animal species and textiles as articulated in lines 77–78. Just as certain species and threads must not be mixed, so too certain classes of humans should not be mixed.[85] Marriage with the unholy (i.e., dissimilar) seed of non-Jews profanes the holy seed of both priests and lay Jews and thus creates what Hayes refers to as "genealogical impurity."[86]

Regarding the application of the prohibition of intermarriage to priests, 4QMMT relies on Lev 21:7, which prohibits priests from marrying a זנה, a term understood by 4QMMT to designate a non-Jewish woman. Lev 21:7 explains this restriction by appealing to the holy status of the priests:

81 Hayes, *Gentile Impurities*, 82–89.

82 Qimron and Strugnell, *Qumran Cave 4.V*, 171 n. 178a.

83 Hayes, *Gentile Impurities*, 84.

84 Hayes, *Gentile Impurities*, 86–87.

85 This same analogical reasoning is found in the *Damascus Document*'s regulations concerning general improper marriages. See 4Q267 7 13; 4Q269 9 2–3; 4Q270 5 15–17; 4Q271 3 9–10. On this "analogical reasoning," see further Bernstein and Koyfman, "Interpretation of Biblical Law," 83. A similar analogy is found in later rabbinic law. See *Pereq 'Arayot* (*Derekh 'Ereṣ Rabbah*) 11, which identifies intercourse with a handmaiden as a violation of the prohibition of mixed species (among other things). See also Josephus, *Jewish Antiquities* 4.229, where he explains that the law of mixed species was enacted because combining unlike agricultural items may lead one to engage in forbidden human "mixtures."

86 Hayes, *Gentile Impurities*, 85.

אשה זנה וחללה לא יקחו . . . כי קדש הוא לאלהיו, "They shall not marry a woman defiled by harlotry ... for they are holy to their God." The extension of this restriction to lay Jews reflects a widespread tendency in the Second Temple period to extend priestly law and practices to lay Jews. Thus, lines 75–76 refer to the "holy" status of all Jews: והמה ב[ני זרע] קדש, "(This practice exists) despite their being so[ns] of holy [seed]." With regard to marriage restrictions, Hayes positions the attempt to "narrow the gap between Israel and priest" in 4QMMT as following a similar trend in *Ezra* and the book of *Jubilees*.[87]

Hayes's explanation of 4QMMT represents the most cogent consideration of the presence of both lay Jews and priests in this passage. She clearly demonstrates the legal and exegetical role of Lev 21:7. While Lev 21:7 is the conceptual underpinning of the entire passage, 4QMMT never cites it or even alludes to it. Two presumed scriptural citations appear earlier in the passage introduced by citation formulae (l. 76: משכתוב, l. 77: כתוב). The citation formula כתוב ("as it is written") in 4QMMT generally does not introduce explicit citations of scripture but is more commonly employed to introduce a general description or paraphrase of scripture.[88] This sense of the citation formula captures well the "citation" regarding mixed species in lines 77–78, which represents a paraphrase of Lev 19:19 and Deut 22:9.[89]

The first citation formula introduces the expression קודש ישראל, "Israel is holy" (l. 76). Consistent with the general sense of כתוב in 4QMMT, Qimron and Strugnell suggest that the "citation" here is merely a general allusion to Israel's sacred status as articulated throughout scripture.[90] In this particular case, however, the expression under consideration finds an exact parallel in a scriptural source, Jer 2:3: קדש ישראל ליהוה ראשית תבואתה, "Israel is holy to the Lord, the first fruits of his harvest." George Brooke further argues that if the passage is merely a general allusion to the scriptural idea that Israel is holy, then no citation formula would be present.[91] Indeed, כתוב otherwise appears in 4QMMT as a citation formula for scriptural paraphrases, not scriptural ideas. The textual agreement suggests that, notwithstanding the general principles of 4QMMT's citation formulae, this is in fact a verbatim citation.[92]

What role does this citation play in the formulation of the law? At first glance, the scriptural citation seems merely to support the general assertion in lines 75–76 that lay Jews are holy and thus should not engage in marriage with unholy non-Jews. While this is indeed a function of the citation, closer examination of the larger literary unit reveals a much more central role for this passage in the legal exegesis. As observed by Hayes, 4QMMT extends priestly

87 Hayes, *Gentile Impurities*, 85. On the influence of the description of intermarriage in Ezra 9:2, see below.

88 Qimron and Strugnell, *Qumran Cave 4.V*, 14–41. For further discussion of scripture in 4QMMT, see Bernstein, "Scripture in MMT"; Brooke, "Scripture in 4QMMT."

89 On these "citations," see Brooke, "Scripture in 4QMMT," 75–76.

90 Qimron and Strugnell, *Qumran Cave 4.V*, 55.

91 Brooke, "Scripture in 4QMMT," 74–75.

92 So also Bernstein, "Scripture in MMT," 45; Loader, *The Dead Sea Scrolls on Sexuality*, 66–67.

law to lay Jews by applying to lay Jews the same expectation of endogamous marriage. 4QMMT infuses this practice with scriptural support. For priests, the restriction on marriage with non-Jews is based on Lev 21:7. 4QMMT engages in a process of analogical reasoning to apply this same restriction to all Israelites. Lev 21:7 requires endogamous marriage because of the "holy" status of priests (כי קדש הוא, "For they are holy"). Jer 2:3 identifies *all* of Israel as holy (קדש ישראל, "Israel is holy"). Thus, the same laws that apply to the *holy* priests are incumbent upon the *holy* Israelites. The keyword קדש, "holy," provides the intertextual link between Lev 21:7 and Jer 2:3, thereby extending the expectation of endogamous marriage to all Jews.

The same concern for holiness likely accounts for the appearance in lines 75–76 and 81 of language from Ezra 9:2: והתערבו זרע הקדש בעמי הארצות, "So that the holy seed has become intermingled with the peoples of the land."[93] The mingling of the "holy seed" in Ezra 9:2 is employed to condemn marriage with non-Jews by both priests *and* lay Jews.[94] Thus, both possess holy seed that should not be mingled with that of outsiders. In spite of the seeming equation of priestly and lay holiness, line 80 affirms that a distinction still exists between the "holy" seed of lay Jews and the "most holy" seed of priests.[95] As noted by Qimron and Strugnell, similar distinctions in the holiness of priests and lay Jews are present in other sectarian texts.[96]

One exegetical issue still remains. Israel's sanctity is articulated numerous times in the Hebrew Bible. Why specifically therefore does 4QMMT draw upon Jer 2:3? The answer is found in the parallel stich in Jer 2:3, which identifies Israel as the "first fruits of his harvest" (ראשית תבואתה). The agricultural tenor of Jer 2:3 was likely attractive to the author of 4QMMT within the context of the analogy that is developed between forbidden marriages and mixed plant species.[97]

Concerning Revenge and Bearing a Grudge: CD 9:2–8 (par. 4Q267 9 i 1–3; 4Q270 6 iii 16–19)[98]

2 ואשר אמר לא תקום ולא תטור את בני עמך וכל איש מביאו[99]
3 הברית אשר יביא על רעהו דבר אשר לא בהוכח לפני העדים

[93] See further Himmelfarb, "Intermarriage," 7–8; Loader, *The Dead Sea Scrolls on Sexuality*, 67, 69.

[94] See Hayes, *Gentile Impurities*, 28–29.

[95] On these distinctions, see fuller treatment in Himmelfarb, "Intermarriage," 10; Hayes, *Gentile Impurities*, 85–86.

[96] Qimron and Strugnell, *Qumran Cave 4.V*, 173.

[97] I am indebted to Professor Devorah Dimant for calling this connection to my attention.

[98] Hebrew text follows Qimron, "CDC," 27. Translation follows Baumgarten and Schwartz, "Damascus Document," 21. For 4Q267 and 4Q270, see Baumgarten, *Qumran Cave 4.XIII*, 105, 158.

[99] 4Q270 has מבאי. As commentators have long noted, the text of CD should be emended accordingly (as in CD 2:2; 6:19; 1QS 2:18).

4 והביאו בחרון אפו או ספר לזקניו להבזותו נוקם הוא ונוטר
5 ואין כתוב כי אם נוקם הוא לצריו ונוטר הוא לאויביו
6 אם החריש לו מיום ליום ובחרון אפו בו דבר בו בדבר מות
7 ענה בו יען אשר לא הקים את מצות אל אשר אמר לו הוכח
8 תוכיח את רעיך[100] ולא תשא עליו חטא

2. And as to that which he said: "You shall not take vengeance nor bear a grudge against the sons of your nation" (Lev 19:18): anyone among those who have entered
3. the covenant who brings (a charge) upon his neighbor without reproof before witnesses,
4. but he brings it in burning wrath or he tells it to his elders in order to shame him, this person is taking vengeance and bearing a grudge.
5. It is only written "He (God) takes vengeance against his adversaries and bears a grudge against his enemies" (Nah 1:2).
6. If he remains silent from day to day and in his burning wrath brought against him a capital charge,
7. his iniquity is upon him on account of the fact that he did not fulfill the command of God, who said to him, "You shall surely
8. reprove your neighbor, in order that you do not bear guilt on account of him" (Lev 19:17).

This passage reformulates the Pentateuchal prohibition regarding revenge and bearing a grudge.[101] In particular, the *Damascus Document* is concerned with how specifically one violates the law of revenge and bearing of grudge as articulated in Lev 19:18. The *Damascus Document* focuses on the juxtaposition of this law in *Leviticus* with the requirement of reproof in Lev 19:17. Thus, the *Damascus Document* asserts that any community member who instigates a charge against his neighbor must first reprove him before witnesses. Failure to do so represents a violation of the prohibition of vengeance and bearing a grudge, presumably because these emotions were the motivating factors in the

[100] 𝔐 Lev 19:17: עמיתך.

[101] On this passage, see Schiffman, *Sectarian Law*, 89–109; idem, "Reproof as Requisite for Punishment in the Law of the Dead Sea Scrolls," in *Jewish Law Association Studies*, volume 2: *The Jerusalem Conference Volume* (ed. B. S. Jackson; Atlanta: Scholars Press, 1986), 59–74; idem, *Reclaiming the Dead Sea Scrolls: The History of Judaism, the Background of Christianity, the Lost Library of Qumran* (ABRL; New York: Doubleday, 1995), 220–21; Devorah Dimant, "The Hebrew Bible in the Dead Sea Scrolls: Torah Quotations in the *Damascus Covenant*," in *"Sha'arei Talmon": Studies in the Bible, Qumran, and the Ancient Near East Presented to Shemaryahu Talmon* (ed. M. Fishbane and E. Tov; Winona Lake: Eisenbrauns, 1992), 113*–22* (116*–18*); Steven D. Fraade, "Looking for Legal Midrash at Qumran," in *Legal Fictions: Studies of Law and Narrative in the Discursive Worlds of Ancient Jewish Sectarians and Sages* (JSJSup 147; Leiden: Brill, 2011), 145–68 (155–57) (1998); Hempel, *Laws*, 32–33, 99–100. Scholars have noted that this passage represents one of the few examples of explicit legal exegesis (*midrash halakhah*) in the Dead Sea Scrolls, in that Lev 19:18 is cited and then expounded (see Fraade, ibid.).

individual's failure to follow judicial procedure.[102] Immediately following this explication of the law, the text cites a verse from Nah 1:2, which is preceded by a citation formula: נוקם הוא לצריו ונוטר הוא לאיוביו, "He takes vengeance against his adversaries and keeps a grudge against his enemies."[103]

The legal-exegetical function of the *Nahum* passage has been debated. Devorah Dimant proposes that the use of על רעהו, "his neighbor," in the formulation of the law in line 3 indicates that this entire law only applies to relationships among members of the community. The sectarian interpretation would therefore seem to be exegetically linked to בני עמך, "the sons of your nation," in Lev 19:18.[104] The passage from *Nahum*, argues Dimant, emphasizes this application of the law of revenge and bearing of a grudge because God only takes revenge and bears a grudge against his *enemies* (i.e., not Israelites).[105] Dimant supports this interpretation by calling attention to a rabbinic parallel in *Genesis Rabbah* 55:3:

> כך אמרו ישראל לפני הקב"ה רבון כל העולמים כתבת בתורה לא תקם ולא תטר ואתה נוקם י"י ובעל חימה נוקם י"י לצריו ונוטר הוא לאויביו אמר להם הקב"ה אני כתבתי בתורה לא תקם ולא תטר לישראל אבל באומות נקם נקמת בני ישראל

> Similarly,[106] Israel asked the Holy One, Blessed be He: "Master of the Universe, you wrote in the Torah, 'Do not take revenge and do not bear a grudge' (Lev 19:18), but you [do thusly, as it says] 'The Lord is vengeful and fierce in wrath. The Lord takes vengeance on his enemies, he rages against his foes' (Nah 1:2). The Holy One, Blessed be He, said, "I wrote in the Torah 'Do not take revenge

102 Schiffman, *Sectarian Law*, 89.

103 Nah 1:2 is not extant in the scriptural Dead Sea Scrolls and does not appear in *Pesher Nahum* (4Q169). 𝔐 has the Tetragrammaton as the subject, while the citation in the *Damascus Document* has the third masculine singular independent personal pronoun. As noted by several commentators, this is a deliberate alteration out of respect for the divine name (Ginzberg, *Jewish Sect*, 40, 197; Rabin, *Zadokite Documents*, 45; Fitzmyer, "Old Testament Quotations," 19 n. 23; Schiffman, *Sectarian Law*, 100–1, n. 16). The third-person masculine singular independent personal pronoun often appears as a substitute for the Tetragrammaton in the sectarian Dead Sea Scrolls corpus. See further Joseph M. Baumgarten, "A New Qumran Substitute for the Divine Name and Mishnah Sukkah 4.5," *JQR* 83 (1992): 1–5, especially 2. On the more general avoidance of the Tetragrammaton, see 1QS 6:27–7:2 and discussion in Patrick W. Skehan, "The Divine Name at Qumran, in the Masada Scroll, and in the Septuagint," *BIOSCS* 13 (1980): 14–44; Schiffman, *Sectarian Law*, 133–36; Emanuel Tov, *Scribal Practices and Approaches Reflected in the Texts Found in the Judean Desert* (STDJ 54; Leiden: Brill, 2004), 218–19, 238–46.

104 Dimant, "The Hebrew Bible in the Dead Sea Scrolls," 117*.

105 Dimant, "The Hebrew Bible in the Dead Sea Scrolls," 117*. A related explanation is offered by R. H. Charles, "Fragments of a Zadokite Work," in idem, ed., *Apocrypha and Pseudepigrapha of the Old Testament* (2 vols.; Oxford: Clarendon, 1913), 2:823.

106 This passage follows after an exposition detailing the different laws regarding lending on interest to Israelites versus non-Israelites. Thus, the connection is distinctions made between the treatment of Israelites and non-Israelites.

> and do not bear a grudge' – against Israel. But, against the nations: 'Avenge the Israelite people [on the Midianites]' (Num 31:2)."[107]

In *Genesis Rabbah*, Israel "asks" God how it is that revenge and bearing a grudge can be prohibited in the Torah (Lev 19:18), yet God is described with these characteristics in Nah 1:2. God responds by asserting that Lev 19:18 only applies to Jews. This notion is supported by a contrasting Pentateuchal passage from Num 31:2, which promotes the act of taking revenge against the Midianites. Two important points emerge from the passage in *Genesis Rabbah*. First, it preserves a tradition that understands Lev 19:18 as only applying to Israelites based on the supporting prooftext of Nah 1:2. Second, *Genesis Rabbah* employs the non-Pentateuchal prooftext from Nah 1:2 alongside the Pentateuchal prooftext from Num 31:2. According to *Genesis Rabbah*, Nah 1:2 affirms the notion that God takes revenge. Yet, Num 31:2 clarifies the precise parameters of the legal position that revenge can only be directed at non-Jews. As in the *Damascus Document*, the citation from Nah 1:2 therefore plays a supporting role.

Lawrence Schiffman, following Ginzberg's earlier comments, proposes a different interpretation of the role of Nah 1:2 in the *Damascus Document*. Schiffman suggests that the *Nahum* passage is furnished in order to stress that only God, not humans, may take revenge and bear grudges.[108] This understanding has support from a similar formulation in Rom 12:19, where Paul cites Deut 32:35 in defense of the idea that God alone may take revenge:

> μὴ ἑαυτοὺς ἐκδικοῦντες ἀγαπητοί ἀλλὰ δότε τόπον τῇ ὀργῇ γέγραπται γάρ· ἐμοὶ ἐκδίκησις ἐγὼ ἀνταποδώσω λέγει κύριος.

> Beloved, never avenge yourselves, but leave room for the wrath of God; for it is written, "Vengeance is mine, I will repay, says the Lord."[109]

Both Ginzberg and Schiffman raise the obvious question of why the *Damascus Document* cites Nah 1:2 instead of Deut 32:35. Ginzberg notes that while the Masoretic Text of Deut 32:35 has לי נקם ושלם ("Vengeance is *mine*, I will repay"), the Septuagint *Vorlage* and the Samaritan Pentateuch reflect a Hebrew text of ליום נקם ושלם ("In the *day* of vengeance, I will repay"). Ginzberg speculates that the sect may have had the latter version of Deut 32:35, which would not lend itself to the legal conclusions articulated in the *Damascus Document*.[110]

107 Hebrew text follows Julius Theodor and Chanokh Albeck, *Midrash Bereshit Rabbah* (3 vols.; Berlin, 1912–36; repr., Jerusalem: Shalem, 1996), 2:586–87 (with parallel traditions listed in notes). The rabbinic parallel is also observed by Ginzberg, *Jewish Sect*, 188.

108 Schiffman, *Sectarian Law*, 89–90; idem, *Reclaiming*, 220. The same argument is advanced in Fitzmyer, "Old Testament Quotations," 18–19.

109 The Fragmentary Targum and Targum Neofiti adduce a similar application of Deut 32:35 (see Schiffman, *Sectarian Law*, 90).

110 Ginzberg, *Jewish Sect*, 41.

Ginzberg's initial speculation still cannot be confirmed. No manuscript containing the critical part of Deut 32:35 is preserved in the Judean Desert corpus. 4QpaleoDeut[r] (4Q45) 41 2 preserves the beginning of the verse, but all that is extant are traces of the *lamed* and *yod*. The manuscript does not preserve enough room to indicate even if there is an additional letter (𝔊 /ܣ: ליום) or a space (𝔐: לי).[111] If we assume that the Masoretic Text version of Deut 32:35 was known to the sectarian community, the choice of Nah 1:2 rather than Deut 32:35 would seem to support Dimant's understanding of the text. For Schiffman, the issue is merely that God alone is permitted to take revenge, a notion expressed by both Deut 32:35 and Nah 1:2. For Dimant, the *Damascus Document* wishes to apply Lev 19:18 exclusively to nonsectarians. This understanding is reinforced by the focus on "enemies" in Nah 1:2, something absent from Deut 32:35.

The intertextual relationship between the Nah 1:2 and Lev 19:18 is much clearer. As Dimant notes, the *Damascus Document* relies upon *Nahum* as the scriptural source neither for the general law against taking revenge and bearing a grudge nor for its sectarian interpretation and application. This role is filled by Lev 19:18 and its exegetical understanding. The *Nahum* passage is introduced to make a secondary point. For Dimant, it is a secondary legal point – to emphasize that the law is restricted to community members. For Schiffman, it is a secondary theological point – only God and therefore not humans may take revenge.

Concerning Acknowledgment of Guilt: 4Q270 7 i 15–20 (par. 4Q266 11 1–5)[112]

15 [אלה המ]שפטים א[שר ישפטו] בם כל המתיסרים כל אי[ש] אשר
16 [יתיס]ר(?) יבוא וידיעהו לכוהן [המ]ופקד על ה[רבים וקב]ל את משפטו מר[צונ]ו כ[א]שר
17 א[מ]ר ביד משה על הנפש אשר תח[טא בשגגה אשר יביאו] את חטאתו ו[את אשמו וע]ל
18 ישראל כתוב אלכה לי אל קצה הש[מים ולא אריח בריח ני]חוח°ם ובמ[קום אחר כתוב
19 קרעו לבבכם ואל בגדיכם וכת[וב לשוב אל אל בבכי ובצום]

15. *vacat* And these are the l]aws by which all who are disciplined [shall be ruled.] Any man who

[111] See Patrick W. Skehan, Eugene Ulrich, and Judith E. Sanderson, "4Q45: 4QpaleoDeuteronomy[r]," in *Qumran Cave 4.IV: Palaeo-Hebrew and Greek Biblical Manuscripts* (ed. P. W. Skehan, E. Ulrich, and J. E. Sanderson; DJD 9; Oxford: Clarendon, 1992), 147. They suggest the ink traces recommend restoring with ליום, but the evidence is equivocal at best.

[112] Text and translation follow Baumgarten, *Qumran Cave 4.XIII*, 163–64. The overlining represents text preserved in 4Q266 (see ibid., 76–77). While this fragment is overall better represented in 4Q266, I present the text here according to 4Q270 because only 4Q270 preserves the first line and a half.

16. is disciplined (?)] shall come and make it known to the priest appoint[ted over the many and acc]ept his judgement [wil]lingly, as
17. he said through Moses, "Concerning the soul that sin[s unwittingly, that they shall bring] his sin-offering and [his guilt-offering" (≈ Lev 4:2, 27 + 4:4, 14, 23, 28; 5:6). And con]cerning
18. Israel it is written, "I will get me to the ends of the hea[vens and will not smell the savor] of your sweet odors" (≈ Deut 30:4 + Lev 26:31). And else[where it is written,]
19. Rend your hearts, not your garments" (Joel 2:13). And it is writ[ten, "To return to God with weeping and fasting"] (Joel 2:12).

This passage forms part of the expanded penal code found in two of the Cave 4 manuscripts of the *Damascus Document* (4QD^a – 4Q266; 4QD^e – 4Q270).[113] It legislates concerning punishment for one who has violated sectarian law. Later, we are informed that this individual is banished temporarily from the community.[114] This particular passage exhorts the guilty party to accept his punishment willingly.

This resolution is supported by two sets of Pentateuchal prooftexts, each of which is introduced by an explicit citation formula. The first is a composite of several passages related to the sacrificial laws of Lev 4–5. The first half of the citation (הנפש אשר תח]טא בשגגה, "The soul that sin[s unwittingly") draws its textual character from the protases in Lev 4:2, 27, which introduce individuals who have inadvertently sinned (נפש כי תחטא בשגגה, "When a person unwittingly incurs guilt").[115] The second half (אשר יביאו] את חטאתו ו[את אשמו, "That they shall bring] his sin-offering and [his guilt-offering") is drawn from the language of the accompanying apodoses that follow in Lev 4:4, 14, 23, and 28, as well as Lev 5:6, which describe the sacrificial procedures that this sinner must undertake.[116] In drawing upon these verses, the *Damascus Document* articulates the notion that sin is traditionally expiated through sacrifice. Simultaneously, however,

113 On which, see Joseph M. Baumgarten, "The Cave 4 Versions of the Qumran Penal Code," *JJS* 43 (1992): 268–76. On this specific passage, see idem, "'Scriptural' Citation," 95–98; Hempel, *Laws*, 178–79. Baumgarten notes that this section would have appeared toward the end of the penal code represented in CD 14:18–22, where the text lists the penalties for violating sectarian laws ("Citation," 95). It likely represents the final section of the entire document (see Hempel, *Laws*, 183–85).

114 See 4Q266 11 5–14 (par. 4Q270 7 i 19–21). See Hempel, *Laws*, 180–82.

115 Lev 4:2 is the general classificatory heading for the three cases that follow (high priest, nation, and prince), all introduced by the subheadings אם or אשר. Lev 4:27 is the specific heading for any individual who has sinned.

116 Because the protasis of Lev 4:2 covers the three cases that follow, it seems that the *Damascus Document* is drawing upon all three of the apodoses in these cases. The specific root employed here (בוא–*hiph'il*) appears only in Lev 4:23, 28; 5:6. Lev 4:4, 14 use קרב–*hiph'il*. The conflation of the guilt offering (אשם) together with the sin offering (חטאת) in the *Damascus Document* is based on the inclusion of the apodosis from Lev 5:6. The initial protasis in this sequence (Lev 5:1: ונפש כי תחטא) only partially parallels the text found here.

the text generates an equivalency between the expiatory force of sacrifice and the acknowledgment of guilt and willful acceptance of punishment.

The next passage is a composite citation of Deut 30:4 and Lev 26:31.[117] The former articulates the future exile that Israel will experience as a result of its sin. The latter describes one of several realities that will exist in such a future time of doom; God will destroy all shrines and no longer be able to accept sacrifices. The two themes in the conflated scriptural citation reinforce the appropriateness of banishment as the punishment for the sectarian transgressor and the justification for a nonsacrificial expiatory rite. Because of its own exilic status, the community promotes banishment for the transgressor in lieu of a sin or guilt offering.[118]

The insistence that acknowledgment of guilt and the associated temporary banishment is equivalent to the expiatory force of sacrifice must be further understood within the context of the sectarian community's critical stance toward the present state of the Temple and sacrificial cult and its promotion of alternative modes of piety and atonement. This secondary feature is what stands behind the introduction of the two passages from Joel 2:12 and 13.[119] These two passages are introduced with the citation formulae "and elsewhere it is written" and "and it is written" that already serve to mark them as secondary elements.[120] Neither of these two passages contains any reference to the expiatory force of sacrifice or the promotion of banishment, acknowledgment of guilt, and acceptance of punishment as equivalent rites, the focus of the Pentateuchal paraphrases.

The conflated citation of Deut 30:5 and Lev 26:31 reflects both a critical stance toward the sacrificial cult and the recognition that communities in exile must seek alternative modes of piety. The *Damascus Document* therefore draws upon Joel 2:12–13 in order to introduce additional alternative means by which

117 Baumgarten, "A 'Scriptural' Citation," 96.

118 Baumgarten, "A 'Scriptural' Citation," 96.

119 4Q266 cites verse 12 followed by verse 13. 4Q270, reproduced above, cites verse 13 prior to verse 12. In 4Q266, the second passage is written supralinear. In both manuscripts, the first cited passage is introduced with "and elsewhere it is written." The second passage, however, is cited differently. 4Q266 has "and in a place it is written" (ובמקום כתוב), while 4Q270 has "and it is writ[ten" (וכת]וב). Baumgarten suggests that "another" should also be assumed in 4Q266 (*Qumran Cave 4.XIII*, 77). Because the text is citing the next verse in *Joel*, however, it seems more likely that the second citation formula is intended to indicate that the quotation is from the same place (i.e., "in the same place, it is written"). See also Hempel, *Laws*, 177, who asserts that [אח]ר is actually present on the manuscript. Why 4Q270 only has "and it is written," however, is less clear.

120 This seems to be the simple sense of the expression "and elsewhere it is written." Hempel proposes that it reflects the "gradual addition" of citations (*Laws*, 179). Unfortunately, the other Dead Sea Scrolls do not provide any comparative evidence for further analysis of this citation formula. The expression is reconstructed in 4Q485 (4QapProph) 1 5: [ובמקו]ם אחר כתוב. See text in Baillet, *Qumrân grotte 4.III*, 4. The reconstruction is suggested in Baumgarten, "A 'Scriptural' Citation," 98 n. 8.

a transgressor can return to God's favor without sacrifice: weeping, fasting (v. 12: לשוב אל אל בבכי ובצום), and rending one's heart and garments (v. 13; קרעו לבבכם ואל בגדיכם).[121] It is all the more suggestive that the text deliberately refrains from citing the conclusion of this literary unit in *Joel*, which refers to bringing meal and drink offerings:

> מי יודע ישוב ונחם והשאיר אחריו ברכה מנחה ונסך ליהוה אלהיכם
>
> Who knows but he may turn and relent, and leave a blessing behind for meal offering and drink offering to the Lord your God?" (Joel 2:14)

The passages from Joel 2:12–13 are not cited in order to prescribe a course of action for the guilty individual. Rather, they merely reinforce the community's preference for nonsacrificial models of expiation and concomitantly the importance of acknowledgment of guilt and the pursuit of proper repentance. In this sense, they fulfill a secondary role relative to the two sets of Pentateuchal citations provided earlier in the passage.

IV. CONCLUSIONS

The eight texts that I have examined in this chapter share a number of features. They all contain a sectarian legal formulation with a non-Pentateuchal passage employed as the scriptural prooftext. In several cases, these passages are introduced with standard citation formulae found elsewhere in sectarian legal texts. As prooftexts, these non-Pentateuchal passages are employed in much the same was as Pentateuchal passages are used in other sectarian legal literature. At times, they are identified as the explicit scriptural source. Elsewhere, the non-Pentateuchal passages are drawn upon as part of the legal hermeneutics of the sectarian law. At times, the legal conclusions are determined through the employment of wordplay with the scriptural passage. At other times, these passages play a critical role in the logical reasoning of the sectarian law. Throughout all these texts, however, there is no hesitation to turn to a non-Pentateuchal passage as a legal prooftext. Indeed, they function in much the same way as Pentateuchal passages are employed in other sectarian legal texts.

[121] The portion of verse 13 that is cited agrees with 𝔐 and other ancient versions. The citation of verse 12, however, contains several variants. The divine first-person speech in 𝔐 and 𝔊 Joel 2:12 (שבו עדי; Επιστράφητε πρός με, "Turn back to me") appears as a third-person reference in the *Damascus Document* (לשוב אל אל, "To return to God"). Moreover, the imperative represented in 𝔐 and 𝔊 appears as an infinitive construct in the *Damascus Document*. The exhortation to return to God בכל לבבכם ("with all your heart") is also absent in the citation. This may be because this notion is expressed in the citation from verse 13. Furthermore, the string of expiatory rites in verse 13 is reproduced without its final element – ובמספד ("mourning"). The Dead Sea Scrolls *Joel* manuscripts do not reflect any significant variants. לב]בכם is preserved in 4QXII[g] (4Q82) 30β, 31α recto, 36–37 14 and ובמספד is found in 4QXII[c] (4Q78) 14–17 3.

As suggested at the outset of this chapter, the combined use of Pentateuchal and non-Pentateuchal passages as prooftexts provides an instructive context for understanding the relative authority assigned to each of these scriptural units. The last three passages treated here freely employ non-Pentateuchal passages as prooftexts. In each case, however, they appear only after the initial Pentateuchal prooftext. Moreover, they fulfill a secondary legal and exegetical function. In each case, the Pentateuchal prooftext is cited as the primary scriptural source, while the non-Pentateuchal prooftext appears with regard to a secondary legal or theological point. To be sure, other sectarian legal texts similarly employ multiple Pentateuchal passages as primary and secondary prooftexts. Yet, in no case does an explicit Pentateuchal prooftext function as secondary to a non-Pentateuchal primary prooftext.

12

Conclusions

This book began with a broad overarching inquiry: In what ways did the sectarian community of the Dead Sea Scrolls adapt and expand legal content preserved in its collection of authoritative scriptural texts? This broad inquiry brings with it an equally wide set of intersecting questions: What constitutes an authoritative text for the sectarian community and what distinctions, if any, exist within collections of authoritative texts? What hermeneutic strategies and exegetical techniques are deployed in the service of reinscribing legal content found in the authoritative scriptural texts? Where does the evidence of the Dead Sea Scrolls fit into the landscape of Jewish law and legal exegesis in ancient Judaism, within both contemporaneous Second Temple Judaism and later rabbinic Judaism?

I noted at the beginning of this study the imbalance that often characterizes these types of questions in Dead Sea Scrolls scholarship. Studies on the contribution of the Dead Sea Scrolls to the origins of the canon and the history of scriptural interpretation are plentiful. After two generations of neglect, the study of Jewish law in the Dead Sea Scrolls has recently begun to flourish. In all settings, scholars have positioned their work on the Dead Sea Scrolls in dialogue with the literary and social worlds of Second Temple Judaism and rabbinic Judaism. Yet, few attempts have been made to explore the intersection of scripture and law in the Dead Sea Scrolls in a systematic way. Moreover, the present state of research on the Dead Sea Scrolls and ancient Judaism demands that any such inquiry be informed by dramatic advances in our understanding of the origins of the canon of the Hebrew Bible, the development of Jewish law, and the history of scriptural interpretation, at the same time as it contributes to this larger set of conversations.

This book represents an attempt to explore a single aspect related to legal hermeneutics in the Dead Sea Scrolls – the degree of legal-exegetical authority ascribed to scriptural material outside the Pentateuch – within the framework of wider questions related to scripture and law in the Dead Sea Scrolls. As noted in Chapter 1, I embarked upon this study based on conclusions reached in earlier research on the relationship between prophecy and law in the Dead Sea Scrolls. If the ancient prophets were conceptualized in the Dead Sea Scrolls as the second phase in the progressive revelation of law, then surely the literary record of their activity (i.e., the prophetic books) could be understood as a literary repository of such legislative activity. Testing this hypothesis has involved examining a set of questions that have long occupied historians of Jewish law, particularly in rabbinic literature. For communities that ground their legislative innovations in creative exegesis of scripture, what authority does non-Pentateuchal scripture possess, and what is the relative authority of Pentateuchal and non-Pentateuchal passages? As noted in Chapter 2, these questions are seemingly already addressed within the classical rabbinic corpus, which explicitly proscribes the application of *midrash halakhah* (legal exegesis) to non-Pentateuchal scripture. Indeed, rabbinic legal exegesis is on the whole Pentateuch centered, though there exist several cases in which non-Pentateuchal scriptural passages are employed.

Prior scholarship on these questions in the Dead Sea Scrolls corpus has been both limited and contradictory. In this study, I have taken advantage of the opportunity to view the full corpus of Dead Sea Scrolls texts. Moreover, I have repeatedly emphasized that law and legal hermeneutics in the Dead Sea Scrolls cannot be understood in literary isolation. Rather, any successful inquiry must place the legal texts of the Dead Sea Scrolls in dialogue with related material in Second Temple Judaism and rabbinic literature. This approach is not merely about drawing upon the comparative material to understand better the often complex legal content in the Dead Sea Scrolls. The evidence treated in this study has demonstrated the degree to which law in the Dead Sea Scrolls is part of a much larger world of law and legal exegesis in ancient Judaism.

Based on the evidence treated here, what can we conclude about the force of non-Pentateuchal scripture in the sectarian legal hermeneutics? The three forms in which we have seen non-Pentateuchal citations all follow the standard uses of scripture in sectarian legal texts – paraphrase, independent prooftexts, and secondary prooftexts. In all cases, the hermeneutic strategies and exegetical techniques match what scholars have observed for legal exegesis of Pentateuchal scripture. This would presumably suggest that the community felt no reluctance to employ non-Pentateuchal passages and therefore assigned them the same authority as the Pentateuch.

A number of considerations, however, recommend against this simple conclusion. The most glaring feature of the passages I have collected is that there are not that many. To be sure, I have noted the lack of explicit legal exegesis in the Dead Sea Scrolls. Thus, we should not expect an abundance of scriptural citations in sectarian legal passages. The *Damascus Document*, however, is often singled out for its overwhelming dependence on scripture, in both the legal and nonlegal portions. Yet, the *Damascus Document* furnishes only five explicit citations and three paraphrases from non-Pentateuchal sources. Furthermore, only one citation of non-Pentateuchal scripture is found in *4QMiqṣat Ma'ase Ha-Torah*. Though this document contains few explicit citations from scripture, it is marked by numerous scriptural paraphrases and allusions with citation formulae, especially in the legal section. Here, however, the Pentateuch represents the near exclusive source. Jer 2:3, moreover, merely fulfills a secondary role in the broader legal exegesis regarding forbidden marriage.

If we turn to the paraphrase of scripture, a ubiquitous form of employing scripture in legal texts, an even greater discrepancy is visible. Isa 58:13 and Jer 17:21–22 are clearly very popular and versatile texts for sectarian legal exegesis. Yet, they stand in relative isolation in contrast to the many paraphrases of Pentateuchal passages that are found in sectarian legal literature. What is more, the clear reliance on Isa 58:13 and Jer 17:21–22 in several sectarian legal texts is ultimately the product of more widespread exegetical and legal traditions in ancient Judaism. As my analysis in Chapters 4, 5, 7, and 9 demonstrates, Isa 58:13 and Jer 17:21–22 clearly are central to the sectarian attempts to expand Sabbath law through legal exegesis of scripture. Yet, my complementary analysis of Second Temple and rabbinic sources in Chapters 6, 8, and 10 reveals that these same two scriptural passages stand at the center of a robust exegetical expansion of Sabbath law in ancient Judaism. Therefore, while the paraphrase of non-Pentateuchal scripture in these few passages is a critical window into sectarian legal exegesis, their contribution to understanding the broader issue of legal hermeneutics must be significantly tempered.

Based on the evidence analyzed in this study, we can conclude that the sectarian community displayed no hesitation in drawing upon non-Pentateuchal passages in legal exegesis. No hermeneutic principles are articulated in the sectarian texts that proscribe this practice, and the few examples treated in this study fit seamlessly with the many examples of exegesis of the Pentateuch. Here, the evidence from rabbinic literature provides a useful comparative data set. Rabbinic legal hermeneutics explicitly proscribes the exegetical use of non-Pentateuchal scripture. To be sure, my discussion of the rabbinic material in this study clearly demonstrates that this principle was far from universally applied. Yet, in all the rabbinic material treated, I detected multiple examples of strands within the rabbinic corpus that deliberately avoid turning to non-Pentateuchal scripture for exegetical support. No such hesitation is found in the Dead Sea Scrolls texts or any of the Second Temple texts.

Thus, the evidence explored in this study has yielded seemingly contradictory results. Wider sectarian legal hermeneutics display limited engagement with non-Pentateuchal scripture. Yet, when non-Pentateuchal scripture is employed, the hermeneutic strategies and exegetical techniques reflect little, if any, distinctions regarding the authority of these texts and their exegetical function. The general avoidance of non-Pentateuchal scripture presumes that these texts are of inferior legal authority at the same time as the few examples of their explicit use indicate that they were seen as just as authoritative for paraphrase and prooftexts. A number of possible answers present themselves in response to this set of questions. One could very easily suggest that the Pentateuch contains the overwhelming majority of the Hebrew Bible's legal content and therefore provides the natural starting point for legal-exegetical activity. While this general observation is indeed true, its implications do not follow. Communities engaged in creative exegesis are rarely limited by the seemingly narrow contents of the scriptural texts. Thus, non-Pentateuchal scriptural passages with very little legal content can very easily be exegetically finessed for the larger legal-exegetical purpose. Moreover, such an explanation does not consider the secondary function of such passages. For example, in Chapter 11, we saw the example of Jer 3:2 employed as part of the logical underpinning of *4QMiqṣat Ma'ase Ha-Torah*'s restriction on intermarriage. Jer 3:2 possesses no direct connection to the legal issue at hand. It is employed secondarily as part of the larger legal argument. For such a scripture-based community, it is therefore all the more surprising that non-Pentateuchal content does not function more often in legal contexts.

In Chapter 3, I suggested that the results of this study could have implications for achieving further clarity in our understanding of the emergence of the canon of the Hebrew Bible and its diverse layers of textual authority. Indeed, my analysis has demonstrated that the sectarian community made a distinction for the purposes of legal exegesis – something not made for nonlegal exegesis – between the Pentateuch and all other scriptural texts. It seems likely, however, that such a distinction was not generated by the community itself but rather would have been part of inherited models of textual authority. As argued at length in Chapter 3, the Pentateuch had already achieved a degree of "canonical" authority in late Second Temple Judaism. Though the precise scriptural text was still not formalized, the Pentateuch as a whole stood in its own class of scriptural authority. Most important, from the Persian period onward, the Pentateuch was viewed as the supreme legal authority within the emerging scriptural texts. In contrast, scriptural material outside the Pentateuch was well suited for other forms of nonlegal exegesis. In particular, the prophetic writings were regarded as repositories of special knowledge concerning the eschatological expectations of the sectarian community. The inspired exegesis in the *Pesharim* and related texts focuses on this collection of scriptural texts.

Non-Pentateuchal scriptural texts – some of which would later become part of the canonical divisions of the Prophets and Writings – were thus regarded as authoritative but clearly of a lesser authority than the Pentateuchal texts. As such, legal exegesis would look in the first instance to the Pentateuch. Non-Pentateuchal passages, by virtue of the sacred status of these books, could likewise be employed for legal exegesis but invariably were not when Pentateuchal material was freely available and applicable. Unlike the rabbis, however, the sectarian community never adapts an exegetically inferior Pentateuchal passage in lieu of the clearly more appropriate non-Pentateuchal passage. Evidence for distinctions in textual authority is further reinforced by the absence of any legal exegesis on scriptural texts that would later fall outside of the canon of the Hebrew Bible. Books such as *Jubilees*, though regarded as authoritative and indeed scriptural for the sectarian community, were nonetheless only drawn upon for nonlegal exegesis. No evidence survives in which the book of *Jubilees* or related "noncanonical" books were employed for legal exegesis.

The conclusions reached here can be profitably applied to the study of the wider development of law and exegesis in ancient Judaism. As discussed in Chapter 2, the role of non-Pentateuchal passages in rabbinic legal exegesis is the subject of much scholarly inquiry. The rabbis make explicit statements rejecting the force of non-Pentateuchal passages for *midrash halakhah*. Occasionally, however, such passages do play a significant (and independent) role in rabbinic *midrash halakhah*. These passages deserve an independent treatment of the role and function of the hermeneutics of *midrash halakhah*. Provisionally, we may suggest that the conclusions of this study can serve to map out larger questions and considerations of such an undertaking. I have suggested that the evidence treated throughout this study must be understood within the context of the canonical process. The sectarian community's legal-exegetical activity was concurrent with the canonical process of the formation of the Hebrew Bible. For the sectarian community, the primary distinction in authority was between the Pentateuch and all other texts. While the issue of textual authority was a major point of distinction between the two scriptural corpora, non-Pentateuchal scripture maintained a heightened degree of textual authority. Accordingly, when appropriate, the community turned to it. Rabbinic legal-exegetical activity comes after the closing of the canon and the formalization of its tripartite division. As observed in Chapter 3, rabbinic Judaism very clearly marks a distinction in authority and sanctity between the Torah (Pentateuch) and the Prophets and Writings. These distinctions are retained in the role of these canonical divisions in legal exegesis.

For rabbinic Judaism, as for the sectarian community, all scriptural books aside from the Torah were regarded as possessing less textual authority. In the case of rabbinic Judaism, however, the full stabilization of the canon and its attendant formulation of acute distinctions among its constituent divisions served to distance the Torah and its legal-textual authority even further from the other scriptural writings. In this sense, the hermeneutics of non-Pentateuchal scripture among the rabbis represents a more fully developed approach to scripture and law that finds its earliest expression in legal texts of the Dead Sea Scrolls and related segments of Second Temple Judaism. This approach extends to individual non-Pentateuchal passages that figure prominently in rabbinic legal exegesis. No treatment of the role of Isa 58:13 or Jer 17:21–22 in rabbinic legal hermeneutics can ignore the prehistory of exegesis on these passages found in Second Temple Judaism. Thus, any discussion of rabbinic legal hermeneutics must take into consideration the broader world of law and legal exegesis from which rabbinic Judaism emerges.

This book has explored several intersecting worlds of scriptural exegesis in ancient Judaism. The main areas of contrast consist of the sectarian community of the Dead Sea Scrolls and related segments of Second Temple Judaism alongside the vast corpus of rabbinic texts. When these texts are placed in dialogue with one another, a shared world of Jewish law and legal exegesis in ancient Judaism is revealed. All of these texts reflect attempts to enliven the legal traditions of ancient Israel for later Judaism in ways that make the sacred texts and their legal content relevant and timely. Many of the same legal issues are addressed in the Second Temple and rabbinic texts. In this sense, the Second Temple and rabbinic evidence should be viewed in terms of continuity. Yet, the evidence examined here highlights the divergent strategies and forms in which this shared enterprise was undertaken. As discussed at length in Chapter 2, scriptural exegesis in Second Temple Judaism adapts the meaning of the text by changing the very text (rewriting), while rabbinic Judaism changes the meaning of the text by commentary that exists outside of the text. The many legal-exegetical traditions from these two corpora treated in Chapters 4 through 11 reinforce this conceptual model.

These two approaches are intimately bound up with the intersection of canon, exegesis, and creativity in Second Temple and rabbinic Judaism. For Jews in the Second Temple period, authoritative scripture was still in formation, with regard to both the specific books and their textual form. The exegetical reformulation of Isa 58:13 and Jer 17:21–22 in the Dead Sea Scrolls, the book of *Jubilees*, and *Nehemiah* employs exegetical techniques such as literary inversion, semantic reformulation, and analogical reasoning to reorient the text *and* meaning of these passages. This phenomenon is further apparent in the prooftexts treated in Chapter 11. One of the features that I observed in many of these prooftexts is the presence of textual modification in order to suit the particular exegetical goals. Thus, even as these texts turn to scriptural material for authority, they are free to change the very wording of the authoritative texts. In so doing, the Second Temple texts are themselves contributing to the formation of the canon and its textual character. In contrast, the rabbinic approaches to many of the very same scriptural passages respect their textual integrity even as they dramatically transform their meaning and practical application through midrashic reformulation.

In spite of the different approaches taken, the end result is the same – scripture is infused with new meaning appropriate to the social world of the exegetes. Through creative exegesis, scripture remains a viable and central text for Jewish law and practice.

Bibliography

"אזהרה ('Azharah)." Pages 517–23 in vol. 1 of *Encyclopedia Talmudica*. Edited by M. Bar-Ilan and S. Y. Yeiven. Translated by H. Freedman. 6 vols. to date. Jerusalem: Yad HaRav Herzog, Talmudic Encyclopedia Institute, 1974–.

"אסמכתא ('Asmakhta)." Pages 515–22 in vol. 2 of *Encyclopedia Talmudica*. Edited by M. Bar-Ilan and S. Y. Yeiven. Translated by H. Freedman. 6 vols. to date. Jerusalem: Yad HaRav Herzog, Talmudic Encyclopedia Institute, 1974–.

"רבדי קבלה." Pages 106–14 in vol. 7 of *Enṣiklopedyah Talmudit*. Edited by M. Bar-Ilan and S. Y. Yeiven. 23 vols. Jerusalem: Mossad ha-Rav Kook, 1947–. [Hebrew]

Adelman, Rachel. *The Return of the Repressed: Pirqe de Rabbi Eliezer and the Pseudepigrapha*. Journal for the Study of Judaism Supplement Series 140. Leiden: Brill, 2009.

Albeck, Chanokh. *Das Buch der Jubiläen und die Halacha*. Berichte der Hochschule für die Wissenschaft des Judentums 47. Berlin: Hochschule für die Wissenschaft des Judentums, 1930.

"The Halakhot and the *Derashoth*." Pages 1–8 in *Alexander Marx: Jubilee Volume on the Occasion of His Seventieth Birthday, Hebrew Volume*. New York: Jewish Theological Seminary, 1950. [Hebrew]

Introduction to the Mishnah. Jerusalem: Bialik Institute; Tel Aviv: Dvir, 1959. [Hebrew]

Shishah Sidre Mishnah, vol. 2: *Seder Mo'ed*. Jerusalem: Bialik Institute; Tel Aviv: Dvir, 1958.

Alexander, Philip S. "The Redaction-History of the *Serekh Ha-Yaḥad*: A Proposal." *Revue de Qumran* 17 (1996; Milik volume): 437–56.

"Retelling the Old Testament." Pages 99–121 in *It Is Written: Scripture Citing Scripture; Essays in Honour of Barnabas Lindars, SSF*. Edited by D. A. Carson and H. G. M. Williamson. Cambridge: Cambridge University Press, 1988.

Alexander, Philip S., and Geza Vermes. *Qumran Cave 4.XIX: Serekh Ha-Yaḥad and Two Related Texts*. Discoveries in the Judaean Desert 26. Oxford: Clarendon, 1998.

Allegro, John M., with Arnold A. Anderson. "4Q158: Biblical Paraphrase: Genesis, Exodus." Pages 1–6 in *Qumran Cave 4.I (4Q158–4Q186)*. Edited by J. M. Allegro with A. A. Anderson. Discoveries in the Judaean Desert 5. Oxford: Clarendon, 1968.

"4Q159: Ordinances." Pages 6–9 in *Qumran Cave 4.I (4Q158–4Q186)*. Edited by J. M. Allegro with A. A. Anderson. Discoveries in the Judaean Desert 5. Oxford: Clarendon, 1968.

Allison, Dale C., Jr. *The New Moses: A Matthean Typology*. Minneapolis: Fortress, 1993.

Amir, Yehoshua. "Authority and Interpretation of Scripture in the Writings of Philo." Pages 421–53 in *Mikra: Text, Translation, Reading and Interpretation of the Hebrew Bible in Ancient Judaism and Early Christianity*. Edited by M. J. Mulder. Compendia rerum iudaicarum ad Novum Testamentum 2/1. Assen: Van Gorcum; Minneapolis: Fortress, 1988.

Arndt, William F., and F. Wilbur Gingrich. *A Greek-English Lexicon of the New Testament and Other Early Christian Literature*. Chicago: University of Chicago Press; Cambridge: Cambridge University Press, 1957.

Aune, David E. "On the Origins of the 'Council of Javneh' Myth." *Journal of Biblical Literature* 110 (1991): 491–93.

Bacher, Wilhelm. *Die Bibelexegetische Terminologie der Tannaiten*. Leipzig: Hinrichs, 1899.

"Zu Schechters neuestem Geniza-Funde." *Zeitschrift für Hebraische Bibliographie* 15 (1911): 13–26.

Baillet, Maurice. "4Q513: Ordonnances (ii)." Pages 287–95 in *Qumrân grotte 4.III (4Q482–4Q520)*. Edited by M. Baillet. Discoveries in the Judaean Desert 7. Oxford: Clarendon, 1982.

Baillet, M., J. T. Milik, and R. de Vaux. *Les "Petites Grottes" de Qumran*. Discoveries in the Judaean Desert 3. Oxford: Clarendon, 1962.

Barton, John. *Oracles of God: Perceptions of Ancient Prophecy in Israel after the Exile*. London: Darton, Longman, and Todd, 1986.

"The Significance of a Fixed Canon of the Hebrew Bible." Pages 67–83 in *Hebrew Bible/Old Testament: The History of Its Interpretation*, volume 1, part 1: *Antiquity*. Edited by M. Sæbø. Göttingen: Vandenhoeck and Ruprecht, 1996.

Baumgarten, Joseph M. "4Q264a: 4QHalakha B." Pages 53–56 in *Qumran Cave 4.XXV: Halakhic Texts*. Edited by J. M. Baumgarten et al. Discoveries in the Judaean Desert 35. Oxford: Clarendon, 1999.

"The Avoidance of the Death Penalty in Qumran Law." Pages 31–38 in *Reworking the Bible: Apocryphal and Related Texts at Qumran: Proceedings of a Joint Symposium by the Orion Center for the Study of the Dead Sea Scrolls and Associated Literature and the Hebrew University Institute for Advanced Studies Research Group on Qumran, 15–17 January, 2002*. Edited by E. G. Chazon, D. Dimant, and R. A. Clements. Studies on the Texts of the Desert of Judah 53. Leiden: Brill, 2005.

"The Cave 4 Versions of the Qumran Penal Code." *Journal of Jewish Studies* 43 (1992): 268–76.

"Damascus Document." Pages 166–70 in vol. 1 of *Encyclopedia of the Dead Sea Scrolls*. Edited by L. H. Schiffman and J. C. VanderKam. 2 vols. Oxford: Oxford University Press, 2000.

"The 'Halakah' in Miqṣat Ma'aśe ha-Torah [Review of DJD 10]." *Journal of the American Oriental Society* 116 (1996): 512–16.

"Halivni's *Mishnah, Midrash, and Gemara*." *Jewish Quarterly Review* 77 (1986): 59–64.

"A New Qumran Substitute for the Divine Name and Mishnah Sukkah 4.5." *Jewish Quarterly Review* 83 (1992): 1–5.

"A Proposed Re-Interpretation of Qumran Shabbat Regulations." Pages 9*–13* in *Zaphenath-Paneah: Linguistic Studies Presented to Elisha Qimron on the Occasion of His Sixty-Fifth Birthday*. Edited by D. Sivan, D. Talshir, and C. Cohen. Beer-Sheva: Beer-Sheva University Press, 2009.

"Qumran and the Halakah in the Aramaic Targumim." Pages 45–60 in *Proceedings of the Ninth World Congress of Jewish Studies: Panels Sessions, Bible Studies and Ancient Near East*. Edited by M. Goshen-Gottstein. Jerusalem: World Congress of Jewish Studies, Magnes, the Hebrew University, 1985.

Qumran Cave 4.XIII: The Damascus Document (4Q266–273). Discoveries in the Judaean Desert 18. Oxford: Clarendon, 1996.

"Sacrifice and Worship among the Jewish Sectarians of the Dead Sea (Qumran) Scrolls." Pages 39–56 in *Studies in Qumran Law*. Studies in Judaism in Late Antiquity 24. Leiden: Brill, 1977. Repr. from *Harvard Theological Review* 46 (1953): 141–59.

"A 'Scriptural' Citation in 4Q Fragments of the Damascus Document." *Journal of Jewish Studies* 43 (1992): 95–98.

Studies in Qumran Law. Studies in Judaism in Late Antiquity 24. Leiden: Brill, 1977.

"Tannaitic Halakhah and Qumran: A Re-evaluation." Pages 1–11 in *Rabbinic Perspectives: Rabbinic Literature and the Dead Sea Scrolls: Proceedings of the Eighth International Symposium of the Orion Center for the Study of the Dead Sea Scrolls and Associated Literature, 7–9 January, 2003*. Edited by S. D. Fraade, A. Shemesh, and R. A. Clements. Studies on the Texts of the Desert of Judah 62. Leiden: Brill, 2006.

"The Unwritten Law in the Pre-Rabbinic Period." Pages 13–35 in *Studies in Qumran Law*. Studies in Judaism in Late Antiquity 24. Leiden: Brill, 1977. Repr. from *Journal for the Study of Judaism in the Persian, Hellenistic, and Roman Period* 3 (1972): 7–29.

Baumgarten, Joseph M., and Daniel R. Schwartz. "Damascus Document (CD)." Pages 4–58 in *The Dead Sea Scrolls: Hebrew, Aramaic, and Greek Texts with English Translations; Damascus Document, War Scroll and Related Documents*. Edited by J. H. Charlesworth. Princeton Theological Seminary Dead Sea Scrolls Project 2. Tübingen: Mohr Siebeck; Louisville: Westminster John Knox, 1995.

Beckwith, Roger. "Formation of the Hebrew Bible." Pages 39–86 in *Mikra: Text, Translation, Reading and Interpretation of the Hebrew Bible in Ancient Judaism and Early Christianity*. Edited by M. J. Mulder. Compendia rerum iudaicarum ad Novum Testamentum 2/1. Assen: Van Gorcum; Minneapolis: Fortress, 1988.

The Old Testament Canon of the New Testament Church and Its Background in Early Judaism. Grand Rapids: Eerdmans, 1985.

Beentjes, Pancratius. "Inverted Quotations in the Bible: A Neglected Stylistic Pattern." *Biblica* 63 (1982): 506–23.

Beer, Georg. *Faksimile-Ausgabe des Mischnacodex Kaufmann A 50*. Haag: M. Nijhoff, 1929. Repr., Jerusalem, 1969.

Belkin, Samuel. *Philo and the Oral Law: The Philonic Interpretation of Biblical Law in Relation to Palestinian Halakhah*. Harvard Semitic Series 11. Cambridge: Cambridge University Press, 1940.

Benovitz, Moshe. "The Origin and Meaning of the Prohibitive Vow in Second Temple and Tannaitic Literature." *Tarbiz* 64 (1995): 203–28. [Hebrew]

Bernstein, Moshe J. "4Q252: From Re-Written Bible to Biblical Commentary." *Journal of Jewish Studies* 41 (1994): 1–27.

"Contours of Genesis Interpretation at Qumran: Contents, Context, and Nomenclature." Pages 57–85 in *Studies in Ancient Midrash*. Edited by J. Kugel. Cambridge: Harvard University Press, 2001.

"The Contribution of the Qumran Discoveries to the History of Early Biblical Interpretation." Pages 215–38 in *The Idea of Biblical Interpretation: Essays in Honor of James L. Kugel*. Edited by H. Najman and J. H. Newman. Journal for the Study of Judaism Supplement Series 83. Leiden: Brill, 2004.

"The Employment and Interpretation of Scripture in 4QMMT: Preliminary Observations." Pages 29–51 in *Reading 4QMMT: New Perspectives on Qumran Law and History*. Edited by J. Kampen and M. J. Bernstein. Society of Biblical Literature Symposium Series 2. Atlanta: Scholars Press, 1996.

"Pseudepigraphy in the Qumran Scrolls: Categories and Functions." Pages 1–26 in *Pseudepigraphic Perspectives: The Apocrypha and Pseudepigrapha in Light of the Dead Sea Scrolls: Proceedings of the International Symposium of the Orion Center for the Study of the Dead Sea Scrolls and Associated Literature, 12–14 January, 1997*. Edited by E. G. Chazon and M. Stone. Studies on the Texts of the Desert of Judah 31. Leiden: Brill, 1999.

"'Rewritten Bible': A Generic Category Which Has Outlived Its Usefulness?" *Textus* 22 (2005): 169–96.

"What Has Happened to the Laws? The Treatment of Legal Material in 4QReworked Pentateuch." *Dead Sea Discoveries* 15 (2008): 24–49.

Bernstein, Moshe J., and Shlomo A. Koyfman. "The Interpretation of Biblical Law in the Dead Sea Scrolls: Forms and Methods." Pages 61–87 in *Biblical Interpretation at Qumran*. Edited by M. Henze. Grand Rapids: Eerdmans, 2005.

Beyer, Klaus. *Die aramäischen Texte vom Toten Meer*. Göttingen: Vandenhoeck and Ruprecht, 1984.

Bickerman, Elias. "Two Legal Interpretations in the Septuagint." Pages 201–24 in *Studies in Jewish and Christian History*. Arbeiten zur Geschichte des antiken Judentums und des Urchristentums 9. Leiden: Brill, 1976. Repr. from *Revue internationale des droits de l'antiquité* 3 (1956): 81–104.

Blenkinsopp, Joseph. *Ezra-Nehemiah: A Commentary*. Old Testament Library. Philadelphia: Westminster, 1988.

Isaiah 56–66. Anchor Bible 19B. New York: Doubleday, 2003.

Judaism, the First Phase: The Place of Ezra and Nehemiah in the Origins of Judaism. Grand Rapids: Eerdmans, 2009.

The Pentateuch: An Introduction to the First Five Books of the Bible. Anchor Bible Reference Library. New York: Doubleday, 1992.

Botterweck, G. J., and H. Ringgren, eds. *Theological Dictionary of the Old Testament*. Translated by J. T. Willis, G. W. Bromiley, and D. E. Green. 15 vols. Grand Rapids: Eerdmans, 1974–2006.

Braude, William G. *Pesiqta Rabbati: Discourses for Feasts, Fasts, and Special Sabbaths*. Yale Judaica Series 18. 2 vols. New Haven: Yale University Press, 1968.

Brettler, Marc Z. *How to Read the Bible*. Philadelphia: Jewish Publication Society, 2005.

Bright, John. "The Apodictic Prohibition: Some Observations." *Journal of Biblical Literature* 92 (1973): 185–204.

Brongers, H. A. "Einige Bemerkungen zu Jes 58 13–14." *Zeitschrift für die alttestamentliche Wissenschaft* 87 (1975): 212–26.

Brooke, George J. "4Q252 as Early Jewish Commentary." *Revue de Qumran* 17 (1996): 385–401.

"Between Authority and Canon: The Significance of Reworking the Bible for Understanding the Canonical Process." Pages 85–104 in *Reworking the Bible: Apocryphal and Related Texts at Qumran: Proceedings of a Joint Symposium by the Orion Center for the Study of the Dead Sea Scrolls and Associated Literature and the Hebrew University Institute for Advanced Studies Research Group on Qumran, 15–17 January, 2002*. Edited by E. G. Chazon, D. Dimant, and R. A. Clements. Studies on the Texts of the Desert of Judah 53. Leiden: Brill, 2005.

"'The Canon within the Canon' at Qumran and in the New Testament." Pages 27–51 in *The Dead Sea Scrolls and the New Testament*. Minneapolis: Fortress, 2005. Repr. from pages 242–66 in *The Scrolls and the Scriptures: Qumran Fifty Years After*. Edited by S. E. Porter and C. A. Evans. Journal for the Study of the Pseudepigrapha Supplement Series 26. Sheffield: Sheffield Academic Press, 1997.

"The Explicit Presentation of Scripture in 4QMMT." Pages 67–88 in *Legal Texts and Legal Issues: Proceedings of the Second Meeting of the International Organization for Qumran Studies, Cambridge, 1995; Published in Honour of Joseph M. Baumgarten*. Edited by M. J. Bernstein, F. García Martínez, and J. Kampen. Studies on the Texts of the Desert of Judah 23. Leiden: Brill, 1997.

"New Perspectives on the Bible and Its Interpretation in the Dead Sea Scrolls." Pages 19–37 in *The Dynamics of Language and Exegesis at Qumran*. Edited by D. Dimant and R. Kratz. Forschungen zum Alten Testament 2/35. Tübingen: Mohr Siebeck, 2009.

"Prophetic Interpretation in the *Pesharim*." Pages 235–54 in *A Companion to Biblical Interpretation in Early Judaism*. Edited by M. Henze. Grand Rapids: Eerdmans, 2012.

"Rewritten Bible." Page 777–81 in vol. 2 of *Encyclopedia of the Dead Sea Scrolls*. Edited by L. H. Schiffman and J. C. VanderKam. 2 vols. Oxford: Oxford University Press, 2000.

Brooke, George J., Hindy Najman, and Loren T. Stuckenbruck, eds. *The Significance of Sinai: Traditions about Sinai and Divine Revelation in Judaism and Christianity*. Themes in Biblical Narrative 12. Leiden: Brill, 2008.

Brooks, Roger. *The Talmud of the Land of Israel: A Preliminary Translation and Explanation*, volume 2: *Peah*. Chicago: University of Chicago Press, 1990.

Brown, F., S. R. Driver, and C. A. Briggs. *Hebrew and English Lexicon of the Old Testament*. Peabody: Hendrickson, 1997.

Buber, Solomon. *Midrash Tanḥuma: Shemot*. Vilna, 1885. Repr., Jerusalem, 1963.

Büchler, Adolph. "Schechter's 'Jewish Sectaries.'" *Jewish Quarterly Review* 3 (1913): 429–85.

Campbell, Jonathan G. "4QMMT[d] and the Tripartite Canon." *Journal of Jewish Studies* 51 (2000): 181–90.

The Use of Scripture in the Damascus Document 1–8, 19–20. Beihefte zur Zeistchrift für die alttestamentliche Wissenschaft 228. Berlin: de Gruyter, 1995.

Carmignac, J. "Les citations de l'Ancien Testament dans 'La guerre des fils de lumière contre les fils de ténèbres.'" *Revue biblique* 63 (1956): 234–60.

Chajes, Zvi H. *Torat Nevi'im ha-mekhuneh Eleh ha-mitsvot* (1836), printed in *Kol Sifre Maharaṣ Chajes*. Jerusalem: Divre Hakhamim, 1958.

Chapman, Steven B. *The Law and the Prophets*. Forschungen zum Alten Testament 27. Tübingen: Mohr Siebeck, 2000.

Charles, R. H. *The Book of Jubilees*. London: Adam and Charles Black, 1902.

"Fragments of a Zadokite Work." Pages 785–834 in vol. 2 of *Apocrypha and Pseudepigrapha of the Old Testament*. Edited by R. H. Charles. 2 vols. Oxford: Clarendon, 1913.

Charlesworth, James H., and Carsten Claussen. "Halakah A: 4Q251." Pages 271–85 in *Dead Sea Scrolls: Hebrew, Aramaic, and Greek Texts with English Translations; Damascus Document II, Some Works of the Torah, and Related Documents*. Edited by J. H. Charlesworth. Princeton Theological Seminary Dead Sea Scrolls Project 3. Tübingen: Mohr Siebeck; Louisville: Westminster John Knox, 2006.

"Halakah B: 4Q264a." Pages 286–89 in *Dead Sea Scrolls: Hebrew, Aramaic, and Greek Texts with English Translations; Damascus Document II, Some Works of the Torah, and Related Documents*. Edited by J. H. Charlesworth. Princeton Theological Seminary Dead Sea Scrolls Project 3. Tübingen: Mohr Siebeck; Louisville: Westminster John Knox, 2006.

Childs, Brevard S. *Isaiah*. Old Testament Library. Louisville: Westminster John Knox, 2001.

Clarke, E. G. *Targum Pseudo-Jonathan of the Pentateuch: Text and Concordance*. Hoboken: Ktav, 1984.

Coffey, Gerard. "Codifying the Meaning of 'Intention' in the Criminal Law." *Journal of Criminal Law* 79 (2009): 394–413.

Cohen, Boaz. *Mishnah and Tosefta: A Comparative Study*, part 1: *Shabbat*. New York: Jewish Theological Seminary, 1935.

"Sabbath Prohibitions Known as *Shebut*." Pages 127–66 in *Law and Tradition in Judaism*. New York: Ktav, 1969. Repr. from *Proceedings of the Rabbinical Assembly* 9 (1949): 123–61.

Collins, John J. *Beyond the Qumran Community: The Sectarian Movement of the Dead Sea Scrolls*. Grand Rapids: Eerdmans, 2010.

Cook, Edward. "Damascus Document." Pages 49–78 in Michael Wise, Martin Abegg Jr., and Edward Cook, *The Dead Sea Scrolls: A New Translation*. 2d ed. San Francisco: HarperSanFrancisco, 2006.

Cothenet, É. "Le Document de Damas." Page 149–204 in *Les Textes de Qumran traduits et annotés*, volume 2. Edited by J. Carmignac, É. Cothenet, and H. Lignée. Paris: Letouzey et Ané, 1963.

Crawford, Sidnie White. "The Pentateuch as Found in the Pre-Samaritan Texts and 4QReworked Pentateuch." Pages 123–36 in *Changes in Scripture: Rewriting and Interpreting Authoritative Traditions in the Second Temple Period*. Edited by H. von Weissenberg, J. Pukkala, and M. Martilla. Berlin: de Gruyter, 2011.

Rewriting Scripture in Second Temple Times. Grand Rapids: Eerdmans, 2008.

"The 'Rewritten Bible' at Qumran: A Look at Three Texts." *Eretz-Israel* 26 (1999): 1*–8*.

"The Use of the Pentateuch in the Temple Scroll and the Damascus Document in the Second Century B.C.E." Pages 301–18 in *The Pentateuch as Torah: New Models for Understanding Its Promulgation and Acceptance.* Edited by G. N. Knoppers and B. M. Levinson. Winona Lake: Eisenbrauns, 2007.

Cross, Frank Moore. *The Ancient Library of Qumran.* 3d ed. Minneapolis: Fortress, 1995.

"The Contribution of the Qumrân Discoveries to the Study of the Biblical Text." Pages 278–92 in *Qumran and the History of the Biblical Text.* Edited by F. M. Cross and Sh. Talmon. Cambridge: Harvard University Press, 1975. Repr. from *Israel Exploration Society* 16 (1966): 81–95.

"The Evolution of a Theory of Local Texts." Pages 306–20 in *Qumran and the History of the Biblical Text.* Edited by F. M. Cross and Sh. Talmon. Cambridge: Harvard University Press, 1975.

"The History of the Biblical Text in the Light of Discoveries in the Judaean Desert." Pages 177–95 in *Qumran and the History of the Biblical Text.* Edited by F. M. Cross and Sh. Talmon. Cambridge: Harvard University Press, 1975. Repr. from *Harvard Theological Review* 57 (1964): 281–99.

"The Stabilization of the Canon of the Hebrew Bible." Pages 219–29 in *From Epic to Canon: History and Literature in Ancient Israel.* Baltimore: Johns Hopkins University Press, 1998.

Cross, Frank Moore, Donald W. Parry, and Richard J. Saley. "4Q51: 4QSam[a]." Pages 1–216 in *Qumran Cave 4.XII: 1–2 Samuel.* Edited by F. M. Cross et al. Discoveries in the Judaean Desert 17. Oxford: Clarendon, 2005.

Dahood, Mitchell. *Psalms 1–50.* Anchor Bible 16. Garden City: Doubleday, 1965.

Danby, Herbert. *The Mishnah.* Oxford: Oxford University Press, 1933.

Dan-Cohen, Meir. "Harmful Thoughts." *Law and Philosophy* 18 (1999): 379–405.

Daube, David. *The Deed and the Doer in the Bible, Gifford Lectures*, volume 1. Edited and compiled by Calum Carmichael. West Conshohocken: Templeton Foundation, 2008.

Davenport, Gene. *The Eschatology of the Book of Jubilees.* Studia post-biblica 20. Leiden: Brill, 1971.

Davies, Philip R. "Halakhah at Qumran." Pages 37–50 in *A Tribute to Geza Vermes: Essays on Jewish and Christian History and Literature.* Edited by P. R. Davies and R. T. White. Journal for the Study of the Old Testament Supplement Series 100. Sheffield: JSOT Press, 1990.

"The Ideology of the Temple in the Damascus Document." *Journal of Jewish Studies* 33 (1982): 287–301.

"The Judaism(s) of the Damascus Document." Pages 27–43 in *The Damascus Document: A Centennial of Discovery: Proceedings of the Third International Symposium of the Orion Center for the Study of the Dead Sea Scrolls and Associated Literature, 4–8 February, 1998.* Edited by J. M. Baumgarten, E. G. Chazon, and A. Pinnick. Studies on the Texts of the Desert of Judah 39. Leiden: Brill, 2000.

Debel, Hans. "Greek 'Variant Literary Editions' to the Hebrew Bible." *Journal for the Study of Judaism in the Persian, Hellenistic, and Roman Periods* 41 (2010): 161–90.

Derrett, J. D. M. "*Beḥuqey hagoyim*: Damascus Document IX,1 Again." *Revue de Qumran* 11 (1983): 409–15.

Dillman, August. *Der Prophet Jesaja*. Handbuch zum Alten Testament. Leipzig: S. Hirzel, 1890.

Dimant, Devorah. "The Hebrew Bible in the Dead Sea Scrolls: Torah Quotations in the *Damascus Covenant*." Pages 113*–22* in *"Sha'arei Talmon": Studies in the Bible, Qumran, and the Ancient Near East Presented to Shemaryahu Talmon*. Edited by M. Fishbane and E. Tov. Winona Lake: Eisenbrauns, 1992. [Hebrew]

"Two 'Scientific' Fictions: The So-Called Book of Noah and the Alleged Quotation of Jubilees in CD 16:3–4." Pages 242–48 in *Studies in the Hebrew Bible, Qumran, and the Septuagint: Essays Presented to Eugene Ulrich on the Occasion of His Sixty-Fifth Birthday*. Edited by P. W. Flint, J. C. VanderKam, and E. Tov. Supplements to Vetus Testamentum 101. Leiden: Brill, 2003.

Dix, G. H. "The Enochic Pentateuch." *Journal of Theological Studies* 27 (1925–26): 29–42.

Doering, Lutz. "The Concept of the Sabbath in the Book of Jubilees." Pages 179–205 in *Studies in the Book of Jubilees*. Edited by M. Albani, J. Frey, and A. Lange. Texte und Studien zum antiken Judentum 65. Tübingen: Mohr Siebeck, 1997.

"Jub 50:6–13 als Schlussabschnitt des 'Jubiläenbuchs' – Nachtrag aus Qumran oder ursprünglicher Bestandteil des Werks?" *Revue de Qumran* 20 (2002): 359–87.

"New Aspects of Qumran Sabbath Law from Cave 4 Fragments." Pages 251–74 in *Legal Texts and Legal Issues: Proceedings of the Second Meeting of the International Organization for Qumran Studies, Cambridge, 1995; Published in Honour of Joseph M. Baumgarten*. Edited by M. J. Bernstein, F. García Martínez, and J. Kampen. Studies on the Texts of the Desert of Judah 23. Leiden: Brill, 1997.

"Parallels Without 'Parallelomania': Methodological Reflections on Comparative Analysis of Halakhah in the Dead Sea Scrolls." Pages 13–42 in *Rabbinic Perspectives: Rabbinic Literature and the Dead Sea Scrolls: Proceedings of the Eighth International Symposium of the Orion Center for the Study of the Dead Sea Scrolls and Associated Literature, 7–9 January, 2003*. Edited by S. D. Fraade, A. Shemesh, and R. A. Clements. Studies on the Texts of the Desert of Judah 62. Leiden: Brill, 2006.

Schabbat: Sabbathhalacha und -praxis im antiken Judetum und Urchristentum. Texte und Studien zum antiken Judentum 78. Göttingen: Mohr Siebeck, 1999.

Doležel, Lubomír. *Heterocosmica: Fiction and Possible Worlds*. Baltimore: Johns Hopkins University Press, 1998.

Dupont-Sommer, A. *The Essene Writings from Qumran*. Translated by G. Vermes. Cleveland: Meridian, 1962.

Ehrlich, Arnold B. *Mikra Kifshuṭoh*. 3 vols. New York: Ktav, 1969.

Eilberg-Schwartz, Howard. *The Human Will in Judaism: The Mishnah's Philosophy of Intention*. Brown Judaic Studies 103. Atlanta: Scholars Press, 1986.

Elgvin, Torleif. "4Q421: 4Q*Ways of Righteousness*[b]." Pages 183–202 in *Qumran Cave 4.XV: Sapiential Texts*, part 1. Edited by J. A. Fitzymer et al. Discoveries in the Judaean Desert 20. Oxford: Clarendon, 1997.

Elman, Yaakov. "Some Remarks on 4QMMT and the Rabbinic Traditions: Or, When Is a Parallel Not a Parallel?" Pages 99–128 in *Reading 4QMMT: New Perspectives on Qumran Law and History*. Society of Biblical Literature Symposium Series 2. Edited by J. Kampen and M. J. Bernstein. Atlanta: Scholars Press, 1996.

Enelow, H. G. *Mishnat Rabbi Eli'ezer: Midrash Sheloshim u-Shetayim Middot*. New York: Block, 1933.

Epstein, Jacob N. "Additional Fragments of the Yerushalmi." *Tarbiz* 3 (1932): 15–26, 121–36, 237–48. [Hebrew]

Introduction to the Literature of the Tanaaim. Tel Aviv: Dvir; Jerusalem: Magnes, 1957. [Hebrew]

"Mishnat Rabbi Eliezer." *Hebrew Union College Annual* 23, part 2 (1950–51): *1–*15. [Hebrew]

Epstein, Jacob N., and E. Z. Melamed. *Mekhilta de Rabbi Shimon ben Yoḥai*. Jerusalem: Mekitse Nirdamim, 1955.

Eshel, Esther, and Hanan Eshel. "Dating the Samaritan Pentateuch's Compilation in Light of the Qumran Biblical Scrolls." Pages 215–40 in *Emanuel: Studies in the Hebrew Bible, Septuagint, and Dead Sea Scrolls in Honor of Emanuel Tov*. Edited by S. M. Paul et al. Supplements to Vetus Testamentum 94. Leiden: Brill, 2003.

Eshel, Hanan. "The Historical Background of the Pesher Interpreting Joshua's Curse on the Rebuilder of Jericho." *Revue de Qumran* 15 (1992): 409–20.

Falk, Daniel K. *Daily, Sabbath, and Festival Prayers in the Dead Sea Scrolls*. Studies on the Texts of the Desert of Judah 27. Leiden: Brill, 1997.

Falk, Ze'ev W. "*Beḥuqey hagoyim*: Damascus Document IX,1." *Revue de Qumran* 6 (1969): 569.

Fernández Marcos, Natalio. *The Septuagint in Context: Introduction to the Greek Versions of the Bible*. Translated by W. G. E. Watson. Leiden: Brill, 2000.

Finkelstein, Louis H. "The Book of Jubilees and the Rabbinic Halakha." *Harvard Theological Review* 16 (1923): 36–61.

"Some Examples of Maccabean Halaka." *Journal of Biblical Literature* 49 (1930): 20–42.

Fishbane, Michael. *Biblical Interpretation in Ancient Israel*. Oxford: Clarendon, 1985.

"Inner-Biblical Exegesis." Pages 33–48 in *Hebrew Bible/Old Testament: The History of Its Interpretation*, volume 1, section 1: *Antiquity*. Edited by M. Sæbø. Göttingen: Vandenhoeck and Ruprecht, 1996.

"Use, Authority, and Interpretation of Mikra at Qumran." Pages 339–77 in *Mikra: Text, Translation, Reading and Interpretation of the Hebrew Bible in Ancient Judaism and Early Christianity*. Edited by M. J. Mulder. Compendia rerum iudaicarum ad Novum Testamentum 2/1. Assen: Van Gorcum; Minneapolis: Fortress, 1988.

Fitzmyer, Joseph A. "The Use of Explicit Old Testament Quotations in Qumran Literature and in the New Testament." Pages 3–58 in *Essays on the Semitic Background of the New Testament*. London: G. Chapman, 1971. Repr. from *New Testament Studies* 7 (1960–61): 297–333.

Flint, Peter. "The Daniel Tradition at Qumran." Pages 329–67 in vol. 2 of *The Book of Daniel: Composition and Reception*. Edited by J. J. Collins and P. W. Flint. The Formation and Interpretation of Old Testament Literature 2. Supplements to Vetus Testamentum 83. 2 vols. Leiden: Brill, 2001.

Fonrobert, Charlotte. "From Separatism to Urbanism: The Dead Sea Scrolls and the Origins of the Rabbinic 'Eruv." *Dead Sea Discoveries* 11 (2004): 43–71.

Fraade, Steven D. "'Comparative Midrash' Revisited: The Case of the Dead Sea Scrolls and Rabbinic Midrash." Pages 261–84 in *Higayon L'Yonah: New Aspects in the*

Study of Midrash, Aggadah, and Piyut in Honor of Professor Yona Fraenkel. Edited by J. Levinson, J. Elbaum, and G. Hasan-Rokem. Jerusalem: Magnes, 2006. [Hebrew] Expanded version of an earlier English article of the same name that appeared as pages 4–17 in *Agendas for the Study of Midrash in the Twenty-First Century*. Edited by M. L. Raphael. Williamsburg: Department of Religion, The College of William and Mary, 1999.

"The Dead Sea Scrolls and Rabbinic Judaism after Sixty (Plus) Years: Retrospect and Prospect." Pages 109–24 in *Legal Fictions: Studies of Law and Narrative in the Discursive Worlds of Ancient Jewish Sectarians and Sages*. Journal for the Study of Judaism Supplement Series 147. Leiden: Brill, 2011.

From Tradition to Commentary: Torah and Its Interpretation in the Midrash Sifre to Deuteronomy. Albany: SUNY Press, 1991.

Legal Fictions: Studies of Law and Narrative in the Discursive Worlds of Ancient Jewish Sectarians and Sages. Journal for the Study of Judaism Supplement Series 147. Leiden: Brill, 2011.

"Looking for Legal Midrash at Qumran." Pages 145–68 in *Legal Fictions: Studies of Law and Narrative in the Discursive Worlds of Ancient Jewish Sectarians and Sages*. Journal for the Study of Judaism Supplement Series 147. Leiden: Brill, 2011. Repr. from pages 59–79 in *Biblical Perspectives: Early Use and Interpretation of the Bible in Light of the Dead Sea Scrolls; Proceedings of the First International Symposium of the Orion Center for the Study of the Dead Sea Scrolls and Associated Literature, 12–14 May, 1996*. Edited by M. E. Stone and E. G. Chazon. Studies on the Texts of the Desert of Judah 28. Leiden: Brill, 1998.

"Qumran *Yaḥad* and Rabbinic *Hăbûrâ*: A Comparison Reconsidered." Pages 125–44 in *Legal Fictions: Studies of Law and Narrative in the Discursive Worlds of Ancient Jewish Sectarians and Sages*. Journal for the Study of Judaism Supplement Series 147. Leiden: Brill, 2011. Repr. from *Dead Sea Discoveries* 16 (2009): 433–52.

"Rewritten Bible and Midrash as Commentary." Pages 381–98 in *Legal Fictions: Studies of Law and Narrative in the Discursive Worlds of Ancient Jewish Sectarians and Sages*. Journal for the Study of Judaism Supplement Series 147. Leiden: Brill, 2011. Repr. from pages 59–76 in *Current Trends in the Study of Midrash*. Edited by C. Bakhos. Journal for the Study of Judaism Supplement Series 106. Leiden: Brill, 2006.

Fraade, Steven D., Aharon Shemesh, and Ruth A. Clements, eds. *Rabbinic Perspectives: Rabbinic Literature and the Dead Sea Scrolls; Proceedings of the Eighth International Symposium of the Orion Center for the Study of the Dead Sea Scrolls and Associated Literature, 7–9 January, 2003*. Studies on the Texts of the Desert of Judah 62. Leiden: Brill, 2006.

Frankel, Yonah. *The Way of Legend and Midrash*. 2 vols. Tel Aviv: Open University, 1991. [Hebrew]

Frankel, Zecharias. *Uber den Einfluss der palästinischen Exegese auf die alexandrinische Hermeneutik*. Leipzig: Verlag von Joh. Ambr. Barth, 1851.

Friedman, Shamma. "The Holy Scriptures Defile the Hands – The Transformation of a Biblical Concept in Rabbinic Theology." Pages 117–32 in *Minḥa le-Naḥum: Biblical and Other Studies Presented to Nahum M. Sarna in Honour of His Seventieth Birthday*. Edited by M. Brettler and M. Fishbane. Journal for the Study of the Old Testament Supplement Series 154. Sheffield: Sheffield Academic Press, 1993.

Friedmann, Meir. *Midrash Pesikta Rabbati*. Vienna, 1880. Repr., Tel Aviv, 1963.

Fuller, Russell E. "4Q82: 4QXII[g]." Pages 271–318 in *Qumran Cave 4.X: The Prophets*. Edited by E. Ulrich et al. Discoveries in the Judaean Desert 15. Oxford: Clarendon, 1997.

García Martínez, Florentino. "The Heavenly Tablets in the Book of Jubilees." Pages 243–60 in *Studies in the Book of Jubilees*. Edited by M. Albani, J. Frey, and A. Lange. Tübingen: Mohr Siebeck, 1997.

"Rethinking the Bible: Sixty Years of Dead Sea Scrolls Research and Beyond." Pages 19–36 in *Authoritative Scriptures in Ancient Judaism*. Edited by M. Popović. Journal for the Study of Judaism Supplement Series 141. Leiden: Brill, 2010.

"The Temple Scroll." Pages 927–33 in vol. 2 of *Encyclopedia of the Dead Sea Scrolls*. Edited by L. H. Schiffman and J. C. VanderKam. 2 vols. Oxford: Oxford University Press, 2000.

García Martínez, Florentino, and Eibert J. C. Tigchelaar. *The Dead Sea Scrolls Study Edition*. 2 vols. Leiden: Brill, 1997–98.

Geiger, Abraham. *Urschrift und Übersetzungen der Bibel in ihrer Abhängigkeit von der inneren Entwicklung des Judentums*. Breslau: Julius Hainauer, 1857.

Gertner, M. "Terms of Scriptural Interpretation: A Study in Hebrew Semantics." *Bulletin of the American Schools of Oriental Research* 25 (1962): 1–27.

Gilat, Yitzḥak D. "Halakhic Interpretation (Midrash Halakha) of Scripture in the Post-Talmudic Period." Pages 374–94 in *Studies in the Development of the Halakha*. Ramat Gan: Bar Ilan University Press, 1992. Repr. from pages 210–31 in *Mikhtam le-David: Memorial Volume for R. David Ochs, z.l.* Ramat Gan: Bar Ilan University Press, 1978. [Hebrew]

"Intention and Action in Tannaitic Literature." Pages 72–84 in *Studies in the Development of the Halakha*. Ramat Gan: Bar Ilan University Press, 1992. Repr. from *Bar Ilan* 4–5 (1967–68): 104–16.

"Regarding the Antiquity of Several Sabbath Prohibitions." Pages 249–61 in *Studies in the Development of the Halakha*. Ramat Gan: Bar Ilan University Press, 1992. Repr. from *Bar Ilan* 1 (1963): 106–20. [Hebrew]

"The Sabbath and Its Laws in the World of Philo." Pages 61–73 in *Torah and Wisdom: Studies in Jewish Philosophy, Kabbalah, and Halacha; Essays in Honor of Arthur Hyman*. Edited by R. Link-Salinger. New York: Shengold, 1992.

The Teachings of R. Eliezer ben Hyrcanus and Their Place in the History of Halakha. Tel Aviv: Dvir, 1968. [Hebrew]

Ginzberg, Louis. *The Legends of the Jews*. 7 vols. Philadelphia: Jewish Publication Society of America, 1908–38.

"Eine unbekannte jüdische Sekte." *Monatschrift für Geschichte und Wissenschaft des Judentums* 55/2 (1911): 666–98; 56 (1912): 33–48, 285–307, 414–48, 664–89; 57 (1913): 153–76, 284–308, 394–418, 666–96; 58 (1914): 16–48, 143–77, 395–429.

Eine unbekannte jüdische Sekte. New York, 1922. Repr., Hildesheim: Olms, 1972.

An Unknown Jewish Sect. Moreshet 1. New York: Jewish Theological Seminary, 1976.

Gladson, Jerry A. "Jeremiah 17:19–27: A Rewriting of the Sinaitic Code?" *Catholic Biblical Quarterly* 62 (2000): 33–40.

Goldberg, Abraham. *Commentary to the Mishna Shabbat*. Jerusalem: Jewish Theological Seminary of America, 1976. [Hebrew]

Goldenberg, Robert. "Commandment and Consciousness in Talmudic Thought." *Harvard Theological Review* 68 (1975): 261–72.

Goodman, Martin D. "Sacred Scripture and 'Defiling the Hands.'" *Journal of Theological Studies* 41 (1990): 99–107.

Grätz, Sebastian. "The Second Temple and the Legal Status of the Torah: The Hermeneutics of the Torah in the Books of Ruth and Ezra." Pages 273–87 in *The Pentateuch as Torah: New Models for Understanding Its Promulgation and Acceptance*. Edited by G. N. Knoppers and B. M. Levinson. Winona Lake: Eisenbrauns, 2007.

Greenfield, Jonas. "The Words of Levi Son of Jacob in Damascus Document IV 15–19." *Revue de Qumran* 13 (1988): 319–22.

Greenspoon, Leonard J. "The Dead Sea Scrolls and the Greek Bible." Pages 101–27 in vol. 1 of *The Dead Sea Scrolls after Fifty Years: A Comprehensive Assessment*. Edited by J. C. VanderKam and P. W. Flint. 2 vols. Leiden: Brill, 1998–99.

Halivni, David Weiss. *Midrash, Mishnah, and Gemara: The Jewish Predilection for Justified Law*. Cambridge: Harvard University Press, 1986.

Hanneken, Todd R. "The Status and Interpretation of *Jubilees* in 4Q390." Pages 407–28 in vol. 1 of *A Teacher for All Generations: Essays in Honor of James C. VanderKam*. Edited by E. Mason et al. 2 vols. Journal for the Study of Judaism Supplement Series 153. Leiden: Brill, 2011.

Harrington, Daniel J. "The Bible Rewritten (Narratives)." Pages 239–47 in *Early Judaism and Its Modern Interpreters*. Edited by R. A Kraft and G. W. E. Nickelsburg. Atlanta: Scholars Press, 1986.

Harrington, Hannah K. "Biblical Law at Qumran." Pages 160–85 in vol. 1 of *The Dead Sea Scrolls after Fifty Years: A Comprehensive Assessment*. Edited by J. C. VanderKam and P. W. Flint. 2 vols. Leiden: Brill, 1998–99.

The Impurity Systems of Qumran and the Rabbis: Biblical Foundations. Atlanta: Scholars Press, 1993.

Hatch, Edwin, and Henry A. Redpath. *A Concordance to the Septuagint*. 2d ed. Grand Rapids: Baker, 1998.

Hayes, Christine. *Gentile Impurities and Jewish Identities: Intermarriage and Conversion from the Bible to the Talmud*. Oxford: Oxford University Press, 2002.

"Legal Realism and the Fashioning of Sectarians in Jewish Antiquity." Pages 119–46 in *Sects and Sectarianism in Jewish History*. Edited by S. Stern. Leiden: Brill, 2011.

Hempel, Charlotte. *The Laws of the Damascus Document: Sources, Traditions, and Redaction*. Studies on the Texts of the Desert of Judah 29. Leiden: Brill, 1998.

"The Place of the Book of Jubilees at Qumran and Beyond." Pages 187–96 in *The Dead Sea Scrolls in Their Historical Context*. Edited by T. H. Lim. Edinburgh: T. and T. Clark, 2000.

Henshke, David. "On the Relationship between Targum Pseudo-Jonathan and the Halakhic Midrashim." *Tarbiz* 68 (1999): 187–210. [Hebrew]

Henze, Matthias. *Jewish Apocalypticism in Late First Century Israel*. Texts and Studies in Ancient Judaism 142. Tübingen: Mohr Siebeck, 2011.

Herr, Moshe D. "Continuum in the Chain of Tradition of the Torah." *Zion* 44 (1979): 43–56. [Hebrew]

Higger, Michael. "Intention in Talmudic Law." Pages 235–93 in *Studies in Jewish Jurisprudence*. Edited by E. M. Gershfield. New York: Hermon, 1971. Repr. from Ph.D. dissertation, Columbia University, 1927.

Himmelfarb, Martha. "Levi, Phinehas, and the Problem of Intermarriage at the Time of the Maccabean Revolt." *Jewish Studies Quarterly* 6 (1999): 1–24.

Hoffmann, David Z. *Die erste Mischna und die Controversen der Tannaim*. Berlin, 1881–82.

Holladay, Carl R. *Fragments from Hellenistic Jewish Authors*, volume 1: *Historians*. Chico: Scholars Press, 1983.

Horgan, Maurya P. *Pesharim: Qumran Interpretations of Biblical Books*. Catholic Biblical Quarterly Monograph Series 8. Washington, D.C.: The Catholic Biblical Association of American, 1979.

Horowitz, H. S., and I. A. Rabin. *Mekhilta' d'Rabbi Ishmael*. Frankfurt: J. Kaufman, 1931. Repr. Jerusalem: Shalem, 1997.

Isaac, Ephraim. "Jubilees." Pages 35–142 in vol. 2 of *The Old Testament Pseudepigrapha*. Edited by J. H. Charlesworth. 2 vols. Anchor Bible Reference Library. New York: Doubleday, 1983–85.

Itzchaky, Efraim. "The Halacha in Targum Jerushalmi I (Pseudo-Jonathan Ben-Uziel) and Its Exegetical Methods." Ph.D. dissertation, Bar Ilan University, 1982. [Hebrew]

Jackson, Bernard S. "Liability for Mere Intention in Early Jewish Law." Pages 202–34 in *Essays in Jewish and Comparative Legal History*. Studies in Judaism in Late Antiquity 10. Leiden: Brill, 1975. Repr. from *Hebrew Union College Annual* 42 (1971): 197–225.

"The Prophets and the Law in Early Judaism and the New Testament." *Cardozo Studies in Law and Literature* 4 (1992): 123–66.

Jacobs, Louis, and Benjamin De Vries. "Halakhah." Pages 251–58 in vol. 8 of *Encyclopedia Judaica*. 2d ed. Edited by M. Berenbaum and F. Skolnik. 22 vols. Detroit: Macmillan Reference USA, 2007.

Japhet, Sara. "'Law' and 'The Law' in Ezra-Nehemiah." Pages 137–51 in *From the Rivers of Babylon to the Highlands of Judah: Collected Studies on the Restoration Period*. Winona Lake: Eisenbrauns, 2006. Repr. from pages 99–115 in *Proceedings of the Ninth World Congress of Jewish Studies, Panel Sessions: Bible Studies and Ancient Near East*. Edited by M. Goshen-Gottstein. Jerusalem: Magnes, 1988.

Jassen, Alex P. "American Scholarship on Jewish Law in the Dead Sea Scrolls." Pages 101–54 in *The Dead Sea Scrolls in Scholarly Perspective: A History of Research*. Edited by Devorah Dimant. Studies on the Texts of the Desert of Judah 99. Leiden: Brill, 2012.

"Law and Exegesis in the Dead Sea Scrolls: The Sabbath Carrying Prohibition in Comparative Perspective." Pages 115–56 in *The Dead Sea Scrolls at Sixty: The Scholarly Contributions of the New York University Faculty and Alumni*. Edited by L. H. Schiffman and S. Tsoref. Studies on the Texts of the Desert of Judah 89. Leiden: Brill, 2010.

Mediating the Divine: Prophecy and Revelation in the Dead Sea Scrolls and Second Temple Judaism. Studies on the Texts of the Desert of Judah 68. Leiden: Brill, 2007.

"The Pesharim and the Rise of Commentary in Early Jewish Scriptural Interpretation." *Dead Sea Discoveries* 19 (2012): 363–98.

"The Presentation of the Ancient Prophets as Lawgivers at Qumran." *Journal of Biblical Literature* 127 (2008): 307–37.

"What Exactly Is Prohibited in the Field? A New Suggestion for Understanding the Text and Context of CD 10:20–21." *Revue de Qumran* 25 (2011): 41–62.

Jastrow, Marcus. *A Dictionary of the Targumim, the Talmud Babli and Yerushalmi, and the Midrashic Literature*. Peabody: Hendrickson, 2005.

Kampen, John. "4QMMT and New Testament Studies." Pages 129–44 in *Reading 4QMMT: New Perspectives on Qumran Law and History*. Edited by J. Kampen and M. J. Bernstein. Society of Biblical Literature Symposium Series 2. Atlanta: Scholars Press, 1996.

Kaufman, Yehezkel. *The History of Israelite Religion*. 4 vols. Jerusalem: Bialik Institute, 1955. [Hebrew]

Kimbrough, S. T., Jr. "The Concept of Sabbath at Qumran." *Revue de Qumran* 5 (1966): 483–502.

Kister, Menahem. "A Common Heritage: Biblical Interpretation at Qumran and Its Implications." Pages 101–12 in *Biblical Perspectives: Early Use and Interpretation of the Bible in Light of the Dead Sea Scrolls; Proceedings of the First International Symposium of the Orion Center for the Study of the Dead Sea Scrolls and Associated Literature, 12–14 May, 1996*. Edited by M. E. Stone and E. G. Chazon. Studies on the Texts of the Desert of Judah 28. Leiden: Brill, 1998.

"Physical and Metaphysical Measurements Ordained by God in the Literature of the Second Temple Period." Pages 153–76 in *Reworking the Bible: Apocryphal and Related Texts at Qumran; Proceedings of a Joint Symposium by the Orion Center for the Study of the Dead Sea Scrolls and Associated Literature and the Hebrew University Institute for Advanced Studies Research Group on Qumran, 15–17 January, 2002*. Edited by E. G. Chazon, D. Dimant, and R. A. Clements. Studies on the Texts of the Desert of Judah 58. Leiden: Brill, 2005.

Kittel, G., and G. Friedrich, eds. *Theological Dictionary of the New Testament*. Translated by G. W. Bromiley. 10 vols. Grand Rapids: Eerdmans, 1964–76.

Klawans, Jonathan. *Impurity and Sin in Ancient Judaism*. Oxford: Oxford University Press, 2000.

Knibb, Michael A. *The Qumran Community*. Cambridge Commentaries on Writings of the Jewish and Christian World 2. Cambridge: Cambridge University Press, 1987.

Koehler, Ludwig, and Walter Baumgartner. *The Hebrew and Aramaic Lexicon of the Old Testament: Study Edition*. 2 vols. Leiden: Brill, 2001.

Kraft, Robert. "'Ezra' Materials in Judaism and Christianity." Pages 119–36 in *Aufstieg und Niedergang der römischen Welt: Geschichte und Kultur Roms im Spiegel der neueren Forschung* II.19.1. Edited by W. Hasse. Berlin: de Gruyter, 1979.

"Para-mania: Beside, Before and Beyond Bible Studies." *Journal of Biblical Literature* 126 (2007): 5–27.

Krochmal, Nachman. *More Nebukhe Ha-Zeman*. Lemberg: Josephi Schnayder, 1851. Repr. in *Kitve Rabbi Naḥman Krokhmal*. Edited by **Simon Rawidowicz**. 2d ed. London: Ararat, 1961.

Kugel, James L. *The Idea of Biblical Poetry: Parallelism and Its History*. New Haven: Yale University Press, 1981.

In Potiphar's House: The Interpretative Afterlife of Biblical Texts. San Francisco: HarperSanFrancisco, 1990.

Traditions of the Bible: A Guide to the Bible as It Was at the Start of the Common Era. Cambridge: Harvard University Press, 1998.

"Two Introductions to Midrash." Pages 77–103 in *Midrash and Literature*. Edited by G. H. Hartman and S. Budick. New Haven: Yale University Press, 1986. Repr. from *Prooftexts* 3 (1983): 131–55.

A Walk through Jubilees: *Studies in the* Book of Jubilees *and the World of Its Creation*. Journal for the Study of Judaism Supplement Series 156. Leiden: Brill, 2012.

Kugel, James L., and Rowan A. Greer. *Early Biblical Interpretation*. Philadelphia: Westminster, 1986.

Labendz, Jenny R. "The Book of Ben Sira in Rabbinic Literature." *Association for Jewish Studies Review* 30 (2006): 347–92.

Lange, Armin. "The Status of the Biblical Texts in the Qumran Corpus and the Canonical Process." Pages 21–30 in *The Bible as Book: The Hebrew Bible and the Judaean Desert Discoveries*. Edited by E. D. Herbert and E. Tov. London: British Library; New Castle: Oak Knoll Press, 2002.

"'They Confirmed the Reading' (y. Ta'an 4.68a): The Textual Standardization of Jewish Scriptures in the Second Temple Period." Pages 29–80 in *From Qumran to Aleppo: A Discussion with Emanuel Tov about the Textual History of Jewish Scriptures in Honor of His Sixty-Fifth Birthday*. Edited by A. Lange, M. Weigold, and J. Zsengellér. Forschungen zur Religion und Literatur des Alten und Neuen Testaments 230. Göttingen: Vandenhoeck and Ruprecht, 2009.

Larson, Eric, Manfred R. Lehmann, and Lawrence Schiffman. "4Q251: 4QHalakha A." Pages 28–30 in *Qumran Cave 4.XXV*. Edited by J. M. Baumgarten et al. Discoveries in the Judaean Desert 35. Oxford: Clarendon, 1999.

Lauterbach, Jacob Z. *Mekilta de-Rabbi Ishmael*. 3 vols. Philadelphia: Jewish Publication Society, 1976.

"Midrash and Mishnah: A Study in the Early History of Halakhah." Pages 163–256 in *Rabbinic Essays*. Edited by S. B. Freehof. Cincinnati: Hebrew Union College, 1951. Repr. from *Jewish Quarterly Review* 5 (1914–15): 503–27; 6 (1915–16): 23–95, 303–23.

Leaney, A. R. C. *The Rule of Qumran and Its Meaning*. New Testament Library. Philadelphia: Westminster, 1966.

Lehrman, S. M. *Midrash Rabbah: Exodus*. London: Soncino, 1939.

Leiman, Sid Z. *The Canonization of Hebrew Scripture: The Talmudic and Midrashic Evidence*. Transactions of the Connecticut Academy of Arts and Sciences 47. 2d ed. New Haven: Connecticut Academy of Arts and Sciences, 1991.

Leiter, Brian. "American Legal Realism." Pages 50–66 in *The Blackwell Guide to the Philosophy of Law and Legal Theory*. Edited by M. P. Golding and W. A. Edmundson. Malden: Blackwell, 2005.

Leslau, Wolf. *Comparative Dictionary of Ge'ez (Classical Ethiopic)*. Wiesbaden: Otto Harrassowitz, 1987.

Lévi, I. "Un Écrit Sadducéen Anterieur a la Destruction du Temple." *Revue des études juives* 61 (1911): 161–205.

Levine, Baruch A. "The Temple Scroll: Aspects of Its Historical Provenance and Literary Character." *Bulletin of the American Schools of Oriental Research* 232 (1978): 5–23.

Levinson, Bernard M. "The Case for Revision and Interpolation within the Biblical Legal Corpora." Pages 201–23 in *"The Right Chorale": Studies in Biblical Law and Interpretation*. Forschungen zur Alten Testament 54. Tübingen: Mohr Siebeck, 2008. Repr. from pages 37–59 in *Theory and Method in Biblical and Cuneiform Law:*

Revision, Interpolation, and Development. Edited by B. M. Levinson. Sheffield: Sheffield University Press, 1994.

Deuteronomy and the Hermeneutics of Legal Innovation. New York: Oxford University Press, 1997.

"The Hermeneutics of Tradition in Deuteronomy: A Reply to J. G. McConville." Pages 256–75 in *"The Right Chorale": Studies in Biblical Law and Interpretation*. Forschungen zur Alten Testament 54. Tübingen: Mohr Siebeck, 2008. Repr. from *Journal of Biblical Literature* 119 (2000): 269–86.

"Is the Covenant Code an Exilic Composition? A Response to John Van Seters." Pages 276–75 in *"The Right Chorale": Studies in Biblical Law and Interpretation*. Forschungen zur Alten Testament 54. Tübingen: Mohr Siebeck, 2008. Repr. from pages 272–325 in *In Search of Pre-Exilic Israel: Proceedings from the Oxford Old Testament Seminar*. Edited by J. Day. Journal for the Study of the Old Testament Supplement Series 406. London: T. and T. Clark, 2004.

Legal Revision and Religious Renewal in Ancient Israel. Cambridge: Cambridge University Press, 2008.

"The Manumission of Hermeneutics: The Slave Laws of the Pentateuch as a Challenge to Contemporary Pentateuchal Theory." Pages 281–324 in *Congress Volume: Leiden, 2004*. Edited by A. Lemaire. Supplements to Vetus Testamentum 109. Leiden: Brill, 2006.

Levinson, Bernard M., and Molly M. Zahn. "Revelation Regained: The Hermeneutics of כי and אם in the Temple Scroll." *Dead Sea Discoveries* 9 (2002): 295–346.

Levinson, Joshua. "Dialogical Reading in the Rabbinic Exegetical Narrative." *Poetics Today* 25 (2004): 497–528.

Lewin, B. M., ed. *Iggeret Rav Sherira Gaon*. Jerusalem: Makor, 1921.

Lewis, Jack P. "Jamniah Revisited." Pages 146–62 in *The Canon Debate*. Edited by L. M. McDonald and J. A. Sanders. Peabody: Hendrickson, 2002.

"What Do We Mean by Jabneh?" Pages 254–61 in *The Canon and Masorah of the Hebrew Bible: An Introductory Reader*. New York: Ktav, 1974. Repr. from *Journal of Bible and Religion* 32 (1964): 125–32.

Licht, Jacob. *The Rule Scroll: A Scroll from the Wilderness of Judaea*. Jerusalem: Bialik Institute, 1965. [Hebrew]

Liddell, Henry C., and Robert Scott, revised and augmented by Henry Scott Jones. *A Greek-English Lexicon: With Revised Supplement*. Oxford: Clarendon, 1996.

Lieberman, Saul. "The Discipline of the So-Called Dead Sea Manual of Discipline." Pages 200–7 in *Texts and Studies*. New York: Ktav, 1974. Repr. from *Journal of Biblical Literature* 71 (1952): 199–206.

"Light on the Cave Scrolls from Rabbinic Sources." Pages 190–99 in *Texts and Studies*. New York: Ktav, 1974. Repr. from *Proceedings of the American Academy of Jewish Research* 20 (1951): 395–404.

The Tosefta: The Order of Mo'ed. New York: Jewish Theological Seminary, 1962.

Tosefta Kifshuṭah, part 3: *Seder Mo'ed*. Jerusalem: Jewish Theological Seminary of America, 1962.

Yerushalmi Kifshuṭoh, volume 1. Jerusalem: Darom, 1935.

Lightstone, Jack N. "The Rabbis' Bible: The Canon of the Hebrew Bible and the Early Rabbinic Guild." Pages 163–84 in *The Canon Debate*. Edited by L. M. McDonald and J. A. Sanders. Peabody: Hendrickson, 2002.

Lim, Timothy H. "The Alleged Reference to the Tripartite Division of the Hebrew Bible." *Revue de Qumran* 20 (2001): 23–37.

"The Defilement of the Hands as a Principle Determining the Holiness of Scriptures." *Journal of Theological Studies* 61 (2010): 501–15.

Loader, William. *The Dead Sea Scrolls on Sexuality: Attitudes towards Sexuality in Sectarian and Related Literature at Qumran*. Grand Rapids: Eerdmans, 2009.

Lohse, Eduard. *Die Texte aus Qumran*. München: Kösel, 1964.

Lucas, Alec J. "Scripture Citations as an Internal Redactional Control: 1QS 5:1–20a and Its 4Q Parallels." *Dead Sea Discoveries* 17 (2010): 30–52.

Lundbom, Jack R. *Jeremiah 1–20*. Anchor Bible 21A. New York: Doubleday, 1999.

Lust, Johann. "Quotation Formulae and Canon in Qumran." Pages 67–77 in *Canon and Decanonization*. Edited by A. van der Kooij and K. van der Toorn. Studies in the History of Religions 82. Leiden: Brill, 1998.

Magness, Jodi. "Communal Meals and Sacred Space at Qumran." Pages 81–112 in *Debating Qumran: Collected Essays on Its Archaeology*. Leuven: Peeters 2004. Repr. from pages 15–28 in *Shaping Community: The Art and Archaeology of Monasticism*. Edited by S. McNally. Biblical Archaeology Review International Series 941. Oxford: Archaeopress, 2001.

"Dogs and Chickens at Qumran." Pages 349–62 in *The Dead Sea Scrolls and Contemporary Culture: Proceedings of the International Conference Held at the Israel Museum (July 6–8, 2008)*. Edited by A. D. Roitman, L. H. Schiffman, and S. Tzoref. Studies on the Texts of the Desert of Judah 93. Leiden: Brill, 2011.

Mandel, Paul. "Midrashic Exegesis and Its Precedents in the Dead Sea Scrolls." *Dead Sea Discoveries* 8 (2001): 149–68.

"The Origins of 'Midrash' in the Second Temple Period." Pages 9–43 in *Current Trends in the Study of Midrash*. Edited by C. Bakhos. Journal for the Study of Judaism Supplement Series 106. Leiden: Brill, 2006.

Margaliot, Mordechai. *Midrash Ha-Gadol: Shemot*. Jerusalem: Mossad ha-Rav Kook, 1956.

Midrash Vayyikra Rabbah. 5 vols. New York: Jewish Theological Seminary, 1993.

Mason, Steve. "Josephus and His Twenty-Two Book Canon." Pages 110–27 in *The Canon Debate*. Edited by L. M. McDonald and J. A. Sanders. Peabody: Hendrickson, 2002.

McCarter, P. Kyle, Jr. *I Samuel*. Anchor Bible 8. Garden City: Doubleday, 1980.

McDonald, Lee Martin. "Appendix A: Primary Sources for the Study of the Old Testament/Hebrew Bible Canon." Pages 580–82 in *The Canon Debate*. Edited by L. M. McDonald and J. A. Sanders. Peabody: Hendrickson, 2002.

McKenzie, John L. *Second Isaiah*. Anchor Bible 20. New York: Doubleday, 1968.

Meier, John P. "Is There *Halaka* (Noun) at Qumran?" *Journal of Biblical Literature* 122 (2003): 150–55.

Meir, Ofra. *The Darshanic Story in Genesis Rabba*. Tel Aviv: Hakibbutz Hameuchad, 1987. [Hebrew]

Metso, Sarianna. "Biblical Quotations in the Community Rule." Pages 81–92 in *The Bible as Book: The Hebrew Bible and the Judaean Desert*. Edited by E. D. Herbert and E. Tov. London: British Library; New Castle: Oak Knoll Press, 2002.

The Serekh Texts. Companion to the Qumran Scrolls 9. Library of Second Temple Studies 62. London: T. and T. Clark, 2007.

The Textual Development of the Qumran Community Rule. Studies on the Texts of the Desert of Judah 21. Leiden: Brill, 1997.

Milgrom, Jacob. "The Levitical 'Aboḏā." *Jewish Quarterly Review* 61 (1970): 132–54.

"The Qumran Cult: Its Exegetical Principles." Pages 165–80 in *Temple Scroll Studies: Papers Presented at the International Symposium on the Temple Scroll: Manchester, December 1987*. Edited by G. J. Brooke. Journal for the Study of the Pseudepigrapha Supplement Series 7. Sheffield: JSOT Press, 1989.

"Qumran's Biblical Hermeneutics: The Case of the Wood Offering." *Revue de Qumran* 16 (1993–94): 449–56.

Studies in Levitical Terminology I: The Encroacher and the Levite, the Term 'Aboda. University of California Publication in Near Eastern Studies 14. Berkeley: University of California Press, 1970.

Milik, J. T. "1Q30–31: Textes liturgiques (?)." Pages 132–34 in *Qumrân Cave 1*. Edited by D. Barthélemy and J. T. Milik. Discoveries in the Judaean Desert 1. Oxford: Clarendon, 1955.

"5Q12: Document de Damas." Page 181 in *Les "Petites Grottes" de Qumran*. Edited by M. Baillet, J. T. Milik, and R. de Vaux. Discoveries in the Judaean Desert 3. Oxford: Clarendon, 1962.

The Books of Enoch: Aramaic Fragments of Qumrân Cave 4. Oxford: Clarendon, 1976.

Milik, J. T., and James C. VanderKam. "4Q217: 4QpapJubilees[b]?" Pages 24–33 in *Qumran Cave 4.VIII: Parabiblical Texts*, part 1. Edited by H. Attridge et al. Discoveries in the Judaean Desert 13. Oxford: Clarendon, 1994.

Morris, Herbert. "Punishment for Thoughts." Pages 1–29 in *On Guilt and Innocence: Essays in Legal Philosophy and Moral Psychology*. Berkeley: University of California Press, 1976.

Najman, Hindy. "Interpretation as Primordial Writing: Jubilees and Its Authority Conferring Strategies." Pages 39–71 in *Past Renewals: Interpretative Authority, Renewed Revelation and the Quest for Perfection in Jewish Antiquity*. Journal for the Study of Judaism Supplement Series 53. Leiden: Brill, 2010. Repr. from *Journal for the Study of Judaism in the Persian, Hellenistic, and Roman Periods* 30 (1999): 380–410.

"Reconsidering Jubilees: Prophecy and Exemplarity." Pages 189–206 in *Past Renewals: Interpretative Authority, Renewed Revelation and the Quest for Perfection in Jewish Antiquity*. Journal for the Study of Judaism Supplement Series 53. Leiden: Brill, 2010. Repr. from pages 229–43 in *Enoch and the Mosaic Torah: The Evidence of Jubilees*. Edited by G. Boccaccini and G. Ibba. Grand Rapids: Eerdmans, 2009.

Seconding Sinai: The Development of Mosaic Discourse in Second Temple Judaism. Journal for the Study of Judaism Supplement Series 77. Leiden: Brill, 2003.

"Torah of Moses: Pseudonymous Attribution in Second Temple Writings." Pages 73–86 in *Past Renewals: Interpretative Authority, Renewed Revelation and the Quest for Perfection in Jewish Antiquity*. Journal for the Study of Judaism Supplement Series 53. Leiden: Brill, 2010. Repr. from pages 202–16 in *The Interpretation of Scripture in Early Judaism and Christianity*. Edited by C. A. Evans. Scripture in Early Judaism and Christianity 7. London: T. and T. Clark, 2004.

"The Vitality of Scripture Within and Beyond the Canon." *Journal for the Study of Judaism in the Persian, Hellenistic, and Roman Periods* 43 (2012): 497–515.

Nelson, W. David. *Mekhilta de Rabbi Shimon bar Yoḥai*. Philadelphia: Jewish Publication Society, 2006.

Neusner, Jacob. *Judaism and Scripture: The Evidence of Leviticus Rabbah*. Chicago: University of Chicago Press, 1986.

"Map Without Territory: Mishnah's System of Sacrifice and Sanctuary." Pages 133–54 in *Method and Meaning in Ancient Judaism*. Atlanta: Scholars Press, 1979.

The Mishnah: A New Translation. New Haven: Yale University Press, 1988.

The Rabbis, the Law, and the Prophets. Lanham: University Press of America, 2008.

The Tosefta: Translated from the Hebrew with a New Introduction. 2 vols. Peabody: Hendrickson, 2002.

Neusner, Jacob, and Alan J. Avery Peck. *Encyclopedia of Midrash*. 2 vols. Leiden: Brill, 2005.

Newsom, Carol A. "4Q378 and 4Q379: An Apocryphon of Joshua." Pages 350–85 in *Qumranstudien: Vorträge und Beiträge der Tailnehmer des Qumranseminars auf dem internationalen Treffen der Society of Biblical Literature, Münster 25.–26. Juli 1993*. Edited by H.-J. Fabry, A. Lange, and H. Lichtenberger. Göttingen: Vandenhoeck and Ruprecht, 1996.

Nihan, Christophe L. "The Emergence of the Pentateuch as 'Torah.'" *Religion Compass* 4 (2010): 353–64.

Nitzan, Bilhah. "The Continuity of Biblical Interpretation in the Qumran Scrolls and Rabbinic Literature." Pages 337–50 in *The Oxford Handbook of the Dead Sea Scrolls*. Edited by T. H. Lim and J. J. Collins. Oxford: Oxford University Press, 2010.

Noam, Vered. "Creative Interpretation and Integrative Interpretation in Qumran." Pages 363–76 in *The Dead Sea Scrolls and Contemporary Culture: Proceedings of the International Conference Held at the Israel Museum (July 6–8, 2008)*. Edited by A. D. Roitman, L. H. Schiffman, and S. Tzoref. Studies on the Texts of the Desert of Judah 93. Leiden: Brill, 2011.

"Early Signs of Halakhic Midrash at Qumran." *Diné Israel: Studies in Halakhah and Jewish Law* 26–27 (2009–10): 3–26. [Hebrew]

"Embryonic Legal Midrash in the Qumran Scrolls." Pages 237–62 in *The Hebrew Bible in Light of the Dead Sea Scrolls*. Edited by N. Dávid et al. Forschungen zur Religion und Literatur des Alten und Neuen Testaments 239. Göttingen: Vandenhoeck and Ruprecht, 2011.

"Ritual Purity in Tannaitic Literature: Two Opposing Perspectives." *Journal of Ancient Judaism* 1 (2010): 65–103.

Noam, Vered, and Elisha Qimron. "A Qumran Composition of Sabbath Laws and Its Contribution to the Study of Early Halakah." *Dead Sea Discoveries* 16 (2009): 55–96. Earlier Hebrew version appeared in *Tarbiz* 74 (2005): 511–46.

Pardo, Rabbi David. *Ḥasde David*, volume 1. Livorno, 1776.

Patrick, Dale. "The Covenant Code Source." *Vestus Testamentum* 27 (1977): 145–57.

Philo, volume 6. Translated by F. H. Colson. Loeb Classical Library 289. Cambridge: Harvard University Press; London: William Heinemann, 1935.

Pérez Fernández, Miguel. *An Introductory Grammar of Rabbinic Hebrew*. Translated by J. Elwolde. Leiden: Brill, 1999.

Puech, Émile. "Notes sur les fragments grecs du manuscript 7Q4 = 1 Hénoch 103 et 105." *Revue biblique* 103 (1996): 592–600.

Pummer, Reinhard. "The Samaritans and Their Pentateuch." Pages 237–69 in *The Pentateuch as Torah: New Models for Understanding Its Promulgation and Acceptance*. Edited by G. N. Knoppers and B. M. Levinson. Winona Lake: Eisenbrauns, 2007.

Purvis, James D. *The Samaritan Pentateuch and the Origins of the Samaritan Sect*. Harvard Semitic Monographs 2. Cambridge: Harvard University Press, 1968.

Qimron, Elisha. "The Text of CDC." Pages 9–49 in *The Damascus Document Reconsidered*. Edited by M. Broshi. Jerusalem: Israel Exploration Society, the Shrine of the Book, Israel Museum, 1992.

Qimron, Elisha, and James H. Charlesworth. "Rule of the Community (1QS; cf. 4QMSS A–J, 5Q11)." Pages 1–107 in *The Dead Sea Scrolls: Hebrew, Aramaic, and Greek Texts with English Translations; Rule of the Community and Related Documents*. Edited by J. H. Charlesworth. Princeton Theological Seminary Dead Sea Scrolls Project 1. Tübingen: Mohr Siebeck; Louisville: Westminster John Knox, 1994.

Qimron, Elisha, and John Strugnell. *Qumran Cave 4.V: Miqṣat Maʿaśe Ha-Torah*. Discoveries in the Judaean Desert 10. Oxford: Clarendon, 1996.

Rabbinovicz, Raphael. *Sefer Dikduke Sofrim = Variae Lectiones in Mischnam et in Talmud Babylonicum*. 2 vols. New York: M. P. Press, 1976.

Rabin, Chaim. *Qumran Studies*. Scripta Judaica 2. Oxford: Clarendon, 1957.

The Zadokite Documents. Oxford: Clarendon, 1954.

Ratner, Baer. *Ahavath Ṣiyyon Vi-Yerushalayim: Shabbat*. Vilna: F. Garber, 1902.

Ravid, Liora. "Sabbath Laws in the Book of *Jubilees* 50:6–13." *Tarbiz* 69 (2000): 161–66. [Hebrew]

Roberts, Alexander, and James Donaldson. *The Ante-Nicene Fathers*, vol. 7. Buffalo: Christian Literature Company, 1886.

Roberts, Bleddyn J. "The Dead Sea Scrolls and the Old Testament Scriptures." *Bulletin of the John Reynolds University Library of Manchester* 36 (1953–54): 75–96.

Rochberg-Halton, Francesca. "Canonicity in Cuneiform Texts." *Journal of Cuneiform Studies* 36 (1984): 127–44.

Rost, Leonhard. *Die Damascusschrift: Neu Bearbeitet*. Klein Texte für Vorlesungen und Übungen 167. Berlin: de Gruyter, 1933.

Roth, Martha T. *Laws Collections from Mesopotamia and Asia Minor*. 2d ed. Society of Biblical Literature Writings from the Ancient World 6. Atlanta: Scholars Press, 1997.

"Mesopotamian Legal Traditions and the Laws of Hammurabi." *Chicago-Kent Law Review* 71 (1995–96): 13–39.

Rubenstein, Jeffrey L. "Nominalism and Realism in Qumranic and Rabbinic Law: A Reassessment." *Dead Sea Discoveries* 6 (1999): 157–83.

Sanderson, Judith A. *An Exodus Scroll from Qumran: 4QpaleoExod^{m} and the Samaritan Tradition*. Harvard Semitic Studies 30. Atlanta: Scholars Press, 1986.

Sarna, Nahum. *On the Book of Psalms: Exploring the Prayers of Ancient Israel*. New York: Schocken, 1993.

Sarna, Nahum, S., et al. "Bible." Pages 572–679 in vol. 3 of *Encyclopedia Judaica*. 2d ed. Edited by M. Berenbaum and F. Skolnik. 22 vols. Detroit: Macmillan Reference USA, 2007.

Schechter, Solomon. *Avoth de-Rabbi Nathan*. New York: Jewish Theological Seminary, 1997.

Documents of Jewish Sectaries, volume 1: *Fragments of a Zadokite Work*. Cambridge; Cambridge University Press, 1910. Repr. with prolegomenon by Joseph Fitzmyer. Library of Biblical Studies. New York: Ktav, 1970.

"Dr. Büchler's Review of Schechter's 'Jewish Sectaries.'" *Jewish Quarterly Review* 4 (1914): 449–74.

Schiffman, Lawrence H. "Codification of Jewish Law in the Dead Sea Scrolls." Pages 170–83 in *Qumran and Jerusalem: Studies on the Dead Sea Scrolls and the History of Judaism*. Grand Rapids: Eerdmans, 2010. Repr. from pages 21–39 in *Discussing Cultural Influences: Text, Context, and Non-text in Rabbinic Judaism*. Edited by R. Ulmer. Lanham: University Press of America, 2007.

"Confessionalism and the Study of the Dead Sea Scrolls." *Jewish Studies: Forum of the World Union of Jewish Studies* 31 (1991): 3–14.

The Courtyards of the House of the Lord: Studies on the Temple Scroll. Edited by F. García Martínez. Studies on the Texts of the Desert of Judah 75. Leiden: Brill, 2008.

"The Dead Sea Scrolls and Rabbinic *Halakhah*." Pages 3–24 in *The Dead Sea Scrolls as Background to Postbiblical Judaism and Early Christianity: Papers from an International Conference at St. Andrews in 2001*. Edited by J. R. Davila. Studies on the Texts of the Desert of Judah 46. Leiden: Brill, 2003.

"Dead Sea Scrolls, Biblical Interpretation in." Pages 40–54 in vol. 1 of *Encyclopedia of Midrash*. Edited by J. Neusner and A. J. Avery Peck. 2 vols. Leiden: Brill, 2005.

"The Deuteronomic Paraphrase of the Temple Scroll." Pages 443–70 in *Courtyards of the House of the Lord*. Edited by F. García Martínez. Studies on the Texts of the Desert of Judah 75. Leiden: Brill, 2008. Repr. from *Revue de Qumran* 15 (1992): 543–67.

"Halakhah and History: The Contribution of the Dead Sea Scrolls to Recent Scholarship." Pages 63–78 in *Qumran and Jerusalem: Studies in the Dead Sea Scrolls and the History of Judaism*. Grand Rapids: Eerdmans, 2010. Repr. from pages 205–19 in *Jüdische Geschichte in hellenistisch-römischer Zeit*. Edited by A. Oppenheimer and E. Müller-Luckner. Schriften des Historischen Kollegs, Kolloquien 44. Munich: Oldenbourg, 1999.

"Halakhah and Sectarianism in the Dead Sea Scrolls." Pages 123–42 in *The Dead Sea Scrolls in Their Historical Context*. Edited by T. Lim. Edinburgh: T. and T. Clark, 2000.

"The Halakhah at Qumran." 2 vols. Ph.D. dissertation, Brandeis University, 1974.

The Halakhah at Qumran. Studies in Judaism in Late Antiquity 16. Leiden: Brill, 1975.

"The Judean Scrolls and the History of Judaism." Pages 542–57 in *The Dead Sea Scrolls Fifty Years after Their Discovery: Proceedings of the Jerusalem Congress, July 20–25, 1997*. Edited by L. H. Schiffman, E. Tov, and J. C. VanderKam. Jerusalem: Israel Exploration Society in cooperation with the Shrine of the Book, Israel Museum, 2000.

Law, Custom, and Messianism in the Dead Sea Scrolls. Jerusalem: Zalman Shazar Center, 1993. [Hebrew]

"The Law of Vows and Oaths (Num. 30:3–16) in the Zadokite Fragments and the Temple Scroll." Pages 557–72 in *The Courtyards of the House of the Lord: Studies on the Temple Scroll*. Edited by F. García Martínez. Studies on the Texts of the

Desert of Judah 75. Leiden: Brill, 2008. Repr. from *Revue de Qumran* 15 (1991): 199–214.

"Ordinances and Rules." Page 145–76 in *The Dead Sea Scrolls: Hebrew, Aramaic, and Greek Texts with English Translations; Rule of the Community and Related Documents*. Edited by J. H. Charlesworth. Princeton Theological Seminary Dead Sea Scrolls Project 1. Tübingen: Mohr Siebeck; Louisville: Westminster John Knox, 1994.

"Pre-Maccabean Halakhah in the Dead Sea Scrolls and the Biblical Tradition." Pages 184–96 in *Qumran and Jerusalem: Studies in the Dead Sea Scrolls and the History of Judaism*. Grand Rapids: Eerdmans, 2010. Repr. from *Dead Sea Discoveries* 13 (2006): 348–61.

"Prohibited Marriages in the Dead Sea Scrolls." Pages 113–25 in *Rabbinic Perspectives: Rabbinic Literature and the Dead Sea Scrolls: Proceedings of the Eighth International Symposium of the Orion Center for the Study of the Dead Sea Scrolls and Associated Literature, 7–9 January, 2003*. Edited by S. D. Fraade, A. Shemesh, and R. A. Clements. Studies on the Texts of the Desert of Judah 62. Leiden: Brill, 2006.

Qumran and Jerusalem: Studies in the Dead Sea Scrolls and the History of Judaism. Grand Rapids: Eerdmans, 2010.

"The Qumran Scrolls and Rabbinic Judaism." Pages 1–11 in *Qumran and Jerusalem: Studies in the Dead Sea Scrolls and the History of Judaism*. Grand Rapids: Eerdmans, 2010. Repr. from pages 552–71 in vol. 2 of *The Dead Sea Scrolls after Fifty Years: A Comprehensive Assessment*. Edited by J. C. VanderKam and P. W. Flint. 2 vols. Leiden: Brill, 1998–99.

Reclaiming the Dead Sea Scrolls: The History of Judaism, the Background of Christianity, the Lost Library of Qumran. Anchor Bible Reference Library. New York: Doubleday, 1995.

"Reproof as Requisite for Punishment in the Law of the Dead Sea Scrolls." Pages 59–74 in *Jewish Law Association Studies*, volume 2: *The Jerusalem Conference Volume*. Edited by B. S. Jackson. Atlanta: Scholars Press, 1986.

Sectarian Law in the Dead Sea Scrolls: Courts, Testimony and the Penal Code. Brown Judaic Studies 33. Chico: Scholars Press, 1983.

"The Septuagint and the Temple Scroll: Shared 'Halakhic' Variants." Pages 85–98 in *The Courtyards of the House of the Lord: Studies on the Temple Scroll*. Edited by F. García Martínez. Studies on the Texts of the Desert of Judah 75. Leiden: Brill, 2008. Repr. from pages 277–97 in *Septuagint, Scrolls, and Cognate Writings: Papers Presented to the International Symposium on the Septuagint and Its Relations to the Dead Sea Scrolls and Other Writings*. Edited by G. J. Brooke and B. Lindars. Society of Biblical Literature Septuagint and Cognate Studies 33. Altanta: Scholars Press, 1992.

"The Temple Scroll and the Halakhic Pseudepigrapha of the Second Temple Period." Pages 163–74 in *The Courtyards of the House of the Lord: Studies on the Temple Scroll*. Edited by F. García Martínez. Studies on the Texts of the Desert of Judah 75. Leiden: Brill, 2008. Repr. from pages 121–31 in *Pseudepigraphic Perspectives: The Apocrypha and Pseudepigrapha in Light of the Dead Sea Scrolls: Proceedings of the International Symposium of the Orion Center for the Study of the Dead Sea Scrolls and Associated Literature, 12–14 January, 1997*. Edited by E. G. Chazon and M. Stone. Studies on the Texts of the Desert of Judah 31. Leiden: Brill, 1999.

"The Temple Scroll and the Systems of Jewish Law in the Second Temple Period." Pages 239–55 in *Temple Scroll Studies: Papers Presented at the International Symposium on the Temple Scroll: Manchester, December 1987*. Edited by G. J. Brooke. Journal for the Study of the Pseudepigrapha Supplement Series 7. Sheffield: JSOT Press, 1989.

"The Temple Scroll in Literary and Philological Perspective." Pages 143–58 in *Approaches to Ancient Judaism*, volume 2. Edited by W. S. Green. Chico: Scholars Press, 1980.

Schmid, Konrad. "The Persian Imperial Authorization as a Historical Problem and as a Biblical Construct: A Plea for Distinctions in the Current Debate." Pages 23–38 in *The Pentateuch as Torah: New Models for Understanding Its Promulgation and Acceptance*. Edited by G. N. Knoppers and B. M. Levinson. Winona Lake: Eisenbrauns, 2007.

Schofield, Alison. *From Qumran to the Yaḥad: A New Paradigm of Textual Development for the Community Rule*. Studies on the Texts of the Desert of Judah 77. Leiden: Brill, 2008.

Schremer, Adiel. "'[T]he[y] Did Not Read in the Sealed Book': Qumran Halakhic Revolution and the Emergence of Torah Study in Second Temple Judaism." Pages 105–26 in *Historical Perspectives: From the Hasmoneans to Bar Kokhba in Light of the Dead Sea Scrolls: Proceedings of the Fourth International Symposium of the Orion Center for the Study of the Dead Sea Scrolls and Associated Literature, 27–31 January, 1999*. Edited by D. Goodblatt, A. Pinnick, and D. R. Schwartz. Studies on the Texts of the Desert of Judah 37. Leiden: Brill, 2001.

Schuller, Eileen. "Women in the Dead Sea Scrolls." Pages 117–44 in vol. 2 of *The Dead Sea Scrolls after Fifty Years: A Comprehensive Assessment*. Edited by J. C. VanderKam and P. W. Flint. 2 vols. Leiden: Brill, 1998–99.

Schwartz, Daniel R. "Law and Truth: On Qumran-Sadducean and Rabbinic Views of Law." Pages 229–40 in *The Dead Sea Scrolls: Forty Years of Research*. Edited by D. Dimant and U. Rappaport. Studies on the Texts of the Desert of Judah 10. Leiden: Brill; Jerusalem: Magnes Press and Yad Izhak Ben-Zvi, 1992.

Segal, Michael. "4QReworked Pentateuch or 4QPentateuch." Pages 391–99 in *The Dead Sea Scrolls Fifty Years after Their Discovery: Proceedings of the Jerusalem Congress, July 20–25, 1997*. Edited by L. H. Schiffman, E. Tov, and J. C. VanderKam. Jerusalem: Israel Exploration Society in cooperation with the Shrine of the Book, Israel Museum, 2000.

"Between Bible and Rewritten Bible." Pages 10–28 in *Biblical Interpretation at Qumran*. Edited by M. Henze. Grand Rapids: Eerdmans, 2005.

The Book of Jubilees: Rewritten Bible, Redaction, Ideology, and Theology. Journal for the Study of Judaism Supplement Series 117. Leiden: Brill, 2007.

"The Text of the Hebrew Bible in Light of the Dead Sea Scrolls." *Materia Giudaica Anno* 12/1–2 (2007): 10–17.

Sharp, Carolyn. "Phinehan Zeal and Rhetorical Strategy in 4QMMT." *Revue de Qumran* 18 (1997): 207–22.

Sharvit, Baruch. "The Sabbath of the Judean Desert Sect." *Immanuel* 9 (1979): 42–48.

Shaver, Judson R. *Torah and the Chronicler's History Work: An Inquiry into the Chronicler's References to Laws, Festivals, and Cultic Institutions in Relationship to Pentateuchal Legislation*. Brown Judaic Studies 196. Atlanta: Scholars Press, 1989.

Shemesh, Aharon. "4Q265 and the Authoritative Status of Jubilees at Qumran." Pages 247–60 in *Enoch and the Mosaic Torah: The Evidence of Jubilees*. Edited by G. Boccaccini and G. Ibba. Grand Rapids: Eerdmans, 2009.

Halakhah in the Making: The Development of Jewish Law from Qumran to the Rabbis. Berkeley: University of California Press, 2009.

"Scriptural Interpretations in the Damascus Document and Their Parallels in Rabbinic Midrash." Pages 161–75 in *The Damascus Document: A Centennial of Discovery: Proceedings of the Third International Symposium of the Orion Center for the Study of the Dead Sea Scrolls and Associated Literature, 4–8 February, 1998*. Edited by J. M. Baumgarten, E. G. Chazon, and A. Pinnick. Studies on the Texts of the Desert of Judah 39. Leiden: Brill, 2000.

Shemesh, Aharon, and Cana Werman. "Halakhah at Qumran: Genre and Authority." *Dead Sea Discoveries* 10 (2003): 104–29.

Silman, Yochanan. "Halakhic Determinations of a Nominalist and Realistic Nature: Legal and Philosophical Considerations." *Diné Israel: Studies in Halakhah and Jewish Law* 12 (1984–85): 249–66. [Hebrew]

Skehan, Patrick W. "The Divine Name at Qumran, in the Masada Scroll, and in the Septuagint." *Bulletin of the International Organization for Septuagint and Cognate Studies* 13 (1980): 14–44.

Skehan, Patrick W., and Eugene Ulrich. "4Q103: 4QProv[b]." Pages 183–86 in *Cave 4.XI: Psalms to Chronicles*. Edited by E. Ulrich et al. Discoveries in the Judaean Desert 16. Oxford: Clarendon, 2000.

Skehan, Patrick W., Eugene Ulrich, and Judith Sanderson. "4Q11: 4QpaleoGen-Exod[l]." Pages 17–50 in *Qumran Cave 4.IV: Palaeo-Hebrew and Greek Biblical Manuscripts*. Edited by P. W. Skehan, E. Ulrich, and J. E. Sanderson. Discoveries in the Judaean Desert 9. Oxford: Clarendon, 1992.

"4Q45: 4QpaleoDeuteronomy[r]." Pages 131–52 in *Qumran Cave 4.IV: Palaeo-Hebrew and Greek Biblical Manuscripts*. Edited by P. W. Skehan, E. Ulrich, and J. E. Sanderson. Discoveries in the Judaean Desert 9. Oxford: Clarendon, 1992.

Qumran Cave 4.IV: Palaeo-Hebrew and Greek Biblical Manuscripts. Discoveries in the Judaean Desert 9. Oxford: Clarendon, 1992.

Skinner, J. *Isaiah: Chapters XL–LXVI*. Cambridge: Cambridge University Press, 1898.

Slomovic, Elieser. "Toward an Understanding of the Exegesis in the Dead Sea Scrolls." *Revue de Qumran* 7 (1969): 3–15.

Smith, Jonathan Z. "Sacred Persistence: Toward a Redescription of Canon." Pages 36–52 in *Imagining Religion: From Babylon to Jonestown*. Chicago: University of Chicago Press, 1982. Repr. from pages 11–28 in *Approaches to Ancient Judaism: Theory and Practice*. Edited by W. S. Green. Brown Judaic Studies 1. Missoula: Scholars Press, 1978.

Smith, Morton. "Pseudepigraphy in the Israelite Literary Tradition." Pages 191–215 in *Pseudepigrapha*, volume 1: *Pseudopythagorica, lettres de Platon, littérature pseudépigraphique juive: Huit exposés suivis de discussion*. Edited by K. von Fritz. Vandœuvres-Genève: Fondation Hardt pour l'Étude de l'antiquité classique, 1971.

Sokoloff, Michael. *A Dictionary of Jewish Palestinian Aramaic*. 2d ed. Ramat Gan: Bar Ilan University Press; Baltimore: Johns Hopkins University Press, 2002.

Stackert, Jeffrey. *Rewriting the Torah: Literary Revision in Deuteronomy and the Holiness Legislation*. Forschungen zum Alten Testament 52. Tübingen: Mohr Siebeck, 2007.

"The Sabbath of the Land in the Holiness Legislation: Combining Priestly and Non-priestly Perspectives." *Catholic Biblical Quarterly* 73 (2011): 239–50.

Staples, W. E. "The Meaning of *ḤĒP̱EṢ* in Ecclesiastes." *Journal of Near Eastern Studies* 24 (1965): 110–12.

Steinmetz, Devora. *Punishment and Freedom: The Rabbinic Construction of Criminal Law*. Divinations. Philadelphia: University of Pennsylvania Press, 2008.

Stern, David. "On Canonization in Rabbinic Judaism." Pages 227–52 in *Homer, the Bible, and Beyond: Literary and Religious Canons in the Ancient World*. Edited by M. Finkelberg and G. G. Stroumsa. Jerusalem Studies in Religion and Culture 2. Leiden: Brill, 2003.

Steudel, Annette. "The Houses of Prostration – CD XI, 21–XII, 1: Duplicates of the Temple." *Revue de Qumran* 16 (1993): 49–68.

Stone, Michael E. "Aramaic Levi in Its Contexts." Pages 307–26 in *Apocrypha, Pseudepigrapha and Armenian Studies: Collected Papers*, volume 1. Orientalia lovaniensia analecta 144. Leuven: Peeters, 2006. Repr. from *Jewish Studies Quarterly* 9 (2002): 307–26.

Strack, H. L., and Günter Stemberger. *Introduction to the Talmud and Midrash*. Translated by M. Bockmuehl. Minneapolis: Fortress, 1996.

Strauch-Schick, Shana. "Intention in the Babylonian Talmud: An Intellectual History." Ph.D. dissertation, Yeshiva University, 2011.

Sullivan, Marbree D. "The Thought Police: Doling out Punishment for Thinking about Criminal Behavior in John Doe v. City of Lafayette." *New England Law Review* 40 (2005): 263–301.

Sussman, Yaakov. "The History of Halakha and the Dead Sea Scrolls: Preliminary Talmudic Observations on *Miqṣat Maʿaśe ha-Torah* (4QMMT)." *Tarbiz* 49 (1992): 11–76. [Hebrew] Expanded version of article by the same name that appeared as pages 99–127 in *The Scrolls of the Judaean Desert: Forty Years of Research*. Edited by M. Broshi et al. Jerusalem: Bialik Institute and Israel Exploration Society, 1992. English translation of the shorter version is found as pages 179–200 in Elisha Qimron and John Strugnell, *Qumran Cave 4.V: Miqṣat Maʿaśe Ha-Torah*. Discoveries in the Judaean Desert 10. Oxford: Clarendon, 1996.

ed. *Talmud Yerushalmi: Yoṣe le-ʿOr ʿal Pi Ketav Yad Skaliger 3 (Or. 4720) Shebe-Sifriyat ha-Universitah shel Laiden ʿim Tashlamot ve-Tiqunim*. Jerusalem: The Academy of the Hebrew Language, 2001.

Swanson, Dwight D. *The Temple Scroll and the Bible: The Methodology of 11QT*. Studies on the Texts of the Desert of Judah 14. Leiden: Brill, 1995.

Talmon, Shemaryahu. "Between the Bible and the Mishna." Pages 21–48 in *The World of Qumran from Within*. Jerusalem: Magnes; Leiden: Brill, 1989.

The Community of the Renewed Covenant: Between Judaism and Christianity." Pages 12–21 in *The Community of the Renewed Covenant: The Notre Dame Symposium on the Dead Sea Scrolls*. Edited by E. Ulrich and J. VanderKam. Christianity and Judaism in Antiquity 10. Notre Dame: University of Notre Dame Press, 1994.

"The Crystallization of the 'Canon of Hebrew Scriptures' in the Light of Biblical Scrolls from Qumran." Pages 419–42 in *Text and Canon of the Hebrew Bible*. Winona Lake: Eisenbrauns, 2010. Repr. from pages 5–20 in *The Bible as Book: The Hebrew Bible and the Judaean Desert Discoveries*. Edited by E. D. Herbert and E. Tov. London: British Library; New Castle: Oak Knoll Press, 2002.

"A Further Link between the Judean Covenanters and the Essenes." *Harvard Theological Review* 56 (1963): 313–19.

"The Textual Study of the Bible: A New Outlook." Pages 321–400 in *Qumran and the History of the Biblical Text*. Edited by F. M. Cross Jr. and Sh. Talmon. Cambridge: Harvard University Press, 1975.

Teeter, David A. "Exegesis in the Transmission of Biblical Law in the Second Temple Period: Preliminary Studies." Ph.D. dissertation, University of Notre Dame, 2008.

Theodor, Julius, and Chanokh Albeck. *Midrash Bereshit Rabbah*. 3 vols. Berlin, 1912–36. Repr. Jerusalem: Shalem, 1996.

Tigchelaar, Eibert J. C. "More on *4Q264a* (*4QHalakha A* or *4QWays of Righteousness*[c]?)." *Revue de Qumran* 19 (2000): 453–56.

"Sabbath Halakha and Worship in 4QWays of Righteousness: 4Q421 11 and 13+2+8 par 4Q264(a) 1–2." *Revue de Qumran* 18 (1998): 359–72.

Tov, Emanuel. "4QJer[a–e]." Pages 145–208 in *Qumran Cave 4.X: The Prophets*. Edited by E. Ulrich et al. Discoveries in the Judaean Desert 15. Oxford: Clarendon, 1997.

"4QReworked Pentateuch: A Synopsis of Its Contents." Pages 21–26 in *Hebrew Bible, Greek Bible, and Qumran: Collected Essays*. Texte und Studien zum antiken Judentum 121. Tübingen: Mohr Siebeck, 2008. Repr. from *Revue de Qumran* 16 (1995): 647–53.

"The Biblical Texts from the Judaean Desert: An Overview and Analysis of the Published Texts." Pages 128–54 in *Hebrew Bible, Greek Bible, and Qumran: Collected Essays*. Texte und Studien zum antiken Judentum 121. Tübingen: Mohr Siebeck, 2008. Repr. from pages 139–66 in *The Bible as Book: The Hebrew Bible and the Judaean Desert Discoveries*. Edited by E. D. Herbert and E. Tov. London: British Library; New Castle: Oak Knoll Press, 2002.

"Excerpted and Abbreviated Biblical Texts." Pages 27–41 in *Hebrew Bible, Greek Bible, and Qumran: Collected Essays*. Texte und Studien zum antiken Judentum 121. Tübingen: Mohr Siebeck, 2008. Repr. from *Revue de Qumran* 16 (1995): 581–600.

"From 4QReworked Pentateuch to 4QPentateuch (?)." Pages 73–91 in *Authoritative Scriptures in Ancient Judaism*. Edited by M. Popović. Journal for the Study of Judaism Supplement Series 141. Leiden: Brill, 2010.

"Hebrew Biblical Manuscripts from the Judaean Desert: Their Contribution to Textual Criticism." *Journal of Jewish Studies* 39 (1988): 5–37.

"The History and Significance of a Standard Text of the Hebrew Bible." Pages 49–66 in *Hebrew Bible/Old Testament: The History of Its Interpretation*, volume 1, part 1: *Antiquity*. Edited by M. Sæbø. Göttingen: Vandenhoeck and Ruprecht, 1996.

"Jeremiah Scrolls from Cave 4." *Revue de Qumran* 14 (1989): 189–206.

"The Literary History of the Book of Jeremiah in Light of Its Textual History." Pages 363–84 in *The Greek and Hebrew Bible: Collected Essays on the Septuagint*. Supplements to Vetus Testamentum 72. Leiden: Brill, 1999. Repr. from pages 211–37 in *Empirical Models for Biblical Criticism*. Edited by J. Tigay. Philadelphia: University of Pennsylvania Press, 1985.

"The Many Forms of Hebrew Scripture: Reflections in Light of the LXX and 4QReworked Pentateuch." Pages 11–28 in *From Qumran to Aleppo: A Discussion with Emanuel Tov about the Textual History of Jewish Scriptures in Honor of His Sixty-Fifth Birthday*. Edited by A. Lange, M. Weigold, and J. Zsengellér. Forschungen zur Religion und Literatur des Alten und Neuen Testaments 230. Göttingen: Vandenhoeck and Ruprecht, 2009.

"A Modern Textual Outlook based on the Qumran Scrolls." *Hebrew Union College Annual* 53 (1982): 11–27.

"Rewritten Bible Compositions and Biblical Manuscripts, with Special Attention to the Samaritan Pentateuch." *Dead Sea Discoveries* 5 (1998): 334–54.

Scribal Practices and Approaches Reflected in the Texts Found in the Judean Desert. Studies on the Texts of the Desert of Judah 54. Leiden: Brill, 2004.

"Scribal Practices Reflected in the Paleo-Hebrew Texts from the Judean Desert." *Scripta Classica Israelica* 15 (1996): 268–73.

"The Socio-Religious Background of the Paleo-Hebrew Biblical Texts Found at Qumran." Pages 353–74 in vol. 1 of *Geschichte – Tradition – Reflexion: Festschrift für Martin Hengel zum 70. Geburtstag.* Edited by H. Cancik, M. Hengel, and H. Lichtenberger. 2 vols. Tübingen: Mohr Siebeck, 1996.

Textual Criticism of the Hebrew Bible. 3d ed. Minneapolis: Fortress, 2012.

"Three Fragments of Jeremiah from Qumran Cave 4." *Revue de Qumran* 15 (1992): 531–42.

"Three Strange Books of the LXX: 1 Kings, Esther, and Daniel Compared with Similar Rewritten Compositions from Qumran and Elsewhere." Pages 283–308 in *Hebrew Bible, Greek Bible, and Qumran: Collected Essays.* Texte und Studien zum antiken Judentum 121. Tübingen: Mohr Siebeck, 2008. Repr. from pages 269–93 in *Die Septuaginta: Texte, Kontexte, Lebenswelten.* Edited by M. Karrer and W. Kraus. Wissenschaftliche Untersuchungen zum Neuen Testament 219. Tübingen: Mohr Siebeck, 2008.

Tov, Emanuel, with the collaboration of Robert A. Kraft and a contribution by Peter Parsons. *The Greek Minor Prophets Scroll from Naḥal Ḥever (8ḤevXIIgr).* Discoveries in the Judaean Desert 8. Oxford: Clarendon, 1990.

Tov, Emanuel, and Sidnie White (Crawford). "4Q364–367: 4QReworked Pentateuch$^{b–e}$." Pages 187–351 in *Qumran Cave 4.VIII: Parabiblical Texts*, part 1. Edited by H. Attridge et al. Discoveries in the Judaean Desert 13. Oxford: Clarendon, 1994.

Trebolle Barrera, Julio C. "A 'Canon Within a Canon': Two Series of Old Testament Books Differently Transmitted, Interpreted and Authorized." *Revue de Qumran* 19 (2000): 383–99.

"Origins of a Tripartite Old Testament Canon." Pages 128–45 in *The Canon Debate.* Edited by L. M. McDonald and J. A. Sanders. Peabody: Hendrickson, 2002.

"Qumran Evidence for a Biblical Standard Text and for Non-standard and Parabiblical Texts." Pages 89–106 in *The Dead Sea Scrolls in Their Historical Context.* Edited by T. H. Lim. Edinburgh: T. and T. Clark, 2000.

Ulmer, Rivka. *Pesiqta Rabbati: A Synoptic Edition of Pesiqta Rabbati Based on All Extant Manuscripts and the Editio Princeps.* 3 vols. Scripta Judaica. Lanham: University Press of America, 2009.

Ulrich, Eugene C. "The Bible in the Making: The Scriptures at Qumran." Pages 17–33 in *The Dead Sea Scrolls and the Origins of the Bible.* Grand Rapids: Eerdmans, 1999. Repr. from pages 77–94 in *The Community of the Renewed Covenant: The Notre Dame Symposium on the Dead Sea Scrolls.* Edited by E. Ulrich and J. VanderKam.

Christianity and Judaism in Antiquity 10. Notre Dame: University of Notre Dame Press, 1994.

"The Canonical Process, Textual Criticism, and Latter Stages in the Composition of the Bible." Pages 51–78 in *The Dead Sea Scrolls and the Origins of the Bible*. Grand Rapids: Eerdmans, 1999. Repr. from pages 267–91 in *"Sha'arei Talmon": Studies in the Bible, Qumran, and the Ancient Near East Presented to Shemaryahu Talmon*. Edited by M. Fishbane and E. Tov, with W. Fields. Winona Lake: Eisenbrauns, 1992.

"Clearer Insight into the Development of the Bible – A Gift of the Scrolls." Pages 119–37 in *The Dead Sea Scrolls and Contemporary Culture: Proceedings of the International Conference Held at the Israel Museum (July 6–8, 2008)*. Edited by A. D. Roitman, L. H. Schiffman, and S. Tzoref. Studies on the Texts of the Desert of Judah 93. Leiden: Brill, 2011.

"The Dead Sea Scrolls and the Biblical Text." Pages 79–100 in vol. 1 of *The Dead Sea Scrolls after Fifty Years: A Comprehensive Assessment*. Edited by J. C. VanderKam and P. W. Flint. 2 vols. Leiden: Brill, 1998–99.

"Double Literary Editions of Biblical Narratives and Reflections on Determining the Form to Be Translated." Pages 34–50 in *The Dead Sea Scrolls and the Origins of the Bible*. Grand Rapids: Eerdmans, 1999. Repr. from pages 101–16 in *Perspectives on the Hebrew Bible: Essays in Honor of Walter J. Harrelson*. Edited by J. L. Crenshaw. Macon: Mercer University Press, 1988.

"Methodological Reflections on Determining Scriptural Status in First Century Judaism." Pages 145–61 in *Rediscovering the Dead Sea Scrolls: An Assessment of Old and New Approaches and Methods*. Edited by M. L. Grossman. Grand Rapids: Eerdmans, 2010.

"Multiple Literary Editions: Reflections toward a Theory of the History of the Biblical Text." Pages 99–120 in *The Dead Sea Scrolls and the Origins of the Bible*. Grand Rapids: Eerdmans, 1990. Repr. from pages 78–105 in *Current Research and Technological Developments on The Dead Sea Scrolls*. Edited by D. Parry and S. Ricks. Studies on the Texts of the Desert of Judah 20. Leiden: Brill, 1996.

"The Non-attestation of a Tripartite Canon in 4QMMT." *Catholic Biblical Quarterly* 65 (2002): 202–14.

"The Notion and Definition of Canon." Pages 22–35 in *The Canon Debate*. Edited by L. M. McDonald and J. A. Sanders. Peabody: Hendrickson, 2002.

"The Paleo-Hebrew Biblical Manuscripts from Qumran Cave 4." Pages 121–47 in *The Dead Sea Scrolls and the Origins of the Bible*. Grand Rapids: Eerdmans, 1990. Repr. from pages 103–30 in *Time to Prepare a Way in the Wilderness: Papers on the Qumran Scrolls*. Edited by D. Dimant and L. H. Schiffman. Studies on the Texts of the Desert of Judah 16. Leiden: Brill, 1995.

"Pluriformity in the Biblical Text, Text Groups, and Questions of Canon." Pages 79–98 in *The Dead Sea Scrolls and the Origins of the Bible*. Grand Rapids: Eerdmans, 1999.

"The Qumran Biblical Scrolls – The Scriptures of Late Second Temple Judaism." Pages 67–87 in *The Dead Sea Scrolls in Their Historical Context*. Edited by T. H. Lim. Edinburgh: T. and T. Clark, 2000.

"The Qumran Scrolls and the Biblical Text." Pages 51–59 in *The Dead Sea Scrolls Fifty Years after Their Discovery: Proceedings of the Jerusalem Congress, July 20–25, 1997*. Edited by L. H. Schiffman, E. Tov, and J. C. VanderKam. Jerusalem: Israel

Exploration Society in cooperation with the Shrine of the Book, Israel Museum, 2000.

Urbach, Ephraim E. "The *Derasha* as the Basis of the Halakhah and the Problem of the *Soferim*." *Tarbiz* 27 (1957–58): 166–82. [Hebrew]

"Law and Prophecy." Pages 21–49 in *The World of the Sages: Collected Studies*. Jerusalem: Magnes, 1988. Repr. from *Tarbiz* 18 (1946–47): 1–27. [Hebrew]

van der Kooij, Arie. "The Textual Criticism of the Hebrew Bible before and after the Qumran Discoveries." Pages 167–77 in *The Bible as Book: The Hebrew Bible and the Judaean Desert Discoveries*. Edited by E. D. Herbert and E. Tov. London: British Library; New Castle: Oak Knoll Press, 2002.

Van Seters, John. "Creative Imitation in the Hebrew Bible." *Studies in Religion/Sciences Religieuses* 29 (2000): 395–409.

VanderKam, James C. "Authoritative Literature in the Dead Sea Scrolls." *Dead Sea Discoveries* 5 (1998): 382–402.

The Book of Jubilees: A Critical Text. Corpus scriptorum Christianorum Orientalium 510–11. Scriptores Aethiopici 87–88. 2 vols. Leuven: Peeters, 1989.

"The End of the Matter? Jubilees 50:6–13 and the Unity of the Book." Pages 267–84 in *Heavenly Tablets: Interpretation, Identity and Tradition in Ancient Judaism*. Edited by L. LiDonnici and A. Lieber. Journal for the Study of Judaism Supplement Series 119. Leiden: Brill, 2007.

"The Manuscript Tradition of Jubilees." Pages 3–21 in *Enoch and the Mosaic Torah: The Evidence of Jubilees*. Edited by G. Boccaccini and G. Ibba. Grand Rapids: Eerdmans, 2009.

"Questions of Canon as Viewed through the Dead Sea Scrolls." Pages 91–109 in *The Canon Debate*. Edited by L. M. McDonald and J. A. Sanders. Peabody: Hendrickson, 2002. Repr. from *Bulletin for Biblical Research* 11 (2001): 269–92.

"Recent Scholarship on the Book of Jubilees." *Currents in Biblical Research* 6 (2008): 405–31.

"Revealed Literature in the Second Temple Period." Pages 1–30 in *From Revelation to Canon: Studies in the Hebrew Bible and Second Temple Literature*. Journal for the Study of Judaism Supplement Series 62. Leiden: Brill, 2000.

"Sinai Revisited." Pages 44–60 in *Biblical Interpretation at Qumran*. Edited by M. Henze. Grand Rapids: Eerdmans, 2005.

"Studies on the Prologue and *Jubilees* 1." Pages 266–79 in *For a Later Generation: The Transformation of Tradition in Israel, Early Judaism, and Early Christianity*. Edited by R. A. Argall, B. A. Bow, and R. A. Werline. Harrisburg: Trinity Press International, 2000.

"The Wording of Biblical Citations in Some Rewritten Scriptural Works." Pages 41–56 in *The Bible as Book: The Hebrew Bible and the Judaean Desert Discoveries*. Edited by E. D. Herbert and E. Tov. London: British Library; New Castle: Oak Knoll Press, 2002.

Veijola, Timo. "The Deuteronomistic Roots of Judaism." Pages 459–78 in *Sefer Moshe: The Moshe Weinfeld Jubilee Volume; Studies in the Bible and the Ancient Near East, Qumran, and Post-Biblical Judaism*. Edited by Ch. Cohen, A. Hurvitz, and S. M. Paul. Winona Lake: Eisenbrauns, 2004.

Vermes, Geza. "Biblical Proof-Texts in Qumran Literature." Pages 56–67 in *Scrolls, Scriptures, and Christianity*. London: T. and T. Clark, 2005. Repr. from *Journal of Semitic Studies* 34 (1989): 493–508.

The Complete Dead Sea Scrolls in English. London: Penguin, 2004.

Scripture and Tradition: Haggadic Studies. Studia post-biblica 4. 2d ed. Leiden: Brill, 1973.

Wacholder, Ben Zion. *The Dawn of Qumran: The Sectarian Torah and the Teacher of Righteousness*. Monographs of the Hebrew Union College. Cincinnati: Hebrew Union College Press, 1983.

The New Damascus Document: The Midrash on the Eschatological Torah of the Dead Sea Scrolls: Reconstruction, Translation, and Commentary. Studies on the Texts of the Desert of Judah 56. Leiden: Brill, 2007.

Watts, J. D. *Isaiah 34–66*. Word Biblical Commentary 25. Waco: Word Books, 1987.

Watts, James W., ed. *Persia and Torah: The Theory of Imperial Authorization of the Pentateuch*. Society of Biblical Literature Symposium Series 17. Atlanta: Society of Biblical Literature, 2001.

Weinfeld, Moshe. "The Counsel of the 'Elders' to Rehoboam and Its Implications." Pages 516–39 in *Reconsidering Israel and Judah: Recent Studies on the Deuteronomistic History*. Edited by G. N. Knoppers and J. G. McConville. Sources for Biblical and Theological Study 8. Winona Lake: Eisenbrauns, 2000. Repr. from *MAARAV* 3 (1982): 27–63. Expanded version of "The Counsel of the 'Elders' to Rehoboam (2 Kgs 12:7)." *Lešonenu* 36 (1974): 3–13. [Hebrew]

Deuteronomy 1–11. Anchor Bible 5. New York: Doubleday, 1991.

"God versus Moses in the Temple Scroll: 'I Do Not on My Own Authority but on God's Authority' (*Sifrei Deut.* sec. 5; *John* 12:48f)." *Revue de Qumran* 15 (1991; Starcky volume): 175–80.

Weiss, Herold. "Philo on the Sabbath." *Studia Philonica Annual* 3 (1991; Hilgert Festschrift): 83–105.

Weiss, Raphael. "Two Notes." *Lešonenu* 37 (1972–74): 306.

Wells, Bruce. "What Is Biblical Law? A Look at Pentateuchal Rules and Near Eastern Practice." *Catholic Biblical Quarterly* 70 (2008): 223–43.

Werman, Cana. "Jubilees 30: Building a Paradigm for the Ban on Intermarriage." *Harvard Theological Review* 90 (1997): 1–22.

Wernberg-Møller, P. *The Manual of Discipline*. Studies on the Texts of the Desert of Judah 1. Leiden: Brill, 1957.

Westbrook, Raymond. "The Laws of Biblical Israel." Pages 317–40 in *Law from the Tigris to the Tiber: The Writings of Raymond Westbrook*, volume 2: *Cuneiform and Biblical Sources*. Edited by B. Wells and R. Magdalene. Winona Lake: Eisenbrauns, 2009. Repr. from pages 99–119 in *The Hebrew Bible: New Insights and Scholarship*. Edited by F. E. Greenspahn. New York: New York University Press, 2008.

"What Is the Covenant Code?" Pages 97–118 in *Law from the Tigris to the Tiber: The Writings of Raymond Westbrook*, volume 1: *The Shared Tradition*. Edited by B. Wells and R. Magdalene. Winona Lake: Eisenbrauns, 2009. Repr. from pages 15–36 in *Theory and Method in Biblical and Cuneiform Law: Revision, Interpolation, and Development*. Edited by B. M. Levinson. Sheffield: Sheffield University Press, 1994.

Westermann, Claus. *Isaiah 40–66: A Commentary*. Old Testament Library. Philadelphia: Westminster, 1969.

Whybray, R. N. *Isaiah 40–66*. NCBC. Grand Rapids: Eerdmans; London: Marshall, Morgan, and Scott, 1981.

Wilson, Gerard H. *The Editing of the Hebrew Psalter*. Society of Biblical Literature Dissertation Series 76. Chico: Scholars Press, 1985.

Wintermute, O. S. "Jubilees." Pages 37–142 in vol. 1 of *Old Testament Pseudepigrapha*. Edited by J. H. Charlesworth. 2 vols. Anchor Bible Reference Library. New York: Doubleday, 1983–85.

Wright, David P. *Inventing God's Law: How the Covenant Code of the Bible Used and Revised the Laws of Hammurabi*. New York: Oxford University Press, 2009.

Yadin, Azzan. "4QMMT, Rabbi Ishmael, and the Origins of Legal Midrash." *Dead Sea Discoveries* 10 (2003): 130–49.

"Resistance to Midrash? Midrash and Halakhah in the Halakhic Midrashim." Pages 35–58 in *Current Trends in the Study of Midrash*. Edited by C. Bakhos. Journal for the Study of Judaism Supplement Series 106. Leiden: Brill, 2006.

Yadin, Yigael. "Is the Temple Scroll a Sectarian Document?" Pages 153–69 in *Humanizing America's Iconic Books: Society of Biblical Literature Centennial Addresses 1980*. Edited by G. M. Tucker and D. A. Knight. Chico: Scholars Press, 1982.

The Temple Scroll. 3 vols. Jerusalem: Israel Exploration Society, the Hebrew University, and the Shrine of the Book, 1983.

Yonge, C. D. *The Works of Philo*. Peabody: Hendrickson, 2000.

Zahn, Molly M. "Genre and Rewritten Scripture: A Reassessment." *Journal of Biblical Literature* 131 (2012): 271–88.

"The Problem of Characterizing the 4QReworked Pentateuch Manuscripts: Bible, Rewritten Bible, or None of the Above?" *Dead Sea Discoveries* 15 (2008): 315–39.

Rethinking Rewritten Scripture: Composition and Exegesis in the 4QReworked Pentateuch Manuscripts. Studies on the Texts of the Desert of Judah 95. Leiden: Brill, 2011.

Zeidel, Moshe. "Parallels between Isaiah and Psalms." *Sinai* 38 (1955–56): 149–72, 229–40, 272–80, 335–55. [Hebrew]

Zeitlin, Solomon. "Midrash: A Historical Study." Pages 41–56 in *Studies in the Early History of Judaism*, volume 4: *History of Early Talmudic Law*. New York: Ktav, 1978. Repr. from *Jewish Quarterly Review* 44 (1953): 21–36.

Studies in the Early History of Judaism, volume 4: *History of Early Talmudic Law*. New York: Ktav, 1978.

Index of Ancient Sources

Ancient Near Eastern Literature

Laws of Hammurabi
- i.27–49, 21
- v.14–24, 21
- xlvii.9–58, 21

Hebrew Bible and Second Temple Period Texts

1 Chronicles
- 28:21 𝔊, 152–53

2 Chronicles
- 6:22, 73
- 9:10, 193
- 9:12 𝔊, 142

1 Enoch
- 103, 52
- 105, 52

1 Kings
- 5:22 𝔊, 142
- 5:22–24 $\mathfrak{T}^{J}$, 143
- 7:2(14) 𝔊, 152, 153
- 7:19(33) 𝔊, 153
- 8:31, 73
- 9:1 𝔊, 153, 156
- 9:11 $\mathfrak{T}^{J}$, 143
- 10:11, 193
- 10(9):22(19) 𝔊, 153
- 17:1 𝔊, 72
- 20:33 𝔊, 72

2 Kings
- 22–23, 22

2 Maccabees
- 2:13–14, 51

1 Samuel
- 16:7, 133
- 25:26, 9, 221–24, 222 (4QSam^{a})
- 25:31 𝔊, 𝔐, 223
- 25:33, 223

2 Samuel
- 14:13 𝔊, 72
- 23:5 𝔊, 142

4 Ezra
- 14, 24
- 14:22–48, 51, 57

Amos
- 5:26–27 𝔊, 𝔐, 65
- 8:5, 148

Daniel
- 1:17, 153
- 4:2, 166
- 6:4 𝔊, 153

Deuteronomy, 19–23, 27–29, 62
- 5:12–14, 179
- 5:13 81–82, 139–40, 151(𝔊)
- 5:18, 132
- 8:1, 34
- 9:10, 33–34
- 15:2, 73, 80
- 17:8, 80–81
- 17:13, 96
- 19:4–5, 132
- 22:9, 237
- 24:10, 73
- 30:4, 243–44
- 30:5, 244

Deuteronomy (*cont.*)
32:35 4QPaleoDeut^{r}, 𝔊, 𝔐, ⅏, 241–42
32:47, 77–78
Ecclesiastes
1:10, 33–34
3:1 𝔊, 70, 142
3:17 𝔊, 70, 142
5:3 𝔊, 142
5:7 𝔊, 70, 142
8:6 𝔊, 70, 142
8:13 𝔊, 142
12:1 𝔊, 142
12:10 𝔊, 142
Exodus
12–40, 34
12:16, 98, 160
16, 177, 186
16:29, 70, 107, 144–45, 173, 176–82, 178 (4QpaleoGen–Exod^{l}), 186–90, 188 (𝔗$^{Ps-J}$), 207–13, 211 (𝔗$^{Ps-J}$), 215
19–20, 22
20:1, 34
20:9, 81–82, 139–40, 157–59
20:10, 120, 122–24, 151 (𝔊), 160, 164
20:11, 200
20:17, 132
20:19–23:33, 19
21:1, 22
21:12–14, 132
22:24, 73
28:11 𝔊, 152
30:25 𝔊, 152
31:14–15, 197
31:17, 159–60
34, 29
34:27, 34
35:2, 113, 120, 122
35:3, 152, 155
36:6, 207, 210, 212
Ezekiel
45:11, 232–33
Ezra
7:6, 23
9:2, 237–38
Genesis, 46–50, 56–57
2:3, 200
6:5, 133
9:25, 13
25:8, 31
35:29, 31
37:25, 13
39:11 𝔐, 𝔗^{J}, 122
49:33, 31–32
50:20 𝔊, 154
Hosea
8:8, 143
8:12, 34
10:4, 72
Isaiah
2, 231
2:22, 229–31, 230 (1QIsa^{a})
9:16 𝔊, 𝔐, 𝔗^{J}, 76, 77
30:7, 78
32:5–7, 76
32:6, 76–77 (𝔐, 𝔗^{J}), 77 (1QIsa^{a}), 78, 80
42:21 𝔊, 154
46:10 𝔊, 143, 154
48:14, 142 (𝔊), 143
55:7–8 𝔊, 154
55:11, 143
58, 75
58:3, 70
58:9, 72 (𝔐, 𝔗^{J}), 75–77, 80
58:13
1QIsa^{a}, 1QIsa^{b} (1Q8), 4QIsa^{n} (4Q67), 69
𝔊, 71–72, 75, 142–43, 155–56
𝔐, 69–72, 74–85, 88–89, 91–117, 119–23, 125–31, 136–40, 142–47, 149–50, 154–63, 165–71, 186–87, 189, 209, 216, 249, 251–52
𝔗^{J}, 72, 75, 120, 142–43, 156
58:13–14, 71, 77, 120, 128, 158
58:14, 77
66:23, 142
Jeremiah
2:3, 234, 237–38, 249–50
17:21–22, 17, 173, 176–94, 196–205, 207, 209–10, 212–13, 215, 216, 249, 251–52
17:21–24 4QJer^{a} 178
17:22 𝔊, 151
17:23–27, 189, 191
17:24, 176–78, 185–88, 190, 192–94
30:10, 31–32
32:44, 39
48:38 𝔗^{J}, 143
49(42):22 𝔊, 154
Job
40:14, 223
Joel
2:12–13, 244–45 (𝔊, 𝔐), 245 (4QXII^{c,g})
Jubilees, 8, 17, 20–21, 26–29, 35, 38, 47–50, 54, 63–64, 66, 69, 104, 125, 130, 172, 190, 195, 213–15, 237, 251–52

2, 195–96, 206
2:27, 82
2:29–30, 105, 194, 196–97, 200–206, 214
50, 195–96, 206
50:6–13, 105, 194–96
50:8, 88, 105–10, 126, 175, 194, 196–200, 204–6, 214–15
50:12, 188

Letter of Aristeas
10, 52

Leviticus
4–5, 243
4:2–28, 243
5:1, 243
5:6, 243
19:17–18, 132, 223, 239–42
19:19, 237
21:7, 236–38
21:14, 234
22:16, 48
23, 144
23:3, 82
23:7–36, 82, 142
23:38, 48
23:39–43, 24
25:8, 142
26:31, 243–44

Micah
7:2, 218–20, 218 (4QXII^g, Mur 88), 220 (𝕿^J)

Nahum
1:2, 239–42

Nehemiah
5:7–10, 73
8, 23
8:8, 23
8:13–18, 24
10:32, 144, 191
13:15–22, 148, 184, 190–94, 200, 214–15

Numbers
15:32–37, 152
24:17, 65
28, 144
28:18–26, 82
29:1–35, 82
30:15, 221
31:2, 241

Proverbs
15:8, 225 (4QProv^b, 𝕲, 𝔐), 227–29
15:29, 225
17:9, 91
19:21, 91
31:13, 70

Psalms
44:4, 223
89:23, 73
140:3, 91

Sirach
10:26, 142–43, 155
11:21, 70
12:16, 91
38:34, 152

Wisdom of Solomon
13:10, 152
13:19, 153
14:2, 153
14:19, 152

Zechariah
7:10, 91
8:17, 91

Dead Sea Scrolls

CD (*Damascus Document*), 7–11, 14, 17, 27, 36–38, 65, 114, 119, 125, 130, 150, 154–56, 160–63, 168–77, 180–89, 190, 196–97, 199, 204–6, 213–14, 218–29, 232, 236, 239–45, 248
2:2, 238
4:15–19, 48
4:20–5:11, 13
5:2–3, 10
6:19, 238
7:14–18, 65
7:19–20, 65
9:1, 220
9:2–8, 221, 223, 238
9:6, 221
9:8–10, 9, 221–24
10:15, 95
10:17, 144
10:17–19, 68–69, 72–85, 88–97, 99–103, 106, 109–10, 126, 129, 136, 145–48, 187, 206
10:17–21, 101–3
10:20–21, 91–92, 101–3, 131, 135–49, 167, 186
10:21, 188
10:22, 144
11:2, 144, 145
11:5, 144
11:7–9, 173–74, 176–78, 180–81, 183, 185
11:9, 144

CD (*Damascus Document*) (*cont.*)
11:10, 144
11:11, 144
11:12, 144
11:13, 144
11:14, 144
11:15, 144
11:17, 144
11:18, 48
11:18–21, 224–29
12:3–6, 197
14:18–22, 243
16:3–4, 47, 109
16:13–15, 217, 219
1QS (*Rule of the Community*), 7–8, 13, 51, 78–79, 224, 230–31
1:3, 51
2:18, 238
3:17, 70
5:7–12, 13, 230
5:14, 83
5:15, 48
5:16–18, 229, 231
5:25–26, 96
6:2, 84
6:6–8, 13
6:17, 230
6:27, 224
6:27–7:2, 240
7:9, 78–80
7:25, 230
8:12–16, 1, 13, 51
8:23, 230
9:4–5, 228
1QSa (*Rule of the Congregation*)
2:5–6, 96
1Q30 (*Liturgical Text? A*)
1 4, 54
1QM (*War Scroll*)
7:4, 96
2Q25 (*Juridical Text*)
1 3, 48
4Q158, 4Q364–397 (*Reworked Pentateuch*), 26–27, 37, 54–55, 63–64
4Q159 (*Ordinances*[a])
1 ii 13, 232
4Q165 (*Pesher on Isaiah E*)
6 3–4, 76–77
6 7–8, 76
4Q174 (*Florilegium*)
21–23, 48
4Q217 (*papJubilees*[b]*?*)
3, 196
4Q218 (*Jubilees*[c])
1 3, 82
4Q228 (*Work with Citation of Jubilees*)
1 i 9, 47
4Q251 (*Halakha A*), 17, 36, 38, 172–77, 180, 186–90, 196, 199, 204–6, 213–14
1–2 1–6, 90, 144
1–2 4–5, 174, 178, 181–82, 184–85
4Q252 (*Commentary on Genesis*), 35–36, 49
4Q256 (*Rule of the Community*[b])
4 ix 10–11, 229, 231
4Q258 (*Rule of the Community*[d])
1a i 229, 231
1a ii 7, 84
1b i 9–10, 229, 231
4Q263 (*Rule of the Community*[i])
3, 84
4Q264a (*Halakha B*), 17, 36, 38, 79, 86–104, 106–12, 114–16, 118–19, 121, 125–31, 148–50, 154–55, 157, 159, 161, 166–68, 170, 175, 187
1, 87
1 i 1, 188
1 i 1–8, 90
1 i 5, 90–92, 115, 126, 145–46, 149, 167
1 i 5–8, 69, 83, 89–103, 136, 145–46
1 i 6–7, 92–97, 109
1 i 7, 187
1 i 7–8, 97–100
1 i 8, 148
3, 175, 188
4Q265 (*Miscellaneous Rules*), 49, 172–73, 177, 182, 187–89, 196, 198, 204–5, 213–14
6 2, 144
6 4, 144
6 4–5, 144–45, 174–76, 178, 180–81, 184–86
6 5, 144
6 7, 144
6 8, 144
4Q266 (*Damascus Document*[a])
6 ii 3–4, 187
8 i 8, 96
10 ii 3–4, 79–80
11 1–14, 242–43
4Q267 (*Damascus Document*[b])
7 13, 236
9 i 1–3, 238
9 i 4–5, 221

4Q269 (*Damascus Document*[d])
9 2–3, 236
4Q270 (*Damascus Document*[e])
5 15–17, 236
6 iii 16–19, 238
6 v, 136
6 v 1, 82
6 v 3–4, 72
6 v 13–14, 172–74
7 i 15–21, 242–43
4Q271 (*Damascus Document*[f])
2 2, 232
3 9–10, 236
4 ii 14–15, 217
5 i 2, 188
5 i 3–4, 172–74
5 i 12–15, 224
4Q274 (*Tohorot A*)
2 i 2, 144
4Q379 (*Apocryphon of Joshua*[a])
22 7–15, 48
4Q384 (*Pseudo-Ezekiel*[a])
9 2, 47
Miqṣat Ma'ase Ha-Torah (composite text), 36–37, 56, 226, 249–50
B 27–33, 13
B 75–82, 13, 233–38
C 7–11, 13
C 9–11, 50
4Q396 (*Miqṣat Ma'ase Ha-Torah*[c])
1–2 iv 4–11, 233
4Q397 (*Miqṣat Ma'ase Ha-Torah*[d])
6–13 12–15, 233
4Q397 14–21 9–11, 50
4Q398 (*Miqṣat Ma'ase Ha-Torah*[e])
14–17 i 2–3, 50
4Q421 (*Halakha B*)
12 6–7, 175, 188
13+2+8, 69, 87–88
13+2+8 1–5, 69, 87–88
4Q485 (*Prophecy*)
1 5, 244
4Q513 (*Ordinances*[b])
1–2 i 4, 232
3–4 3, 144
5Q12 (*Damascus Document*)
1 3–4, 221
11QT[a] *(Temple Scroll*[a]), 2, 27–29, 37–38, 54, 62–64
14:10, 82
17:11, 82
17:16, 82
19:8, 82
25:9, 82
27:6, 82
27:7, 82
27:10, 82
43:17, 144
50:6, 96
51:7, 29
52:10, 96
54:19–20, 96
55:17–18, 96
64:7–8, 220
11QT[b] (*Temple Scroll*[b])
III 3ii, 5–7 25, 82

Philo and Josephus
Philo
Life of Moses
2.31, 52
2.211–20, 151–54
On the Contemplative Life
25, 51
On the Eternity of the World
19, 55
On the Migration of Abraham
91, 73, 152
The Special Laws
2.59–66, 151–52
2.250–51, 152

Josephus
Against Apion
1.37–43, 5, 55, 57
2.217, 133
Jewish Antiquities
4.229, 236
18.18–19, 226
Jewish War
2.147, 176

New Testament and Early Christian Texts
2 *Timothy*
2:4, 153
John
5:10, 213
Luke
24:44, 51
Mark
9:47, 133
Matthew
5–7, 29
5:22, 78
5:27–28, 133

Romans
12:19, 241
Apostolic Constitutions
VII.36, 72
Jerome
Adversus Helvidium de Mariae virginitate perpetua
7, 24
Tertullian
De cultu feminarum
1.3, 24

Rabbinic Texts
Mishnah
'Abot
1:1, 33
5:22, 1
Baba Meṣi'a
7:2–8, 218
Beṣah
5:2, 73, 118
'Erubin
4:1, 5, 211
Miqva'ot
8:3, 167
Nazir
9:4, 167
'Ohalot
4:3, 133
Shabbat
1:1, 206–12
7:1, 82
7:2, 207
11:1–4, 211
23:3, 108, 110, 166
Yadayim
3:5, 58
Zavim
2:2, 167

Tosefta
Beṣah
4:2, 118
Megillah
4:20, 59
Sanhedrin
4:7, 24
Shabbat
16:21–22, 114, 118
17:5, 115
17:9, 90, 113, 116, 122
17:11, 112

Palestinian Talmud
Ḥagigah
1:8 76d, 34
Megillah
1:1 70d, 59
1:11 71b, 24
4:1 74a, 34
Pe'ah
2:6 17a, 33
Shabbat
1:1 2b, 207, 212
15:3 15a–c, 114, 123–25, 164
Shebu'ot
1:1 32c, 212

Babylonian Talmud
'Abodah Zarah
58b, 64
Baba Batra
14b–15a, 51
Baba Qamma
2b, 39
'Erubin
17b, 188, 208–10
38b, 141, 161, 164
48a, 211
51a, 188, 211–12
Giṭṭin
36a, 39
Horayot
4a, 207, 210, 212
Ḥagigah
10b, 39
Ḥullin
37b, 167
Menaḥot
65a, 64
Niddah
13b, 167
23a, 39
Sanhedrin
21b, 24
Shabbat
2a–b, 207–8
12a–b, 114, 118, 124
39b, 212
96b, 212
113a–b, 117–20, 128
118b, 167
150a–b, 112–18, 162, 165–66
153b, 211

Sukkah
20a, 24
Yoma
29a, 167

Midrash and Other Rabbinic Texts
'Abot de-Rabbi Nathan
B 21, 159–60
Pereq 'Arayot (Derekh 'Ereṣ Rabbah)
11, 236
Ecclesiastes Rabbah
1.9.2, 34
Exodus Rabbah
47, 34
Genesis Rabbah
55:3, 240–41
Leviticus Rabbah
22:1, 34
34:16, 119, 123, 125, 161–62
Mekhilta de-Rabbi Ishma'el
Ba-Ḥodesh 7, 158, 160
Shabbata 1, 159–60
Wa-Yassa 6, 188
Mekhilta de-Rabbi Shim'on b. Yoḥai
Exodus 12:16, 160
Exodus 20:10, 160
Exodus 35:2, 122, 128–29
Midrash Ha-Gadol
Exodus 20:10, 122–23, 164
Midrash on Psalms
1, 55
90:4, 59
Midrash Tanḥuma
Shemot Ki Tissa 17, 34
Mishnat Rabbi Eli'ezer
20, 120–21, 128, 161–62
Pesiqta Rabbati
23:8, 123, 164
Sifra
Be-Ḥuqotai 12, 219
Yalquṭ Shim'oni
Exodus 31:17, 159, 162

Medieval Jewish Literature
Sherira Gaon
Epistle, 36
Rashi (Shlomo Yitzḥaki)
Commentary on the Babylonian Talmud
Shabbat 12a, 113
Shabbat 113b, 118
Shabbat 150a, 111–12, 115
Abraham ibn Ezra
Exodus 16:29, 188
Isaiah 58:13, 71
Maimonides (Moshe ben Maimon)
Mishneh Torah
Hilkhot Shabbat 24:1, 167
Commentary on the Mishnah
Shabbat 1:1, 207
David Kimḥi
Isaiah 58:13, 70–72
Tosafot
Commentary on the Babylonian Talmud
'Erubin 17b, 188
Shabbat 2a, 207–8
Shabbat 113a, 118
Obadiah of Bertinoro
Commentary on the Mishnah
Shabbat 1:1, 208
Yosef Caro
Shulḥan 'Arukh
'Oraḥ Ḥayyim 306:1–8, 167

Index of Modern Authors

Adelman, Rachel, 30
Albeck, Chanokh, 36, 68, 105, 106, 108, 111, 172, 188, 198, 200, 208, 241
Alexander, Philip S., 26, 229–31
Allegro, John M., 54, 232
Allison, Dale C., Jr., 29
Anderson, Arnold A., 54, 232
Amir, Yehoshua, 155
Arndt, William F., 78, 152–54
Aune, David E., 44
Avery Peck, Alan J., 30

Bacher, Wilhelm, 23, 78
Baillet, Maurice, 52, 232, 244
Barton, John, 51, 58–59
Baumgarten, Joseph M., 2–3, 12, 15–16, 37, 72–74, 79, 86–90, 97, 98, 136, 140, 173–74, 176–77, 186, 197–98, 217, 219–21, 223–27, 232–33, 235, 238, 240, 242–44
Baumgartner, Walter, 142
Beckwith, Roger, 43–44, 51, 55–58
Beentjes, Pancratius, 84
Beer, Georg, 111, 206
Belkin, Samuel, 151–52
Benovitz, Moshe, 217, 219
Bernstein, Moshe J., 4–5, 11, 14–15, 26–28, 35, 37, 49, 74, 76, 223, 227, 235–37
Beyer, Klaus, 49
Bickerman, Elias, 25
Blenkinsopp, Joseph, 23–24, 52, 54, 70–71, 191
Botterweck, G. J., 70–71
Braude, William G., 123, 164–65
Brettler, Marc Z., 21
Bright, John, 187–88
Brongers, H. A., 69–71
Brooke, George J., 27, 35, 37, 42, 48, 63, 66, 74, 76, 233, 237
Brooks, Roger, 34
Buber, Solomon, 34, 119
Büchler, Adolph, 9

Campbell, Jonathan G., 14, 50
Carmignac, J., 49
Chajes, Zvi H., 39
Chapman, Steven B., 43
Charles, R. H., 9–11, 14, 73–74, 78, 80, 105–8, 140, 177, 200, 202, 240
Charlesworth, James H., 86–87, 89–90, 174, 177, 229, 231
Childs, Brevard S., 71
Clarke, E. G., 211
Claussen, Carsten, 87, 89–90, 174, 177
Coffey, Gerard, 132
Cohen, Boaz, 68, 78, 116, 118
Collins, John J., 5
Cook, Edward, 141, 143
Cothenet, É., 143, 228
Crawford, Sidnie White, 25–27, 47, 49, 51, 54–56, 63
Cross, Frank Moore, 42, 45, 51, 222, 226

Dahood, Mitchell, 54
Danby, Herbert, 208

Dan-Cohen, Meir, 134
Daube, David, 132
Davenport, Gene, 195–96
Davies, Philip R., 12, 226–27
Debel, Hans, 46
Derrett, J. D. M., 220
Dillman, August, 71
Dimant, Devorah, 13–14, 47
Dix, G. H., 55
Doering, Lutz, 3, 15–16, 68–69, 72–74, 79, 86, 88–90, 95, 97–98, 105–7, 115, 136, 151–52, 172–77, 186–88, 195–98, 200, 207–8, 214
Doležel, Lubomír, 61
Donaldson, James, 72
Dupont-Sommer, A., 140

Ehrlich, Arnold B., 71
Eilberg-Schwartz, Howard, 133
Elgvin, Torleif, 86, 90
Elman, Yaakov, 135
Enelow, H. G., 120, 122, 161
Epstein, Jacob N., 23, 120–22, 124, 128, 160, 164
Eshel, Esther, 53
Eshel, Hanan, 48, 53

Falk, Daniel K., 228
Falk, Ze'ev W., 220
Fernández Marcos, Natalio, 52
Finkelstein, Louis H., 105–6, 108, 195
Fishbane, Michael, 4, 14, 20, 22–25, 28, 70, 74, 76, 179, 190–92
Fitzmyer, Joseph A., 14, 48, 218–19, 222, 227, 230, 240–41
Flint, Peter, 49
Fonrobert, Charlotte, 172–73
Fraade, Steven D., 2–4, 12–16, 30, 33, 74, 239
Frankel, Yonah, 30
Frankel, Zecharias, 25–26
Friedman, Shamma, 58
Friedmann, Meir, 164
Fuller, Russell E., 218

García Martínez, Florentino, 28–29, 35, 42, 48, 65, 88, 90, 143
Geiger, Abraham, 25
Gertner, M., 23
Gilat, Yitzḥak D., 16, 36, 68, 72, 78, 114, 116, 118, 128, 133, 151–52, 198
Gingrich, F. Wilbur, 78, 152–54
Ginzberg, Louis, 1–2, 9–11, 24, 33, 39, 68, 73–74, 78, 136–37, 141–44, 161, 172, 177, 217–20, 222, 224–26, 240–42
Gladson, Jerry A., 179
Goldberg, Abraham, 111, 206
Goldenberg, Robert, 133
Goodman, Martin D., 58
Grätz, Sebastian, 51
Greenfield, Jonas, 48
Greenspoon, Leonard J., 52
Greer, Rowan A., 23

Halivni, David Weiss, 24, 36–37
Hanneken, Todd R., 47, 109–110
Harrington, Daniel J., 27
Harrington, Hannah K., 3, 12, 235
Hatch, Edwin, 151–52
Hayes, Christine, 135, 233–38
Hempel, Charlotte, 47, 177, 220, 225, 227, 232, 239, 243–44
Henshke, David, 25
Henze, Matthias, 21
Herr, Moshe D., 33
Higger, Michael, 133
Himmelfarb, Martha, 235, 238
Hoffmann, David Z., 36
Holladay, Carl R., 52
Horgan, Maurya P., 77
Horowitz, H. S., 158–59, 165

Isaac, Ephraim, 106
Itzchaky, Efraim, 25

Jackson, Bernard S., 29, 132–34
Jacobs, Louis, 1
Japhet, Sara, 25
Jassen, Alex P., 2–3, 6, 8, 10, 22–23, 30, 35, 65, 135–38, 141, 143, 175
Jastrow, Marcus, 142, 160
Jones, Henry Scott, 151–54

Kampen, John, 235
Kaufman, Yehezkel, 23–24, 36
Kimbrough, S. T., Jr., 68, 74, 78, 172, 177
Kister, Menahem, 4, 35, 195, 233
Klawans, Jonathan, 227
Knibb, Michael A., 230
Koehler, Ludwig, 142
Koyfman, Shlomo A., 5, 11–12, 14–15, 74, 76, 223, 227, 236
Kraft, Robert, 23, 52, 67
Krochmal, Nachman, 36

Kugel, James L., 15, 23, 29, 34, 105–6, 108, 195–96

Labendz, Jenny R., 59
Lange, Armin, 42–43, 48–50, 60
Larson, Eric, 174, 177, 186
Lauterbach, Jacob Z., 36, 158–59
Leaney, A. R. C., 230
Lehmann, Manfred R., 174, 177, 186
Lehrman, S. M., 34
Leiman, Sid Z., 43–44, 54, 56–59
Leiter, Brian, 135
Leslau, Wolf, 107, 197, 199, 201
Lévi, I., 73
Levine, Baruch A., 28
Levinson, Bernard M., 19–22, 27–29, 61–62
Levinson, Joshua, 30–32, 61, 64
Lewis, Jack P., 44
Licht, Jacob, 2, 222, 224, 230
Liddell, Henry C., 151–54
Lieberman, Saul, 2, 113, 115, 124–25
Lightstone, Jack N., 57–58
Lim, Timothy H., 50–51, 54, 58
Loader, William, 235, 237–38
Lohse, Eduard, 143
Lucas, Alec J., 231–32
Lundbom, Jack R., 24, 190–91
Lust, Johann, 48

Magness, Jodi, 226
Mandel, Paul, 4, 31
Margaliot, Mordechai, 119, 122–23, 162, 164
Mason, Steve, 57
McCarter, P. Kyle, Jr., 222–23
McDonald, Lee Martin, 51, 56
McKenzie, John L., 70–71
Meier, John P., 1
Meir, Ofra, 30
Melamed, E. Z., 122, 160
Metso, Sarianna, 230–31
Milgrom, Jacob, 5, 12, 83
Milik, J. T., 52, 54–55, 196, 221
Morris, Herbert, 134

Najman, Hindy, 21–25, 28–29, 35, 47, 67
Nelson, W. David, 160
Neusner, Jacob, 30, 33, 113, 119–20, 162, 206, 227
Newsom, Carol A., 48
Nihan, Christophe L., 21, 52
Nitzan, Bilhah, 35

Noam, Vered, 3, 5, 14–16, 36, 68, 87–91, 93, 97, 109, 134, 175, 188, 217

Pardo, Rabbi David, 113
Parry, Donald W., 222
Parsons, Peter, 52
Patrick, Dale, 22
Pérez Fernández, Miguel, 121
Puech, Émile, 52
Pummer, Reinhard, 53
Purvis, James D., 53

Qimron, Elisha, 16, 37, 50, 68, 72, 87–91, 93, 97, 109, 136, 173, 175, 188, 217, 221, 224, 229, 231, 233–38

Rabbinovicz, Raphael, 210
Rabin, Chaim, 2, 65, 73, 74, 78–79, 136–37, 143, 172, 177, 199, 207–8, 218–19, 221–22, 225–26, 228, 240
Rabin, I. A., 158–59, 165
Ratner, Baer, 124
Ravid, Liora, 105, 195–96
Redpath, Henry A., 151–52
Roberts, Alexander, 72
Roberts, Bleddyn J., 49
Rochberg-Halton, Francesca, 20
Rost, Leonhard, 73–74, 78, 177, 217, 222
Roth, Martha T., 21
Rubenstein, Jeffrey L., 135

Saley, Richard J., 222
Sanderson, Judith A., 52–53, 55, 178, 242
Sarna, Nahum, 24, 55
Schechter, Solomon, 8–11, 73–74, 78, 80, 109, 136–37, 140–43, 145, 160, 218, 222, 226
Schiffman, Lawrence H., 2–6, 11–13, 15–16, 23, 25, 27–28, 36–37, 42, 68–69, 72–80, 136, 143, 172–74, 177, 186–88, 207, 221–22, 224, 226–27, 232, 235, 239–42
Schmid, Konrad, 52
Schofield, Alison, 79
Schremer, Adiel, 12
Schuller, Eileen, 235
Schwartz, Daniel R., 73–74, 134–36, 140, 220, 225, 238
Scott, Robert, 151–54
Segal, Michael, 25, 27, 29, 63, 195
Sharp, Carolyn, 235
Sharvit, Baruch, 68, 78, 143
Shaver, Judson R., 25

Shemesh, Aharon, 3–4, 6, 13–14, 16, 28, 47, 49, 74, 135, 170, 219–20
Silman, Yochanan, 135
Skehan, Patrick W., 52–53, 178, 225, 240, 242
Skinner, J., 70–71
Slomovic, Elieser, 4, 69, 73–74, 76, 78, 80
Smith, Jonathan Z., 60–62, 64
Smith, Morton, 20, 22
Sokoloff, Michael, 72, 120, 153
Strugnell, John, 37, 50, 233–38
Stackert, Jeffrey, 20, 22, 160
Staples, W. E., 70
Steinmetz, Devora, 208
Stemberger, Günter, 30, 34, 36, 120, 122, 157
Stern, David, 58
Steudel, Annette, 228
Stone, Michael E., 48
Strack, H. L., 30, 34, 36, 120, 122, 157
Strauch-Schick, Shana, 133
Sullivan, Marbree D., 134
Sussman, Yaakov, 2, 33, 124
Swanson, Dwight D., 27

Talmon, Shemaryahu, 19, 29, 42, 58, 62, 64, 83–84
Teeter, David A., 26–27
Theodor, Julius, 241
Tigchelaar, Eibert J. C., 86–90, 109, 143
Tov, Emanuel, 25, 27, 43–45, 52–54, 56, 60, 63, 66, 178, 240
Trebolle Barrera, Julio C., 42, 46, 48, 50–51, 56

Ulmer, Rivka, 123–24, 164
Ulrich, Eugene C., 5–6, 22–23, 41–47, 50–56, 60, 63, 178, 225, 242
Urbach, Ephraim E., 36, 39

Van Seters, John, 20
van der Kooij, Arie, 45
VanderKam, James C., 28–29, 41–43, 46–51, 54, 56–58, 105–6, 108–9, 195–97, 200
Vaux, Roland de, 52, 221
Veijola, Timo, 20
Vermes, Geza, 14, 26–27, 49, 140, 229–31

Wacholder, Ben Zion, 28, 68, 73–74, 78–79, 136
Watts, J. D., 70
Weinfeld, Moshe, 22, 28, 70–72, 78, 107
Weiss, Herold, 152
Weiss, Raphael, 71, 74
Wells, Bruce, 19
Werman, Cana, 3, 13–14, 28, 235
Wernberg-Møller, P., 224
Westbrook, Raymond, 19–20
Westermann, Claus, 70–71
Whybray, R. N., 70
Wilson, Gerard H., 55
Wintermute, O. S., 200
Wright, David P., 21–22, 83

Yadin, Azzan, 4, 37
Yadin, Yigael, 2, 15–16, 27–28
Yonge, C. D., 151

Zahn, Molly M., 26, 28–29, 54, 63
Zeidel, Moshe, 84, 96, 103, 110, 158, 183, 185, 201
Zeitlin, Solomon, 36, 133

Subject Index

analogical reasoning, 236, 238, 252
apodictic law, 36–39, 75, 81, 88, 111–13, 138, 161, 165, 187–88, 216, 229
asmakhta, 10
azharah (warning), 208

banishment, 244
bans (on food), 219–20
business speech, prohibition of
  biblical referents, 69–72
  in Dead Dea Scrolls, 73, 79–80, 83–85, 88–89, 91–94, 96–101, 103, 104–5, 107–110, 145, 147–48, 168, 170
  in rabbinic literature, 110–18, 121, 125–29, 166
  in Philo, 154, 168, 170

canonization, 42–60
  bipartite vs. tripartite canon, 50–51
  of the Pentateuch, 50–55
  of Prophets, 55–56
carrying, prohibited on Sabbath
  biblical referents, 177–80, 190–94
  in Dead Dea Scrolls, 171–89, 194–206
  in rabbinic literature, 206–15
Covenant Code, 19–20, 22, 27, 62
cuneiform law, 20–22

diversity, canonical and textual, 24, 46, 50, 55, 60, 62, 67

eating and drinking on Sabbath, 77, 97–98, 123–24, 148, 229
Essenes, 226

financial dealings/speech, prohibited on Sabbath. *See* business speech, prohibition of
food. *See* eating and drinking on Sabbath
formal structure of law in Dead Sea Scrolls, 91–92, 101–3, 105–7, 129, 137, 187, 200–202

gezera shawah, 76
guilt, 133, 239, 242–45

Hagu, book of 222
halakhah, 3–4, 16, 36, 38, 59, 87, 127
hermeneutical method
  Dead Sea Scrolls, 3–5, 11–14, 18
  rabbinic developments in, 34–35, 38–40
Hillel, School of, 114, 133–34

idle speech, prohibition of
  biblical referents, 71
  in Dead Dea Scrolls, 78–79, 99, 125–29
  in rabbinic literature, 110, 116–21, 123, 125–29
intention in law, 106, 116, 132–34, 166, 198
inversion (literary), 84, 96, 101–3, 109–10, 158, 183–85, 201, 252

Jamnia. *See* Yabneh, council of

Jesus, 29, 133, 213

Karaites, 9

law
  ancient Israel, 3, 18–21, 29, 35, 132–33, 213
  comparative history of, 4–5, 15–16, 35–40
  Dead Sea Scrolls, 1–8, 12–15, 18–29
  rabbinic, 29–35
  Second Temple Judaism, 7–8, 15–16, 18–29
legal-exegetical method, 4–5, 12–17, 25–27, 103

marriage, 118, 233–38, 249–50
measurements, 211, 232–33
midrash (as a method), 4, 32–34, 36
midrash halakhah, 4, 13, 23–24, 36–39, 239, 248, 251
Moses, 1, 28, 48, 50–53, 55, 151, 177, 212
  as legal authority 6–7, 22–25, 28–29, 31–34, 65, 155, 243
muqṣe, 176, 198

nominalism vs. realism
  in Jewish law, 134–35, 170–71
non-Pentateuchal scripture, appeal to, 5–12, 17, 39, 57, 129–30, 209, 213, 216–46, 248–51
  rabbinic rejection of, 8–11, 39–40, 121–25, 129–30, 209, 213, 248–51

oaths, 219–24
Oral Torah, 30–31, 35

paleo-Hebrew, 53–54
paraphrase, 37, 48, 56, 79, 84, 125, 176–77, 210, 216, 221, 237, 244, 248–49
Pesharim, 30, 35–36, 76–77, 240, 250
Pharisees, 9–10, 37, 218
  Pharisaic literature, 10, 37
physical labor, prohibited on Sabbath, 74, 83–84, 95, 137–43, 153–54, 158, 161
prayer, 90, 97–98, 114, 119, 148, 225, 227–29
priests, 9, 23, 33, 155, 234–238, 243
prooftexts, 14, 37–39
  non-Pentateuchal, 10–11, 17, 130, 158–60, 216–46, 248, 250, 252
  Pentateuchal, 17, 129, 216–17, 241, 243, 245–46, 248, 250
prophets, prophecy, 5–7, 10, 22–23, 33, 45, 51, 65, 100, 155, 248, 250
Prophets (Nebi'im; canonical division), 9–11, 43–44, 50–51, 55–57, 59, 65, 250–51
proto-Masoretic Text, 60
purity/impurity, 133, 225–27, 236

revenge, 223, 238–42
rewritten scripture, 49, 56, 84
  as an exegetical technique, 26–27, 29, 63
  as a genre, 26–27, 30, 35, 66
  of legal material, 27, 38
  as a marker of authority, 27–29, 49–50, 62
  and rabbinic literature, 30, 39

Sabbath boundary, 107, 188, 211. *See also* carrying, prohibited on Sabbath
Sabbath Code, 83, 144, 147, 188, 225, 229
sacrifice, 225–29, 243–45
  sectarian substitutes for, 228
Sadducees, 9, 37, 56
Samaritan Pentateuch, 25–27, 44–45, 52–53, 55, 63, 241
Scripture, definition of, 5–6, 22–23, 34, 60
semantic reformulation, 92, 101, 107, 139–40, 143, 146, 155–56, 252
Septuagint, 25, 44–46, 49, 52, 55, 63, 71–72, 75, 77, 81, 84, 100, 142–143, 151–53, 155–56, 160, 225, 230, 241
Shammai, school of, 114, 133–34
Sinai, 22, 24, 28–29, 179
  rabbinic appeal to, 30–34

Targum, 25, 71–72, 75–77, 81, 84, 98, 100, 119, 121–22, 142–43, 156, 160, 211–212, 220, 225, 241
Temple (Jerusalem), 226
textual authority, 6, 20–22, 27–28, 246–52
  in Dead Sea Scrolls, 6, 27–29, 41, 46–50, 54, 57, 97, 217
  divinely granted, 6, 22, 28–29, 31, 57
  in the Hebrew Bible, 24–25, 250
  in rabbinic texts, 10, 29–33, 37–38, 42, 47, 57–60
theory of local texts (Cross), 45
thoughts, prohibition of
  and American law and legal theory, 134
  biblical referents, 137, 139
  in Dead Dea Scrolls, 91–92, 101–2, 126, 131–49, 167–71
  in Philo, 150–56, 167–71

thoughts, prohibition of (*cont.*)
in rabbinic literature, 112, 117–18, 156–71, 209
travel on Sabbath, 70, 83, 88, 91, 93, 107, 136, 138, 141, 147, 187–88, 208–12

variant literary editions, 45–46, 63

Writings (Ketubim; canonical division), 10, 43–44, 59, 250–51

Yabneh, council of, 44, 58

Zadokites, 9, 37
"Zeidel's law." *See* inversion (literary)

Printed in the United States
By Bookmasters